D0208655

The Investments Reader
The Investments Reader
The Investments Reader
The Investments Reader
The Investments Reader
The Investments Reader
The Investments Reader
The Investments Reader
The Investments Reader
The Investments Reader
The Investments Reader
The Investments Reader

Robert W. Kolb

The Investments Reader

Edited by

Robert W. Kolb

School of Business Administration
University of Miami

K KOLB Kolb Publishing Company   Miami, Florida

RANDALL LIBRARY UNC-W

A list of sources appears on pages 311–313 at the end of this text.

Copyright © Kolb Publishing Company, Inc., 1991.
All rights reserved.

Printed in the United States of America.

Library of Congress Catalog Card Number   91–90018

ISBN: 1–878975–05–6

Kolb Publishing Company
7175 S.W. 47th Street, Suite 210   Miami, Florida 33155
(305) 663-0550   FAX (305) 663-6579

HG
4508.3
.I 58
1991

Preface

In many respects, the 1980s was the decade of finance, and even more the decade of securities investing. The decade saw one of the longest sustained economic expansions in history, the stock market achieved new highs, and the financing of America's corporations was transformed through a wave of mergers and the issuance of tremendous amounts of risky debt. However, this same period brought the most dramatic stock market crash in history when the market fell about 25 percent in a single day in October 1987. Also, individuals grabbed the spotlight of the financial press and seemed to stir the envy of millions. Many of these same apparently blessed individuals fell from grace. Donald Trump, a great financier by his own account, now tries to keep his tattered empire from the jaws of bankruptcy. Rupert Murdoch built a world-wide media empire that now finds itself uncomfortably strapped for cash to service its debt. Perhaps most dramatically, Michael Milken, the junk bond king who made hundreds of millions for himself while he helped issue debt and transform corporations, now stands as an admitted felon and faces a lengthy jail sentence.

The Investments Reader attempts to provide the background to help make sense of the contemporary drama of the investments world. The 30 articles in this book span the range of investment topics, with a strong emphasis on policy issues currently being debated. The articles are arranged into the following sections:

Section I	**An Overview of Securities Markets**
Section II	**Debt, Inflation, and Macroeconomic Forecasts**
Section III	**Equity Market Linkages and Market Volatility**
Section IV	**The Stock Market**
Section V	**The Bond Market**
Section VI	**Derivative Instruments**
Section VII	**Global Investing**
Section VIII	**The Investor–Broker Relationship**

To illustrate the focus of the book, consider the fact that technology is transforming the securities and brokerage business and making the securities market truly global. Section I, *An Overview of Securities Markets*, reflects this trend by its emphasis on technology and the changing system for paying for securities transactions. Similarly, Section VI, *Global Investing*, focuses on the international linkages that are knitting all securities markets together.

The linkages between the stock market and the equity derivatives markets is currently under close scrutiny, with many observers believing that those linkages contribute to stock market volatility. Already, there have been significant changes in the operation of these markets in response to the Crash of 1987 and the Mini-Crash of 1989. Section III, *Equity Market Linkages and Market Volatility*, includes articles that focus on the nature and importance of those linkages.

The text is intended to serve as a course supplement for investment courses at either the undergraduate or MBA level. While it is quite comprehensive, the text does not provide coverage of every area of investments. Instead, the articles in *The Investments Reader* attempt to compensate for a necessary weakness of most investments textbooks: Investments texts must cover the entire domain of securities investing, without undue emphasis on certain features merely because of timeliness. By contrast, the readings in this book deal with the topics that are timely and most clearly before the mind of the investments community and the informed public. This focus helps students to understand the dynamic and contemporary nature of the subject matter of investing.

A special word of thanks goes to the authors represented in the pages that follow. Without their creativity and labor, this book could never have appeared. We also want to thank the publications where these articles were originally published for allowing the articles to be collected in *The Investments Reader*. While it is customary to praise others for making a book possible, such praise has a special meaning for this book. The original work by the authors represented in this text really did make this book possible.

Robert W. Kolb
University of Miami

Contents

Section I
An Overview
of Securities Markets

Section I introduces some current topics of debate in securities markets. It considers the large issues of the social role of securities markets. Whom do these markets serve and how? Articles in this section also deal with some of the current issues that confront ever-evolving markets. In the 1990s, technological advances will play a critical role in transforming markets. For example, it is already possible for an individual to enter orders to trade securities from a home computer. This trend will accelerate in the 1990s. Also, financial markets are becoming more fully global. Today traders in one country freely execute orders in foreign markets. This raises issues of tracking capital flows around the world.

The first article, "What Securities Markets Do-And for Whom," was prepared by the Office of Technology Assessment (OTA) of the U.S. Congress. The article investigates whether securities markets do a good job of raising capital, whether the markets promote efficient resource allocation, and whether the markets benefit ordinary citizens. The article also considers the different types of investors that participate in the market. As the article shows, there has been an important transformation in the market as financial institutions have come to dominate the market at the expense of individual shareholders.

"How Technology is Transforming Securities Markets," also by the Office of Technology Assessment (OTA) briefly reviews the information mechanisms that have been used in the stock market since the early 1800s. As the article notes, Wall Street first received electric lights in 1882. After this brief review, the article focuses on recent and current innovations. The article features a treatment of information service vendors for news, stock quotations, foreign exchange data, and bond data. In addition, the article provides an inside look at how technology affects brokerage houses. The discussion covers trading support, back-office support, surveillance activities, and customer support. Finally, the article assesses global trading systems, including those now in place and those likely to develop in the future.

"Payments System Issues in Financial Markets That Never Sleep," by Herbert L. Baer and Douglas D. Evanoff, refers to the insomniac world securities markets, because there is always some security market in operation somewhere in the world. The payments system is the mechanism used for settling securities transactions. For the most part, the payments system operates through electronic means. For example, a financial institution in the United States might sell a security on the German stock exchange. Most likely, the stock will be shown electronically on the firm's books and the settlement will consist of adjusting the institution's computer records, along with a wire transfer of money from the buyer to the selling institution. The article considers the various risks that beset the global payments system. For example, one kind of risk arises because one party might not pay as promised. A more serious risk arises if a group of parties has simultaneous difficulties. This system-wide difficulty is critical, because it could cause disaster for markets around the world. Baer and Evanoff explore these potential difficulties and suggest regulatory practices that may help to reduce risks of system-wide failure.

Article 1

What Securities Markets Do—And For Whom

Securities markets have five basic functions in a capitalistic economy:

1. they make it possible for corporations and governmental units to raise capital;
2. they help to allocate capital toward productive uses;
3. they provide an opportunity for people to increase their savings by investing in them;
4. they reveal investors' judgments about the potential earning capacity of corporations, thus giving guidance to corporate managers; and
5. they generate employment and income.

How important are these functions, and how well do securities markets, in 1990, perform them? Who benefits?

DO SECURITIES MARKETS DO A GOOD JOB OF RAISING CAPITAL?[1]

Corporations raise new capital by issuing stock (i.e., selling ownership shares) or by borrowing through bonds, notes, and related debt instruments.[2] State and local governments and the U.S. Government also issue debt securities.

Both stocks and bonds can be sold to investors directly or through underwriters. This is the primary market. It converts household and business savings into investments, to the benefit of both the savers and the corporation.[3] The secondary securities markets, the subject of this report, are for the reselling of stocks and bonds. People would be less likely to invest in securities, even with high dividends or interest, without assurance that they can sell their investments for cash when they wish to.

A decision about which stocks or bonds to buy is supposedly based on information that an investor has about the issuing firm's assets, markets and customer base, future earnings and growth potential, and management skills. Past performance is therefore important in evaluating established firms. Evaluation of new firms is, by comparison, difficult. For startup firms, public stock and bond offerings are often not an effective mechanism for raising capital, and venture capital specialists are more likely to provide it.[4] At some later point, successful growing firms often move to public sale of equities or bonds.

A market, whether physical or electronic, is a meeting place for potential buyers and sellers. A market that attracts many buyers and sellers is said to be "liquid" or to have liquidity. In a liquid market, selling or buying can be done with minimal effect on the prevailing competitively established price. The advantage of a liquid market for customers is "immediacy," the ability to sell quickly when the customer needs his assets, or buy quickly when there is a chance for profit, and to clear and settle the trade quickly. Some markets attempt to assure immediacy by designating certain traders as market-makers, with an affirmative obligation to buy shares at a price close to the last sale price, or to sell from inventory when there is an eager buyer. Other markets depend on the interaction of bids and offers from customers and market professionals to provide liquidity and immediacy.

Another desirable characteristic of securities markets is "efficiency." This means that changes in investors' collective judgment about the fundamental value of corporations are accurately and swiftly reflected in the prices at which stocks and bonds are bought and sold, with minimum distortion from transaction costs, regulations, or other external factors. Information technology should speed up the process of registering changes in investors' judgment, and both information technology and deregu-

---

[1]Parts of this chapter draw on an OTA contractor report: James L. Butkiewicz (University of Delaware), *The Role of the Stock Market in the U.S. Economy*, May 3, 1989; and on a workshop by the same name held at OTA on Apr. 5, 1989.

[2]The bond is a contract obligating the borrower to repay the debt principal at a specified time and also to make interest payments to the bondholder at a specified rate and time.

[3]Alternatively, savings may go into other kinds of investment (e.g., real estate), or into various kinds of bank accounts which banks then use to make loans to individuals, corporations, or governments. Corporations also use retained earnings and depreciation as sources of capital for growth.

[4]The U.S. Small Business Administration is studying the feasibility of special regional stock exchanges to handle issues of small companies. The International Stock Exchange in London set up such a market for small or startup firms in 1987; it trades stocks of about 50 firms.

lation should tend to lower transaction costs. Some people believe, however, that as a result of technology and deregulation market prices have recently become too volatile, and that transaction costs should be deliberately raised by taxing, to discourage "in and out" trading.

New equity issues in public markets are not the major source of funding for corporate investment.[5] From 1952 through 1981, the proportion of funds raised by American non-financial corporations through stock issues ranged from an occasional high of 7 percent to a low of 0.2 percent in 1980-81. From 1982 through 1988, new stock issues made no net contribution to capital formation. As corporations bought back and withdrew stock, there was in fact a net loss of 14.7 percent. The percent of corporate funds exclusive of bank loans supplied by bonds and notes grew from 10.5 percent in 1980-81 to 19.6 percent during the rest of the 1980s. The proportion of all corporate funds supplied by both equity and debt securities averaged about 16 percent from 1952 to 1982, and has been much less since then.[6]

This has led some people to believe that financial markets "may have deteriorated over time in performing their social functions of spreading risk and efficiently guiding the allocation of capital."[7] John Maynard Keynes said, over 50 years ago, "As the organization of investment markets improves, the risk of the predominance of speculation does increase."[8] Today, some critics perceive that more efficient markets (in part a result of information technology) have encouraged a kind of speculation that drives stock prices away from fundamental values and leads to misallocation of financial resources. Other people argue, however, that securities markets work far better than they have in the past, and without them the growth of today's multinational enterprise would not be possible.

DO STOCK MARKETS DO A GOOD JOB OF RESOURCE ALLOCATION?

In addition to facilitating capital formation, securities markets are assumed to allocate capital to its most productive uses, by allowing stocks (and other securities) to compete for the investor's money. Stock market prices theoretically reveal the relative values placed on ownership in a corporation ("price discovery"). Market efficiency in performing this function is essential, according to many main-stream economists. They say that a stock price is the collective best estimate by investors of the present value of future earnings, reflected in prices that are set by people bidding against each other, each using incomplete but overlapping information. The interaction of supply, demand, and price is assumed to be the best signal for allocation of resources.

Taxes and regulations affect market pricing by altering the rewards for risk taking. When that effect is deliberate and desired, tax and regulatory policies are working as intended. When the outcomes are unintentional and undesirable, taxes and regulations may cause capital to be misallocated. Efficient-market theorists tend to see most market regulations and taxes as harmful.

Changes in stock prices are also affected dramatically by mergers, acquisitions, takeovers, and leveraged buyouts that may have unpredictable affects on corporate values and corporate performance for reasons not related to market valuation.

Efficient-market theory emphasizes the importance of information in market behavior. It is therefore not considered possible to "outperform the market" over time, even by studying all available information, because, in an efficient market, all information about stock value is presumably already reflected in market prices. The only "special"

---

[5] In the first 6 months of 1989, 1,955 new securities issues were offered on American domestic markets, valued at $142 billion; but only 4 percent were initial public offerings of new stock. Junk bonds accounted for 11 percent, other bonds for 40 percent, convertible debt and preferred stock for 5 percent, and mortgage- and asset-backed securities (which are pools of loans packaged and resold by banks) accounted for the other 40 percent. Kevin Winch, "Growing Risk in Corporate Finance," *CRS Review*, October 1989, pp. 20-21. Data from Investment Dealers' Digest. This does not count the implicit change in net equity from earnings retention, used as a method of shielding dividends from higher income tax rates.

[6] Board of Governors of the Federal Reserve System, *Flow of Funds Accounts*. During this period the percent of corporate funding supplied by retained earnings and depreciation ranged from a low of 62 percent (1970-73) to a high of 81.3 percent (1982-88), with the rest accounted for by loans.

[7] Lawrence H. Summers (Harvard University) and Victoria P. Summers (Hale Dorr), "When Financial Markets Work Too Well: A Cautious Case for a Securities Transactions Tax," presentation at the Annenberg Conference on Technology and Financial Markets, Washington, DC, Feb. 28, 1989, p. 2.

[8] John Maynard Keynes, *The General Theory of Employment, Interest, and Money* (New York, NY: Harcourt Brace, 1936).

information is knowledge that is available only to "insiders" (i.e., corporate officials, regulators, etc.), in which case its use is illegal. Many large investors, because they believe that one cannot outperform the market except in very brief instances, hold "indexed" portfolios that contain all of the stocks used in computing the Standard and Poor 500 index or another standard market index. (The index is the weighted average price of a basket of selected stocks that are assumed to represent the market as a whole.) The indexed portfolio, by definition, should appreciate or depreciate just as the overall market does. These investors may also use "passive" trading techniques aimed only at reflecting general market trends.

Some people dispute the claims that markets are efficient, that investor behavior is rational, and that the price investors are willing to pay represents any judgment about fundamental values.[9] Economist Joseph Stiglitz said the market is "a gambling casino for the rich,"[10] and John Maynard Keynes likened it to a beauty contest in which:

> . . . it is not a case of choosing which [faces] are really the prettiest, nor even those which average opinion genuinely thinks the prettiest [but] . . . we devote our intelligences to anticipating what average opinion expects average opinion to be.[11]

Many empirical studies, especially since the market crash of 1987, have cast doubt on efficient market theory.[12] They ask whether corporate assets really declined in value by one-third between October 13-19, or what new information caused investors to collectively revise their previous judgment so quickly. Alternative explanations of "excessively volatile" stock prices vary from large swings in the discount rate that people use in valuing future earnings streams, to the blind following of perceived trends in general investor behavior, to mass hysteria, or the actions of those who seek to profit by anticipating changes in "market psychology."[13]

Many people have concluded that price jumps caused by large block trades, by new computerized trading strategies, and by professional "speculators" make stock prices excessively volatile. This, they say, endangers financial systems, causes instability in the economy, and imposes unnecessary risks on small investors. Others blame excessive volatility on arbitraging, hedging, and manipulation (although critics sometimes confuse these behaviors in discussing volatility). These arguments are considered in chapters 3, 4, and 5, which describe stock, futures, and options markets.

There is, in short, little consensus about whether investor behavior, even in the extreme circumstances that result in a market crash, is rational or irrational. If investors do behave irrationally a significant portion of the time, then prices may not reflect fundamental values, and investment decisions may be based on inappropriate prices. But even if stock markets are efficient and investors behave rationally, the allocation of investment capital is affected by more than securities prices. It is also affected by banking decisions, interest rates, the mortgage market, and the domestic money markets;

---

[9]See Michael C. Jensen et al., "Some Anomalous Evidence Regarding Market Efficiency," *Journal of Financial Economics* 6, 1978; Robert J. Shiller, "Do Stock Prices Move Too Much To Be Justified by Subsequent Changes in Dividends?" *American Economic Review* 71, June 1981, pp. 421-436; Lawrence Summers, "Does the Stock Market Rationally Reflect Fundamental Values," *Journal of Finance* 41, July 1986, pp. 591-601. There are many articles by economic historians on "bubbles," panics, and crashes in the past, but no consensus is apparent on the extent of investor irrationality. A number of recent papers along this line were presented at a Salomon Brothers Center Conference on *Crashes and Panics in Historical Perspective*, New York University, Oct. 19, 1988.

[10]Joseph Stiglitz, "Comment on Robert Schiller," *Keynes' Economic Legacy: Contemporary Economic Theories*, James L. Butkiewica et al. (eds.) (New York, NY: Praeger, 1986).

[11]John Maynard Keynes, op. cit., footnote 8.

[12]The most vocal proponents of the irrationality of markets at present are Prof. Robert Schiller of Princeton and Prof. Lawrence Summers of MIT. See op. cit., footnote 9. David M. Cutler, James M. Poterba, and Lawrence H. Summers examined news events on the 20 days over the last 50 years when the largest market moves occurred and concluded that it was not possible to relate the events convincingly to price movement. ("What Moves Stock Prices," *Journal of Portfolio Management*, 1989.) Richard Roll examined the futures market in frozen orange juice in the context of predictions about the weather in Florida and reached similar conclusions. ("Orange Juice and Weather," *American Economic Review*, 1984, pp. 861-880.) Kenneth French and Richard Roll compared price movements during and between trading sessions and found no evidence that they reflected information bearing on fundamental values. ("Stock Return Variances: The Arrival of Information and the Reaction of Traders," *Journal of Financial Economics*, 1987, pp. 5-26.)

[13]A psychologist argues that panics become almost inevitable when bull markets continue for a long time. Participation in markets becomes very high and "there are no new believers to be recruited"; "slight tilts in trends will destroy faith that a trend will continue," causing investors to flee from the market. Donald C. Hood, "Toward Understanding Stock Market Movements: A Marriage of Psychology and Economics," presented in a Science and Public Policy Seminar held by the Federation of Behavioral, Psychological, and Cognitive Sciences, Washington, DC, July 1, 1988.

and increasingly, it is affected by markets, currencies, economic conditions and policies in other countries. At best, increased efficiency of the stock market may not improve, or may only slightly improve, the allocation of corporate capital.

DO SECURITIES MARKETS BENEFIT ORDINARY AMERICANS?

A third function of securities markets is to provide opportunities for people to invest and increase their savings, and thus to encourage overall savings and investment. Public policy has traditionally focused on encouraging small investors by protecting them against market fraud and manipulation. But trading on stock exchanges is increasingly dominated by large investment funds. Only about 18 percent of trades in 1988 were made on behalf of individual investors.[14]

Most stock—about 59 percent—is still owned directly by individuals and households.[15] Even more people own stock indirectly through pension funds and mutual funds. The rest is owned by banks, insurance companies, foreign owners, and broker-dealers.

It may be misleading to think of individual investors as "small investors." While about 19 percent of American households own some stock,[16] 43 percent of stock shares and 31 percent of mutual fund shares is owned by wealthy families—those with incomes higher than that of 99.5 percent of American households.[17]

The largest group of individual investors—which is, however, shrinking in numbers—are those who have a few thousand dollars invested in securities; this generally does not represent a large proportion of their household assets. Most of these investors probably seldom trade their stocks; some trade them almost as a "dabble", not as a livelihood. A much smaller class of individual investors have securities that average $75,000 to $100,000; these wealthier Americans are probably much more frequent and sophisticated traders.

Small investors have been leaving the stock market for about 20 years, a trend that accelerated in 1987. In early 1989, individual investors were net sellers of stock at the rate of an average 3.5 million shares per day, according to the Securities Industry Association. In the last 5 years, individual investors decreased their direct holdings by more than a third.[18] The "small investor" will increasingly be found mostly under the umbrella of large investment funds with professional investment managers, and individual investors still directly in the market are increasingly less likely to be the traditional small investors.

Pension funds now give more Americans, and less wealthy Americans, a stake in the markets.[19] Pension plans cover more than 57 million people. Before the late 1940s, pension plans were rare, and pension reserves did not show up in accounting for household assets. Even in 1950, pension reserves constituted only 2.6 percent of household assets. By 1987 this had risen to 15.1 percent of household net worth.[20] In 1955, pension plans owned only 2 percent of corporate securities, in 1988 they owned

---

[14]Securities Industry Association, *Trends*, Mar. 16, 1989. This is an estimate; other estimates vary according to how shareholders are categorized.

[15]According to the Securities Industry Association in its publication *Trends* (Mar. 16, 1989), direct individual ownership of equities fell from 82.2 percent in 1968 to 58.5 percent in 1988. Ownership of securities, both direct and through mutual funds, makes up a decreasing share of household assets; it was 10.6 percent in 1988, compared to over 18 percent in 1958 and 1969. Bonds constituted 6 percent of household assets in 1988, compared to 6.7 percent in 1958 and 6.8 percent in 1969. Edward N. Wolff, "Trends in Aggregate Household Wealth in the United States, 1900-1983," *The Review of Income and Wealth* 35(1), March 1989:1-29.

[16]Robert B. Avery (Cornell University) and Arthur B. Kennickell (Federal Reserve Board), "Rich Rewards," *American Demographics*, June 1989, pp. 19-22. Based on 1983 and 1986 Surveys of Consumer Finance conducted by the University of Michigan, Survey Research Center, for the Federal Reserve Board. The median value of stock owned by households was reported as $6,000, and the average value as $81,300. Stocks, on average, constitute about 9 percent of household assets, according to this report.

[17]For comparison, the top half of 1 percent of families by income distribution own 3 percent of savings accounts, 5 percent of owner-occupied houses, 14 percent of IRA and Keoghs, 28 percent of corporate and Treasury bonds, and 69 percent of trust accounts. Robert B. Avery and Gregory E. Elliehausen, "Financial Characteristics of High-Income Families," *Federal Reserve Bulletin* 72, March 1986, pp. 164-175. This data is probably from 1985; since small investors have been leaving the markets at a high rate since then, the concentration of ownership in the top 0.5 percent of households is probably understated.

[18]Michael C. Jensen, "Eclipse of the Public Corporation, *Harvard Business Review*, September-October 1989, p. 61.

[19]As first pointed out by Peter Drucker, *The Unseen Revolution: How Pension Fund Socialism Came to America* (New York, NY: Harper & Row, 1976).

[20]Mark J. Warshawsky, "Pension Plans: Funding, Assets, and Regulatory Environment," *Federal Reserve Bulletin* 74, November 1988, p. 725.

25 percent. Pension plan investments have become a major force in the securities markets.[21]

Two-thirds of these pension plan investments, however, are held by defined-benefit plans.[22] When the market value rises, this reduces the contribution the corporation has to make to the plan, but does not increase the wealth of the workers, whose retirement benefits are already specified. Such plans cover 72 percent of all covered workers. Only one-third of the securities owned by pension plans (approximately 9 percent of all securities) are owned by defined-contribution pension plans, in which workers directly own the assets and thus benefit directly by market gains. Defined-contribution plans also make those people directly vulnerable to market declines. The proportion of people covered by defined-contribution plans is growing rapidly and thus the number of people potentially directly affected by market losses will grow.

Policymakers and regulators must take these complexities into account. The traditional public policy focus on "the small investor" may not in the future be as realistic or useful as in the past. The interests of securities owners and of securities traders are not always the same. The interests of wealthy speculators and small investors are not always the same. The needs of individual investors and investment fund money managers may be different. Technology for trade support may not meet the needs of these groups equally. Exchange rules and government regulations may not affect them the same way. Understanding the benefits and costs to all parties is important in framing public policy.

DOES PUBLIC OWNERSHIP IMPROVE CORPORATE MANAGEMENT?

A fourth function of securities markets is to control corporate management, or provide it with guidance. First, the prices at which shares trade in the market should indicate to managers the public's judgment about the earnings prospects of the corporation and thus about the quality of their manage-ment. Second, shareholders have the rights of owners to exercise control through voting in shareholder meetings and elections. The question is, how effective are these controls now?

Monitoring management performance is difficult and time-consuming. Since each shareholder has one voice among many thousands, there is a vanishingly small amount of leverage, and little incentive for most shareholders to vote. One school of thought says that the separation of ownership and control in publicly held corporations may result in a misallocation of resources and is a serious problem.[23] Among these critics, some see a basic conflict of interest between shareholders and corporate managers. It is assumed to be in the shareowners' interest to maximize company profits and pay them out as dividends; and in the interests of corporate management to enlarge the corporation through developing new products, entering new markets, spawning new divisions, acquiring other companies, investing in research and development, etc. This may defer the paying out of profits to shareholders. Some argue that managers will seek to further the long-term growth of the corporation from a spirit of healthy entrepreneurship, or from a feeling of responsibility to the workforce and the surrounding community; others say that managers will be motivated chiefly by the need to justify large salaries or bonuses for themselves. In either case, shareholders are (according to this school of thought) deprived of immediate possession of their profits.

Takeovers are seen as the way to enforce these alleged rights to immediate profits. In a takeover, an individual or group acquires enough shares to exert control, install new management, and change corporate policy. After a takeover, "excess" corporate resources—labor, facilities, products, divisions, or subsidiaries—can be sold and the proceeds paid out to shareholders for re-investment.

Critics of takeovers say that the fear of takeovers discourages managers from investing in long-range productivity improvements such as research, development of new products, and ventures into new markets. The threat of a takeover encourages strategies aimed at short-term profits rather than long-

---

[21] "The Power of the Pension Funds," *Business Week*, Nov. 6, 1989, p. 154.

[22] Mark J. Warshawsky, op. cit., footnote 20, pp. 717.?

[23] Adolf A. Berle and Gardiner C. Means were perhaps the first to identify this problem, in *The Modern Corporation and Private Property* (Chicago, IL: Commerce Clearing House, 1932). See also Hal R. Varian et al., "Symposium on Takeovers," *Journal of Economic Perspectives* 2, Winter 1988, pp. 3-82.

term growth that would strengthen American industry's competitive position in world markets. At their worst, takeovers may destroy jobs, hurt local communities, and often weaken or destroy the corporation. At least 39 States have passed laws to discourage hostile takeovers.[24]

There is disagreement about whether takeovers result in more efficient and profitable firms. There is also little agreement as to whether or when a corporate emphasis on short-term profits, if it exists, is attributable to fear of takeovers.[25] A short-term focus can also result from high real interest rates.[26] Advocates and critics of takeovers often agree, however, that securities markets may not exert strong discipline over very large corporations. This may be due to the proportionate decrease in the influence that can be exerted by even the larger shareholders, as corporations and corporate assets have increased in scale. Another reason may be that the indexed portfolios and program trading strategies of large investment funds have blurred the relationship between stock prices and public judgments about the fundamental value of corporations. Some people advocate public policy incentives to encourage the long-term holding of large blocks of stock and the active exercise of shareownership rights in corporate governance by large institutions (e.g., pension funds' corporate sponsors), or other mechanisms for stronger shareholder control.

An internal defense against acquisition or takeover is the "buyout," in which a corporation buys back much of its own stock, removing it from the public market. Most buyouts are highly leveraged, that is, they are accomplished by borrowing heavily and committing the corporation to very high interest payments. The acquired corporation will often sell assets, pare down staff and workforce, cut other costs, and pay out the proceeds as interest and as dividends to the remaining (internal) shareholders. Leveraged buyouts are usually funded by issuing "junk bonds"—i.e., debt that is not given an investment-grade rating, but carries a high interest rate."[27]

Michael Jensen claims that "privatization of equity" is becoming the central characteristic of corporate activity today, signaling the "eclipse of the public corporation."[28] This privatization is being carried out by the switch to public and private debt instead of equity, by the concentration of shareownership in large institutional investors, and even more strikingly by the wave of hostile takeovers and leveraged buyouts. If Jensen is right that "privatization of equity" is the wave of the future, then the role of securities markets in the American economy could decline in importance even more. This is a minority viewpoint, but it is likely to be widely debated in the future.

DOES STOCK MARKET IMPROVEMENT ENCOURAGE SAVINGS AND INVESTMENT?

The behavior of the stock market is assumed to influence the level of investment and possibly the

---

[24]Investor Responsibility Research Center, Washington, DC.

[25]David J. Raverschraft and F.M. Scherer studied 95 firms before and after takeovers, and found that their profitability did not significantly change. ("Life After Takeover," *Journal of Industrial Economics* 36, December 1987, pp. 147-156.) See also, F.M. Scherer, "Corporate Takeovers: The Efficiency Arguments," *Journal of Economic Perspectives* 2, Winter 1988, pp. 69-82. Frank R. Lictenberg and Donald Siegel studied manufacturing establishments taken over from 1972 through 1981 and found that their productivity did increase significantly. ("Productivity and Changes in Ownership of Manufacturing Plants," *Brookings Papers on Economic Activity* 3, 1987, pp. 643-673.) In subsequent studies they found that managerial employment growth in these acquired firms was less than industry averages, resulting in cost savings; that there was no significant difference in R&D employment between acquired firms and industry averages; and that growth in wages and benefits was 12 percent lower in acquired than non-acquired firms ("The Effect of Takeovers on the Employment and Wages of Central-Office and Other Personnel," 1988, National Bureau of Economic Research Working Paper No. 2895).

[26]Real interest rates are market rates less the expected rate of inflation. If one assumes that "expected" inflation rates approximate real inflation rates, then real interest rates in the 1980s have still been higher than in recent decades. At a 5 percent rate of interest, the present value of a dollar of profits to be realized 10 years in the future is 61.4 cents. At a 10 percent rate of interest, it is only 38.5 percent. Thus long-term investments that seem reasonable at periods with relatively low interest rates, may not appear justified at periods such as the present, with higher interest rates.

[27]Junk bonds are sometimes considered "quasi-equity" because unlike conventional bonds they are "less a bet on interest rates than on a given company's earning power and . . .on its ability to meet interest payments out of cash flow." "Junk Bonds: Last Resorts," *The Economist*, Sept. 2, 1989, p. 75. Companies with large debt and interest burdens are vulnerable to small setbacks as well as to general economic recessions, and may be at a competitive disadvantage relative to other companies. The junk bond market grew very rapidly in the 1980s, to about $200 billion, but began to decline rapidly in 1988 and 1989. Some companies that used junk bonds for leveraged buyouts were unable to either meet interest payments or refinance their debt.

[28]Michael C. Jensen, "Eclipse of the Public Corporation," *Harvard Business Review*, September-October 1989, pp. 61-99.

savings rate.[29] The availability of capital for industry (and thus the cost of capital) is the product of the multiple decisions of individuals to save or to spend.[30] The American rate of saving is considered low compared to that in other developed nations, and personal saving has declined in recent years.[31] Many explanations have been offered for this: people may feel less need to save for retirement because of insurance coverage and pension plans; large purchases can be financed by borrowing rather than saving; the baby boom generation until recently was in the youthful low-savings phase of their lifecycle; and two-income households engenders confidence that reduces the need to save.

It may be that saving in the United States is neither low or declining.[32] Economists count only private savings, not the purchase of a home, pension contributions, and insurance policies that many Americans think of as their life savings. Pension plans, insurance, and homeownership represent long-term, predictable investment, and public policies that encourage their growth might yield more capital for investment, in the long run, than a cut in the capital gains tax. Some people assume that increasing the income of upper-income households will tend to increase savings more than would income redistribution downward, which would tend to increase consumption. Others argue that the wealthy need not invest most of what they have in order to generate more income than they can consume, and therefore have relatively little incentive to seek productive investments.

The relationship between income, return on investment, and savings is not empirically well-established. The extent to which the saving rate is responsive to rates of return is still doubtful.[33] Continuing debate about the taxation of securities markets transactions or of income derived from securities markets cannot be resolved on these grounds. Nearly all of the possible public policy approaches to encourage saving and investment in productive capital are highly controversial from a social or political standpoint.

HOW MUCH EMPLOYMENT IS GENERATED BY SECURITIES MARKETS?

Gross revenues for the securities industry tripled between 1980 and 1986, reaching a high of $50 billion. Revenue was flat in 1987 and 1988, and probably declined in 1989. Employment for New York securities firms reached a high of 262,000 just before the 1987 crash, and declined to 227,000 by September 1989, a drop of 13 percent. There have been further cuts since then, accelerating with the bankruptcy of the large firm of Drexel Burnham Lambert in early 1990.[34] Total employment nationwide is estimated, on the basis of Labor Department and Census figures, at 641,000.

The National Association of Securities Dealers has 6,148 member firms, with 29,235 branch offices. These firms have altogether 438,701 registered representatives. The number of support staff is unknown, but total employment can be estimated at approximately 530,000. However, there is some double-counting between this and the earlier figure of 641,000. A loose estimate of 1 million jobs related to securities markets sounds realistic.

---

[29]There are various economic models of investment behavior, including the neoclassical model, James Tobin's "q theory of investment," the internal cash flow model, etc. The role of securities markets is explained somewhat differently in each model. For an econometric evaluation of these models, see Richard W. Kopcke, "The Determinants of Investment Spending," *New England Economic Review*, Federal Reserve Bank of Boston. July/August 1985, pp. 19-35.

[30]There are several theoretical explanations of how individuals decide when to consume and when to save. The "permanent income" model developed by Milton Friedman says that consumption decisions depend on the level of income expected over long periods of time, so that temporary fluctuations in income—e.g., loss of employment, or the fear of it—have only marginal effects on decisions to save or not save. The lifecycle model developed by Modigliani, Brumberg, and Ando says that people attempt to stabilize consumption over their lifetime, including retirement, so that they tend to be net borrowers in early adulthood, net savers during the later working years, and "dissavers" or net consumers during retirement. Other theories emphasize the effects of inflation-adjusted rates of return on savings and changes in government or business-sector savings rates.

[31]Annual average personal savings declined by half from 1981 to 1989. This is about one-third the average for other industrialized nations.

[32]Robert Kuttner, *The Economic Illusion: False Choices Between Prosperity and Social Justice* (Boston, MA: Houghton Mifflin, 1984).

[33]See for example, Martin Felstein, "Social Security, Induced Retirement and Aggregate Capital Accumulation," *Journal of Political Economy* 82, September/October 1974, pp. 905-926; Lawrence Summers and Chris Carroll, "Why Is U.S. National Saving So Low," *Brookings Papers on Economic Activity*, 1987: pp. 607-635; Gregory V. Jump, "Interest Rates, Inflation Expectations, and Spurious Elements in Measured Real Income and Saving," *American Economic Review* 70, December 1980, pp. 990-1004.

[34]Data from the Securities Industries Association, by telephone and published in *Trends*, December 1989.

There are 362 firms of futures commission merchants. They include (as of Jan. 31, 1990) 37,240 "Associated Persons"; 13,638 principals (who are not themselves registered to sell); and 24,184 "introducing brokers," commodity trading advisers, and commodity pool operators. There are also 7,470 futures floor brokers. This is 82,532 jobs—with support staff, total employment might be estimated as 100,000.

These estimates indicate that employment in securities and futures markets accounts for, at most, one-tenth of one percent of U.S. employment. The majority of these jobs are probably concentrated in New York and Chicago; only in those cities would they have a perceptible effect on the local economy.

THE INVESTORS

Institutional Investors

Institutional investors now are the dominant users of U.S. financial markets in terms of trading on exchanges, ownership of equity ownership, and total assets invested in equities. Their assets grew from $2.1 trillion in 1981 to $5.2 trillion in 1988.[35] (See table 2-1.) This amounts to a 14 percent compound annual growth rate for the period. The New York Stock Exchange (NYSE) says that about 10,000 institutions, representing 150 million Americans, use its services.[36]

Corporate pension funds managed more than $1 trillion in 1988; public (governmental) pension funds held more than $600 billion and were growing faster than corporate plans. The 500 largest corporate pension plans together had over $640.2 billion invested in securities in 1988. The four largest—General Motors, AT&T, General Electric, and IBM—each have assets of more than $26 billion. There are also very large public pension funds, e.g., New York City Employees Retirement Fund has over $30 billion and California's employee fund had over $50 billion invested in 1988.[37]

Table 2-1—Institutional Investors

Category	Total assets ($, end 1988)	Percent of assets[a]	% average annual growth (1981-88)
Pension funds	2,240	43.0	14.3
Insurance companies ...	1,259	24.0	12.3
Investment companies ..	816	15.5	18.5
Bank trusts	775	15.0	12.7
Foundations & other	133	2.5	13.2
Total	5,223	100.0	

[a]Percentage of all institutional investment holdings.
SOURCE: Columbia Institutional Investment Project, Columbia University, Center for Law and Economic Studies.

U.S. insurance companies also manage over $1 trillion in securities investments.[38] Historically, stocks were only a small part of insurance company assets, for reasons rooted both in the industry's investment philosophy and in laws regulating the industry.[39] State laws now commonly allow some investment in stocks, often requiring them to be maintained in a separate account.

In the last few decades, mutual funds became popular. A mutual fund, often set up by a financial management services company to invest in securities, might have growth, income, or other objectives. It might focus on securities that are either all or mostly domestic, foreign, or international. Customers, including many small investors, buy shares of the funds, and share in the funds' profits or losses. Mutual funds' assets grew at a rate of nearly 27 percent per year from 1975 to 1987, when for a time after the market crash of 1987 the industry had net redemptions. Historical ownership patterns suggest that institutional investing has broadened the base of participation in markets. (See table 2-2.) By 1989, the total number of mutual fund accounts, including money market funds, was 36 million. Their total value by April 1990 had grown to $1 trillion ($554 billion of which was in stock, bond, and income mutual funds).[40]

[35]Carolyn Kay Brancato and Patrick A. Gaughan, *The Growth of Institutional Investors in U.S. Capital Markets: 1981-1987*, The Institutional Investor Project, Columbia University School of Law, New York City, November 1988, and *The Growth of Institutional Investors, Updated Data: 1981-1988*, Jan. 12, 1990.

[36]NYSE *Annual Report*, 1989, p. 16. These data, however, appear to come from a 1985 NYSE survey of investors.

[37]"1989 Pensions Directory," *Institutional Investor Magazine*, January 1989, p. 131.

[38]Information from the American Council of Life Insurance, courtesy of Paul Reardon.

[39]In the 19th century, common stock was regarded as a speculative investment and avoided by insurance funds. Often this avoidance was written into law. For example, until 1951 life insurance companies operating in New York State were prohibited from investing in common stock.

[40]Data from the Investment Company Institute, June 1990.

Table 2-2—Volume of Stock Trading on the NYSE[a]

Year	Institute	Retail	Member firms
1969	42.4%	33.4%	24.2%
1980	47.4	25.7	26.9
1988	54.6	18.2	26.2

[a]These SIA estimates were revised in 1990 to adjust for NYSE-provided data on the contribution of program trading to the volume of trading by institutions.

SOURCE: Securities Industry Association, *Trends*, Mar. 16, 1989.

Institutional ownership of NYSE-listed stocks has increased from 13 percent in 1949 to nearly 50 percent. Institutional funds do about 55 percent of all NYSE trades; another 26 percent are done by exchange member firms for their own accounts; and only 18 percent are done for individuals.[41] (See table 2-2.) According to the Securities Industry Association, less than 50 percent of institutional trades are in blocks smaller than 900 shares. Institutions own about 39 percent of the stocks listed on NASDAQ.[42] They also dominate the market for privately placed corporate securities.

Individual Investors

Individual investors now own just over 50 percent of American equity and account for less than one-fifth of all trading. Over half the population owns some type of equity investment, although for most it is through participation in institutional investments, such as mutual, pension, and insurance funds. Direct ownership is concentrated among a relatively small proportion of investors. The United States, nevertheless, has the highest level of individual participation in the securities markets of any country in the world. Less than 25 percent of British citizens hold stock investments.[43]

In 1985, the NYSE conducted its 11th survey of Americans who own stock in public corporations.[44] (The NYSE has not published more recent data and uses this data in its annual reports and Fact Books through 1989.) The number of respondents who only owned mutual funds increased from 4.5 million (10.8 percent) in 1983 to 8.0 million (17.1 percent) in 1985.

Figure 2-1—Mutual Funds Net Capital Flows

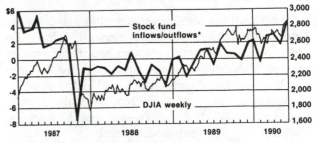

Investors yanked money out of stock mutual funds after the October 1987 market crash. But with the DJIA hitting record highs before the market drop in mid-1990, money began once again pouring in; monthly, in billions (left scale) v. the DJIA, weekly close (right scale).

*New stock fund sales less redemptions, plus the net effect of switches within the same fund family between stock funds and other mutual funds.

SOURCE: Investment Company Institute.

It is commonly said that individual investors are "leaving the market" because they have been net sellers for 5 years and their holdings are decreasing. The number of Americans owning stock actually increased at least until 1985, growing from 42 million to 47 million in the preceding 5 years.[45] However, nearly all of the increase was in ownership of shares of mutual funds. (See figure 2-1.) The number of Americans directly owning stock has almost certainly decreased since 1985, although the numbers are hard to pin down. In 1969, shares of common stock represented 36 percent of personal financial assets, but by 1979, that figure dropped to 25 percent, and to about 20 percent by 1989. Individual shareholders' median income was $36,800 in 1985, a 5.3 percent annual increase over 1983.[46] The median size of their stock portfolios increased from $5,000 to $6,200 in that same period.

Income and investment patterns suggest that individual investors can be grouped into three sets. The first includes people who have less than $5,100 directly invested in the stock market. This is about 45 percent of all individual investors. Approximately 35 percent of individual investors had portfolios of between $5,000 to $25,000. These are the traditional small investors. Approximately 20

---

[41]In contrast, about 55 to 60 percent of the volume of trading of NASDAQ stock is attributed to individuals, according to NASD officials.

[42]Information provided by the National Association of Securities Dealers.

[43]North American Securities Administrators Association, Inc.

[44]New York Stock Exchange, *Shareownership*, 1985.

[45]Ibid.

[46]The U.S. median income, in comparison, increased from $20,200 to $22,400 during the same time, a 5.5 percent annual increase.

percent of individual investors had portfolios in excess of $25,000. (See table 2-3.)

The 37 million small investors, although probably better off than the "average American," clearly do not depend on securities markets profits for a major part of household income, and probably do little trading. The other 20 percent of individual investors—9 million people whose average portfolio is estimated at $78,000 to $94,000—are wealthier Americans who may trade more frequently.[47]

Table 2-4 shows the historical pattern of ownership of equity in the population.

BROKERS

The Industry

Major changes have occurred in the operations and structure of the brokerage industry during the past few decades; contributing factors were the paper-work crisis of the late 1960s, the unfixing of commission rates in 1975, the departure of many retail investors from direct investments in common stock, the increasing dominance of institutional investors, and more attractive returns for brokerage firms from "risk-based" businesses. This has resulted in floundering and uncertainty for many brokerage firms. Other changes include cyclical impacts on the industry's employment and profit levels and increased concentration in the industry. The long-term effects on small investors have not all been beneficial.

The "back office" overload of the late 1960s accelerated the introduction of computers into brokerage firms. Since then, computers have increasingly permeated most of their operations, from

Table 2-3—Size of Individual Portfolios, 1985

Percent of individual portfolios	Number of investors (millions)	Portfolio ($ value)
45	21.1	less than 5,000
35	16.5	5,000 to 25,000
20	9.4	over 25,000

SOURCE: Data from New York Stock Exchange, *Share Ownership, 1985.*

recordkeeping to order entry, transaction confirmation, client report preparation, client account analysis, and clearing and settlement.

Competition for commission rates led to substantial rate reductions for institutional customers and kept rates on small orders from rising. Between 1970 and 1989, for example, commissions on institutional investors' transactions dropped from 26 cents to between 4 and 7 cents per share.[48] Pension funds, which in mid-1985 paid little attention to transaction costs, now look hard at ways to reduce them.[49] Based on a survey conducted by the *Institutional Investor* in 1989, 99 percent of responding pension plan sponsors monitored their commission costs, 50 percent monitored soft-dollar[50] usage, 45 percent monitored market price impact, and almost half reported that they have cost-cutting programs or are planning to start them.[51]

In spite of the growth of stock trading volume, commission revenues in the brokerage industry have declined as a proportion of total revenue.[52] Institutional and retail trading volume both have fallen below record peaks in 1987.[53] The combined effect of this trend (and the rapid growth of other businesses), is that commissions from equities transactions have declined from over 60 percent of all revenues in 1965 to under 17 percent in the first half

---

[47]The U.S. public equity markets have a capitalization of about $2.5 trillion. Conservatively estimating that one-half of this is owned by 47 million individuals ($1.25 trillion), then the *average* stock portfolio is $27,000. Yet, 45 percent of stock portfolios are $5,000 or less. Assume that these $5,000 accounts collectively amount to between $59 billion and $106 billion of stock owned by individuals. Stock owners with portfolios of $5,000 to $25,000 account for an additional $247 to $411 billion of individual stock ownership. Therefore, the remaining 10 million (one-fifth of 47 million) investors has between $733 billion and $944 billion of the $1,250 billion of equity owned by individuals, or an average portfolio of $78,000 to $94,000.

[48]About 70 percent of pension plan sponsors responding to a survey reported that their commission costs were between 4 and 7 cents per share. "The Drive To Cut Transaction Costs," *Institutional Investor*, May 1989, pp. 125-126.

[49]Ibid. Transaction costs consist of commissions, market impact, portfolio turnover, futures trading costs, and soft-dollar usage.

[50]Soft dollars is a means of paying brokerage firms for their services through commission revenue, rather than through direct payments, or hard dollar fees. For example, a mutual fund may offer to pay for the research of a brokerage firm by executing trades generated by that research through the brokerage firm. The brokerage firm may agree to this arrangement if the fund manager promises to spend at least $100,000 in commissions with the broker that year.

[51]*Institutional Investor*, op. cit., footnote 48.

[52]Brokers' large transactions—more than 50 percent were from using risk and index arbitrage—receive few commissions per share relative to smaller transactions.

[53]Trading averaged 189 million shares per day in 1987, a record year for the New York Stock Exchange, and 165 million shares in 1989. *NYSE 1990 Fact Book*, p. 80. Trading averaged 156 million shares per day by mid-June 1990, according to the NYSE.

Table 2-4—Individual Equity Investment

Year	Number of equity owners	Percentage of population	Owned mutual funds only	Percentage of equity owners
1956	8,630,000	5.20	935,000	10.83
1962	17,010,000	9.20	2,165,000	12.73
1970	30,850,000	15.10	3,977,000	12.89
1980	30,200,000	13.50	2,231,000	7.39
1985	47,040,000	20.10	6,219,000	13.22

SOURCE: New York Stock Exchange Shareholder Surveys.

of 1989.[54] (See figure 2-2.) The trend also has affected large, full, service brokers. At Merrill Lynch, for example, commissions were about 53 percent of total revenues in 1972, while by 1988 they had fallen to 15 percent.[55] The securities industry also has undergone considerable concentration. In 1973 the top 10 industry firms accounted for 33 percent of the industry's share of capital. By September 1989 their share had increased to 61 percent.

Even though cyclical trends, e.g., large-scale swings of employment and profits, are not uncommon in the industry,[56] capital increased fivefold from 1980 to midyear 1989 from $7 billion to $39 billion.[57] Another key long-term trend is diversification through financing principal transactions, many of which have become large revenue earners. (See figure 2-3.) These include proprietary trading, merchant banking, bridge loans, sole-managed underwritings, and participation in ownership of commercial enterprises. These are areas in which the industry is risking its own capital, in contrast with its historical tendency to provide services for clients' fees. Risk-based revenues in the securities industry accounted for 64 percent of all revenue in 1989 v. 42 percent in 1980.[58]

A Tiered Client Structure

Some brokerage firms have begun to treat all but their largest institutional clients like "retail" cus-

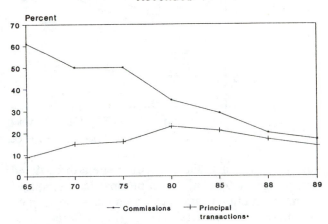

Figure 2-2—Share of Domestic Broker-Dealer Revenues

Percent

— Commissions   —+— Principal transactions*

*Principal transactions are revenues from trading and investments.

SOURCE: Securities Industry Association, *Trends, An Analysis of Emerging Trends in the Securities Industry*, vol. XV, No. 4, May 30, 1989, p. 9, updated by SIA, July 1990.

tomers. One firm found that 150 of its clients were contributing 90 percent of its revenue, while the remaining approximately 700 institutions contributed about 10 percent. Only the 150 largest institutional clients now get lower commissions, access to the firm's research, and direct access to its analysts. Another firm has similar plans; these disadvantage clients whose accounts generate less than $60,000 in commissions per year.[59] Medium-sized institutions and large retail clients, however, still receive better service than do small retail clients. If this trend

---

[54]Securities Industry Association, *Trends*, Dec. 29, 1989, vol. XV, No. 7, pp. 7-8.

[55]Data from Merrill Lynch's 1972 and 1988 annual reports.

[56]For example, at least 35,000 jobs in the industry have been cut in the 2 years following the October 1987 stock market crash, although total employment grew by 62 percent from the end of 1980 to the third-quarter of 1989. Securities Industry Association, *Trends*, vol. XV, No. 7, Dec. 29, 1989, p. 3. At least another 10,000 jobs may be cut in New York during 1990 alone. "Wall Street's Mediocre Managers Again Lurch From Binge to Bust," *Wall Street Journal*, Feb. 1, 1990, p. C1.

[57]See SIA, *Trends*, op. cit., footnote 56, p. 3.

[58]SIA, *Trends*, Oct. 20, 1989, p. 1.

[59]"PaineWebber Puts Squeeze on Clients That Don't Trade," *Wall Street Journal*, Jan. 11, 1990, p. C 1. Shearson, Lehman, Hutton, for example, offers "preferred client" status to customers based on assets in their accounts of at least $200,000 and account activity which generates $1,000 in annual commissions. Shearson, Lehman, Hutton, *The FMA Journal*, Apr. 2, 1990.

Figure 2-3—Securities Industry Main Revenue Sources

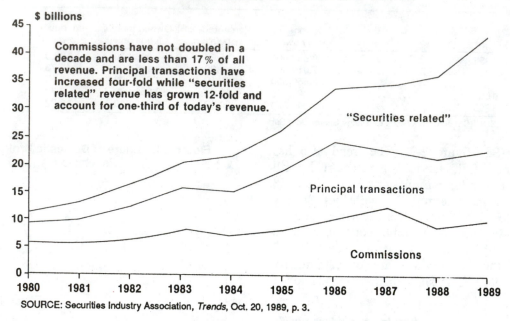

$ billions

Commissions have not doubled in a decade and are less than 17% of all revenue. Principal transactions have increased four-fold while "securities related" revenue has grown 12-fold and account for one-third of today's revenue.

"Securities related"

Principal transactions

Commissions

SOURCE: Securities Industry Association, *Trends*, Oct. 20, 1989, p. 3.

becomes industry-wide, it will create a three-tiered brokerage system, with institutional investors, medium institutional and large retail customers, and small retail customers each paying different rates and receiving different services by full-service brokers. The emergence of the discount brokerage industry represents still another level of treatment. This could mean higher costs and fewer services for small investors from major brokerage firms.

Stockbrokers in the past were generally paid commissions based on sales volume. They were motivated to encourage clients to buy and sell securities and, later, an expanding array of other products. Commissions are higher for sales of a firm's proprietary products. Stockbrokers typically had some measure of independence. For example, they might or might not recommend to clients the same stocks or other products that their employers recommended. The key factor that distinguished stockbrokers from most other sales workers was their personal relationship to clients. If a stockbroker became a trusted adviser to clients, those clients often could be lured away when the stockbroker changed employers. These relationships made possi-

ble frequent job changes to other brokerage firms. One of the effects of the introduction of brokerage firms' proprietary products—mutual funds, real estate limited partnerships, and cash management accounts—was to strengthen the relationship between the client and firm, while weakening the stockbroker-client relationship.[60]

By the mid-1980s, computer terminals and workstations had become commonplace for most brokers. They are valuable for keeping track of customer accounts and providing rapid access to securities prices and other market news. Computerization also made it easier for employers to audit stockbrokers' performance and productivity.[61] New software made it possible for brokerage firms to standardize certain customer services. Many firms broadened the scope of their brokerage business to add personalized financial consulting, relating their clients' broader financial interests to financial securities, real estate, annuities, college and retirement planning, mutual funds, and life insurance investments, some of which were proprietary. Some of these products are particularly profitable for the firm, because they generate underwriting fees and commissions in addition to

---

[60]Garson, Barbara, "The Electronic Sweatshop" (New York, NY: Simon & Schuster, 1988), Ch. 5, *The Wall Street Broker: Decline of a Salesman*, p. 128.

[61]Ibid.

annual management fees.[62] There is a conflict of interest between selling those products that generate the highest commissions and helping clients find the investments best suited to their needs.

The terms "registered representative" and "stockbroker" were replaced by "Account Executive," which, in turn, was largely replaced with "Financial Consultant" (FC). FCs increasingly are being encouraged to use their employer's specialized software packages to enter data on clients and to analyze clients' needs for products offered by the brokerage firm. This leads to standardized recommendations to clients and a closer relationship between the firm and the client; proprietary products may be difficult to transfer to another brokerage firm. There is also a trend toward replacing FCs with lower paid employees, sometimes salaried, who are less well-trained and even less independent than brokers.[63]

Many midsize investors who need professional help in managing their assets are unwilling to be dependent solely on FCs. They may manage substantial amounts of funds (typically between $100,000 and $10 million, representing perhaps a family's assets or a small business' pension fund)—yet the amount may not be sufficiently large to qualify for the management services of a large investment house that manages only bigger portfolios. Brokerage firms began to bring these clients together with outside portfolio managers, who make investment decisions for the client for a fee.[64] The brokerage firm executes transactions, arranges depository services and keeps records of transactions, and provides independent reports on the performance of the manager. For this the brokerage firm receives a separate fee. This has become one of the fastest growing parts of the investment business. Competitive commission rates have facilitated the unbundling of investment advice and brokerage.

For large investors, the long-term collective effects of these changes in the brokerage industry are probably positive. They may be less so for midsized investors. The small investor benefits from the larger range of products available, the greater competitiveness of the industry, and the availability of discount brokers.[65] In other ways, however, the small investor may become worse off because some brokerage houses may not give their interests high priority due to the difficulty of profiting from small transactions. Moreover, the competitive economic forces unleashed by the unfixing of commission rates and the unbundling of services mean that services for small investors may be becoming less subsidized by large investors.

Some FCs say[66] that their office managers no longer inquire about how well they are serving the firm's clients, but instead use computer printouts to monitor the commission revenues each FC has generated on a daily basis.

These trends indicate an ongoing restructuring in the brokerage industry with greater concentration, realignment of business focus away from retail sales, continued pressure on floor brokers for lower commissions, and different treatment of investors according to the commissions generated. For small investors the question arises: where may they get good advice and how much will it cost?

---

[62]Some products, such as some closed-end funds of stocks or bonds, are sometimes offered to clients at "no commission," which is misleading. When the brokerage firm is one of the lead underwriters, the broker may receive between 4 and 5 percent of the amount of these sales.

[63]Garson, op. cit., footnote 60, pp. 145-154.

[64]The annual fee either is a fixed ("wrap") fee or variable percentage of the total value of the client's portfolio, e.g., 2 percent of the first $30,000, 1.8 percent of the next $20,000, and 1.5 percent of the amount exceeding $50,000. Fees vary among portfolio managers.

[65]The discount brokerage industry also has been undergoing concentration. Some estimates are that the number of independent discounters has shrunk by as much as 25 percent since 1983 to about 100 by early 1990, and is still shrinking as the industry remains competitive. One comparison of commissions notes that full-service brokers' commissions may be about two to three times or more as much as those of the big three discounters, and even greater than deep-discount brokerages. One discount broker recently announced a three-tier commission structure for traders ranging from 2 cents per share to 5 cents per share, depending on their trading volume. "Now Fewer Firms Are Chasing Small Investors," The New York Times, June 17, 1990, sec. 3, p. 10.

[66]OTA interviews.

Article 2

How Technology Is Transforming Securities Markets

In the early 19th century, delivery of a message (or a market quote) from New Orleans to New York took from 4 to 7 days. The telegraph was first demonstrated in 1844. By January 27, 1846, telegraphic communication linked New York and Philadelphia, via Newark. Until direct lines were installed a few months later, messengers ran between the telegraph office and Wall Street. It was 2 years more before the New York and New Orleans foreign exchange markets could directly communicate, but then message time was nearly instantaneous.[1] Financial markets were quick to realize the possibilities. The New York Herald of March 3, 1846, mentioned that "certain parties in New York and Philadelphia were employing the telegraph for speculating in stocks." The use of the telegraph greatly reduced price differences between the participating markets.

A successful trans-Atlantic cable was completed on July 27, 1866. Four days later the New York Evening Post published price quotations from the London exchange. The first cable transfers occurred about 1870 and arbitrage between the London and New York exchanges began immediately. This led to further reductions in price differences between markets.

The third invention that revolutionized the exchanges was the stock ticker, introduced in 1867. Before that, reports of transactions were recorded by "pad shovers"—boys who ran between the trading floor and the brokers' offices with messages. Several ticker companies had men on the trading floor to type results directly into the ticker machine. These reports went to the ticker companies' headquarters and were retyped to activate indicator wheels at local tickers, which then printed the results on paper tape.

In 1878, the telephone, successfully tested 2 years earlier by inventor Alexander Graham Bell, reached Wall Street. Until then, a messenger carrying a customer's order could take 15 minutes to get to the floor; with the telephone, it took 60 seconds. By 1880, most brokers had telephones linked directly to trading floors, and in the next few years, telephones were installed by the thousands. Finally, in 1882, the Edison Electric Illuminating Co. gave Wall Street electric lights.[2]

By 1880 there were over a thousand tickers in the offices of New York banks and brokers. In 1885, the New York Stock Exchange (NYSE) began to assemble the information for ticker company reporters to ensure consistency. The New York Quotation Co. was created by NYSE members in 1890 to consolidate existing ticker companies and integrate the information distribution. This did not eliminate "bucket shops," where the ticker tape output was rigged to swindle investors.

TWENTIETH CENTURY MARKET TECHNOLOGY

Trading Support Systems

Fully electronic transmission and storage of trading information began in the 1960s. Quotation devices were first attached to ticker circuits to provide bid and ask quotations and prices. An improved stock ticker was introduced in 1964 that could print 900 characters per minute and report transactions without delay up to 10 million shares per day. The pneumatic tube carried information to the ticker and quotation system, until it was replaced with computer-readable cards in 1966. Reporters on the floor recorded the transaction on a card and put it into an optical scanner. The scanner read the information into a computer where it entered the ticker system. At about this time the Central Certificate Service was created as an exchange subsidiary, to computerize the transfer of security ownership and reduce the movement of paper. In 1973, this became the Depository Trust Company. The computer display of dealers' bids and offers, described in chapter 3 and called NASDAQ (National Association of Securities Dealers Automated Quotations), began to operate in 1971.

Despite these technologies, the securities industry had a severe back-office paper-work crisis during

---

[1]Kenneth D. Garbade and William L. Silber, "Technology, Communication, and the Performance of Financial Markets," *The Journal of Finance*, vol. XXXIII, No. 3, June 1978, pp. 819-832.

[2]Deborah S. Gardner, "Marketplace: A Brief History of the New York Stock Exchange," for The New York Stock Exchange, Office of the Secretary, 1982.

the 1960s. Brokerage houses could not keep up with paper-work for the high transaction volume. Finally, in April of 1968, the crisis forced trading hours to be curtailed so that the back-offices could catch up. This led to development of automated systems for back-office processing. In 1972 the Securities Industry Automation Corp. (SIAC) was established by the NYSE and the American Stock Exchange (AMEX) to coordinate the development of their data processing.

Three systems were introduced by SIAC during the 1970s: the Market Data System (MDS), the Designated Order Turnaround System (DOT) and the Common Message Switch (CMS). The MDS, originally introduced in 1964, was improved in the 70s to process last-sale information. DOT, introduced in 1973, automated the delivery of small orders (fewer than 199 shares) from member-firm offices to exchange floors. The CMS let member firms communicate with the other SIAC systems.

Since the 1970s these trading support systems have been improved in speed, accuracy, and efficiency. Regional exchanges have developed comparable systems. In many cases the regional exchanges led the way—e.g., in continuous net settlement (the Pacific Stock Exchange) and bookkeeping systems (the Midwest Stock Exchange). As early as 1969, the Pacific Stock Exchange (PSE) automated some trade execution. This meant that unless halted by the specialist, a trade was completed by a computer without human intervention. This first-of-its-kind system was called COMEX.

In 1979 the PSE introduced an improved version of COMEX, called the Securities Communication Order Routing and Execution (SCOREX). When an order reaches the SCOREX system, the current Intermarket Trading System (ITS) price is determined, and the order and price are displayed at the appropriate PSE specialist post. The specialist has 15 seconds to better the price for market orders, before the order is automatically executed by the computer, at the ITS price, for the specialist's account. For a limit order, the specialist also has 15 seconds to accept, reject or hold the order in his electronic book. If the order is rejected, it is routed back to the member-firm. Otherwise, when the

order's designated price coincides with an ITS bid or offer, the specialist executes the order.

Most stock exchanges now have small order execution systems similar in function to SCOREX. There are also systems for small orders in options contracts, and in NASDAQ for small orders of over-the-counter stocks. These electronic small order execution systems were introduced with relative ease despite the reduction in the services of the "two-dollar broker,"[3] but electronic systems for executing larger orders threaten the livelihood of more powerful professionals on the exchange floor, and thus are controversial.

Technology may reshape the entire exchange structure. The Cincinnati Stock Exchange and the London International Stock Exchange (ISE) do not use physical trading floors but operate through computer rooms. The ISE and NASDAQ combine screen-based quotation systems with telephone negotiation. Exchanges in Toronto, Madrid, Brussels, Copenhagen, Zurich, and Frankfurt are also essentially "floorless." For the time being, most U.S. exchanges have chosen to maintain their automatic trading support systems at a level that preserves the roles of specialists, floor brokers, and other intermediaries. Enhancements now usually mean faster computers or new devices that work around the traditional trading infrastructure and established participants.

Market Surveillance Systems

Today's financial environment has increased securities markets' vulnerability to illegal activity, even as today's technology has increased the ability to monitor markets. The magnitude and frequency of mergers and acquisitions and other major corporate transactions, and the allure of staggering profits increase the market's susceptibility to insider trading. The addition of new derivative products and new players around the globe further complicates surveillance.

Manual processes for detecting illegal activity are no longer adequate. People are not fast enough to inspect and evaluate the enormous volumes of information. Computers can improve detection of some kinds of illegal activity. They are less effective against the illegalities that occur in the least auto-

---

[3]"The Two-dollar broker" or "Broker's broker" executes overflow trades for other floor brokers too busy to execute them personally. These free agents were once paid $2 for every round lot executed, thus the name.

mated trading arenas—the Chicago trading pits—and insider trading in securities markets. For example, to detect insider trading, exchanges must obtain information from broker/dealers (as well as from the Securities and Exchange Commission (SEC)).[4] Some of them are not yet able to transmit trade data automatically, and paper-based data are difficult to work with.[5]

Surveillance in Self Regulatory Organizations (SROs) (i.e., exchanges, NASD) follows three general steps. First, the SROs monitor market data using computerized systems, to detect unusual price and/or volume fluctuations. Second, when an unusual trading pattern is detected, the SRO's staff conducts analyses to determine the probable cause of the fluctuation. If a satisfactory answer is not found, the staff conducts further investigations, using automated systems and analytical tools.[6] SROs maintain large computer databases of historical information about trades, personal background of traders, news, and past case materials, to identify, compare, and probe suspicious trends.

Market surveillance may be further improved by several emerging technologies, including expert systems (computer programs that incorporate the decision rules and judgment criteria of many human experts). The thrust has been to build systems and databases with great analytical power, to enable market analysts to sift through large amounts of data. If an expert system can give the analyst an advanced starting point in an investigation, the rest of the job can be done faster and more effectively.

Personal computers and ''intelligent'' workstations are replacing dumb terminals in market surveillance. Although interactive computing requires greater technical expertise, such as a database query language, it also enables analysts to retrieve information faster and integrate applications more effectively. Data feeds and programs from many sources can be combined locally, and better analytical tools can be applied to real-time market information. The emerging trends in software and hardware are entwined. The ability to manipulate data locally is also important for the development of expert systems for recognizing trends and abnormalities in market surveillance.[7] Until recently, market surveillance systems lagged behind the technology for trading support. Now computers offer critical tools such as expert systems, artificial intelligence, voice response, and complex relational databases for further improving market surveillance.

Clearing and Settlement Systems

Clearing and settlement (ch. 6) is the process whereby ownership of a security or options contract is transferred from the seller to the buyer and payment is made. The participants in this process are the principals to the trade (investors or broker/dealers and banks), the market places, clearing organizations, and settlement organizations. In the case of futures, the clearing and settlement process also involves the posting of margin by both the buyer (long) and the seller (short) to the accounts of the clearinghouse.

Banks transfer funds from the buyer to the seller. The 12 Federal Reserve Banks, their 24 branches, the Federal Reserve Board in Washington, D.C., the U.S. Treasury offices in Washington, D.C., and the Chicago and Washington, D.C., offices of the Commodity Credit Corporation are all connected by the Fedwire, a high-speed, computerized communications network over which banks transfer reserve balances from one to another for immediately available credit. The depositories and registrars are involved in the transfer of ownership. Depositories register all securities in the name of the depository as nominee and then transfer ownership via book-entry. Transfer agents physically transfer ownership by creating new registered certificates.

---

[4]The SEC has also applied automation to its task of financial filings and registration. The Electronic Data Gathering Analysis and Retrieval system (EDGAR) is designed to receive and display financial filings. When the project is completed it is expected that over 11,000 publicly traded companies and 2,700 investment firms will submit their required filings and disclosures electronically.

[5]As of August 1989, 373 broker-dealers were submitting automated data to the New York Stock Exchange, according to exchange officials, August 1989.

[6]For example, they may monitor the covariance between securities to capture their price interrelationship and hypothesize the correct price probability distribution for the securities. The parameters are set by computers using a moving average algorithm or standard deviation to determine the ''acceptable'' ranges of price movement and volume activity. When these limits are violated the staff is alerted by the computer to investigate unusual activity.

[7]In general, an expert system is a computer program that attempts to replicate, to some degree, human logic and decision processes. The long range benefits of using such systems are many, including better utilization of professional time, cost savings and improved quality and consistency of decision making.

Participants are linked by paper, tape, electronic systems, and direct computer-to-computer links. For example, the Options Clearing Corp. (OCC) in Chicago receives taped data from nine exchanges,[8] and has some direct computer-to-computer linkage with them. OCC also has electronic feeds to market data vendors. Communication with banks is via paper and facsimile, and with regulators it is through paper transactions. Clearing members are linked by dial-up capabilities, leased lines, microfiche, tape, and paper media. Clearing corporations communicate with OCC with magnetic tape transfer as well as some direct computer-to-computer linkage. The Depository Trust Co., the Midwest Securities Trust Co. and the Philadelphia Depository Trust Co. are all linked to the OCC via direct computer-to-computer connection.

Since 1982, trade volume has surged. Critical problems can occur in trade matching when heavy volume, manual entry, and tight time constraints combine to strain the system. Continuous net settlement (CNS)[9] and electronic book-entry systems have allowed the processing of these high transaction volumes, as have faster, higher capacity mainframe computers. The critical element in handling rising trade volume on a sustained basis, however, is the first step in processing the trade, i.e., the trade entry or trade capture component. Manual trade entry processes are prone to error and result in a disproportionately high rate of unmatched trades as trade volume rises.

The development, operational and maintenance costs of automation have risen over the past two decades. Rapid technological obsolescence in management information systems and technical infrastructures implies high reengineering costs. Regulatory rules often influence or even dictate specific technologies that must be used. In many cases such rules have had a positive impact. For example, NYSE Rule 386 requires all members to use the Depository Trust Co's. automated Institutional Delivery system or its equivalent. The Municipal Securities Rule-making Board's rules G12 and G15 require municipal bond clearinghouse members to use a municipal bond comparison system. The rules go so far as to define the output specifications for the system.

On the other hand, there are also regulatory, legislative, and political factors that inhibit automation. These include domestic disputes over regulatory jurisdiction, resistance to change, tradition, and customs; and overseas, legislation prohibiting dissemination of some data.

In hopes of achieving a competitive edge, firms are evaluating new relational database management systems and communication systems of copper, fiber-optics, and microwave. Communications networks such as LANs (local area networks), hypernets, and shared terminal networks will also be increasingly used in clearance and settlement. Higher density storage media will be needed to accommodate anticipated increases in on-line storage requirements. As an alternative to the direct access storage devices in use today, optical disk storage technology may have greater use. Optical disk is also an effective data distribution medium; for example, Lotus sells a service providing historical price information on securities on CD for use with the Lotus 1-2-3 spreadsheet. Today's systems are being designed with several levels of backup, fault-tolerant redundant hardware, and data storage backup.

INFORMATION SERVICES VENDORS

As early as 1850 Paul Julius Reuter first used carrier pigeons to fly stock market quotations between Brussels and Aachen, Germany. One year later, an underwater telegraph cable opened between Dover and Calais. Reuter then began delivering news and market quotes from London to Continental Europe. Reuters is, 150 years later, still one of the dominant market information services vendors.

The market for financial information can be broadly divided into three categories—news, data on exchange-traded instruments, and data on over-the-counter instruments. The market structure is different for each of these.

---

[8]The PHLX, PSE, NASD, PBOT, ACC, NYFE, CBOE, AMEX and NYSE. The PBOT is the Philadelphia Board of Trade, the ACC is the AMEX Commodities Corp. and the NYFE is the New York Futures Exchange.

[9]CNS was developed by the Pacific Stock Exchange in the late 1960s and is much more effective than settling on a trade-for-trade basis, which is probably not viable with today's volumes.

Financial News

Financial news may be gathered by information vendors themselves, or they may carry reports from leading news organizations. Dow Jones & Co. Inc., is the leading provider of financial news in the United States. Dow Jones has tried to extend its dominant position in equities news to the fixed-income bond market through the Dow Jones Capital Markets Report, but in-depth news is not as essential for the bond trader as it is for the stock trader.

Reuters has an edge over Dow Jones in news that affects foreign exchange and fixed-income prices because of its vast international communications network. Reuters is also a strong competitor in delivering news about U.S. commodity markets, but Knight-Ridder is a major presence in this market through its Commodity News Service, and has also made headway in supplying news concerning financial futures and underlying cash markets. Other providers of online financial news include the Associated Press, McGraw-Hill Inc., Financial News Network, and Market News Service.

Stock Quotations

Five companies dominate the market for securities and futures quotations in the United States—Reuters Holdings PLC, Quotron Systems Inc., Automatic Data Processing Inc. (ADP), Telerate Inc. (now owned by Dow Jones), and Knight-Ridder Inc. These five companies had a total of approximately 426,000 terminals worldwide as of February 1989.[10] For most stocks, all commodity and financial futures, and all options, the market data—bids, offers, last-sale prices, and volume information—are generated by exchanges and the over-the-counter market and delivered to vendors. In foreign exchange and fixed-income markets, where there is no central exchange, price information is contributed by banks and securities firms to vendors.

Quotron Systems Inc. has long dominated the market for U.S. stock quotations, but this market is now in ferment.[11] ADP is a strong competitor. Outside the United States, the leading position is held by Reuters, which recently entered the U.S. market for stock prices. In the past, Reuters supplied quotes and news for foreign exchange, money market instruments, and commodities in this country, but not equities.

The internationalization of the securities markets has prompted foreign vendors such as Reuters and Telekurs of Switzerland to enter the U.S. market, while American companies such as Quotron and ADP have been expanding their operations overseas. The growing links between the equities, futures, fixed-income and foreign exchange markets have also led to diversification among vendors who traditionally specialized in one market. Telerate Inc., which holds a near monopoly in the market for U.S. government securities prices, has entered the equities market through acquisition of CMQ Communications Inc., the leading stock quote provider in Canada. It remains to be seen whether Reuters and Telerate can replace Quotron and ADP, or will merely add equities quotes to their existing terminal base. There are about 200,000 terminals receiving real-time prices from U.S. stock exchanges, and some industry observers are skeptical that the pie will become bigger with the entrance of new players.

Nevertheless, the relative ease of acquiring and distributing prices for exchange-traded instruments has attracted several new competitors in recent years, including PC Quote Inc., and ILX Systems, a new venture backed by International Thomson Organization. Despite the competitive conditions in the securities quotation business, there is always room for new ''niche'' companies offering innovative products, such as proprietary analytics.

Value-Added Products

The relative ease with which any vendor can obtain data from American stock markets and many of their foreign counterparts has made the market for

---

[10]Eric Philo and Kenneth Ng, ''Reuters Holdings PLC,'' Goldman, Sachs & Co., New York, NY, February 1989, p. 5. There may be some double-counting here due to screens displaying more than one vendor's data.

[11]Following Quotron's acquisition by Citicorp in 1986 for $680 million, two major firms—Merrill Lynch & Co., Inc. and Shearson Lehman Brothers, Inc., now known as Shearson Lehman Hutton Inc.—announced they would not renew their contracts with Quotron because they consider Citicorp a competitor. ADP has recently begun installing a personal computer-based stock quotation system for registered representatives at Shearson and Merrill. If these installations are completed, and ADP achieves a one-for-one replacement of the terminals at both Merrill and Shearson, Quotron's network of approximately 100,000 terminals could be reduced by up to 30 percent and ADP could surpass Quotron as the leading stock quotation provider in the U.S. (Waters Information Systems, Transcript of Quotron-Reuters-Telerate Conference, New York, NY, November 1988, p. 19.) To date, ADP's conversion of terminals at Merrill and Shearson is running behind schedule, and Quotron has added more terminals than it has lost. (Roxanne Taylor, Quotron, Los Angeles, CA, personal communication, August 1989).

exchange trade data into a "commodities" market, in the sense of highly standardized products competing on price or value-added features. In order to maintain their profit margins, vendors are trying to add value through new technology or exclusive products, and to generate as much revenue per terminal as possible. This has encouraged third-party suppliers to offer historical information, research, analytics and tailored news services through the terminals of vendors such as Quotron, Reuters and Bridge Brokerage Systems. Vendors that control the distribution network typically keep 30 to 40 percent of the revenue generated by third-party products.[12]

Foreign Exchange Data

The commoditization of exchange trade data has no parallel in markets where there are significant barriers to entry for vendors. Reuters created the market for real-time foreign exchange data in 1973 when it first put computer terminals on the desks of traders and convinced them to enter their rates into the system. Reuters charges subscribers a flat monthly fee but does not pay banks for contributing their quotes to the service. Reuters also launched the Monitor Dealing Service in 1981, allowing traders to negotiate transactions over their terminals instead of telephones. This system has been successful in part because of its built-in audit trail. In 1989, between 30 and 40 percent of the $640 billion traded each day in the interbank foreign exchange market took place on the Monitor Dealing Service.[13]

While Reuters is the best established in the foreign exchange market, Telerate is a competitive alternate service. Traders probably like having a backup quotation system, and also like the idea of competition for Reuters. It was nevertheless difficult for Telerate to gain a place in foreign exchange ("forex") until Reuters agreed to permit its subscribers to install "binco boxes"—bank in-house computers—that let them simultaneously update their rates on Reuters and Telerate. Until then, Telerate's forex market coverage was often slightly behind because dealers posted their rates on Reuters first. Other reasons for Telerate's success in penetrating this market are the availability of AP-Dow Jones foreign exchange news on Telerate, and traders' need for U.S. interest rate data.

Telerate did not until recently offer dealers a transactional system such as Reuters' Monitor Dealing Service. It has now launched a foreign exchange conversational (on-line) dealing system through a joint venture with AT&T. Known as The Trading Service, this service allows dealers to talk to several dealers at once, unlike the Monitor Dealing Service. Now Reuters in turn is taking another step forward with an enhanced version of the Monitor Dealing Service and a centralized order database facility. While the original Dealing Service facilitates one-on-one negotiation between two traders, Dealing 2000 will emulate an auction market where bids and offers from multiple parties are exposed. This is designed to replace "blind" brokers, who act as middlemen in foreign exchange trading. The system will display the aggregate size of all bids and offers at each price, but will not disclose the identities of the dealers participating.

U.S. Government Bond Data

Telerate is currently the only vendor broadly distributing prices in the government securities market. Under an exclusive agreement scheduled to expire in 2005, Telerate disseminates bids, offers and last-sale prices from Cantor Fitzgerald Securities Corp., the only major inter-dealer broker serving both primary dealers and retail customers. Other brokers provide price information only among the primary dealers, those who are authorized to deal directly with the Federal Reserve Bank of New York.[14] In a 1987 study, the General Accounting

---

[12]Among companies successfully exploiting demand for third-party services is MMS International, which delivers analysis and commentary on Telerate, Bridge and Reuters. MMS was recently acquired by McGraw-Hill Inc. Another third-party provider is First Call, part of International Thomson's InFiNet group, along with ILX Systems. Jointly owned by Thomson and a group of securities firms, First Call is a leading provider of on-line research produced by Wall Street analysts. Both Quotron and Reuters have tried to compete against First Call's research distribution service, but Reuters recently discontinued its own service and signed an agreement to offer First Call to its subscribers.

[13]Speech by Robert Ethrington, international marketing manager for transaction products, Reuters Holdings, PLC, New York, NY, July 1988.

[14]Prices from one or more primary dealers are not as representative of current market conditions as are those from inter-dealer brokers, who receive quotes from all the dealers. One vender, Bloomberg (30 percent owned by Merrill Lynch), packages quotes entered by Merrill's primary dealer operation with proprietary analytics that can help traders spot arbitrage opportunities. Bloomberg also delivers versions of this that include inter-dealer broker prices, but only to dealers authorized to see these quotes. If wider distribution of inter-dealer broker prices does come about, Telerate could be hurt financially. Under its agreement with Cantor Fitzgerald, it cannot carry quotes from any other inter-dealer broker. Telerate also distributes information provided by Market Data Corp.. It is possible Market Data Corp. could be used as the distributor of bids, offers, and last-sale prices from other dealers.

Office encouraged brokers to distribute quotations to non-primary dealers within 2 years.[15] In April 1989, major government bond dealers reportedly pressured a large government bond broker into abandoning a controversial effort to broaden access to bond-trading information by offering its electronic trading information screens to a wider group of customers.[16]

Reuters, Quotron, and Knight-Ridder have periodically held talks with individual brokers about disseminating their quotes, and three inter-dealer brokers have discussed distributing consolidated last-sale prices, but none of these efforts have reached fruition. When they do, "commoditization" will probably also occur in the market for U.S. government securities prices. Vendors would have to compete by providing proprietary analytics or news, or by specializing in a particular area of the Treasury market.

Reuters and Quotron are likely to try to expand into the fixed-income information business. Since its acquisition by Citicorp, Quotron has been developing information and transactional services in both foreign exchange and fixed-income markets. However, Quotron faces the same obstacles here as do Reuters and Telerate in equities: lack of critical mass and a shortage of space for terminals on the already crowded desks of traders.

Competition and Technological Change

Since the financial information business is still growing, it continues to attract aggressive competitors. This may eventually bring down prices for information services, but some observers report that customers who complain about the high costs of the established vendors often ignore lower cost firms who lack track records. Several securities brokers have tried to use raw data directly from exchanges and process this information in-house using customized software. They were largely unsuccessful, having underestimated the time and expense of becoming self-suppliers.

Technological change is creating upheaval and uncertainty among financial information vendors. As recently as 5 years ago, an equities trader typically had one terminal on his desk—probably a

Quotron—which carried Dow Jones News Service and gave the trader access to prices for U.S. securities only. In the fixed-income department of the same firm, each trader would have a Telerate terminal. In the foreign exchange area, each desk would have a Reuters terminal, and perhaps one from Telerate. Because markets did not greatly affect one another, there was no need for most traders in one market to be watching other markets.[17]

The technology used by the vendors was essentially the same, a dumb terminal connected to a host computer by dedicated telephone circuits. But as a number of niche services sprung up, traders ended up with more and more dedicated terminals on their desks. The use of single dumb terminals declined sharply when the PC permitted local storage and manipulation of price information. Now, because of digital technology, the way vendors transmit the data is becoming less important than what data they transmit.

Several other technological advances in the early and mid-1980s also irrevocably changed the delivery of financial information. The video switch, long used in the broadcast industry, reduced the clutter of terminals on traders' desks by allowing several screens to be controlled by a single keyboard. They became an important part of trading rooms, and were also responsible for the rapid rise of two companies that installed thousands of new trading room systems integrators worldwide. There were also rapid changes in the manner in which stock quotations were transmitted from vendors to customers. In addition to delivering prices over dedicated telephone lines, vendors began exploring other alternatives, such as broadcasting data by FM sideband and satellite. Midwestern commodity market data vendors began in 1981 to use small, low cost, receive-only satellite dishes which were particularly effective for one-way broadcast communications such as financial quotations. They now distribute financial data for vendors such as ADP, Dow Jones, Knight-Ridder, PC Quote, Reuters, and Telerate. Although dedicated interactive networks remain the primary delivery mechanism of financial information vendors, financial data accounts for 63 percent of the

---

[15]U.S. General Accounting Office, *U.S. Government Securities: Expanding Access to Interdealer Brokers' Services* (Washington, DC: 1987).

[16]Tom Herman, "Big Dealers Keep Monopoly on Bond Data," *Wall Street Journal*, Apr. 11, 1989.

[17]However, fixed-income traders always needed to follow the foreign exchange markets since currency prices and interest rates are closely linked.

114,000 data broadcasting satellite receiving sites currently in operation.[18]

Digital Data Feeds

To satisfy the demand for analytical tools, vendors have begun to offer their data in digital as well as analog form. Digital data gives users more flexibility in viewing and using data, such as the ability to create customized composite pages. This has created a dilemma for financial information vendors and their customers because neither exchanges or vendors are sure how best to price digital information. The fees paid by customers have in the past been based on the number of terminals or display devices authorized to receive information. This created some inconsistencies; for instance, a workstation with four separate screens will be charged four exchange fees while a workstation with one screen and four windows will be charged one exchange fee. Many users will not tell vendors the number of screens on which their data are displayed. Several industry efforts are under way to address the issues raised by digital data: the Financial Information Services Division of the Information Industry Association has formed a subcommittee on digital data feeds and workstations, and the Financial Industry Standards Organization, a user group, is also doing analysis.

It is now often cheaper for securities firms to buy hardware off the shelf than it is for them to lease equipment from vendors. In addition, the securities firms want to be able to choose whether they get a dumb terminal, a PC, or a UNIX-based workstation, and they would like industry-standard hardware that can be integrated with the firms's other systems. In recognition of this, Reuters recently stopped manufacturing terminals and Quotron plans to sell off-the-shelf equipment. ADP is also moving to industry-standard hardware.

Diversification Into Transactional Services

With data treated as a commodity and a diminished role as systems providers, financial information vendors may move toward offering transactional services, using automated execution systems. Citicorp and McGraw-Hill failed with the GEMCO electronic commodity trading system a few years ago. In the futures market, the World Energy Exchange and the International Futures Exchange of Bermuda (INTEX) both failed to convert open outcry traders to screen-based trading. Security Pacific Corp. has not had much success in automating the front office. But these failed ventures in automated trading have not deterred Reuters, which owns Instinet Corp., a registered broker/dealer offering an electronic securities trading system. Instinet began in the 1970s, but was acquired by Reuters in 1987. The company is now executing an average of 13 million share-trades a day (including both over-the-counter and exchange-listed stock), a volume still dwarfed by the 150 million or more shares traded by NYSE on an average day, but Reuters hopes that exchanges will begin using Instinet during the hours when their trading floors are closed.

It remains to be seen whether the foreign exchange market will accept the automated trading Reuters is offering through Dealing 2000, but the technology used in that system was adapted for GLOBEX, an electronic 24-hour futures trading system jointly developed by Reuters and the Chicago Mercantile Exchange and the Chicago Board of Trade, and projected to be ready for use in 1990-91. MATIF, the French financial futures exchange, has already agreed to use GLOBEX for after-hours trading and other foreign futures exchanges may also participate.

The Chicago Board Options Exchange (CBOE) and the Cincinnati Stock Exchange have agreed to form a joint venture with Reuters and Instinet to create a worldwide system for entering, routing, and executing trades of options listed on the CBOE and equities traded by the Cincinnati Stock Exchange, the only fully automated securities exchange in the Intermarket Trading System.

Quotron has not moved as rapidly as Reuters, but reportedly has electronic execution facilities in development for both foreign exchange and fixed-income markets. It has been aggressively marketing Currency Trader, which allows corporate customers of Citicorp to execute automatically foreign exchange trades of $500,000 or less.

Telerate is licensing software from INTEX and they are working together to offer exchanges and exchange members automated order-routing and execution facilities. In the fixed-income market, INTEX has licensed the rights to its order-matching software to Security Pacific Corp., and ADP is collaborating with a municipal bond broker on an automated trading system.

If this kind of competition from vendors is not successful, Reuters may acquire a near-monopoly in automated execution systems as it did in the foreign exchange market. This would mean that the after-hours transactions, and possibly all transactions, of the Nation's futures and options (and perhaps later stock markets) would be processed by a single vendor, and that a foreign one. About 46 percent of Reuters' stock is held by Americans, and 25 percent of its employees are American, but by Reuters' charter it will remain a British company.

Reuters' emergence as the leader in providing exchanges with trading infrastructure is surprising because other vendors have closer relationships to exchanges. ADP and Quotron, through the latter's Securities Industry Software (SIS) subsidiary, have extensive networks that route orders from brokerage firm offices to exchanges. These networks were installed in the stock market following the paper crunch of 1968, but are only recently being adopted by futures exchanges. The Chicago Board of Trade (CBOT) has selected Bridge Brokerage Systems, a unit of Bridge Information Systems, to build its order processing network, while the Chicago Mercantile Exchange (CME) went to SIS for its order-routing network. Since the futures exchanges contend that automated execution during regular trading hours does not provide the same liquidity as pit trading, they do not see automatic execution as becoming integrated with order-routing.

ADP has been dominant in securities order-routing through its Data Network Services subsidiary and the BTSI unit that it acquired from Control Data Corp. There are also Tandem-based order-routing systems offered by SIS and Bridge Brokerage Systems. Many operating order-routing systems were overwhelmed during the 1987 stock market crash, although most have since been upgraded and enlarged. Several industry observers believe however that brokerage firms' back-office infrastructure is outmoded, in part because securities firms have concentrated during the 1980s on installing video switches and personal computers in their trading

rooms. Because of lower volumes since the crash, those firms appear less concerned about capacity shortages and are reluctant to make large investments in order-routing and back-office systems.

REGULATION OF INFORMATION SERVICES

So far, the financial information vendors have not been subject to much Federal regulation. Under Federal law, the SEC has jurisdiction over companies that distribute and publish securities transaction data and quotations and over companies that collect, process or prepare this information for distribution or publication. To date, the SEC has registered only those organizations that process information on an exclusive basis for a securities exchange or association— the Securities Industry Automation Corp., the National Association of Securities Dealers Automated Quotation System, and the Options Price Reporting Authority. But it has been keeping close watch over vendors since the stock market crash of 1987.[19]

Options markets are particularly sensitive now. Many quote vendors were overwhelmed by the proliferation of options series and strike prices. They were not prepared to handle the increased number of different strike prices when volume shot up on October 19 and 20, 1987. They could be further overwhelmed in the future with multiple-trading of options, introduction of automated trading systems, and 24-hour trading.

Most options are now traded exclusively on one exchange, but this is to change over the next 2 years (see ch. 5). The trading of options on several exchanges (''multiple-trading'') will require an expansion of capacity by financial information vendors. The SEC has been working closely with options data vendors on their plans to handle this problem. The introduction of automated trading systems for after-hours trading by futures and options exchanges is expected to provide quote vendors with a glut of information to package and sell. Smaller vendors are also concerned about the potential for discrimination in favor of their large competitor, Reuters, who is helping exchanges to build the trading systems.[20]

---

[19]''SEC Expresses Concern About Vendor Capacity,'' *Trading Systems Technology*, Sept. 26, 1988, p. 6.

[20]After Reuters built a real-time price reporting service for the London Metal Exchange (LME), the exchange proposed a pricing structure that favored large vendors such as Reuters. Each vendor would have had to pay a sign-up fee of 50,000 pounds sterling regardless of how many users were taking that vendors' quotes. After protests by vendors with small subscriber bases, the LME withdrew the plan and is formulating a new one.

The transactions systems of securities information processors are not now subjected to SEC regulation as exchanges. The SEC has in the past issued no-action letters exempting proprietary trading systems from registering as exchanges. No-action letters have been issued for 11 proprietary trading systems to date, with the understanding that the operators of automated trading systems would keep the SEC informed of their progress. The agency is still using the no-action approach, but is working on a new rule after several sponsors ignored Commission requests for information; it wants to prevent possible abuses by foreign counterparties and ensure that access to the systems is fair and open.[21]

The agency recently proposed a rule requiring sponsors of proprietary trading systems to file a financial and operational plan with the Commission.[22] Proposed Rule 15c2-10 also gives the SEC authority to examine all books and records of both the sponsor and the trading system.

In January 1990 SEC again considered the question of what constitutes an exchange.[23] Delta Government Options Corp. had applied for registration as a clearing agency, to issue, clear, and settle options on Treasury securities, executed through an over-the-counter options trading system operated by RMJ Securities, Inc. This was granted temporarily in 1989, with a concurrent ''no-action'' letter saying that the system need not register as an exchange. CBOT and CME challenged in court the view that the trading system was not an exchange. The court returned the case to the SEC for reconsideration and the SEC reaffirmed its decision after hearing arguments from those opposed to requiring the system to register as an exchange, and those in favor.

Those opposed to registration argued that to constitute an exchange, there must be members with a proprietary interest and representation in the administration of the exchange, a trading floor to which orders are routed, listing of securities, an auction process, a limit order book, and execution of trades. They further argued that exchange registration of proprietary trading systems would serve no regulatory purpose and would deter development of innovative trading systems.

Those advocating a registration requirement (the CBOT, CME, and CBOE) argued that an exchange was any mechanism that affords to prospective buyers and sellers advantages in ''finding a market, obtaining a price, and saving time''; establishes criteria for admission and discipline of members; sets margin requirements and trading and position limits; and has the discretion to terminate trading. Characteristics such as a system of specialists with market-maker obligations, a trading floor, and member ownership and representation, they argued, are historical rather than fundamental attributes of an exchange.

The SEC, in reaching its decision not to require exchange representation, said that the fundamental characteristic of an exchange is its centralization of trading and the fact that it provides quotations ''on a regular or continuous basis so that those purchasers and sellers have a reasonable expectation that they can regularly execute their orders at those price quotations.'' The means employed to do this, the SEC acknowledged, might range from a physical floor or trading system to other means of intermediation such as a formal market-making system or a consolidated limit order book or single price auction. The bulletin board established by the RMJ System, the SEC said, does not meet this central characterization.

No clear definition of a ''bulletin board'' was offered, although it was incidently described as ''a mechanism whereby indications of interest may be displayed by participants'' (a function subject to regulation as part of the government securities brokerage function), and again as ''for the episodic display, by broker-dealers and institutions, of buying and selling interest.'' Such bulletin boards were not clearly distinguished from either a NASDAQ-like system or a GLOBEX-like system, if such

---

[21]On July 19, 1985, the SEC issued a no-action letter to Security Pacific National Bank concerning their options on government securities on-line trading system. Concerned about competition, and customer protection and financial integrity in the unregulated system, The Chicago Mercantile Exchange brought their concerns to the attention of the Federal Reserve Board and Cong. John D. Dingell. Convinced that banking could be adversely effected by such an unregulated exchange, Mr. Dingell urged further consideration by the SEC. Security Pacific sold the system to RMJ.

[22]Proposed Rule 15c2-10 would apply to Reuters' Instinet subsidiary, but would not affect GLOBEX, since the CFTC, not the SEC, has jurisdiction over futures trading. The CFTC has already reviewed and approved GLOBEX.

[23]SEC Release No. 34-27611. Self-Regulatory Organizations: Delta Government Options Corp.; Order Granting Temporary Registration as a Clearing Agency, Jan. 12, 1990.

distinction was intended. The SEC said that an "overinclusive" approach to its prerogative of determining what constitutes an exchange "would place those evolving systems within the 'strait jacket' of exchange regulation" or force it "into a regulatory scheme for which it is ill-suited. . . ."

As financial information vendors increase their presence in transactional services, they will have to deal with regulation for the first time. Even if they do not enter the transactional business, information providers may face growing government involvement in their markets because of technological changes occurring in the industry. If vendors, exchanges, and customers fail to come to terms on a pricing structure for digital data transmissions, customer use of data received from vendors, and proprietary rights to financial information, these issues may ultimately be resolved by a government agency or by the courts.[24]

U.S. BROKERAGE HOUSES

Brokerage houses use computers to assist in four major functions of the firm: data compilation and analysis, trading support, back-office functions, and surveillance activities.

Data Compilation and Analysis

Brokerage houses receive and monitor market information via electronic news wire services that provide the broker with market price information. In the retail branch offices of U.S. stock brokerage firms, 90 percent of information services are provided by Quotron and ADP;[25] but increasingly emerging as strong contenders are Reuters, Telerate, CMQ, Bridge Information Systems, Knight-Ridder Financial Information, Beta Systems, and Standard & Poor. Other vendors include Shark (Wang) and PC Quote. The annual expenditure for information services is forecast to increase to about $3 billion by 1991.[26]

A great deal of computing power is spent in analyzing and formatting raw data for decision support. Since all brokerage houses have access to basically the same information, the analytical software and graphics packages they apply to this data is thought to determine their competitive edge.[27] Individual brokers analyze and use the information differently, so the firm's computer facility must support many types of analytical software.

Trading Support

Brokerage houses were once called "wire houses" because of their use of leased wire systems and their function as a collection point for orders to be wired to the floor of an exchange. Individual and institutional customers still telephone their broker, but today orders are then collected by computers and sent via dedicated lines to trading departments and exchange floors. Every major wire house has some type of electronic order entry and routing system. Program trading (buying and selling diversified portfolios or baskets of stock) uses computers to track market movements and enter simultaneous buy/sell orders according to an algorithm (see chs. 3 and 4).

There are thousands of commercial software packages available to brokers and traders that focus on tasks such as portfolio management and risk assessment.[28] Many of these packages are "projective";[29] they use statistics to predict the price of a stock or derivative product in a certain time frame. There are also commercially available pocket-pagers, or "electronic watchdogs," often offered by information services vendors, that offer a variety of services including alerting brokers to stock price movements, news events, or SEC filings.

Back-Office Functions

Since the back-office crisis of the 1960s, when brokerage houses were overwhelmed by paper work, the back-offices have relied on computers. To aid in

---

[24]Potential regulation of financial information vendors will become a larger issue as digital data becomes the significant portion of information cost. The present trend is towards unbundled costs; one price for view only, another for cut and paste capabilities and another for data manipulation rights.

[25]Terry Landi, IBM Securities Application Systems, New York, NY, personal communication, February 1989.

[26]Henry Fersko-Weiss, "The Battle for the Broker's Desk," *High Technology Business*, September 1988, p. 30.

[27]"As Telerate and Reuters move toward elementized digital feeds, the way they display the data will no longer be as important as what they display," says Robert Mark in Marine Midland Bank's capital markets sector, "because software is able to grab specific data elements and create customized pages."

[28]Risk assessment encompasses the analysis of both market risk and credit risk. Credit risk is the risk that a counterparty will go bankrupt whereas market risk is the risk that market prices will move adversely (away from you).

[29]Grant J. Renier, "The Electronic Investment System," *The Futurist*, vol. 16, April 1982.

clearing and settlement of accounts, brokerage houses batch-process massive amounts of data. Trade confirmation reports from the exchange floors and information from the clearinghouses must be reconciled to complete the transaction. Some brokerage houses process these in-house, some use service vendors. Much of this batch-processing goes on in the evening hours, or all night, and this will be a problem for 24-hour trading. In many cases, the computers used to support trading during trading hours are used as batch processors in the evening. This could be remedied with the purchase of additional machines, but most clearing programs are designed to run in a batch mode rather than on-line. The conversion into on-line processing will be costly, time-consuming, and technologically difficult, considering the massive databases which will have to be maintained and updated concurrently. Although 24-hour/global trading may be the strong impetus, on-line processing has other benefits. Risk could be greatly reduced by more timely and accurate characterization of investment positions.

Surveillance Activities

Brokerage houses monitor trading patterns and investor positions for indications of fraud, violations of firm policies or other improper activities by brokers servicing customer accounts and employees with "information sensitive" jobs (e.g., research analysts) who may be the source of information leaks. Compliance efforts also emphasize educating employees as a deterrent to illegal activity,[30] but surveillance and auditing activities are now among the more technologically advanced aspects of financial institutions' technology. Analysts often have the capability for on-line query or real-time market surveillance activity. But human analysts are still the crucial factor; computers merely indicate where further attention should be directed.

Customer Services

Many brokerage houses lease or sell personal computer investment systems to small investors. For example, a personal computer dial-up service lets people in their homes receive market information, conduct analysis, and enter buy and sell orders. One such service has no annual sign-up fee but can cost the user 27.5 to 44 cents per minute. A large discount broker serves over 26,000 customers through its computerized trading system.[31] With these systems individual investors feel "in control" and may feel able to compete with institutional investors. On the other hand, many argue that when telephone lines are jammed on a busy trading day, an investor is no more likely to get through to a broker on his computer than he is on his telephone.[32] Most systems are equipped with "fail-safe" techniques to protect the investor, such as requiring second confirmations, or stopping them from selling stock they don't own or buying more than their margin limit. Virtually all mechanisms a firm uses for entering customer orders have a human review element to protect the firm from error, liability and loss.[33] Thus, regardless of the transmission details, there is still a "gatekeeper" that can become a bottleneck during heavy trading. The function of the gatekeeper could be an application for expert systems.

TECHNOLOGY FOR THE INDIVIDUAL INVESTOR

Of the 40 million individual investors in the United States, an estimated 2 million use PCs, and the securities industry claims that perhaps 100,000 are using them to manage portfolios.[34] In the near future, individual investors should have the technology available on home workstations to incorporate on-line trading, real-time quotes, graphics, portfolio management, on-line news, reports on investment activity, and historical data. Some of these services are now available, but not readily accessible; "windowing" software to split the screen and merge these services may be expensive and difficult to operate.

Largely within the last 5 or 6 years, individual investors have begun to use at-home trading systems based on a personal computer. Many of them have

---

[30]Ray Vass, "Detection of Illegal Trading; Systems and Realities in a Large Firm," presented at the Securities Industry Association Forum on the Prevention of Insider Trading in New York, NY, June 23, 1987.

[31]Earl Gottschalk, "Computerized Investment Systems Thrive as People Seek Control Over Portfolios," *Wall Street Journal*, Sept. 27, 1988.

[32]However, ISDN and Broadband ISDN via intelligent networks could provide network services to help surmount traditional telecommunications problems.

[33]T. Williams, Information Industry Association, discussion with OTA staff.

[34]Lee Siegfried, "Investing in the Year 2000," *Financial World*, Feb. 21, 1989, p. 56.

been quoted as saying that these systems give them a feeling of being "in control" (although none of the systems provides automated execution) and better equipped to compete with the institutional funds' professional investment managers. This perception is encouraged by the brokers who provide the systems, and who have been alarmed by the perceived "flight of the small investor."[35] The industry estimates that 400,000 individual investors will be using home trading systems by 1992.[36] Such estimates sometimes display more enthusiasm than analysis, but it appears that the number of users could have tripled in the last 3 years.

The most widely used home trading system, provided by the largest discount broker, claims approximately 50,000 users. Several similar systems claim about 10,000 to 12,000 customers each.[37] These trading systems offer similar services. They allow the investor, at his computer, to:

- access research databases,
- receive real-time quotes,
- place orders and receive confirmations,
- track the progress of a portfolio, and
- set up dummy portfolios and track their progress.

Trades ordered through one of these systems go to a broker who routes the order to an exchange.[38] The customer usually gets immediate confirmation of a trade, or if there is to be a delay of a minute or longer a confirmation is left in a "mailbox" in the system. The advantages to the investor are access to information before the trade, greater ease in tracking the portfolio after the trade, the ability to place orders 24 hours a day (but they can only be executed when the exchange is open), and a slight reduction in transaction time, chiefly because there is no wait on the telephone for a broker. (Trades are said to take 15 to 20 seconds, in most cases.) The feeling of "greater control," although it may exist, is not highly justified.

THE FUTURE: STRATEGIC TECHNOLOGIES AND THEMES

Expert Systems

An expert system is a computer program that attempts to replace a human decision process by using several primary components.[39] The first component is the experiential knowledge of an expert expressed as a set of rules and facts (if/then statements), more commonly referred to as the knowledge base. Second is the inference engine, or the computer program that sorts through the knowledge base and decides which rules apply. With the inference engine go the user interfaces, an explanation subsystem and a knowledge acquisition subsystem. Respectively, these "front end" components communicate with the user of the expert system, reconstruct the reasoning of the system for inspection, and allow the expert or knowledge engineer to add new or modified rules and facts. The potential long-range benefits of using expert systems include savings of professional time, cost savings, and improved quality and consistency of decisionmaking.

There were early high hopes for applying expert system (ES) technology to many brokerage house activities, even possibly replacing the trader, but users today generally have more conservative expectations.[40] ES applications for financial firms are made more difficult both because it is difficult to formulate real rules for investment decisions and because there is little agreement on who the experts are. Systems designed to make investment *suggestions* are controversial, but have sometimes been successful. Systems designed to make investment *decisions* are met with great resistance from traders, who trust their instincts to set them apart from other traders. Only a handful of companies are experimenting with expert systems to "replace" traders.

Two areas in which ES technology is rapidly developing are data compilation and analysis and

---

[35]The "small investors" do 18.2 percent of the trading, down from 19.7 percent in 1987, according to a study by the Securities Industries Association. This has been decreasing for years.

[36]OTA discussions with various company representatives.

[37]The systems identified by OTA are those of Charles Schwab, Inc., Fidelity Investments, and Quick & Reilly. There may be others with comparable level of use.

[38]The Fideliy Express Service says that trades are checked within the system without human intermediaries and go directly to the exchange floor.

[39]Paul Harmon and David King, *Expert Systems* (New York, NY: John Wiley & Sons, Inc., 1985).

[40]Jonathon Friedland, "The Expert Systems Revolution," *Institutional Investor*, July 1988, p. 107.

market surveillance. A common example of the first is a "news wire sifter." One security firm's new workstation will include an expert system that sorts through the news wire information to determine whether a user should be alerted to news of an event or impending event. The New York Stock Exchange has a similar expert system to sort and analyze news for market surveillance purposes.

Another application of ES is risk assessment, i.e., a rule-based system to analyze the risk of a firm's position in rapidly changing markets. For example, one firm has a risk management system for corporate and municipal bond trading, running on a Compaq 386, that sorts through massive amounts of trading data and asks for additional information when necessary, to produce a statement of risk for management's review.

Brokerage house surveillance is beginning to use rule-based systems to identify trends and anomalies in trade information. One already in use, that runs on a PC, has a set of 25 rules; it analyzes trade data and may suggest that a study should be made of a particular firm, broker or customer.

Hardware

The strategic initiatives described above are pushing firms towards faster and better hardware. Computer industry experts expect that brokerage houses may buy supercomputers before exchanges do. Mini-supercomputers are popular but are already being challenged as having insufficient power to meet the expanding needs of brokerage houses. Until April 1989, when Control Data's ETA Systems division was closed, Wall Street firms could rent time on the ETA 10P, the first air-cooled supercomputer that was running portfolio analysis software and complex fixed-income analytics.[41] An analysis of 150 stocks, each with 15 options, for 500 accounts that would normally take 6 hours on a 386 (20 mhz)

computer would take only a few minutes on a supercomputer. However, not many firms utilized this service.

FURTHER TRENDS

Some industrywide trends are:

- *Firm-wide system integration*—Firms are moving towards workstation integration with windowing, so that a user can reach many systems and information services through distributed processing. Relational databases are replacing hierarchical or flat file architectures.[42]
- *More end-user computing*—This will ease the burden of the central data processing department and makes system development for user needs more cost-efficient.
- *More automation of the back-office*—The off-floor support functions have the greatest percentage of labor which could be made more efficient by automation.
- *Flexibility to allow for multiple vendors*—With UNIX and OS/2[43] becoming more nearly standard as operating systems, this task is becoming easier.
- *New tools for easier, faster program writing*—One example is Computer Aided Software Engineering, CASE. Although firms continue to buy information services and integration software, they are increasingly choosing to build rather than buy their trading room systems.[44]
- *Emerging telecommunications capabilities*—ISDN and fiber optic networks are the keys in this area.[45]
- *Cross-training of technical and "business" side staff*—This is increasing and has been found especially useful in systems development.[46]

---

[41]"Frontline," *Wall Street Computer Review*, November 1988, p. 7.

[42]Saul Hansell, "The Moving Target," *Institutional Investor*, January 1989, p. 79.

[43]A relational database is a data schema in which the data is stored in tables and the associations between the tables are represented within the data itself, as opposed to the schema defining the relationships as in hierarchical or flat file architectures. David M. Kroenke and Kathleen A. Dolan, *Database Processing*, 3d ed., (Chicago, IL: Science Research Associates, Inc., 1988).

[44]The market penetration of OS/2 has been somewhat slow, and its probability for success is a continuing debate.

[45]Ivy Schmerken, "To Build or Buy?" *Wall Street Computer Review*, January 1989, p. 33. Peter Penczer, "Wall Street Rolls Out CASE Technology," *Wall Street Computer Review*, February 1989, p. 55.

[46]Discussions with J.W. Palmer, AT&T Bell Laboratories, Holmdel, NJ. New York Telephone recently announced that it will develop an independent fiber optic network for securities firms in the New York City area. As of October 1989, 27 firms had agreed to purchase voice and data services off of the network. In the future this network could serve as a platform for other developments such as trading, clearing and settlement processes. New York Telephones public network will serve as a backup to the private network.

• *Increased obstacles*—Technological advances in brokerage houses may be proceeding faster than at exchanges, but they will increasingly be hampered by an aging computer infrastructure that has grown difficult to manage.[47]

The strategic automation initiatives of today's brokerage house are being driven by four major forces: 1) customer demand for service and efficiency; 2) regulatory pressure to maintain a fair and orderly market; 3) domestic competition and the resurgence of program trading, which demands faster computers with more capacity; and 4) fear of Japanese competition.

There are two major differences in the approach to automation of the Japanese "Big Four" securities firms (Nomura, Daiwa, Nikko, and Yamaichi) and American firms.[48] The Japanese appear to take a more unified, standardized, long-term approach, probably because of comparatively loose Japanese antitrust laws and the influence of the Ministry of Finance. Japanese firms also appear to plan for 5 to 10 years, unlike the shorter term but more varied plans of American securities firms.[49]

For example, the Japanese have standardized home trading system software on the Nintendo Family Computer. The Big Four have also issued magnetic identification cards to customers that enable them to transfer funds from and to stock trading accounts at automated teller machines. They have agreed on protocol, architecture, and command standards for lap-top computers.[50]

Although the Japanese seem to be making faster technological progress with respect to customer service and hardware, they have lagged behind in software for analytics and investment strategies. However, this may not be true with the next generation of software.

THE MARKETS AND TECHNOLOGICAL PROGRESS

Technological progress in securities related organizations is subject to two opposing factors: the urge to use technology for competitive advantage and resistance from established, powerful market participants whose role is threatened. Brokerage houses, regional exchanges, and other organizations in which automation is a strategic necessity may be technologically progressive, because they have the benefit of strong trade-room and executive level support.[51]

Research and development on leading-edge technologies in the financial industry are often behind the technical advances and enthusiasm of universities and other industry research laboratories. In July 1988, Coopers & Lybrand estimated that only 50 percent of the major financial services firms in the United States either used or were developing leading-edge technology, such as expert systems.[52]

For example, in 1988, Ford spent approximately $200 million on expert systems research and development, while the entire financial services industry spent only $50 million. Competitive secrecy is perhaps part of the reason that universities and electronics research and development facilities are not utilized for joint financial information projects. It may also be that the right financial incentives for, or vehicles to establish, cooperative efforts are lacking or not known to the financial industry. Many States have started technology transfer centers, which facilitate industry and university consortia. The long-run benefits of being on the leading edge of technology may make it worth efforts to utilizing them.

Standards for Automation

Standards are needed for securities industry automation in three categories: data, technology, and operational standards. Data standards apply to the definition, form, and transmission of data. Technol-

---

[47]Discussions with Joseph Rosen, Rosen Kupperman Associates, Riverdale, NY.

[48]Pavan Sahgal, "Automation at the 'Big Four' Securities Firms," *Wall Street Computer Review*, January 1989, p. 22. These Japanese firms are much larger than the biggest five U.S. firms combined.

[49]"The U.S. short-term focus is hurting our technological prowess," according to Robert Mark, Manufacturers Hanover.

[50]See Sahgal, op. cit., footnote 48.

[51]The U.S. futures and options exchanges' recent technological progress with GLOBEX (MERC) and AURORA (CBOT) was reportedly resisted by floor brokers until competitive pressures forced the systems' acceptance for off-hours trading.

[52]According to Fred Clowney, Drexel Burnham Lambert, Inc., New York, NY, personal communication, March 1989.

ogy standards apply to the hardware, software, and communications aspects of automation. Operational standards apply to the way inter-professional transactions are handled. Currently the sea of "standards" includes AT&T/Sun, IEEE (Institute of Electrical and Electronic Engineers), CCITT (Comite Consultatif Internationale de Telegraphique), POSIX (Portable Operating System Interface Specification), X/OPEN, and OSF.[53]

In general, standardization in the securities-related industry is driven by two pressures: normal attrition in the computer/electronics industry, which leaves the survivors as market leaders the "preferable" companies from which to buy, and the industry-wide need to integrate diverse systems. Attrition is a double-edged sword, as it intensifies competition in the computer industry, making standards resolution even more difficult. During the 1970s and 1980s, as volume increased, Wall Street firms used high profits to acquire systems of all makes and models with little concern that they might be incompatible, or would have a short economic life.

Although competition in the vendor community is still fierce, these two pressures toward standardization are prompting vendors of software, market information, hardware, and other systems to form strategic alliances to solve automation needs. Tighter Wall Street budgets are also forcing firms to look to integration rather than replacement. Those companies specializing in systems integration platforms are currently very important to the industry. However, this requires software vendors to expand their hardware compatibility and the hardware vendors to expose their proprietary architecture. Although more established standards may begin to appear, systems builders will still incorporate sufficient flexibility and variation in the systems to enable organizations to create their own competitive advantage.

It may be that market forces could produce data standards in a reasonable length of time. However, the road to technology standards is much longer, and, given the competitive computer industry, is less likely to be brought about by market forces. Proprie-

tary (provider-controlled) technology standards setting could be bad not only for the U.S. computer/electronics industry, but also for the securities-related industry. Progress and innovation in technology are more likely to be fueled by a competitive environment.

On the other hand, "open" technology standards, which allow multiple suppliers to furnish systems elements and enhance their ability to work cooperatively, may promote this competition and improve system efficiency and productivity. Standardization will certainly be necessary for the United States to move further toward an integrated national market system. Such open standards could be developed by broad-based industry groups, standards organizations, and/or government.

By comparison, data standards could be established more easily and would also increase productivity and U.S. competitiveness. Beyond the issue of U.S. data standards, is the issue of global standards. The array of considerations necessary when attempting to set such global standards range from language agreements to holidays.[54] The development of securities-related industry data standards could, however, give the United States an early advantage in non-U.S. markets, such as Japan and 1992 Europe. As an example, the development, deployment, and acceptance of broadband, or even narrowband, Integrated Services Digital Network (ISDN) would increase productivity and efficiency by integrating voice with high-speed computer-to-computer communications and video for complex analysis graphics capabilities.

Currently, telecommunications domestically (T1, ANSI, and IEEE) and internationally (CCITT and ISO) are progressing towards broadband ISDN standards.[55] However, to achieve real standards, a serious industry-wide effort must be made which targets coordination of U.S. with global standards. A standing committee with a charter and discipline might be an effective way to approach data standards-setting.[56] The committee members would have to be influential and committed to a long-term effort.

---

[53]Victor Kulkosky, "Strategic Alliances Buoy New Technology Boom," *Wall Street Computer Review*, May 1989, p. 19.

[54]Consider the scenario of the Oct. 19, 1987 market break occurring 1 week earlier, on Columbus Day, when the exchanges were open but the banks were closed.

[55]The State Department, Communications and Information Policy/Technical Standards Development Bureau (CIP/TSD) has been active in coordinating the U.S. position on broadband ISDN and related work.

[56]Useful areas of inquiry could include standardizing order message and execution report formats and a symbol scheme for fixed-income and money market instruments (very complex).

Government oversight, perhaps including the State Department and National Institute of Standards and Technology, may be the most effective method of ensuring implementation of such an entity and charter. Another alternative would be an industry driven approach such as the Securities Industry Association (SIA) or the Futures Industry Association (FIA).

24-Hour Global Trading Systems

There are financial centers in Aukland, London, Paris, Frankfurt, Zurich, Hong Kong, Tokyo, Singapore, and Sydney, all of which now operate futures and options exchanges as well as stock exchanges. Because foreign exchanges began to offer their own versions of U.S. contracts, investment firms were able to offer products to customers without regard to trading hours in the United States. U.S. futures exchanges began to suffer volume losses. This trend originally drove the exchanges to consider accommodating 24-hour trading.[57] The first attempts to meet this need took the form of mutual offset agreements, such as the one between The Chicago Mercantile Exchange (CME) and the Singapore International Monetary Exchange (SIMEX) for Eurodollar and foreign currency contracts. Of the many offset agreements attempted by exchanges, SIMEX was for a time one of the most successful, although only marginally so.

In September of 1987, CME announced that it had developed, together with Reuters, the Post (Pre) Market Trade System, later renamed GLOBEX for "global exchange." With the assurance that GLOBEX was strictly an off-hours system, and in exchange for receiving a portion of the revenues generated by GLOBEX, CME members accepted the idea.

In 1989 The Chicago Board of Trade (CBOT) unveiled plans for another off-hours global system, "AURORA." The GLOBEX system is an automatic order matching system, while AURORA attempted to emulate the traders in the pit with icons that offered the ability for traders to select the counterparty to their trade. However, there were complaints from the financial community about the necessity of installing two terminals, and in late May 1990, the CME and the CBOT announced they would merge GLOBEX and AURORA. In fact, the GLOBEX system was the victor. Despite the fact that Reuters is a British company, this is a strategic move for the preservation of the U.S. position in commodities and futures trading.[58]

There are many risks and barriers involved with implementing 24-hour global trading systems. Some foreign countries still restrict access to their markets. Involving the country's own securities exchange is in that case often seen as a good entry strategy.[59] Clearinghouses in moving into 24-hour operation may incur large costs in changing operations and practices. However, clearing in a shorter time frame should reduce traders financial risk.[60] "Fedwire"[61] does not operate 24 hours a day; other methods of money transfer will need to be devised, some of which may not be as secure. Communications outages, in general, are an important factor. Line outage contingency plans, which must coordinate several countries, different languages, staggered time zones and varying numbers of telephone companies, are difficult to formulate.[62] Lastly, there is a management barrier: 24-hour operations require competent and experienced management at all levels around the clock.

Electronic 24-hour global trading, regardless of product, has several barriers yet to be conquered. The first pertains to basic global data standards, as addressed above. There is also the issue of international regulation. In order to control market and credit risk globally, there will have to be an international government/industry effort.[63] This is also true of coordinating post-trade practices, which could prove to be difficult, considering that some foreign exchanges presently remain with a 2-week or

---

[57]Karen Pierog, "How Technology Is Tackling 24-Hour Global Markets," *Futures*, June 1989, p. 68.

[58]William Crawford, Jr., "MERC, CBOT Plan After-Hours Trade System," *Washington Post*, May 27, 1989, p. D11.

[59]For example, the MERC-Osaka joint effort on the Nikkei index facilitated workings with the Japanese Ministry of Finance.

[60]GLOBEX has a parallel "Guard" system, which monitors positions real-time and prevents participants from entering into certain unsafe transactions.

[61]For further information on Fedwire, see ch. 6.

[62]For example, to maintain a dedicated circuit from New York to Tokyo can involve from five to seven telecommunications companies.

[63]In the case of GLOBEX, the Commodity Futures Trading Commission (CFTC) asserting jurisdiction was a major enticement to Sydney and the MATIF to join. However, the CFTC alone may have limited jurisdiction over foreign participants in the instance of a crisis.

longer settlement cycle. It is not, in other words, technological capabilities that can hold back the movement toward 24-hour global trading, but policy problems such as data standards, regulation, and post-trade activities. Additionally, international competition is also a major force. These are all areas in which the private sector can do only so much and government participation may increasingly be crucial. These international issues are discussed in an OTA Background Paper, *Trading Around the Clock: Global Securities Markets and Information Technology.*

Article 3

Payments system issues in financial markets that never sleep

Herbert L. Baer and
Douglas D. Evanoff

Financial market participants rely heavily on the payments system to control risk arising out of the trading or exchange process. Because of this reliance, changes in the nature of financial transactions may necessitate changes in the payment systems that support them.

The last decade has witnessed a dramatic change in the nature of financial transactions. In particular, today's financial markets are globally intertwined and function on a 24-hour basis. For example, foreign currency trading has been growing at nearly 40 percent annually. The resulting risks associated with the settlement of foreign currency contracts are perceived by many market participants to be significant. Major changes are also occurring in the futures and options markets, which may lead to increased payments activity during nontraditional hours. The Philadelphia Stock Exchange and the Chicago Board of Trade have introduced nighttime trading hours, and the Chicago Mercantile Exchange is promoting the introduction of its GLOBEX system, which will allow electronic trading at night. Moreover, the customer base for these instruments is significantly more international today than it was five years ago. During this same period, foreign countries have developed competing exchanges on which many U.S. customers desire to participate. Finally, the growth of cross-border holdings of securities, and the associated increase in the demand for cross-border security lending, will also create a demand for changes in the payments system.

Given the changing financial markets, many market participants and central bankers are concerned that existing payment systems do not provide adequate means for market participants to control the risks emerging from these transactions. In particular, while an increasing number of financial markets operate on a 24-hour basis, national payment systems generally continue to operate for eight hours a day. This makes the control of certain types of risks difficult and costly. This paper describes the types of risks that are encountered in financial transactions, discusses how changes in payment systems can be used to control or eliminate these risks, and provides estimates for the demand for nighttime operation of a dollar-based payment system. The final section summarizes and offers policy options.

Risks and payments systems: An overview

Trading financial contracts creates two types of risk. *Market risk* arises because a party to the contract may incur costs when seeking to replace a defaulted agreement because the market value of the contract has changed. *Delivery risk* (or principal risk)

The authors are assistant vice president and senior economist, respectively, at the Federal Reserve Bank of Chicago. Helpful comments on earlier drafts by John Davidson, George Juncker, John McElravey, John McPartland, Jeffrey Marquardt, Larry Mote, Janet Napoli, Patrick Parkinson, and Don Wilson are acknowledged. The authors also thank the numerous individuals who participated in background interviews. However, the views expressed are those of the authors and may not be shared by others.

arises because one party may default on a contract after the other has already performed its obligations. By moving cash and collateral, netting payment obligations, and facilitating settlement in a delivery vs. payment network, the payments system allows market participants to manage these risks.

While financial instruments are increasingly being traded on a continuous basis around the world, payment systems have remained more parochial. The problems caused by this parochialism can best be appreciated by considering how clearance and settlement of obligations would occur, and risk would be managed, in a world in which transaction costs were unimportant. In this world, trades could be instantly transmitted to the clearing system. Any credit exposure due to market risk could be instantaneously eliminated through posting cash or collateral on a real-time basis. Any delivery risk could be eliminated through the use of delivery vs. payment mechanisms. (Payment system risk definitions and means to manage risk are presented as background material in the Box).[1]

It is unlikely that this system will ever be achieved. Participants would incur considerable transaction costs in the form of wire fees, accounting costs, and forgone interest on cash balances. However, today's global payments system is further removed from this situation than many market participants find desirable. For much of the 24-hour day, elimination of emerging market risk through the transfer of dollar-denominated currency or collateral is either awkward or impossible. Procedures to counteract the resulting risk on transfer networks have frequently not been adopted. Delivery risk is also substantial in many markets, and the development of formal netting agreements and effective delivery vs. payment mechanisms to counteract this has not occurred.

Below we detail potential payments problems that are emerging as a result of the rapid growth of cross-border trading of securities, interbank trading of foreign exchange obligations, cross-border and nighttime trading of derivative products such as futures and options, and offshore clearing of dollar payments. As these problems are analyzed, we also attempt to reflect the likely impact of anticipated market changes such as adjustments to procedures on CHIPS (Clearing House Interbank Payments System), the introduction of delivery vs. payment arrangements, and the introduction of multilateral netting of foreign currency contracts.[2]

International securities trading

Cross-border secondary market trading of U.S. government securities has grown rapidly—in recent years the average annual growth rate has been 22 percent (Pavel and McElravey 1990)—and is now conducted on a 24-hour basis.[3] In 1988, trading by nonresidents in these securities reached $3 trillion, or roughly $12 billion per day. Nighttime trading of Treasury securities is also becoming more important. While there are no good estimates of the volume of off-hours trading of Treasury securities, an analysis of futures trading data suggests that 15 percent of trades take place during these hours. This would suggest a daily nighttime volume of U.S. government securities trading of approximately $53 billion. This growth has led to the development of off-hours trading of Treasury bond futures contracts at the Chicago Board of Trade (CBOT), the Tokyo Stock Exchange, and the London International Financial Futures Exchange (LIFFE). In response to this growth in 24-hour trading of U.S. government securities, the Public Securities Association has recently announced a plan to disseminate pricing data on a 24-hour basis. Although the current volume of trading in private securities is much smaller, that market has registered more dramatic growth rates. Foreign transactions in private sector U.S. bonds currently approach $640 billion per year, and trading volumes have increased at an average annual rate of approximately 80 percent.

Similar trends have been observed in other countries (see Table 1). In Germany, for example, bond transactions have increased at a 43 percent annual rate over the 1985-89 period and accounted for over one-third of the value of all transactions in German bond markets. Foreign investment in equity markets has also increased dramatically. For instance, foreign transactions in U.S. markets grew at nearly 30 percent annually to $650 billion in 1989 (see Table 2).

To a significant extent, the growth in cross-border trading is likely to create relatively few demands on the global payments system that cannot be handled by existing

Payments system risk and means to manage it

The increase in the number and dollar volume of international financial transactions is giving financial market and payment system participants the incentive to reduce both the costs and risks involved in these transactions. To understand the deficiencies in existing payment systems, as well as the implications of proposed changes, it is necessary to have an understanding of the nature of the risks involved and means to address them. We briefly discuss these aspects of payment and clearing arrangements, and in the process introduce the terminology used throughout the article.

The major risks involved with financial transactions are liquidity, credit, and systemic risk. *Liquidity risk* results from the possibility that payments will not be made when due, but will be forthcoming at a later date. *Credit risk* results from the possibility that full payment may not be possible at any date. Credit risk can be separated into two components. If a counterparty defaults on the obligation before it is due, the contract may only be replaceable at a higher cost. This is *market risk*. It is a function not of the gross value of the contract, but of the difference between the original cost of the defaulted contract and the current cost of obtaining the same contract. Parties to transactions are also subject to *delivery risk*, the risk that one party will fulfill his settlement obligations while the counterparty does not. Unlike market risk, delivery risk applies to the gross value of the obligation. It is a major problem in cross-border or multicurrency transactions.

Systemic risk occurs when a large number of parties find it so difficult to value the direct and indirect credit risks associated with the clearing and settlement of transactions that they simply abandon the market. In the market for bank deposits this is manifested in a run from deposits into currency. In a securities or derivative products market it is manifested in a cessation of trading through conventional channels. Although regulators are concerned with risk in general, it is systemic risk that concerns them most and that drives most policy decisions.

Market participants have developed certain practices to control payment system risks and costs. For example, in certain markets, such as foreign exchange, participants have a large number of contracts with one another that may be offsetting over the course of the trading day. To reduce transaction and accounting costs on the delivery day, the parties may use a *position netting* procedure in which the net position of parties is summarized. One payment covering the net position therefore replaces all the individual transactions. Position netting can be either bilateral (between any two parties) or multilateral (a single net position between all market participants). However, position netting does not reduce risk. Risk can be reduced when netting procedures are employed by introducing *novation*. With this legal device, each trade creates a new contract or obligation for the resulting net position and previous contracts are discharged. Thus, participants are contractually obligated to a running position. To further reduce risk and potential counterparty squabbles, market participants can have the entity that serves as the central accountant in the multilateral netting arrangement (frequently a clearinghouse) substitute as a counterparty for all trades. Thus, with multilateral netting with novation and *substitution*, market participants trade with indistinguishable counterparties, are legally obligated to the substitute for the net position owed as a result of trades with all participants, and delegate risk management to the substitute.

The lag between initiation and final settlement of the transaction, especially troublesome in cross-border transactions, can increase liquidity, market, and delivery risk. This can be eliminated by introducing *delivery vs. payment structures* in which both sides of the transactions occur simultaneously. This would be particularly useful in the cross-border trading of securities where depositories can be created that house the securities and act in conjunction with the payments system to transfer payment and ownership simultaneously. Other commonly used payments system risk-management tools include frequent scrutiny of the financial viability of clearinghouse participants, limits or caps on intraday exposure to individual counterparties or groups of counterparties, and collateralization of debit positions.

TABLE 1		
Foreign transactions in domestic bond markets (billions of dollars)		
	1985	1989
U.S.	1263.5	4835.3
Government sector	968.0	4153.7
Private sector	295.5	681.6
Canada	43.4	134.7
Germany	55.6	366.6
Japan	197.9	527.2
SOURCE: Various central bank statistical releases.		

TABLE 2			
Foreign transactions in U.S. equity markets (billions of dollars)			
	Transactions in U.S. securities	Transactions in foreign securities	Total
1982	79.9	15.7	95.6
1983	134.4	30.2	164.6
1984	62.2	15.8	78.0
1985	159.0	45.8	204.8
1986	277.5	100.2	377.7
1987	481.9	189.3	671.2
1988	364.4	152.7	517.1
1989	416.7	232.4	649.1
SOURCE: Federal Reserve Bulletin (1990).			

institutions and arrangements. Participants in these markets typically have several days to complete the settlement process. Consequently, problems commonly associated with moving cash between parties in some financial transaction arrangements are generally unimportant in these markets. Indeed, because securities traded through exchanges are generally subject to netting, these markets account for a relatively small portion of international payment activity. For markets with a netting mechanism in place, the major problem involves the movement of paper-based securities and the introduction of delivery vs. payment arrangements. Both of these problems can be ameliorated by the introduction of book-entry securities depositories. Even after implementation of recommendations to move from a five-day to a three-day settlement of securities transactions, limits on the timely movement of cash will not in general be a constraining factor.[4]

The timely movement of funds may become a problem, however, in payments associated with the lending of securities to facilitate settlement and the delivery of U.S. government securities. It is becoming increasingly common for U.S. and foreign investment banks to borrow securities from U.S. institutional investors. Typically, these investors seek immediate reinvestment of the proceeds of the transaction in dollar-denominated assets and are not interested in maintaining a large number of offshore bank accounts. At the same time, neither the institutional investors nor the investment banks are interested in maintaining an unsecured credit exposure against the other for any length of time. Under the current system, securities lent to facilitate settlement in Tokyo are particularly troublesome, since "good" or "final" dollars do not flow into U.S. accounts until 5 p.m. eastern time the next day (via CHIPS).[5] While there are no hard numbers, several financial firms indicated in interviews that these types of transactions had grown significantly in the past two years. Payments arising from the settlement of these transactions could be as high as $1 billion a day. The proposed three-day settlement deadlines for securities transactions could well accelerate the demand for such services as market participants are forced to rely more heavily on securities borrowings to meet settlement guidelines.

The current arrangements for settling transactions in U.S. government securities also may be inadequate to meet the needs of the international marketplace. Unlike other markets of its size, a large proportion of transactions in U.S. government securities are not subject to netting. Instead, most Treasury securities are immobilized on the books of the Federal Reserve, and a large proportion of purchases are settled by a delivery vs. payment settlement process. The structure of the settlement process in the U.S. government securities market arises in part from the fact that it provides an excellent source of liquidity. This means that settlement procedures in the Treasury market are more focused on providing rapid availability than on minimizing transaction costs through netting. Because Treasury securities are used as short-term investment vehicles, the growing importance of trading in Treasuries at night may also be an indication of a growing demand for liquidity outside of traditional trading hours. Without the operation of a nighttime book-entry system, the marketplace's ability to provide this liquidity may be limited.

Interbank foreign exchange markets

Based on the volume of transactions, foreign exchange trading is the largest single international financial activity. The Bank for International Settlements estimated that the 1989 daily turnover in the foreign exchange market was about $650 billion. It has been growing at approximately 40 percent annually during the 1980s (Pavel and McElravey 1990).

Foreign exchange products—such as spot, forward, option, and swap instruments—specify a settlement or ''value date'' in the future on which the exchange of currencies will be completed. Spot contracts are usually value-dated two days from the initiation date. Forward, option, and swap transactions are value-dated for longer periods, as specified by the transacting parties. These foreign exchange transactions are initiated through informal, over-the-counter interbank markets. In most cases the market risk inherent in these products is not collateralized. Instead, risk is controlled by setting exposure limits to individual counterparties. The risks inherent in the foreign exchange markets have recently been exacerbated by the somewhat deteriorating creditworthiness of some of its participants.

Today, most foreign exchange obligations are subject only to position netting (not novation). This occurs when final delivery instructions are entered into the relevant payments system (for example, CHIPS for the dollar leg of a transaction). The reliance on position netting and the lack of delivery vs. payment leaves market participants with temporary exposures which are large relative to their capital. This risk is particularly important in settling dollar-yen transactions because of the 14-hour gap between the final payment of yen in Tokyo and the final payment of dollars in New York. One way to reduce this delivery

risk is to close the settlement gap by making it possible to transfer dollars and yen simultaneously.

Another way to reduce delivery risk is to introduce netting by novation. The foreign exchange market has several characteristics that make it a candidate for the introduction of netting by novation. The largest participants enter into numerous transactions that ultimately offset one another. As a result, gross exposures are often large relative to the participating banks' capital, exposing banks to delivery risk. Since the net exposures are small, much of this risk could be avoided if netting by novation were implemented. Given the large number of value dates, currencies, and participants, multilateral netting would lead to greater reductions in transactions volume and risk than would bilateral approaches. In addition, since most participants deal with a wide array of parties, indirect credit risk is significant and a participant can find it extremely difficult to assess accurately its exposure to other parties.

The private marketplace took the first step toward netting foreign exchange transactions with the formation of FXNET, a bilateral netting by novation system that began operation in London in 1987. However, because the system does not provide delivery vs. payment, it only reduces delivery risk and does not eliminate it. The major benefit of FXNET is that it should significantly reduce transaction volume—by an estimated 50 percent (Bartko 1990)—which could lead in turn, to significant reductions in transaction costs and both liquidity and credit risks.

A multilateral netting procedure would reduce the costs of foreign exchange transactions even more. With this arrangement losses are allocated according to a pre-arranged formula. Risk levels are controlled by setting strict entry requirements and demanding frequent demonstrations of financial strength by group participants. This allows traders to view all counterparties as homogeneous. This approach has worked particularly well in the futures market where the clearinghouses have enforced strict entry requirements and margin requirements, and stand as the counterparty to all trades. Simulations conducted in 1990 by International Clearing Systems and 13 banks suggested that multilateral netting by novation would reduce the credit risk associated with foreign exchange trading by 70-75 percent. It was projected that payment transactions would be reduced by more than 95 percent.

What has worked so well for the futures market, however, may not apply to other markets. Conversations with investment bankers and large international bankers concerning the various netting proposals for foreign exchange activity suggest that they see these netting schemes as a leveling influence that would reduce the advantage of firms doing the best job of evaluating and bearing risk. Moreover, some firms are concerned that these proposals place them in the undesirable position of being unable to control or monitor counterparty risk. As a result, some of the major firms may be unwilling to sacrifice their ability to evaluate and select counterparties individually.

Recent proposals for multilateral netting attempt to address this problem by tying a party's exposure to the value of transactions it originated with the failing counterparty. In the event of the failure of a member of the clearinghouse, only those losses in excess of each originating party's capital would be mutualized. It is hoped that this procedure will maintain incentives for individual members to monitor and control risk, and will protect the competitive advantage of those members with greater expertise in risk analysis.

On the surface, the delivery risk associated with the settlement of foreign exchange trades would appear to make this market an important factor in any decision to extend existing payments system hours. However, the adoption of multilateral netting would significantly reduce this delivery risk, in turn reducing the need for extended hours. Nevertheless, should multilateral netting systems fail to develop, demand for improvements to the existing payment services would increase.

Derivative products

Derivative products are financial instruments whose value is tied to an underlying instrument. Examples of exchange-traded derivative products include futures and options tied to Treasury bonds, Eurodollar interest rates, the S&P 500 stock index, or the Japanese yen. A futures contract is an agreement to buy or sell a commodity at a later date under terms specified by the exchange at a price determined today. Options contracts provide

the owner with the right to buy or sell a financial instrument under the terms of the contract. The contracts are standardized with respect to the underlying commodity, the posting of initial and variation margin, the method of delivery, and the value date.

Globalization has spurred the creation and rapid growth of futures and options on international financial products (see Table 3). For example, futures contract trading on Eurodollar interest rates increased almost 55 percent annually since 1984, reaching almost 47 million in 1989. Moreover, combining futures and options, nearly 40 million contracts on various foreign currencies were traded worldwide in 1988, up from 14 million in 1983.[6] Open interest, which is more closely associated with clearinghouse risk and payments, has also grown (see Table 4).

Globalization has also led to the establishment of futures and options exchanges worldwide. Once the exclusive domain of U.S. markets, particularly in Chicago, derivative products are now traded in significant volumes throughout Europe and Asia. Between 1985 and 1989, 20 new formal exchanges were established, bringing the worldwide total to 72 (*Euromoney* 1989). Obviously, competition in this business line has increased as exchanges in London, Tokyo, and Singapore trade contracts that compete directly with those offered on U.S. exchanges. In addition, foreign membership on many exchanges is considerable. For example, over two-thirds of LIFFE's members are based outside of the United Kingdom (Thagard 1989). As a result of growth overseas, the share of exchange-traded futures and options volume commanded by the U.S. exchanges dropped from 98 percent in 1983 to about 80 percent in 1988 (Pavel and McElravey 1990).

U.S. derivative product exchanges are responding to the increased interest in round-the-clock trading as well as to the increased competition from foreign exchanges. The Chicago Mercantile Exchange and the Chicago Board of Trade have made plans to extend their normal trading hours through computerized systems. The Chicago Board Options Exchange (CBOE) is planning a 24-hour electronic trading system. The trading hours for foreign currency options on the Philadelphia Stock Exchange and Treasury bond futures on

TABLE 3

Futures contract volume

Number of contracts traded on Eurodollar interest rate futures and selected foreign exchange futures contracts

	1984	1985	1986	1987	1988	1989
Australian Dollar					99,948	118,702
British Pound	1,444,492	2,799,024	2,701,330	2,592,177	2,646,849	2,545,160
Canadian Dollar	345,875	468,996	734,071	914,563	1,418,065	1,270,192
Deutschemark	5,549,150	6,620,223	6,795,907	6,168,972	5,813,868	8,326,020
Japanese Yen	2,334,764	2,415,094	4,081,116	5,454,578	6,701,474	8,190,280
Swiss Franc	4,129,881	4,758,159	4,668,430	5,268,276	5,363,232	6,156,064
French Franc					3,932	2,030
Total foreign exchange	13,804,162	17,061,496	18,980,854	20,398,566	22,047,368	26,608,448
Eurodollar	5,248,531	10,488,514	12,388,763	23,682,773	25,237,481	46,846,982
U.S. T-Bond	30,130,943	41,079,396	54,183,691	68,413,062	73,764,578	72,611,890

SOURCE: Futures Industry Association.

the CBOT have already been expanded to provide greater overlap with the London and Tokyo business days.

Settlement procedures in futures markets

Derivative product markets control the credit risk created by the lag between initiation and settlement of contracts through the use of netting by novation, initial margin, variation margin, and loss-sharing arrangements.[7] One or more times a day futures positions are marked to market. At this time losers are required to pay in cash to the clearinghouse a *variation margin* equal to the decline in the value of the contract. The clearinghouse, in turn, passes these payments on to the winners. The payment of variation margin eliminates existing credit risk from the system and signals that participants are sufficiently sound to maintain their position and continue trading. Because winners and losers need not have accounts at the same clearing bank, interbank funds transfers are an integral part of the futures variation margin process. Thus, the futures clearinghouses prefer a rapid, reliable electronic payments system to facilitate the transfer of ''good'' variation margin.

A futures clearinghouse also collects *initial margin* from all clearing members which, in turn, collect initial margin from their cus-

tomers. This margin is employed to guarantee that counterparties meet their contractual obligations to make variation margin calls. Currently, initial margin must first be posted in cash; however, it may later be replaced with acceptable securities or standby letters of credit. In principle, there is no reason why initial margin could not be met by posting acceptable securities or standby letters of credit. Thus, futures clearinghouses need not be dependent on the payments system to receive initial margin payments.

Settlement procedures in options markets

In options markets cleared by the Options Clearing Corporation (OCC), the distinction between variation and initial margin is not so clear. When a short position is opened, a margin must be posted based on the current value and volatility of the option. The margin requirement is updated each day to reflect the opening and closing of positions, as well as changes in the value of existing short positions, that is, the value of contracts sold. The process is similar to that employed in the futures market. First, payments to meet increased margin requirements are made with cash, securities, or standby letters of credit. Second, short positions are marked to market daily. If the short position suffers a loss, addi-

TABLE 4

Futures contract open interest

	Open interest on Eurodollar interest rate futures and selected foreign exchange futures contracts					
	1984	1985	1986	1987	1988	1989
Australian Dollar					1,519	2,557
British Pound	18,385	25,082	23,145	28,589	16,442	20.208
Canadian Dollar	7,058	13,929	14,937	14,908	22,062	23,573
Deutschemark	35,506	53,830	44,911	35,502	36,572	58,987
Japanese Yen	14,083	28,058	23,868	44,524	33,840	50,971
Swiss Franc	18,920	27,351	23,138	24,298	21,956	32,698
French Franc					59	25
Total foreign exchange	93,952	148,250	129,999	145,821	132,450	189,019
Eurodollar	95,673	141,831	251,830	332,960	588,827	671,853
U.S. T-Bond	203,866	303,048	233,297	268,361	373,972	295,446

SOURCE: Futures Industry Association.

tional payments must be made to the clearinghouse. If the short position gains, the clearing member's margin requirement is reduced, permitting it to withdraw funds from the OCC.

Since the options settlement process does not move funds from winners to losers, it is, in theory, less dependent on the payments system than are the futures clearinghouses. The value of payments to the OCC clearing members never exceeds the member's margin deposits, and payments to the clearinghouse *could* be—and in many cases are—made with securities and standby letters of credit rather than cash. However, OCC clearing members frequently find it convenient to post securities and standby letters of credit *after* cash has been supplied. In contrast, the only way that a futures clearinghouse could execute a variation margin call without the payments system being open would be to have a single clearing bank.

Variation margin in derivative products in a global market

Derivative product exchanges located in the United States are seeking to expand their customer base in East Asia and Europe and are rapidly moving towards 24-hour trading. Meanwhile, U.S. firms are making increased use of products offered on foreign markets. These business development strategies will have a significant impact on the settlement process in the futures and options industry.

Most of the problems faced by the OCC could be dealt with by setting up overseas depositories, using standby letters of credit, and having U.S. depositories execute securities transfers 24 hours a day. The problem of effecting settlements during nontraditional banking hours is more complex for the futures clearinghouses and their clearing members. As business in Asia expands, the clearing members of these exchanges must confront the difficulties of levying cash variation margin calls on Asian customers during the U.S. business day. If the margin call is issued during Chicago business hours, the Japanese banking system is not open. Therefore, the only resources available to a Japanese customer are deposits and lines of credit with banking offices in the United States. Clearing members currently make up any customer shortfalls out of working capital until the end of the next U.S. business day. As the volume of business from the Far East increases, this intraday exposure due to the time zone differences may grow large relative to clearing members' capital, making them less willing to continue this practice.

By increasing the expense of dealing with East Asian customers, the existing payment systems may be making it difficult for U.S.

exchanges to penetrate further into the Asian markets. However, interviews with a number of clearing members suggest that most foreign customers had U.S. balances arising from other activities that were large relative to their futures activities in the United States. Where this was not the case, payments problems were typically resolved using foreign exchange services provided by the clearing member. Because of the smaller size of the typical U.S. customer and the deficiencies of many foreign payment systems and money markets, most clearing members seemed more concerned about the funds movements of U.S. customers dealing overseas than with the U.S. activities of foreign firms.

Round-the-clock trading creates additional problems for futures clearinghouses and their members. For example, the substantial overnight price movement in a number of contracts creates the potential need for intraday margin calls between 5:00 p.m. and 7:00 a.m. eastern time. Indeed, the yen-dollar contract experiences more price movement overnight than during the U.S. business day (Lane 1989). Therefore, the ability to levy a nighttime margin call would be particularly useful for these contracts. However, the margin call could be completed only if the relevant institutions (U.S. banks) and their payment system were open during nighttime hours and had a means of transferring value. When the payments system is not operating, a clearing member would be exposed to increased risk commensurate with the additional time necessary to complete the margin call (that is, the additional time to confirm the customers' ability to cover their positions).

Derivative product markets can and do function at night even though the clearinghouses lack the ability to levy margin calls and receive payments during these hours. However, a large nighttime price move would create significant credit exposures between clearing members or between clearing members and their customers. If the resulting exposures were large relative to the resources of the clearinghouse, trading would slow and perhaps cease as clearing members became unwilling to bear additional clearinghouse risk. Trading would resume only after the existing credit risk had been eliminated by the transfer of cash or securities from losing clearing members. Such a trading halt would be the market-

based analog to a regulatory circuit breaker. This market-induced trading halt, like its regulatory counterpart, would be a nuisance rather than a disaster once the payment system opened, since payments and settlement would still take place.[8] However, to the extent that such halts are the result of deficiencies in payment systems, market participants can be made better off by altering payment practices.

In summary, as the trading hours and customer bases expand in derivative product markets, the desire to move margin monies around the world and around the clock will increase. This in turn will lead market participants to seek ways to execute cross-border variation margin calls outside of traditional business hours. While the critical pressure is likely to come from clearinghouses associated with exchanges, the growing collateralized over-the-counter market could also be a source of demand.

Offshore dollar clearings

Offshore dollar clearing arrangements have been introduced in foreign countries to meet the demand of local institutions for dollar transactions with (local) same-day value. U.S. banks commonly serve as the clearing entity—they determine positions of the participating parties and serve as the settling bank once the U.S. markets open. Given the trend toward globalization and the imposition of daylight overdraft limits on U.S. domestic transfer networks, the role of offshore dollar clearing arrangements may increase in the future. It was this potential which lead the Federal Reserve to issue its policy statement emphasizing the need for risk control measures on these arrangements (Board of Governors 1989).[9]

These clearing arrangements involve additional risk when the operating hours of the host country's banking system do not overlap with the U.S. banking day. The resulting local same-day value is essentially a credit extension by the settlement bank. For example, these arrangements commonly have transactions netted and "provisionally" settled during the local business day, with final settlement in "good" funds at the end of the U.S. business day through the account of the U.S.-based clearing bank via CHIPS. Although a loss-sharing arrangement may be in place, there may be no collateral backing the agreement, and nothing dictates that the positions are legally binding, although customers may act as if they were. This may be particularly troublesome during times of crisis. If settlement were to occur over CHIPS, the clearing bank could face significant problems if a participant in a debit position failed to make payment before the end of the U.S. banking day. The bank probably would have already initiated irreversible credits on CHIPS (to the remaining clearing arrangement members) and may have difficulty meeting its settlement requirements. Thus, CHIPS' settlement could be impaired. Alternatively, the clearing bank could provide the necessary credit and, during the next business day, could request that participants unwind credits received the previous day. While small reversals may be made to maintain the dollar clearing system, reversals of large positions during a time of crisis would be unlikely. Institutions would probably simply defer until more information were available on the defaulting participant. Therefore, the lack of overlapping business hours creates account overdrafts and temporal risk for the U.S. bank organizing the dollar clearing arrangement.

Improvements could be made in the current clearing arrangements. First, legally binding agreements that make the allocation of credit and liquidity risk explicit and which guarantee finality could be initiated. The guarantee could be backed by collateral or the capital of the participants. Movement toward this goal appears in prospect on some of the arrangements. Second, adjustments to the payments system could be introduced so that a dollar-based funds transfer network with finality operates during the U.S. nighttime hours. This would directly address problems evolving from the lack of overlapping business days.

Nighttime transactions and the potential demand for payments activity

Emerging stresses on the global payments system arise from several sources: the increasing importance of cross-border securities lending, growth in the nighttime trading of U.S. government securities, significant risk in the foreign exchange markets resulting from the lack of netting or delivery vs. payment mechanisms, rapid growth of offshore dollar clearings, and the attempt by futures and options exchanges to expand their trading hours and customer base.

The objectives in evaluating alternative ways to improve current means of transferring value during nontraditional U.S. banking hours are twofold: to increase efficiency and to improve risk management. Since the level of risk resulting from payments activity during these hours is closely correlated with payment volume, the demand for nighttime transactions is thought to depend critically on the level of activity in the nighttime market.

What is the current level of demand for nighttime transactions? We attempt to generate a rough estimate based on the assumption that the bulk of the activity will be generated from the sources discussed above.

As noted earlier, there are no publicly available estimates of the volume of off-hours trading in Treasury securities. However, reasonable approximations can be generated. If we assume that the hourly ratio of nighttime to total trading is the same for the cash securities as for the futures contracts, then we can project that approximately 15 percent of total trading in Treasury securities occurs at night. However, only a portion of these transactions would be for same-day settlement. The general rule-of-thumb is that about 50 percent of transfer instructions received by the Federal Reserve are for the settlement of trades made earlier in the day. Given this assumption, about 7.5 percent of the Treasury transactions crossing the books of the Federal Reserve on a given day would arise from trades entered into the previous night for same-day delivery. This suggests a daily volume of approximately $26 billion.

In contrast, transactions from margin calls for futures and options contracts are likely to be relatively modest. On a typical day the derivative product markets create perhaps $12 billion in payments traffic.[10] Typically about 70 percent of this represents variation margin with the remaining portion meeting initial margin requirements. During times of extreme volatility like October 19, 1987, total payments volume associated with the derivative markets might well exceed $30 billion. However, only part of this total would shift to nighttime trading.

Based on Chicago Board of Trade experience, nighttime trading constitutes about 15 percent of daytime volume. Thus, we could expect that payment of initial margin associated with the opening and closing of positions would approximate 15 percent of the current daily total of approximately $3.6 billion—or $500 million. Since average nighttime price movements for derivative products is about 40 percent of the total daily movement (Lane 1989), nighttime variation margin payments would approach 40 percent of the daily total of $8.4 billion—or $3.3 billion. Summing these two components, the total nighttime payments arising from margin calls would be approximately $3.8 billion. A more conservative scenario, and perhaps more realistic, would have payments restricted to transactions between the clearinghouses and their clearing members and would exclude payments between clearing members and their customers. These payments, which would only encompass variation margin calls, currently account for approximately 20 percent of the total $3.8 billion variation margin. This would produce a conservative nighttime estimate of approximately $800 million. Rapid growth of the dollar-denominated contracts in London and Singapore could cause this to grow, as could a shift in variation margin practices of Japanese futures exchanges which currently give participants three days to meet a margin call on dollar-denominated contracts.

Payment flows related to the settlement of foreign exchange contracts are the most difficult to predict. Demand will depend critically on whether, and how, multilateral netting is introduced into this market. In the absence of a system of multilateral netting, contracts involving European currencies would probably settle at the close of the European business day (12 noon to 2 p.m. eastern time) and, thus, would not contribute to the U.S. nighttime volume. Similarly, movement toward a single monetary unit for Europe after 1992 could lead to reductions in foreign exchange activity involving these countries.

In the absence of multilateral netting, therefore, the primary source of nighttime foreign exchange transactions would be contracts involving the Japanese yen. The Bank for International Settlements (1989) estimated that dollar-yen trading averaged $162 billion a day in 1989. Of this, perhaps $25 billion is netted away through existing offshore clearing arrangements. Thus, in the absence of any contract netting, dollar volume could average $137 billion a day. However, netting is ex-

pected to occur. The introduction of bilateral netting on a currency pair basis could reduce the $162 billion to $81 billion (Bartko 1990). Since bilateral netting should continue to proliferate, this approximation should provide an upward bound on the demand for transactions.

The introduction of a multilateral foreign exchange clearinghouse could dramatically reduce the volume of payments associated with the settlement of dollar-yen transactions. International Clearing Systems, Inc. estimates that multilateral netting reduces dollar volume by approximately 95 percent, leaving us with a conservative revised total nighttime volume of about $8 billion. However, existing multilateral netting proposals would net dollar payments associated with dollar-yen transactions against dollar payments associated with other foreign currency transactions. To eliminate delivery risk completely, all currencies would need to move at the same time. A logical time for this to occur would be early in the U.S. morning when the other two payments systems are open. However, even this would require changes in payments system practices in Europe and Japan. With global foreign exchange trading currently running at $650 billion a day, multilateral netting would reduce the daily dollar settlement by 95 percent to roughly $32.5 billion.

Summing these sources of demand, estimated nighttime transactions would run somewhere between $27 and $110 billion a day, depending on the assumptions employed (see Table 5).[11] The lower figure is comparable to the Federal Reserve's 1968 electronic funds transfer volume; in today's terms, it equals approximately 2 percent of current volume on CHIPS and FedWire combined. However, if past growth trends are any indication, we can expect transaction volume to increase substantially in the future.

Summary and policy implications

During much of the 24-hour day, financial market participants find it difficult or impossible to eliminate market risk by transferring cash or collateral. In many cases participants do not have the option of settling transactions on a delivery vs. payment basis. Additionally, in contrast with domestic transactions, it is difficult for participants to limit the delivery risks inherent in international transactions by having settlement occur relatively soon after

TABLE 5
Potential nighttime transaction demand (billions of dollars)

Treasury securities	26
Derivative products[a]	.8 to 3.8
Foreign exchange[b]	0 to 81
Total	26.8 to 110.8

[a]The low end of the range assumes that the only payments made are between the clearinghouse and its members; the high end assumes that clearing members attempt to collect from and pay to customers at night.

[b]The low end of the range represents the case of multilateral netting with delivery vs. payment implemented during daytime hours; the high end represents an environment with bilateral netting and nighttime settlement of dollar-yen transactions only.

NOTE: See text for citations.

the initiation of payment. Ten years ago these problems were less important. However, the financial markets have changed significantly since then. The hours during which markets are active have been extended for some financial products and will be extended for others in the immediate future. Financial transaction activity has grown exponentially. These changes have occurred without many corresponding changes in the payments system.

This study has reviewed trends in the flow of international payments, the characteristics of existing payment system arrangements, and the problems inherent in these arrangements. Such recent changes in payment system practices as the movement toward netting arrangements and implementation of loss-sharing agreements allowing for settlement finality will lead to significant cost savings and reductions in payments system risk. However, given the changing financial markets and the growing demand for transfers of value during nontraditional business hours, the changes to date may be inadequate. Discussions with financial market participants as well as estimates based on what we believe to be realistic assumptions suggest a potentially significant demand for nighttime payments arising from the market for U.S. government securities, cross-border securities lending, offshore dollar clearing systems, settlement of foreign exchange activity, and margin calls for exchange-traded derivative products. Exclud-

ing offshore dollar clearing arrangements, we estimate the potential demand for nighttime transactions currently to be between $27 and $110 billion a day, or 1.5 percent of current daytime volume. Even at the low end of this range, the resulting risk from using current payments arrangements is thought by many market participants to be significant. Additionally, the evidence suggests that in the future, transactions during this period will continue to increase.

How can the demand for these transactions best be met? In our opinion, the bulk of the solution should come from the private sector. Similarly, the bulk of the risks resulting from payment system activity should be borne by financial institutions and their customers. However, for these solutions to be implemented efficiently and effectively, the private sector needs the tools to manage nighttime risk. The central bank has the ability to provide those tools without distorting the marketplace. Thus, a combination of public and private sector initiatives would appear to be appropriate. This approach is based on two propositions. First, the private sector has demonstrated that it has both the ability and incentives to evaluate and to manage risk, and an incentive structure that balances the benefits of risk reduction against its costs. Second, as a result of investments made to service daytime demand, the Federal Reserve may well have a cost advantage in providing the tools to manage nighttime risks. Likely private sector initiatives include the extension of netting by novation and substitution to new markets, the creation of new clearinghouses, improved finality on private sector payments arrangements, and extended operating hours for private payments systems and securities depositories. Likely central bank initiatives include additional net settlement services and extended hours of operation for funds and securities transfer systems.

By opening the book-entry and funds transfer services earlier and offering an additional early net settlement service, the Federal Reserve would make it possible for private sector transfer networks to decrease temporal risk.[12] While proposed plans to enhance the degree of finality on private transfer networks should reduce the need for FedWire finality, offering the additional settlement could decrease the monitoring cost incurred by banks in controlling temporal risk. These risks would otherwise exist until settlement at the end of the day on FedWire.

Market participants may advocate the extension of *existing* daytime Federal Reserve services to cover the full 24-hour day. However, we believe this approach has at least two problems. First, should the central bank simply expand *existing* operations to the nighttime market, there would be significantly less incentive for the private sector to make needed changes in its operations. Second, we know that the central bank's presence in the provision of payments, if not properly structured, can distort market behavior and can lead to the creation of excessive risk exposures. However, having a *modified* version of FedWire and book-entry services operating *in conjunc-* *tion* with private firms during the nighttime hours may still be desirable, given that it already operates during the daytime.[13]

Any extension of Federal Reserve hours, however, should be preceded by the implementation of modifications to eliminate the distortions induced by current operating practices. These would include the full collateralization of overdrafts and the elimination of the below market interest rates currently charged for emergency loans at the discount window. Of course, strong consideration should be given to making these changes even if the Federal Reserve continues to operate only in the daytime market. At issue, obviously, and a topic beyond the scope of this paper, is whether or not the central bank should have an operational presence in the daytime market.

FOOTNOTES

[1]For a more complete description of payments system risk and costs and alternative means to manage them, see Bank for International Settlements (1989), Parkinson (1990), or Baer and Evanoff (1990).

[2]CHIPS is a private clearing system located in New York and operated by the New York Clearinghouse Association. It is a dollar-denominated network specializing in international payments. Payments undergo multilateral position netting (without novation) and settlement occurs at the end of the U.S. day over the books of the Federal Reserve Bank of New York. CHIPS is currently taking steps to improve its risk management procedures.

[3]The reader is referred to Pavel and McElravey (1990) for a more complete discussion of recent trends in international financial activity.

[4]A report by the Group of 30 (1989) recommended the proposed change. The report also seeks the creation of delivery vs. payment settlement systems where feasible and encourages securities lending as a means of expediting settlement.

[5]By ''good'' or ''final'' funds we mean the security of receivers that funds transferred to them via electronic transfer networks will actually be delivered. The degree of security depends on the characteristics of the sender and the network on which the funds were transferred. For example, funds transferred over FedWire are considered ''final'' because the Federal Reserve guarantees them. Thus, to the extent the Federal Reserve can and will deliver on the guarantee, the transfer is considered final. Other networks may declare all transfers final, but the claim is only as good as the credibility of the network.

[6]See Pavel and McElravey (1990).

[7]For a discussion of the various settlement systems in the derivative product markets, see Rutz (1988).

[8]See Moser (1990) for a discussion of circuit breakers for the U.S. stock market and financial derivatives market.

[9]When daylight overdraft caps were originally placed on CHIPS and FedWire there was concern that certain business and payments activities would shift offshore. Partly in response to this concern, the Federal Reserve issued its policy statement

[10]The $12 billion figure and the other percentages used in this analysis are approximations based on discussions with several bank and clearinghouse representatives; alternative sources suggest similar figures.

[11]No publicly available information exists on the dollar flows through offshore dollar clearing arrangements. Since our estimates cover a relatively broad range it is doubted that the exclusion of this sector appreciably affects our projections.

[12]These alternatives are currently being evaluated by the Federal Reserve System.

[13]For a more thorough discussion of policy options to manage payments system risk, see Baer and Evanoff (1990).

REFERENCES

Baer, Herbert L., and Douglas D. Evanoff (1990). "Payments system risk issues in a global economy." Federal Reserve Bank of Chicago Working Paper Series WP:90-12 (August).

Bank for International Settlements (1989). *Report on netting schemes*. Basle: BIS.

Bartko, Peter (1990). "Foreign exchange and netting by novation." Paper presented at the Federal Reserve System symposium on international banking and payment services, Washington, D.C., June 7-9, 1989. Summarized in *Payment Systems Worldwide*, pp. 48-51 (Spring).

Board of Governors of the Federal Reserve System (1989). *Proposals to Modify the Payments System Risk Reduction Program*. Press Release—Request for Comment and Policy Statement. Docket Numbers R0665-R0670, Washington, D.C. (June 16)

Chicago Mercantile Exchange (1989). "Clearing House Banking Interfaces." White paper (February).

Euromoney (1989). "U.S. exchanges fight for market share." Special issue, pp. 9-12 (July).

Group of Thirty (1989). "Clearance and settlement systems in the world's securities markets." New York/London (March).

Lane, Morton (1989). "Blue print for the global broker." Research Paper, Discount Corporation of New York Futures.

Moser, James (1990). "Circuit breakers." Federal Reserve Bank of Chicago, *Economic Perspectives*, pp. 2-13 (September/October).

Parkinson, Patrick (1990). "Innovations in clearing arrangements: A framework for analysis." *Proceedings of a Conference on Bank Structure and Competition*. Federal Reserve Bank of Chicago (forthcoming).

Pavel, Christine, and John McElravey (1990). "Globalization in the financial services industry." Federal Reserve Bank of Chicago, *Economic Perspectives*, pp. 3-19 (May/June).

Rutz, Roger D. (1988). "Clearing and settlement systems in the futures, options and stock markets." Paper presented at the Regulatory Issues in Financial Markets Conference sponsored by the Chicago Board of Trade, Washington D.C. Summarized as "Background paper: Clearance, payment, and settlement systems in the futures, options, and stock markets." *The Review of Futures Markets*, pp. 346-370 (November).

Thagard, Elizabeth R. (1989). "London's jump." *Intermarket*, pp. 22-24 (May).

Section II
Debt, Inflation, and Macroeconomic Forecasts

In Section II, we consider the macroeconomic issues critical to securities investing. In general, these issues concern factors that affect the economy as a whole, such as changing attitudes toward debt, inflation, and the prediction of broad economic movements.

In his article, "The Changing American Attitude Toward Debt, and Its Consequences," Frank E. Morris focuses on the debt of the U.S. government. Stemming from the continuing budget deficits, the large increase in Treasury debt has helped transform the United States from the largest net creditor nation in the world to the largest debtor nation. Thus, the movement toward increasing levels of debt has characterized both the public and private sectors. Morris draws some potentially grim implications of this public debt for firms and society at large. Morris fears that high governmental debt can lead to increases in interest rates, higher inflation, and reduced real investment. Therefore, continuing budget deficits have a fairly direct impact on the securities investor. Based on the arguments advanced by Morris, the federal debt presents a problem of substantial magnitude that will affect the economy in the years ahead.

The next three articles consider different aspects of inflation. In "The Costs of Anticipated Inflation," Adrian W. Throop utilizes the key distinction between anticipated and unanticipated inflation. Unanticipated inflation is an unexpected change in price levels, and this kind of inflation can cause wealth transfers among different sectors of society. By contrast, inflation is anticipated when the market as a whole correctly expects the inflation that actually happens. While some argue that anticipated inflation has little cost, Throop shows that there are some important costs associated with inflation even when it is fully anticipated.

The Iraqi invasion of Kuwait led to a tremendous increase in the price of oil. In a second article, "Oil Prices and Inflation," Adrian W. Throop considers how changing oil prices affect inflation. Typically, inflation is regarded as a change in the overall price level in the economy. Thus, a price increase for a single commodity would not generally affect inflation. Oil is a special kind of commodity, however, because oil is such a key ingredient in so many final goods and services in the economy. Thus, oil pervades the entire economy, rather than being a single and separate commodity, like wheat. Therefore, Throop attempts to assess the inflationary impact on the economy of the large oil price increase caused by the Iraqi invasion of Kuwait. By implication, the price drop resulting from the coalition's early successes against Iraq should help to dampen inflation.

To place the entire issue of inflation in perspective, David P. Ely and Kenneth J. Robinson review the evidence on inflation and the stock market in their paper, "The Stock Market and Inflation: A Synthesis of the Theory and

Evidence." Ely and Robinson begin from the well-accepted observation that stock prices perform poorly during inflationary periods. They attempt to evaluate two main competing explanations for this regularity. One view traces this poor performance to a inflation-induced rise in the real tax burden of corporations, while a second suggests that Federal Reserve policy may be the ultimate cause of the poor performance.

The last two articles of this section consider the ability of forecasting devices to predict macroeconomic variables. One possible forecasting tool is the index of leading economic indicators. Gerald H. Anderson and John J. Erceg explore whether leading economic indicators can predict recessions and recoveries in their paper, "Forecasting Turning Points with Leading Indicators." Leonard Mills asks "Can Stock Prices Reliably Predict Recessions?" Stock market performance is itself a leading indicator. Therefore, Anderson and Erceg examine leading indicators in general, while Mills focuses on a single, but very important indicator. Regrettably, leading indicators do not seem to provide useful forecasts of macroeconomic performance. However, understanding why this is the case helps to develop our understanding of the economy as a whole.

Article 4

The Changing American Attitude toward Debt, and Its Consequences

The Congress and the President have been struggling with the federal government budget deficit for six years, thus far with little result. The fundamental reason for their failure is the fact that the American people no longer view the deficit as a significant problem. This represents a radical change in the attitude of Americans from thirty years ago, when even small deficits were viewed with great concern. People are not much concerned about our long string of trade deficits, either. Those working in industries affected by foreign competition are, of course, worried about their jobs; others may feel uneasy about Mitsubishi buying Rockefeller Center; but people in general are not clamoring for the steps needed to eliminate the trade deficit. Moreover, there is no perception of the linkage between the federal budget deficit and the trade deficit.

This article will describe the factors that have produced this change in American values and assess the consequences, both past and future. Although society's values most often refer to social issues, they also help to shape the macroeconomic options open to a democratic government.

Early Influences

Dean Acheson chose as the title for his autobiography *Present at the Creation*. He was referring, of course, to the creation of the Marshall Plan, NATO and other aspects of U.S. foreign policy in the years following World War II. I was present at the creation of the changed American attitude toward national debts.

It began in the Kennedy Administration in the early 1960s. The President had run on a platform of getting the American economy going again. His principal economic advisers, Walter Heller, Chairman of the Council of Economic Advisers, and Douglas Dillon, Secretary of the Treasury, argued that the way to achieve that objective was through a

Frank E. Morris

Peter F. Drucker Professor of Management Science, Wallace E. Carroll School of Management, Boston College, and former President of the Federal Reserve Bank of Boston. This article is based on his remarks at his installation, February 12, 1990.

major tax cut, which would stimulate economic growth and, in the process, increase Treasury revenues sufficiently that the tax cut would not result in any substantial increase in the federal deficit.

This was a radical idea in those days and President Kennedy was quite conservative in fiscal matters. It took a long time for his advisers to persuade the President that it made economic sense to cut taxes even though the government was already running a deficit. It took much longer to persuade the Congress. One of the key features of the Kennedy tax program was the investment tax credit. I remember being stunned to learn that the leading business organizations had testified against the investment tax credit. In part it was due to a preference for accelerated depreciation, but in part it reflected an uneasiness with the general idea of cutting taxes when the government budget was in deficit.

The popular view of the day was the view of President Eisenhower—that the federal budget was akin to a family budget and if the government ran deficits, trouble was certain to ensue. Walter Heller complained that what he called the "Puritan Ethic," an unreasoning fear of deficits, was keeping the government from following sound economic policies. And so a big educational effort was undertaken to deal with the "Puritan Ethic."

My small role was to talk to the banking groups that regularly visited the Treasury. We argued that there certainly were times when an increase in the

---

The popular view of the day was that if the government ran deficits, trouble was certain to ensue.

---

deficit would be inappropriate. If the economy were operating close to capacity, an increase in the deficit could be inflationary, and would raise interest rates and squeeze out private investment. But in the conditions of 1962 and 1963, when the economy was operating well below capacity, a tax cut would raise total output and increase private investment, without enlarging the deficit significantly.

In the event, the Kennedy tax cut was a triumph.

In the first three years that the tax cut was in effect, 1964–66, the growth rate of real GNP averaged 5.6 percent, federal government revenues rose by 23 percent, and the fiscal 1966 deficit was slightly less than in fiscal 1963.

This was the first of five factors that changed American attitudes toward the federal debt, and perhaps the most important, because if the Kennedy tax cut had been viewed as a failure, subsequent U.S. fiscal history would have been very different and the "Puritan Ethic" might be alive and well today.

Theoretical Justifications

The second factor changing attitudes was the emergence of the doctrine that large deficits were needed to control federal government spending. A principal advocate of this position was Milton Friedman. He argued that deficits were not important; what was important was the percentage of the GNP absorbed by federal government spending. Government deficits would not be inflationary if the Federal Reserve refused to monetize the debt, and the presence of large deficits would constrain spending. What Friedman did not emphasize was that this combination of a loose fiscal policy and a tight monetary policy would, in an economy operating close to capacity, drive up interest rates, squeeze out private investment, and make American industry less competitive in world markets.

The large deficits have had the effect that Friedman anticipated. Because of the rise in military spending, total federal government spending as a percent of the GNP was higher in the last year of the Reagan administration than it was in Carter's last year. However, excluding the military, entitlement programs, and interest costs, the remainder of the budget declined as a percentage of the GNP. More important, the deficits have restrained the Congress from initiating new social programs. President Bush has been talking about establishing a new space program, improving the educational system, initiating a war on drugs, and aiding the Eastern European countries. Because of the deficit, however, only nominal amounts of money are being allocated to these programs. The United States is not in a financial position to undertake new initiatives or address new challenges. Because of the restraint on spending, conservatives who traditionally have opposed government deficits are now comfortable in defending a policy of continuing deficits.

The *Wall Street Journal* has been a constant advocate of this position on its editorial pages. The following is from an editorial of January 31, 1990:

Spending measures the government's real command over resources; it's a secondary matter whether it's financed by taxes, by borrowing or by even higher taxes with a budget surplus. While we'd like something a lot more surgical, an item veto for example, the deficit has been the only spending restraint we've had. The inexorable climb of outlays as a percent of GNP was checked by holding the line on taxes even at the expense of a budget deficit. Revenues are already climbing back toward their postwar high. On that ground alone it's time to cut them again, letting the people who earned the money decide how to consume, save and invest.

Other Contributing Factors

The third factor affecting attitudes has been the massive net inflow of foreign savings, totaling about $800 billion during the past seven years, which has mitigated the effect of the deficits on interest rates and private investment. Without this $800 billion in foreign savings, interest rates in the United States would have been much higher and the man in the street would be much less complacent about the deficits than he is today.

The fourth factor changing attitudes toward debt is the apparent success of the Reagan economic policies. I say "apparent" because we lack historical perspective, but without question a good feeling is widespread in the country. The unemployment rate is low. The inflation rate and interest rates are high by historical standards, but they are so much lower than they were in the early years of the decade that they seem quite satisfactory. For example, students today cannot relate to the fact that the mortgage rate on a house built in 1970 is 5½ percent—they think anything below 10 percent is pretty good. The very fact that the economy is in the eighth year of economic expansion with no recession in sight has caused people to discount concerns about the deficits.

The fifth and a very important factor changing attitudes toward debt, is the fact that the United States has not had a major depression in fifty years. This has made people much less cautious in financial matters. The clearest examples are in corporate finance, with many major companies taking on levels of debt that would not permit them to survive a serious depression. Some are even having trouble

dealing with a slower growth rate. The top managers of American companies in the 1950s and 1960s were people who had come to maturity during the Great Depression. The willingness of today's managers to leverage their companies must seem to them to be reckless behavior, and the willingness, until recently, of investors to buy the bonds of such highly leveraged corporations must seem to them to be naive. The fact that nobody under the age of sixty has any memory of the Great Depression has contributed substantially to the new attitudes about debt.

The massive net inflow of foreign savings has mitigated the effect of the deficits on interest rates and private investment.

The Consequences

Having discussed the reasons for the changed American attitude toward debt, I would like to turn to the consequences of that change. Economic theory tells us that if the government runs large deficits when the economy is running close to capacity, the result will be high interest rates, the squeezing out of private investment, and a slower rate of growth in productivity and real income. All of these consequences are clearly apparent in the 1980s, mitigated only by the large inflows of foreign capital.

Since World War II the U.S. economy has had two economic expansions that lasted more than seven years. It may be instructive to compare the first seven years of the present expansion (1983–89) with the first seven years of the earlier expansion (1961–67).

During the 1961–67 period the federal government budget deficits averaged 0.8 percent of the GNP versus 4.5 percent in the 1983–89 period, almost six times as large. At the same time, the gross private savings rate dropped from 17.2 percent during the 1961–67 period to 15.8 percent during 1983–89, which means that the burden of the deficits on our capital markets in the 1980s was even greater than the ratios of the deficits to the GNP would suggest. During the 1961–67 period, U.S. government long-term bond yields averaged 4.25 percent and the bank prime lending rate averaged 4.8 percent. These interest rates seem almost impossibly low today, but they are not very low relative to the rates that have prevailed in recent years in Japan and Germany, our major competitors.

Given the high cost of capital, it is not surprising that the investment performance of the United States in the 1980s was the poorest of any decade since

---

One of the most worrisome aspects of the large international deficit is that the United States has lost sovereignty over its financial markets.

World War II and that the rate of growth of productivity and real income was also the poorest. Net fixed domestic investment as a percentage of GNP during the 1983–89 period was only 72 percent of the 1961–67 level, and net fixed nonresidential domestic investment as a percentage of the GNP was only 58 percent of the 1961–67 level. We shall note later that the rate of growth of output per person in the nonfarm business sector during 1983–89 was 56 percent of the 1961–67 level. These domestic investment figures tell only part of the story. During the 1961–67 period the United States invested more abroad than foreigners invested in the United States, in an amount averaging 0.8 percent of the GNP. Net foreign investment during 1983–89 averaged a *negative* 2.7 percent of the GNP.

Since 1983 the level of investment in the United States has clearly been subpar despite the fact that in the past seven years the economy has enjoyed net imports of foreign savings totaling more than $800 billion. If this inflow had been associated with an exceptionally high level of investment in state-of-the-art plant and equipment, this country's future prospects would be greatly enhanced, but the facts clearly indicate that this inflow was consumed rather than invested.

While a national budget deficit is clearly not like a family's budget deficit, an international deficit is very similar. A family can consume beyond its in-

come as long as its credit remains good. The same is true of a nation in international transactions. The credit of the United States has been amazingly strong during the past seven years. This has led one prominent economist to argue that the United States can sustain current account deficits indefinitely at around the $100 billion level. I am skeptical of this proposition. My experience suggests that the fact that something has gone on for several years is no basis for assuming that it can go on forever.

When I was a graduate student in the 1950s, a common theme was that the world was going to have a perpetual shortage of dollars. When I arrived in the Treasury in 1961, I found that the dollar shortage was over. Foreign central banks had more dollars than they wanted to hold. The span of time between perpetual dollar shortage and dollar glut was very short.

One of the most worrisome aspects of the large international deficit is that the United States has lost sovereignty over its financial markets. The year 1987 was a case in point. In the spring of 1987 the inflow of private foreign capital suddenly dried up. Private foreign investors were unwilling to finance our deficit at prevailing interest rates and exchange rates. The dollar dropped and the deficit was financed entirely by an inflow of foreign central bank funds, as these banks sought to dampen the rate of decline of the dollar. While private foreign investors had been absorbing 30 percent or more of our new bond issues, central banks do not buy bonds; they invest short-term. As a consequence long-term bond yields rose by 150 basis points and this, in turn, triggered the great stock market collapse of 1987.

Prospects

The United States is currently vulnerable to another financial shock stemming from any change in the attitudes of private foreign investors. The major interest rate advantage that the United States offered in earlier years has largely been eliminated for German investors and is very much smaller for Japanese investors. The dollar has fallen by 18 percent against the deutsche mark since September, although it has thus far been steady against the yen. There could well be ahead of us another period in which the demand for U.S. assets by private foreign investors dries up. Again the United States would experience a sharp decline in the dollar and a rise in long-term interest rates. Despite an easing in Federal Reserve policy, long-term government bond yields have increased 75 basis points since December 20. At least in part, this rise in long-term yields reflects a recognition by the market that U.S. assets may be less attractive to foreign investors than they have been in the past. This is a matter of concern, since the economy in 1990 may be less capable of absorbing financial shocks than it was in 1987.

In 1981 the United States had net investment income of $34 billion, meaning that income on U.S. foreign investment exceeded income on foreign investment in the United States by that amount. This was a substantial American asset, the product of decades of heavy investment abroad. It permitted the country to run a trade deficit that in 1989 dollars would amount to $700 for every American family, and still balance its international accounts. In seven years this asset was dissipated; net investment income turned negative in 1989. At some point in the future, the United States will have to run a trade surplus in order to cover the interest payments due on the debt that we incurred so that we could consume more than we produced in the 1980s.

It should not be surprising that the poor investment performance of the 1980s has been associated with a poor productivity performance, the poorest of any major industrial country. Productivity growth during this expansion has been only 56 percent of the level of 1961–67, roughly the same proportion as the relative rates of growth of fixed nonresidential investment. Real compensation per hour in the nonfarm business sector rose by 20 percent during the expansion in the 1960s but only by 5 percent during this expansion.

With such an abysmal record of real income growth, why do Americans feel good about the 1980s? I think there are four reasons. First, the almost negligible real income growth dates back to 1973, the year of the first oil price shock. During the previous twenty-six years, 1947–73, real compensation per hour doubled. During the following sixteen years it rose by only 5 percent. Americans no longer expect a rapid rise in real income, as they did in the 1960s. Second, the decline of the inflation rate and interest rates from the high double-digit levels of the early 1980s is viewed, quite properly, as a success of economic policy. But there is no perception that the current levels of the inflation rate and interest rates are very high by historical standards. Young people find the cost of housing to be very high, and it is much higher in real terms than it was for my generation; but they do not understand that it is the higher

mortgage rates rather than the higher purchase price of housing that is the source of the problem. Third, the labor force participation rate for women has risen by almost 30 percent since 1973. The United States has many more two-earner families, and this has helped to mask the fact that real income per person has made little progress. Fourth, the poor U.S. economic performance was also masked by the large trade deficits that permitted us to consume more than we as a nation produced.

A prolonged reluctance of private foreign capital to finance our trade deficit would produce a declining dollar and sharply higher long-term interest rates.

Americans are a much less compassionate people than we were in the 1960s. We are now much less willing to sacrifice for the benefit of the disadvantaged, at home or abroad. The reason, I believe, is that with real incomes rising at 3 percent a year during the 1960s, Americans felt affluent. Today after sixteen years of little growth in real incomes the sense of affluence has gone and along with it some of our compassion for others.

In the American democracy, with all of its checks and balances and diffused power, we are often not able to act except in a crisis environment. While the economic policies of the 1980s have carried with them considerable costs, the costs are long-term in their impact, not the stuff to generate crises. The most likely disturbance to capture the attention of the American people would be a prolonged reluctance of private foreign capital to finance our trade deficit, which would produce a declining dollar and sharply higher long-term interest rates. We had a taste of this in 1987. More may come.

In the early 1960s economists of all persuasions agreed with President Kennedy's theme of the need to get the economy going again. In a congressional hearing in 1964, Keynesians argued that fiscal policies were too restrictive in the 1950s and monetarists complained that the Federal Reserve had not permitted the money supply to grow fast enough. They agreed on the need for more expansionary policies to enable the economy to reach its full potential. I shared this conventional wisdom.

President Eisenhower and William McChesney Martin, Jr., who presided over fiscal and monetary policies during most of the 1950s, were indeed conservative men. However, if we look at the economic statistics of the 1950s in the perspective of history, we might wonder why economists of that era were so unanimously dissatisfied with the results. During the 1950s we had an average rate of growth of real GNP of 4.1 percent, the unemployment rate averaged 4.5 percent, the increase in the Consumer Price Index averaged 2.3 percent per year. Not too shabby, but the dramatic numbers were those for productivity and real incomes. During the decade of the 1950s, output per hour rose by almost 30 percent, an average of 2.6 percent per annum, and real compensation per hour rose by almost 37 percent, averaging 3.2 percent per annum. We are unlikely to achieve that kind of economic performance in the 1990s.

In retrospect, I have reluctantly come to the conclusion that the country would be a lot better off today if we in the Kennedy Administration had failed to destroy the "Puritan Ethic" in the early 1960s.

Article 5

The Costs of Anticipated Inflation

"Our strategy continues to be centered on moving toward, and ultimately reaching, stable prices, that is, price levels sufficiently stable so that expectations of change do not become major factors in key economic decisions."
Alan Greenspan, in testimony to the House Committee on Banking, Finance, and Urban Affairs on January 24, 1989.

Inflation can distort economic decision making. In this regard, it is important to distinguish between the effects of anticipated and unanticipated inflation. Some of the more serious costs arise from inflation that is not fully anticipated. As discussed in the *Letter* of March 2, 1990, these include arbitrary transfers of wealth between creditors and debtors and difficulty in distinguishing between absolute price changes and movements in relative prices. Inflation uncertainty also hampers long-term planning by business and labor, and increases uncertainty about the real returns to saving and investment, thereby reducing economic growth.

In contrast, many argue that when inflation is fully anticipated, there is little or no cost to the economy since nominal interest rates will adjust to maintain real returns. However, with a tax system that is not indexed to inflation and loan instruments that generally do not allow households to borrow against anticipated increases in future income, even anticipated inflation can have distortionary effects. This *Letter* discusses the major effects of anticipated inflation, and presents some quantitative estimates of these effects on the allocation of resources in the U.S. economy. These estimates show that even fully anticipated inflation is significantly non-neutral in its impact.

Anticipated inflation and taxes
Irving Fisher provided the classic analysis of the effects of anticipated inflation in his *Theory of Interest* over a half century ago. Fisher argued that borrowers and lenders base their decisions on real interest rates, and that nominal interest rates adjust to compensate for anticipated infla-

tion. Moreover, in a world in which interest income is taxable and the costs of borrowing are tax deductible, the Fisherian model suggests that borrowers and lenders base their decisions on *after-tax* real interest rates.

Thus, for example, when the marginal income tax rate is 50 percent and the equilibrium real after-tax rate of interest is three percent, the nominal interest rate will settle at six percent, assuming anticipated inflation is zero. But if anticipated inflation rises to five percent, the nominal interest rate will rise to 16 percent to give the same real after-tax return of three percent.

The key insight of the Fisherian model is that anticipated inflation should have no impact on the real economy as long as nominal rates adjust fully to preserve real rates of return. In practice, however, certain aspects of the U.S. tax code interact with inflation in such a way that real rates are affected. First, although the tax code allows businesses to provide for the replacement of worn-out capital stock through a depreciation allowance, it specifies allowable depreciation in terms of the historical cost of the capital, not its current replacement cost. Thus, when prices rise due to inflation, the effective tax rate on business profits also rises because the base for depreciation is not increased accordingly. As a result, business investment tends to fall relative to other kinds of spending in an inflationary environment.

The U.S. tax code also may discourage inventory investment during inflationary periods. Seventy percent of U.S. firms value inventories on a first-in, first-out basis (FIFO). When these firms sell goods out of inventory in an inflationary period, they incur a taxable capital gain since the goods are sold at inflated prices but are valued for tax purposes at old, lower prices.

LIFO accounting, in which valuation is on a last-in, first-out basis, largely avoids this tax because the cost of goods sold is measured in terms of more recent prices. However, it is more complex than FIFO, and it has the disadvantage of reducing reported pre-tax profits, something publicly-held firms may be reluctant to do. To the extent that firms use the FIFO method, then, anticipated inflation raises the after-tax cost of holding inventories, which, in turn, may reduce inventory investment.

Liquidity constraints
In addition to the way anticipated inflation interacts with the tax code to alter real investment decisions, rising nominal interest rates associated with anticipated inflation tend to exacerbate liquidity constraints on households. Even in a noninflationary environment, households may be liquidity constrained in the sense that they are unable to borrow against rising real incomes to alter their current spending and investment patterns.

Anticipated inflation exacerbates this constraint because it raises nominal interest rates immediately, while increases in household nominal incomes occur only gradually. Because lenders are averse to high ratios of current debt service to current income, households are not able to borrow against the anticipated increases in future income, making it more difficult for them to qualify for loans. As a result, borrowing by households for expenditures on housing and consumer durables tends to be more sensitive to nominal after-tax interest rates than to real after-tax rates. And although capital gains on housing assets are given favorable tax treatment, which tends to increase the demand for housing when inflation and nominal interest rates rise, the effect of liquidity constraints tends to dominate, so that expenditures on residential investment vary inversely with nominal interest rates.

In contrast, this type of liquidity constraint is less important for businesses. The typical business has both old and new capital stock. When expected inflation rises, the cashflow (net of debt service) on the existing capital rises as well, and offsets the low initial net cashflow on new capital investment. As a result, business borrowing tends to respond more to real interest rates than to nominal interest rates.

Estimating the costs
To estimate the costs of anticipated inflation, I have simulated its effects on the U.S. economy using a medium-scale structural econometric model. In the simulation, money growth was permanently raised by five percentage points, thus generating a permanent increase in the inflation rate of five percentage points. Nominal interest rates were allowed to rise by the amount required to keep the aggregate demand for goods and services equal to long-run potential output.

The Fisher effect suggests that nominal interest rates should rise by more than the five-percentage point increase in the anticipated rate of inflation to compensate for both the increase in inflation and the increased tax liability associated with the higher nominal interest payments. However, as discussed above, the use of historical cost depreciation in an inflationary environment increases the effective tax rate on business profits and, therefore, raises the real cost of capital for business. This tends to reduce business borrowing, thereby reducing the upward pressure on nominal interest rates. Similarly, the inflation-related increase in liquidity constraints on households tends to depress household borrowing, which further limits the rise in nominal interest rates.

The simulation shows that these two influences more than offset the Fisher effect; nominal interest rates in the economy rise by only seven tenths of a percentage point for each one percentage point increase in the steady-state rate of inflation. This estimate is similar in magnitude to other estimates that have been obtained using alternative approaches.

Consequently, this simulation suggests that a rise in expected inflation reduces real after-tax interest rates. This means that when expected inflation rises, sectors that tend to respond to real interest rates will gain relative to those that respond to nominal interest rates.

The accompanying table shows the changes in resource allocation caused by a five-percentage point increase in anticipated inflation. Some of the largest impacts are on household investment in consumer durables and residential structures. Because of liquidity constraints, households respond more strongly to changes in nominal interest rates than to changes in real interest rates. Thus, although real interest rates fall in the simulation, higher nominal interest rates reduce household investment in durables by 10 percent and residential investment by 7.5 percent.

Because of the increased costs of investing in consumer durables and housing, households increase their expenditures on nondurables and services by 1.5 percent.

Estimated Effects of 5 Percent Anticipated Inflation

	Percent Change in Sector	Percent Contribution to Real GNP
Consumption		
Durables	−10.0	−1.0
Nondurables and Services	1.5	1.0
Residential Investment	−7.5	−0.4
Nonresidential Investment	−1.0	−0.1
Inventory Investment	0.0	0.0
Government Spending	0.0	0.0
Net Exports	30.5	0.5
		Sum 0.0

Business investment

As previously discussed, the business sector of the economy is not liquidity constrained the way households are. Business investment therefore responds primarily to changes in real after-tax interest rates, rather than to changes in nominal interest rates. The decline in real after-tax interest rates associated with the five-percentage point increase in anticipated inflation tends to stimulate business investment in plant and equipment.

At the same time, however, the higher inflation also increases the effective rate of taxation on business investment, an effect which tends to work in the opposite direction. As it turns out, the latter effect dominates slightly, and nonresidential fixed investment drops by one percent.

Similar tax and real interest rate effects may be present for inventory investment. But like other studies that have investigated this issue, this study did not find a statistically significant relationship between inventory investment and the after-tax cost of capital. Therefore, the impact of inflation on inventory investment is estimated to be nil.

National saving and investment

Although investment spending by households and businesses declines as a result of anticipated

inflation, net investment in foreign assets rises. This occurs because the decline in U.S. real interest rates makes investing abroad more attractive. These larger capital outflows act to depreciate the dollar and raise net exports. Net exports are estimated to rise by 0.5 percent of GNP.

The increase in net investment in foreign assets is not enough to offset the decline in investment in domestic assets, however. As a result, the overall rate of saving and investment in the economy falls. As noted above, because consumption becomes relatively less expensive than investment in durables and housing, household spending on nondurables and services rises by 1.5 percent. As a result, national saving (including the saving implied by households' investment in consumer durables) falls by an equal amount. This reduction in saving amounts to one percent of GNP.

The decline in saving is matched by an equal reduction in national investment. Total domestic investment falls by 1.5 percent of GNP, while net foreign investment rises by 0.5 percent of GNP, causing a net decline in national investment equal to one percent of GNP.

Significant distortions

Some of the most widely recognized costs of inflation arise when it is not anticipated. It is less well recognized, however, that even when inflation *is* anticipated, it significantly distorts economic decisions. Increases in anticipated inflation in the U.S. economy raise nominal interest rates and reduce real rates. This raises net foreign investment at the expense of domestic investment, and favors business investment over household investment, even though the effective tax rate on business investment rises. Increases in anticipated inflation also tend to reduce the economy's overall rate of saving and investment. Heightened liquidity constraints created by loan market imperfections primarily are responsible for this shift in resource use, although an increase in the effective tax rate on business investment also plays a role. As a result, the allocation of resources is less efficient than if prices were stable.

Adrian W. Throop
Research Officer

Article 6

Oil Prices and Inflation

The price of oil rose 35 percent immediately following Iraq's invasion of Kuwait—from about $20 a barrel to $27. Since then, prices have been relatively high and volatile, and an outbreak of armed conflict could send the price of oil even higher. Thus, even though other OPEC producers expect eventually to make up most of the shortfall in oil supplies resulting from the embargo against Iraq, it is possible that higher oil prices will persist, providing a sustained shock to the U.S. economy.

This *Letter* examines the effects of such a shock on price inflation in the U.S. A rise in the price of oil has a direct effect on the prices of final goods and services, as higher energy costs are passed through to consumers. Whether higher oil prices lead to a permanent increase in either the price level or the rate of inflation, however, depends on both the response of the Federal Reserve and the effect on expectations of future inflation.

To ensure that the price level does not remain permanently higher as a result of a rise in oil prices, the Federal Reserve would have to allow non-oil prices to adjust to offset the effects of higher oil prices. Such an adjustment would require the economy to grow more slowly for a time. Furthermore, if expectations of higher inflation generate higher wage inflation, temporarily slower growth also would be required to prevent a permanent increase in the *rate* of inflation.

To estimate the inflationary consequences of the recent 35 percent increase in oil prices, this *Letter* examines both the direct effect on overall prices and the indirect effect operating through inflation expectations.

The direct effect
A change in the price of oil has both direct and indirect effects on overall prices. These effects can be understood in terms of a simple model of the inflationary process that describes overall price movements as a function of changes in the price of non-labor inputs, wages, and inflation

expectations. In this model, final goods prices are equal to the sum of the cost of the labor required to produce a unit of output ("unit labor cost") plus a mark-up to cover the costs of non-labor inputs, including energy.

This mark-up changes as the costs of non-labor inputs change. Thus, a rise in oil prices raises the mark-up and, therefore, the prices of final goods and services. Historically, a 35 percent increase in the price of oil has raised the level of the GNP price index by about 1¼ percent through this direct channel. The effect on consumer prices is about 50 percent larger because this index includes the prices of imports (including the higher prices of imported oil), while the GNP price index does not include imports.

The direct effects of higher oil prices on the price level will not persist, however, as long as the Federal Reserve does not accommodate these higher prices by allowing an increase in the stock of money. In this case, higher oil prices will cause economic activity to slow and unemployment to rise temporarily. Wage inflation will moderate and offset the increase in the mark-up associated with higher oil prices. However, if the Federal Reserve attempts to counter the weakening in economic activity with a larger stock of money, an oil price increase can have a permanent effect on the price level.

Indirect effect of expectations
In addition, if expectations are affected, higher oil prices can permanently raise the *rate* of price inflation through higher wage inflation. In the model, the rate of wage inflation is a function of the unemployment rate and the expected rate of price inflation. The unemployment rate provides a measure of demand pressure in labor markets. When the demand for labor is strong, as measured by a low unemployment rate, wages will tend to rise because firms will bid them up trying to attract workers.

Competition in the labor market also occurs against the background of workers' and firms' expectations regarding the future rate of overall price inflation. Workers will demand higher wages to compensate them for higher expected prices in the future. For this reason, when there is neither excess demand nor excess supply in the labor market, wages will tend to rise at a rate equal to the expected rate of price inflation plus the expected growth in labor productivity. As a result, expected real (inflation-adjusted) wages will rise only as fast as productivity. The expected rate of price inflation will be realized as this rate of wage inflation is passed through to higher prices.

However, when the unemployment rate is low, and job vacancies exceed the number of unemployed, competitive pressures will push up wages at an even faster rate than the expected rate of price inflation plus the growth in productivity. These higher wage costs are then passed through to prices, and actual inflation will exceed expected inflation until firms and workers raise their expectations of future inflation. However, once they revise their expectations, and these expectations get reflected in wages and ultimately in prices, there is a further rise in actual inflation. Thus, in this situation, a wage-price spiral can occur, whereby inflation continues to accelerate as long as the demand for labor exceeds the supply of workers.

Because inflation expectations cannot be observed directly, in most models, including the one used here, expected inflation usually is represented by the rate of inflation over the recent past. Empirically, past inflation has an influence on current and future inflation. This may arise because market participants form their expectations adaptively, by extrapolating past inflation forward. Alternatively, expectations may be more forward-looking than this, but staggered, multi-year labor contracts introduce an element of inertia in the wage-setting process so that past inflation has an influence on the current and future rate of wage inflation.

Oil prices and expectations
How does an oil price shock affect expectations of future inflation? Labor market participants may realize that an oil price "shock" represents a one-time change in a relative price that need not affect the rate of overall price inflation in the long run. As such, wages would not need to rise to compensate for it.

However, labor market participants may not be able to discriminate perfectly between a one-time shock to the price level and other developments that would lead to a permanent increase in the rate of inflation. If they cannot or do not do so, higher oil prices may raise expectations of future inflation, leading to extra wage inflation, and therefore additional price inflation.

The extent to which expectations of future inflation are affected also depends, in part, on the credibility of the Federal Reserve's commitment to maintaining price stability. If labor market participants believe that the Federal Reserve will accommodate the pressures from oil prices, a wage-price spiral could ensue even though the initial shock was only transitory in nature. On the other hand, if the market believed the Federal Reserve would not accommodate a transitory shock, there would be no effect upon inflation expectations, and wage inflation would not augment the direct effect of higher oil prices.

Combining the two effects
To see how an increase in oil prices might affect long-run inflation, consider the following simple example. Suppose there is a permanent increase in the price of oil that causes the mark-up and overall price inflation to rise by one percentage point this year. This is the direct effect of a rise in oil prices. Wage inflation this year would be unaffected by this price rise. However, assuming that the rate of inflation that is observed this year is fully reflected in expectations of future inflation, wage inflation and hence price inflation will be one percentage point higher next year even though the direct effects of the higher price of oil will have gone away.

Moreover, to the extent the Federal Reserve accommodates these expectations by allowing the money supply to grow more rapidly, these expectations will be self-perpetuating, and wage and price inflation will be permanently higher. In this way, a temporary oil shock can permanently raise the rate of inflation.

This is a simple example. In practice, it is likely that labor market participants distinguish among the causes of price movements better than this example suggests. It also is likely that market participants expect the Federal Reserve to attempt to avoid accommodating the rise in oil prices. Both of these observations suggest that the response of wage inflation to an oil price shock is likely to be smaller than in the example. The long-run impact of a rise in oil prices, therefore, will be muted.

Econometric estimates of the inflation model described here suggest that the market has indeed tended to discount the influence of past oil-price and other supply shocks in forming its expectations of future inflation. Consequently, both wage and long-run price inflation have not been fully responsive to these supply shocks.

Interestingly, the estimates also show that the degree of discount has increased over time. It is estimated that 75 percent of past inflation associated with the direct effects of supply shocks was passed through to expectations of future inflation from the major oil shocks in 1974 and 1979, while only 35 percent was passed through from subsequent shocks during the 1980s. This change is most likely due to an increased awareness that such shocks change relative prices and equilibrium real wages, but need not affect the price level in the long run. This change also reflects a stronger faith in the Federal Reserve's commitment to maintaining stable prices.

Simulation results
To put the current oil shock into perspective, the accompanying chart shows the simulated time path of inflation in the GNP price index following a permanent 35 percent increase in the real price of oil. The direct effect from the increase in the mark-up is shown along with the estimate of the total response in both the 1970s and 1980s. The simulation assumes an accommodative monetary policy that keeps the unemployment rate unchanged. The simulation shows that through its direct effect on the mark-up, an oil price shock increases the inflation rate an average of 0.86 percentage points in the six quarters following the shock. However, after the price level has adjusted to the higher oil prices, there is no further increase in the inflation rate from this source.

Nonetheless, the simulation shows that because of the effect on expectations and wage inflation, the rate of inflation will continue to be higher even after the direct effects of the price shock

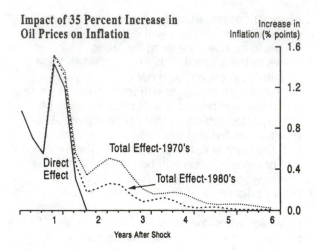

Impact of 35 Percent Increase in Oil Prices on Inflation

Increase in Inflation (% points)

Years After Shock

have been completed. The extra wage inflation operating through this indirect channel is at its highest in the third year, where, on average, it contributed 0.44 percentage points to the inflation rate during the 1970s, and 0.23 percentage points in the 1980s. But in either case this extra wage inflation becomes insignificant after the fourth year or so.

Conclusion
The direct effect of the current oil-price hike on the price level can be offset gradually by a non-accommodative policy on the part of the Federal Reserve. The negative effects on economic activity resulting from such a gradual approach need not be large as long as expectations do not change and cause wage inflation to magnify and perpetuate the inflationary pressure.

The estimates presented here reveal that the response of wage inflation to supply shocks, such as the current boost to oil prices, tends to be small and to die out fairly quickly. Moreover, the wage response has fallen over time as the market has become more accustomed to fluctuations in the price of oil and as the Federal Reserve's commitment to maintaining price stability has become more credible. As a result, the current oil price shock is not likely to set off a significant wage-price spiral.

Adrian Throop
Research Officer

Article 7

David P. Ely
Assistant Professor
San Diego State University

Kenneth J. Robinson
Economist
Federal Reserve Bank of Dallas

The Stock Market and Inflation: A Synthesis of the Theory and Evidence

One of the more puzzling anomalies found in financial markets is the poor performance of the stock market during periods of inflation. The failure of equities to maintain their value during inflationary time periods is considered anomalous as stocks, representing claims to *real* assets, should provide a good hedge against inflation. Moreover, if the so-called "Fisher" effect holds, stocks should be positively related to measures of expected inflation as well.

As shown in Chart 1, during the rapid inflation years of the 1970s, movements in U.S. stock prices failed to keep pace with movements in the general level of prices. This pattern has also been found in a number of other countries. Table 1 contains correlation coefficients between real stock returns and inflation for the Group of Seven countries using monthly data over the period 1950–1986. As that table shows, a significant negative relationship holds during at least one extended subperiod for all except one of the countries listed. And a significant negative relationship is found in four of the seven countries for the overall period of 1950–1986. Against this backdrop, it is not surprising that "inflation fears" were cited as a possible contributing factor to the stock market crash of October 1987.[1]

A number of studies have documented the inverse relationship between real common stock returns and various measures of both actual and expected inflation.[2] The literature is generally divided, however, over the reasons why equities might fail to maintain their value during periods of inflation. This paper surveys the two main arguments that have been advanced as possible explanations for this observed anomaly in the U.S. stock market. First, the so-called "tax-effect" hypothesis is examined. This hypothesis focuses on the treatment of depreciation and the valuation of inventories in periods of inflation. Particularly, share prices fail to keep pace with inflation because inflation increases corporate tax liabilities and thus reduces after-tax earnings. Here, inflation can be said, in an econometric sense, to "cause"—or more precisely to temporally precede—movements in stock prices.

The "proxy-effect" hypothesis is the alternative explanation for why real stock returns are negatively correlated with inflation. In its current form, this hypothesis involves two assumptions—one that cyclical variations in output and earnings growth are positively correlated, and the other that monetary policy is countercyclical. The central tenet here is that lower stock returns signal lower expected future output and earnings growth, which, in turn, initiates a countercyclical policy response by the central bank. Individuals anticipate the expansion in the money supply and thus anticipate future inflation, which leads to an increase in *current* inflation. So, when stock re-

The authors would like to thank Mike Cox, Joe Haslag and Scott Hein for helpful comments without implicating them in our conclusions.

[1] The Report of the Presidential Task Force on Market Mechanisms *(1988, p. I-13)* states that *"It is meaningless whether or not these inflation fears were justified, for it is clear that for as long as financial authorities were responding to the inflation threat—whether real or imagined..."* the equity market might suffer.

[2] See Bodie *(1976)*, Nelson *(1976)*, and Fama and Schwert *(1977)*.

Chart 1
Annual CPI and S&P 500
Common Stock Price Index

1970 = 100

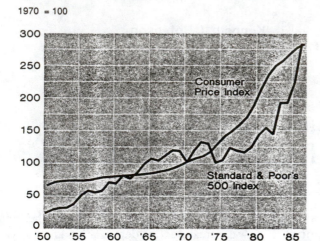

Sources of Primary Data: Standard & Poor's Corporation.
U.S. Bureau of Labor Statistics.

Table 1
Real Stock Returns and Inflation:
Various Periods

Country	1950-1959	1960-1969	1970-1979	1980-1986	1950-1986
United States	−0.05	−0.28*	−0.24*	−0.34*	−0.25*
Japan	−0.08	−0.21*	−0.33*	−0.26*	−0.20*
West Germany	−0.05	−0.19*	−0.02	−0.12	−0.09
France	−0.24*	−0.12	−0.005	−0.15	−−0.13*
United Kingdom	−0.02	−0.16	−0.06	−0.08	−0.04
Italy	−0.26*	−0.16	−0.29*	−0.09	−0.20*
Canada	−0.06	−0.12	−0.04	−0.26*	−0.03

* Significant at the 1-percent level.

turns fall, inflation increases. Although inflation in this case, is negatively correlated with stock returns, more precisely, stock returns temporally precede inflation. Thus, in an econometric sense, they are said to "cause" inflation.[3]

In the following analysis, a simple model of stock-price determination is offered. (*See the accompanying box for a description.*) This model can be used to highlight the role that inflation has played in determining both stock prices and stock returns in the U.S. economy. In the context of this model, the tax-effect hypothesis is first examined, with emphasis on particular features of the U.S. Tax Code that may have given rise to inflation's adverse effect on equity markets. This is followed by an exposition of the proxy-effect hypothesis, which shows how monetary policy may have historically contributed to the anomalous relationship between stock returns and inflation.

Tax-effect hypothesis: the firm's perspective

Adherents of the tax-effect hypothesis argue that the adverse effect of inflation on share prices stems primarily from two sources—inflation's effect on after-tax earnings of firms and inflation's effect on individuals' portfolio allocation. This section considers the first of these two sources.

From the standpoint of firms, inflation has a detrimental effect due primarily to two features of the U.S. Tax Code. The first of these features is the treatment of depreciation. Traditionally, the value of the depreciation deduction allowed for firms has been based on the original or "historic cost" of an asset, and *not* on its full replacement value. In a period of rising prices, then, the value of the depreciation allowance becomes inadequate and real corporate tax liabilities increase. In this way, inflation leads to a reduction in real after-tax earnings of firms and a consequent reduction in real dividends and stock prices.

Also contributing to the adverse effect of inflation on the firm is the treatment of inventory valuation under U.S. tax laws. When inventories are valued under FIFO (or first-in-first-out) accounting, inflation leads to an understatement of the costs of replacing these inventories. As is the case under the use of historic-cost accounting for depreciation charges, inflation raises the effective corporate tax burden, thus depressing net earn-

ings. Each of the above two factors—depreciation allowances and inventory valuation—acts to make inflation a penalty to firm profitability; consequently, inflation penalizes a firm's dividends and share prices.

There is, however, one potential *benefit* to firm profitability from rising prices. Namely, at higher rates of inflation, nominal interest rates are higher. And, since firms are allowed to deduct the full nominal interest payments on debt, accounting profits are in this regard reduced by inflation.

The net corporate tax burden caused by inflation thus depends on a comparison of the *penalty* arising from historic-cost accounting methods to the *benefit* arising from the deductibility of nominal interest payments on debt. Using simulation analysis, Hasbrouck (1983) finds that, under tax laws in effect through 1980, the loss due to historic-cost accounting outweighs the leverage gain at low inflation rates. Hasbrouck estimates that the corporate tax-maximizing inflation rate is in the range of 7–9 percent. Beyond these rates, inflation actually reduces the corporate tax burden since gains resulting from the use of debt financing outweigh the effects of historic-cost accounting.[4] It is worth noting that from 1973 to 1980, when real stock prices tended to fall, the rate of inflation averaged 9.2 percent per year. Interpreted in light of Hasbrouck's esti-

---

[3] Modigliani and Cohn (1979) offer a third explanation. Investors commit two "major errors" in evaluating stocks during periods of inflation. First, investors are said to be unable to distinguish between real and nominal rates of return in the valuation of equities. Second, market participants fail to realize the gain that flows from a depreciation in the value of corporate debt outstanding in a time of inflation. In essence, Modigliani and Cohn argue that investors suffer from a form of "money illusion." This framework is ignored in the current analysis as it is outside the generally accepted paradigm of market efficiency and thus has not generated much interest.

[4] Maher and Nantell (1983) argue that there is no offset possible from debt usage as the premium that must be paid to bondholders in the face of inflation exceeds the tax advantages of debt financing. The crucial assumption for this result to hold is that the bondholder's marginal tax rate must exceed the corporate tax rate.

A Model of Share Price Determination

This box outlines a simple model of stock-price determination helpful for illustrating the relationship between stock prices and inflation. In order to focus attention on the issues considered in this article—specifically, on the tax-effect hypothesis and on the proxy-effect hypothesis—certain simplifying assumptions are made.

In general, the price of a firm's stock today can be expressed as the present discounted value of expected future dividends (Brealey and Myers 1984, Chap. 4). That is,

$$(1) \qquad V_t = \sum_{i=1}^{\infty} \frac{DIV_{t+i}^e}{(1+R)^i}$$

where V_t equals the dollar price of the firm's stock today, DIV_{t+i}^e equals the firm's nominal expected future dividend (dividend in period $t+i$), and R represents the nominal rate (presumed constant over time) at which market participants discount these expected future cash flows (or the rate of return required by investors).

Consider first the numerator of this expression. There are essentially two ways that expected dividends can grow over time. One of these is through growth in expected *real* earnings, and the other is through inflation. That is, $DIV_{t+i}^e = div_{t+i}^e * P_{t+i}^e$ where div_{t+i}^e represents real earnings of the firm in period $t+i$ and P_{t+i}^e is the expected price level in period $t+i$. Since the purpose of this paper is to investigate the relationship between *inflation* and the stock market, both actual and expected real earnings will be provisionally treated as constant over time. This allows div_{t+i}^e to be expressed simply as div in all periods.

For simplicity, it is also assumed that inflation, π, is constant over time and fully anticipated. Under these assumptions, P_{t+i}^e can be rewritten simply as $P_t(1+\pi)^i$. This allows expected nominal dividends to be separated into its two components, real dividends and the general level of prices, so $DIV_{t+i}^e = div * P_t(1+\pi)^i$.

Turning now to the denominator of this expression, the nominal rate of discount can be separated into its two components—inflation and the (constant) real rate of discount (r)—by making use of the Fisher relationship. That is, $1+R$ equals $(1+r)(1+\pi)$.

With these simplifications, the value of the firm's stock can then be expressed as:

$$(2) \qquad V_t = \sum_{i=1}^{\infty} \frac{div^* P_t \,(1+\Pi)^i}{(1+r)^i \,(1+\Pi)^i},$$

which, upon simplification, reduces to:

$$(3) \qquad V_t = \frac{div \cdot P_t}{r}$$

As equation 3 makes clear, stock prices will not increase proportionately with an increase in the general price level if inflation is associated with either (1) a reduction in real dividends of the firm, or (2) an increase in individuals' discount rate. Equation 3 is thus helpful in explaining both the tax-effect hypothesis and the proxy-effect hypothesis. The tax-effect hypothesis, for example, is represented in equation 3 as the case where either (1) div is reduced, or (2) r is increased due to an increase in P_t. The proxy-effect hypothesis, on the other hand, is represented as the case where an anticipated reduction in GNP growth causes a reduction in div and V_t, which is associated with an increase in P_t. In the text we will discuss more fully the underlying bases for each of these hypotheses.

mates, stock prices fell during a period in which inflation had risen to roughly its corporate tax-maximizing rate, indicating the possibility of an adverse tax-effect at work.

Tax-effect hypothesis: individuals' perspective

The foregoing discussion pertains to the adverse effect that inflation can have on stock prices due solely to its direct effect on firms' profitability. Inflation was shown to potentially lower firms' real dividends which, as seen from Equation 3, prevents stock prices from keeping pace with the general level of prices. Chart 2 illustrates this hypothesized link between inflation and stock prices.

There are, however, other methods by which taxes and inflation can interact to lower firms' stock prices. One of these methods, as outlined by Martin Feldstein (1980 a & b), pertains to the manner in which tax rules and inflation interact to raise individuals' effective rate of discount. Feldstein's argument relies principally on the assumption that individuals invest in a wide range of alternative assets (stocks, bonds, land, gold, owner-occupied housing, tax-free instruments, etc.). Furthermore, although inflation generally reduces firm profitability and thus reduces the rate of return on stocks, it tends to raise the relative return offered on a variety of other assets. (In fact, as Feldstein points out, individuals may actually experience an increase in their net real yield on some assets during inflation).

Therefore, since they: (1) must pay income tax on both dividends and capital gains; (2) must pay taxes on nominal interest income from corporate bonds; and (3) may invest in a much wider range of alternative investments, individuals will substitute out of corporate stocks and bonds in times of rising prices. The effect of this substitution is to increase the real cost to firms of raising capital or, viewed alternatively, to increase the real rate at which individuals discount their before-tax dividends received from firms (r). As seen in equation (3), this effect of inflation on individuals' rate of discount reinforces that outlined previously on firms' dividends, so that real stock prices would be further depressed in periods of inflation.[5] Chart 2 illustrates this added effect of inflation on stock prices.

Tax-effect hypothesis: empirical evidence

While the theoretical justification for the tax-effect hypothesis is generally acknowledged, formal empirical evidence is more problematic. As shown previously, when firms' computation of taxes is based on historic-cost accounting methods for both depreciation and cost of goods sold, tax-deductible firm costs differ from the current costs of factors of production. It follows that real *aggregate* corporate tax liabilities, then, should vary directly with the rate of inflation. Following this line of reasoning, Gonedes (1981) attempts to assess the impact of both expected and unexpected inflation on various measures of the aggregate real corporate tax burden over the period 1929–1974. Contrary to expectations, Gonedes presents evidence that appears to be inconsistent with the tax-effect hypothesis.[6] Specifically, aggregate corporate tax liabilities over the period from 1929–1974 are found to be unrelated to various measures of inflation——rather than positively affected by inflation—and thus not in support of the tax-effect hypothesis.

Gonedes attributes the lack of empirical verification of a tax effect at work to an implicit "indexing" that has occurred over the period 1929–1974. Indexing the tax code with respect to both depreciation and inventory charges would eliminate the effect of inflation on share prices. Gonedes argues that de facto indexation has been

[5] *Friend and Hasbrouck (1982) criticize the ad hoc nature of Feldstein's approach to share-price determination. Using a model based on expected utility maximization, along with different values of the tax and risk parameters, Friend and Hasbrouck arrive at the same qualitative conclusions as Feldstein. That is, inflation places downward pressure on share prices due to tax effects, but the magnitude of the effect is discovered to be much smaller than what follows from Feldstein's model. Feldstein (1982) acknowledges the usefulness of deriving the price investors are willing to pay per share on the basis of expected utility maximization, but rejects as "implausible" some of the parameter values assumed by Friend and Hasbrouck.*

[6] *Gordon (1983) also finds little evidence in support of a tax effect at work.*

Chart 2

Tax-Effect Hypothesis

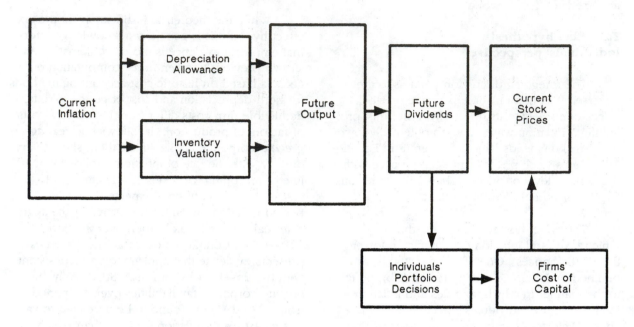

Proxy-Effect Hypothesis

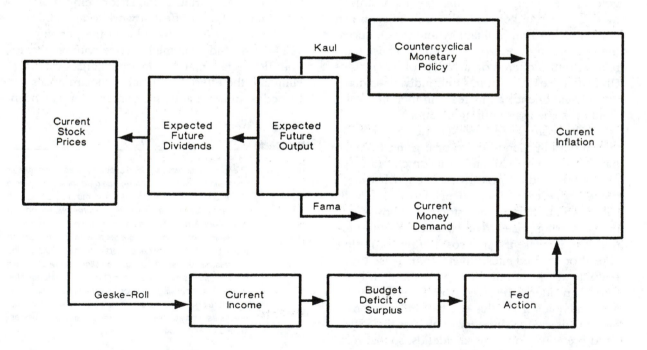

achieved through such factors as: (1) The implementation of accelerated depreciation schedules; (2) Various subsidies, such as the Investment Tax Credit; and (3) Decreasing the service lives on depreciable assets, all of which occurred simultaneously over the period 1929-1974.

Recall that, during times of inflation, the *net* corporate tax burden depends on both a penalty arising from historic-cost accounting methods and a benefit arising from the deductibility of nominal interest payments on corporate debt. If inflation is unanticipated, an additional benefit is available from the unforeseen decline in the real value of a firms'outstanding debt. Over the time period November 1977 through December 1982, Pearce and Roley (1988) examine the impact of unanticipated inflation on firms' share prices by considering these potential penalties and benefits. Historic-cost accounting of inventories is found to adversely affect stock prices. But, depreciation expenses are not a significant factor in explaining movements in share prices. Finally, the magnitude of a firms' outstanding debt is found to have a positive affect on share prices, indicating that inflation, in part, reduced the real value of firms' liabilities.

Tax-effects hypothesis: recapitulation of theory and evidence

The failure of changes in share prices to keep pace with movements in the overall level of prices could be attributed to certain features of the tax system. Particularly, the use of historic-cost accounting drives a wedge between tax-deductible costs and current costs of the factors of production. As a result, taxable profits increase at a faster pace than inflation, which puts downward pressure on equity prices. Empirical evidence of a tax effect at work is mixed and does not generally come out in support of the tax-effects hypothesis. Also, evidence that relies on simulation analysis is usually quite sensitive to the assumptions regarding the *effective* corporate tax burden.[7] Further, if it *is* the tax structure which is the driving force behind the seemingly anomalous relationship between inflation and stock prices in the U.S., then it is puzzling to observe (*see Table 1*) basically the same phenomenon across countries despite variation in tax laws.

An alternative framework: the proxy-effect hypothesis

In view of the criticisms of the tax-effect hypothesis, an alternative framework has developed to explain why inflation and stock values are inversely related. This explanation—known as the proxy-effect hypothesis—argues that expected future output growth and current inflation are inversely correlated. Inflation is said to be merely "proxying" for expected output or earnings growth in statistical tests of the relationship between stock returns and inflation. According to the proxy-effect hypothesis, any significant inverse relationship between these two variables is spurious, because it is induced by a *direct* relationship between stock returns and expected output growth together with an *inverse* relationship between expected future output growth and inflation. In contrast to the tax-effect hypothesis, the proxy-effect hypothesis claims that inflation has not been a causal factor in the performance of real stock prices but, rather, the relationship between inflation and stock prices is spurious.

Understanding the proxy-effect hypothesis requires exposition of the purported links in two contemporaneous chains of causality. Each chain begins with an increase or decrease in the rate of growth of expected future output. In one case this chain runs to expected future dividends and thus to current stock returns and in the other case, to expected future inflation and thus to current inflation. The link between expected future output growth and current stock returns is straightforward and requires little explanation. The purported link between expected future output growth and current inflation is not commonly acknowledged and requires further elaboration. In what follows, three explanations are reviewed to show how movements in expected future output may be related to current inflation.

---

[7] *See the discussion in Friend and Hasbrouck (1982) and Feldstein (1982) for an example of the importance of assumed parameter values.*

The proxy-effect hypothesis: linkage through money demand

The proxy-effect hypothesis was first introduced by Eugene Fama (1981). Fama's explanation for the inverse relationship between expected economic activity and current inflation follows from two key assumptions—(1) that individuals are "rational" in the sense of making use of all available current information relevant to their money and financial decisions, and (2) that individuals' current demand for money is related to future real economic activity and current interest rates.[8] Then, assuming that the money supply, real economic activity, and interest rates are exogenous, this demand for money, in effect, becomes a vehicle for the transmission of expected future inflation to current inflation.

In order to explain this more fully, consider the case where individuals' expectations of future output growth are revised downward. The lowering in expected future output growth leads to a lowering in expected future dividends and has the direct and immediate effect of reducing current stock returns. But also, the decline in expected future output growth leads to a decrease in

money demand currently and thus an excess supply of money. Following Fama's assumption that interest rates and the money supply are exogenous, the excess supply of money is accompanied by an increase in the price level to restore monetary equilibrium. Essentially, the forward-looking nature of individuals' money demand generates an inverse relationship between current inflation and expected future growth in GNP. This enables a decrease in future output growth to cause *both* a decline in current stock returns and an increase in current inflation.

In terms of the model developed earlier, and summarized in equation 3, a reduction in expected future output and earnings growth lowers *div* with the direct effect of lowering V_t.[9] But also, the reduction in anticipated future output growth raises P_t. Chart 2 outlines this purported linkage of the proxy-effect hypothesis (identified as the Fama scenario). Any observed relation between stock returns and current or expected inflation then, according to this theory, is purely spurious, with no causal chain from inflation to stock returns.[10]

The proxy-effect hypothesis: linkage through debt monetization

Geske and Roll (1983), who relax the assumption of an exogenous money supply, have suggested an extension of Fama's argument. These authors posit, in fact, that a "reverse causality" actually drives the inverse relationship between stock returns and inflation. In contrast to earlier work which hypothesized a causative influence of inflation on stock returns (and in contrast to Fama's model in which inflation and stock returns are spuriously related), it is stock returns which "cause" inflation.[11]

Geske and Roll weave a sequence of events by which this reverse causality comes about. In order to illustrate the Geske-Roll hypothesis, consider the case where expectations regarding future GNP growth are lowered. Stock prices decrease in response to projections of slower growth which leads to a decline in both personal and corporate income. Government tax revenues then decline which leads to a deficit in government revenue. That is, Geske and Roll suggest that a decline in expected future economic activity should be fol-

---

[8] It should be pointed out that it is not common in economic models to assume that the demand for money currently is related to future economic activity, and, on this basis, Fama has been criticized. It is worth noting, however, that Fama's results could also be obtained in a more standard framework where, instead of Fama's assumption (2), current money demand is assumed to be related to current income and current interest rates, but with individuals being forward looking in decisions regarding interest rates. In this case, a decline in expected future output growth would lead to a perceived future excess supply of money and thus to a perceived increase in future inflation and interest rates (equivalently a decrease in future bond prices). Expecting such an increase in future interest rates, individuals may bid up interest rates today (bond prices fall) as they sell bonds in order to avoid a future capital loss. Again, the demand for money currently would fall leading to an excess supply of money and inflation.

[9] This application of the proxy-effect hypothesis assumes that the expected growth rate of future output was initially zero, so that a decline in the growth rate amounts to an anticipated contraction in GNP.

lowed both by a decline in government revenue *and* by an increase in the federal budget deficit. The next step in the Geske-Roll model involves the central bank. When deficits begin to grow, government debt outstanding increases. The central bank chooses to monetize a portion of this debt, thus leading to inflation. Since this debt monetization is anticipated by rational individuals, a decline in the stock market will cause an increase in expected future inflation. Therefore, stock returns are inversely correlated with expected future inflation.

Geske and Roll point out that changes in expected inflation tend to be highly correlated with unexpected inflation. This explains the negative association between stock returns and unexpected inflation which Fama (1981) found puzzling. Finally, through individuals' forward-looking behavior, the increase in expected future inflation is transmitted to current inflation as well. It is through this extended chain of causality, then, that lower current stock returns cause an increase in current inflation. In terms of the model developed earlier, *div* first falls (due to an anticipated cyclical contraction in output). The reduction in *div* drives V_t down, which ultimately leads to an increase in P_t. Chart 2 shows this hypothesized chain of events (identified as the Geske-Roll scenario).

The proxy-effect hypothesis: linkage through countercyclical monetary policy

The Fama model excludes any response by the monetary authority while Geske and Roll stress a policy response of debt monetization. An extension of these arguments is developed by Kaul (1987) who agrees that the relationship between stock returns and inflation is spurious. Following Fama, Kaul stresses the importance of the money demand linkage in his analysis but is also willing to incorporate a response of the monetary authorities. Unlike Geske and Roll, however, this response does not hinge exclusively on the practice of debt monetization. Rather, Kaul presumes that the central bank follows a *countercyclical* money supply process.

The full sequence of events as viewed by Kaul occurs as follows. First, expected future output declines which is signaled by a fall in

stock prices. The Fed then responds with a countercyclical policy which results in an increase in the money supply. This causes both an increase in current inflation and an upward revision in inflation expectations. As a result, there is an observed inverse relationship between stock returns and both actual and expected inflation.

Kaul's version of the proxy effect hypothesis thus incorporates two commonly accepted effects of a perceived reduction in future GNP growth. For one, the anticipated slowing lowers current stock returns. For another, the anticipated slowing causes a current monetary expansion, and thus inflation. These two alone are sufficient to generate the inverse relationship often found between stock returns and inflation. The inverse relationship between expected future GNP growth and current inflation now is the result of the equilibrium process in the monetary sector. In terms of the model developed earlier, *div* first declines (due to an anticipated decline in GNP) which lowers V_t. But also, the decline in *div* stimulates a countercyclical response on the part of the monetary authorities which raises P_t. Chart 2 shows this hypothesized connection between stock prices and inflation (identified as the Kaul scenario).

[10] Benderly and Zwick (1985) agree with Fama that the relationship between stock returns and inflation is spurious. Unlike Fama though, Benderly and Zwick argue that the relationship runs from inflation to expected output growth. These authors base their conclusion on a real balance model of output in which changes in aggregate demand are related to lagged changes in real money balances.

[11] One should take note of the subtle distinction in Geske and Roll's use of the term "cause" here. Really, there is not reverse causality in the sense previously described for the tax-effect hypothesis because the sequence of events does not begin with stock prices. It begins with movements in expected future output. Actually, then, the relationship between current inflation and stock returns is here, too, spurious because both inflation and stock returns are ultimately driven by a decline in expectations of future GNP growth. Movements in stock prices, however, do precede movements in inflation and in this sense can be said to cause inflation.

Proxy-effect hypothesis: the empirical evidence

Empirical evidence on the proxy-effect hypothesis is extensive and generally may be delineated into the categories outlined above in reviewing the theoretical linkages between stock returns and inflation. In what follows, we will review the empirical evidence on the proxy-effect hypothesis beginning with the evidence on the linkage through money demand, as theorized by Fama.

Recall that the key to the spurious relationship between inflation and stock returns in Fama's hypothesis is that movements in expected future economic activity cause movements in both expected and current inflation. Empirical evidence relating real stock returns to both expected and unexpected inflation reveal a significant negative relationship. However, in multiple tests which also include real expected output growth, expected inflation looses its significance in explaining stock returns. This evidence suggests a spurious relationship between expected future inflation and current stock returns. Note also that *unexpected* inflation remains significant in nearly all of Fama's tests (all but those using annual data), and the expected inflation term looses significance in explaining real stock returns only when the growth rate of the monetary base is added to the set of explanatory variables. Fama points out that his measure of expected inflation is highly correlated with monetary base growth. Therefore, it is possible that one proxy for expected inflation has simply replaced another and the puzzling relationship between stock returns and inflation remains.

Turning now to empirical evidence on other views of the proxy-effect hypothesis, recall that Geske and Roll view current stock prices as driving current inflation through a practice of debt monetization by the central bank. Geske and Roll offer as empirical evidence a series of "transfer-functions" which purport to establish the linkage between stock prices and inflation in their model. For the most crucial element of this linkage, however—the practice of debt monetization—Geske and Roll do not offer compelling evidence. Empirical verification of the existence of debt monetization by the Federal Reserve is mixed, at best.[12] Geske and Roll point out that "...the detectable effect of Federal Reserve System Treasury debt holdings on the Fed's issuance of base money is very small in estimated magnitude; however, it *is* significant." The failure to discover a very substantial degree of debt monetization is blamed on "the incredible short-term churning of the Fed's asset portfolio."[13]

Kaul (1987) presents empirical evidence for the United States, as well as for Canada, the United Kingdom and Germany, consistent with the central tenets of the proxy-effect hypothesis. Regression results indicate a positive relationship between stock returns and expected real activity. Inflation and expected real activity are found to be negatively related, Kaul argues, due to both a countercyclical monetary policy response and to the practice of debt monetization.

Just as Geske and Roll's results hinge on the practice of debt monetization, Kaul's conclusions rely on a consistent countercyclical policy response which is anticipated by individuals. In estimates of both base-growth and monetary-aggregate growth equations, Kaul includes the unemployment rate to capture this policy response. In the four countries analyzed, however, the unemployment rate is generally insignificant in explaining money growth.

Evidence of central bank behavior from reaction functions casts doubt about the consistency of Federal Reserve policymaking, making it difficult to derive a generally accepted model of central-bank behavior.[14] Moreover, throughout most of the 1970's, the Fed engaged in federal funds rate targeting, which tends to result in a *procyclical* policy. Also, the current procedure of targeting on borrowed reserves, in effect since the fall of 1982, represents a return to funds rate targeting.[15] Clearly, a procyclical policy results in either a *positive* relationship between stock re-

---

[12] See Allen and McCrickard (1988) and Joines (1988). For additional support of the inconclusive evidence of debt monetization, see the references in McMillin (1986).

[13] Geske and Roll (1983, p. 22)

[14] For a summary of the reaction function literature, see Barth Sickles and Wiest (1982).

[15] See Gilbert (1985) and Thornton (1988).

turns and inflation or, at best, no relationship. Yet there has been an inverse relationship between stock returns and inflation in the United States during the 1970's and 1980's, as Table 1 shows, despite evidence of a procyclical policy stance by the central bank. These findings cast further doubt on the validity of Kaul's hypothesis.

Summary and conclusions

Equities, representing claims to real assets, should prove to be good hedges against inflation. Moreover, if future inflation can be at all foreseen, stock-market returns should be positively related to expected inflation as well. During much of the post-war time period, however, a well-documented tendency exists for equities to perform poorly during periods of inflation. Two main schools of thought have arisen to explain this anomaly.

The first of these appeals to particular features of the tax code in the United States as the primary factor behind the failure of equities to maintain their value during inflation. Historic-cost accounting for both depreciation and inventories results in an overstatement of corporate profits during periods of inflation. As a result, real corporate tax liabilities increase, which decreases net earnings. A simple model of share price determination then predicts downward pressures on real equity values during periods of inflation. While theoretically valid, empirical evidence for a tax effect at work is inconclusive.

The second school of thought appeals to the monetary sector as a vehicle through which the inverse stock return-inflation relationship occurs. A combination of money demand effects, along with both the practice of debt monetization and countercyclical monetary policy responses by the central bank is said to give rise to an inverse relationship between stock returns and inflation. Again, empirical evidence for this model is problematic.

References

Allen, Stuart D., and Donald L. McCrickard, (1988), "Deficits and Money Growth in the United States: A Comment," *Journal of Monetary Economics* 21 (January): 143–153.

Barth, James, Robin Sickles, and Philip Wiest, (1982), "Assessing the Impact of Varying Economic Conditions on Federal Reserve Behavior," *Journal of Macroeconomics* 4 (Winter): 47–70.

Benderly, Jason, and Burton Zwick, (1985), "Inflation, Real Balances, Output, and Real Stock Returns," *American Economic Review* 75 (December): 1115–1123.

Bodie, Zvi (1976), "Common Stocks as a Hedge Against Inflation," *Journal of Finance* 31 (May): 459–470.

Brealey, Richard, and Stewart Myers (1984), *Principles of Corporate Finance* (New York: McGraw-Hill).

Fama, Eugene F. (1981), "Stock Returns, Real Activity, Inflation and Money," *American Economic Review* 71 (September): 545–565.

———— and G. William Schwert, (1977), "Asset Returns and Inflation," *Journal of Financial Economics* 5. (November): 115–146.

Feldstein, Martin (1980a), "Inflation, Tax Rules and the Stock Market," *Journal of Monetary Economics* 6 (July): 309–331.

———— (1980b), "Inflation and the Stock Market," *American Economic Review* 70 (December): 839-847.

———— (1982), "Inflation and the Stock Market: Reply," *American Economic Review* 72 (March): 243–246.

Friend, Irwin, and Joel Hasbrouck (1982), "Inflation and the Stock Market: Comment," *American Economic Review* 72 (March): 237–242.

Geske, Robert, and Richard Roll (1983), "The Fiscal and Monetary Linkage between Stock Returns and Inflation, "*Journal of Finance* 38 (March): 1–33.

Gilbert R. Alton, (1985), "Operating Procedures for Conducting Monetary Policy," Federal Reserve Bank of St. Louis *Review*, (February): 13–21.

Gonedes, Nicholas J. (1981), "Evidence on the 'Tax Effects' of Inflation under Historical Cost Accounting Methods, "*Journal of Business* 54 (April): 227–270.

Gordon, Myron G. (1983), "The Impact of Real Factors and Inflation on the Performance of the U.S. Stock Market from 1960-1980," *Journal of Finance* 38 (May): 553–563.

Hasbrouck, Joel (1983) "The Impact of Inflation Upon Corporate Taxation," *National Tax Journal* 36 (March): 65–81.

Joines, Douglas H. (1988), "Deficits and Money Growth in the United States: Reply, *Journal of Monetary Economics* 21 (January): 155–160.

Kaul, Gatam (1987), "Stock Returns and Inflation: The Role of the Monetary Sector," *Journal of Financial Economics* 18 (June): 253–276.

Maher, Michael, and Timothy J. Nantell (1983), "The Tax Effects of Inflation: Depreciation, Debt and Miller's Equilibrium Tax Rates," *Journal of Accounting Research* 21 (Spring): 329–340.

McMillin, W. Douglas (1986), "Federal Deficits, Macrostabilization Goals, and Federal Reserve Behavior," *Economic Inquiry* 24 (April): 257–269.

Modigliani, Franco, and Richard A. Cohn (1979), "Inflation, Rational Valuation and the Market," *Financial Analysts Journal* (March/April): 24–36.

Nelson, Charles R. (1976), "Inflation and Rates of Return on Common Stocks, *Journal of Finance* 31, no. 2, (May): 471–483.

Pearce, Douglas K., and V. Vance Roley (1988), "Firm Characteristics, Unanticipated Inflation, and Stock Returns," *Journal of Finance* 43 (September): 965–981

Report of The Presidential Task Force on Market Mechanisms (1988) (Washington, D.C.: Government Printing Office, January).

Thornton, Daniel L. (1988), "The Borrowed-Reserves Operating Procedure: Theory and Evidence," Federal Reserve Bank of St. Louis *Review*, (January/February): 30–54.

Article 8

Forecasting Turning Points With Leading Indicators

by Gerald H. Anderson
and John J. Erceg

A major topic of current interest to economic forecasters is whether the U.S. economy is headed for recession in the near future. Some have concluded that recession is on the horizon, or has already begun. One piece of evidence offered to support that view is the Composite Index of Leading Indicators (ILI), which reached a peak in January 1989, and by mid-August was reported to have fallen in four of the last five months.

Generally speaking, a major task in economic forecasting is to anticipate turning points in economic activity — points when a business expansion will reach its zenith, or peak, or when a business contraction will reach its nadir, or trough. A reliable method for forecasting turning points has continued to elude forecasters, despite advances in mathematical and statistical techniques.

The financial news media frequently refer to "leading" indicators of economic activity as clues, if not predictors, of changes in activity. The media commonly report the magnitude of an increase or decline in the ILI, which, they conclude, implies continued growth or contraction in economic activity. Some reports also claim that the ILI is the government's "chief economic forecasting gauge."[1]

This *Economic Commentary* discusses the composition and ostensible purpose of the ILI and examines its record as a forecasting tool. We conclude that, while the ILI *can* provide useful information to forecasters, it is by no means a foolproof tool for forecasting peaks or troughs in business activity. We also conclude that the ILI does not yet appear to be signaling the approach of a business peak.

■ **The ILI: A Historical Perspective**
Economic data series that might be helpful in identifying changes in aggregate economic activity have been studied by researchers at the National Bureau of Economic Research (NBER), a private, nonprofit economic research organization, since the 1930s. Of the hundreds of economic series examined, some were found to precede or lead, others to coincide, and still others to follow or lag turning points in the direction of overall economic activity, as determined by the NBER.

The first notable use of leading indicators occurred in 1937, when Secretary of the Treasury Henry Morgenthau asked the NBER to compile a list of economic series that would best indicate when the 1937-38 recession would end.[2]

In October 1961, the Bureau of Economic Analysis (BEA) of the U.S. Department of Commerce began to publish leading, coincident, and lagging indicators in its then-new monthly publication, *Business Conditions Digest*.

■

The financial news media frequently point to the movement of the Composite Index of Leading Indicators (ILI) as proof of impending growth or contraction in economic activity. A closer look indicates, however, that while the ILI can provide a great deal of useful information, its value as a forecasting tool is limited. Its usefulness increases when it is used in combination with other indexes.

■

From among the leading indicators originally selected by the NBER, the BEA selected the 12 best on the basis of six criteria: economic significance; statistical adequacy; timing at troughs and peaks of aggregate economic activity; conformity to past business expansions and contractions; smoothness; and frequency and timeliness. The 12 individual series were combined into a composite index, which was first published in November 1968.

The BEA has revised the list of components of the composite index from time to time, as the usefulness of some series waned, and new or improved series became available. The composition of the ILI was last changed in January 1989 and now includes 11 series.[3]

The ILI as a Forecaster of Business Peaks

There have been eight business peaks since World War II. The ILI has peaked prior to each one by periods ranging from two to 20 months, making it a potentially good tool for forecasting business peaks. However, closer analysis reveals that the ILI has serious shortcomings as a forecasting tool.

The usefulness of the ILI as a forecaster of business peaks depends on avoiding false signals of peaks, avoiding the failure to forecast peaks, and providing ample but not excessive warning of peaks. The ILI exhibits some substantial failings when judged by these criteria.

First, the ILI has given from three to seven false signals of peaks, depending on the number of consecutive months of decline that is taken to be a signal of a peak. If a seven-month decline is taken as a signal, there were false signals in 1951, 1966, and 1984, when the ILI declined for seven, nine, and seven consecutive months, respectively. If a five-month decline is considered to be a signal, the ILI also gave a false signal at the start of 1988. The financial news media sometimes say that a three-month decline in the index usually indicates a recession. If so, there was also a false signal in 1962, and perhaps also at the beginning of 1979 and the beginning of 1981.

Second, it is stretching things to say that consecutive monthly declines in the ILI forecast the July 1981 peak, because the ILI had declined from its peak for only two months before the business peak, according to the BEA. A less restrictive statement of that episode is that the ILI declined in five of the eight months before the business peak, which could be taken as a reasonable signal.

Two of the leads reckoned by the BEA include periods when the decline in the ILI was interrupted by rises of two or more months. The 20-month lead before the August 1957 peak includes three gaps of two months each. Excluding those gaps, there was an uninter-

rupted lead of nine months. The 15-month lead before the January 1980 peak includes a gap of two months, and three gaps of one month each. Excluding those gaps, there was no lead.

A forecasting rule using the ILI must specify how many months of decline constitutes a signal of a business peak, while also taking into account interruptions in the downward movement of the ILI. An example of such a rule is that the ILI is forecasting a recession if the index falls in four out of six months. That rule would have yielded false signals in 1951, 1966, 1984, and 1987, and would have failed to forecast the peak of July 1981.

Any forecasting rule based on the ILI must accept some trade-off between false signals and failures to forecast a business peak. We tested several rules based on the experience of the last 42 years. The least restrictive rule that would not have given any false signals is that the ILI must fall for 10 consecutive months. However, with that rule, the ILI would have failed to anticipate all of the peaks. The least lenient rule that would have forecast all of the peaks is that the ILI must fall in four out of seven months. With that rule, the ILI would have given four false signals.

Considering failure to forecast a peak, and a false signal of a peak, as equally egregious errors, two rules appear to minimize the total errors. One is that a recession is forecast if the ILI falls in any four of seven months. The other rule uses a test of falling in any four of eight months. Both rules would have made four errors, giving four false signals. However, neither would have failed to forecast any business peak. The first of the two rules seems preferable because it provides a longer average warning time and has a shorter average duration of false signals.

Another shortcoming of the ILI is the variability of its warnings of business peaks. As reckoned by the BEA, the ILI peaks from two to 20 months before a business peak. What is more relevant is the range in length of the

periods between the time the ILI signals an impending business peak and the peak itself. The rule selected here on the basis of minimizing forecast errors provides leads ranging from one to 14 months.

This analysis indicates that any statement suggesting that the ILI always turns down before the economy turns down would be true, but misleading. It is misleading because it implies that the ILI can be used to *forecast* business peaks, when in fact the index is quite unreliable for that purpose. Any forecasting rule based on the ILI will give either some false signals of business peaks, or will fail to forecast peaks, or will do both. Moreover, the correct forecasts exhibit highly variable lead times.

The most accurate rule identified in this analysis can be said to offer the following guidance to an analyst using the ILI to help forecast the next business peak: If the ILI has declined in four of the last seven months, the chances are two out of three that a business peak will occur sometime within the next 14 months.[4]

The foregoing analysis uses a historical series for the latest composition of the ILI, calculated after all of the revisions of the basic data had been made. However, when actually using the ILI to forecast, an analyst first receives an unrevised figure for the ILI for a particular month. That figure could then be revised in each of the next five months, which adds to the uncertainty confronting the analyst. Consequently, the probability of false signals and failures to forecast might be even greater than is implied by this analysis.

Finally, this analysis assumes that the ILI is available during the month for which it is issued. In fact, it is published about four or five weeks following the end of the month. Therefore, the ILI gives forecasters that much less lead time.

■ The ILI as a Forecaster of Business Troughs

The ILI has turned upward prior to each of the last eight business troughs. By the reckoning of the BEA, the spans between the low points of the ILI and the troughs of the business cycles ranged from one month to 10 months. For six of the eight troughs, the span was from one month to six months.

Unfortunately, it is not uncommon for the ILI to give a false signal of the approach of a trough. In six of the eight contractions, the ILI gave a false signal by rising and then declining again. For example, in the 1960-1961 recession, the ILI rose in five consecutive months following the business peak but then flattened for three months, which at the time could have been interpreted as canceling the signal that a trough was at hand. Again, during the 1981-1982 recession, the ILI advanced in four months of a six-month period and then declined, before rising again to signal an impending end to the recession.

A rule that a one-month rise in the ILI forecasts a trough is clearly too lenient because it would have given false signals in six of the eight recessions. A rule with a three-consecutive-month criterion is probably too strict, because while it would have given no false signals, it would have failed to anticipate the troughs in 1958, 1970, 1975, and 1980.

The rule that seems to balance best the risks of the two types of error states that two consecutive rises in the ILI forecasts a business trough. That rule would have given two false signals and would have failed to forecast the troughs of 1970 and 1975. The forecasts of impending troughs given by the two-consecutive-month rule would have preceded the troughs by periods ranging from one month to nine months, and averaging 4.7 months.

Thus, the foregoing analysis can be said to offer the following guidance to an analyst using the ILI to help forecast the end of a recession: If the ILI has risen for two consecutive months, the experience of the last 42 years suggests that the chances are three to one that a trough will be reached in the next one to nine months. But if the ILI has *not* risen in both of the last two months, the analyst must nevertheless keep in mind that the rule has failed to forecast two of the last eight business troughs. If the ILI has risen for three consecutive months, the experience of the last 42 years suggests that a trough will be reached within the next six months or has already occurred within the last two months.

■ Forecasting Business Peaks Using Other Indexes in Combination With the ILI

In addition to the ILI, three other composite indexes of leading indicators are published in *Business Conditions Digest*. They are the ratio of the Composite Index of Coincident Indicators to the Composite Index of Lagging Indicators (the Ratio), the Long-Leading Index, and the Short-Leading Index.[5]

Rules based on these measures have the same shortcomings as the ILI: a rule lenient enough to predict all business peaks will also give false signals, and a rule strict enough to avoid false signals will fail to forecast most of the peaks. If four declines in the last seven consecutive months is considered a forecast of a business peak, the three alternative indexes would have forecast all of the last eight peaks, with one exception: the Short-Leading Index would have failed to forecast the July 1953 peak. However, the Ratio, the Long-Leading Index, and the Short-Leading Index would have given false signals nine, five, and eight times, respectively.

Despite the shortcomings of the alternative indexes, analysts can improve their forecasts to some extent by using the alternative indexes in conjunction with the ILI. A rule for doing so is to say that the ILI is forecasting a peak only when two conditions are met: (1) the ILI has declined in four of the last seven months, and (2) at least two of the alternative indexes are also signaling a peak by the same four-out-of-seven test.

Using that rule, the ILI would have forecast all eight peaks. The average lead time falls slightly to 4.4 months from the 5.6 months obtained by using the ILI alone. However, the range of lead times is narrowed to one to nine months from one to 14 months, thereby reducing the uncertainty about when the peak will arrive.

The rule also would be somewhat better in that it would have given three false signals instead of the four that are given by forecasting with the ILI alone. The false signal of a business peak following the stock market collapse in October 1987 would have been avoided. The rule does not reduce the nine-month average duration of the false signals.

■ Forecasting Business Troughs Using Other Indexes

We used two rules to examine the forecasting accuracy for business troughs of both the ILI and the alternative indexes. Because recessions have been much shorter than expansions, the forecasting rules can be much simpler than those used to forecast peaks. The two rules tested are (1) a one-month rise in a measure forecasts a trough, and (2) rises in two consecutive months forecast a trough.

The Long-Leading Index with the two-month rule would have given the best performance during the last eight recessions in terms of minimizing forecast errors. It forecast all eight troughs and gave only one false signal. Its range of lead times, one to nine months, is wider than some of the other choices, but that greater variability seems a small price to pay for its much greater forecasting reliability.

Thus, the Long-Leading Index appears to be superior to the ILI, which gave two false signals and failed to forecast two troughs with the two-month rule, and gave seven false signals with the one-month rule. The Ratio and the Short-Leading Index are much less reliable measures for forecasting troughs, making 10 and nine errors, respectively, with the one-month rule, and five and six errors, respectively, with the two-month rule.

■ Implications for the Current Outlook

As of August 31, it appeared that the ILI had declined in February, March, May, and June 1989, thereby satisfying the criterion of falling in four of the last seven months. Thus, taken by itself, the ILI began forecasting a business peak when the ILI figure for June 1989 was released on August 4. But this forecast was confirmed by only one of the alternative indexes, so a peak was *not* being forecast by the more complete rule, which requires confirmation by *two* of the alternative indexes.

On September 1, the ILI for June was revised upward to no change, and the ILI for July was reported to have risen. This new information, in effect, canceled the ILI's forecast of recession, because the ILI then appeared to have fallen in only three of the last seven months.

This episode illustrates how the possibility of data revisions reduces the usefulness of the ILI as a tool for forecasting business peaks. It also illustrates the value of using the more complete rule, which had not signaled and still does not signal a peak.

■ Conclusions

The Composite Index of Leading Indicators is often used by analysts seeking to forecast business peaks and troughs. It can provide useful information, but its value as a forecasting tool is quite limited.

The ILI has a good record in turning down and up before business peaks and troughs. Forecasters, however, do not have the luxury of knowing the future path of the ILI—they only know where it has been, subject, of course, to revisions. Moreover, the ILI's value as a forecasting tool is limited by its tendency to give false signals.

For the purpose of forecasting peaks, the ILI can be used with a four-months-out-of-seven rule, supplemented by the requirement that two of the alternative indexes confirm the forecast. For forecasting troughs, the ILI should be discarded in favor of the Long-Leading Index, using a two-month rule.

Based on these rules, the ILI, which has not declined in four of the last seven months, is not signaling a recession.

■ Footnotes

1. For examples, see Hilary Stout, "Leading Indicators Fell Sharply During May, Darkening Outlook," *The Wall Street Journal*, June 29, 1989, page A2; and "Leading Indicators Down 0.1%," *The New York Times*, August 4, 1989, page 25.

2. Geoffrey H. Moore, *Business Cycles, Inflation, and Forecasting*, National Bureau of Economic Research Studies in Business Cycles, No. 24, Ballinger Publishing Company, Cambridge, Mass., 1983, page 370.

3. See Marie P. Hertzberg and Barry A. Beckman, "Business Cycle Indicators: Revised Composite Indexes," *Business Conditions Digest*, BEA, January 1989, pages 97-102.

4. The criterion of four declining months in a seven-month period was met 12 times in periods of expansion during the last 42 years. Four of these episodes were false signals, while the other eight correctly signaled impending business peaks. Thus, the rule was correct only two-thirds of the time.

5. Strictly speaking, the Ratio is not an index of leading indicators. The Long-Leading Index and the Short-Leading Index were developed by Columbia University's Center for International Business Cycle Research (CIBCR). Although they have been calculated back to January 1948, they were first published by CIBCR on October 6, 1987, and have been published in *Business Conditions Digest* only since April 1989.

Gerald H. Anderson is an economic advisor and John J. Erceg is an assistant vice president and economist at the Federal Reserve Bank of Cleveland. They wish to thank Susan Byrne for her research assistance.

The views stated herein are those of the authors and not necessarily those of the Federal Reserve Bank of Cleveland or of the Board of Governors of the Federal Reserve System.

Article 9

Can Stock Prices Reliably Predict Recessions?

Leonard Mills*

The stock market crash of October 19, 1987, has had its impacts on Wall Street—including congressional calls for more regulation of the financial markets, the New York Stock Exchange's proposals for limits on trading, and reduced volume and liquidity in the financial markets. The expected impact on Main Street, however, never seemed to materialize. Immediately following the crash, predictions of

*Leonard Mills is an Economist in the Macroeconomics Section of the Research Department of the Federal Reserve Bank of Philadelphia. The author extends special thanks to Tom Stark and Henry Min for valuable research assistance.

recession—or, reminiscent of 1929, depression—were rampant. But overall the economy remained strong in the fourth quarter of 1987 and the first half of 1988, and fears of recession soon dissipated.

The economy's resilience in the wake of the crash has surprised many observers. Some have argued that the time between a decline in stock prices and a recession is so long that we have yet to see the upcoming recession. But others claim to be not surprised, arguing that stock prices have never been a reliable indicator of impending recessions. This view is summarized in the often-quoted quip by Paul Samuelson: "The stock market has predicted nine of the last five recessions!"[1]

To be fair, however, no indicator of future economic activity is infallible, and the October crash may be just one of those rare occasions when the stock market made an incorrect prediction. In short, the issue that the crash has resurrected is whether stock prices, by themselves, are a reliable leading indicator of recessions. Theory alone cannot provide the answer; it is an empirical issue. But analysts looking at the same set of numbers do not always reach the same conclusions. So we should first try to quantify objectively the stock market's performance as a leading indicator. One statistical technique, recently developed by Salih Neftci and one that has been applied to other economic indicators, can provide a helpful perspective when applied to stock prices. The results of the Neftci technique suggest that though stock prices alone offer some indication of the economy's future, broader indicators, such as the Index of Leading Indicators, are more reliable.

DECLINING STOCK PRICES COULD SIGNAL RECESSIONS

There are sound economic reasons for thinking that a fall in stock prices would be a good leading indicator of recessions. One reason is that declining stock prices may have direct effects on consumer spending because falling stock prices lower the financial wealth of stockholders. This decline in wealth may induce them to decrease their spending on goods and services. Consumers who do not own stock also could be affected by falling stock prices because they may lose confidence in the economy and feel their own income prospects are dimmer. Hence, they may become more cautious in their current spending. For businesses, lower stock prices raise the cost of acquiring equity funds to pur-

chase new plant and equipment, so investment spending could be reduced when stock prices fall. And as investment and consumer spending decrease because of declining stock prices, the economy could grow at a slower rate and perhaps slip into a recession.

The 1987 stock crash, however, seemed to have only modest effects on consumer spending and investment. After slowing in the fourth quarter of 1987, consumption and business investment came back in the first half of 1988. In a recent study, Alan Garner concludes that "this relatively small effect is consistent with empirical studies showing that the stock market has only a modest impact on consumer spending."[2] Likewise, in an earlier study, Douglas Pearce finds that most empirical studies have concluded that decreases in stock prices lead to decreases in investment, but that the size of the effect is uncertain.[3]

Even if the direct impact of stock price declines is small, stock prices may still be a good leading indicator. The conventional view is that stock prices reflect firms' expected future earnings. According to this view, a general decline in stock prices means that market participants have lowered their expectations of firms' future earnings, presumably because they foresee a downturn in the economy. If the expected downturn actually occurs, the decline in stock prices will have preceded it. So to the extent that an economic downturn, whatever its cause, can be foreseen, its onset should be forewarned by the stock market.

An alternative view is that stock prices sometimes fluctuate for reasons unrelated to the economic fundamentals. In particular, the stock market may be subject to speculative bubbles. In a bubble, speculators bid up the current prices

[1]Paul A. Samuelson, "Science and Stocks," *Newsweek*, September 19, 1966.

[2]C. Alan Garner, "Has the Stock Market Crash Reduced Consumer Spending?" Federal Reserve Bank of Kansas City *Economic Review* (April 1988) pp. 3-16.

[3]Douglas K. Pearce, "Stock Prices and the Economy," Federal Reserve Bank of Kansas City *Economic Review* (November 1983) pp. 7-22.

of stocks simply because they expect to sell the stocks at still higher prices in the future, even though expectations of future earnings remain unchanged. For a while, the expectations of higher prices are self-fulfilling. A second group of buyers is willing to pay more than the first because it expects to get even higher prices from a third group, and so on. But at some point in time, people lose faith that prices will go any higher—an expectation that is likewise self-fulfilling. The bubble then bursts and stock prices come tumbling down. In this circumstance, a decline in stock prices is *not* the result of lowered expectations of future earnings. Some analysts have argued that the October crash, which followed a steep run-up in stock prices earlier in 1987, was just such an episode and that the crash did not mean that market participants had foreseen an economic downturn.[4]

Casual observation of stock prices over the postwar period reveals that they do seem to be a leading indicator of recessions, though an imperfect one. Since 1947 the S&P 500-stock index, shown in Figure 1 (p. 6), has often declined just before the onset of recessionary periods (depicted by the vertical bars). The recessions of 1959 and 1973 are examples. But stock prices do not seem to be completely reliable as a leading indicator. Sometimes, as in 1962, a bear market cried wolf: stock prices fell dramatically, but no recession followed. Ideally, a leading indicator would not generate these false signals. Other times, as in 1980, a recession started without a decline in stock prices: that is, the stock market gave no advance warning. An ideal leading indicator would anticipate all recessions.

In practice, there is no leading indicator that meets the ideal standard of emitting no false signals and anticipating every recession. And a precise answer to how many errors are acceptable for an indicator depends on the costs of these errors. Nevertheless, the number of false signals and the number of unanticipated recessions are useful quantitative measures in assessing a leading indicator's reliability.

THE NEFTCI RULE HELPS EXTRACT THE SIGNALS

Evaluating an indicator's success or failure as a predictor requires some method of determining when the indicator is signaling recession. One method is the x-month rule. If the indicator decreases for x consecutive months, then it is said to be predicting that a recession is imminent. This kind of rule has been applied primarily to the Index of Leading Indicators by analysts who say that three consecutive monthly declines in this index presage a recession. Another method is the x-percent rule. In this rule, if the indicator declines by x percent, then it is said to be signaling a recession. This kind of rule has often been applied to stock prices by analysts who say that a 10 percent decline in stock prices, for example, signals a recession.[5] But any x-month or x-percent rule is somewhat arbitrary and may not take full advantage of the information provided by the indicator. An alternative approach for extracting a turning-point signal is to apply a more sophisticated statistical rule called Neftci's optimal prediction rule.

How the Neftci Rule Works. The Neftci rule starts with the same assumption underlying the more popular rules: that a substantial downturn in an indicator presages an upcoming recession. After each new reading of the indicator, an

[4]For a discussion of experimental evidence suggesting that bubbles are possible, see Herbert Taylor, "Experimental Economics: Putting Markets Under the Microscope," this *Business Review* (March/April 1988) pp. 15-25, and the references therein. However, evidence that the run-up in stock prices in 1986-87 was not the result of a speculative bubble is presented in Gary Santoni, "The Great Bull Markets 1924-29 and 1982-87: Speculative Bubbles or Economic Fundamentals?" Federal Reserve Bank of St. Louis *Review* (November 1987) pp. 16-30.

[5]For applications of the x-percent rule to stock prices as a leading indicator, see Bryon Higgins, "Is a Recession Inevitable This Year?" Federal Reserve Bank of Kansas City *Economic Review* (January 1988) pp. 3-16, and Alfred Malabre, "As Economy Goes, So Goes Stock Market," *Wall Street Journal*, February 9, 1987.

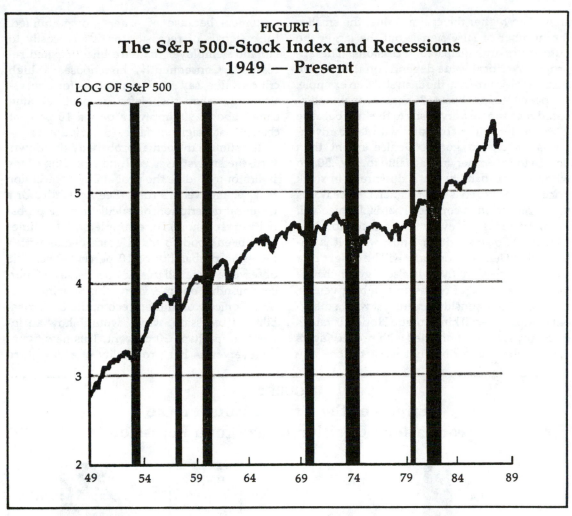

FIGURE 1
The S&P 500-Stock Index and Recessions
1949 — Present

LOG OF S&P 500

analyst using the Neftci rule would assess the probability that the indicator has gone into a "down" phase. When this probability climbs above a critical value prespecified by the analyst, the indicator is interpreted to be signaling a coming recession. Taking stock prices as an example, each month the Neftci procedure will calculate a probability that the stock market has entered a "bear" market. If that probability is higher than the critical value, the analyst will interpret this to mean that the stock market is calling for a recession.

The critical probability value that must be reached before a recession is signaled also determines the probability of false signals that the analyst is willing to accept. For instance, suppose an analyst—call her Denice D'spair—sets her critical probability at 75 percent. When the probability that the indicator has entered a down phase increases to .75 or higher, Denice warns that a recession is imminent. At this critical probability value, Denice is willing to accept the 25 percent probability that the indicator has not entered a down phase and hence that the prediction of recession is wrong.

In general, choosing the critical value involves a trade-off between the number of false signals and the number of unanticipated recessions that arise. The higher the critical value, the smaller the number of false signals but the larger the number of unanticipated recessions. The appropriate critical value depends on the relative costs of these errors to the analyst. As an example, suppose Denice's boss tells her that an unanticipated recession is very costly to the firm because it would leave the company with large inventories of unsold goods. Denice might then decide to lower her critical value to, say, .50. So when the probability that a downturn in stock prices has occurred is .50 or higher, Denice warns that a recession is coming. That is, Denice will predict a recession every time a recession is at least a 50-50 proposition. Thus, while it is unlikely that Denice's company will be caught by a surprise recession, there is also a good chance that a false signal of recession will be given.

For contrast, consider an analyst with a different company—call him Horatio Hope. Horatio's company is more concerned with preserving its market share and does not want to lose any customers because of orders going unfilled. False signals of recession are more costly to Horatio's employer than are unanticipated recessions. Consequently, he chooses a high critical value, say .90. Horatio calls for a recession only when the Neftci probability value climbs above .90, implying only a 10 percent chance that a signal is false. (See Figure 2.)

To estimate the actual probability of a downturn, the analyst uses each new reading of the indicator to update the probability of recession by applying Neftci's rule. (See Appendix for a technical description of calculating the probability of recession.) For example, suppose times have been good so that Denice begins with a recession probability of 10 percent. Then she observes a large fall in stock prices, say a 7 percent monthly decline. Using this new information, Denice would then recompute the probability of recession, which would show an increase to perhaps 30 percent. This new figure then serves as her probability of a downturn

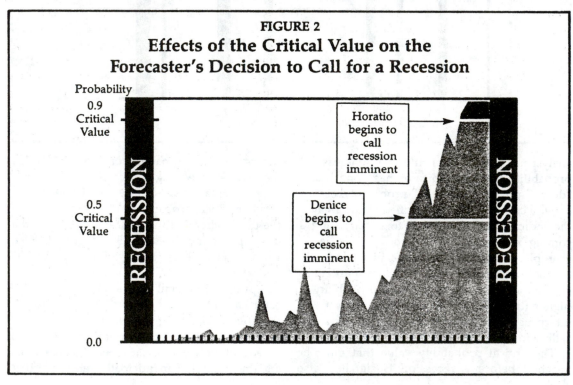

FIGURE 2

Effects of the Critical Value on the Forecaster's Decision to Call for a Recession

until her next observation of the indicator. So suppose in the next month Denice observes a 15 percent increase in stock prices. Using the Neftci rule to combine the previous estimate of a 30 percent probability of a downturn with this new observation would produce a lower probability of recession, say 12 percent. Thus, as new information on stock prices becomes available, Denise's assessment of the probability of recession is revised based on both current and past movements in stock prices.

The updating aspect of the Neftci procedure takes the advantages of the x-month and x-percent rules and improves upon them. Like the x-month rule, the Neftci rule includes information from previous movements in stock prices. Like the x-percent rule, the Neftci rule also uses the information revealed by the magnitude of the change in stock prices. That is, a large decline in stock prices will raise the probability of recession more than a small decline will. But the x-month and x-percent rules allow only the crude statements that a recession is either likely or unlikely. There will always be some uncertainty in any economic forecast, but the popular rules do not quantify the degree of uncertainty. The Neftci rule improves on the popular rules because it produces probability statements, such as "the recent decline in the stock market implies that the probability of a coming recession is 67 percent," thus indicating the analyst's degree of uncertainty.

Using the Neftci Rule to Count Errors. Any leading indicator can be evaluated by comparing its signals of recession with the dates of actual recessions. To define what he means by a correct signal, however, the analyst must define an acceptable lead time. The lead time is the number of months between the time the indicator flashes the signal and the onset of the recession. For our purposes a lead time of 12 months or less may be considered acceptable. The shortest expansion in the postwar period lasted 12 months. Since we will compute the probability of a recession only while we are in an expansion, 12 months is the longest lead time

possible for all of the expansions.[6]

With the prespecified critical probability and a lead time that is considered acceptable, we can label every signal of recession as either correct or false and every recession as either anticipated or unanticipated. If the indicator gave a probability of recession above the critical value sometime within the 12 months prior to the recession, then the indicator correctly anticipated the recession. The top panel in Figure 3 gives an example of a correct signal. In contrast, if the indicator switched on, and then off, more than 12 months prior to the recession, then it gave a false alarm, as shown in the middle panel. Finally, if the signal was never on within the 12 months prior to the recession, then the indicator failed to anticipate the recession. The bottom panel of Figure 3 illustrates this type of error.

HOW RELIABLE ARE SIGNALS FROM STOCK PRICES?

The Historical Record. Applying the Neftci rule to the monthly growth rate in the S&P 500-stock index during the 1947-82 period produced the probabilities of recession shown in Figure 4 (p. 10). Clearly, stock prices contain some information about the economy's future direction; the probability of recession climbed before each of the seven recessions that occurred between 1949 and 1982 (represented by the vertical bars). Before five of the seven recessions, the probabilities based on the stock market rose above the 50 percent critical value within 12 months of the economic downturn. These five successful predictions of recession all occurred before 1975. The lead times of the five correct predictions ranged from one to 11 months. Although all of the recessions were anticipated during this period, stock prices did emit some false signals. Using the 50 percent critical value resulted in four false signals before the December 1969 peak and one false signal before

---

[6]A lead time of zero months—or no lead time—is considered to be a useful signal because it usually takes several months to recognize that a recession has in fact occurred.

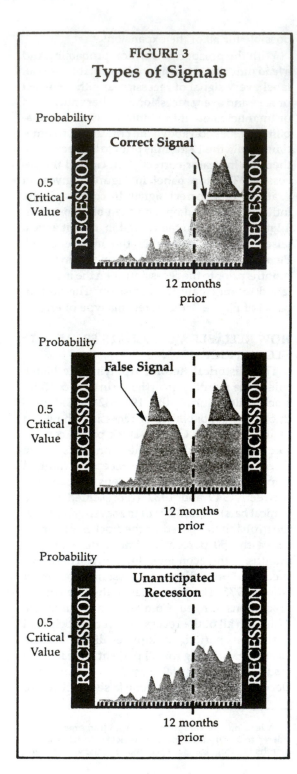

FIGURE 3
Types of Signals

Probability

Correct Signal

RECESSION

0.5
Critical
Value

RECESSION

12 months
prior

Probability

False Signal

RECESSION

0.5
Critical
Value

RECESSION

12 months
prior

Probability

Unanticipated
Recession

RECESSION

0.5
Critical
Value

RECESSION

12 months
prior

the November 1973 peak.[7] Thus, of the 10 recession signals given before 1975, five were false and five were correct.

Unfortunately, the two recessions in the 1980s were cases in which the stock market failed to provide a useful signal. Before the recession that began in January 1980, the stock market sent a signal that was considerably earlier than our 12-month lead time. The probability of a downturn climbed above 50 percent in April 1977 and stayed there for the remaining 33 months of the expansion. This type of signal is considered correct, even though its lead time is greater than 12 months, because the probability never fell below the 50 percent critical value prior to the recession. But the severe prematurity of this signal, relative to the lead times of the previous correct signals, means that stock prices had little value in predicting the timing of the 1980 recession. Before the recession that began in July 1981, the stock market did not send any signal at all; stock prices failed to push the probability of recession above the 50 percent level. In short, using the .50 critical value for extracting recession signals from the stock market worked reasonably well through the 1970s, but the stock market's performance as an indicator seems to have deteriorated in the 1980s.

In Figure 4, raising the critical value for recession signals to .90 reduces the number of false signals slightly, from five to four over the entire postwar period. But the number of unanticipated recessions increases dramatically, from one to six. Apparently, we cannot presume that a high probability of a stock market downturn is associated with a high probability of recession. We should certainly be suspicious, then, of claims that stock prices have always been a reliable leading indicator.

The Crash of 1987. The stock market crash of

---

[7]In fairness to stock prices, some of these false signals were associated with pronounced economic slowdowns that were not quite severe enough to be labeled recessions; an example is 1966-67.

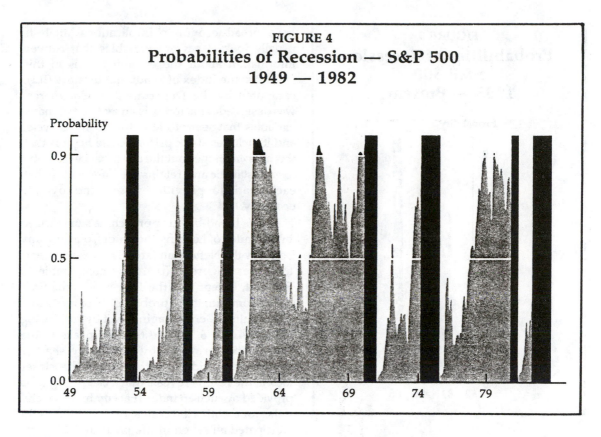

FIGURE 4
Probabilities of Recession — S&P 500
1949 — 1982

1987 can now be interpreted with the benefit of this historical perspective. Figure 5 shows the probabilities of recession given by stock prices since the beginning of the current expansion in December 1982. Stock prices generated false signals early in this expansion: at the .50 critical value, they flashed a recession warning between February and December of 1984. Thereafter, generally rising stock prices reduced the probability of recession to very low levels. The low point was achieved at the stock market peak, in August 1987, when the probability of recession was only about 5 percent. After climbing to 14 percent in September, the probability of recession shot up to 88 percent after the crash in October. Thus, the probability of recession as determined by stock prices was certainly increased by the crash. Since stock prices subsequently fell further and have yet to fully recover, the current probability of recession is even higher, 98 percent as of May 1988. But as we have seen, probabilities of a downturn exceeding 90 percent have turned out, more often than not, to be false signals of recessions. Thus, while it may be too early to tell whether stock prices will accurately predict the next recession, it would not be too surprising if even this strong signal turned out to be false.[8]

A BROADER INDICATOR SENDS A CLEARER SIGNAL

Because stock prices may move for reasons

---

[8]In a recent article, Joe Peek and Eric S. Rosengren, "The Stock Market and Economic Activity," *Federal Reserve Bank of Boston New England Economic Review* (May/June 1988) pp. 39-50, suggest that real stock prices are more reliable than nominal prices in predicting economic slowdowns. Applying the Neftci rule to real stock prices (measured as the S&P 500 divided by the CPI), however, did not improve the stock market's recession predictions.

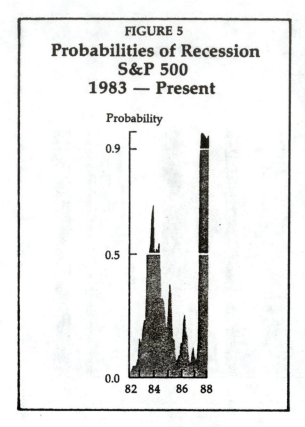

FIGURE 5

**Probabilities of Recession
S&P 500
1983 — Present**

unrelated to the economic fundamentals, the information that these prices provide may be noisy. Our statistical analysis certainly indicates this. But many other economic statistics are subject to the same criticism. For example, measures of the money stock may exhibit this noise problem as well. Dramatic changes in the public's demand for money, such as those that occurred during the period of deposit deregulation in the early 1980s, can distort the signal the money supply provides about the economy's future direction.[9]

Because any single economic statistic is subject to idiosyncratic movements that may not have broad economic implications, analysts usually look at several variables that convey information about the economy. It is in this spirit that the Index of Leading Indicators (ILI), computed by the Department of Commerce, was designed. This index is an average of many variables that seem to lead the business cycle, and it includes stock prices.[10] The hope is that this index averages out the disturbances specific to each statistic and retains the information that each statistic provides about the overall economy.

Does a broad-based approach, as summarized by the Index of Leading Indicators, perform any better by the Neftci standard? The answer seems to be yes. Figure 6 (p. 12) is comparable to Figure 4, except that the ILI replaces the S&P 500 in computing the probabilities of recession. The results are encouraging. Just by comparing Figures 4 and 6, we see that the peaks in the probabilities provided by the ILI are sharper than those provided by stock prices.[11] A closer look at the results reveals that a clearer signal is provided by such an index that combines several indicators. With a .50 critical probability, the ILI anticipated all seven of the postwar recessions and sent only four false signals. Choosing the higher .90 critical value reduced the number of false signals to two, but at the cost of two unanticipated recessions. Finally, the range of lead times seems narrow enough for the ILI to provide a useful signal; lead times ranged from two to 15 months with the .50 critical value and from zero to eight months with the .90 cutoff.

"Sure," someone might say, "but what has this

[9]See Herbert Taylor, "What Has Happened to M1?" this *Business Review* (September/October 1986) pp. 3-14, for a discussion of the deterioration of the relation between M1 and future GNP movements.

[10]Gary Gorton, "Forecasting With the Index of Leading Indicators," this *Business Review* (November/December 1982) pp. 15-27, describes the Index of Leading Indicators in more detail and discusses its usefulness.

[11]Stock prices are clearly a superior leading indicator with respect to timeliness. In particular, stock prices are observed instantaneously and are not subject to revision. The Index of Leading Indicators, like several other indicators, is observed with a one-month lag and is subject to several revisions.

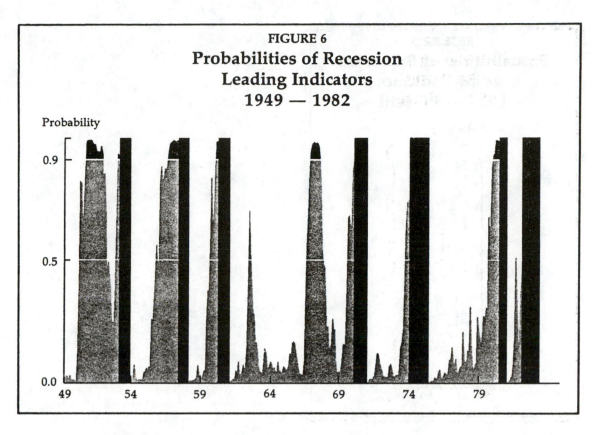

FIGURE 6
Probabilities of Recession
Leading Indicators
1949 — 1982

index done for me lately?" Figure 7 shows the probabilities of recession generated by the ILI since December 1982. Like stock prices, the ILI generated some false recession signals early on in the current expansion. But the important difference between the ILI and stock prices is in the recent behavior of both. While the likelihood of a recession is almost certain if we use stock prices as a leading indicator, the likelihood is much smaller using the ILI. Although the probability of a recession based on the ILI increased after October 1987, it remained below even the .50 critical value. The probability based on the ILI peaked at 45 percent in January 1988 and has since fallen to 31 percent in May.[12] In contrast, the probability based on stock prices soared above the .90 critical value and has remained

[12]Based on preliminary data released June 29, 1988.

there. Given the relative performance of these two indicators in the past, the prediction from the Index of Leading Indicators seems more reliable.

CONCLUSION

While economists are always looking for clues about the economy's future course, no indicator has proven infallible in its predictions. Sometimes an indicator will fail to signal an upcoming recession. Sometimes it will send false signals. Stock prices have proven to be a particularly unreliable leading indicator in recent years, and the stock market crash of 1987 may prove a telling example. Movements in stock prices do seem to offer some information about the economy's future. But our analysis suggests that a combination of various indicators, such as the Index of Leading Indicators, provides more reliable signals of future economic activity.

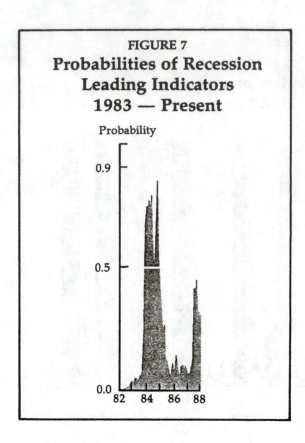

FIGURE 7
Probabilities of Recession
Leading Indicators
1983 — Present

APPENDIX

Estimating the Probability of Recession

The Neftci approach to estimating the probability of recession from observing a selected indicator, such as a stock price index, builds on two assumptions. The first is that the indicator is always operating under one of two regimes: an upturn regime, during which we are more likely to see increases in the indicator, or a downturn regime, during which we are more likely to see the indicator decline. The second assumption is that the probability of the indicator being in its downturn regime is related to the probability of the economy as a whole going into a recession.

The analyst begins computing the probability of an upcoming recession in the first month of the expansion. At that point the initial probability of a downturn in the indicator (and the economy) is equal to zero. Then, each month, as the analyst gets a new reading on the indicator, he revises his probability that the indicator (and hence the economy) is in its downturn regime by applying the Neftci rule:

$$\Pi_t = \{[\Pi_{t-1} + P(1-\Pi_{t-1})]p_t^d\}/\{[\Pi_{t-1} + P(1-\Pi_{t-1})]p_t^d + (1-\Pi_{t-1})p_t^u(1-P)\}$$

where Π_t = the conditional probability that the indicator is in the downturn regime;

p_t^u, p_t^d = the probability that the observed movement in the indicator came from the upturn regime and downturn regime, respectively;

P = the unconditional probability that a switch from an upturn regime to a downturn regime will occur in the current period.

This rule produces the best estimate of the probability that the indicator has entered its downturn regime. Salih Neftci shows that using this rule minimizes the average delay in signaling a downturn for a given critical value.[a] We use a procedure that is similar to that used by Francis Diebold and Glenn Rudebusch in implementing the Neftci rule.[b]

p_t^u and p_t^d are the probability densities for the event that an observed change in the indicator variable was drawn from the upturn regime and downturn regime, respectively. Estimation of these densities requires some judgment on the dating of the downturn and upturn regimes for the indicator variable. Because the expansions have lasted about four times as long as recessions, we define a downturn regime as one year (the shortest expansion in the sample) prior to the business cycle peak through three months prior to the business cycle trough. This dating captures the major movements in both the S&P 500 and the Index of Leading Indicators. Alternative dates for the regimes using shorter lead times did not alter the results. The probability densities, p_t^u and p_t^d, were assumed to be normally distributed using the mean and standard deviation of the monthly growth rates estimated for each regime. These parameters were estimated from the 1948-82 period. Thus, the Neftci probabilities for the period 1949-82 are analogous to within-sample predictions, and the probabilities for the period 1983-88 are analogous to out-of-sample predictions.

P is the unconditional transition probability, that is, the probability that a switch from a downturn regime to an upturn regime will occur in the current period given that it has not yet occurred. P is an unconditional probability because it is not based on the movement of the indicator variable. In Neftci's original application, this transition probability was determined by the length of the expansion because of an assumption that expansions "age" and become weaker. This assumption has recently been questioned and was not used in this application so that we might focus more sharply on the proposed indicators.[c] Instead, a constant transition probability of switching from the upturn to the downturn regime was used. This probability was estimated to be .029 by following the procedure outlined in J. Huston McCulloch.[d] Further, the hypothesis that this probability is a constant could not be rejected at usual significance levels.

---

[a]For derivations of the Neftci rule, see Salih Neftci, "Optimal Prediction of Cyclical Downturns," *Journal of Economic Dynamics and Control* 4 (1982) pp. 225-41, and Francis X. Diebold and Glenn D. Rudebusch, "Scoring the Leading Indicators," Federal Reserve Board *Special Studies Paper No. 206* (1987). Carl J. Palash and Lawrence J. Radecki, "Using Monetary and Financial Variables to Predict Cyclical Downturns," Federal Reserve Bank of New York *Quarterly Review* (Summer 1985) pp. 36-45, use the Neftci rule to evaluate the leading indicator properties of other financial variables.

[b]Francis X. Diebold and Glenn D. Rudebusch, "Scoring the Leading Indicators."

[c]Studies that find that business expansions do not become weaker with age include J. Huston McCulloch, "The Monte Carlo Cycle of Business Activity," *Economic Inquiry* 13 (September 1975) pp. 303-21, Francis X. Diebold and Glenn D. Rudebusch, "Does the Business Cycle Have Duration Memory," Federal Reserve Board *Special Studies Paper No. 223* (1987), and Victor Zarnowitz, "The Regularity of Business Cycles," National Bureau of Economic Research *Working Paper No. 2381* (1987). This issue has not been settled, however; see Frank de Leeuw, "Do Expansions Have Memory?" Bureau of Economic Analysis *Discussion Paper 16* (1987).

[d]J. Huston McCulloch, "The Monte Carlo Cycle of Business Activity."

Section III
Equity Market Linkages and Market Volatility

Prior to the 1970s, stocks were traded on exchanges and through the over-the-counter market, and these venues comprised the entire equity market. In the 1970s, this began to change with the introduction of exchange-traded options on individual stocks. The 1980s brought a rush of innovation as other equity related products began to trade. In the early 1980s, stock index futures contracts were introduced. These contracts provided for the trading of entire baskets of stocks, such as the S&P 500. Other products followed, with options trading on the index and options trading on stock index futures. Collectively these products (options, stock index futures, options on indexes, and options on stock index futures) are called *derivatives*. In this section we focus on the linkages between the equity market and the various markets for equity derivatives.

Many observers believe that the flourishing of equity derivatives has stimulated market volatility, while others deny any such connection. This section explores this issue by considering market volatility in greater detail and by examining the linkages between the equity market and the markets for equity derivatives.

On October 19, 1987 the stock market lost about 25 percent of its value. In the 1980s, other days of great drama also helped call the investor's attention to financial market risk, or volatility. Sean Becketti and Gordon H. Sellon address the changing risk of financial markets in their paper, "Has Financial Market Volatility Increased?" They consider stocks, interest rates, and exchange rates. They find that stock market volatility did not increase during the 1980s. While this might seem surprising given some of the dramatic events, the results of Becketti and Sellon corroborate a number of other studies. Regarding interest rates and exchange rates, however, they reach a different conclusion. The volatility of both interest and exchange rates did increase during the 1980s.

Even if overall volatility has not increased, some observers believe that the proper focus should be on episodic volatility. For example, the October 1987 Crash was an episode of great volatility that some observers believe to have originated from the linkages between the equity market and the market for equity derivatives. To explore this issue more carefully, we begin with an article, "The Operation of Stock Markets," by the Office of Technology Assessment (OTA) of the U.S. Congress. This article reviews the organization of equity markets in the United States and distinguishes between the exchanges and the over-the-counter market. Attention soon turns to the 1987 Crash. Attention there focuses on the linkage between the stock market and the market for stock index futures. One problem that perhaps exacerbated the Crash was a failure of market makers on the stock exchanges and in the over-the-counter market. The article assesses this issue and closes by considering technological problems in handling the tremendous order flow that occurs in periods of high price volatility.

A continuing issue in the debate about the influence of equity derivatives on the stock market focuses on the question of margin. In the stock market, a trader can buy stock on margin. The margin payment that the purchaser puts down acts as a down payment on the stock, and the purchaser borrows the rest of the funds from the broker. In the stock market, the purchaser must pay at least half of the cost of the stock with his or her own funds. In the derivatives market, margin rules are different. For example, in the futures market, the margin is much less than half of the price of the underlying assets. However, futures margins play a fundamentally different role than stock market margins. In the futures market, the margin payment is merely a good faith deposit, or performance bond. Futures margin is not a down payment on the contract. George Sofianos, in his article "Margin Requirements on Equity Instruments," carefully discusses margin levels and rules on stocks, stock index futures, stock options, stock index options, and options on stock index futures. Understanding these rules is important for fully comprehending the relationships between the equity market and the market for equity derivatives.

The price of a stock index futures contract depends very closely on the price of the underlying stocks. Traders in both markets constantly watch for deviations between the two prices. If the deviation does not match the theoretically prescribed difference, an opportunity for index arbitrage arises. For example, if the futures price is too high relative to the price of the stocks themselves, index arbitrageurs will sell the futures contract and buy the stocks. Index arbitrage has become big business and a cause of concern over market volatility. Because of the intimate linkage between prices in the two markets, there is concern that a disruption in one market could lead to a disruption in the other. Some observers maintain that index arbitrage activity played an important role in the Crash of 1987. Since that time, exchanges have developed rules for trading halts to create a cooling-off period and to de-couple the stock market and the stock index futures markets. These rules are known as *circuit breakers*, and James T. Moser explores these rules in his paper "Circuit Breakers." Circuit breakers were implemented after the Crash of 1987 and received a good workout in the Mini-Crash of October 1989. Moser finds that circuit breakers have some good features, but the benefits they might bring come at the cost of reducing access to markets.

Article 10

Has Financial Market Volatility Increased?

By Sean Becketti and Gordon H. Sellon, Jr.

There is a widespread perception that financial market volatility has increased during the 1980s. While the collapse in stock prices in October 1987 has drawn the most attention, many investors and financial market analysts believe that the volatility of interest rates and exchange rates has risen as well.

If financial market volatility has increased, there may be important consequences for investors and policymakers. Investors may equate higher volatility with greater risk and may alter their investment decisions in light of increased volatility. Policymakers may be concerned that financial market volatility will spill over into the real economy and harm economic performance. Alternatively, policymakers may feel that increased financial volatility threatens the viability of financial institutions and the smooth functioning of financial markets.

Sean Becketti is a senior economist at the Federal Reserve Bank of Kansas City and Gordon H. Sellon, Jr. is an assistant vice president at the bank. Deana VanNahmen, a research associate at the bank, provided research assistance.

The purpose of this article is to examine the claim that financial volatility has increased in the 1980s. That is, are the volatilities of returns on stocks, bonds, and exchange rates historically high in the 1980s? The article finds that financial market volatility has indeed increased; yet the nature of the volatility, its magnitude, and its persistence are very different across markets.

The first section of the article examines why financial market volatility is important to investors and policymakers. The second section provides statistical evidence on the volatility of returns in the stock, bond, and foreign exchange markets. The third section discusses the response of investors and policymakers to increased financial volatility.

Why volatility matters

Financial markets and institutions play a key role in the economy by channeling funds from savers to investors. Some volatility in the prices of financial assets is a normal part of the process of allocating investable funds among competing uses. Excessive or extreme volatility of stock prices, interest rates, and exchange rates may be detrimental, however, because such volatility may impair the smooth functioning of the financial system and adversely affect economic performance.

Stock market volatility

Much of the recent concern over financial market volatility has centered on the stock market and the collapse in stock prices that occurred on October 19, 1987. The 508 point drop in the Dow-Jones average on October 19 was the largest one-day percentage drop in history. Stock market volatility of this magnitude could harm the economy through a number of channels.[1]

One way that stock price volatility hinders economic performance is through consumer spending. For example, immediately after the October 19 drop in stock prices, economic forecasters predicted sharply weaker economic growth. These analysts believed that the fall in stock prices would reduce consumer spending. The sizable fall in consumer wealth was expected to directly lower consumer spending. In addition, a weakening in consumer confidence could contribute to a further spending reduction.[2]

Stock price volatility may also affect business investment spending. Investors may perceive a rise in stock market volatility as an increase in the risk of equity investments. If so, investors may shift their funds to less risky assets. This reaction would tend to raise the cost of funds to firms issuing stock. Moreover, small firms and new firms might bear the brunt of this effect as investors gravitated toward the purchase of stock in larger, well-known firms.[3]

Extreme stock price volatility could also disrupt the smooth functioning of the financial system and lead to structural or regulatory changes. For example, the commissions studying the October 19 stock price collapse focused their attention on the stock-order execution and market-making systems. Systems that work well with normal price volatility may be unable to cope with extreme price changes. Indeed, the system itself may contribute to volatility if investors are unable to complete stock transactions. Changes in market rules or regulations may be necessary to increase the resiliency of the market in the face of greater volatility.[4]

Interest rate volatility

The 1980s have also seen increased concern over interest rate volatility. In the early 1980s, rising inflationary expectations, restrictive monetary policy, and removal of interest rate ceilings contributed to high and volatile interest rates. Like stock market volatility, extreme interest rate volatility may hurt economic performance and disrupt the smooth functioning of the financial system.

One way in which interest rate volatility may harm the economy is through business investment spending. Investors may see an increase in the volatility of interest rates as an increase in the risk of holding bonds and other debt instruments. If investors shift their portfolios toward lower risk assets, firms may find it more costly to fund investment projects. The resulting fall in investment spending would reduce economic growth.

Interest rate volatility could also have a direct impact on monetary policy. If higher rate volatility causes investors to change their investment portfolios, the demand for money may also change. To the extent that monetary policy is based on an assumed stable relationship between money and economic activity, changes in money demand due to rate volatility could complicate monetary policy.[5]

Greater interest rate volatility could also weaken the financial system if this volatility threatens the viability of financial intermediaries.[6] Increased interest rate volatility is a serious problem for depository intermediaries, such as savings and loans, that have long-term assets and short-term liabilities.[7] An increase in rate volatility can lead to periodic liquidity crises for some of these institutions and may threaten the solvency of others. Regulatory actions, such as an increase in capital requirements, may be necessary to protect these institutions from increased volatility of interest rates.

Exchange rate volatility

In 1973 the major industrialized countries abandoned the Bretton Woods system of fixed exchange rates in favor of a floating rate system. Since 1973 there has been continuing concern that exchange rate volatility under the new system might adversely affect international trade and capital flows.[8]

Like volatility in the stock market and interest rates, exchange rate volatility may create uncertainty about future profits, which impairs long-term investment decisions. Companies involved in international trade may be reluctant to commit to long-term investment projects if they fear that exchange rate changes might significantly reduce profits.

A second way that exchange rate volatility might impede international trade is through higher prices for exports and imports. If companies add a risk premium to the prices of internationally traded goods because of exchange rate uncertainty, consumers may reduce the amount of the higher priced goods they demand and slow the growth of world trade.

Finally, exchange rate variability may alter international capital flows. Long-term capital flows may be reduced by greater exchange rate uncertainty, impeding the efficient flow of resources in the world economy. At the same time, increased exchange rate volatility may promote short-term, speculative capital flows. These speculative capital flows may complicate monetary policy. Central banks may be forced to intervene frequently in exchange markets or to adjust monetary policy to prevent these capital flows from having adverse effects on the domestic economy.

Measuring financial market volatility

Because financial volatility matters to investors and policymakers, it is important to examine the claim that volatility has increased during the 1980s. This section presents evidence supporting the view that volatility has increased across financial markets in the 1980s. However, the nature, the magnitude, and the persistence of the increase in volatility differ across markets.

Stock market volatility

Most discussions of stock market volatility center on the large price movements on and around October 19, 1987. To put these events in proper perspective, however, it is useful to examine stock market volatility over a longer time span.

Viewing the stock market over a longer time horizon, some observers have concluded that the volatility of stock returns in the 1980s is not

CHART 1
Volatility of stock returns, 1918-88

Standard deviation

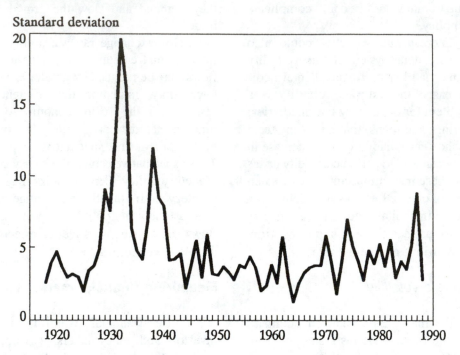

Note: In this chart, volatility is measured by the annual standard deviation of monthly stock returns. See endnote 9 for details.

Source: Center for Research in Security Prices.

unusual. For example, Chart 1 shows the volatility of stock returns from 1918 to 1988. The measure of volatility used in this chart is the annual standard deviation of the monthly returns in the Standard and Poor 500 Composite Stock Price Index.[9] According to this chart, record stock market volatility occurred in the 1930s. Compared with the 1930s, stock market volatility in the 1980s does not appear abnormal.[10]

The relevance of this extended historical comparison is open to question, however. Most observers regard the economic turbulence of the 1930s as an extraordinary historical episode, one unlikely to be repeated. Thus, a more recent perspective on volatility may be in order. Examining Chart 1 from 1950 to 1988 shows that stock market volatility in 1987 was the highest in the postwar period.

Focusing on October 19, 1987, suggests a way of resolving these differing opinions on stock market volatility. The key feature of the October 19 period is the sharp one-day movements in stock prices. Stock prices fell 108 points on Friday, October 16, and an additional 508 points on October 19 before rising 102 points on October 20. In each case, stock price changes were considerably above normal daily price movements.

CHART 2
Normal volatility of stock returns, 1918-88

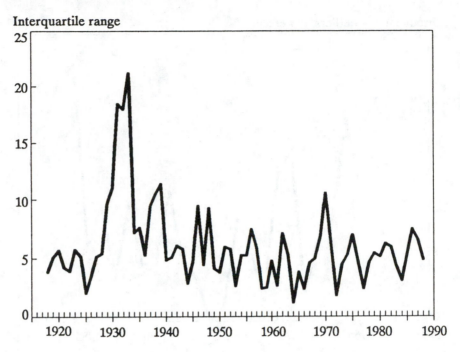

Interquartile range

Note: In this chart, volatility is measured by the annual interquartile range of monthly stock returns. See endnote 11 for details.

Source: Center for Research in Security Prices.

It is possible to think of stock market volatility as including two parts, normal volatility and jump volatility. Normal volatility refers to the ordinary variability of stock returns, that is, the ordinary ups and downs in returns. Jump volatility, on the other hand, refers to occasional and sudden extreme changes in returns.

An analogy may be useful in showing the distinction between normal volatility and jump volatility. The tidal rise and fall of the ocean resembles the normal volatility of stock returns. Tidal swings may be more or less pronounced at different times of the year, but tidal changes have a regularity and smoothness that capture the idea of normal volatility. Occasionally, however, violent weather or offshore earthquakes suddenly produce extreme changes in the level of the water and in the severity of wave actions. These disruptions are like jump volatility. In this analogy, the collapse of stock prices on October 19, 1987, was like a tidal wave.

Using a measure of normal volatility, there is no evidence that normal stock market volatility has increased in the 1980s. Chart 2 shows a measure of normal volatility that excludes extreme price changes.[11] By use of this measure, the volatility of stock prices is not historically high. Indeed, with this measure, peak stock

CHART 3

Frequency of jumps in stock returns, 1962-88

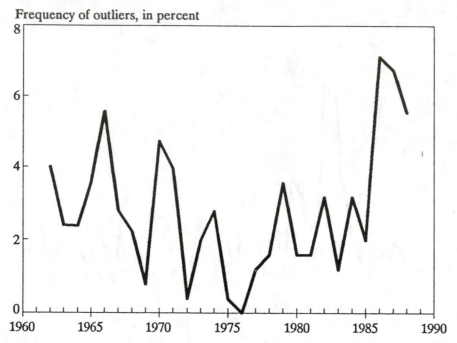

Frequency of outliers, in percent

Note: In this chart, volatility is measured by the percentage of days in each year that experienced unusually large daily stock returns, either negative or positive. See endnote 12 for details.

Source: Center for Research in Security Prices.

market volatility in the postwar period occurs in 1970, not 1987.

Jump volatility in the stock market, as measured by the frequency of extreme price changes, does seem to be higher in the 1980s, however. Chart 3 shows the percentage of daily stock returns that are extremely high or low in a given year.[12] According to this measure of volatility, the frequency of large stock price movements in 1987, as well as in 1986 and 1988, is considerably greater than in any other year since 1966. Thus, this measure of volatility suggests that jump volatility in stock returns may

have risen in the 1980s.[13] However, it should be noted that with only three years of increased volatility, additional evidence would be needed to support the view that there has been a permanent change in the jump volatility of stock returns.

Interest rate volatility

Unlike the mixed evidence regarding volatility in the stock market, all measures of interest rate volatility show sharply higher volatility in the 1980s. In the early 1980s, financial markets

CHART 4
Volatility of Treasury bill yields, 1926-87

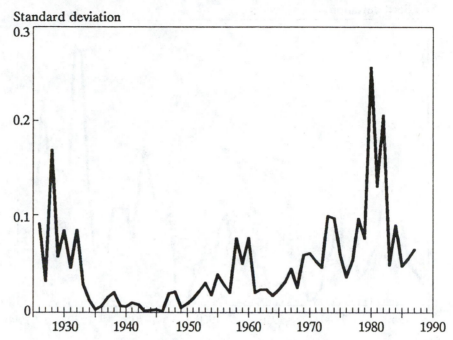

Standard deviation

Note: In this chart, volatility is measured by the annual standard deviation of monthly returns of a one-year Treasury bill index.

Source: Center for Research in Security Prices.

experienced large shifts in inflationary expectations, a change in monetary policy procedures that permitted greater short-term interest rate volatility, and widespread deregulation. These factors contributed to greater volatility of interest rates at all maturities.

The dramatic increase in the volatility of short-term interest rates during the 1980s is illustrated in Chart 4. This chart shows the annual standard deviation of the monthly returns on a one-year Treasury bill index from 1926 to 1987. As seen in this chart, short-term interest rate volatility reached record levels in the early 1980s. However, since 1982 volatility appears to have subsided to more normal levels. Thus, the increase in the volatility of short-term interest rates in the early 1980s appears to have been a temporary phenomenon.

In contrast, the increased volatility of long-term interest rates in the 1980s has been sustained. Chart 5 shows the volatility of returns on 20-year Treasury securities from 1926 to 1987.[14] According to this chart, the volatility of long-term interest rates shifted upward once in the late 1960s and early 1970s, and volatility increased again in the early 1980s. Moreover,

CHART 5

Volatility of Treasury bond yields, 1926-87

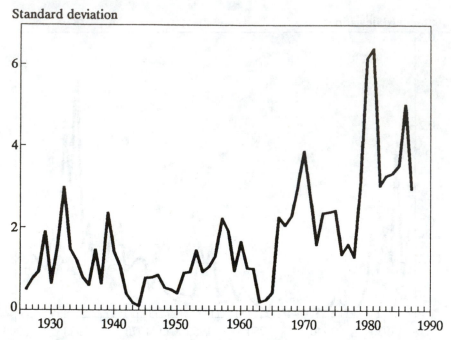

Standard deviation

Note: In this chart, volatility is measured by the annual standard deviation of monthly returns of a 20-year Treasury bond index.

Source: Center for Research in Security Prices.

although volatility has fallen from the 1981-82 peak, it remains historically high. Unlike volatility of short-term interest rates, the volatility of long-term rates in the 1980s seems to be permanently higher.

Exchange rate volatility

The measurement and interpretation of exchange rate volatility are more complicated than for stock and bond markets. Historically, exchange rates have been subject to considerable governmental controls. In the postwar period, for example, there have been two major exchange rate regimes, the Bretton Woods system of fixed exchange rates from 1946 to 1972, and a system of floating exchange rates since 1973. Moreover, during the floating-rate period, governments have intervened at times to stabilize foreign exchange markets or to realign currency relationships.

In moving from a fixed to a flexible system of exchange rates, exchange rate volatility should rise. Indeed, as shown in Chart 6, volatility after 1973 is significantly greater than in the earlier postwar period.[15] However, many analysts

CHART 6
Volatility of the dollar/pound exchange rate, 1950-88

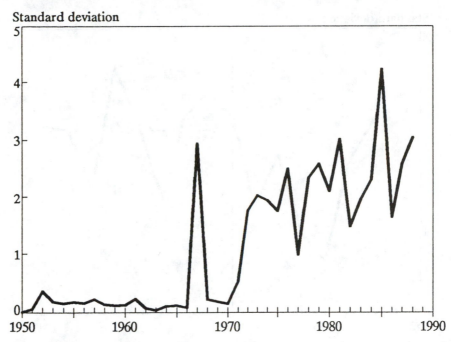

Standard deviation

Note: In this chart, volatility is measured by the annual standard deviation of monthly percentage changes in the nominal U.S. dollar/pound sterling exchange rate.

Source: Board of Governors, Financial Markets section.

expected increased volatility to be temporary until foreign exchange traders adapted to the new system. Chart 6 shows that, contrary to expectations, exchange rate volatility has shown no tendency to diminish after 1973.

A closer look at the 1973-88 floating-rate period suggests that exchange rate volatility actually increased further during the 1980s. Chart 7 shows the volatility of the trade-weighted value of the dollar.[16] Dividing the period at 1980 demonstrates that the average volatility of the dollar, shown by the horizontal line, is higher in the 1980s than in the 1970s.[17]

Thus, in the foreign exchange market as in the stock and bond markets, there is evidence of greater financial volatility in the 1980s.

Responses to increased financial volatility

In the presence of increased financial market volatility, investors may alter their investment strategies, and policymakers may pursue regulatory reforms. Investors have two options to cope with greater volatility. They can shift their investment portfolios toward less risky assets,

CHART 7

Volatility of the trade-weighted dollar, 1974-88

Standard deviation

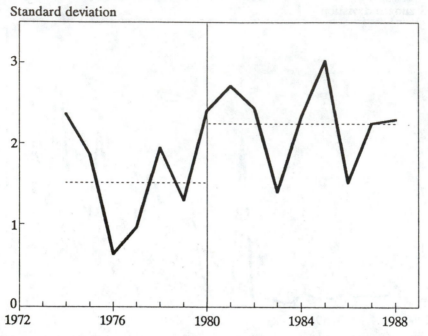

Note: In this chart, volatility is measured by the annual standard deviation of monthly percentage changes in the index of the nominal trade-weighted value of the dollar published by the staff of the Board of Governors. The horizontal dashed lines show the average volatility of the dollar before and after 1980.

Source: Board of Governors, Financial Markets section.

or they can attempt to immunize the value of their portfolios. Policymakers can also pursue either of two options. They can try to reduce volatility directly, or they can assist financial markets and institutions in adapting to increased volatility. Some investors have attempted to adjust to volatility by restructuring their portfolios. An example is the sharp drop in stock purchases by individual investors after October 19, 1987. Individual investors reduced their direct purchases of stocks and also shifted away from stock mutual funds. As a consequence, retail stock brokerages and mutual funds have experienced reduced profitability and have scaled back operations and employment.

In the face of a general increase in financial volatility, however, investors may find it difficult to protect themselves through portfolio restructuring. For example, investors have generally considered bonds to be less risky than stocks. With increased stock market volatility, investors might prefer to shift into bonds. However, as shown in the previous section, bond market volatility has increased dramatically in the 1980s. Indeed, as shown in Chart 8, the unprecedented upsurge in volatility in the 1980s

CHART 8
Volatility of stock returns and Treasury bond yields

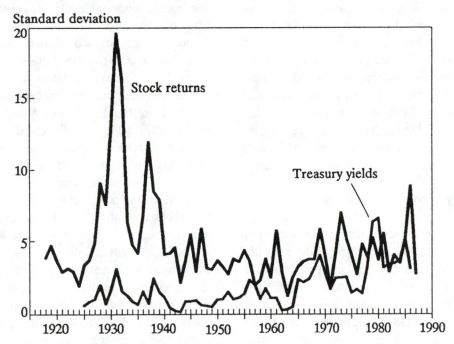

Standard deviation

Stock returns

Treasury yields

Note: In this chart, volatility is measured by the annual standard deviations of monthly stock returns and 20-year Treasury bond returns.

Source: Center for Research in Security Prices.

has made fixed income investments as risky as stocks. In this environment, risk averse investors may be inclined to move away from any type of long-term investment.

The 1980s have also seen explosive growth in hedging and immunization strategies by individual and institutional investors. Individual investors, corporations, and financial institutions are increasingly using interest rate futures, swaps, and options for protection against greater interest rate volatility.[18] Similarly, stock index futures and options are now widely employed to manage stock market volatility.[19] And, cor-

porations and other institutions involved in international trade now use similar instruments to reduce their exposure to exchange rate volatility.

For the most part, policymakers have shown little inclination to attempt to reduce financial volatility directly. For example, proposals to reduce interest rate volatility and stock market volatility through regulation have received little support. Moreover, although governments have intervened in foreign exchange markets to prevent disorderly markets, they have generally rejected proposals to return to a system of fixed exchange rates.

In contrast, policymakers have attempted to increase the ability of financial markets and institutions to adapt to greater volatility.[20] For financial institutions directly exposed to increased volatility, such as depository institutions and market makers, policymakers have encouraged greater capitalization. Increased capital allows these institutions to weather greater financial volatility without incurring the liquidity and solvency problems that might disrupt the functioning of financial markets.

Summary and conclusions

The 1980s have seen increased volatility in many financial markets. The nature of the volatility, its magnitude, and its persistence differ across markets. In the stock market, there is no evidence that normal stock return volatility is different in the 1980s than in previous periods. The frequency of large one-day price movements, however, is considerably higher in each of the past three years.

The volatility of interest rates at all maturities increased sharply at the beginning of the 1980s. The volatility of short-term rates has since declined to historical levels. However, the volatility of long-term rates has continued to be unusually high. Indeed, during the 1980s the volatility of returns on long-term Treasury securities has been as great as stock volatility.

Exchange rate volatility has been considerably higher during the flexible-rate system than under the pre-1973 regime of fixed exchange rates. Even so, exchange rate volatility during the 1980s is generally higher than in the early years of floating exchange rates.

Investors and policymakers have had to adapt to increased financial volatility. Investors have shown some evidence of shifting toward less risky, short-term assets. Investors have also made increasing use of hedging and other portfolio immunization strategies. For the most part, policymakers have resisted pressures to reduce financial volatility directly through increased regulation. Instead, policymakers have attempted to improve the ability of financial markets and institutions to weather increased volatility.

Endnotes

[1] For an overview of some of the channels by which the stock market might affect the economy, see Bryon Higgins, "Is a Recession Inevitable This Year?" *Economic Review*, Federal Reserve Bank of Kansas City (January 1988), pp. 3-16.

[2] For evidence on the impact of the fall in stock prices on consumer spending, see C. Alan Garner, "Has the Stock Market Crash Reduced Consumer Spending?" *Economic Review*, Federal Reserve Bank of Kansas City (April 1988), pp. 3-16.

[3] A discussion of how financial fluctuations affect the economy is found in Mark Gertler and R. Glenn Hubbard, "Financial Factors in Business Fluctuations," *Financial Market Volatility* (Federal Reserve Bank of Kansas City, 1989), pp. 33-72.

[4] Two widely cited reports on the October 1987 stock market decline are: U.S. Presidential Task Force on Market Mechanisms, *Report of the Presidential Task Force on Market Mechanisms*, Washington, D.C., January 1988; and Working Group on Financial Markets, *Interim Report of the Working Group on Financial Markets*, Washington, D.C., May 1988.

[5] For evidence on the linkage between interest rate volatility and money demand, see C. Alan Garner, "Does Interest Rate Volatility Affect Money Demand?" *Economic Review*, Federal Reserve Bank of Kansas City (January 1986), pp. 25-37.

[6] The implications of greater interest rate volatility for financial institutions are discussed in Charles S. Morris, "Managing Interest Rate Risk with Interest Rate Futures," *Economic Review*, Federal Reserve Bank of Kansas City (March 1989), pp. 3-20. Potential costs of interest rate volatility are also discussed in Raymond Lombra and Frederick Struble, "Monetary Aggregate Targets and the Volatility of Interest Rates: A Taxonomic Discussion," *Journal of Money, Credit and Banking* (August 1979), pp. 284-300.

[7] A more detailed discussion of interest rate risk and savings and loans is contained in Charles S. Morris and Thomas J. Merfeld, "New Methods for Savings and Loans to Hedge Interest Rate Risk," *Economic Review*, Federal Reserve Bank of Kansas City (March 1988), pp. 3-15.

[8] See, for example, Keith E. Maskus, "Exchange Rate Risk and U.S. Trade: A Sectoral Analysis," *Economic Review*, Federal Reserve Bank of Kansas City (March 1986), pp. 3-15.

[9] The data in Chart 1 are obtained from the Center for Research in Security Prices (CRSP). These returns are the nominal monthly percentage capital gain in the Standard & Poor's index of 500 stocks. These returns exclude dividend yields. Statistics for the returns including dividend yields are virtually identical to those displayed in Chart 1.

The measure of volatility pictured in Chart 1 and in most of the succeeding charts is the annual standard deviation of monthly returns. This is a measure of the dispersion of monthly returns about the average return for each year. More precisely, if $r_{i,t}$ is the return for month i in year t and $\bar{r}_t$ is the average monthly return in year t, then the annual standard deviation of monthly returns for that year is

$$\sigma_t = \left(\frac{\sum_{i=1}^{12} (r_{i,t} - \bar{r}_t)^2}{11} \right)^{\frac{1}{2}}$$

For a more detailed look at the distribution of stock returns after 1949, see *"Stock Market Volatility,"* Carolyn D. Davis and Alice P. White, Staff Study No. 153, Board of Governors of the Federal Reserve System, August 1987.

[10] This finding that the stock market volatility of the 1980s is not unusually high when compared with the volatility of the 1930s is also reported in Robert J. Shiller, "Causes of Changing Financial Market Volatility," with *Financial Market Volatility* (Federal Reserve Bank of Kansas City, 1989), pp. 1-22.

[11] To measure normal volatility, what statisticians call a robust measure of scale is required. The statistic displayed in Chart 2 is the fourth spread, a statistic that is essentially the same as the interquartile range, the distance between the 25th and 75th percentile of the monthly returns within the year. For an explanation of the fourth spread and of its superiority to the standard deviation in measuring normal volatility, see Boris Iglewicz, "Robust Scale Estimators and Confidence Intervals for Location," *Understanding Robust and Exploratory Data Analysis*, edited by David C. Hoaglin, Frederick Mosteller, and John W. Tukey (New York: John Wiley & Sons, Inc., 1983). Note that in the special case where returns are normally distributed,

$$\text{fourth spread} \approx 1.35\sigma_t.$$

[12] The measure of jump volatility depicted in Chart 3 is related to the measure of normal volatility shown in the previous chart. First, the fourth spread of the daily returns for each year is calculated. Then, two critical values, the upper and lower adjacent values, are calculated as follows:

upper adjacent value = 75th percentile + 1.5 (fourth spread)
lower adjacent value = 25th percentile − 1.5 (fourth spread)

Any daily returns that are either higher than the upper adjacent value or lower than the lower adjacent value are classified as outliers, that is, as extremely high or low returns relative to the rest of the daily returns in that year. Chart 3 displays for each year the number of outliers divided by the number of trading days in the year, that is, the percentage of daily stock returns that are unusually high or low. The statistical justification for this measure of outliers is discussed in David C. Hoaglin and Boris Iglewicz, "Fine-Tuning Some Resistant Rules for Outlier Labeling," *Journal of the American Statistical Association*, vol. 82 (December 1987), pp. 1147-49.

[13] This finding is consistent with the statistics reported in Steven P. Feinstein, "Stock Market Volatility," *Economic Review*, Federal Reserve Bank of Atlanta (November/December 1987), pp. 42-47. Feinstein finds no evidence for a recent increase in the volatility of stock returns when the measure of volatility is the absolute monthly return. On the other hand, when the measure of volatility is the monthly standard deviation of daily returns, the 13 months from October 1986 through October 1987 do exhibit abnormal volatility. It is well known that the standard deviation is extremely sensitive to outliers, in this case, to jumps in daily returns.

[14] The volatility of Treasury bonds is measured as the annual standard deviation of the monthly returns on a 20-year con-stant maturity Treasury bond index.

[15] The volatility of exchange rates in this chart is measured as the annual standard deviation of the monthly return on the U.S. dollar/pound sterling exchange rate.

[16] The volatility of the exchange rate in this chart is calculated using the index of the trade-weighted value of the dollar published by the staff of the Board of Governors. Because this measure begins in 1967, it was not used to make the longer historical comparison in Chart 6.

[17] The difference in average volatilities of the trade-weighted dollar pictured in Chart 7 is statistically significant at the 5 percent level. Greater exchange rate volatility in the 1980s is also reported in Jacob A. Frenkel and Morris Goldstein, "Exchange Rate Volatility and Misalignment: Evaluating Some Proposals for Reform," *Financial Market Volatility* (Federal Reserve Bank of Kansas City, 1989), pp. 185-219.

[18] See, for example, Morris, "Managing Interest Rate Risk . . . "; Morris and Merfeld, "New Methods for Savings and Loans . . . "; and Gregg Whittaker, "Interest Rate Swaps: Risk and Regulation," *Economic Review*, Federal Reserve Bank of Kansas City (March 1987), pp. 3-13.

[19] For an introduction to stock index futures and their use as hedging instruments, see Charles S. Morris, "Managing Stock Market Risk with Stock Index Futures," *Economic Review*, Federal Reserve Bank of Kansas City (June 1989), pp. 3-16.

[20] There has also been increased recognition by policymakers that stable macroeconomic policies contribute to financial market stability. See, for example, Craig Hakkio, "Exchange Rate Volatility and Federal Reserve Policy," *Economic Review*, Federal Reserve Bank of Kansas City (August 1984), pp. 18-31.

Article 11

The Operation of Stock Markets

A securities market is at core a communication system and a trading mechanism. Its functions are: 1) to communicate orders for securities and the prices bid or offered for them (''quotes''), and 2) to match those orders and transform them into trades. Because of this, communication and computer technology (''information technology'') not only can, but inevitably will, change the nature and operations of securities markets. Their performance and efficiency must be evaluated in the light of what could be achieved with advanced information technology.[1]

The stock market crash in 1987 highlighted three problems that could cause future disasters—excessive short-term volatility, technological risk, and strains on the abilities of market-makers to perform their functions under stress. Neither the markets nor their regulators have completely solved those problems in the intervening 3 years.

Stocks are traded in two different kinds of markets—exchanges and over-the-counter (OTC) markets. These markets differ in several important respects. In exchange markets, member firms act for themselves and as agents (brokers) for customers, bringing their orders to a central facility—a ''floor''— to be executed. These member firms are large securities companies such as Merrill Lynch or Goldman Sachs. Orders can be executed in two ways: against other orders—i.e., a bid to buy matching an offer to sell; or if there is no such order at an acceptable price, by a sale to or purchase from the ''specialist''—a member designated by the exchange to be the sole market-maker for that stock.[2]

The largest U.S. exchange, by far, is the New York Stock Exchange (NYSE). Approximately 1,740 companies' stocks are listed on the NYSE. The smaller American Stock Exchange (AMEX) lists approximately 860 stocks. In general, the stocks of the larger and better-known corporations are traded on the NYSE, which has more stringent listing requirements. The NYSE-listed stocks account for almost 95 percent of the trading volume in all exchange-listed stocks.

There are also five regional exchanges—the Midwest, Pacific, Philadelphia, Boston, and Cincinnati Stock Exchanges—that serve as alternative markets for stocks listed on the NYSE and the AMEX (and a few stocks listed solely on the regional exchanges).[3] Exchange-listed stocks are also traded over the counter. This is the so-called ''third market,'' which accounts for about 3.2 percent of the volume in NYSE-listed stock.

Many stocks do not trade on stock exchanges. They are traded only in the OTC market, operated by the National Association of Securities Dealers (NASD) as a self-regulatory organization. In this market securities firms can act as brokers (agents) or dealers (principals) with respect to any stock.[4] A firm receiving a customer's order to buy stock can either sell the stock to the customer from the firm's own inventory (if it is a dealer in that stock) or act as broker in purchasing the stock from another dealer. In this market, nearly every transaction involves a dealer as one party, whereas in exchanges, customer buy and sell orders can be matched. OTC orders are not routed to a central physical facility but handled by dealers working over the telephone or through a computerized small order execution system. About 4,900 actively traded OTC stocks are listed, and bids and offers for them are displayed, on NASD's

---

[1]Some of the material in this chapter draws on an OTA contractor report, Joel Seligman, ''Stock, Options, and Stock-Index Futures Trading,'' University of Michigan Law School, August 1989. For further background on the issues discussed in this chapter, see Joel Seligman, ''The Future of the National Market System,'' 10 *Journal of Corporate Law* 79, 1984; Macy and Haddock, ''Shirking at the SEC: The Failure of the National Market System,'' 1985 *University of Illinois Law Review* 315; and Normon Poser, ''Restructuring the Stock Markets: A Critical Look at the SEC's National Market System,'' 56 *New York University Law Review* 883 (1981). See also U.S. Congress, *Progress Toward Developing a National Market System*, Report of the Subcommittees on Oversight and Investigations and Consumer Protection, Committee on Interstate and Foreign Commerce, U.S. House of Representatives, No. 96-89, Sept. 24, 1979. Contributions to this chapter were also made by contractors Professor David Ratner, Georgetown University School of Law, and Junius Peake, Peake/Ryerson Consulting Group, Inc.

[2]NYSE rules technically allow for competing specialists, but there have been none since 1967, and exchange procedures (including those procedures for disciplining specialists by reallocating stock assignments) are framed around the assumption that there will be only one specialist per stock.

[3]Share volume in NYSE-listed stocks in 1989 was: Midwest, 5.6 percent; Pacific, 3.1 percent; Philadelphia, 1.8 percent; Boston, 1.6 percent, Cincinnati, 0.5 percent.

[4]New York Stock Exchange member firms are, however, forbidden by NYSE rules to do so (Rule 390, discussed later).

Automated Quotation system, NASDAQ. Corporate bonds, municipal bonds, American Depository Receipts, and U.S. Treasury bonds and notes are also traded in the OTC market. Figure 3-1 and box 3-A illustrate the mechanics of a stock trade.

OPERATION OF THE EXCHANGE MARKETS

A key function of securities markets is to facilitate capital formation by providing liquidity, i.e., to enable investors to buy and sell securities when they wish to do so. Many (not all) securities markets use intermediaries or professional market-makers to increase liquidity by helping would-be traders find each other or by themselves trading. Stock exchanges in the United States have a specialist, or designated market-maker, for each listed stock.[5]

U.S. stock exchanges are continuous auction markets. Members of the exchange bring their own or customers' orders to the exchange floor and, in face-to-face negotiations, offer to sell a specified number of shares at a specific price ("an offer") or to buy a specified number of shares at a designated price ("a bid").

The customers served by exchange members are increasingly institutional investors (e.g., pension funds, mutual funds, insurance funds). Over 55 percent of NYSE trading is for these institutions; another 26 percent is for securities firms' proprietary accounts, including those of specialists. Only 18 percent of trades are for individual investors.[6]

Stock exchange specialists act as both brokers and dealers. As brokers, specialists buy and sell for the public, by executing limit orders that are brought to them on behalf of customers by floor brokers; they also execute market orders that reach them through the automated order routing system, SuperDOT.[7] (A limit order specifies the price at which an investor is willing to buy or sell. Limit orders are put in the specialist's "book" until they can be executed at the designated price or a better price.[8] A market order is an order to buy or sell immediately, at the prevailing price.) Specialists are prohibited by law from handling customer orders other than limit orders.[9] The specialist's book was once a looseleaf notebook but now it is, for most NYSE stocks, a computer screen. The specialist is not, with some exceptions, required to show this screen to other traders, exchange members, or the public, although he must disclose aggregate price information.[10]

As dealers, specialists buy and sell for their own account. They have an "affirmative obligation" to do so when it is necessary to provide liquidity. Specialists provide liquidity by buying or selling when there are no other bidders or offerers at or near the market price. The specialist tries to keep prices from making big jumps, by making a bid or offer that acts as a bridge when there is a wide gap between bids and offers. The specialist also has a "negative obligation," *not* to trade for his own account when there are already customers wanting to trade at or near the market price.[11]

Specialists participate in a substantial proportion of NYSE trades. NYSE figures in 1990 show that specialists' purchases and sales as dealers account for 19 percent of all sales and 9 percent of all transactions (purchases and sales) on the exchange. One study in 1985 concluded that specialists might

---

[5]The exception is the Cincinnati Stock Exchange, which is completely computerized and uses "designated dealers." In other U.S. exchanges, the specialist is part of a specialist firm, or unit, that is a member of the exchange. Historically, specialist firms tended to be small, well-capitalized firms, distinct from the large broker-dealer firms that are better known to the general public; more recently, a few of the specialist firms are owned by brokerage houses such as Merrill Lynch. At the end of 1989, the NYSE had 52 specialist firms with 434 individual specialists making markets in 1,712 common stocks. [Source: NYSE, February 1990]

[6]Securities Industry Association, *Trends*, Mar. 16, 1989.

[7]Also as brokers, specialists "stop" market orders when they see that the order may be executed at a better price later (e.g., when a block trade is being negotiated). The specialist guarantees that the order will receive at least the price available at the time the order was stopped.

[8]A special kind of limit order is a stop order, with which a customer specifies that the order should be executed when the stock price drops to a certain price level, or rises to a certain price level.

[9]Securities Exchange Act, sec. 11 (b), 1934.

[10]The NYSE is filing with the SEC a proposal for "A Look at the Book" Pilot Program, whereby limit orders for 50 stocks will be made available to the public through vendors. Information provided by the NYSE, July 16, 1990.

[11]Besides acting as brokers and dealers, specialists have a third function, which is to begin each trading session by overseeing or orchestrating the determination of the opening price.

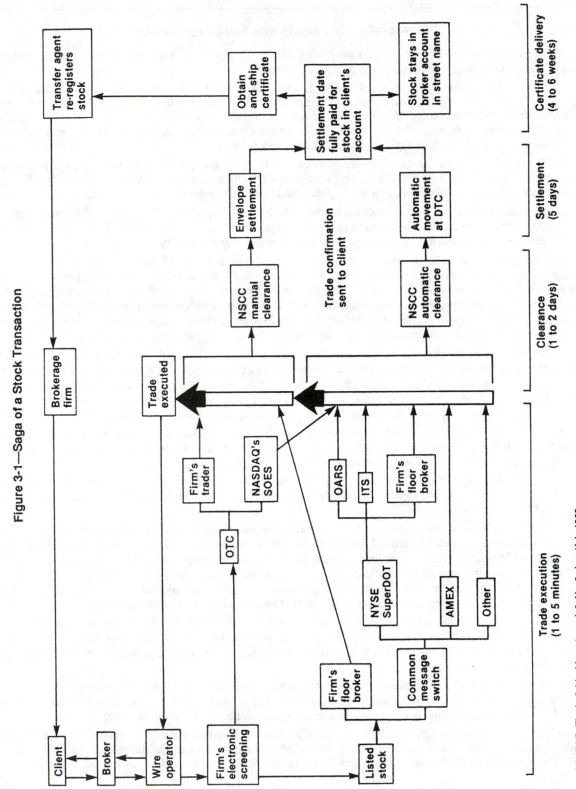

Figure 3-1—Saga of a Stock Transaction

SOURCE: *The Individual Investor*, vol. 3, No. 3, June/July 1989.

Box 3-A—The Mechanics of a Stock Transaction[1]

What happens when you visit or call a stock broker to buy or sell stock? The following description traces the chain of events that results in a transaction by a small investor.

A. When you decide to buy or sell stock, an Account Executive writes an order ticket, filling in the details—whether to buy or sell, the name of the security, how many shares, whether the order is to be executed at the market price or is a limit order (an order to buy or sell when the price reaches a specified level). The market order is passed to a teletype operator who keyboards the information and sends it immediately to an electronic system linking the broker to the various exchanges and over-the-counter dealers.

B. If the order involves an exchange-listed stock and there are no special instructions routing it to another market center, the order will enter the Common Message Switch, an electronic pathway linking brokerage firms and trading floors. This is the beginning of a journey that could carry the order to several alternative destinations.

C. Most orders in NYSE-listed stocks are routed to the NYSE's SuperDOT 250 system, where orders of fewer than 2,000 shares are executed. These orders can go either to the specialist's post on the floor of the exchange, or to the brokerage firm's floor booth (although with a small order, that is unlikely).

What happens next depends on the timing. On a typical day, between 15 and 20 percent of all orders are executed at the market opening. Through SuperDOT, *market orders* to buy or sell, routed to the specialist post prior to the market opening, are automatically paired with opposing orders. The specialist, after matching buy and sell market orders and checking outstanding *limit orders* and larger opening orders, sets an opening price for the stock. The specialist then executes all paired orders at one price and sends confirmation notices to originating brokers within seconds of the market opening, through the Opening Automated Reporting System (OARS).

Orders that arrive at the specialist's post through SuperDOT after the opening can be filled in several ways. Orders of up to 2,099 shares are usually filled at the best quoted price or better in the Intermarket Trading System (ITS). This system connects NYSE, AMEX, five regional exchanges, and NASD's Computer Assisted Execution System (CAES). ITS quotes are displayed at the NYSE specialist's post for all floor traders to see. An order sent to ITS will be filled within 1 or 2 minutes at the best price among any of these markets.

For larger orders, or when a wide spread exists between bid and asked prices, the specialist will execute a SuperDOT order in the traditional way (see D). He can also execute the trades from limit orders in his "book." The specialist is obligated to get the best price available at that moment for the client.

D. Some orders are not handled electronically but rather by the broker firm's floor broker. Wire orders reach floor brokers when they are too large for SuperDOT (see C above) or are larger than the broker's chosen parameters for direct routing through SuperDOT.

At the broker's floor booth, these orders are translated into floor tickets containing the essential buy/sell information necessary to make the trade. Floor clerks pass the details to floor brokers by hard copy (or through hand signals at the AMEX). The floor broker then presents the order at the specialist's post. There the stock is traded with another brokerage firm, or with the specialist, who may be acting as agent for a client on his books, or who may be acting for his own account. Or the floor broker may execute the trade on another exchange, if there is a better price posted on the ITS screen over the specialist's post. The above applies to exchange-traded stock.

E. If the stock is traded over the counter, and the quantity is more than 1,000 shares, the wire order goes to one of the broker's OTC traders at its main office. There, a computer on the OTC trader's desk displays the identities of all market-makers for that stock and their current bids and asked prices. The trader telephones the market-maker with the best price, and executes the trade.

If the brokerage firm itself makes a market in that stock, and the broker's OTC trader is willing to match the best price shown on NASDAQ, the trader can buy or sell it as principal. In either case, at the press of a button on the trader's keyboard, the trade is executed and a confirmation notice is sent to the originating office.

If the OTC order is for 1,000 shares or less, and the stock is listed on NASD's "National Market System," it will be automatically routed via NASDAQ's Small Order Executive System (SOES) to the market-maker with the best price at the time of order. (If the stock is not on the National Market System, it must be for 500 shares

---

[1]Adapted from "The Saga of a Stock Transaction," *The Individual Investor* vol. 3, No. 3, June-July 1988 (American Association of Individual Investors).

maximum to go through this system.) Trades executed through SOES take less than 90 seconds from order wire to confirmation.

F. What happens next is "after the trade" activities, and the process depends on whether the trade was executed manually or electronically. Generally, the trade confirmation is sent back to the broker through the same pathway by which the order arrived, and the broker calls the customer to confirm the transaction.

Executed trades are also reported immediately to the brokerage firm's purchase and sales department and to the exchange, so that the transaction will go on the Consolidated Ticker Tape. Once on the tape it is visible to the investor community, and to the exchange's and regulatory agency's surveillance analysts.

G. On or before the day following a trade, the brokerage firm sends its customer a written confirmation showing the details of the transaction. The customer has five business days from the trade date to pay for purchases delivery (i.e., to settle). About 95 percent of trades are settled through the National Securities Clearing Corp.

The Depository Trust Company (DTC) stores stock and other certificates and maintains records of ownership for brokerage firms and banks. Under normal circumstances, your stock certificate will be registered in DTC's nominee name—"held in street name"—for you as the beneficial" or real owner. Or you may choose to request physical delivery of the stock to you.

For customers who want physical possession of their stock certificates, these shares are registered in the customer's name by the transfer agent of the issuer. Errors and delays can occur in the paperwork trail from brokerage firm to NSCC, NSCC to DTC, DTC to transfer agent, transfer agent back to DTC, DTC to brokerage firm, brokerage firm to customer. For this reason (and other good reasons) there is considerable interest in eliminating paper certificates ("dematerialization") and replacing these with electronic records, as some countries have already done.

be involved, either as dealers or brokers, in more than 70 percent of all NYSE trades at that time.[12]

THE OTC MARKET AND NASDAQ[13]

Until 1939, the OTC market was largely unorganized and unregulated. In that year the Maloney Act Amendments to the Securities Exchange Act allowed the creation of the National Association of Securities Dealers as a self-regulating organization with responsibilities in the OTC market like those of securities exchanges.

Stocks traded in the OTC market are divided into two tiers—the 4,900 NASDAQ stocks, and 40,000 others. NASDAQ includes the more active stocks;

for these, the bids and offers of all registered market-makers (dealers) are shown and continuously updated on the automated quotation system, so that the broker or customer can identify the dealer offering the best quote. A NASDAQ market dealer can become a market-maker in a security merely by notifying NASDAQ operations of intent. There were an average of 10.6 market-makers per security in the NASDAQ market at the end of 1989.[14]

For 40,000 less active stocks, until mid-1990 dealers could advertise their prices only by printed quotations (the "Pink Sheets"). On June 1, NASD opened an electronic "Bulletin Board," on which dealers may post and update quotes for these stocks.

---

[12]Hans R. Stoll, *The Stock Exchange Specialist System: An Economic Analysis.* New York University, Salomon Brothers Center for the Study of Financial Institutions: Monograph Series in Finance and Economics, Monograph 1985-2, p. 15. This was based on analysis of SEC data indicating that limit orders left with the specialist are involved in approximately 24 percent of all purchases and sales. Since the specialist would not be on both sides of a single transaction, this would mean that limit orders were behind 48 percent of total trades (24 percent of purchases added to 24 percent of sales). These figures will be somewhat different from year to year.

[13]Market data in this section supplied by NASD.

[14]National Association of Securities Dealers, Inc., 1989 *Annual Report.*

The Bulletin Board can be accessed by 2,700 terminals in the trading rooms of member firms.[15]

Until 1971, all OTC stock quotations were reported only in daily Pink Sheets, which listed bid and ask prices of each dealer for each stock for the previous trading day. To get up-to-the-minute quotations and meet commonly accepted "best execution" standards, a stockbroker had to telephone at least three dealers and compare their quotes. The time and effort involved in contending with busy signals and wrong numbers made this an ideal situation for using computer and telecommunications technology.[16] Since the introduction of the NASDAQ system in 1971, the volume of trading in NASDAQ securities has grown rapidly. In 1976 NASDAQ share volume was 31 percent of NYSE share volume. In 1989 it was 76 percent of NYSE share volume.[17] Now the NASDAQ market is the second largest stock market in the country. In the first half of 1989 daily volume was more than 134 million shares, up from 123 million at the end of 1988.[18] Increasingly the NASDAQ market is used by institutional investors as well as small investors, and block trades now account for 43 percent of total volume. This growth is largely due to technology; as computer systems supplement telephones, dealers can handle larger volumes and provide immediate automated execution for many trades, and customers can receive more competitive prices.

The NASDAQ-listed stocks are further divided. National Market System or "NMS" stocks are the most widely held and actively traded stocks, for which transactions are reported as they occur. Of the 4,500 stocks in the NASDAQ system, approximately 2,800 are NMS securities.

NASD is basically a telephone market supported by a computer screen quotation-display system (and the automatic execution system for small orders). Quotations are collected and disseminated by leased telephone lines from the NASDAQ Central Processing Complex to dealers' desktop terminals. For NMS securities, OTC dealers must provide last sale data within 90 seconds of a trade. For the second-tier stocks dealers need report only the aggregate trading volume at the end of the day.

NASDAQ quotations are indicative rather than firm for lots over 100 shares, except for orders eligible for small order automated execution, for which prices must be firm up to 1,000 shares.[19] In other words, NASDAQ market-makers do not disclose how many shares of stock (over 100 shares) that they are willing to buy or sell at their quotation prices.[20] The OTC dealers continue to display the minimum size (100 shares) required by NASDAQ rules. The price for transactions over that size must be negotiated.

Market-makers are required by now-mandatory SOES participation in the Small Order Execution System (SOES) to execute public small orders up to 1,000 shares in NMS stocks (the number varies by stocks) at market prices, and to maintain minimum SOES exposure limits up to five times that amount. However, SOES trades are less than 2 percent of NASDAQ volume.[21] The Securities Exchange Commission (SEC) has repeatedly encouraged NASD to change its NASDAQ requirements. An NASD proposal, submitted to the SEC on March 20, 1989 and not yet acted on at mid-1990, would require a NASDAQ market-maker's size display to be at least

---

[15]In the first week of operation, over 100 OTC dealers advertised prices for about 3,000 domestic and foreign securities. NASD says that 7,235 market-making positions were displayed. The Bulletin Board differs from the NASDAQ quotation system in several ways: 1) there are no listing standards; 2) dealer quotations need not be firm quotations, and can even be unpriced indications of interest; 3) the Bulletin Board does not transmit data to press wire services or to information services vendors, as does NASDAQ; 4) it has no equivalent of the NASDAQ's Small Order Execution System.

[16]For history of OTC trading, see Joel Seligman, 1982, op. cit., footnote 1; and Simon and Colby, "The National Market System for Over-the-Counter Stocks," 55 *George Washington Law Review* 17, 19-34, 1986.

[17]About 27 percent by dollar volume, because the average price of OTC stock is much lower than the average price of NYSE stock.

[18]Source: NASD, February 1990.

[19]Professional-proprietary (dealer) orders, and customer orders over 1,000 shares, are not eligible for SOES.

[20]NASD points out that in NASDAQ stocks, where dealers are exposed on an identified basis to both automated execution and other real-time quotation-execution processes, the display of size has impacts on dealers that do not exist in other markets. In NASDAQ each dealer quotation is displayed and the identity of each market-maker firm is disclosed. Actual execution size is as large, above the displayed minimum, as the quantity all competing dealers are willing to take into inventory at a particular time and price. Size in individual dealer quotations contains inventory-related information, and it requires additional resources to update on a continuous basis. In simpler terms, if a dealer is offering the lowest offer, a competing dealer could "pick him off," i.e., buy all of his stock and then resell it at the second dealer's own (higher) price.

[21]A number of proprietary automated systems at dealer firms' also execute such small order trades.

the SOES required order size in the stock (i.e., up to 1,000 shares).

THE NATIONAL MARKET SYSTEM

In the early 1970s and again in the late 1980s, the operation of American stock markets aroused congressional and regulatory concern. In 1969 to 1970, a series of operational and financial crises caused the collapse of a number of securities firms, and thereby provoked studies of the securities industry and markets by both Houses of Congress and by the SEC. These studies ultimately led to the passage of the Securities Acts Amendments of 1975, which included the most far-reaching revisions of the Securities Exchange Act of 1934 in more than 40 years.

A more recent wave of congressional and regulatory concern followed the October 1987 market crash. A number of reform proposals were made by special commissions, regulatory agencies, and Senators and Representatives. More were proposed after disclosure in 1988 and 1989 of a string of stock market abuses and frauds, and a near crash in October 1989. A few of these reform proposals were implemented by self-regulatory organizations, some are still before Congress or regulatory agencies, and some have been dropped for the time being.

The 1975 Amendments directed the SEC to "facilitate the establishment of a national market system for securities" and to order the elimination of "any . . . rule imposing a burden on competition which does not appear to the Commission to be necessary or appropriate in furtherance of the purposes" of the Act.[22] The basic objective of the 1975 Amendments was the development of a more efficient, fair, and competitive national market system that could provide:

- economically efficient execution of transactions;
- fair competition among brokers, dealers, exchange markets, and other markets;
- availability to brokers, dealers, and investors of information about quotations and sales;
- practicability of brokers executing customers' orders in "the best market," and

- "an opportunity, consistent with [other] provisions. . . for investors' orders to be executed without the participation of a dealer."

Congress said that these objectives were to be achieved through "the linking of all markets for qualified securities through communication and data processing facilities. . ..," but it did not specify the exact nature of these systems and facilities.

There is disagreement over whether the objectives of the Amendments, as subsumed in the phrase "a national market system," have been fully achieved. The nature of the basic objective seemed to call for some necessary steps:

- a consolidated quotation and price dissemination system, so that market-makers could compete with each other to make better bids and offers;
- electronic order routing and execution systems, to speed up transactions, reduce transaction costs, and assure customers that their bids and offers are taken in order by price and time of arrival;
- a way of efficiently directing orders to the market or market-maker with the best quotation at that moment; and
- a national clearing and settlement system, making effective use of information technology.

The SEC's efforts to develop a markets-wide communication system predated the 1975 Amendments. Until 1972, NYSE and AMEX ticker tapes and electronic displays gave a continuous report of transactions on those two exchanges. They did not report transactions in the same securities on regional exchanges or in the OTC market. Under SEC prodding, a consolidated *last-sale* reporting system was established in 1972 by the Securities Industry Automation Corp. (SIAC). SIAC is the central trade price processor and reporter for exchange-listed securities for the NYSE, AMEX, the five regional exchanges, and the NASD.

But a consolidated quotation system that would allow brokers to check all markets for the best price to execute a customer order was still not available for exchange-listed stocks at the time of the 1975 Amendments. In 1978, the SEC proposed requiring

---

[22]Securities Exchange Act, sec. 11A(a)(1). The Amendments also extended the Act to cover clearing agencies and information processors, and increased the SEC's oversight powers over the Self-Regulatory Organizations (SROs) in the securities industry.

a universal message switch, a broker-to-market link through which a customer's order would automatically be routed by a broker to the market or dealer showing the best quote. The exchanges objected, and the next year the SEC shelved its proposal.[23] It approved, instead, the development of a market-to-market link—the Intermarket Trading System or ITS—as proposed by the exchanges. The ITS enables specialists and floor brokers on one exchange—not customers or non-member retail brokers—to transmit orders to market-makers on another exchange floor or operating over-the-counter, who have posted a better price on the consolidated quotation system. The market-maker receiving the order must respond within 1 or 2 minutes or the order expires.

The ITS does not require that an order be routed to the market with the best quote. The order can be executed in the market in which it is received, provided the specialist or a floor broker matches the best quote available elsewhere. The regional markets, most of the time, match NYSE quotes; i.e., their prices are derivative of those on the NYSE.

The Securities Acts Amendments of 1975 sought to increase competition by having the SEC review exchange rules "which limit or condition the ability of members to effect transactions in securities otherwise than on such exchanges." The SEC was to report its findings within 90 days and begin a proceeding "to amend any such rule imposing a burden on competition which does not appear to the Commission to be necessary or appropriate in furtherance of the purpose of this title."[24] A "fail-safe" provision authorized the SEC to limit trading in listed securities to exchanges, but only if it were necessary to protect investors and maintain an orderly market, and after public hearings.

The most significant restraint on market-making in exchange-listed securities is NYSE Rule 390 (originally Rule 394), which prohibits members from making markets off-exchange in listed stocks (i.e., they can act as dealer only as a specialist on an exchange). In a proceeding to determine whether it should eliminate Rule 390, the Commission found that the "off-board trading rules of exchanges impose burdens on competition" and that the SEC was "not now prepared to conclude that these burdens are necessary or appropriate for the protection of investors." It proposed repeal of the rule. However, after 4 years of deliberation and hearings, the Commission announced in 1979 that it was withdrawing its proposal. It instead adopted an experimental rule, 19c-3, that allows NYSE members to make OTC markets in stocks first listed on an exchange after April 26, 1979.

A number of major stock exchange members then started making markets in newly listed exchange stocks, about 10 percent of the 100 most actively traded NYSE stocks, including the "Baby Bell" companies spun off in the split-up of AT&T. This market-making proved unattractive or unprofitable, either because of the small number of stocks or because of the competition, or for other unrevealed reasons. By 1983 member firms had largely withdrawn from that activity, although a few have since resumed marking markets.[25]

There are several arguments against abolishing Rule 390. Large member firms might internalize their trading by executing orders upstairs. This would, critics say, fragment the market for those securities, with none of the upstairs or off-exchange markets being liquid or deep enough to keep the spread narrow. However, it could also cause a screen-based market for those securities to develop, with competing market-makers providing good liquidity.

Critics also argue that abolishing Rule 390 could lead firms to execute customer transactions at less favorable prices than could be found on the exchange floor.[26] This is, however, also true for orders

---

[23]Sec. Ex. Act Rels. 14, 416, 14 SEC Dock. 31, 1978; 14, 805, 14 SEC Dock. 1228, 1978; 14, 885, 15 SEC Dock. 139 1978. See also: Norman Poser, "Restructuring the Stock Markets: A Critical Look at the SEC's National Market System," 56 *N.Y. University Law Review* 883, 923, (1981); Joel Seligman, "The Future of the National Market System," 10 *Journal of Corporate Law* 79, 136-137, 1984.

[24]Securities Exchange Act, sec. 11A(c)(4). These provisions were deleted from the Act in 1987, as "obsolete," on the ground that "these requirements were met several years ago." Senate Rep. No. 100-105 at pp. 20-21, 1987. The 90-day provision was obsolete but there is not complete agreement that the substantive intent of the requirement had been met.

[25]Merrill Lynch dropped out in April 1983, followed by Paine Webber and Goldman Sachs.

[26]"Trade-through" rules could forbid brokers from executing orders at a price less favorable than that offered on any exchange or NASDAQ; but when trades are made on the floor the price is sometimes better than the published quotation—i.e., the trade is made "between the quotes" as a result of floor negotiation. There have been several proposals of various kinds of order-exposure rules, which would require orders to be exposed for a length of time before transactions; this could add to transaction costs or to dealers' risks.

sent automatically by many brokers to one exchange (usually the NYSE); they may miss better prices off the exchange. The SEC has been reluctant to force the NYSE to change the rule on the basis that market participants—the members of the exchange—are best able to determine the effects of this NYSE rule.

Competition from overseas markets makes it important that Rule 390 be reexamined. With global securities trading,[27] Rule 390 is becoming increasingly burdensome. Many trades by large investors in 89 of the 100 most actively traded exchange-listed stocks are done after NYSE closing in the London market. (As discussed later, the NYSE is planning limited actions to try to recapture these trades with electronic trading mechanisms. These are likely to be ineffective if large investors want to trade these stocks "around the clock.") The SEC has been criticized for this hands-off attitude toward Rule 390. Congress may soon find it necessary to direct SEC to reconsider.

Another major barrier to competitive trading among markets has been the rule preventing exchange specialists from competing with OTC market-makers in trading unlisted stocks. The 1975 Amendments directed the SEC to grant unlisted trading privileges where "consistent with the maintenance of fair and orderly markets and the protection of investors."

For 10 years the SEC made only tentative moves to meet the intent of the 1975 amendments. In 1987, the SEC allowed exchanges, as a trial, to trade up to 25 NASDAQ securities. Only the Midwest Stock Exchange took advantage of this, and it captured only about 1 percent of the volume in those shares. On June 1, 1990, the SEC expanded this trial into a pilot program that will (in 9 months) allow up to 100 selected OTC stocks to be traded by the Midwest, Philadelphia, Boston, and American exchanges. Because it relies heavily on listing fees for revenue, the NYSE refused to participate. Companies might be reluctant to list with the NYSE if their stocks could be traded on the exchange without listing.

Some large corporations now traded only over the counter (e.g., Apple and Nike) may benefit by the added exposure, and investors may get better prices

because of increased competition. However, these stocks already have competing market-makers on NASDAQ, and it is uncertain how much additional exposure the smaller exchanges will provide.

CHALLENGES TO THE SPECIALIST SYSTEM

Changes in Trading Patterns

The stock exchanges and the NASDAQ system were organized to deal with moderate-sized orders based on a "round lot" of 100 shares. With the growing importance of institutional investors, this system became strained.[28] Institutional trading grew rapidly in the 1960s and thereafter. Institutions increasingly traded in large blocks (10,000 shares or more), that require special techniques because large volumes are difficult to handle in the usual manner. Between 1975 and 1988, the average size of an NYSE transaction increased from 495 shares to 2,303 shares. Comparable increases occurred in other markets. Brokers' commissions were deregulated in 1975. Small individual orders (less than 1,000 shares) became too expensive to handle in the traditional manner. Techniques had to be developed to funnel these orders to the market-maker in a more efficient manner. Traditional techniques based on specialists became increasingly unsatisfactory for both small and large orders.

Small Orders

Faced with either losing money on small-order transactions, or charging high commissions and driving away the small investor, the exchanges and NASDAQ developed automated order routing and execution systems for orders over a specified size.

The NYSE's Designated Order Turnabout System (DOT, later called SuperDOT), began in 1976. In 1988 the order routing system handled 128,000 orders a day. Orders are sent to the specialist post, where they are announced to the floor brokers, executed, and reported back. SuperDOT reduces the costs and eliminates most of the errors in executing, transferring, or reporting trades.

The AMEX Post Execution Reporting is much like DOT, allowing members to electronically route

---

[27]See OTA Background Paper, *Trading Around the Clock: Securities Markets and Information Technology*, OTA-BP-CIT-66 (Washington, DC: U.S. Government Printing Office, July 1990).

[28]In early 1990, institutional investors accounted for 45.3 percent of NYSE trading. The annual average, however, has been 55 percent by share volume.

orders up to 2,000 shares directly to the specialist. Routing may be done from the member's trading room or from the broker's desk on the floor, with an execution report generated automatically.

Four regional exchanges have developed small-customer-order-execution systems that operate as derivative pricing mechanisms, basing prices on NYSE quotes. (The fifth, The Cincinnati Exchange, is completely automated.) Brokers or trading rooms can electronically route an order to a specialist at a regional exchange. The specialist must accept the order at the best price available in the Consolidated Quotation System, or at a better price. (The Philadelphia system does not allow the specialist to better the price.) If the specialist does nothing, at the end of 15 seconds these systems execute the order automatically on behalf of the specialist and report it back. These systems have helped the regional exchanges to increase their share of NYSE-listed volume.[29]

On NASDAQ's small order execution system, SOES, orders of up to 1,000 shares are automatically executed at the best market price.[30] No telephone contact with a dealer is needed. At the end of 1988 only about 9.4 percent of NASDAQ transactions by value (1.4 percent by volume) were being handled through SOES. However, SOES is the standard for a number of proprietary automated execution systems in NASDAQ stocks. About 70 percent of NASDAQ trades are "SOES eligible" (i.e., within SOES size limits), so this allows the automatic execution of a large proportion of NASDAQ trades.

Block Trading

The big problem with trading large blocks is not cost, but liquidity. Big blocks usually have to be broken up, and their execution often sharply changes the prevailing market price. Neither the specialist system on the exchanges nor the NASDAQ system in the OTC market were designed to provide instant liquidity for very large transactions near current market price.

Block trades involve 10,000 or more shares, or have a market value of $200,000 or more.[31] Transactions of this size were rare 25 years ago. They

increased rapidly because of the growth of large investment funds with large assets for investment and trading. Block trades made up only 3.1 percent of reported NYSE share volume in 1965, with an average of 9 block trades a day. In 1988, more than 54 percent of reported share volume on the NYSE involve block trades, with an average of 3,141 block trades per day. About 20 percent of these block trades involve over 250,000 shares. Block trades accounted for 43 percent of share volume on NASDAQ in NMS stocks in 1988, and on the AMEX they accounted for 42 percent.

Specialists were increasingly strained to fulfill their affirmative obligations to provide liquidity and smooth out price jumps when these large blocks came to the floor. The NYSE responded by developing procedures for "upstairs" trading of blocks.

Under these procedures, an institutional investor goes to an exchange member (a large securities firm such as Goldman Sachs or Merrill Lynch) that has registered as a "block positioner."[32] The block positioner usually commits itself to execute the entire block at a specific price, itself taking all of the shares that it cannot sell to others. The positioners primarily work "upstairs" in their trading rooms rather than on the exchange floor. They are, in effect, making markets, although they have no affirmative obligation to do so as does the specialist.

A positioner who receives an order for the purchase or sale of a block is required by NYSE Rule 127 to "explore in depth the market on the floor," and must "unless professional judgment dictates otherwise," ask the specialist whether he is interested in participating in the transaction. Rule 127 also requires the specialist to "maintain the same depth and normal variations between sales as he would had he not learned of the block," in other words, to act as though he has not been warned.

In advertising the block, the positioner may find additional interest on the same side as well as on the other side—i.e., in the case of a block to be sold, additional sellers as well as potential buyers—and may agree to handle these shares also. Once the positioner has put together as many buyers and

---

[29]CTS Activity Report, December 1989. NYSE Strategic Planning and Marketing Research.

[30]These limits vary according to the security—they may be 200 shares, 500 shares, or 1,000 shares.

[31]*New York Stock Exchange Guide* (CCH) Rule 127.10, sec. 2127.10.

[32]In October 1989 there were 57 firms registered with NYSE as block positioners (source: NYSE) as compared to 66 in 1986, according to the Brady Report, VI-9.

sellers as it can find, the positioner may buy for its own inventory any shares left over, or the specialist may do so when the block is taken to the floor.

When the order is carried to the floor, the negotiated price may be above the current offer or below the current bid. There are elaborate rules to make sure that customers with limit orders on the book at or near the current price will not be disadvantaged, as they could be if their orders were executed just before the price moved as a result of the block trade. Instead, their orders are supposed to be executed at the "cross" price (i.e., the block trade price).

Because of strong competition among the block positioners, institutional customers pay very low broker commissions. Possibly for this reason, securities firms now appear increasingly unwilling to risk their capital in block positioning. The block positioners have no affirmative obligation to make markets. SEC officials assert that while these block procedures worked well in addressing the volatility encountered with block trading in the late 1960s, they do not handle progam trading well, and there is evidence that liquidity for the large blocks may now be decreasing.[33]

There is currently a tendency for large institutional trades to be executed on regional exchanges rather than the NYSE. According to the Midwest Stock Exchange, the reasons are to suppress advance information about the impending trade, and to make it less likely that "others will intervene before the institutional trader can play out a particular (positioning) strategy."[34] Brokers like to put together "crosses" (i.e., to match buyers and sellers) without going through the specialist or the floor crowd so that they can collect commissions on both sides. They may go to a regional exchange to avoid the NYSE limit order book, because in New York "the block probably would have gotten broken up," or a specialist may "try to come in late on a deal that's already established."[35]

COMPETITION IN STOCK MARKETS

Assessing competition in the stock markets is difficult because of several structural features. First, stock markets involve many services, including execution of transactions, market-making, and information processing and dissemination. Competitors may provide one or more of these services, and a firm that provides one service may either provide or be a customer for another service. Second, the nature of trading requires that competing firms cooperate with one another by adopting standardized procedures that enable the market to function. Finally, the exchanges and the NASD are membership organizations whose goals and practices reflect the interests of their members. The membership of these organizations overlaps. A firm that is a member of all or most of these organizations may oppose practices in one organization that adversely affect the firm's operations in another.

The three areas of competition which have been most controversial since the 1975 amendments are: 1) competition among market-makers, 2) competition among market facilities, and 3) competition among customer orders.

Competition Among Market-Makers

The SEC has been strongly criticized for not moving toward a national market system by forcing the repeal of NYSE Rule 390. That would permit NYSE member firms to compete in OTC markets in listed stocks. This would in turn encourage the development of proprietary electronic trading systems that could become, in a sense, competing exchanges.

There are reasons to approach such radical change cautiously. There is experience with exchange (specialist) markets and with competing dealer (OTC) markets. There is no real experience with a market where traditional floor-based specialists

---

[33]"Ketchum Says Stock Firms Are Balking at Putting Capital in Block Positions," 21 *Sec. Reg.& L. Rep. (BNA)* 547, 1989.

[34]Midwest Stock Exchange brochure: *Institutional Traders and Regional Exchanges.*

[35]Ibid.

compete with multiple dealers or automated execution systems.[36]

The closest approach to competition of this kind is the "third market" (non-members of exchanges dealing in listed stocks over-the-counter) and the "fourth market" (trading between investors on proprietary electronic trading systems). But these do not show how such a market might develop if the dominant large brokers of listed stocks become market-makers. Experience with Rule 19c-3 indicates that most firms will not make markets in a small number of stocks. If they were able to route orders in all stocks to themselves as market-makers (or even to a neutral electronic facility), market-making might be more attractive.

Some people predict that if Rule 390 were rescinded it would have a negligible impact on the market. Others argue that exchanges would be abandoned and all trading shifted to an OTC market modeled on NASDAQ or on the International Stock Exchange in London. There is disagreement about whether investors are best served by an exchange or an OTC market.

While NYSE members cannot compete on the exchange in market-making for NYSE-listed stocks, there is competition between the NYSE and other markets. Trading of NYSE-listed stocks on regional exchanges, NASDAQ, proprietary trading systems such as Instinet, and overseas markets now accounts for 30 percent of all trades in those stocks and more than 15 percent of the share volume. The third market alone—OTC dealers—accounts for 3.2 percent of volume in NYSE-listed stock. Some dealers now pay brokers for directing order flow to them rather than to exchanges (where the broker would pay a transaction cost).

The NYSE also must compete with the NASD for listings. It has successfully retained almost all of its listed companies (it is nearly impossible for a corporation to "delist" from the NYSE),[37] and has even lured some large companies from NASDAQ. NASD, on the other hand, has been successful in holding many large companies that qualify for NYSE listing. One measure of NASDAQ's success is that on many days there are almost as many stocks that trade more than 1 million shares on NASDAQ as on the NYSE.[38]

There were once competing specialists within the NYSE, but the last disappeared in 1967.[39] Now NYSE procedures, customs, and technology are geared to a single market-maker. Another way to get internal competition would be for member firms to compete for the privilege of being the specialist in a particular stock, but the turnover in specialist assignments is very low.

Competition Among Market Facilities

The SEC has also been criticized for not insisting on more competition among market facilities. It approved the ITS instead of pressing for a universal message switch (UMS) that would automatically route brokers' orders to the market where the best price was being displayed. The critics' assumption is that a UMS would encourage the regional exchange specialists to more effectively compete by offering better prices than offered by the NYSE or AMEX specialist. The regional systems compete with the NYSE and AMEX through speed and transaction costs under the ITS, but there is no inducement to compete by bettering NYSE prices. They need only match the NYSE price.

The regional exchanges warmly defend ITS.[40] In 1989 the Midwest received more than 10 percent of its trades (15 percent of its share volume) from ITS. The number of stocks listed on ITS has grown from 300 in 1978 to 2,082 (of which all but 300 are NYSE-listed). The number of shares traded on ITS

---

[36]The American Stock Exchange and the Philadelphia Stock Exchange have a specialist and competing dealers (on the floor) in certain of the options which it trades. However, because of the complexity of options (puts and calls, different prices, and different expiration dates), this may be more an example of sub-markets than a model which would work in the single market for the single class of stock.

[37]To delist its stock voluntarily, a corporation must have two-thirds of the shares voted to delist and no more than 10 percent of the shareholders opposed to delisting.

[38]NYSE and NASDAQ volume figures are not completely comparable, since all NASDAQ trades involve a purchase or sale by a dealer while some NYSE trades involve a direct transaction between two investors. Customer to dealer to customer is two sales; customer to customer is one sale.

[39]In 1933, there were 466 NYSE stocks with competing specialists, in 1963 there were 37.

[40]For example, a vice president of the Midwest Stock Exchange says that ITS "is vital to the continued competitive viability of all market centers that compete with NYSE. . . . Without ITS there would be insufficient liquidity on markets other than on NYSE to adequately service most investor needs." Allan Bretzer, Oral Statement before the OTA Advisory Panel on Securities Markets and Information Technology, Jan. 22, 1990. Text provided by Mr. Bretzer.

annually has grown from 42,000 in 1978, its first year, to 2.3 billion in 1989.

ITS is not sophisticated; it is simply a communication system. After the 1987 market crash, the SEC concluded that "the present configuration of ITS is not designed to perform efficiently in high volume periods."[41] ITS has been modernized and expanded since the crash; some of its critics have moderated their criticism. Other critics say that one of the objectives of a national market system is not being fully met—that of inter-market competition.[42] It is still much simpler for brokers to route orders routinely to the NYSE than to spread them among exchanges, especially if the price differences are small or nonexistent. Only with automatic routing of customers' orders to the market with the best price will regional and OTC market-makers have a full incentive to provide competing quotations. This is a chicken-or-the-egg situation.

Is real market-making competition among *exchanges* (as they are currently organized) either a realistic or desirable expectation? The benefits of a central market, with a physical floor and specialists to whom all orders are routed, are touted by those who think an electronic market would be fragmented and less liquid. There is some inconsistency in extending this defense to five or six competing floors with specialists, each receiving a portion of the order flow. The regional exchanges have chosen to compete: 1) by offering less expensive service to brokers for the automatic execution of small trades, and 2) enabling block positioners to complete crossed transactions without exposing orders to the NYSE specialist or customer orders on the NYSE floor. Less expensive services may pressure the major exchanges to reduce the costs of executing small transactions,[43] but their services to block positioners may result in denying to customers whose orders have been routed to the NYSE floor an opportunity to participate in the crossed transaction.

The advantages of the regional exchanges for small orders or for block trades might or might not ensure their competitive survival if a UMS routed orders to the market with the best price. A UMS might not strengthen the regional exchanges as competitors with the NYSE but might instead create an integrated electronic market in which all of the exchanges would become only service centers for brokers and issuing companies, and perhaps regional regulatory organs.[44]

Competition Among Customers' Orders

The most far-reaching criticism of the failure of the SEC to "facilitate the establishment of a national market system" is that it has not pushed for the establishment of a single system in which:

1. all customer orders would have an opportunity to meet,

2. customers' orders could be executed against one another without the participation of a dealer, and

3. any dealer would be permitted to make markets.

Such a system would differ from today's stock exchange system (which does not meet the first and third criteria), and from today's OTC market (which does not meet the first or second). Some experts argue that this would require the SEC to replace the exchanges and NASDAQ with a computerized system in which all orders and quotes would be inserted and all transactions would be executed. Such a system is technically feasible and it would hold the promise of cost reductions in trading securities. The basic questions are: Would it work? Would it be an improvement over the current system? What are the risks? Other possibilities are discussed later in this chapter.

---

[41]SEC Division of Market Regulation, *The October 1987 Market Break*, 1988; Report of the Presidential Task Force on Market Mechanisms, 1988 [the Brady Commission Report]. The NYSE acknowledged that extremely high trading volumes generated backlogs of orders. According to the Brady Report, SEC suggested that ITS might adopt default procedures ensuring that if a commitment to trade was not accepted or rejected during the specified time period, execution would automatically occur.

[42]Seligman, contractor report to OTA, op. cit., footnote 1.

[43]The success of the regional exchanges in this competition can be gauged by the fact that they currently account for more than 30 percent of the *trades* (not volume) in NYSE-listed stocks, most of their activity being in small trades.

[44]France plans to integrate its regional bourses with an electronic network, and officials anticipate an outcome such as sketched here. See OTA background paper, op. cit. footnote 27.

THE 1987 MARKET BREAK AND THE PROBLEM OF VOLATILITY

The stock market crash in 1987 focused attention on three important problems—volatility, technological risk, and market-maker performance. Several times in 1986 and 1987 there was extraordinary short-term volatility in the stock market.[45] The break came in October 1987. From the close of trading on October 13, to close of trading on October 19, the Dow fell 769 points, or 31 percent. In the first hour of trading on October 19, the Dow fell 220 points, or over 11 percent. In all, the drop on that day was 508 points, nearly 23 percent, with a record volume of 604 million shares. On the next day, October 20, there was great volatility, with the market rising nearly 200 points in the first hour, declining more than 200 points in the next 2 hours, and rising again by 170 points just before closing, with a new volume record of 608 million shares. On the third day the market rose 10.1 percent, the largest one-day rise in history; but there was another one-day fall of 8 percent the following week. These losses were paralleled by similar declines in the U.S. regional exchanges and OTC markets, and in stock exchanges around the world.

Several special studies by task forces, regulatory agencies, and exchanges reached different conclusions about the cause of the 1987 crash.[46] In the following 2 years no general consensus has emerged. Blame has been placed on rising interest rates, trade and budget deficits, decline in value of the dollar, new financial instruments such as stock-index futures, program trading for portfolio insurance, too much and too little inter-market linkage, discussions in Congress about changing tax laws, investor irrationality, overreliance on computer systems, and under-use of computer systems.

It is also possible that increasing volatility is nearly inevitable given the increased volume of trading, coupled with computerized trading. The average daily volume has increased from about 30 million shares in the mid-1970s to 165 million in 1990. Peaks in volume can go much higher; on October 19, 1987, 604 million shares were traded. The NYSE said at that time that it was preparing—technologically—for a billion share day. The rate of turnover (number of shares traded as a percentage of total number of shares listed) has also been increasing. Between 1951 and 1966, the turnover rate never exceeded 20 percent. Between 1967 and 1979, turnover ranged between 20 and 30 percent; it then began to increase rapidly. Since 1983, turnover has exceeded 50 percent every year, reaching a peak of 73 percent in 1987. This is one of the forces that raises doubts about the continued capability of traditional trading mechanisms to cope with increased pressure.

The Debate About Volatility

Whatever the cause of the 1987 market break, a more persistent concern is the appearance of excessive short-term volatility in the stock market before and since the crash. By some estimates the 1987 volatility was roughly twice the level of volatility over the preceding 4 years.[47] On at least four occasions in April, 1988, there were abrupt rises and falls; for example, on April 21, 1988, the Dow fell 36 points in 30 minutes. On October 13, 1989, the market dropped about 190 points, or 7 percent, most of it in the last hour of trading.

Many experts nevertheless deny that there is excess volatility. There is disagreement over how much is "excessive" or how volatility should be measured (e.g., changes in price from day to day,

---

[45]On Sept. 11 and 12, 1986, the Dow declined 6.5 percent with daily volume of 238 and 240 million shares. On Jan. 23, 1987, it fell 5.4 percent in 1 hour.

[46]Brady Report, VI-47; SEC Market Break Report, 7-48; U. S. Congress, General Accounting Office, *Preliminary Observations on the October 1987 Crash*, 1988; N. Katzenbach, *An Overview of Program Trading and Its Impact on Current Market Practices*, Dec. 21, 1987 [the Katzenbach Report]; Commodity Futures Trading Commission, Divisions of Economic Analysis and Trading and Markets, *Final Report on Stock Index Futures and Cash Market Activity During October 1987*, 1988.

[47]Report of the Presidential Task Force on Market Mechanisms, 1988, pp. 2-4. This did not, however, approach the volatility of 1933, when on 10 percent of all trading days there were moves of over 5 percent.

during the day, during half-hour periods, etc.).[48] If stock prices actually reflect "fundamental values," how much up-and-down movement is inevitable as the market homes in on a consensus about value? Professor G. William Schwert of the University of Rochester concludes that the volatility of rates of return to broad market portfolios of NYSE-listed common stocks has not been unusually high in the 1980s, except for brief periods such as October 1987.[49] Volatility has seemed high to the public, Schwert says, because the level of stock prices has risen over the last 20 years, and a drop of many points is actually a relatively small percentage drop.

Some theorists contend that any attempt to curb volatility makes markets less efficient and is undesirable. But the historical objective of "fair and orderly markets" implies that at some level volatility becomes excessive. Fast rising markets raise fears of "bubbles," and sudden unexplained drops cause many investors to withdraw from the market.

The Debate Over Program Trading

Many people who are concerned about excessive short-term volatility place the blame on portfolio trading, program trading, portfolio insurance, or index arbitrage. These terms are often loosely used by the media, with considerable overlap. This gives rise to much public confusion. Generally, portfolio trading means the buying or selling in a single order or transaction of a large mixed group (portfolio) of stocks. Some trades involve hundreds of different stocks. "Program trading" means the same thing. It is defined by the NYSE, Rule 80A, as either: a) the buying or selling of 15 or more stocks at one time or as part of a single maneuver, when such trades involve at least $1 million; or b) index arbitrage. The term usually also means that a computer program is used to guide trading decisions and to route the orders.

Portfolio insurance is a kind of program trading designed for hedging (protecting one's investment by an offsetting investment or transaction). Portfolio insurance calls for balancing transactions in several markets (e.g., the stock and futures markets) in order to reduce risk. (When the average price of a basket of stock changes adversely, an investor holding a stock-index futures contract covering that basket has locked in the more advantageous price. See ch. 4.) With "passive hedging," there is relatively little turnover of stock. "Dynamic hedging" portfolio insurance can lead to many large institutional investors deciding to sell baskets of stock (and large blocks of each stock) at the same time, when the stock prices are already declining. This can make the decline even more precipitous.

Several forces caused program trading and associated trading strategies to increase in the mid-1980s: 1) the growth of investment funds with very large portfolios and a legal obligation to make prudent profitable investments; 2) computers and telecommunications for making complex, multi-asset transactions simultaneously; 3) the development of computer algorithms for managing dynamic trading strategies; and 4) the invention of stock-index futures.

Institutional investors often hold an "index" of stocks, i.e., a portfolio matched to the stocks used in an indicator index such as the Standard and Poors 500 (S&P 500). In this way, fund managers can be sure that their investment fund does at least as well as the market average (and usually no better). About 20 percent of all stock owned by pension funds, for example, is in indexed funds.[50] These institutional investors often use hedging techniques involving stock-index futures (as described in ch. 4) to protect the value of their portfolios. Some of these strategies require rapid switching of assets among stocks, stock-index futures or options, cash, or other markets. They may turn over every share in the portfolio

---

[48]See, for example: Merton H. Miller, *Financial Innovations and Market Volatility*, Mid America Institute for Public Policy Research, 1988; Theodore Day and Craig M. Lewis, "The Behavior of the Volatility Implicit in the Prices of Stock Index Options," Owen Graduate School of Management, Vanderbilt University, June 1988; Steven P. Feinstein, "Stock Market Volatility," Federal Reserve Bank of Atlanta, *Economic Review*, December 1987; James F. Gammill, Jr., and Terry Marsh, "Trading Activity and Price Behavior in the Stock and Stock Index Futures Markets in October 1987," *Journal of Economic Perspectives*, vol. 2, No. 3, Summer 1988, pp. 25-44; G. William Schwert, "Why Does Stock Market Volatility Change Over Time," 1989, and other papers on volatility, University of Rochester Bradley Policy Research Center; Robert J. Shiller, "Causes of Changing Financial Market Volatility," presentation at Federal Reserve Bank of Kansas City Symposium on Financial Market Volatility, Aug. 17-19, 1988; Adrian R. Pagan and G. William Schwert, "Alternative Models for Conditional Stock Volatility," University of Rochester Bradley Policy Research Center, BC-89-02.

[49]Schwert, "Stock Market Volatility," New York Stock Exchange Working Paper No. 89-02, December 1989.

[50]The largest pension fund indexed investors are now TIAA-CREF ($26 billion), New York State and Local ($15.9 billion), New York State Teachers Fund ($13.7 billion), California Public Employees ($13 billion), and California State Teachers Fund ($12.7 billion). One hundred percent of these portfolios are indexed (1989). *Pensions & Investment Age Magazine*, Jan. 22, 1990, p. 38.

several times in a year. The effect of program trading on stock price volatility is related to the strategy used to direct the switching of assets. If the strategy calls for selling stock when the price is declining and buying when the price is rising, this "positive feedback" will accelerate price movements and increase volatility. This is particularly so if very large blocks of shares are traded and if many investment funds are using similar trading strategies.

Program trading of all kinds accounts for about 21 million shares a day on the NYSE,[51] about 13 or 14 percent of NYSE trading.[52] About half of the program trading on the exchange is in the form of index arbitrage (trading in order to profit by temporary discrepancies or mispricing between stock and stock-index futures prices). Much of the rest is various hedging behaviors for the purpose of risk management rather than profit on trading volume, but they sometimes lead to behavior similar to profit strategies—rapid shifting of assets.

Just before the 1987 market break, the use of portfolio insurance was increasing rapidly. It is likely that when stock prices fell rapidly on October 19, this triggered selling of stock-index futures, causing their price to fall. This in turn led arbitragers to sell stock in order to buy futures, causing stock prices to fall more rapidly. (As discussed in ch. 4, this thesis is still a subject of controversy, and is challenged by the futures industry and its regulators.) The SEC reported that at least 39 million shares were sold by institutions on that day because of portfolio insurance strategies that called for stock sales either in lieu of futures transactions or as a supplement to them.[53]

On October 19, 1987, portfolio insurance sales accounted for only 15 percent of total sales. The effect may have been magnified for two reasons.[54] First, about half of reported sales are accounted for by direct and indirect market-making (specialist activities, block positioners, arbitrageurs, etc.), so that the portfolio insurer sales were about 30 percent of "true sales." The volume of such attempted sales was perhaps twice the volume that insurers were able to complete, again doubling the perceived demand for liquidity. Secondly, market participants could not know how persistent these sales would be, or how far they might go. Specialists saw that their firms' capital could quickly be exhausted.

Many market participants say that "portfolio insurance" of the kind that provides strong positive feedback loops has been largely abandoned and is unlikely to become popular again, since it failed to protect portfolios. Other observers are skeptical of this conclusion. The more one believes that others have given up portfolio insurance, the more strongly one may be tempted to try to beat the market by using it.[55] Many firms said they were giving up program trading, or some forms of program trading, after the 1987 break, but gradually resumed it. After sharp declines on the afternoon of Friday, October 13, 1989, there were renewed demands for "abolishing" or "controlling" program trading, with little attempt to distinguish among the kinds of program

---

[51]See monthly NYSE Program Trading Releases. In September 1989 program trading amounted to 13.8 percent of NYSE trading; this is about the level of early October 1987, prior to the crash. In 1988, program trading was down somewhat, to about 8 to 13 percent depending on the month. There is large variation from week to week, however.

[52]There is much argument over how program trading volume should be calculated. The NYSE calculates it as the sum of shares bought, sold, and sold short in program trading, divided by total reported volume. Some experts think this is double-counting (the same shares are bought and sold), and would prefer to calculate program purchases as percentage of total purchases, or program sales as percentage of total sales, or program purchases and sales as percentage of twice total volume. However, many transactions do not involve program trading on both sides of the trade; and program trading may have one leg in stock markets and one in futures markets; therefore the NYSE believes that its method is a more reliable indicator of the contribution of program trading to volume.

[53]Securities Exchange Commission, *The October 1987 Market Break*, p. 1.

[54]According to R. Steven Wunsch, then Vice President of Kidder Peabody, in discussions with OTA project staff and in "Phoenix Rising From the Crash," *Institutional Investor*, December 1988, p. 25. Wunsch also notes that most specialists stayed at their post, ". . .and many probably deserve medals for doing so, particularly stock specialists who in many cases suffered severe financial and personal strain living up to their affirmative obligations to make markets. . .."

[55]A substitute for portfolio insurance developed in the form of brokers writing put options for institutional investors to "insure" their stock portfolios. When stock prices declined on Oct. 13, 1989, these brokers attempted to hedge, or adjust their hedges, by selling stock. This was identified as a contributor to the rapid price decline. CFTC, Division of Economic Analysis, *Report on Stock Index Futures and Cash Market Activity During October 1989*, May 1990, p. 3; SEC, Division of Market Regulation, *Trading Analysis of Oct. 13 and 16, 1989*, May 1990, p. 5.

trading or determine exactly how it could be controlled.[56]

To the extent that "program trading" means the trading of diversified portfolios or "baskets" of stock simultaneously (with or without the assistance of computers), it is probably an essential procedure for institutional investors trying to manage very large portfolios. A "blue ribbon panel," established by the NYSE to consider the problem after the 1989 market break, did not recommend restraints on program trading.[57] Significant restraints on the practice would certainly run the risk of driving institutional funds into off-exchange or foreign markets where much program trading is already done. According to the NYSE, in a recent week, 78 percent of program trading (in equities) took place on that exchange, 5.2 percent in other domestic markets, and 16.8 percent in foreign markets.[58] Some of this program trading was done in the "fourth market"[59] on two electronic, off-exchange, trading systems: Instinet's "Crossing Network" (owned by the British company, Reuters), and "Posit," a system operated by a Los Angeles brokerage firm.[60] Currently only about 400 institutions trade over these systems. Many of the large program trades cannot be executed on these systems because of limited liquidity. However, if program trading were to be forbidden on the exchange, these systems could become a preferred alternative.

Whether it is possible or wise to reduce program trading by abolishing stock-index futures, by adjusting their margin requirements, or by changing the way in which they are regulated, is another question, which is considered further in chapter 4. The question here is whether or how markets can be helped to cope with the problems that arise when many large investors make instantaneous sales (or purchases) of large baskets of stock. One approach is the increased use of "circuit breakers"—techniques for halting trading when prices move rapidly.

The Debate About Circuit Breakers

The perception of excessive short-term volatility raises the issue of circuit breakers, which were first widely advocated after the 1987 crash, especially by the Brady Report. Circuit breakers are procedural or operational ways of halting trading when there is an abrupt or sustained decline in market prices and a volume of trading that threatens to overload the markets' capacity. Circuit breakers may be designed to be triggered by price limits, volume limits, order imbalances, or trading halts in a related market.

Critics, including free-market advocates, claim that circuit breakers unfairly prevent some investors from leaving the market when they are frightened. This, they say, makes panic worse, and sell orders pile up until the dam breaks. Circuit breakers also inhibit use of some hedging and arbitrage strategies.

Proponents say that circuit breakers allow time for people to consider fundamental values, for traders to determine who is solvent, for credit to be arranged, and for imbalances to be advertised so that bargain hunters can be located and get into the market. Circuit breakers could counter the "illusion of endless liquidity" that tempts institutional investors to try to sell huge amounts of stock quickly.

Market breaks produce ad hoc circuit breakers, in any case. Technological systems overload and break down; some market-makers abandon their posts; communications become chaotic. But to be effective, circuit breakers must be mandatory, be in place

---

[56]Shearson Lehman Hutton announced in October 1987 that it would not do program trading for itself, and announced in October 1989 that it would do no program trading for customers. Many other securities firms took similar actions. Several stock-issuing companies were reported to be putting pressure on securities firms to end program trading; the chairman of Contel Co. said program trading was turning the NYSE into "a gambling casino." William Power, "Big Board Faces Fight on Trading," *Wall Street Journal*, Nov. 30, 1989. See also, Sarah Bartless, "Wall St.'s 2 Camps," *New York Times*, Oct. 23, 1989, D1; Alan C. Greenberg, Chairman of Bear, Stearns, & Co., "How To Reduce Stock Market Injury Potential," letter to the editor, *New York Times*, Nov. 14, 1989. In May 1990 Kidder Peabody resumed program trading.

[57]The panel was made up of 19 corporate executives and business leaders chaired by Roger B. Smith, chairman of General Motors Corp. It reported to the exchange on June 12, 1990.

[58]In the preceding weeks, the comparable percentage figures were 78, 8.7, and 13.3. NYSE Weekly Program Trading Data, Mar. 20, 1990; data was for the week of Feb. 20-23.

[59]"Fourth market" refers to off-exchange (i.e., directly between institutions) trading of stock that is listed on an exchange, Exchanges are the first market and OTC dealers make up the second market; OTC trading of listed stock is the third market.

[60]About 13 million shares are sold daily on Instinet, according to Reuters; the number sold on Posit is not known. Most of the "fourth market" program trading does not involve stock-index futures, but is for the purpose of liquidating or balancing a portfolio after exchange closing. All of Instinet's Crossing Network trades and 10 percent of Posit trades are executed after NYSE's close-of-business, at closing prices.

ahead of time and hence predictable, and be coordinated across stock, futures, and options markets.

Some circuit breakers were put into effect by exchanges following the crash, and others have been proposed. Under specified conditions, the stock exchanges and futures exchanges execute coordinated halts for 1 or 2 hours. This formalizes ad hoc procedures used during the crash (when, for example, the Chicago Mercantile Exchange (CME) suspended trading of stock-index futures in reaction to halts of trading of individual stocks on the NYSE). Some circuit breakers are designed to interrupt program trading rather than halting all trading. The NYSE has adopted a circuit breaker that is activated if the Dow declines or advances 50 points or more in 1 day. It prohibits members from entering program trading orders into the, SuperDOT system. When it was first applied on a voluntary basis, 13 of 14 exchange members then engaged in index arbitrage continued program trading manually instead of by computer. More arbitrage selling was done for customer accounts during this voluntary restraint than before it was imposed.[61] Under an NYSE rule that replaced the voluntary collar, when the stock-index future traded on CME (S&P 500) falls a certain amount, program trading orders will be automatically routed by SuperDOT into a separate file (a "sidecar") for delayed matching and execution.

An NYSE panel, created after the October 1989 market break to consider the problems of program trading and excessive volatility, has recommended new and stronger circuit breakers to halt equity trading in all domestic markets when the market is under pressure.[62] A movement in the Dow Industrial Average of 100 points (up or down) from the previous day's close would call for a 1-hour halt; 200 points would call for 90 minutes, and a 300 point movement would call for a 2-hour pause.

The proposed Stock Market Reform Act (H.R. 3657) would give the SEC authority to suspend trading in stocks and options for up to 24 hours during a "major market disturbance."[63] With Presidential approval, the SEC could extend this for two additional days. (Congress is considering whether the SEC should be given regulatory authority over stock-index futures. Such authority would enable the SEC to coordinate trading halts across markets.) The Market Reform Act would also give the SEC authority to require large-trader reporting, that would improve the Commission's ability to monitor inter-market trading and effectively analyze the results of program trading.

In the meantime, the SEC is being urged to reconsider the oldest form of circuit breaker, the "short sale" rule. Rule 10a-1, adopted in 1938, prohibits traders from selling stocks short[64] when the price is falling. If prices fall and traders believe that the price will continue to fall, they can profit by selling short. This would accelerate a price decline. Efficient-market theorists and many practitioners argue that Rule 10a-1 keeps market professionals from immediately expressing new information, thereby distorting the market function of price discovery. They say, moreover, that the rule is ineffective against panic selling and can be circumvented by trading stock in London. Defenders of the rule point out that negative expectations are not "new information," and that selling short on down-tick merely manipulates the price to the practitioner's advantage. The SEC last reviewed the rule in 1976 but declined to abolish it, and is not expected to do so in the immediate future.

THE 1987 MARKET BREAK AND THE PERFORMANCE OF MARKET-MAKERS

The 1987 market break also exposed problems with the ability of market-makers to respond to the challenges of rapid downward price movement and unprecedented high volume. The performance of exchange specialists and OTC market-makers was criticized. One lesson that may be drawn from the market break, however, is that neither the specialist system nor a system of competing market-makers

---

[61]Memorandum to SEC Chairman Ruder from Richard G. Ketchum, Director of SEC Division of Market Regulation, July 6, 1988. The event described was on Apr. 14, 1988.

[62]See footnote 57 for the makeup of the panel.

[63]The Commodity Futures Trading Commission, which regulates futures markets, already has this power. The SEC can now suspend trading for 24 hours but only with prior Presidential approval.

[64]Selling short is the practice of selling borrowed stock, or stock that one does not yet own. It is done in the belief that one can, before settlement, buy the stock to be delivered at a lower price than one has sold it for, thus making an instant profit.

can assure liquidity in a period of intense selling pressure caused by aggressive trading institutions.

NYSE Specialists

NYSE specialists were net buyers of 9.7 million shares between October 14 and 16, 1987, and made net purchases of 21.2 million shares on October 19, in a futile effort to stem the tide. They were "often the primary, and sometimes the only, buyers" during the crash.[65] By the end of trading on October 19, however, 13 of the 55 specialist units had no buying power left. On the next day, October 20, specialists were net sellers of 9.1 million shares.[66] By contrast, "upstairs firms" (non-specialist members) sold a net 7.6 million shares from their own inventory from October 14-16, and were net sellers of 4.5 million shares on October 19 and 9.6 million shares on October 20.

The President's Task Force on Market Mechanisms (the Brady Task Force) evaluated the NYSE specialists' performance during the crash. It reported that as the market collapsed, most specialists "were willing to lean against the downward trend in the market at a significant cost to themselves."[67] But there were exceptions. Of 50 specialists, 30 percent were net sellers on October 19. Of 31 stocks on October 20, specialists contributed to, rather than countered, the market's fall in 39 percent. The Brady Report acknowledged that some of the poor performance by specialists may have been caused by "exhaustion of their purchasing power following attempts to stabilize markets." For others, however, it seemed hopeless to attempt "to stem overwhelming waves of selling pressure."

Studies after the 1987 market break confirmed that the performance of specialists is highly variable. Some specialists fulfill their obligations to "lean against the market" more aggressively than others. The SEC criticized the NYSE for not using its power to punish specialists for poor performance during the preceding 10 years by reallocating their stock to other specialists.[68] After the crash, however, the NYSE reallocated 11 stocks from 7 specialist units, and in 1989 reallocated stock from another specialist unit.[69] The SEC, in its report on the market break, suggested that the NYSE develop regular comparative evaluations with a view to reassigning stocks from less effective to more effective specialists. The NYSE rejected this suggestion at the time. However, in 1990, the exchange began an experiment with a specialist performance questionnaire system, scored entirely on the basis of relative ranking of specialist units' performance. After further experience, the exchange intends to develop formal performance standards.[70]

In June 1988 capital requirements for specialist firms were substantially increased over those that prevailed during the 1987 crash. Each specialist unit or firm must be able to buy or sell 15,000 shares of each common stock in which it is the registered specialist. Each must have additional net liquid assets equal to 25 percent of those position requirements or $1 million.[71] Some market professionals conclude that the capitalization of specialist firms—in the context of growth in market volume and market capitalization—is inadequate and will become more inadequate. Stanley Shopkorn, Vice Chairman of Salomon Brothers, Inc., says:

> New York Stock Exchange specialists in the aggregate have slightly over a billion dollars of capital. . . . [T]his capital cannot make a meaningful contribution to stability on days when $15-25 billion in stock changes hands on the exchange.[72]

---

[65]SEC Division of Market Regulation, *The October 1987 Market Break*, February 1988, pp. 4-24 to 4-26.

[66]Data in this paragraph on specialists' and upstairs firms' performance was supplied to OTA by the NYSE, Apr. 17, 1990.

[67]Report of the Presidential Task Force on Market Mechanisms, op. cit., footnote 41, pp. 49-50.

[68]SEC, *The October 1987 Market Break*, op. cit., footnote 41, p. 4-29. When in 1972 the SEC assembled evidence of poor performance by 14 specific specialists, the Exchange Committee on Floor Affairs (of whose 11 members 7 were specialist) refused to take disciplinary action, citing as extenuating circumstances "unusual market conditions" or "thinness of the book." This is summarized in U.S. Congress, Senate Committee on Banking, Subcommittee on Securities, 4 *Securities Industry Study Hearings*, 92d Cong. 2d sess., 1972, pp. 34-46.

[69]Between 1984 and 1989, the NYSE censured, suspended, and/or fined 28 specialists, and barred 4 specialists either permanently or conditionally from membership, employment, or association with any member firm. Source: New York Stock Exchange.

[70]Correspondence from the NYSE, July 1990.

[71]Note that upstairs firms on Oct. 19, 1987, were net sellers of 4.6 million shares; if the average price at sale were $30, it would require $138 million to offset these one-day sales, averaging $3 million per specialist firm. On Oct. 20, upstairs firms sold yet another 9.6 million shares.

[72]From a letter signed by Mr. Shopkorn and sent to clients of Salomon Brothers, Inc., and reprinted with permission in *Commodities Law Letter*, November-December 1989.

In 1986, before the crash, the NYSE and AMEX had implicitly acknowledged strains on the specialist system by requesting and getting SEC approval for rule changes to encourage large broker-dealer members to become (buy or affiliate with) specialist firms.[73] The Commission hoped that:

> The financial backing of well-capitalized upstairs firms would serve . . . to strengthen the financial resources available to specialists to withstand periods of market volatility.

However, no broker-dealer acquired a specialist firm until the crash, when Merrill Lynch acquired the financially troubled A.B. Tompane, Inc. Acquisitions were later approved for Bear Stearns & Co. (already a specialist firm), for Drexel Burnham Lambert, Inc. (now bankrupt), and for Smith New Court, Carl Marks, Inc., only four approvals since the rule change.

Both SEC and NYSE reports on the 1987 crash noted the problem of the market's ability to absorb institutional portfolio trading. The reports recommended developing a "basket-trading product" that could restore program trades to more traditional trading techniques. Such a product could provide better information "by identifying program trade executions and overhanging program orders in individual stocks, and provide an efficient mechanism for trading, clearing, and settling baskets [of stock] in a cost-efficient way."[74]

A basket product was approved for trading in late 1989. "Exchange Stock Portfolios" or ESPs are standardized baskets of stocks traded at an aggregate price in a single execution on the exchange's stock trading floor. The initial contract contains the 500 stocks represented in the Standard and Poor 500 Index, and is designed to sell for about $5 million. It is subject to normal margin requirements.[75]

The NYSE elected not to use the traditional specialist system to trade ESPs. Instead, it developed a special adaptation that makes use of advanced information technology. The ESPs, or basket contracts, are assigned to "competitive basket market-makers" (CBMMs) who are not required to be on the floor, as are specialists. They operate upstairs, using special terminals. They do have affirmative obligations as do specialists.[76] However, there has been almost no trading in ESPs since their introduction.

Block trading procedures, the 1986 rule change and the increased specialist capitalization requirements, and the competitive market-maker arrangements for ESPs, are all intended to reduce the strains on the specialist system, as markets try to adapt to increasing pressures.

OTC Market-Makers

The competitive OTC market-makers also performed poorly during the market break. Volume on NASDAQ jumped to 223 million shares on October 19, and reached record levels of 284 million and 288 million on October 20 and 21. (However, NASDAQ share volume on October 19 increased only 49 percent over its average daily volume of the preceding 9 months.)[77] This points to differences in the functioning of the exchange and OTC markets. The NYSE had to halt trading in many stocks for long periods on October 19 and 20. On the other hand, the Brady Task Force found that there were trades reported in 36 of the 50 leading NASDAQ stocks during each quarter-hour on those 2 days and for the remainder of those 50 stocks, trades were not reported in only one or two 15-minute periods. However, the volume of trading that customers were able to do in the OTC market was far less than the volume on the exchanges, as many market-makers either withdrew, ignored telephone calls, or only traded the 100-share minimum they are required to accept.

Prior to the break, 46 of the 50 top NASDAQ market-makers participated in the Small Order Execution System (SOES), in which they are obli-

---

[73]This had not been prohibited before, but was discouraged by prohibitions or restrictions on member firms trading securities that were assigned to specialist firms affiliated with them. See SEC Release No. 34-23765, Nov. 3, 1986.

[74]SEC Rel. 34-27382, Proposed Rule Changes Related to Basket Trading, approved Oct. 26, 1989.

[75]That is, users must put up 50 percent initial margin and maintain 25 percent maintenance margins, as with other stock transactions.

[76]CBMMs may make proprietary bids and offers only in a manner consistent with maintaining a fair and orderly market, must help alleviate temporary disparities between supply and demand, and must maintain a continuous two-sided quotation in the basket product subject to a specified bid-ask parameter. CBMMs must meet a $10 million capital requirement over and above other capital requirements. They are treated as specialists for margin purposes.

[77]NASDAQ share volume, which was equal to more than 80 percent of NYSE volume in the weeks prior to the market break, was equal to only 37 percent of NYSE trading on Oct. 19, 47 percent on Oct. 20, and 64 percent on Oct. 21. Brady Report at VI-50.

gated to buy or sell up to 1,000 shares. (Participation in SOES was then voluntary.) At times during the break, up to one-third of these firms completely withdrew from SOES (thus reducing their exposure to the 100 shares mandated by NASDAQ for non-SOES transactions) and others reduced the number of securities in which they were SOES participants.[78]

Non-SOES trading also became difficult, because market-makers' telephone lines were overloaded and some market-makers simply stopped trading. Market-makers withdrew from 5,257 market-making positions (over 11 percent), according to the SEC.[79] NASD maintains that these may have been inactive positions that were abandoned to allow market-makers to concentrate on more important active positions. The average spread of NASDAQ quotations expanded by over 36 percent.

THE 1987 MARKET BREAK AND THE LIMITATIONS OF TECHNOLOGY

Experience during the market break indicates that information technology, if not developed and utilized wisely, can worsen imbalance and volatility instead of correcting them. All markets had pile-ups of sell orders that could not immediately be executed and therefore overhung the markets for long periods. The NYSE's SuperDOT system, designed to make trading by small investors more economical, was overwhelmed by institutions executing their program trades. However, the order pile-ups could have been worse without the technology. Almost certainly clearing and settlement mechanisms would have failed.

The NASDAQ Small Order Executive System (SOES) was disabled by "locked" or "crossed" quotations (i.e., bid quotes equal to or higher than asked quotes). SOES was programmed to require human intervention when that occurred.

The consolidated tape system became overloaded and there were several computer breakdowns at SIAC. These were mostly isolated incidents that were quickly remedied.[80] But prices of derivative products such as stock-index futures depend on last transaction prices for stocks. Even short delays in reporting those prices can lead to spurious discounts of index futures prices to stock prices. This could cause volume surges on one or the other markets, generated by computer-trading strategies.

After October 1987, the exchanges and the NASD increased the capacity of their systems and took steps to prevent repetition of the practices which made it impossible for public customers to get their orders executed. The NYSE increased the capacity of its SuperDOT system and the number of electronic display books, increased the capacity of the Intermarket Trading System, and constructed a second SIAC data processing facility. The NYSE says it could now handle 800 million trades in 1 day. It now gives small orders of individual investors priority in routing to the specialist when markets are stressed. The NASD made SOES participation mandatory for all market-makers in National Market System securities. The system was modified so that it will continue to execute orders even when quotations are locked or crossed. An order confirmation and transaction service (OTC) was put in place so that dealers can negotiate trades and confirm executions through NASDAQ when they cannot do so by telephone. Other forms of automation have also been put in place, including an Automated Confirmation Transaction service that allows telephone-negotiated trades to be "locked in" through automatic reporting, comparison, and routing to clearing organizations.

AUTOMATION AND STOCK MARKETS: THE FUTURE

The fundamental problems with technology during the crash may have resulted from the fact that the automated systems currently in use in the securities markets were designed for the purpose of facilitating, not replacing, preexisting trading practices. The Brady Report stated in assessing the performance of the NASD's automated system, but in language that is equally applicable to the automated systems on the exchanges:

Many of the problems emanated from weaknesses in the trading procedures and rules which were programmed into the automated execution sys-

---

[78]Brady Report, op. cit., footnote 41, VI-53.

[79]SEC, October 1987 Report, op. cit., footnote 41, pp. 9-19.

[80]*The October 1987 Market Break*, op. cit., footnote 41, pp. 7-3 to 7-7.

tems... From the beginning ... each advance in automating the market was greeted with apprehension by many if not most of the market makers ... To ease that apprehension and, more importantly, to sell the systems to its membership, the NASD found it necessary to build in trading procedures and rules which were not necessarily aimed at achieving the most efficient trading system but were believed necessary by the membership to protect their economic interests... Unfortunately many of these compromises came back to haunt the over-the-counter market during the October market break.[81]

This judgment applies to exchanges as well as OTC dealers. The American stock markets have by and large used technology to facilitate and support, rather than replace, traditional trading methods and practices. The exchanges and OTC markets have each automated some of their functions (order routing, data display and communication, monitoring and analysis, and small order execution), but they have preserved the central role of the market-maker.

Domestic Exchanges of Tomorrow

The capabilities of information technology in data collection, matching, aggregation, manipulation, storage, and dissemination have enormously increased over the last four decades and can reasonably be expected to make comparable advances over the next four decades. The limitations and vulnerabilities of information technology are also becoming better known. Information technology could be used more extensively for automatically routing orders among market-makers, matching like-priced bids and offers, automatically executing and recording the transaction, carrying it through the clearing and settlement process, and providing an audit trail for regulatory purposes.

Alternatively, technological and personal-intermediation trading systems might be operated in parallel, with the customer and/or broker given a choice. Technology might be used to change the nature of exchanges from continuous auctions to periodic single-price auctions, or to offer other alternative trading mechanisms—some of which are growing up around and outside of traditional securities markets, as proprietary trading systems. The fundamental policy question is whether it is desirable to encourage and facilitate the replacement of the

current exchange and OTC market structures with fully automated trading systems, or to allow this to happen incrementally, slowly, or not at all. There are assuredly risks in either course.

Proponents of computerized trading systems say that they provide more information more equally to all participants, reducing the advantage that market professionals have over public investors, and that they would provide better liquidity by encouraging bids and offers anonymously from all geographical locations and aggregating them for all to see—thus encouraging new buyers (or new sellers) to enter the market when an imbalance exists and bargains are to be found.

Opponents of computerized trading systems extol the advantages of personal presence on the floor for both stimulating and gathering or perceiving information (i.e., better price discovery), and providing the incentives for vigorous trading. They stress the advantage to investors of the obligation of the specialist to assure liquidity and immediacy, and the specialist's ability to negotiate prices. Opponents of electronic markets also insist that specialists (or other intermediaries and market-makers) are uniquely able to position and manage large block trades.

The SEC has approved Rule 144a, to allow institutional investors to trade unregistered securities (usually corporate bonds) without the financial disclosure otherwise required. In the past, investors who bought private placement securities often had to hold them. Now the market should be more liquid, and many foreign corporations may participate. But there is a real risk that such developments may accustom institutional investors to using electronic trading systems off-exchange, and in so doing create a two-tiered market where the best prices and deals occur in an electronic market for institutions only, while individuals are left in outmoded physical markets.

The only example of a fully automated trading system in the United States is the Cincinnati Stock Exchange. Its National Securities Trading System is a "black box" that lets brokers instantly execute orders up to 2,099 shares through the computer. Bids or offers are entered automatically, the highest bid or lowest offer is filled first, and identical bids/offers are taken in the order in which they arrived, except that public orders take precedence over specialist or

---

[81]Brady Report, op. cit., footnote 41, VI-52-53.

dealer orders. However, the Cincinnati Stock Exchange failed to attract customers and does little business (0.46 percent of trades in NYSE-listed securities in 1989). The Exchange is now only a computer at the Chicago Board Options Exchange, of which it has become an affiliate.

A number of securities markets in other countries have recently installed computerized trading systems. The Toronto Stock Exchange has a Computer Assisted Trading System, or CATS. This is an order-driven system. Those wishing to trade put their orders (with price and size of the order) into a computer that establishes a queue of bidders and offerers arranged first by price, and then by the time of arrival of each order at that price. The computer also displays the number of shares offered or bid for. When the order at the top of the queue is filled (that is, when the offer is taken or the bid accepted) it is replaced by the next order at the same (or the next best) price. A complete record of all trades is automatically generated. In this system, there is still a "registered trader" who is committed to buy or sell for his own account when the size of orders does not match—i.e., when the number of shares offered at the best price is not sufficient or is in excess of the number of shares bid at the matching price. Equity, futures, and options "floor traders" use CATS to maintain their responsibilities for designated stocks and to trade on their firm's or their own behalf. Other users are upstairs traders, with CATS terminals on their desks.[82]

CATS now handles about half of Toronto-listed stocks and 22 percent of the total trading volume on the exchange. Toronto also has an electronic execution system for small-sized floor transactions. As a result, automated assistance applies to at least 75 percent of Toronto trading. The volume of trading in Toronto is, however, extremely small compared to that at the NYSE. Only about 50,000 trades a day, on average, are done on CATS, with a projected maximum trading capability of 250,000 trades.

Interviews at the Toronto Exchange indicate a high degree of support and enthusiasm for the automated systems, as allowing the exchange "to be more competitive in the cost and level of service. . ."[83] Some skeptics feel that the CATS will not be able to handle the needs of traders for the kind of information that they think comes only from perceptive observation on the trading floor. Others are concerned that an attempt to improve market quality and service might have an opposite effect. It could give people with sophisticated computer support an unfair advantage over others, and encourage institutional dominance of the market. Some are concerned that computer techniques could encourage market manipulation (in Canada, surveillance has historically not had adequate computer support).[84] Finally, there is a concern that a failure in computer systems could cause catastrophic losses.

Other foreign exchanges are also automating. The Paris Bourse, the Belgian Bourse, the Spanish exchanges, and the Sao Paolo exchange in Brazil have all adopted CATS. The Copenhagen stock exchange is being restructured and will eventually include three automated trading systems, one based on CATS.

As another possible alternative to the current systems in the United States, several experts argue that a computerized single-price auction should either supplement or replace the continuous auction market and the specialist function.[85] In a single-price auction, trading takes place at specific times, as contrasted with a continuous auction market. All outstanding bids and offers are collected, compared by computer, and executed at the price that will come closest to clearing the market. Bids above or offers below the clearing price are held for the next round. A single-price auction might be held once or twice during a trading day, with a continuous auction on the side for those who want to trade immediately. It would provide an automated and open display of the specialist book. It might replace the specialist system, because "a continuous market requires the participation of a dealer who is willing to trade

---

[82]Contractor Report on Canadian Market Systems, prepared for OTA by Digital Equipment of Canada, Limited (Robert G. Angel, marketing manager, Capital Markets), July 24 1989. Hereafter cited as "Digital Report to OTA."

[83]Ibid. The report also describes extensive upgrading and enhancement in the Montreal Exchange, with introduction of a FAST automated trading system which includes a screen based limit order book with executable orders.

[84]Digital Report to OTA, op. cit., footnote 82, p. 4.

[85]Steven Wunsch, in written communication to OTA, February 1990; see Steven Wunsch, "SPAworks—The Single Price Auction Network: Question-and-Answer Series," manuscript provided by author; and Joel Chernoff, "Trading Plan Stirs Debate," Investment Age, July 25, 1988.

immediately, while a call market can operate without dealers.''[86]

It may also be necessary to consider whether the national market system that might evolve because of current economic pressures should be a unitary system, or should include ''subsystems for particular types of securities with unique trading characteristics,'' as contemplated by the 1975 amendments.[87] The NYSE and the AMEX use the same trading system for all listed stocks, regardless of the level of trading activity, even though this varies from fewer than five trades per day for some stocks to several hundred, or more than a thousand, trades in a day for others. On the Tokyo Stock Exchange, by contrast, the trading of the 150 most active stocks is done though a continuous auction process (without the intervention of dealers), while 2,000 less active stocks are traded by matching orders through computer terminals. The early development of proprietary trading systems operated by market data service vendors (and soon by U.S. futures exchanges) is discussed in chapter 7.

Around-the-Clock, Around-the-Globe Trading

U.S. OTC dealers, through the National Association of Securities Dealers, have begun several initiatives aimed at competing in international markets. NASD is installing computer facilities in London to extend the NASDAQ network to the United Kingdom. In September 1990 NASDAQ will begin ''dawn trading sessions,'' beginning at 3:30 a.m. e.s.t., to coincide with the London opening and continuing until just before the regular NASDAQ trading day begins at 9:30. In addition, NASD has opened the ''PORTAL'' system for electronic trading by institutional investors of private placement stock issues around the globe.

Until mid-1990, there was no discernible movement by security exchanges to recognize the growing international securities markets, or to prepare for 24-hour trading.[88] In June 1990 the NYSE announced that it was planning a five-step process ''to prepare for continuous 24-hour trading by the year 2000.'' The NYSE's plan is conservative, cautious, and limited in scope.

The first step consists of proposed rule changes filed with the SEC a year ago. It would extend pricing procedures now used on ''expiration Fridays,''[89] which guarantee that already-paired orders received at ''close-of-market'' will be executed at the market's closing price. These trade executions can be done within a few minutes after the exchange closes. This change, to be implemented as soon as approved by the SEC, merely seeks to recapture some of the trades now done in Tokyo or London after the NYSE closes.

The second step would involve a 45-minute ''crossing session'' immediately after the end of the trading session, using SuperDOT. Members could, as the market closes, submit either matched or unmatched orders, to be executed on a first-in, first-filled basis at the closing price. This step too is intended to recapture trades now lost to London, by letting index arbitragers rebalance or close-out their positions. A third step would add to this a second ''crossing session'' of about 15 minutes, in which paired orders that are part of inter-market trading strategies (i.e., related stock/stock-index futures or options transactions) could be completed rather than being done on the domestic fourth market (i.e., Instinet or Posit).

The fourth, and comparatively more daring, step could involve several single-price auctions—as described above—in which all 1,700 listed stocks might trade. These computer-assisted auctions might occur, for example, at 8 p.m., midnight, and 5 a.m. e.s.t. The NYSE says that these ''pricing sessions'' would be essentially the same procedures now used by the specialists to open each day's trading system; but it is not yet clear whether they would involve a dealer or even the daytime specialist firm.

Only the fifth step, which the NYSE does not envision occurring for another decade, would allow continuous 24-hour trading, possibly but not surely from remote locations. NYSE officials are not convinced that there is or will be any real demand for such trading until 2000.

---

[86]Stoll, op. cit., footnote 12, p. 3.

[87]Securities Exchange Act 11A(a)(2).

[88]See OTA background paper, op. cit., footnote 27.

[89]The last Friday in each annual quarter, on which stock-index futures and stock-index options expire—the ''triple witching hour.''

Immediately after the NYSE announcement of its plans, which would not have been made so soon except that they were prematurely disclosed by the press, three other stock exchanges (the AMEX, the Cincinnati, and the Chicago Board Options Exchange) announced that they were working with Reuters to develop plans for systems for eventual 24-hour trading. U.S. futures exchanges and Reuters have already developed a system (GLOBEX, described in ch. 4) for global trading of futures contracts. The NYSE strategy emphasizes the need to encourage many brokers and vendors to plan ways to supply the services NYSE would need for providing global access to investors, to avoid "becoming the captive of one vendor." The suggestion here is that when the original contract between exchange or exchanges and a vendor expires, exchanges could be left without a viable mechanism for serving (and monitoring) remote members. With the NYSE strategy, however, vendors may decide independently to offer transaction services before the NYSE target year of 2000. These risks have to be compared in planning strategy for the future.

Article 12

Margin Requirements on Equity Instruments[1]

The stock market crash of October 1987 focused considerable attention on the adequacy and consistency of margin requirements on U.S. equity-related products. The analysis of these issues is difficult because of the complexity of U.S. margin rules. To help clarify the discussion, this article outlines the margin rules in the markets for stocks, stock index futures, stock options, stock index options, and stock index futures options.[2]

The general principle behind margin requirements is simple. Margin requirements oblige investors who undertake contractual obligations to deposit and maintain a minimum amount of cash or securities with their counterparties. Margin requirements in different markets serve several different goals,[3] but in all cases margin deposits reduce counterparty losses whenever contractual obligations are not fulfilled: if the investor defaults, the counterparty at the very least retains the margin deposit.

This principle applies in all markets, even though the underlying contractual obligations that create the need for margin requirements may differ. These contractual obligations are outlined in Table 1. In practice, margin requirements modify these obligations, since investors must satisfy the margin rules on a continuous basis.

As described in the table, the contractual obligations of short and long positions in the *stock index futures market* are to receive or make payments sometime in the future. Both long and short positions are required to put up and maintain minimum margin deposits with their counterparties. In *options markets,* the basic contractual obligation of the short position is to purchase or deliver the underlying security if and when the long position exercises the option. The short position is required to put up and maintain a minimum margin deposit with the counterparty. Finally, in the *stock market,* contractual obligations arise in two distinct transactions: buying stock on margin and selling stock short. Investors buying stock on margin take out a loan and use the proceeds together with their own funds to buy stock. The stock is then deposited as collateral with the lender. The basic contractual obligation of each investor is to repay the loan. Margin requirements oblige investors to deposit and maintain stock collateral at a specified minimum level above the face value of the loan. In short sales, investors sell borrowed stock, so their basic contractual obligation is to return the stock to the lender. Each short seller is required to put up a minimum deposit with the stock lender.

Describing the margin rules governing transactions in the U.S. financial markets is a difficult task. Different margin systems have developed for different markets and, even within individual markets, the rules may vary depending on the type of investor and transaction. The purpose of this article is to identify the appropriate margin-setting authorities, to sort out the rules apply-

[1]This article is intended only to provide a brief overview of margin regulations and related topics. It is not designed to be used, and should not be used, as a substitute for the appropriate regulations and published interpretations thereof. Questions concerning margin regulations should be addressed to your legal counsel.

[2]A more detailed description of margin requirements can be found in George Sofianos, "Description of Margin Requirements," Federal Reserve Bank of New York, Unpublished research paper, September 1988.

[3]See the discussion in Arturo Estrella, "Consistent Margin Requirements: Are They Feasible?" in this issue of the *Quarterly Review.*

Table 1

Summary of Basic Contractual Obligations*

Stocks

Buying stock on margin: Investors buying stock on margin take out a loan and use the proceeds together with their own funds to buy stock. The stock then serves as collateral for the loan. Such loans are known as margin loans. The basic contractual obligation of each investor is to repay the margin loan plus interest. In general, margin loans carry no stated maturity. The counterparty is the provider of the margin loan.

Selling stock short: In short selling, investors sell borrowed stock. The basic contractual obligation of each short seller is to return the stock to the counterparty, the stock lender. Stock lending agreements are usually of indefinite duration, but they are subject to call by the lender.

Stock index futures

Long positions: The contractual obligation of the long position is to receive on settlement date a multiple (usually $500) times the underlying stock index minus the futures price. (Negative receivables denote a payment.)

Short positions: The contractual obligation of the short position is to make a payment on settlement date equal to the multiple times the underlying stock index minus the futures price. (Negative payments denote receivables.)

Because all positions must be marked to market and losses and gains realized daily, the settlement date differs from other days only in that positions are marked to market for the last time and then closed.

The ultimate counterparty for both short and long positions is the clearinghouse associated with each exchange.

Stock options

Long positions: The long position in an option contract has the right to exercise the option some time in the future and purchase (call option) or sell (put option) the underlying stock at the strike price fixed when the position is opened. Because the long position has a right but not an obligation, once the option premium is fully paid, no contractual obligations remain.

Short positions: The contractual obligation of the short position is to sell (call option) or buy (put option) the underlying stock at the strike price if the long position exercises the option.

The ultimate counterparty in all stock option transactions is the Options Clearing Corporation (OCC).

Stock index options

The contractual obligations are the same as for stock options except that the underlying "security" is a multiple (usually $500) times a stock index. The ultimate counterparty is the OCC.

Stock index futures options

The contractual obligations are the same as for stock options except that underlying a stock index futures option is a stock index futures contract. The ultimate counterparty is the clearinghouse associated with each exchange.

*This table summarizes the *basic* contractual obligations in the absence of margin requirements. The presence of margin requirements changes the contractual obligations of investors because the margin requirements must be satisfied on an ongoing basis. For example, when investors buy stock on margin from broker-dealers, they are required by the margin rules to maintain a specified level of equity in the margin account at all times.

ing to particular parties in particular situations, and to outline each set of rules briefly.

In describing the rules, the article focuses on five features that together determine the amount of protection provided to counterparties:

● *Initial margin requirements* set the minimum margin deposit with which a position can be opened.

● *Maintenance margin requirements* set a floor below which margin is not allowed to fall as long as the position remains open.

● *Variation margin* refers to the flow of payments from losers to gainers that results from the daily or intraday reevaluation of positions in futures markets.

● *Posting period* is the amount of time an investor is given to satisfy the initial, maintenance, and variation margin requirements. If the investor fails to satisfy the requirements within the allowable time, the counterparty can close the undermargined position. The length of the posting period is important because as it increases, counterparty losses may cumulate. In practice, posting periods range from as many as 15 days to a few hours.

● *Allowable form of margin* refers to the type of securities other than cash that can be used as margin. In some cases only cash is allowed as margin; in other cases securities and letters of credit can also be used. The form of margin influences the cost of maintaining a margined position and determines how easily the margin deposit can be converted into cash if needed.

The following sections examine the margin requirements in each market. Table 2 lists the markets that will be discussed, the main contracts, and the various margin-setting bodies. The table also identifies the clearinghouses that play an important role in the margin process for futures and option transactions.

Throughout, the article focuses on the margin requirements imposed by the regulatory bodies cited in the table. It is important to remember that these are minimum requirements. Counterparties, such as broker-dealers, often impose more stringent requirements.

Stocks

The Federal Reserve Board divides stocks into margin and nonmargin groups. Margin stocks consist of all U.S. exchange-traded stocks and some but not all over-the-counter (OTC) stocks. Broker-dealers are not allowed to use nonmargin stock as collateral in making loans. By contrast, banks and other lenders can lend any amount they like on nonmargin stock. Both margin and nonmargin stocks can be sold short.[4] The following sections describe the rules established by the Board and the New York Stock Exchange (NYSE) for buying margin stock using a margin loan and for short selling.[5]

[4]It is likely that some thinly traded nonmargin stocks are not sold short because no stock is available to borrow, but the Board does not prohibit such a sale.

[5]The margin rules of the various exchanges and the National Association of Securities Dealers (NASD) are similar. This is partly the result of a 1975 amendment of the Securities Exchange Act

Buying stock on margin

Margin requirements for buying margin stock using a margin loan differ depending on the source of the loan. Margin loan sources—the lenders—fall into three groups: broker-dealers, banks, and other lenders. Regulation T of the Federal Reserve Board determines the

Footnote 5 continued
of 1934, which prohibits the use of margin rules to get a competitive advantage. The rules of the various exchanges and the NASD apply to each organization's members.

Table 2

Instruments, Markets, Clearing, and Margin Setting*

Stocks

Markets	Margin-setting Bodies
New York Stock Exchange Over-the-Counter Market American Stock Exchange Midwest Stock Exchange Pacific Stock Exchange Philadelphia Stock Exchange Boston Stock Exchange Cincinnati Stock Exchange	Federal Reserve Board, Regulations T, U, G, X (initial margins†) Exchanges and the National Association of Securities Dealers (NASD) (maintenance margins) The Securities and Exchange Commission (SEC) must approve exchange and NASD margins

Stock Index Futures

Main Contracts	Markets	Clearing	Margin-setting Bodies
S&P500 NYSE Composite Major Market Value Line	Chicago Mercantile Exchange (CME) New York Futures Exchange (NYFE) Chicago Board of Trade (CBOT) Kansas City Board of Trade (KCBOT)	CME Clearinghouse Intermarket Clearing Corp.‡ CBOT Clearing Corp. KCBOT Clearing Corp.	Exchanges and clearinghouses The Commodities Futures Trading Commission (CFTC) can impose emergency margins§

Stock Options

Main Markets	Clearing	Margin-setting Bodies
Chicago Board Options Exchange American Stock Exchange Philadelphia Stock Exchange Pacific Stock Exchange New York Stock Exchange	Options Clearing Corp. (OCC)	Federal Reserve Board‖ Exchanges and the OCC SEC must approve exchange and OCC margins

Stock Index Options

Main Contracts	Markets	Clearing	Margin-setting Bodies
S&P 100 Value Line Major Market S&P 500 NYSE Composite	Chicago Board Options Exchange Philadelphia Stock Exchange American Stock Exchange Chicago Board Options Exchange New York Stock Exchange	Options Clearing Corp.	Same as for stock options

Stock Index Futures Options

Main Contracts	Markets	Clearing	Margin-setting Bodies
S&P500 NYSE Composite	Chicago Mercantile Exchange New York Futures Exchange	CME Clearinghouse Intermarket Clearing Corp.	Same as for stock index futures

*For each instrument, markets are ranked according to average daily share or contract volume in March 1988 (greatest volume first).

†Although the Board has the authority to set maintenance margins, it has chosen not to exercise it.

‡The Intermarket Clearing Corporation is a wholly owned subsidiary of the Options Clearing Corporation.

§The exchanges and clearinghouses do not have to get CFTC approval for changes in the level of margin requirements. Major changes in margin systems, however, must be approved by the CFTC.

‖Since September 1985, the Board has allowed the exchanges to set their own margins. Nevertheless, the Board prohibits banks from making margin loans using options as collateral; only margin loans to specialists are exempted from this rule.

initial margin requirements on margin loans provided by broker-dealers, and the NYSE determines the maintenance margin requirements on loans provided by its members. Margin loans from banks and other lenders are regulated exclusively by the Federal Reserve Board through Regulations U, G, and X.[6]

Margin requirements also differ depending on the destination of the loan. Margin loan destinations—the borrowers—fall into three groups: public customers, market makers, and broker-dealers other than market makers.[7] Diagram 1 shows the nine resulting combinations of lenders and borrowers. Because the rules are the same for some combinations, only six distinct cases are discussed.

Margin loans from broker-dealers to public customers. A public customer wishing to borrow from a broker-dealer to buy margin stock must open a margin account with the broker-dealer. The account is debited with the face value of the margin loan and credited with the market value of the stock. The market value of the stock minus the face value of the loan is the net equity in the account. The initial margin requirement sets the minimum acceptable net equity level at the beginning of the transaction at 50 percent of the stock value.[8] Equivalently, the investor cannot borrow more than 50 percent of the market value of the stock; that is, the loan value of the stock is 50 percent.[9] To satisfy this requirement, the investor can make a cash down payment equal to 50 percent of the market value of the stock. For example, to buy a stock worth $100, the investor can put up $50 in cash and borrow $50. The margin account will be credited with $100 worth of stock and debited with the $50 margin loan.[10] Regula-

[6] The Board regulations cover only those loans that are (a) extended for the purpose of purchasing, carrying, or maintaining margin stock ("purpose credit") and (b) secured by margin stock. A purpose loan secured with a bond or with a mortgage on the borrower's home is not covered. Also, a loan secured by margin stock that is used to buy a bond or a house ("nonpurpose credit") is not covered.

[7] There are no margin requirements on loans to non-U.S. borrowers outside the United States. In many cases, however, U.S. citizens are covered by the margin regulations even if they borrow offshore.

[8] NYSE rules also require that a minimum net equity of $2,000 be maintained in the account at all times.

[9] In general, the loan value of a security equals one minus the margin requirement. For example, Treasury bills are subject to a 1 percent NYSE-determined initial margin requirement and consequently have a loan value of 99 percent. Nonmargin OTC stock has zero loan value at broker-dealers.

[10] Alternatively, the investor can deposit in the margin account a fully owned security, borrow an amount equal to the loan value of the security, and use this amount as the cash down payment. For example, the investor can deposit $100 in Treasury bills, borrow $99,

Diagram 1

Sources and Destinations of Margin Loans

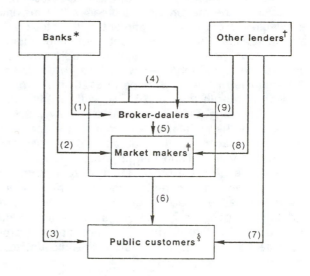

*Banks include member banks of the Federal Reserve System and nonmember banks that have signed a special agreement with the Federal Reserve Board.

†Other lenders include savings and loan associations, credit unions, finance companies, insurance companies, and foreign sources of margin loans.

‡Market makers consist of specialists, odd-lot dealers, OTC market makers, third market makers, and block positioners.

§Public customers include all investors except market makers and broker-dealers.

Distinct Cases for Margin Requirements

(i) Loans from broker-dealers to public customers (arrow 6).
(ii) Loans from banks and other lenders to public customers (arrows 3 and 7).
(iii) Loans from banks and broker-dealers to market makers (arrows 2 and 5).
(iv) Loans from banks to broker-dealers (arrow 1).
(v) Loans from broker-dealers to other broker-dealers (arrow 4).
(vi) Loans from other lenders to broker-dealers and market makers (arrows 8 and 9).

Footnote 10 continued
and use this dollar amount as the cash down payment together with a $99 margin loan to buy $198 worth of stock. The margin account will have $298 in assets (bills and stock) and $198 in liabilities. Because the account also includes Treasury bills, net equity is less than 50 percent.

tion T gives investors up to seven business days to make this down payment.[11]

The initial margin requirement also determines the amount an investor can withdraw from the account. As the price of the margin stock increases, the maximum allowable margin loan (50 percent of the stock value) also increases. The difference between the outstanding margin loan and the maximum allowable loan is an unused credit line that the investor can draw down. In the example, if the stock rises to $120, the maximum allowable margin loan is $60, so with a $50 margin loan outstanding, the investor can withdraw $10.[12]

To satisfy the maintenance margin requirements, the equity in the account must not fall below 25 percent of the market value of the margin stock.[13] If equity falls below 25 percent, the broker must make a margin call asking the investor to restore the account to at least the *maintenance* level. Margin calls must be met "as promptly as possible and in any event within 15 business days."[14] If the margin call is not met, the broker must sell enough stock to restore the account to the maintenance level.

Margin loans from banks and other lenders to public customers. Loans in this category cannot exceed the maximum loan value of the margin stock securing the loan. This maximum loan value is set at 50 percent of the market value of the stock; consequently, it is equivalent to the initial margin requirements for broker-dealer loans. There is no explicit maintenance margin requirement. Margin loans to customers outside the United States, to other domestic and foreign banks, and to qualified employee stock ownership plans may be made on a good faith basis. The phrase "on a good faith basis" means that banks and other lenders, "exercising sound banking judgement," can lend any amount they like against margin stock.[15]

Margin loans from banks and broker-dealers to market makers. The Board allows banks and broker-dealers to make margin loans to market makers on a good faith basis. These loans can be made to registered exchange specialists, odd-lot dealers, and dealers certifying that they are qualified OTC-market makers, qualified third-market makers, or qualified block positioners as defined by the rules of the Securities and Exchange Commission (SEC).[16] Market makers must certify that the loans will be used solely for financing their market-making activities.

Margin loans from banks to broker-dealers other than market makers.[17] Loans in this category may be used for financing proprietary margin buying or for financing broker-dealer margin loans to customers. Regulation U treats bank loans to broker-dealers for financing proprietary margin buying the same way as bank loans to public customers: such loans cannot exceed the 50 percent loan value of margin stock. Several "special purpose loans," however, are exempted and can be made on a good faith basis. Special purpose loans include arbitrage loans, intraday loans, loans for securities in transit or transfer, temporary advances in payment-against-delivery transactions, and distribution loans.[18]

When bank loans are used to finance broker-dealer margin loans to customers, the broker-dealer acts as an intermediary between the banks providing the funds and the margin customers.[19] Regulation U allows broker-dealers to borrow from banks up to the total indebtedness of their customers on a good faith basis, pledging customers' securities. For example, a broker-dealer that provided $1 million in margin loans to its customers to buy $2 million worth of stock could use this stock as collateral to borrow at most $1 million on a good faith basis.[20]

Margin loans from one broker-dealer to another. The

---

[11]Broker-dealers often give investors less time to make the down payment.

[12]In general, if on day one the initial margin requirement is just satisfied and on day two the stock price increases, the investor can withdraw half of the increase.

[13]All exchanges and the NASD impose the same 25 percent maintenance margin requirement. Broker-dealers can impose higher maintenance margins on their customers, just as they can impose higher initial margins.

[14]NYSE Rule 431(f)(6). Broker-dealers usually allow only one to two days for a call to be met. The Securities and Exchange Commission's capital rules require that broker-dealers take capital charges for any maintenance margin deficiencies (less than 25 percent equity) that persist for more than five days. Margin calls can be met by depositing cash or securities.

[15]The quotation is from Regulation U. The good faith loan should not exceed 100 percent of the value of the collateral.

[16]Only banks may provide good faith margin loans to block positioners.

[17]Margin loans to broker-dealers are not the only loans made by banks to securities firms; only margin loans, however, are subject to the Board's margin requirements. Banks regularly provide securities firms with other types of loans, including unsecured loans and loans for financing activities unrelated to the broker-dealer function.

[18]For a loan to qualify as a special purpose loan, the borrower must state in writing the purpose of the loan.

[19]The broker-dealer is not a mere pass-through between the bank and the margin customers. If a customer defaults, the broker-dealer must use its own capital to repay the lending bank.

[20]Loans to broker-dealers secured by customer securities are called hypothecation loans. Written certification of their purpose is required. SEC rules stipulate that a broker-dealer cannot pledge more than its aggregate customer indebtedness but can pledge up to 140 percent of the debit balance in an individual margin account.

Board does not allow margin loans from one broker-dealer to another for financing proprietary buying of stock. Certain other loans between broker-dealers can be made on a good faith basis. These include loans for the purchase of securities for customer accounts[21] and loans by a broker-dealer to any of its partners or stockholders for the purchase of its own stock, the stock of an affiliated corporation, or the stock of another broker-dealer.

Margin loans from other lenders to broker-dealers. The Board does not allow margin loans from other lenders to broker-dealers, including market makers.[22] The only exceptions are emergency and capital contribution loans. Unsecured loans to broker-dealers are theoretically possible.[23]

Selling stock short

In general, a short sale consists of two distinct transactions, each subject to different requirements. One transaction is between a customer and the customer's broker-dealer. In this transaction the broker-dealer provides the stock that the customer sells short. The stock comes from the broker-dealer's own inventory, from other customers of the broker-dealer, from other broker-dealers, or from other institutions.[24] If the stock does not come from the broker-dealer's own inventory, then there is a second transaction—in this case, between the broker-dealer and the stock lender.

Consider first the transaction between broker-dealer and stock lender. According to Regulation T, the broker-dealer must deposit with the stock lender cash or other acceptable collateral equal to 100 percent of the stock's current market value.[25] The broker must adjust or mark to market the amount of collateral daily so that it is at all times equal to 100 percent of the stock value at the close of the preceding business day. For example, if the stock closes $10 higher than the

previous closing, the broker must deposit $10 with the stock lender by the next day's opening.

Consider next the transaction between customer and broker-dealer. The short sale must take place through a margin account. The value of the stock sold short appears as a debit in the account. The proceeds from the short sale are retained by the broker-dealer and credited to the customer's margin account. According to Regulation T, the customer then has seven business days to deposit in the account an additional amount equal to 50 percent of the value of the stock. This additional deposit need not be in cash; securities can be used instead. Once this deposit is made, the account will show a credit equal to 150 percent of the stock value, a debit equal to the market value of the borrowed stock, and net equity equal to 50 percent of the stock value.

The account is marked to market daily so that a change in the value of the stock will lead to an equal and opposite change in the account's equity position, all else equal. For example, a $10 increase in stock value will reduce the equity in the account by $10. The customer need not deposit additional funds unless the account drops below the maintenance level. The NYSE requires customers to maintain net equity at a level equal to at least 30 percent of the market value of the borrowed stock.[26] The customer must restore an undermargined account to the required level promptly, and in no more than 15 days—the same requirement that applies to customers who buy stock on margin.

Finally, two special cases must be mentioned. First, for market-maker short sales that are related to market making, only good faith margin is required. Second, because proprietary broker-dealer short sales involve a single transaction—that between the broker-dealer and the stock lender—the broker-dealer is only subject to the requirements for this transaction: 100 percent collateral marked to market daily.[27]

Stock index futures

In the stock index futures market, a clearinghouse interposes between customers with long and short positions. The clearinghouse is the ultimate counterparty in all trades and guarantees all transactions. Customer transactions entail an additional layer of intermediation: a clearing member comes between the customer and the clearinghouse. A clearing member is an exchange member firm that is also a member of the

---

[21] These loans are subject to the same rules as bank loans to broker-dealers used to purchase securities for customer accounts.

[22] Non-broker-dealer affiliates of securities firms are also not allowed to make margin loans to broker-dealers.

[23] Nevertheless, because virtually all of a broker-dealer's assets are securities, it is difficult to argue that any loan to a broker-dealer is not secured directly, or indirectly, by securities and hence exempt from the Board's lending restriction. One example of a permitted unsecured loan is subordinated debt that complies with SEC rules.

[24] To borrow stock from a customer, a broker-dealer must have the customer's written consent. The broker-dealer cannot borrow more than the debit in a customer's margin account.

[25] As usual, this is a minimum requirement; in practice more collateral may be put up. Acceptable collateral includes Treasury securities, negotiable bank certificates of deposit, banker acceptances, and irrevocable letters of credit.

[26] Maintenance margins for low-priced stocks are slightly higher.

[27] If the proprietary short sale has to be done through an account with another broker-dealer (because the short selling broker-dealer is not self-clearing), then it is subject to the 50 percent initial and 30 percent maintenance margin requirements.

clearinghouse. Clearing members accept financial responsibility for the performance of their customers.[28] Customers include public customers, nonclearing broker-dealers, and the floor traders or "locals." Only proprietary trades of clearing members clear directly through the clearinghouse.[29]

Customers deposit margin at clearing members, and clearing members deposit margin at the clearinghouse. Each clearing member maintains two separately margined accounts with the clearinghouse: a house account for proprietary trades and a customer account for the trades of its customers. The exchanges determine the customer margin rules, and the clearinghouses determine the rules for the deposit of margin by the clearing members in their house and customer accounts.[30]

For both customers and clearing members, there are two distinct sets of margin flows: those associated with the deposit of initial and maintenance margin and those associated with the payment of variation margin. The payment of variation margin is important because once such a payment has been made, future counterparty losses depend on the change in the value of the futures position till the next variation margin payment is due on the following day. As a result, margin deposits are required to protect counterparties against the possible *one-day* loss in the value of futures positions.

The next two sections examine the requirements for both types of margin flows, focusing on the rules of the Chicago Mercantile Exchange (CME) and its clearinghouse. The most popular futures contract, the S&P 500, trades on this exchange.

Initial and maintenance margin requirements. Initial and maintenance margin requirements are specified in fixed dollar amounts to be deposited per contract. As of August 22, 1988, customers are required to deposit with clearing members $20,000 per S&P 500 contract if they are classified as speculators, and $10,000 per contract if they are classified as hedgers.[31] These dol-

lar figures translate to 15.6 percent and 7.8 percent, respectively, of the value of the contract on August 22, 1988. The maintenance margin is $10,000 per contract for both speculators and hedgers. To be classified as hedgers, customers must convince clearing members that they have a need to hedge. For example, customers will qualify as hedgers if they hold diversified baskets of stock and take short futures positions (so-called bona fide hedging). Customers may also qualify as hedgers if they anticipate future capital flows and want to lock in prices (anticipatory hedging). In practice, the criteria used in making the classification vary from clearing member to clearing member; the majority of customers put up hedger margins. Table 3 lists the current margin requirements for the main stock index futures contracts.

The clearinghouse requires clearing members to pass the maintenance portion of customer initial margin on to their customer accounts with the clearinghouse. For example, a speculator opening a single position will deposit at least $20,000 with the clearing member. The clearing member will then forward $10,000 to the clearinghouse and retain the balance. For a hedger, the required initial and maintenance margins are the same, so unless the clearing member asks

Footnote 31 continued
opposite positions in contracts on the same index but with different settlement days; *intermarket* spreaders take opposite positions in contracts based on different stock indexes. Intramarket spreaders have margin requirements as low as $200 per contract.

Table 3

Margin Requirements for Stock Index Futures
(As of August 22, 1988)

	Initial		Maintenance	
	In Dollars	In Percent	In Dollars	In Percent
Chicago Mercantile Exchange (S&P 500)				
Speculators	20,000	15.6	10,000	7.8
Hedgers	10,000	7.8	10,000	7.8
Chicago Board of Trade (Major Market)				
Speculators	15,000	15.5	10,000	10.3
Hedgers	10,000	10.3	10,000	10.3
New York Futures Exchange (NYSE Composite)				
Speculators	6,000	8.2	4,000	5.5
Hedgers	4,000	5.5	4,000	5.5
Kansas City Board of Trade (Value Line)				
Speculators	7,500	6.4	7,500	6.4
Hedgers	5,000	4.3	5,000	4.3

The percent requirements are the dollar requirements as a fraction of the appropriate multiple times the August 22, 1988 value of each index (500 × 257.0 for the S&P 500, 500 × 145.9 for the NYSE Composite, 500 × 234.1 for the Value Line, and 250 × 387.4 for the Major Market).

[28]For example, if a customer defaults, then the clearing member must use its own capital to honor the defaulter's obligations to the clearinghouse.

[29]In practice, the structure of the market is more complicated. Public customers and nonclearing broker-dealers (but not the locals) must trade through a futures commission merchant (FCM). Some FCMs are clearing members and some are not. Moreover, not all clearing members are FCMs. Nonclearing FCMs must clear both customer and proprietary trades through a clearing member—a requirement that adds an extra step in the whole process. This extra step is ignored here. For more details, see Sofianos, "Description of Margin Requirements."

[30]The CME clearinghouse simply determines what portion of the initial margin deposit required by the exchange should be forwarded to the clearinghouse and when this must be done.

[31]There are two other classifications: *intramarket* spreaders take

for more than the required $10,000, the whole of the deposit must be forwarded to the clearinghouse. The total margin each clearing member must have on deposit in its customer account at the clearinghouse equals the total number of open positions it carries times the maintenance margin per position. The CME clearinghouse requires clearing members to make this deposit based on the gross positions of their customers. For example, a clearing member whose customers are long 100 positions and short 99 positions in the same S&P 500 contract must have at least $1,990,000 in its customer account at the clearinghouse.[32]

For proprietary positions, clearing members are subject only to the $10,000 maintenance margin because they clear directly through the clearinghouse.[33] Clearing members must deposit this amount in their house account at the clearinghouse. Because the maintenance level is the same for hedgers and speculators, this distinction is irrelevant for clearing member proprietary positions.

The exchange requires clearing members to collect initial margin from customers in advance of opening a position. The clearinghouse has the following timetable for collecting margin from clearing members: every day, after trading stops, it calculates the number of open positions in each clearing member's accounts, and early every morning it notifies members of their total margin requirements. If a clearing member has on deposit with the clearinghouse more margin than is required, it can withdraw the excess.[34] If the margin on deposit is not sufficient, then the system generates a cash margin call. For example, if open positions increase from 199 to 200 and only $1,990,000 is on deposit, the clearing member will get a call for an extra $10,000. By 7:00 a.m. a bank acting on behalf of the clearing member must confirm that it will meet the call within the same day.[35] In emergencies the clearinghouse may call for additional margin to be deposited, possibly within an hour.

Clearing members can accept as margin from customers cash, U.S. Treasury securities, letters of credit, and listed securities.[36] The clearinghouse, however, is more restrictive in what it accepts as margin from clearing members. The first $25,000 of margin assets per member account must be in cash, after which Treasury securities are acceptable.[37] Letters of credit can be used after $50,000 in cash and Treasury securities have been deposited. The letters of credit must be irrevocable and callable within 60 minutes. The clearinghouse does not accept listed securities.

Variation margin. After the end of the trading day, the clearinghouse marks to market each position in a member's house and customer accounts.[38] It then forwards this information to the clearing members ahead of the next day's opening. Variation margin flows between customers and clearing members and between clearing members and the clearinghouse.

Consider first the flows between customers and clearing members. Each clearing member typically has some customers that lose and some that gain on their S&P 500 futures positions. Using the information provided by the clearinghouse, each member credits the accounts of the gainers with the gain in their positions and debits the accounts of the losers with the loss. Customers whose accounts have been credited can withdraw any gains in excess of the initial margin. Customers whose accounts have been debited will get a margin call if the loss pushed the account balance below the maintenance level.[39] An investor who gets a margin call has to replenish the account, restoring it to the *initial* margin level. Consider the speculator who originally deposited $20,000—$10,000 with the clearinghouse and a $10,000 buffer with a clearing member. A $7,000 loss in the position may be met out of the buffer. No margin call has to be made, but the buffer will be reduced to $3,000. A further loss of $4,000 will leave the account undermargined by $1,000 and will lead to a margin call for $11,000 to restore the account to the initial level. Clearing members determine the time allowed customers to meet a margin call. According to the CME rules, "if within a reasonable time the customer fails to comply with such demand (the clearing member may deem one hour to be a reasonable

---

[32]The example assumes that the maintenance margin is $10,000 for each of the 199 positions. The other three clearinghouses (see Table 2) require clearing members to forward maintenance margin based on the *net* positions of their customers. The netting is done not only for each customer (opposite positions in the same contract cancel each other out) but also across customers. In the example, clearing members would forward the maintenance margin on only one position.

[33]The required margin is lower for intermarket or intramarket spreads.

[34]An excess will occur if the clearing member experienced a net closing of positions.

[35]Even though the bank makes a commitment at 7:00 a.m. to meet the margin call, the clearing member need not put up the cash till some time later in the day.

[36]The securities must be listed on the NYSE or American Exchange and are accepted at 70 percent of market value.

[37]Treasury notes and bonds are subject to at least a 5 percent haircut.

[38]In marking to market, the clearinghouse uses closing settlement prices.

[39]In practice investors whose accounts have been debited may get a margin call even if the account is above the maintenance level.

time), the clearing member may close out the customer's trades or sufficient contracts thereof to restore the customer's account to required margin status."[40]

The clearinghouse calculates variation margin separately for each clearing member's customer account and house account. Customer account variation margin depends on the net gains or losses of each clearing member's customers. A member whose customers experienced more losses than gains will make a cash payment to its customer account at the clearinghouse equal to the net loss. For example, a member with 10 customers losing $4,000 each and 5 customers gaining $4,000 each must pay the clearinghouse $20,000. A member that experienced net losses on its proprietary positions will have to make a payment to its house account at the clearinghouse. The clearinghouse will forward these payments to clearing members whose accounts are experiencing net gains.

Banks acting on behalf of clearing members must confirm by 7:00 a.m. that the variation margin will be posted with the clearinghouse sometime later the same day. Table 4 summarizes the timing of margin flows between clearing members and the clearinghouse. In times of extreme price volatility, the clearinghouse may ask clearing members to make intraday payments of variation margin, usually within an hour. The CME clearinghouse recently introduced a regular 2:00 p.m. intraday variation margin call.[41]

Stock options

The institutional arrangements for stock options are similar to those for futures. The ultimate counterparty in all stock option transactions is the Options Clearing Corporation (OCC). For customer transactions, a clearing member always interposes between the customer and the OCC. Only proprietary trades of clearing members clear directly through the OCC. Public customers, nonclearing broker-dealers, and market makers must clear through a clearing member.

The option exchanges determine the minimum margin to be deposited by customers to clearing members, and the OCC determines the minimum margin to be deposited by clearing members to the OCC.[42] The OCC uses a margining system that differs from the one used

by the exchanges. The next two sections describe the NYSE rules for the deposit of margin by customers to clearing members[43] and the OCC rules for the deposit of margin by clearing members.

Deposit of margin by customers to clearing members.[44] Option buyers—that is, the long positions—must pay the full premium in cash; they are not allowed to buy options on margin.[45] Once the premium is paid, the

[43]The margin rules of the option exchanges are very similar. This similarity enabled the NYSE to specify a uniform set of option rules for all its members, irrespective of where options are listed. The NYSE rules cover most of the market participants.

[44]Option transactions usually, but not necessarily, take place through a margin account. Options may be both held and written in a cash account. This section describes the requirements for margin account option transactions. Writing options through a cash account is subject to a variety of restrictions: most important, the account must hold either (a) the underlying stock in the case of a call option, or (b) cash or money market instruments in the amount of the exercise price in the case of a put option.

[45]Equivalently, the loan value of options is zero. This restriction applies only to borrowing for the purpose of buying options (or stock). It is possible to use the value of long option positions as collateral to borrow for other purposes.

Table 4

Timing of Margin Flows between Clearing Members and Clearinghouse (Chicago Mercantile Exchange, S&P 500 Futures Contract)

Chicago Time

3:15 p.m.	Trading ends.

9:00 p.m.	The clearinghouse begins final trade reconciliation. After it is completed, the clearinghouse calculates two sets of margin flows:
	    (a) the amount of margin each member should deposit or can withdraw to keep total margin in its customer and house accounts at the required level (number of open positions times maintenance margin);
	    (b) the amount of variation margin each member should pay or receive (the net loss or gain in each account).

Early morning	The clearinghouse informs clearing members of the two sets of margin flows.
7:00 a.m.	The clearinghouse receives irrevocable commitments from banks acting on behalf of the clearing members that both sets of margin payments will be made within the day. The timing of the actual cash flows between clearing members and their banks and between the banks and the clearinghouse varies from case to case.
8:30 a.m.	Trading in the S&P 500 futures contract begins.

Source: Chicago Mercantile Exchange, Clearing Division, "Clearing House Banking Interface," White Paper Series, December 1987.

[40]CME rulebook, chap. 8, section 827(D). The clearing member may also lend the required margin to the customer.

[41]The CBOT Clearing Corporation has had a regular 2:00 p.m. intraday variation margin call since before the October 19 stock market crash.

[42]The Board has the authority to set option margin requirements. Since September 1985 the Board has allowed individual exchanges to determine the margin requirements on the options that they list. Nevertheless, the Board's Regulation U prohibits banks from making margin loans against options.

option buyer has no remaining contractual obligations and so is not required to put up and maintain a margin deposit.

Margin requirements on option issuers—the short positions—consist of a set of basic requirements for naked (uncovered) positions. These requirements are reduced for covered positions. Table 5 summarizes the requirements.[46] For a naked position, the issuer must deposit as margin all the proceeds from the sale of the option. If the option is in the money, the issuer must also deposit extra margin equal to 20 percent of the underlying stock price. If the option is out of the money, the extra margin required is 20 percent of the stock price minus the out-of-the-money amount but no less than 10 percent of the stock price.

There are three types of covered short positions: hedges, spreads, and combinations. To hedge a short call (put), the issuer has to be long (short) in the underlying stock.[47] No margin is required for the hedged short option.[48] Spreads combine short with long positions in a given call or put option. The positions can have different expiration dates, different exercise prices, or both. Combinations consist of short puts and short calls on the same underlying stock, possibly with different expiration and exercise prices. The rules for spreads and combinations are summarized in Table 5.

Maintenance margin requirements on short options are the initial requirements marked to market daily. If stock and option prices move favorably, funds will be freed to support other investments. For unfavorable moves, additional funds will be required to support option positions. For example, if the underlying stock price increases by $5 and the premium of an in-the-money naked short call option increases by $1, the margin requirement will increase by $2.

With options, as with stock margin transactions, initial margin must be deposited within seven business days from the trade date, and margin calls must be met promptly.[49] Margin stock and U.S. government securities, valued at their loan value, can be used to satisfy option margin requirements.

The only groups exempted from the customer margin rules are stock specialists, option specialists,[50] and other registered market makers. The NYSE allows its members to carry long and short option positions of these groups on "a margin basis satisfactory to the concerned parties."[51] In the case of option market makers, this special treatment applies only to positions in the options in which they are making markets. In the case of stock market makers, the special treatment applies only to positions in options overlying the stock in which they are making markets. When market-maker positions in other options are allowed, they are subject

[50]In addition to the option specialists, competitive option traders who qualify as specialists under SEC rules are also exempted.

[51]NYSE Rule 431 (f)(2)(J). Moreover, the Board's Regulation U allows banks to lend against long option positions to stock and option specialists on a good faith basis. Such loans must be used to finance narrowly defined "permitted offset positions."

Table 5

Customer Margin Requirements on Stock Options

(As of July 11, 1988)

Long options:	Premium must be paid in full
Naked short options	
In-the-money:	$\pi + (0.20 \times S)$
Out-of-the-money:	$\pi + MAX[(0.20 \times S) - T, 0.10 \times S]$
Hedges	
Short call, long stock:	0 for call
	$0.50 \times S$ for stock
Short put, short stock:	0 for put
	$1.50 \times S$ for stock
Spreads	
Long expires before short:	Premium must be paid in full for long
	Short treated as naked
Long does not expire before short	
Call spreads:	Premium must be paid in full for long
	$MAX[E(long) - E(short), 0]$ for short
Put spreads:	Premium must be paid in full for long
	$MAX[E(short) - E(long), 0]$ for short
Short combinations:	The greater of the naked short put or the naked short call requirement plus π for the option with the lower requirement

Explanations:
π Option premium
S Value of underlying stock
E Exercise price of option
T Out-of-the-money amount $= MAX[E-S,0]$ for a call
                                       $= MAX[S-E,0]$ for a put

[46]Table 5 shows the minimum amounts that must be in deposit at clearing members for each customer short position. In all cases the out-of-pocket payment of an option issuer is the required deposit minus the proceeds from issuing the option.

[47]For example, issuers of IBM calls must hold the underlying IBM stock so that their ability to deliver the stock, whenever the calls are exercised, is assured.

[48]If the stock hedging a short call is not owned outright, it is subject to the usual stock initial and maintenance margin requirements. The same applies for stock sold short to hedge a put.

[49]As in the case of stocks, the NYSE permits members to give customers as many as 15 business days to meet a call. In practice, broker-dealers usually give much less time.

to the customer margin rules.[52]

Proprietary positions of broker-dealers that are neither market makers nor clearing members of the OCC are treated like those of any other customer. The proprietary positions of OCC clearing members are only subject to the OCC requirements.

The deposit of margin by clearing members to the OCC. Each clearing member must maintain separate customer, house, and market-maker accounts with the OCC. These accounts are margined separately. Total margin for the customer account is calculated differently from total margin for the house and market-maker accounts.

The rules for the house and market-maker accounts are examined first. Within each account, the OCC pairs all long positions in an option class with short positions in the same option class.[53] Each option class now consists of some paired long and some paired short positions, and in most cases, either some unpaired long or some unpaired short positions.[54] Concentrating on the paired positions, the OCC subtracts the aggregate value of the paired long options from the aggregate value of the paired short options.[55] A positive balance is called excess short value and a negative balance is called excess long value. There are now four possibilities for each option class:

• Excess short value, unpaired short positions. Total margin is 130 percent of the excess short value plus 130 percent of the value of the unpaired short positions.[56]

• Excess short value, unpaired long positions. Total margin is 130 percent of the excess short value minus 70 percent of the value of the unpaired long positions.

• Excess long value, unpaired short positions. Total margin is minus 70 percent of the excess long value plus 130 percent of the value of the unpaired short positions.

• Excess long value, unpaired long positions. Total margin is minus 70 percent of the excess long value minus 70 percent of the value of the unpaired long positions.

If an option class ends with a margin credit, 50 percent of this credit can be applied against the margin required in other option classes within the same account.

Margin for the customer account is calculated more conservatively. All long positions in an option class are classified as unsegregated or segregated. Unsegregated positions form the long leg of an identified spread in the account of an individual customer. The OCC then follows the same procedure used for the house account, but with two differences: only the unsegregated long positions are paired with short positions,[57] and segregated long positions and excess long values are set to zero.[58] The end result is that clearing members must deposit 130 percent of the aggregate value of customer short positions, with some short positions offset by the value of unsegregated longs. Option classes never end with a margin credit in the customer's account.

The calculations described above are repeated every day after trading stops. By 7:00 a.m. every morning, clearing members get a report stating the aggregate required margin on short positions that must be in deposit with the OCC by 9:00 a.m. Margin must be deposited in the form of cash, U.S. government securities, bank letters of credit, or margin stock at 50 percent of market value. For short calls, the clearing member can deposit the underlying security rather than deposit the margin. The OCC has the authority to change margin requirements at short notice if market conditions make this necessary.

Stock index options
The same institutional arrangements are used for stock index options as for stock options: the OCC is the ulti-

---

[52]Market makers' allowable option transactions are narrowly defined. Stock specialists can only hold options overlying their specialty stock, any option position established must be on the opposite side of the market from the stock position, and the range of permissible hedge ratios is limited.

[53]An option class consists of either puts or calls on the same stock, possibly with different expiration dates and strike prices. The pairing is done as follows: positions in the same option series are paired first, then the highest priced longs are matched with the highest priced shorts, and so on till either the long or the short positions run out.

[54]For example, if an option class consists of two long and three short positions, there will be two paired long, two paired short, and one unpaired short position.

[55]Values are based on the option premium at the close of trading.

[56]Consider an option class consisting of two long options—one $5 and the other $6—and three short options—one $5, one $7, and one $8. The $5 long will be paired with the $5 short (same option series) and the $6 long will be paired with the $8 short, leaving the $7 short unpaired. Subtracting the paired longs from the paired shorts will give $2 excess short value (($5 + $8) − ($5 + $6)). Total margin will be $2.60 (130 percent of the excess short value) plus $9.10 (130 percent of the unpaired short).

[57]Moreover, unsegregated longs cannot be paired with shorts with longer expirations.

[58]Segregated long positions are set to zero because if one customer defaults, the OCC cannot seize the long positions of another customer. The customer account of a clearing member at the OCC consists of the positions of the clearing member's many customers. Even though the clearing member has a lien on the positions of each of its customers, the OCC does not have an indiscriminate lien on all the positions in the customer account.

mate counterparty but clearing members interpose between customers and the OCC. The rules for the deposit of margin by customers to clearing members are almost identical to the corresponding rules for stock options: long options cannot be bought on margin, and the margin deposit on naked short positions is calculated in the same way. For naked short positions in broad-based index options, however, the investor is required to deposit extra margin equal to 15 percent—instead of 20 percent—of the underlying index.[59] Spreads and combinations are given the same treatment as in stock options, but hedged index option positions are treated the same as naked positions. Posting periods are the same as for stock options.

The rules governing the deposit of margin by clearing members in their customer, house, and market-maker accounts at the OCC are different from the corresponding stock option rules.[60] The most interesting feature of these rules is the use of an option-pricing model to estimate the net cost (or value) of liquidating all positions in an account that belong to the same option group.[61] For each option group, the OCC has specified a range, known as the margin interval, that

reflects the likely one-day change in the underlying index. Table 6 lists the current margin intervals for all stock index options. For example, the margin interval for the S&P 100 index is 16 points. Every day, after trading stops, the OCC calculates the current liquidation cost using the closing option premia and estimates the liquidation cost under the assumption that the current closing index value increases and decreases by the full margin interval. If the closing value of the S&P 100 is 250, the OCC will estimate the liquidation cost at 234 and 266.[62] The required margin is equal to the maximum of the estimated and current liquidation costs.[63] With stock index options, as with stock options, the OCC calculates margin for customer accounts more conservatively than for house accounts. The main difference is that the OCC assigns zero value to segregated long positions in a customer account. Posting periods for house, market-maker, and customer accounts are the same as for stock options.

Stock index futures options

Stock index futures options trade on futures exchanges and clear in the same way as futures. The most popular contract is the S&P 500 futures option. Like its underlying futures contract, this option contract trades on the CME and clears through the CME clearinghouse.[64] This section describes the rules of the CME and its clearinghouse.

The rules for the deposit of margin by customers to clearing members are similar to the corresponding stock option rules: both sets of rules are strategy-based. A set of basic requirements applies to naked short positions; these requirements are reduced for hedges, spreads, and combinations. To calculate margin, clearing members use the margin requirements for stock index futures, so the classification of customers as speculators or hedgers carries over to stock index futures options. Table 7 lists customer margin requirements for a sample of positions in the S&P 500 futures option. For example, a customer with a naked long position must pay the premium in full. A customer with a naked in-the-money short position must deposit the premium plus the margin for the underlying futures contract (either $20,000 or $10,000). If the position is

---

[59] Broad-based index options include those on the S&P 500, S&P 100, Major Market, Value Line, and NYSE Composite indexes.

[60] The OCC margins all nonequity options (for example, options on government securities or foreign currencies) in the same way as index options.

[61] An option group consists of all positions (long or short, put or call, at any strike price and any expiration date) on the same underlying index. Long positions give rise to liquidation value while short positions represent a liquidation cost.

Table 6

OCC Stock Index Option Margin Intervals
(As of July 11, 1988)

Option	Margin Interval In Points	Margin Interval In Dollars	Percent of Index
S&P 100	16.00	1,600	6.19
S&P 500	16.00	1,600	5.91
AMEX Major Market	24.00	2,400	5.86
NYSE Composite	8.00	800	5.23
AMEX Institutional	16.00	1,600	5.99
PSE FNN Composite	10.00	1,000	5.34
PHLX National OTC	15.00	1,500	5.77
Value Line Composite	12.00	1,200	4.89
AMEX Computer Tech.	6.00	600	5.16
PHLX Gold and Silver	11.00	1,100	10.48
AMEX Oil	8.00	800	4.54
PHLX Utility Index	7.00	700	3.80

Source: OCC Information Memo, April 11, 1988, updated. Index percentages are based on the closing values of the underlying indexes on July 11, 1988.

---

[62] The OCC also estimates the liquidation cost at all strike prices between these two extremes.

[63] This is a simplified representation of the rules. For more details, see Sofianos, "Description of Margin Requirements." Another interesting feature of these rules is that options based on broad-based indexes form a single "product group" and are margined as an integrated portfolio.

[64] One advantage of this arrangement is that it facilitates the cross-margining of S&P 500 futures option positions and S&P 500 futures positions.

out of the money, less margin is required. Customers can deposit securities and letters of credit as margin instead of cash—the same alternatives open to futures customers. Positions are marked to market daily. Customers must pay any additional required margin in cash, daily, and no later than 10 minutes before the market opens.

The clearinghouse uses a delta-based margin system to calculate the margin to be deposited by clearing members. Everyday it estimates the delta for each option position.[65] The daily margin requirement for each

[65]The option delta is the rate at which the option premium changes as the underlying futures price changes. Deltas range from −1 to +1.

Table 7

Customer Margin Requirements on S&P 500 Futures Options

(Selected Positions; As of September 1, 1988)

Long options:	Premium must be paid in full
Naked short options	
In-the-money:	$\pi + M$
Out-of-the-money:	$\pi + MAX[M - (0.5 \times T), 2,250]$
Option-futures spreads (hedges)	
Short call/long futures	$\pi + MAX[m - (0.5 \times N), 2,250]$
Short put/short futures	on combined position
Long call/short futures	$MAX[m - \pi, 0]$ for futures
Long put/long futures	Premium must be paid in full for long options
Option-option spreads	
Horizontal*	
Long expires before short:	$\mu + MAX[\pi \text{ (short)} - \pi \text{ (long)}, 0]$ for short
	Premium must be paid in full for long
Short expires before long:	0 for short
	Premium must be paid in full for long
Short combinations	
Straddles†:	$\pi(\text{put}) + \pi \text{ (call)} + m$

Explanations:
- π Option premium
- M   Margin on S&P 500 futures contract (20,000 or 10,000)
- m   Hedge margin on S&P 500 futures contract (10,000)
- μ Spread margin on S&P 500 futures contract (400)
- S   Value of underlying index
- E   Exercise price of option
- T   Out-of-the-money amount = $MAX[E - S, 0]$ for a call
  - = $MAX[S - E, 0]$ for a put
- N   In-the-money amount = $MAX[S - E, 0]$ for a call
  - = $MAX[E - S, 0]$ for a put

*Horizontal spreads: one short plus one long, call or put, same exercise price, different expiration date.

†Short straddles: one short put plus one short call, same exercise price, same expiration date.

short position is the current option premium plus the $10,000 maintenance margin requirement for the underlying S&P 500 futures contract multiplied by the relevant delta. There is a minimum margin charge of $475 per naked short option. As in the case of futures positions, clearing members can deposit Treasury securities and letters of credit as margin. Because both the option premium and the delta can vary from day to day, the total margin that must be on deposit with the clearinghouse will change daily even if the number of open positions does not change.[66] The clearinghouse uses the same timetable for calculating and collecting margin on options that it uses for futures.

The CME is currently replacing both its strategy-based and its delta-based margin systems with a new system called Dollars-at-Risk.[67] It will use the new system to calculate the margin that must be deposited both by customers to clearing members and by clearing members to the clearinghouse. The new system is similar to the OCC margin system for stock index options. Under the new system, the CME will be using an option-pricing model to obtain daily estimates of the liquidation cost of a portfolio of positions on the S&P 500 index under a variety of assumptions about the underlying futures price and its volatility. It will set margin to cover the maximum estimated liquidation cost. The portfolio may consist of positions on S&P 500 futures and options on these futures, so that estimated gains (losses) on the futures can offset (augment) estimated losses on the options. The CME will impose additional margin charges for spread positions with different settlement dates, and there will be a minimum margin charge for short options.[68]

Summary

The differences in margin requirements examined in this article can be summarized briefly. The margin rules on U.S. equity-related products differ depending on the product and the identity of the parties in the transaction. Often, for a given product and investor, the requirements will also depend on the investor's combination of positions. Differences in margin requirements go beyond simple variations in margin levels; there are differences in the way margin is calculated, the length of the posting period, and the form margin can take.

Investors buying stock on margin face different

[66]For stock index futures contracts, the total margin that must be on deposit with the clearinghouse changes only if the number of open positions changes.

[67]The new system will be used for S&P 500 futures options and all other CME options on futures.

[68]A more detailed description of the new Dollars-at-Risk system can be found in Sofianos, "Description of Margin Requirements."

requirements depending on whether the source of the margin loan is a broker-dealer, a bank, or some other lender. The requirements also depend on whether the margin borrower is a public customer, a market maker, or a broker-dealer. For short sales, the identity of the short seller is important: the short seller may be a public customer, a market maker, or a broker-dealer, and the requirements vary in each case.

In the stock index futures market, one set of rules governs the deposit of initial, maintenance, and variation margin by customers to clearing members. Initial margin is higher if the customer is classified as a speculator rather than a hedger. Another set of rules governs the deposit of margin by clearing members to the clearinghouse. Each clearing member maintains one customer account and one house account with the clearinghouse, and the two accounts are margined separately.

For options, there are again two sets of rules: one for the deposit of margin by customers to clearing members and another for the deposit of margin by clearing members to the clearinghouse. For stock options, stock index options, and stock index futures options, customer margins are strategy-based: in all cases margins vary depending on whether short positions are naked, or whether they are hedges, spreads, or part of some other combination. For each of these three types of options, a completely different margining system is used to calculate clearing member margins. In all cases, clearing members maintain separate customer and house accounts with the clearinghouse. The two accounts are margined separately using different rules.

George Sofianos

Article 13

Circuit breakers

These safety mechanisms are triggered by rapid or heavy market changes, and they can have unintentional effects on the financial system

James T. Moser

The "circuit breakers" that have gradually been added to financial markets since 1987 got their toughest test of the year yesterday. They passed.

—Wall Street Journal, July 24, 1990.

The limits "did exactly what they were supposed to do," he said.

—New York Times, July 24, 1990, quoting a trader.

Press reports describing the markets' encounter with circuit breakers on July 23, 1990, regarded them as successful. Their apparent criterion for success is the fact that the Dow Jones Industrial Average rose 60 points after encountering the circuit breaker. The experience from other markets suggests that circuit breakers do not usually produce dramatic price reversals. But, they do have effects. This article examines these effects.

Circuit breakers are mechanisms used by management to control activity in capacity-constrained systems. The term circuit breaker originates in electrical engineering to describe a pre-set switch that shuts down electrical activity in excess of a system's design capacity. The activation level of the breaker reflects an *ex ante* decision on the capability of the system.

Circuit breaker activation is inherently costly. The system engineer designing a circuit-breaker makes an *ex ante* choice between temporary loss of the use of the system and reductions in the likelihood of permanent dam-

age to system integrity. Activation of a circuit breaker intentionally imposes costs that are expected to be less than losses realized by exceeding the system's capacity. Cost considerations naturally focus on the value the intended users can expect to obtain through their use of the system.

Activation of circuit breakers can also have unintentional costs. These have two sources. First, activation of circuit breakers can lead to unanticipated convenience losses. For example, system engineers may undervalue some activities lost when a circuit breaker is activated. Therefore, system users with a financial stake in its operation have incentives to increase system capacity by allowing increases in the activation levels of circuit breakers. It is these incentives that produce pressure to re-allocate financial resources toward increased investment in the system. Thus, when private interests are involved, the ability to re-allocate resources insures that unanticipated convenience losses will be infrequent and temporary.

Second, costs are also incurred when unplanned uses of the system are disrupted. System engineers focusing on anticipated uses will not incorporate the value of unanticipated uses into their circuit-breaker decisions. These value losses are recognized only when service interruption motivates increased investment by such users. When value losses fail to attract investment, system engineers are not moti-

James T. Moser is a senior economist at the Federal Reserve Bank of Chicago.

vated to include these losses in the circuit-breaker decision. I refer to these interests as *public*, to distinguish them from *private* interests that do lead to increased investment in the system.

In financial markets, the intended effect of circuit breakers is to halt trading when activity levels threaten market viability. Earlier circuit breaker policy was determined within the affected market by parties having private rather than public interests in the activation of circuit breakers. Exchanges, responding to these interests, developed three separate circuit breaker mechanisms. *Order-imbalance* circuit breakers are intended to protect the interests of market makers in specialist markets. *Volume-induced* circuit breakers are intended to protect the viability of back-office operations. *Price-change* circuit breakers are intended to bring excessive volatility under control.

Recent developments in financial markets have elevated the importance of public interests. Markets are increasingly characterized as inter-related. This inter-relatedness increases the importance of price information flowing between markets. This is particularly true between the stock markets and the markets for financial derivatives—options and futures.

Futures exchanges have developed standardized contracts for a variety of financial assets. Value changes in these contracts are closely linked to developments in their related asset markets. Thus, asset prices serve the public purpose of determining gains and losses in futures contracts. Futures exchanges and their customers have benefitted from the price information generated by asset markets. Activation of circuit breakers interrupts this information flow, decreasing the public value of the services rendered by asset markets.

Futures markets offer a distinct set of services including opportunities to manage risks and additional routes to price discovery. Circuit breakers activated in these markets similarly disrupt these services, lessening their value. The stock-index futures contract illustrates this. Prices for these futures contracts are for hypothetical baskets of stocks. Thus, a single quote determines the price of the futures basket, whereas in the asset market cash prices must be aggregated to produce a cash index. In addition, daily settlement in the futures market is in cash, greatly simplifying order processing. The simplicity of stock-index futures contracts produces an ideal instrument for institutions to manage systematic risk levels through simultaneous trading in asset markets and futures. Circuit breakers disrupt the normal synchronization of price changes between futures contracts and asset prices. This disruption amplifies the risk that gains realizable in one market may be unavailable to offset losses in the other market.

The current proliferation of derivative-asset markets with differing capacity constraints, combined with intensive intermarket trading, raises coordination issues that were less crucial in the past. Circuit breakers activated in one market now can affect several markets, not only the market in which they were activated. Thus, circuit breakers in financial markets can influence public interests. These public costs are realized in two ways. First, circuit breaker interruption of private markets serves to shift trading into markets that remain open. Such interruptions initiate a chain of events that ultimately generates demand for a lender of last-resort to supply liquidity to the financial system. Second, price-change circuit breakers shift credit risk to gaining positions that implicitly extend credit to loss positions. Their creditworthiness may decrease the quality of exchange guarantees of performance.

The next section describes the three types of circuit breakers. Then, I examine the history of circuit breaker activity. An analysis of the unintended result of price limits on liquidity demands and the quality of nonperformance guarantees follows.

Classification of circuit breakers

Circuit breakers are of three types. Each addresses a different design-capability issue. The first, the order-imbalance circuit breaker, occurs in specialist markets. Inequalities in the number of buy and sell orders are balanced by specialists trading for their own accounts. These trades maintain orderly markets by smoothing short-run order imbalances. Substantial order imbalances increase the risk born by specialists. This, in turn, jeopardizes orderly markets. The second type, volume-induced, occurs when order processing becomes uneconomic. At low volume, order processing does not meet costs. High volume impedes the ability of the exchange to effectively process orders. Markets close when either volume effect pushes trading costs to uneconomic levels. The third type, the price-triggered circuit breaker, closes markets when a given price level is reached. This last type originated in the futures markets. Such circuit breakers are called "price limits." Justifications of price limits are couched in terms of controlling "excessive" volatility.

Order-imbalance circuit breakers

Stock markets activate order-imbalance circuit breakers at the request of a specialist. The specialist asks for a suspension of trade in an individual stock when an order imbalance occurs. In these cases, suspension gives the specialist time to determine a market-clearing price based upon information obtained off the exchange floor. Following the price determination period, the market re-opens with the specialist taking a position at the newly determined price. The purpose of this circuit breaker is to protect the specialist from large losses.

Order imbalances were a problem in both the 1987 and 1989 breaks. In 1987, selling pressure at the October 19 opening prevented trading in 140 of the NYSE-listed stocks in the S&P 500 during the first half hour. In 1989, openings on October 16, 1989 were similarly delayed. (Most stocks were reported not opened during the first fifteen minutes of trading. Beginning 8:45 CT, stocks began opening and trading was reported at 9:15.) In both cases, the intended effect of the order-imbalance circuit breakers was to protect specialists from losses incurred by purchases in declining markets.

Activation of these circuit breakers have unintentional effects. Trading halts in individual stocks create uncertainty about the correct level of the aggregate indexes. This, in turn, tends to be reflected in the futures contract. As a result, the futures contract becomes more likely to encounter a price limit. (On October 16, 1989, it did hit the open limit—5 points down.) When a price limit is reached futures trading stops, shifting some trades to the stock exchange. These trades tend to aggravate any existing order-imbalance problems.

Volume-induced circuit breakers

The cost-effectiveness of order processing depends on the level of trading volume. At low trading levels, breakeven costs are not met. The determination of exchange trading hours recognizes that the fixed costs of operations must be covered by revenues generated from trading activities. Exchanges schedule closings based on expectations that additions to these fixed costs will not be adequately compensated. Thus, daily closes can be construed as activation of a circuit breaker.

Trading volume can surpass the ability of exchange back offices to process the paperwork required to document executed trades. When this happens, the effectiveness of order processing is reduced, producing additional costs as the need for correcting orders rises. These costs are expected to rise with trading volume. With these additional costs, exchange operations can become uneconomic and the exchange closes.

In 1968, the stock exchanges instituted a temporary four-day week during the last half of the year, closing on Wednesdays to increase the time available to process paperwork. Heavy volume in the period prior to the four-day week had led to increases in errors executing orders. These midweek closings insured that each five-trading-day delivery period included at least one nontrading day, allowing the back offices to catch up.

More recently, heavy volume appears to have complicated the order-matching activity of the specialists. Stock trading volume during the 1987 price break surpassed the ability of specialists to match orders. As a result, executions were not timely and the ticker lagged current trades. Changes instituted after 1987 substantially increased the capacity of the exchange to process orders to an estimated one billion shares daily. However, the trading suspensions that resulted from the volume on October 13, 1989, suggest a lower capacity. At the rate of trading in the last hour of October 13, daily volume would have been just over 703 million shares. Volume on October 16, 1989, the heaviest day of trading since October 1987, was 416 million shares. After processing the overhang from the previous Friday (most stocks were trading by 10:15), stock trading proceeded smoothly all day.

Price-limit circuit breakers

In futures markets, price limits restrict trading to a band of prices generally symmetrical above and below the previous trading day's settlement price.[1] The stated goals of circuit breaker policies have historically been to control volatility. More recently, price limits on stock index contracts have been set to coordinate price movements in the cash and futures markets. Price limits serve as market-closing rules because:

1) short trades (sales of futures contracts) are not offered on up-limit days—the market clearing price is higher; and

2) long trades (buying futures contracts) are not offered on down-limit days—the market clearing price is lower.

Historically, the rules committees of the futures exchanges incorporated price limits into trading rules in response to threatened regulatory intervention. That pattern suggests that price-triggered circuit breakers would not exist without potential regulatory intervention.

Past circuit breaker experience

This history of the price-limit form of circuit breaker demonstrates that price limits appear to resolve "political" volatility.[2] The imposition of price limits, an apparent impediment to the price discovery purpose of futures exchanges, coincides with threats to the independence of the exchanges. Rather than face increased regulatory oversight and lose their ability to resolve disputes internally, the exchanges accommodated pressures for regulation by self-imposing price limits.

Early history of price limits

The earliest occurrence of a price limit in futures trading was at the Dojima exchange in Japan during the early 18th century. Settlement in the *koku* "small futures" contract for rice was determined by the average of the previous three days' forward-closing prices. If this price deviated by more than a fixed amount from the cash price for rice, all contracts were either reversed out or delivered. This effectively discontinued trading in the contract by eliminating all futures positions. Also, the futures price was tied to the cash market, avoiding the potential criticism that futures trading caused problems in cash markets. Imposition of the rule came during a time when rice markets were described as "deteriorating." Deteriorating markets are often characterized by price volatility.

The first instance of a price limit rule in the United States came during the First World War. On February 1, 1917, Germany announced that its submarines would sink all ships found in the major Atlantic shipping lanes. Cotton prices for May delivery on the New York Cotton Exchange closed down by a record of over five cents a pound. By the following Monday, however, the market had recovered to within one and one-half cents of the earlier price. In subsequent weeks, futures prices continued to be extremely volatile. The threat of attacks on shipping continued to run down prices as traders feared lost access to the European markets. Cotton prices rose as markets responded to news of potentially large purchases of cotton for military uniforms. Congress responded by supplying flat-rate three percent war loss insurance—a substantial discount from the then-current Lloyd's of London quote of ten percent. Cotton prices reached an all-time high following the introduction of this subsidized insurance.

The futures exchanges trading cotton responded to this volatility in two ways. On June 20, 1917, the British Board of Trade closed down cotton futures trading and the New York Cotton Exchange increased margin requirements. Separately, the U.S. government requested a price limit on the cotton contract. On August 22, 1917, a three-cent price limit was imposed. This limit remained in effect for the duration of the war. Interestingly, there is no record of a limit day during this period.

Also during the First World War, the Food Administration froze prices on wheat to prevent profiteering in that commodity. This action closed down trading in wheat futures at the Chicago Board of Trade. However, other grain prices were not frozen and their corresponding futures contracts traded freely. Since these grains are partially substitutable for wheat, government policy regarding wheat induced volatility in other grains. Futures prices for these commodities reflected this volatility, attracting the attention of the Food Administration. As a result of this scrutiny, the Board of Trade instituted a two-cent per day price limit on the oat contract and the New York Mercantile Exchange introduced a three-cent per day price limit on soy bean oil contracts. These price limits were removed once trading in wheat futures resumed after the war.

Price limits were formalized in 1925 at the Chicago Board of Trade. The 1925 Annual Report reported a modification to all contracts allowing the Board of Directors to set price-change limits of five percent of the preceding day's average closing price, following a ten-hour notice period. (For comparison, a five percent limit on wheat in today's wheat contract comes to 18.9 cents per bushel. The present limit is twenty cents per bushel.) Determination of an emergency was left to the Board. Nevertheless, price limits retained their temporary character, to be used only in emergency situations.

Direct federal intervention in agricultural markets during peace time began in the early 1930s under the authority of the Agricultural Adjustment Act. The Federal Farm Board, attempting to maintain prices in spite of large supplies of wheat, opened long futures contracts in May 1931 and 1932 wheat. Uncertainty about government policy (including complaints that officials were manipulating prices in their own interests) increased the frequency of emergency use of price limits.

(A recent proposal by Robert Heller makes similar use of futures markets. He argues the current policy of supplying liquidity during a market break disrupts monetary policy. Instead he suggests the Fed supply liquidity directly by taking long futures positions. His use of futures contracts is reasoned from the same basis as the Federal Farm Board policy of six decades ago—both approaches avoid the problem of the federal government holding and disposing of assets. The experience of the 1930s suggests that careful consideration should be given to the problem of contract expiration.)[3]

Passage of the National Industrial Recovery Act in July 1933 opened the way for trade associations to enforce price stabilization agreements, with the federal government acting both as architect and enforcing partner. Application for these partnerships was made through the National Recovery Administration (NRA) with the agreements chartered through Executive Orders by President Franklin Roosevelt. The agreements came in the form of codes for fair competition.

Grain price volatility continued to be high after the Farm Board ceased its price manipu-

lations. The drought of the period and uncertainty about government policy were contributing factors. This high volatility led to Department of Agriculture pressure in July 1933 for a fair-trade agreement among the grain exchanges. Pressure on the exchanges to comply came in the form of a proposal by the Agricultural Adjustment Administration and the Grain Futures Administration that would have empowered the Secretary of Agriculture to modify and enforce trading rules at the futures exchanges. The proposed authority included limits on individual trading, limits on daily price changes, and margin setting. The futures exchanges complied with the request and Executive Order No. 6648, entitled "Code of Fair Competition for Grain Exchanges and Members Thereof", was signed by President Roosevelt on March 20, 1934. The agreement, implemented the next day, included price limits which could not be exceeded, but did permit exchanges to set limits below the prescribed maximums.

The Supreme Court ruling in the Schechter Poultry Corporation case on May 27, 1935, declared the NRA codes unconstitutional. Following the Schechter decision, Congressional hearings began on the Commodity Exchange Act to broaden the scope of federal regulatory powers over the futures exchanges. These powers had previously been lodged within the Grain Futures Administration. Congressional discussion indicated the proposed Act would institutionalize the defunct NRA codes.

To thwart increased regulation, the Chicago Board of Trade incorporated permanent price limits on all its contracts. (At the same time, the Board of Trade also eliminated trading of options on futures, then called "priviledges [sic]." These were also targeted in Congressional hearings.) The action began the use of price limits as a standard contract feature. The Commodity Exchange Act later passed specifying only regulatory review, rather than expanded powers, over contract details—including price limits.

Circuit breakers in the 1980s

In 1982, futures contracts on stock indexes were introduced. The initial contracts, keeping with standard practice, were introduced with price limits. However, for the first time since the 1930s, these limits were dropped on objections from New York stock trading interests. In late 1984, price limits were dropped on all International Monetary Market contracts for foreign exchange.

The movement away from price limits continued until the market break of October 1987, when price limits were instituted on the S&P 500 contract. Three of the six commissions studying issues of the market break recommended significant regulatory changes. With regard to price limits the recommendations differ substantially. The Brady Commission recommended coordinated trading halts. While no specific method was proposed, the Commission indicated that price limits should be considered among the possible mechanisms. The NYSE "Katzenbach" study group said that price limits will not resolve market break issues. Their proposals focused on increasing the cost of trading to prevent speculation. They specifically proposed requiring delivery of stocks on stock-index futures contracts--increasing the cost of trading futures. The SEC study recommended against price limits on stock-index contracts. The SEC proposal suggested optional delivery of stock on index contracts, again increasing the cost of trading futures.

After the 1987 break, price limits were imposed on stock-index futures. The stated reason for these limits was to synchronize futures and cash prices. In 1988, the S&P 500 contract traded with a level-determined price limit. At levels below 275, the limit was 15 index points ($7500 per contract); between 275.05 and 325, the limit was 20 index points ($10,000 per contract); and, above 325, the limit was 25 index points ($12,500 per contract). Initial margins on these contracts were $15,000, twice the pre-break amount. In addition, a five-point limit was established at market opening. On reaching an opening limit, trading is suspended for two minutes and reopened at a new opening level. The opening limit rule holds only for the first ten minutes of trading.

The 1987 market break also led to introduction of price-triggered circuit breakers on the New York Stock Exchange. After a fall of 25 points in the Dow Jones Industrial Average (DJIA), the Sidecar program re-prioritized orders, giving priority to small (less that one million dollars) orders. After a decline of 250 points in the DJIA, the stock market would be closed for one hour. After a 400-point decline in the DJIA, the stock market would be closed for two hours. In addition, the DOT (Designated Order Turnaround) program would be shut down after a 50-point decline in the DJIA.

The mini-crash of October 1989

Recalling that the intent of these circuit breakers is to synchronize cash and futures markets, the events of October 13, 1989, provide a gauge for the usefulness of circuit breaker mechanisms. The evidence suggests that price limits did not synchronize these markets and may have routed dynamic-hedge trades into the stock market.

At 1:43 (CDT) negotiators announced the failure of financing for the proposed UAL buyout. The announcement sent the stock and index-futures markets into a steep decline. At 2:00 the DJIA was down 55 points. This corresponds to a 7.3 point drop in the S&P. Seven minutes later, the S&P futures contract hit its limit—12 points down. With futures trading suspended, the DJIA at 2:30 was down 114.76 points or roughly 15.3 S&P points. At 2:30, the futures contract reopened, but closed again fifteen minutes later—down 30 points. At the close of trading (3:00), the DJIA was down 190 points, or 25.3 S&P points. Quotes from the stock market clearly lagged behind those from the futures market. The circuit breakers do not appear to have kept prices in line.

Trading volume was affected by the circuit breakers. Figure 1 shows NYSE volume for half-hour intervals for 10/13/89 and 10/16/89. Volume at 1:30 on 10/13 was 125.52 million shares for the day, or 12.55 million shares per half-hour interval. The market response to the UAL announcement in the 1:30-2:00 interval increased volume to 17.48 million shares, or 39 percent above the average prior to 1:30 but still less than two of the previous half-hour intervals.

At 2:07 CDT futures trading was suspended for the remainder of the half-hour period. Minutes later Chicago Board Options Exchange (CBOE) closed without re-opening. Volume during that period was 45.86 million shares, 265 percent above the average and more than twice the busiest previous period. During the last half-hour of trading. volume was 396 percent above the average—nearly

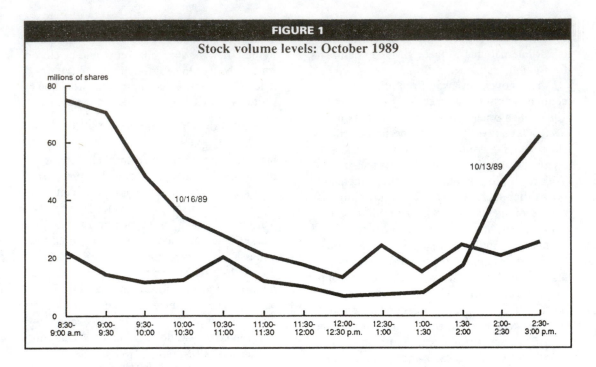

FIGURE 1

Stock volume levels: October 1989

millions of shares

10/16/89

10/13/89

8:30-9:00 a.m. | 9:00-9:30 | 9:30-10:00 | 10:00-10:30 | 10:30-11:00 | 11:00-11:30 | 11:30-12:00 | 12:00-12:30 p.m. | 12:30-1:00 | 1:00-1:30 | 1:30-2:00 | 2:00-2:30 | 2:30-3:00 p.m.

four times the busiest period before 1:30. This trading might be explained as a response to new information and, therefore, independent of the incidence of circuit breakers but evidence in the Index futures pit suggests more was involved.

After limits were hit in the S&P 500 pit for the second time, a limited number of sell orders were executed at the limit price despite the disadvantageous price obtained there. Further, at the official 3:15 close of index trading, 2,000 sell orders worth $330 million were said to be outstanding. The pattern of selling in the Index pit indicates that traders were searching for reliable executions. The closest available substitute to selling stock-index futures is the sale of stock holdings. Thus, the substantial increase in stock volume can be related to the incidence of the CME circuit breaker. (See Figure 2).

The consequence of the volume increase may have been an increased difficulty in keeping up with the flow of orders. Heavy selling after 1:30 CDT produced suspensions in ten stocks with seven not re-opening. This suggests that stock markets were unable to handle the increased volume.

Finally, the evidence from the 1989 price break reveals three weaknesses. First, volume increases after price limits were encountered suggest these circuit breakers routed trades from the futures markets to the stock markets.

This is a serious concern. There is good evidence from the 1987 break that order imbalances are positively correlated with price changes. Policies tending to exacerbate the order-imbalance problem are likely to increase price volatility during price swings encountered in the future. Second, both the price lags reflected in the DJIA and the suspensions in stock trading indicate that the circuit breakers did not keep prices in line. Third, taking the $330 million overhang in the futures market to be intended to cover stock positions of institutional traders, at least one-third of a billion dollars went unhedged.

New circuit breakers in place

After the 1989 market break, price limits were revised. The following describes current limit procedures for the S&P contract. The five-point opening limit is retained. After the opening interval and at all levels of the index, current levels are: On a 12-point drop in the index prior to 2:30 PM (Central Time), trading is suspended for thirty minutes; on a 20-point drop in the index prior to 1:30 PM, trading is suspended for one hour; on a 30-point change (up or down), trading is suspended until 50 percent of S&P stocks (by capitalized value) are open for trading.

The NYSE also revised its circuit breakers to restrain program trading. After a 30-point drop in the DJIA, incoming orders are routed into the Sidecar for fifteen minutes. After a 75-point drop trading orders are Sidecar'd for thirty minutes. In addition, the CME rejects incoming S&P 500 contract orders after a 12-point drop in the S&P.

The emphasis on drops clarifies the purpose of recent price-linked, circuit-breaker policies. They do not resolve cash flow problems for the futures exchanges—else limits would be imposed on the upside as well. Nor do they control volatility—for the same reason. They do shield the futures exchanges from the criticism that futures trading pulls down stock prices.

Circuit breakers and the market for liquidity

Liquidity is the relative ease of matching buy and sell orders at recently observed prices. Sellers can always obtain liquidity by lowering offers to sell. The difference between the price they obtain and the previously observed prices they expected can be construed as the cost of liquidity. Buyers recognize that for some assets these costs may be high. Thus, their offers to buy incorporate the risk of encountering a high liquidity cost on the eventual sale of the asset. Buyers respond by adjusting bids downward.

Markets respond by organizing to keep liquidity costs low. They accomplish this through efficient matching of buy and sell orders backed up by methods to handle any order imbalances that may arise.

The market-making activity

Market making refers to the activity of matching buy and sell orders. In specialist markets such as the stock exchanges, orders to buy or sell arrive at a central post, are matched up by a specialist, and are posted as transactions. The specialist's order book is unbalanced when the number of buy and sell orders at the most recent price are unequal. When these order imbalances occur, exchange rules require the specialist to trade for his own position—buying in a declining market or selling in a rising market. Since these trades are aimed at re-balancing the order book, they may be loss trades for the specialist; that is, buying above the correct market price in a declining market or selling below in a rising market. These trades produce a balance of buy and sell orders and fulfill the specialist's re-

sponsibility of maintaining an orderly market. To facilitate this role, dealers have exchange-required capitalization and minimum inventories for their stock listings.

Under an interest-rate targeting policy, the Fed acts as a marketmaker in markets directly linked to reserve assets. Reserve policy effects credit levels so that a stable monetary policy depends on a stable market for reserves. To maintain this stability, the Fed acts as a specialist in reserves—both buying and selling to prevent order imbalances.

Links between financial markets

The Federal Reserve is affected by circuit breakers because markets for stocks, bonds, and futures contracts are fundamentally linked through the payments system and the market for reserves. To see this, consider the problem faced by the specialist after a steep decline in stock prices. In the process of buying stock to maintain an orderly market, losses have been encountered. In addition, inventories of stock, generally purchased on margin, have been marked down and require additional financing. Summing the financing needs of many specialists after declines of the magnitude experienced during the breaks of 1987 and 1989, one will generally observe a large increase in the demand for loanable funds. Institutions supplying funds to specialists respond by selling short-term Treasury securities to meet reserve requirements. Thus, the demand shock in the loanable funds market tends to destabilize markets for Treasury securities—orders to sell Treasury securities exceed buy orders.

Shocks to the loanable funds market are also felt as the margin accounts of mark-to-market assets are adjusted. Dynamic hedge trades in a declining market increase demand for Treasury securities placed in the initial margin accounts of long and short futures positions. Long and short positions marked to market add further shocks as losing positions sell Treasuries to generate funds required to cover calls for variation margin and winning positions invest cash balances in Treasuries. Over a period of time these shocks will net out. Nevertheless, lack of synchronicity induces short-term swings in the supply of liquidity.

Combining with these separate effects, stock-market specialists encountering losses from their market-making activities are seek-

FIGURE 2

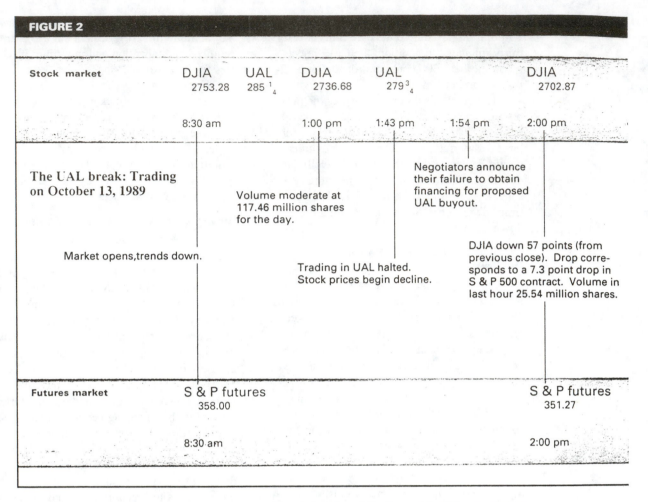

The UAL break: Trading on October 13, 1989

ing funds in a market subjected to volatile levels of liquidity. In its capacity as reserve specialist, the Federal Reserve supports liquidity by maintaining a balance between buy and sell orders for reserves and Treasury securities. This activity prevents short-run order imbalances from wringing liquidity from the system. The credit-demand shock from specialists' needs for funds are supported as the Fed adds reserves to the system.

Importantly, Fed policy must first distinguish between the real and monetary components of these shocks in the market for reserves. Facilitating the liquidity demands of a financial shock need not have real effects. Liquidity can be increased through purchases of Treasuries. Once the short-term credit needs of the payments system subside, reserve levels can then be reduced. These financial shocks can be identified by sharp market declines accompanied by volume and order-balancing problems. The timing of this credit accommodation requires consideration.

Circuit breakers interfere with trades needed to generate liquidity. The appropriate time for the Fed to begin the supply of liquidity is at the point when trading halts create an imbalance of buy and sell orders for reserves and Treasury securities.

Policy considerations for mixed real-monetary shocks differ. In these events, the Fed must consider both the need for credit accommodation through its order-matching activity and its monetary policy which is implemented through reserve-level choices. For example, liquidity operations after the 1987 break produced significant decreases in short-term rates. Reserves were left in the system after October 1987, giving permanence to the October liquidity operations. The 1989 break was followed by reports that the Fed would supply liquidity as in 1987. These reports were later disavowed. However, open market operations on October 16, 1989, did effect a modest temporary increase in the reserve base.

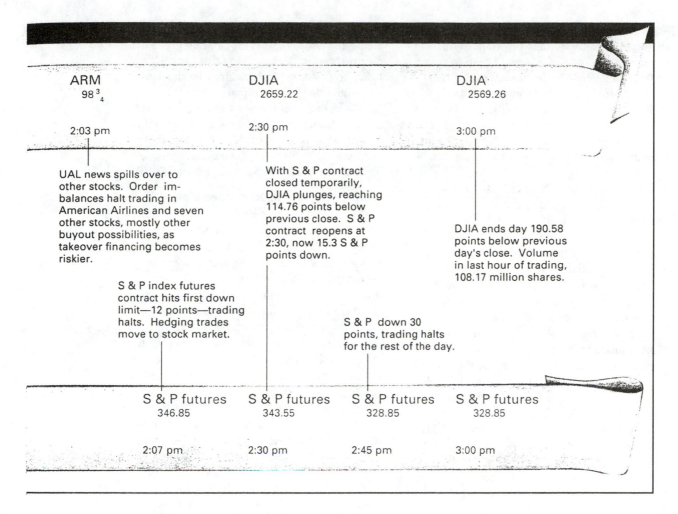

ARM
98 3/4

2:03 pm

UAL news spills over to
other stocks. Order im-
balances halt trading in
American Airlines and seven
other stocks, mostly other
buyout possibilities, as
takeover financing becomes
riskier.

S & P index futures
contract hits first down
limit—12 points—trading
halts. Hedging trades
move to stock market.

S & P futures
346.85

2:07 pm

DJIA
2659.22

2:30 pm

With S & P contract
closed temporarily,
DJIA plunges, reaching
114.76 points below
previous close. S & P
contract reopens at
2:30, now 15.3 S & P
points down.

S & P futures
343.55

2:30 pm

S & P down 30
points, trading halts
for the rest of the day.

S & P futures
328.85

2:45 pm

DJIA
2569.26

3:00 pm

DJIA ends day 190.58
points below previous
day's close. Volume
in last hour of trading,
108.17 million shares.

S & P futures
328.85

3:00 pm

In terms of the effect on credit markets, the expectation of increased credit availability is key. Interest rates fell on October 16, evidencing market anticipation of increased purchases of Treasuries. Interest rates rose shortly afterwards as the Fed's response and its disclaimers became known.

Identification of a real component to a shock suggests consideration of a less temporary adjustment to the reserve level. Accommodation of temporary liquidity needs facilitates the allocation of capital. Failure to accommodate liquidity tends to hinder the reallocation of capital, delaying recovery from the real shock. Once temporary liquidity needs are met, reserve policy should then focus on real, relatively permanent aspects.

Effect of circuit breakers

Circuit breakers alter the effect of a market move on credit markets by altering cash flows. Trading halts have three effects on the flow of funds.

First, amounts marked to market based on prices recorded when trading was halted do not reflect market values—short positions record less gain in a price decline, long positions record less loss. Provided trading halts are synchronized across markets, amounts marked to market for related securities are similar causing no excess demand for loanable funds. Unsynchronized trading halts, on the other hand, tend to produce asymmetry in that losses and gains on related assets are unequal. The liquidity needs produced by losses incurred in one market cannot be covered by recognition of gains in related markets. Thus, nonsynchronized trading halts increase the demand for loanable funds and shift liquidity trades into those markets which remain open. This places greater stress on these markets.

Consider, for example, a specialist hedging his equity position with a short futures position in an index contract. A trading halt in the index futures contract can result in equity losses exceeding gains on futures. In an unrestricted market, the futures position, in this example, would generate needed cash to cover the financing needs of the stock position. A halt in futures trading reduces the flow of funds to the specialist, increasing dependance on borrowed funds. Inventory financing needs that cannot be met with gains from the futures contract must be covered by increased borrowing.

Second, positions not marked to market are affected like marked-to-market accounts. The difference is one of form, not result. Gains and losses on stocks or options are realized by unwinding the position. Circuit breakers halt trading and prevent unwinding of contracts. This restricts access to invested balances required to cover losses, realized elsewhere, increasing the demand for credit.

For example, traders holding UAL on 10/13 attempted to sell out after the 1:43 announcement. The halt in trading of that stock initiated a search for close substitutes for UAL stock. The nearest substitutes were other takeover stocks and transportations, particularly airlines. Order books for these stocks quickly became unbalanced. Three Big Board stocks halted trading temporarily: USAir Group, Delta Air Lines, and Philips Industries. Seven Big Board stocks halted and remained closed for the day: UAL, AMR, BankAmerica, Walt Disney, Capital Cities/ABC, Philip Morris, and Pacific Telesis. Sales again shifted; first to index futures, then to a broad range of stocks after the 15-point limit halted futures trading.

These first two effects of price limits derive from restrictions on investor access to liquidity. During market breaks when liquidity is most valuable, circuit breakers reduce the number of routes available for private resolution of liquidity needs. This tends to increase demand for a source of last resort to supply liquidity—a role many expect to be taken up by the Fed.

A third effect derives from responses to price uncertainty as clearinghouses re-consider prudential margin levels. The trade halt produced by a circuit breaker creates uncertainty about the market's actual volatility. Since margin levels are determined in response to estimates of price volatility, risk-averse clearinghouses are forced to estimate margin needs on a worst-case basis. This will tend to increase the margin levels required by prudent clearinghouses. Recognizing that further losses to customer accounts may be substantial, initial and variation margin levels are increased to prevent losses from spilling over from customer accounts into clearing-member accounts. This effect tends to decrease the supply of loanable funds by increasing use of Treasury securities to meet margin obligations.

Credit risk due to loss financing

The previous comments on circuit breakers emphasize problems induced by disruption to the flow of funds. Circuit breakers can also be viewed as shifting credit risk. Failure to record the full loss amount in a marked-to-market account implicitly extends an interest-free loan for a portion of the loss amount to the losing position. The amount of this loan is the difference between the amount marked to the settlement price and the amount marked to the true market price. The loan is extended to losing positions from gaining positions.

The amount of credit extended by these loans can be considerable. To illustrate, I will use the October 1989 market break. Taking the true futures price to be roughly the 10/16/89 opening, the true settlement price for the 117, 202 December contracts outstanding should have been 323.85. The difference between the actual settlement of 328.85 and the estimate of the true settlement is 5 S&P points. The amount of credit implicitly extended to short positions over the weekend of 10/14-10/15 was, therefore, $58.6 million or 3.3 percent of the value marked to market on 10/13.[4]

To gauge the risk to the financial system, we need to recall that futures clearinghouses provide performance guarantees for contracts trading on their affiliated exchanges. The quality of these guarantees depends on the amount of potential loss relative to equity. As potential losses increase relative to a fixed level of equity, the possibility of default rises, diminishing the quality of any guarantees. Book equity balances for the CME at the end of 1988 were $79.3 million. The $58.6 million implicitly lent to short positions is 73.9 percent of book equity.

The full implication for contract performance guarantees is not known. Threats to these guarantees will tend to shift trading away from the futures markets as the perceived quality of the guarantees declines. This tends to increase the credit needs of specialists operating in stock markets, requiring increases in reserves to meet these demands. Thus, the significance of the credit balance implied by price limits bears investigation. The policy issue is the viability of contract performance guarantees provided by the futures exchanges.

Conclusion

This article examines the effects of circuit breakers on the stability of the financial markets. Circuit breakers are classified into three types based on capacity issues: volume-triggered circuit breakers halt trading when volume exceeds order-processing capacity; order-imbalance circuit breakers halt trading when orders to buy or sell threaten the viability of the specialist; and price-limit circuit breakers halt trading when price changes are regarded as excessive. The history of price limits suggests they are introduced when futures exchanges are threatened with greater regulatory oversight.

This paper argues that circuit breakers reduce access to markets. This reduces the ability of markets to resolve needs for liquidity. Second, price limits extend credit to loss positions in futures and options markets. Since clearinghouses guarantee contract performance, these guarantees may be threatened by large credit balances.

On several recent occasions, circuit breakers have proved of some value in market crises. But it must be remembered that their value is not costless, nor their benefits without limit.

FOOTNOTES

[1]A notable exception to price-limit symmetry is found in the stock-index contracts. These are discussed in the next section.

[2]This term is from Joseph A. Grundfest, Commissioner of the Securities and Exchange Commission.

[3]The Heller proposal is in Heller, R., "Have the Fed Support Stock Market, Too," *Wall Street Journal*, October 27, 1989, p. A14. An analysis of the 1930s experience is in

Moser, James T., "Public Policy Intervention Through Futures Market Operations," forthcoming in the *Journal of Futures Markets*.

[4] The 10/16 open price is probably too high. Opening contract prices on that date encountered the CME open limit of five points, preventing realization of a lower price on the S&P contract. Thus, our estimate may significantly underestimate the amount of credit extended.

Section IV
The Stock Market

Articles in this section focus on investing in the stock market. They range from a consideration of the features of successful stocks of the past to the way in which stocks react to special events. Other articles consider the pricing efficiency of the stock market and the pricing of new issues of stock.

In "Characteristics of Stock Market Winners," Marc Reinganum examines 222 successful stocks from an investments point of view. Reinganum's evidence suggests that it may be possible to create computer screens to identify stocks that will perform well in the future. In creating these screens, he uses publicly available data to identify firms with desirable investment characteristics and details the investment performance of the selected stocks.

For more than twenty years, scholars have examined stock market performance using a technique called an *event study*. This type of study examines how stock prices react to a special kind of event, such as a dividend cut, the announcement of a new stock issue, or a pending merger. In his paper, "How Do Stock Returns React to Special Events," Robert Schweitzer explains this methodology in a non-technical way and reviews some of the many applications of the event study methodology. As Schweitzer concludes, the event study methodology is a powerful tool to increase investors' understanding of the factors that influence stock returns.

Anthony Saunders' article "Why Are So Many New Stock Issues Underpriced?," considers the pricing of newly issued shares. By "new stock" Saunders refers to stock that is newly issued, as opposed to existing shares. Considerable evidence suggests that newly issued stock is underpriced because the stock price increase after issuance exceeds the appropriate risk-adjusted return. Saunders reviews the evidence supporting this view and asks a deeper question: What does this underpricing suggest about the regulation of investment banking firms and commercial banks? (Currently, the Glass-Steagall Act limits commercial bank participation in issuing new stock.) Saunders concludes that repeal of Glass-Steagall could result in fairer pricing for newly issued stock.

A market is efficient with respect to some information set if prices in that market fully reflect the information. Economists study whether particular markets reflect different kinds of information. An efficient market is desirable because prices that reflect information lead to better allocation of scarce resources and can increase the general level of well-being in an economy. Stephen F. Leroy reviews some recent challenges to market efficiency in "Capital Market Efficiency: An Update." While economists have long tended to accept market efficiency for major U.S. capital markets, Leroy joins the growing chorus of economists that find fault with the model of efficiency.

Intimately related to the issue of efficiency is the question of the risk-premium on equity. In capital market theory, the risk-free asset, such as a

Treasury bill, has no default risk. Other assets have risk and are priced to give a higher expected return to compensate for the risk associated with holding the security. This higher expected return is the risk-premium. Comparing stocks with T-bills, we see that stocks are definitely riskier and should offer a higher expected return to attract investors. Chan Huh considers 100 years of stock market evidence in his paper "The Equity Risk-Premium Puzzle." As his paper explains, the risk-premium actually earned by stocks has been quite large. The puzzle is that the earned risk-premium seems to be too large. Huh considers some possible solutions to the puzzle, but it remains an impediment to our complete understanding of equity markets.

Article 14

Investment Characteristics of Stock Market Winners

By Marc Reinganum

For many years, academic research supported the idea that investors cannot consistently outperform a simple strategy of buying and holding a diversified portfolio of common stocks without taking on greater risk. This implies that technical and fundamental research based on publicly available information would, at best, improve investment performance only marginally, and throwing darts to select stocks would most likely be just about as effective.

Serious chinks in this investment view have appeared recently, as several studies have found stock market anomalies—investment characteristics that consistently produce returns above those that would be expected based on the investment's level of risk. For instance, studies have indicated that stocks with low price-earnings ratios outperform those with high price-earnings ratios, and stocks with small market capitalizations outperform large-capitalization companies. Other anomalies characterizing peculiar patterns in the timing of stock returns also emerged, ranging from a month-of-the-year effect to a week-of-the-month effect to a day-of-the-week effect and even down to an hour-of-the-day effect. [For more on market anomalies, see John Markese's Investor Workshop in the April 1989 issue of the *AAII Journal*.] These anomalies point to a similar conclusion: Investors may be able to beat stock performance benchmarks using publicly available information.

Stock market winners may also yield some insights into anomalies. For this study, we singled out stocks with exceptionally high returns to see whether these firms share any common attributes. If history does repeat itself, these common attributes may suggest some

Marc Reinganum is the Phillips professor of finance in the College of Business Administration at the University of Iowa. This article was adapted from an article that appeared in the March-April 1988 issue of the Financial Analysts Journal.

profitable investment strategies.

The Study

The companies chosen for the study were based on companies in "The Greatest Stock Market Winners: 1970-1983," published by William O'Neil & Co. To be considered a great winner, a company typically had to at least double in value within a calendar year, although there were a few exceptions to this guideline, and not all companies that doubled in value were selected. Historical fundamental and technical information on these firms was taken from the Datagraph books (also published by William O'Neil & Co. and sold primarily to institutional investors).

Returns were measured based on the price appreciation of the winners between their buy and sell dates. On average, the 222 winners increased in value by 349%. While this average was buoyed by a few winners with astronomical increases, more than half the firms increased in value by at least 237%.

The variables we examined were divided into one of five categories. The first, "smart money," includes the behaviors of professionally managed funds and corporate insiders. The second contains valuation measures such as price-to-book-value and price-earnings ratios. The third grouping includes the technical indicator of relative strength. The fourth consists of accounting earnings and profitability measures. The final group contains miscellaneous variables that did not fit into the other four groups.

Smart Money Variables

The smart money variables reveal the stock holdings of professionally managed investment funds and corporate insiders. Even if they are not clairvoyants, money managers and corporate insiders are probably well-informed. We broke professionally managed funds down into four groups—investment advisers, banks, mutual funds and insurance companies. For each of these groups, Datagraph reports the number of institutions holding a particular issue as well as the aggregate holdings of these institutions as percentages of the outstanding common stock.

Table 1 summarizes the results. We can draw several general observations from the professionally managed funds as a whole. If hindsight were foresight, one would like to know of impending significant increases in the sponsorship of stock held by banks, mutual funds and investment advisers. Between the buy and sell dates, these three groups of professionally managed funds increased their average ownership stakes in the 222 winners by 25%, 60% and 107%, respectively. At least at the conclusion of the rapid price advance, these funds were where the action was. Prior to the buy quarter, the ownership claims of these managed funds tended to rise only slightly. Thus professional money managers may participate in, but do not prophesy, extraordinary price appreciation.

Corporate insiders form another group that may be privy to information about a company's prospects. Will tracking their transactions lead to profitable trading? Several prior studies have suggested that it may. However, the data among the winning stocks does not indicate any great changes in the pattern of insider trading.

For most companies, no corporate insiders bought stock either prior to the large price advance or after it. Selling transactions seem equally uninformative. One might expect insider selling to subside prior to the major price advance. In fact, insider selling of these 222 companies actually increased slightly before the advance, rising from an average of 0.84 insider sales per company to 1.38.

While the smart money variables may reflect the actions of well-informed investors, the evidence suggests that they do not predict major price advances.

Valuation Measures

Five different valuation variables were examined: price-to-book-value ratio, price-earnings ratio, stock price level, stock market capitalization, and beta. Table 1 provides a brief summary of the findings.

Price-to-book-value ratio compares the market value of the stock to its book value. A ratio less than 1.0 indicates that the market value of a company is less than its book value, suggesting that the stock is underpriced.

Among the 222 winners, 164 were selling for less than book value in the quarter in which the buy occurred. The median price-to-book-value ratio was 0.60, while the average ratio was 0.95. (The median is the exact mid-point, where half of all ratios fall above and half fall below; it is used because it is less influenced by extreme values.) While a price-to-book-value ratio of less than one may not be a perfect indicator of a stock

market winner, it does seem to be a common characteristic. This suggests an investment strategy that isolates firms selling below book value.

The distribution of price-earnings ratios provided quite different results. In the buy quarter, the average price-earnings ratio equaled 13.6, while the median was 10. In general, the price-earnings ratios for the set of winners do not tend to be very small. In fact, only one out of every 10 of these firms had price-earnings ratios of less than 5 in the buy quarter. This indicates that very low price-earnings ratios are not a necessary ingredient of a successful investment strategy.

The results also indicated that the winners are not characterized by either low stock prices or small stock market capitalizations (number of shares times price per share). The median share price on the buy date was $24.07, while the average was $27.69. The median market capitalization was $120.1 million—a figure that falls in the upper half of New York Stock Exchange and American Stock Exchange-listed stocks. Only one of the 222 winners had a market capitalization less than $10 million, and only 12 had capitalizations less than $20 million. This suggests that small size, whether measured by share price or stock market capitalization, is not a necessary component of a successful investment strategy.

The betas of the stock market winners were examined to see if their extraordinary rates of return might be compensation for riskiness. Beta measures the variation of a stock relative to the stock market. The stock market has a beta of 1.00; a beta greater than 1.00 implies that when the stock market changes, the stock will change to a greater degree and is therefore riskier [for more on beta, see this month's Editor's Choice, starting on page 16]. The average and median beta of these firms was 1.14, and fewer than 5% had betas greater than 2.00. While the firms as a group were slightly riskier than the market as a whole, the additional stock market risk cannot account for the extraordinary returns of these winners.

Technical Indicators

The technical indicator measured among the stock winners was relative strength (see Table 1). The relative strength of a stock is the average of quarterly price changes during the previous year, but giving more weight (40%) to the most recent quarter and less weight (20% each) to the three other quarters; these average changes are then ranked among all stocks, ranging from 1 (lowest) to 99 (highest). Among the winners, the median rank in the buy quarter was 93; fully 212 of the 222 firms possessed relative-strength rankings of greater than 70. In addition, the relative-strength rankings for 170 of the 222 winners increased between the quarter prior to the buy and the quarter during which

Table 1.
Characteristics of Stock Market Winners on the Buy Date

Smart Money Variables	Average	Median
Number of Investment Advisers Owning Shares	9.3	0
Percent of Outstanding Stock Held by Investment Advisers	7.2	0
Number of Insiders Buying Stock	0.37	0
Number of Insiders Selling Stock	1.38	1
Valuation Measures		
Price/Book Value	0.95	0.60
Price/Earnings	13.6	10.0
Share Price ($)	27.69	24.07
Stock Market Capitalization ($ millions)	484.3	120.1
Stock Beta	1.14	1.14
Technical Indicators		
Relative Strength Rankings (99 = Highest, 1 = Lowest)	90.2	93.0
Earnings and Profitability Measures		
Pretax Profit Margins (%)	12.7	11.2
Changes in Quarterly Earnings (%)	45.9	7.4
Changes in Quarterly Sales (%)	9.5	7.3
Five-Year Earnings Growth Rates (%)	23.0	17.0
Miscellaneous Variables		
Common Shares Outstanding (in thousands)	13,885	5,740
Ratio of Buy Date Price to Maximum Price During 2 Previous Years	0.899	0.922

the stock was purchased. These findings have two implications for investment strategy: First, investors should seek out firms with high relative-strength rankings; and second, investors should try to identify firms that exhibit a positive change in their relative-strength ranking from the prior quarter.

Earnings and Profitability Measures

Several measures of earnings and profitability among the stock market winners were examined: pretax profit margins, changes in quarterly earnings, changes in quarterly sales, and five-year quarterly earnings growth rates. Table 1 provides a summary of the results.

The average pretax profit margin in the buy quarter was 12.7%. In the quarter prior to the buy, the profit margin was slightly smaller, while by the sell quarter, the average profit margin had increased to 14.5%. In fact, the nearly 2% increase in the pretax profit margins may have contributed to the significant price appreciation of these firms. Fully 216 of the 222 winners had positive pretax margins in the buy quarter and 215 had positive pretax margins in the quarter prior to the purchase. This evidence clearly indicates that a high, pos-

itive pretax profit margin should be one of the selection screens in an investment strategy.

On average, quarterly earnings in the buy quarter rose nearly 45.9% from the previous quarter; these were not seasonally adjusted and they represent changes in the raw accounting earnings. Interestingly, quarterly earnings in the quarter prior to the buy increased an average of 60.8%, while in the quarter prior to that they increased an average of 50.4%—in other words, there was an acceleration in quarterly earnings. Thus, another investment rule suggested by the winners is to seek out firms with a positive change in quarterly earnings—earnings acceleration.

The pattern of changes in quarterly sales closely parallels that of changes in quarterly earnings. During the two quarters prior to the buy, quarterly sales were positive and increasing. During the buy quarter, quarterly sales on average increased 9.5%.

A longer-term picture of earnings growth was gleaned from the five-year quarterly earnings growth rates. These rates were determined using five years of quarterly earnings data that were annualized. In the buy quarter, the earnings growth rates averaged 23.0% while in the quarter prior to the buy, they averaged 21.6%. By the sell quarter, the average earnings growth rate increased dramatically, to 38.2%. This is most likely due to the method of calculating the growth rates, which discards the low rates from the prior years and replaces them with the high earnings growth rates experienced during the period of dramatic stock price appreciation. During the quarters prior to the quarter just before the buy, the average five-year rates remained stable. However, during the quarter just before the buy, over 85% of the firms exhibited positive five-year earnings growth rates. This suggests that investors should select companies that have positive five-year quarterly earnings growth rates.

Miscellaneous Variables

Two variables that didn't fit into the other categories

were also examined: the number of common shares outstanding and the ratio of the price on the buy date to the maximum price during the two previous years.

The average stock market winner had 13.8 million outstanding shares during the buy quarter; the median was a much lower 5.7 million. During the sell quarter, the average and median number of outstanding shares nearly doubled, most likely indicating that many of the firms split their shares of stock during the time of rapid share price increases. However, the most meaningful statistic for investors is that nearly 90% of the firms had fewer than 20 million shares of stock outstanding. Investors may want to select companies with fewer than 20 million outstanding shares of stock.

The ratio of the price on the buy date to the maximum price during the two previous years provides a measure of whether these firms had fallen out of favor among investors. This ratio measures the extent to which the extraordinary success of these 222 winners might have been captured by a contrarian investment strategy of selecting stocks that have suffered substantial price declines. However, the results indicate that a contrarian rule would not have led to the selection of these stocks. On the buy date, more than half the winners were selling within 8% of their previous two-year highs, and only one was selling at a price of less than half its previous two-year high. More than 80% of the firms were selling within 15% of their previous two-year highs. Thus, an investment strategy that selects stocks selling within 15% of their two-year highs would capture a common characteristic of these winners.

A Test of Possible Screens

Given the number of variables examined, there are myriad potential investment strategies that could be developed. To get an idea of the usefulness of some of these screens, we tested one strategy that employed four of the variables. The four chosen were those variables that produced the highest median returns when each of the variables were used as screens for the 222 winners. The four screens were:

- A price-to-book-value ratio of less than 1.0;
- Accelerating quarterly earnings;
- A relative-strength ranking of the stock in the current quarter greater than the ranking in the previous quarter;
- Fewer than 20 million common shares outstanding.

These screens were applied against a universe of 2,057 stocks listed on the New York Stock Exchange and the American Stock Exchange over the 1970 through 1983 period; the 222 winners were excluded from this list. Stocks were "purchased" 63 days after a buy signal, which ensured that accounting information assumed known had actually been released. The stock was held for two years, and cumulative holding period returns for each stock were determined and compared against the cumulative returns for the S&P 500 over the same time period. The difference between the stock return and the S&P 500 return is the "excess" return generated by the screen.

Table 2 provides the performance results for this strategy, which did quite well relative to the S&P 500. After one year, the selected firms on average provided holding-period returns that were 16.67% above those of the S&P 500; after two years they provided on average holding-period returns that were 37.14% above those of the S&P 500.

Other tests implied that increasing the number of investment rules suggested by our investigation of stock market winners would improve performance.

These results should not be construed to mean that these four investment screens are the best four filters. They do, however, illustrate that the lessons learned from an examination of the biggest winners may be profitably applied to a broader universe of firms. In addition, it seems unlikely that any one of the investment rules will yield better performance than all jointly.

Investors may also want to take note of the absence of certain characteristics from the trading strategies mentioned. These strategies do not exploit characteristics that prior research has revealed to be associated with superior performance. The strategies are not tilted in favor of stocks with very small market capitalizations. Nor are firms with low share prices singled out, or those with low price-earnings ratios. The strategies are not contrarian in the sense that companies with substantial previous price declines are selected. Despite the absence of these characteristics, the trading strategies produce excess returns that are economically significant. This suggests that there may be more than one way to skin the performance cat!

Table 2.
The Four-Screen Investment Strategy

Cumulative Excess Holding-Period Returns*	Average	Median
First Quarter following purchase	3.04%	1.4%
Second Quarter following purchase	8.19	4.4
Third Quarter following purchase	12.65	7.3
One Year following purchase	16.67	9.7
Fifth Quarter following purchase	20.84	12.7
Sixth Quarter following purchase	26.10	15.6
Seventh Quarter following purchase	31.13	18.5
Two Years following purchase	37.14	22.3

*An excess return is the difference between the holding-period return on the security and the S&P 500 over the same time.

Article 15

How Do Stock Returns React to Special Events?

Robert Schweitzer

Investors expect stock prices to react to some special events as a matter of course. They're rarely as certain, however, about the timing and magnitude of that reaction, and sometimes they aren't even sure of the direction.

This much, however, is known: unexpected events can change the stock prices of a firm by changing the profit potential or riskiness of that firm. And if the financial markets pick up information about an impending event, that event can change stock prices days or weeks

before it actually occurs—and continue to influence stock prices for some time thereafter.

That stock markets quickly digest all new public information about firms and transmit it rapidly into changes in stock prices underlies a methodology now being used frequently in financial analysis. To provide some insights into how the equities market reacts to new information, financial economists have conducted "event studies," statistical techniques for analyzing the pattern of stock prices and returns when a special event occurs.

Event studies offer insight into such issues as the extent to which shareholders of acquired firms gain abnormal returns during mergers, and the extent to which bad news affects banks'

*Robert Schweitzer is an Associate Professor of Finance at the University of Delaware. He wrote this article while he was a Visiting Scholar in the Research Department of the Federal Reserve Bank of Philadelphia.

stock returns. Some of these studies have implications for how forthcoming regulatory and market changes will affect banking firms.

The methodology of event studies may appear complicated, but the basic idea is quite simple. Many such studies have been conducted to analyze specific events in both the corporate finance and banking fields. A review of some of these studies shows how much stock returns can change in response to new information about a group of firms or a particular industry.

THE METHODOLOGY
OF EVENT STUDIES

Event studies examine the stock returns for some specific firms (or for an industry) before and after the announcement of a special event—a merger, say. The returns for a certain holding period are calculated by adding the stock's dividend for the period to the change in the stock's price (a capital gain or loss) and dividing by the initial stock price. The capital gain (or loss) is included, since the investor could realize this gain (or loss) by selling the stock. Changes in the stock's price, then, have a major effect on the stock's returns.

News of a significant event could alter the pattern of stock returns for a firm (or industry). Suppose an event is taken as good news—that is, investors believe the event portends a bright future for the firm. The firm's stock price will increase as a result. This price increase represents a capital gain, which raises the return on the firm's stock.

But the stock returns might have changed for other reasons. The stock's price, and hence the returns, could have changed just from the overall movement in the stock market itself. The magnitude of this change will depend on the degree to which the firm's stock moves with the overall market. Stock analysts report that some stocks move almost in a one-to-one relationship with the stock market, while others do not move with the market at all. The

difficult part of event studies is to make adjustments for overall movements of the stock market, as well as for other events unrelated to the specific announcement under study. To do so, event studies follow four basic steps.

Identification of the Event. The first step is to identify the event and the date on which it occurred. Usually, the event of interest is a single, one-time occurrence—a merger of two firms, for example. Other event studies investigate the impact on a group of firms (or on a specific industry) of a frequently occurring event, such as earnings announcements. Compared to studies of one-time events, this second type usually provides more reliable results because it covers a group of companies over different periods. If the results are the same for different firms at different points in time, we can be more confident of the event's impact.

Estimation of Abnormal Returns. The event-study methodology calls for examining the returns on a firm's stock around the date selected and separating out the portion of the total returns that is a reaction to the event. Part of the returns on a firm's stock reflects ups or downs in the overall stock market. The remainder reflects the unexpected event.

To separate the general movement of stock returns from an individual stock's return, economists calculate what are called "abnormal returns." Abnormal returns, also called "excess returns," represent the firm's return after subtracting out returns attributable to overall movements of the stock market.

Statistical models of the firm's stock returns are used to determine "normal returns"—an estimate of the firm's returns in the absence of the event. The estimated normal returns are subtracted from the actual returns, with the difference being the abnormal returns. (For details on the approaches to estimating normal returns, see *Estimating Returns*, p. 25.) The pattern of the abnormal returns should show the event's impact, if there is one.

Grouping of the Abnormal Returns. Once obtained, the abnormal returns for the firms under study are grouped for analysis. The usual approach is to calculate the cross-section average and cumulative abnormal returns for the firms. The cross-section average abnormal returns are calculated by summing the abnormal returns and dividing by the number of firms in the study; the averages take into account the possibility that the event may have different impacts on the firms in the sample. (Using data for many firms provides evidence as to whether the impact of the event is more than just a one-time occurrence for a single firm.) Cumulative abnormal returns, representing the sum of the average abnormal returns to a point in time, show the impact of the event over time. If the equities market does not anticipate an event, the cumulative average abnormal returns up to the event date should be approximately zero.

In Figure 1, Panel A shows what the cumulative abnormal returns would look like for an event that has a one-time positive impact on stock returns. The cumulative abnormal returns are zero until the event date, plotted as Day 0; on the event date, the abnormal returns jump. Panel B, on the other hand, shows the event having a one-time negative impact. In both panels, however, the event has a lasting effect in that the cumulative abnormal returns do not return to zero. If the event is anticipated, the pattern of cumulative abnormal returns would look like Panel C; here, the returns start to move up several days before the event date, then jump on the event date.

Analysis of the Data. The final step in the event-study process is to interpret the abnormal returns data. The examples plotted in Figure 1 are not taken from actual data. But the data plotted in Figures 2 and 3 (pp. 20 and 21) are from actual, and fairly typical, event studies. In Figure 2, we see the impact of a decision in a major lawsuit on two firms' abnormal returns. In Panel B, the cumulative abnormal

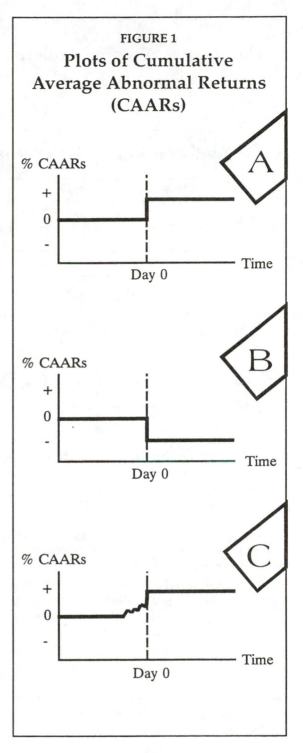

FIGURE 1

Plots of Cumulative Average Abnormal Returns (CAARs)

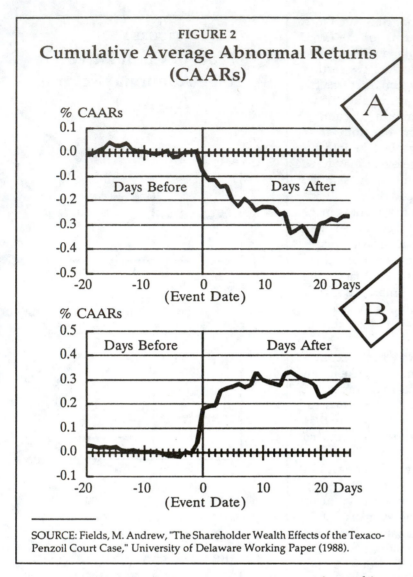

FIGURE 2
Cumulative Average Abnormal Returns (CAARs)

SOURCE: Fields, M. Andrew, "The Shareholder Wealth Effects of the Texaco-Penzoil Court Case," University of Delaware Working Paper (1988).

turns indicating that the event has a positive effect on stock returns for one group of banks. Focusing on the event date, Day 0, we see that the returns tend to increase about 27 days before the event and that the positive effect is still present 30 days after the event. That the pattern of returns increases before the event indicates that the market anticipated this event.

The bottom panel of Figure 3 shows the pattern of returns that might develop if the event had a negative impact on the stock of another group of banks. Note that the cumulative returns drop sharply before the event date. This pattern indicates that the market reacted negatively to the event even before it was announced.

After examining the plot of the abnormal returns, financial economists then ask whether the pattern of returns is statistically significant or whether it is attributable to chance. To arrive at this answer, economists perform statistical tests on the abnormal returns data, seeking evidence to support their financial theories about the event's economic significance.[1]

Shortcomings of the Event-Study Approach. The event-study approach is not without its

returns show that the decision has a positive impact on the one firm's stock. On the other hand, Panel A shows a negative impact on the stock of the other firm.

Figure 3 shows the impacts, on two different groups of banks, of a regulatory change—an anticipated event. The cumulative abnormal returns are plotted for 30 days before and after the event, itself shown as Day 0. The top panel of Figure 3 shows cumulative abnormal re-

---

[1]The details of the statistical tests are presented in Brown and Warner (1980) and (1985).

critics. Financial economists cite several shortcomings. First, if researchers are unable to identify the exact event date, they could end up looking at the wrong pattern of abnormal returns and attribute, incorrectly, a stock's response to a specific event. Then again, they may not observe any trend in the pattern of returns at all.

In some event studies, establishing the exact date of the event can be very difficult. In studies of legislative events, for example, financial economists generally have trouble determining which date to focus on. New laws are often discussed before they are introduced, and there is usually a considerable period of debate. Moreover, the impact of the legislative change, because of its newsworthiness, will be recognized by investors and affect stock prices even before the bill actually becomes law. A way around this problem is to look at an event "window" framing the possible event date within a period of several days.

A second shortcoming is data contamination by other events, which makes the results of event studies difficult to interpret. The confounding of several events often enters into event studies, particularly when the event date is difficult to determine. For example, we might study the effect on firms' stock prices of announcements of unexpected earnings changes. But if some of the firms were involved in

FIGURE 3
Cumulative Average Abnormal Returns (CAARs)

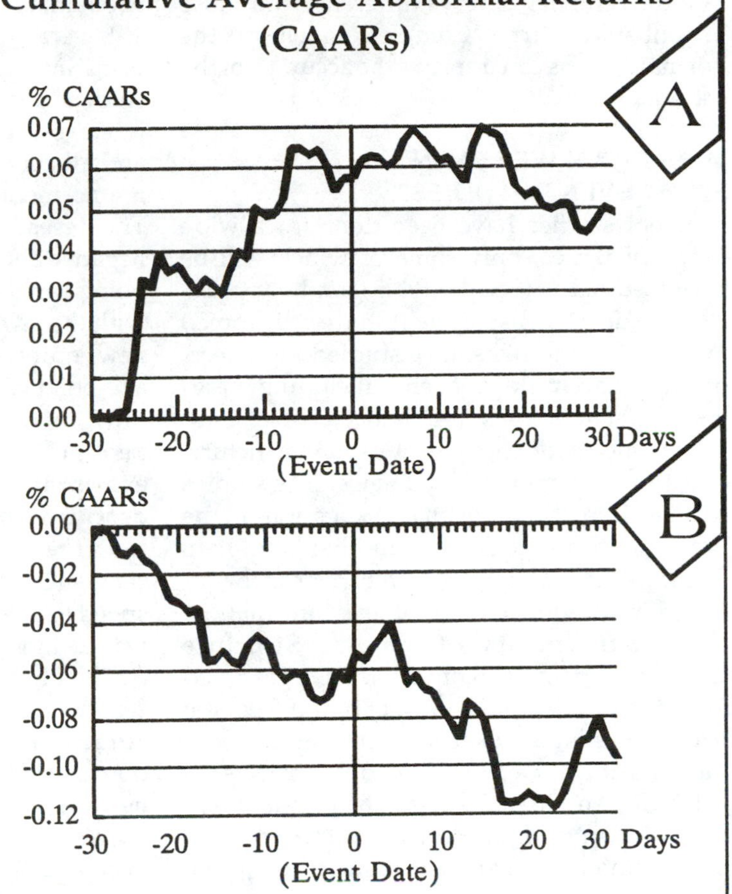

SOURCE: Black, Harold, M. Andrew Fields, and Robert Schweitzer, "Changes in Interstate Banking Laws: The Impact on Shareholder Wealth," Working Paper #88-16, Federal Reserve Bank of Philadelphia (November 1988).

mergers around the same time as the unexpected earnings announcements, it would be difficult to determine if the abnormal returns were attributable to the merger or to the unexpected earnings announcements.

The third shortcoming is the difficulty of estimating what the firm's normal returns would be in the absence of the event itself. The firm's stock price could have changed because of factors unrelated to the market's movement or to the event itself. For example, banks' stock prices may change because of general interest-rate movements in ways different from those of nonbanking firms. Complex modeling of the normal returns can improve the accuracy of the estimates.[2]

WHAT CAN WE LEARN FROM EVENT STUDIES?

Event studies have been done for a wide range of issues, only some of which will be reviewed here. (See the Bibliography, pp. 27-29, for a detailed list of event studies, by topic.) Financial economists have studied the effects of single and multiple events, including mergers and acquisitions, regulatory changes, announcements of changes in capital structure, and announcements of bad news. The studies covered here, focusing on investigations in the fields of corporate finance and banking, help illustrate how much stock returns can be affected by announcements of new information.

Announcements of Capital Structure Changes. Financial economists have grappled for some time with the issue of optimal capital structure—that is, whether a firm's capital structure (its mix of equity and debt) affects its value. Recent financial research indicates there might be an optimal capital structure for the firm.[3] Thus, changes in capital structure, which represent changes in a company's leverage position, could be reflected in a firm's stock returns. Firms employ financial leverage when they use debt, which has a fixed interest cost, rather than equity (common stock) to finance their operations. A firm's announcement of its intentions to issue new debt or equity therefore signals information to the financial markets about that firm to which investors might react.

Several event studies examine the impact of firms' intentions to issue new securities.[4] These studies test the impact on stock returns of leverage-changing capital structure adjustments, and all conclude that the market sees the announcement to issue new equity as bad news. The research shows statistically significant negative abnormal returns (about 3 percentage points, on the announcement date) associated with the leverage-decreasing events of selling new equity or repurchasing debt. A 3-percentage-point change would mean, for example, a drop in returns from, say, 11 percent to 8 percent. The research on leverage-increasing events, such as the announcement to issue new debt, is inconclusive. Most of these studies report results that are not statistically significant, suggesting that the market does not respond to leverage-increasing events in the same way as it does to leverage-decreasing events.

The impact of capital structure changes on stock returns for bank holding companies has attracted recent attention because of the adoption of risk-based capital standards. These new capital standards will require bank holding companies (BHCs) to hold different amounts of capital based on the riskiness of their assets and off-balance-sheet activities.[5] To meet these new capital-to-asset ratio standards, some BHCs will be required to issue new equity.

---

[2]Kane and Unal (1988) discuss the problems of estimating normal returns and offer solutions involving more advanced techniques.

[3]For more details on the optimal capital structure literature, see Thomas Copeland and Fred Weston, *Financial Theory and Corporate Policy*, 3rd edition, chapters 13 and 14 (Reading, MA: Addison-Wesley Publishing Co., 1988).

[4]See Kolodny and Suhler (1985), Masulis and Korwar (1985), Asquith and Mullins (1986), and Mikkelson and Partch (1986).

[5]The details of the new risk-based capital standards are presented in Robert Avery and Allen Berger, "Risk-Based Capital and Off-Balance-Sheet Activities," Finance and Economics Discussion Series (FEDS) #35, Board of Governors of the Federal Reserve (1988); and Jeffrey Bardos, "The Risk-Based Capital Agreement: A Further Step Towards Policy Convergence," Federal Reserve Bank of New York *Quarterly Review* (Winter 1987-88) pp. 26-34.

Applying the event-study approach to returns for 36 major bank holding companies, James Wansley and Upinder Dhillon (forthcoming) tested the impact of announcements by major bank holding companies about adjustments in their capital structure. Their results showed that banks' stock returns display the same negative reaction to new equity issues that was found for industrial firms. However, the negative reaction reported for banks was only around 1.5 percentage points, compared to 3 percentage points for industrial firms. The size of the negative reaction for banks, though, is closer to the negative reaction of almost 1 percentage point that Paul Asquith and David Mullins (1986) reported for utility firms.

Mergers and Acquisitions. Event studies have also been used to analyze the impact of mergers on firms' returns. Research by Michael Jensen and Richard Ruback (1983) shows that the shareholders of targeted firms gain substantial, and statistically significant, positive abnormal returns of almost 30 percentage points. In the case of unsuccessful merger attempts, shareholders of targeted firms gained some positive returns when the merger was initially announced, but lost these gains when it became clear that the merger would not go through. As for the bidding or acquiring firms, studies yield no evidence that mergers increase their returns.

The effect of interstate bank mergers on banks' stock returns was investigated by Jack Trifts and Kevin Scanlon (1987), who report significant positive abnormal returns for the acquired or target banks. The share prices of acquired banks, in fact, were found to increase around 20 percent. For the acquiring banks, however, the research failed to show significant abnormal returns, as was the case for industrial firms.

In a study that used a sample larger than that of Trifts and Scanlon, Marcia Cornett and Sankar De (1988) studied 153 bank merger bids and reported significant positive abnormal returns both for the target bank and for the bidding bank. They reported a gain of 9 percent for shareholders of the acquired banks—not nearly as large as the 20 percent increase in share price reported by Trifts and Scanlon. Nonetheless, the evidence is strong and very convincing that shareholders of acquired banks do gain in interstate bank mergers.

Bank Regulatory Changes. Because changes in laws and regulations can influence the way firms operate and thus affect firms' earnings, they could alter firms' abnormal returns. Larry Dann and Christopher James (1982) investigated the removal of deposit interest rate ceilings on the stock prices of stock-owned S&Ls. They detected a negative cumulative abnormal return of 8 percentage points 15 days after the change in interest rate ceilings. This is not surprising, since thrift institutions received net benefits from regulated deposit rates in the form of a lower cost of funds. As a result, the benefits of these reduced-cost deposits should have been capitalized in thrifts' share prices; thus, when deposit rate ceilings were removed, thrifts' share prices fell.

In another study focusing on the banking industry, Michael Smirlock (1984) examined the removal of the ceilings on deposit interest rates in the 1970-78 period to see if bank stock returns reacted to this deregulatory event. Using a data set of 17 large banks listed on the major stock exchanges, Smirlock found that bank stock returns were unaffected by the removal of interest rate ceilings. This finding is in contrast to the Dann and James results for S&Ls; however, we must remember that this study focused on larger banks, which were not as dependent on rate-ceiling-protected deposits for funding.

Bad-News Announcements in Banking. When a firm faces some bad news that substantially alters the prospects for its earnings or its riskiness, investors typically react quickly by bidding down the price of its stock. But not all bad news affects firms' stock prices to the same degree. Analysts have begun to use event studies to determine the extent of stock returns' reactions to announcements of bad news. Many examples of bad-news events can be found in the banking literature. Looking at three different bank failures—U.S. National Bank of San Diego in 1973, Franklin National Bank of New York in 1974, and Hamilton National Bank of Tennessee in 1976—Joseph Aharony and Itzhak Swary (1983) assessed the reaction of bank stock returns using a data sample of other banks' stock returns. The sample included 73 commercial banks: the 12 money-center banks, 31 medium-sized banks (with total deposits of around $5 billion), and 30 smaller banks (total deposits around $1 billion). The stock prices of these banks showed little response to the announcement of the three bank failures.

Later, Robert Lamy and G. Rodney Thompson (1986) studied the announcement effects associated with the 1982 failure of Penn Square Bank of Oklahoma. They reported a significant negative abnormal return of about 1 percentage point, on the day Penn Square was closed, for a sample of 54 major banks all traded on the New York or American stock exchanges—a result that could be linked to the market's perception that Penn Square, at the time of its failure, had complex lending relationships with many money-center banks. Thus, the failure of Penn Square, though only a medium-sized bank, had adverse implications simply because of its relationships with other, much larger banks.

In another study, Swary (1986) investigated the market's reaction to the bad-news announcement in 1984 that Continental Illinois National Bank was in financial distress. This event study, conducted on a portfolio of large banks, found significant negative abnormal returns (approximately 3 percentage points) following the news of Continental's problems. These returns could be explained by investors' downward valuation of other banks' stock. This revaluation might have occurred because in-vestors believed that depositors, especially uninsured depositors, would have less confidence in major banks, and this loss of confidence would increase the cost of funds for these banks. An increase in their cost of funds would put downward pressure on banks' earnings.

Another bad-news event that attracted considerable attention was Citicorp's announcement in 1987 that it had increased its loan-loss reserves to offset potential defaults on its Latin American loans. Theoharry Grammatikos and Anthony Saunders (1988) studied the impact of this event and the announcements made subsequently by other major American banks having large Latin American loan portfolios. Using a sample of 112 U.S. banks, the researchers found that the Citicorp announcement had only a weak negative effect on other banks' returns.[6]

Meanwhile, another study, conducted on the 12 major money-center banks by Jeff Madura and William McDaniel (forthcoming), showed that the market for bank stocks had anticipated the Citicorp announcement. In yet another study, by James Musumeci and Joseph Sinkey (1988), the effect of the announcement was found to be significantly positive for Citicorp and a sample of 25 large bank holding companies. All these studies show that Citicorp's announcement had effects on other major banks much like previous studies showing the news of bank failures in the 1980s having an effect on major banks.

SUMMARY

Event studies such as those just described provide investors, financial managers, and regulators with new data about how firms' stocks behave and about how quickly new

---

[6]The effect of subsequent announcements by other banks, however, was found to differ across banks in the sample; some experienced large negative abnormal returns while others had positive abnormal returns. The study therefore reports that no general conclusions can be drawn.

information affects firms' stock returns. Such studies have helped document the extent to which the shareholders of acquired firms or acquired banks gain abnormal returns in mergers. They also have helped identify and quantify cases in which bad news affecting one bank or group of banks has had so-called contagion effects on other banks.

Event-study research might prove useful as well in helping to assess the impact on bank holding companies' stock prices when some BHCs issue new capital to meet the new risk-based capital standards. All these examples of event studies suggest that the methodology will likely continue to have widespread uses in the fields of banking and finance.

Estimating Returns

To conduct an event study, the analyst must measure a security's performance against a benchmark. The benchmark is usually the return that the security would have achieved had the event not occurred. Thus, the key to this analysis is to determine a model of the return-generating process for the security in question.

Several methods have been used to model the return-generating process. The simplest way is by mean-adjusted returns. Under this approach the abnormal returns would be:

$$AR_{jt} = R_{jt} - \bar{R}_j \tag{1}$$

where:

AR_{jt} is the abnormal return on the security of firm j in time period t,

R_{jt} is the observed return on the security of firm j in time period t, and

$\bar{R}_j$ is the mean return for the security of firm j over a given sample period.

This technique assumes that the expected returns for a firm's security are constant and equal to the historical average return and, thus, that any changes from the mean should be abnormal returns.

Another simple approach involves market-adjusted returns. Here it is assumed that the abnormal returns are those that are above the market return. Under this approach the abnormal returns would be:

$$AR_{jt} = R_{jt} - R_{mt} \tag{2}$$

where R_{mt} is the return on the market portfolio in time period t. Financial economists usually use an index return, such as the Standard & Poor's 500-stock index, for the market return.

Most event studies employ a more complicated return-generating process called the market model. In this model the returns for a security are assumed to be linearly related to the returns on the market. The market model requires the analyst to estimate the parameters of the following equation using regression analysis:

$$R_{jt} = \alpha + \beta R_{mt} + \varepsilon_{jt} \tag{3}$$

where α, β are regression parameters, and ε_{jt} is the error term for time period t. Once these regression parameters are estimated, the security's normal returns (called $\hat{R}_{jt}$) are then estimated using the estimated parameters $(\hat{\alpha}, \hat{\beta})$ and the return on the market by substituting into equation (3)

$(R_{jt} = \hat{\alpha} + \hat{\beta} R_{mt})$. The abnormal returns are the difference between the estimated normal returns to the actual:

$$AR_{jt} = R_{jt} - \hat{R}_{jt} \qquad (4)$$

where $\hat{R}_{jt}$ is the estimated return for time period t from the regression equation.* This approach recognizes that few stocks move one-for-one with the overall market.

Once the abnormal returns have been estimated, the cross-section average abnormal returns are then calculated. They are:

$$AAR_t = \sum_{j=1}^{N} AR_{jt} / N \qquad (5)$$

where AAR_t is the average abnormal return for time period t, and N is the number of firms in the study. The average abnormal returns are then summed to find the cumulative average abnormal returns. They are:

$$CAAR_t = AAR_t + CAAR_{t-1} \qquad (6)$$

where $CAAR_t$ is the cumulative average abnormal return for time period t.

---

*For more details on these approaches, see Brown and Warner (1980) and (1985).

Selected Bibliography

This selected bibliography includes examples of event studies from the corporate finance and banking literature. The selections are organized by type of event.

Bad-News Events

Grammatikos, Theoharry, and Anthony Saunders. "Additions to Bank Loan-Loss Reserves: Good News or Bad News?," New York University Working Paper (March 1988).

Madura, Jeff, and William McDaniel. "Market Reaction to Increased Loan-Loss Reserves at Money-Center Banks," *Journal of Financial Services Research* (forthcoming).

Musumeci, James, and Joseph Sinkey. "The International Debt Crisis and the Signalling Content of Bank Loan-Loss-Reserve Decisions," University of Georgia Working Paper (August 1988).

Pruitt, Stephen, and David Peterson. "Security Price Reactions Around Product Recall Announcements," *Journal of Financial Research* 9 (Summer 1986) pp. 113-22.

Capital Structure

Asquith, Paul, and David Mullins. "Equity Issues and Offering Dilution," *Journal of Financial Economics* 15 (January/February 1986) pp. 61-89.

Keeley, Michael. "The Stock Price Effects of Bank Holding Company Securities Issuance," Federal Reserve Bank of San Francisco *Economic Review* (Winter 1989) pp. 3-19.

Kolodny, Richard, and Diane Rizzuto Suhler. "Changes in Capital Structure, New Equity Issues, and Scale Effects," *Journal of Financial Research* 8 (Summer 1985) pp. 127-136.

Masulis, Ronald, and Ashok Korwar. "Seasoned Equity Offerings: An Empirical Investigation," *Journal of Financial Economics* 15 (January/February 1986) pp. 91-118.

Mikkelson, Wayne, and M. Megan Partch. "Valuation Effects of Security Offerings and the Issuance Process," *Journal of Financial Economics* 15 (January/February 1986) pp. 31-60.

Modigliani, Franco, and Merton Miller. "The Cost of Capital, Corporation Finance, and the Theory of Investment," *American Economic Review* 48 (June 1958) pp. 261-97.

Modigliani, Franco, and Merton Miller. "Corporate Income Taxes and the Cost of Capital: A Correction," *American Economic Review* 53 (June 1963) pp. 433-43.

Wansley, James, and Upinder Dhillon. "Determinants of Valuation Effects for Security Offerings of Commercial Bank Holding Companies," *Journal of Financial Research* (forthcoming).

Dividends and Earnings Announcements

Aharony, Joseph, and Itzhak Swary. "Quarterly Dividend and Earnings Announcements and Stockholders' Returns: An Empirical Analysis," *Journal of Finance* 35 (March 1980) pp. 1-12.

Asquith, Paul, and David Mullins. "The Impact of Initiating Dividend Payments on Shareholders' Wealth," *Journal of Business* 56 (January 1983) pp. 77-96.

Brickley, James. "Shareholder Wealth, Information Signaling and the Specially Designated Dividend: An Empirical Study," *Journal of Financial Economics* 12 (August 1983) pp. 187-209.

Fama, Eugene, and others. "The Adjustment of Stock Prices to New Information," *International Economic Review* 10 (February 1969) pp. 1-21.

Keen, Howard. "The Impact of a Dividend Cut Announcement on Bank Share Prices," *Journal of Bank Research* 13 (Winter 1983) pp. 274-81.

Myers, Stewart, and Nicholas Majluf. "Corporate Financing and Investment Decisions When Firms Have Information That Investors Do Not Have," *Journal of Financial Economics* 13 (June 1984) pp. 187-221.

Pettit, R. Richardson. "Dividend Announcements, Security Performance, and Capital Market Efficiency," *Journal of Finance* 27 (December 1972) pp. 993-1007.

Event-Study Methodology

Bowman, Robert. "Understanding and Conducting Event Studies," *Journal of Business Finance and Accounting* 10 (December 1983) pp. 561-84.

Brown, Stephen, and Jerold Warner. "Measuring Security Price Performance," *Journal of Financial Economics* 8 (September 1980) pp. 205-58.

Brown, Stephen, and Jerold Warner. "Using Daily Stock Returns: The Case of Event Studies," *Journal of Financial Economics* 14 (March 1985) pp. 3-31.

Kane, Edward, and Haluk Unal. "Change in Market Assessments of Deposit-Institution Riskiness," *Journal of Financial Services Research* 1 (June 1988) pp. 207-29.

Madura, Jeff. "Banking Event Studies: Synthesis and Directions for Future Research," Florida Atlantic University Working Paper (1988).

Mergers and Acquisitions

Cornett, Marcia, and Sankar De. "An Examination of Stock Market Reactions to Interstate Bank Mergers," Southern Methodist University Working Paper (September 1988).

Jensen, Michael, and Richard Ruback. "The Market for Corporate Control: The Scientific Evidence," *Journal of Financial Economics* 11 (April 1983) pp. 5-50.

Trifts, Jack, and Kevin Scanlon. "Interstate Bank Mergers: The Early Evidence," *Journal of Financial Research* 10 (Winter 1987) pp. 305-11.

Problem Banks

Aharony, Joseph, and Itzhak Swary. "Contagion Effects of Bank Failures: Evidence from Capital Markets," *Journal of Business* 56 (July 1983) pp. 305-22.

Lamy, Robert, and G. Rodney Thompson. "Penn Square, Problem Loans, and Insolvency Risk," *Journal of Financial Research* 9 (Summer 1986) pp. 103-11.

Swary, Itzhak. "Stock Market Reaction to Regulatory Action in the Continental Illinois Crisis," *Journal of Business* 59 (July 1986) pp. 451-73.

Regulation

Aharony, Joseph, and Itzhak Swary. "Effects of the 1970 Bank Holding Company Act: Evidence from Capital Markets," *Journal of Finance* 36 (September 1981) pp. 841-53.

Binder, John. "Measuring the Effects of Regulation with Stock Price Data," *Rand Journal of Economics* 16 (Summer 1985) pp. 167-83.

Dann, Larry, and Christopher James. "An Analysis of the Impact of Deposit Rate Ceilings on the Market Values of Thrift Institutions," *Journal of Finance* 37 (December 1982) pp. 1259-75.

Smirlock, Michael. "An Analysis of Bank Risk and Deposit Rate Ceiling: Evidence from the Capital Markets," *Journal of Monetary Economics* 13 (March 1984) pp. 195-210.

Strategic Decisions

Eisenbeis, Robert, Robert Harris, and Josef Lakonishok. "Benefits of Bank Diversification: The Evidence from Shareholder Returns," *Journal of Finance* 39 (July 1984) pp. 881-92.

Hite, Gailen, and James Owers. "Security Price Reactions Around Corporate Spin-off Announcements," *Journal of Financial Economics* 12 (December 1983) pp. 409-36.

McConnell, John, and Chris Muscarella. "Corporate Capital Expenditure Decisions and the Market Value of the Firm," *Journal of Financial Economics* 14 (September 1985) pp. 399-422.

Saunders, Anthony, and Michael Smirlock. "Intra- and Interindustry Effects of Bank Securities Market Activities: The Case of Discount Brokerage," *Journal of Financial and Quantitative Analysis* 22 (December 1987) pp. 467-82.

Schipper, Katherine, and Abbie Smith. "Effects of Recontracting on Shareholder Wealth: The Case of Voluntary Spin-offs," *Journal of Financial Economics* 12 (December 1983) pp. 437-67.

Zaima, Janis, and Douglas Hearth. "The Wealth Effects of Voluntary Selloffs: Implications for Divesting and Acquiring Firms," *Journal of Financial Research* 8 (Fall 1985) pp. 227-36.

Article 16

Why Are So Many
New Stock Issues Underpriced?

*Anthony Saunders**

Each year hundreds of small firms approach the capital market to issue equity for the first time. These firms are usually growing so fast, or have so many profitable investment projects available to them, that traditional sources of funds (bank loans, retained earnings, and the owners' own equity) are often insufficient to finance their expansion.

Because of this need for finance at a crucial stage in their growth, it is important for these firms that the prices of their shares reflect the

*Anthony Saunders is a Professor of Finance at New York University's Stern School of Business. He wrote this article while he was a Research Adviser to the Federal Reserve Bank of Philadelphia.

true value of company assets or growth opportunities. In particular, if their shares are sold too cheaply, these firms will have raised less capital than was warranted by the intrinsic values of their assets. In other words, their shares will have been "underpriced."

Considerable evidence shows that new or initial public equity offerings (IPOs) are underpriced on *average*. That is, the prices of firms' shares offered to the public for the first time are, on average, set below the prices investors appear willing to pay when the stocks start trading in the secondary market. That is, in the parlance of investment bankers, small firms appear to leave behind considerable "money on the table" at the time of a new issue.

Why small firms raise fewer funds in the new-issue process than the market indicates they should is a crucial public policy issue. Clearly, some degree of market imperfection or lack of competition could cause such an outcome. For example, if, by restricting commercial banks' participation in the market, the Glass-Steagall Act of 1933 has allowed investment bankers to enjoy a type of monopoly (market) power over new equity-issuing firms, then this would suffice to explain underpricing. Alternatively, underpricing may be the premium the issuing firm must pay for having little information about itself to offer potential investors. In that case, underpricing would have little to do with the regulatory structure of the investment banking industry.

Let's examine the reasons for IPO underpricing and evaluate the degree to which underpricing is due to Glass-Steagall restrictions. What is the evidence on the degree of underpricing of U.S. IPOs? What are the various explanations for underpricing? And what are the implications of these explanations, and of the associated empirical evidence, for commercial and investment bank regulation?

EVIDENCE ON UNDERPRICING

In "firm commitment" underwriting ("firm" in that the investment banker guarantees the price), an investment banker (and his syndicate) will undertake to buy the whole new issue of a firm at one price (the *bid* price, or BP) and seek to resell the issue to outside investors at another price (the *offer* price, or OP). In doing so, the investment banker offers a valuable risk-management service to the issuing firm by guaranteeing to purchase 100 percent of the new issue at the bid price (BP). The return for the investment banker in bearing underwriting risk—that is, the risk that investors will demand less than 100 percent of the issue when it is reoffered for sale to the market—is the spread between the public offer price and the bid price (OP - BP) plus fees and commissions. (Here,

and throughout this article, the term "investor" refers to those who buy shares through the investment banker at the offer price.) Thus, the investment banker's spread plus fees and commissions may be viewed as the *direct* cost of going public.

However, there is also potentially an *indirect* cost of going public, measured by the degree to which the issue is underpriced. For example, if the BP is $5 per share and the OP is $5.25 per share, then the underwriter's spread is 25 cents per share. However, suppose that on the first day of trading in the secondary market the share price (P) closes at $7 per share. This indicates that the share has been underpriced in the new-issue process and that, potentially, the firm might have raised as much as $7 per share had it been priced "correctly." This implies that the issuing firm has borne an additional *indirect* new-issue cost of $1.75 per share ($7.00 - $5.25), because the investment banker has set the offer price below the price the market was willing to pay on the first day of trading.

Thus, more formally, the "raw" percentage degree of underpricing (UP) of an IPO can be defined as:

(1) $UP = [(P - OP) / OP] \times 100$

where:

> OP = offer price of the IPO
> P = price observed at the end of either the first trading day, week, or month

If UP is positive, the issue has been underpriced; if UP is zero, the issue is accurately priced; and if UP is negative, it has been overpriced. The expression for UP is also the expression for a percentage rate of return. Thus, equation (1) can be viewed as the one-day (or one-week or one-month) *initial* return on buying an IPO (that is, UP = R, the initial return on the stock).

Returns calculated by equation (1) are deemed raw returns. However, researchers also compute excess (market-adjusted) returns, as well. The reasons for this are easy to see. Given a lag between the setting of the offer price and the beginning of trading on an exchange (anywhere from one day to two weeks or more), the price observed in the market on the first day of trading may be high (low) relative to the offer price simply because the stock market as a whole has risen (fallen) over this period. Thus, in analyzing underpricing, reseachers need to control for the performance of the stock market in general. More specifically:

$$(2) \qquad R_m = [(I_1 - I_0) / I_0] \times 100$$

where:

R_m = return on the market portfolio

I_1 = level of the general market share index at the time of listing (first day, first week, or first month)

I_0 = level of the market share index at the time offer is announced

If R_m is positive, the market has been going up in the time between the setting of the offer price and the listing of the stock on the stock exchange. If R_m is negative, the market has been falling. Excess market or risk-adjusted initial returns (EX) can therefore be defined as:[1]

$$(3) \qquad EX = R - R_m$$

According to equation (3), underpricing occurs only when R is greater than R_m.

The findings of 22 studies that examine the degree of underpricing are summarized in the table on p. 10. Although the time periods, sample sizes, and ways of calculating initial returns (especially raw versus market-adjusted) differ widely across these studies, each finds underpricing on average. For example, studies that use a one-week period to calculate the difference between the offer price and the market price of an IPO find underpricing ranging from 5.9 percent to as much as 48.4 percent.[2]

Thus, an important empirical fact is that U.S. IPOs are underpriced on average, resulting in small firms raising less capital than is justified by the markets' ex post valuation of their shares.

WHY ARE NEW ISSUES UNDERPRICED?

Several reasons have been proposed in the institutional, finance, and economics literature as to why underpricing occurs. Although this article will not discuss all the proposed reasons, it concentrates on four views that have received much publicity. The first view attributes underpricing to "monopoly power" enjoyed by investment bankers. The second regards Securities and Exchange Commission regulations as the primary cause. And the third and fourth see underpricing as a problem of imperfect information among contracting parties—especially between investors and issuers.

---

[1] For a detailed discussion of excess returns, see Robert Schweitzer, "How Do Stock Returns React to Special Events?" this *Business Review* (July/August 1989) pp. 17-29. For IPOs, researchers adjust the initial return on the stock by deducting the return on the market. This is equivalent to assuming that a new IPO's returns move exactly with the market's. That is, they have a unit degree of systematic risk (or their β is 1). The reason for this assumption is that since IPOs have no past history of returns, one cannot estimate directly the IPO's β at the time of issue. The only researcher

who has tried to address this problem was Ibbotson (1975), who developed an ingenious method of constructing synthetic β's for IPOs.

[2] It should be noted that these are one week's returns and are thus very large. These underpricing "costs" swamp the direct costs of a new issue, which are, on average, in the range of 2 to 5 percent of the issue's dollar size.

The Monopoly Power of Underwriters. One possible explanation for pervasive underpricing is the monopoly power the investment banker enjoys over the issuer.[3] Given that commercial banks are barred from entering into corporate equity underwriting (a result of the Glass-Steagall Act, which effectively separated commercial banking from investment banking), investment bankers may have a degree of monopoly power that they use to earn "rents" by underpricing new issues. Of course, competition among investment banks would limit the extent of this monopoly power.

But how real is this monopoly power? Compared to U.S. commercial banks, U.S. noncommercial banking firms and foreign banks have always faced fewer restrictions on entry into investment banking. Moreover, thrifts also can enter investment banking. In recent years, for example, nonbank firms such as General Electric and Prudential have entered the investment banking industry via acquisitions, as has Franklin Savings Bank, a thrift. This potential competition presumably places a limit on the degree of monopoly power enjoyed by investment bankers.

In addition, foreign banks were not subject to Glass-Steagall regulations until passage of the International Banking Act of 1978. Even then, those already possessing investment banking powers had them grandfathered. The emphasis on investment banks is due to their traditional dominance of the underwriting market and to their potential economies of scope (cost savings from offering a combination of services) in extending to their underwriting customers a broader range of financial services.

If investment bankers have monopoly power

over the new issuer, they might use it to increase both the spread between the offer price and bid price (the underwriters' spread) as well as the degree to which the offer price is set below the markets' true valuation (P). A monopolist investment banker might have the incentive to underprice, since by doing so he can increase the probability of being able to sell the whole issue to outside investors (thereby minimizing his underwriting risk) while earning a high investment banking spread (OP - BP) on the issue.[4]

Clearly, if this was the prime reason for underpricing, it would tend to make a case for allowing commercial banks into the underwriting business. This argument would be based on the expectation that pro-competitive effects would reduce the average degree of underpricing.[5] But this argument would, of

---

[3]For a discussion of the reasons for and effects of investment bankers' potential monopoly power, see Ibbotson (1975) and Pugel and White (1984).

---

[4]Implicitly, this argument presumes that investment bankers are risk-averse. This is reasonable, given the private nature of many companies, their limited capital bases, and the potential for a large loss if they take a "big hit" (loss) on an underwriting. For example, many U.S. investment bankers suffered significant losses in underwriting an issue of British Petroleum shares at the time of the October 1987 stock market crash.

[5]A different monopoly-based argument, advanced in Baron (1982), is that investment bankers possess monopoly power through their private access to *information* about the likely size of the demand for a new issue. Since issuers are viewed as being relatively uninformed about the nature of this demand, they can easily be exploited by the investment banker. Indeed, since the issuer has no way of knowing ex ante the size of investor demand, the underwriter has an incentive to save resources on distribution and search ("shirking") by simply underpricing enough to ensure that the whole issue is sold. In this context, the presence of potential competitors, such as commercial banks, and the importance of maintaining a reputation might be viewed as potential controls on the investment bankers' temptation to shirk. This presumes, however, that commercial banks, if they entered into underwriting, have the same abilities to "place" (sell to investors) a new issue as investment bankers do. In reality, it might take commercial bankers a number of years to build up the same placement powers.

course, be tempered by the need to maintain safety and soundness of the banking system, which could be lessened if the spread (P - OP) is small enough to risk inability to sell the entire issue.[6]

Due-Diligence Insurance. A second reason given for why underwriters underprice IPOs is the fear of potential legal problems stemming from overpriced issues. Underwriters, along with company directors, are required to exercise "due diligence" in ensuring the accuracy of the information contained in the prospectus they offer to investors.[7] Since passage of the Securities Acts of 1933 and 1934, both underwriters and directors may be held legally responsible under SEC regulations for the accuracy of this information.

Investors who end up holding heavily overpriced issues may well have an incentive to sue the underwriter and/or the company directors for publishing misleading or incomplete information in the prospectus. The investors could contend they were misled into believing this was a "good" issue rather than a "bad" one. To avoid any negative legal effects, as well as adverse publicity and damage to reputation, a risk-averse underwriter may try to keep investors happy by persistently underpricing IPOs. Hence, some researchers believe that the legal penalties for due-diligence failures are what have created incentives for investment bankers to underprice.

The Problem of the "Winner's Curse." The academic literature has paid a great deal of attention to a theory first advanced by Rock (1986) and extended by Beatty and Ritter (1986) and McStay (1987), among others. This theory considers underpricing as a competitive outcome in an IPO market in which some investors are viewed as informed while a larger group is viewed as uninformed. As a result, underpricing is directly related to the degree of information imperfection—or, more specifically, information asymmetry—in the capital market and to the costs of collecting information. Both this theory and the one that follows view underpricing as a way of resolving the problem of costly information collection.

In Rock's model, there are two types of IPOs: good issues and bad issues. Informed investors, defined as those who expend resources collecting information on IPOs, will bid only for those issues that are good. (This search effort is assumed to allow the informed investor to assess exactly the true value of the IPO.) Those investors who are uninformed, however, will not engage in expensive search, but rather will bid randomly across all issues, good and bad. It is further assumed that informed investors are never sufficiently large as a group to be able to purchase a whole issue.

First, consider a good issue. In this case, both informed and uninformed investors will bid for the issue (the uninformed in a random manner). Because both groups bid for the issue, it is likely to be oversubscribed, so that any single *individual* bidder (informed or uninformed) will get fewer shares than he bid for. Thus, for good issues, uninformed investors get only partial allotments.

Next, consider bad issues. In this case, informed investors will not bid at all. The only bidders will be the uninformed. Moreover, owing to the absence of competing informed bidders, any individual bidder will more likely achieve his full allotment (or a higher probability of an allotment). That is, the uninformed bidder suffers from the problem of the "winner's curse": he achieves a large allotment for bad IPOs and a small allotment for good IPOs.

Rock's argument is that, because of the winner's curse, IPOs have to be underpriced on average so as to produce an expected return for

---

[6] Since P is not known with certainty, a small spread (P - OP) risks occasional negative spreads, in which case the underwriting firm suffers a loss.

[7] See, for example, Tinic (1988).

the uninformed investor that is high enough to attract investment in IPOs regardless of whether the issue is good or bad.[8] That is, underpricing is a phenomenon perfectly consistent with competitive market conditions in a world of imperfect information flows. Thus, monopoly power is rejected as an argument explaining underpricing.

Underpricing as a Dynamic Strategy. In the most recent literature, underpricing is seen as a dynamic strategy employed by issuing firms to overcome the asymmetry of information between issuing firms and outside investors.[9] Implicitly, underpricing is viewed as a cost to be borne by the issuing firm's insiders to persuade investors to collect (or aggregate) information about the firm and in that way establish its true value in the secondary market. Moreover, the better the firm (a "good" issue), the more it will be underpriced relative to the bad issue.

Specifically, a good firm will underprice its issue to attract outside investors.[10] Investors (such as analysts) collect information about the firm and, in the secondary market, establish its true value above its offer price. The owners of the firm benefit from this strategy because once the true (higher) market value is established, the owners have an incentive to "cash in" by coming out with new (further) secondary offerings at the higher market price. Thus, the cost or losses of underpricing the IPO are offset by the benefits from cashing in on the secondary offering.[11]

By comparison, a bad firm—one that knows it is a bad firm—will have the opposite incentives. In particular, the firm may seek to price the IPO as high as possible, since it knows that once investors collect information and discover that it is a "bad" firm, its stock's price will fall on the secondary market.[12]

As in the Rock model, these types of dynamic-strategy models view underpricing as a phenomenon that is consistent with competition in a world of imperfect information among issuing firms and investors. The difference is that, here, IPO underpricing is viewed as a cost to be borne by good firms, which is offset by the revenue benefits from making a secondary ("seasoned") offering later on at a higher price.

IMPLICATIONS FOR BANK REGULATION

What do these models imply for bank regulation and, in particular, the Glass-Steagall Act? If underpricing is indeed due to information imperfections in the capital market—especially between firms and investors—it is difficult to see how commercial banks' entry into underwriting will have much effect, unless these banks somehow collect more information and alleviate the degree of information imperfection in the market. Since the modern theory of banking views banks as major collectors and users of information, increased production of information about small firms may indeed be a benefit from repealing Glass-Steagall.

However, a better test of whether Glass-

---

[8] Technically, the *conditional* expected return for the uninformed investor, across both good and bad issues, must be at least as great as the risk-free rate.

[9] See, for example, Chemmanur (1989) and Welch (1988).

[10] In these models, the investment banker plays a largely passive function, operating as an agent on behalf of the principal (the firm). The failure of the investment banker to take a more active role may be seen as a weakness of these information-based models.

---

[11] Welch (1988) offers preliminary evidence that these issues that are more underpriced tend to follow up more quickly with a secondary (seasoned) offering.

[12] This is not to imply that the bad firms necessarily overprice. However, the theory has the *aggregate* implication that the greater the porportion of good to bad issues in the market, the greater the degree of underpricing on *average*.

Steagall has undesirable costs is whether it confers monopoly power on existing investment banks that is reflected in the degree of underpricing. That is, what, if any, is the empirical evidence linking underpricing to the monopoly power of investment banks?

One implication of the monopoly-power hypothesis[13] is that an underwriter, because of his expertise and more precise knowledge of the issuing firm's true value, can save effort (shirk) by ensuring maximum sales through underpricing while still earning a high underwriting spread (OP - BP). However, even in a world of asymmetric information, presumably firms would learn that they are being exploited and, if competition exists, would switch to other underwriters. In contrast, monopoly power would imply that issuing firms would fare as well with one investment bank as with another and that underwriters could ignore all problems or considerations related to maintaining a reputation.

Beatty and Ritter (1986) have sought to test this reputation–monopoly power effect. That is, do investment bankers who heavily underprice in one period lose business from issuing firms in the next? Beatty and Ritter's results tended to confirm that the more an investment banker underpriced in one period, the greater his loss of business in the next—a result suggesting that monopoly power is temporary at best.

A second implication of the monopoly-power hypothesis is that the investment banker—to avoid risk—will have a greater incentive to underprice relatively risky issues so as to ensure maximum sales. For example, it can be argued that the more uncertain are firms' uses of the proceeds of the issue (for example, to pay

off existing debt, to develop new projects, and so on), the riskier the issue. Or, alternatively, the more variable the after-market returns on an issue—measured by the standard deviation of returns over a period subsequent to listing on the stock exchange—the riskier the issue. Thus, we would expect underpricing to increase as the number of potential uses of proceeds, and the volatility of its (expected) price in the after-market, grows.

Beatty and Ritter (1986) found a positive relationship between number of uses of proceeds and underpricing; Ritter (1984) and Miller and Reilly (1987) found a positive relationship between the standard deviation of after-market returns and the degree of underpricing. Both these results are consistent with the monopoly-power hypothesis; however, it *must* be noted that both findings are also consistent with the competitive-market, information-imperfection "winner's curse" theory of Rock (1986).[14]

A third potential implication of the monopoly-power model is that the degree of underpricing should have been less prior to passage of Glass-Steagall—that is, the pre-1933 *average* degree of underpricing should have been less than the post-1933 average degree. In a recent study, Tinic (1988) tested the degree of underpricing in the period 1923-30 and compared it with the period 1966-71. He found that underpricing was higher in the 1966-71 period. While Tinic interpreted these results as consistent with the due-diligence-insurance hypothesis—that is, the passage of the Securities Act of 1934, which forced investment banks to underprice to avoid potential lawsuits—they are also consistent with the monopoly-power hypothesis. That is, in a period preceding Glass-Steagall (when commercial banks had greater power to

---

[13] See Baron (1982), who developed a theory of investment banker monopoly power based on the inability of issuers to accurately monitor the investment bankers' effort in placing new shares with investors.

[14] That is, the greater the risk or uncertainty about the issue, the greater the cost of becoming informed and thus the greater the degree of underpricing required in equilibrium.

underwrite corporate securities),[15] the degree of underpricing was less than in a period following the Glass-Steagall separation of powers.

A fourth implication of the monopoly-power hypothesis is that IPOs of investment banks (for example, Morgan Stanley going public) should *not* be underpriced, since the investment bank brings its "own firm" public. Looking at 37 IPOs of investment banks that went public in the 1970-84 period and participated in the distribution of their own issues, Muscarella and Vetsuypens (1987) find an average degree of underpricing of *8 percent* on the first day of trading. At first sight this tends to contradict the monopoly-power hypothesis as the sole reason for underpricing; however, it could be argued that 8 percent underpricing is less

than the median or mean underpricing found in the majority of studies listed in the table below and that monopoly power may offer a partial explanation for underpricing.

Nevertheless, the results favoring monopoly power as the major determinant of new-issues underpricing appear somewhat weak. Indeed, the evidence is largely consistent with the existence of competitive markets in which investors have incomplete or imperfect infor-

[15]This was particularly true in 1927-33, when commercial banks had the same powers as investment banks. Since technology and the structure of the financial services industry are continuously changing, a more valid test might have been to compare underpricing in the period *immediately following* passage of the Glass-Steagall Act.

Initial Returns, According to Various Studies

Study	Sample Period	Sample Size	Initial Returns 1 Week	Initial Returns 1 Mo.
Reilly/Hatfield (1969)	1963-65	53	9.9%	8.7%
McDonald/Fisher (1972)	1969-70	142	28.5%	34.6%
Logue (1973)	1965-69	250	—	41.7%
Reilly (1973)	1966	62	9.9%	—
Neuberger/Hammond (1974)	1965-69	816	17.1%	19.1%
Ibbotson (1975)	1960-71	128	—	11.4%
Ibbotson/Jaffe (1975)	1960-70	2650	16.8%	—
Reilly (1978)	1972-75	486	10.9%	11.6%
Block/Stanley (1980)	1974-78	102	5.9%	3.3%
Neuberger/LaChapelle (1983)	1975-80	118	27.7%	33.6%
Ibbotson (1982)	1971-81	N/A	—	2.9%
Ritter (1984)	1960-82	5162	18.8%	—
	1977-82	1028	26.5%	—
	1980-81	325	48.4%	—
Giddy (1985)	1976-83	604	10.2%	—
John/Saunders (1986)	1976-82	78	—	8.5%
Beatty/Ritter (1986)	1981-82	545	14.1%	—
Chalk/Peavy (1986)	1974-82	440	13.8%	—
Ritter (1987)	1977-82			
Firm commitment		664	14.8%	—
Best efforts		364	47.8%	—
Miller/Reilly (1987)	1982-83	510	9.9%	—
Muscarella/Vetsuypens (1987)	1983-87	1184	—	7.6%

mation about new firms. While new issues did appear to be *less* underpriced before Glass-Steagall (consistent with the monopoly-power hypothesis), evidence suggests that those investment banks that excessively underprice today lose future business from prospective issuing firms and that investment banks' own IPOs are also underpriced on average (although less so than those of other firms). The gains from allowing commercial banks to compete directly with investment banks for corporate equity underwritings may come less from creating more potential competition than from collecting, producing, and disseminating more information about small firms in the new-issue process. This conclusion suggests that allowing banks into investment banking activities may indeed bring about price changes that benefit the public; however, those changes may be smaller and occur for different reasons than once thought.

REFERENCES

Baron, D.P. "A Model of the Demand for Investment Banking and Advising and Distribution Services for New Issues," *Journal of Finance* (1982) pp. 955-77.

Beatty, R., and J. Ritter. "Investment Banking, Reputation, and the Underpricing of Initial Public Offerings," *Journal of Financial Economics* (1986) pp. 213-32.

Block, S., and M. Stanley. "The Financial Characteristics and Price Movement Patterns of Companies Approaching the Unseasoned Securities Market in the Late 1970s," *Financial Management* (1980) pp. 30-36.

Chalk, A.J., and J.W. Peavy. "Understanding the Pricing of Initial Public Offerings," Southern Methodist University Working Paper 86-72 (1986).

Chemmanur, T.J. "The Pricing of Initial Public Offerings: A Dynamic Model With Information Production," mimeo, New York University (1989).

Giddy, I. "Is Equity Underwriting Risky for Commercial Bank Affiliates?" in I. Walter, ed., *Deregulating Wall Street* (New York: John Wiley, 1985).

Ibbotson, R.G. "Price Performance of Common Stock New Issues," *Journal of Financial Economics* 3 (1975) pp. 235-72.

Ibbotson, R.G. "Common Stock New Issues Revisited," Graduate School of Business, University of Chicago, Working Paper 84 (1982), unpublished.

Ibbotson, R.G., and J.J. Jaffe. "'Hot Issue' Markets," *Journal of Finance* 30 (1975) pp. 1027-42.

John, K., and A. Saunders. "The Efficiency of the Market for Initial Public Offerings: U.S. Experience 1976-1983," unpublished (1986).

Logue, D.E. "On the Pricing of Unseasoned New Issues, 1965-1969," *Journal of Financial and Quantitative Analysis* (1973) pp. 91-103.

McDonald, J.G., and A.K. Fisher. "New-Issue Stock Price Behavior," *Journal of Finance* (1972) pp. 97-102.

McStay, K.P. *The Efficiency of New Issue Markets*, Ph.D. thesis, Department of Economics, U.C.L.A. (1987).

Miller, R.E., and F.K. Reilly. "An Examination of Mispricing, Returns, and Uncertainty for Initial Public Offerings," *Financial Management* (1987) pp. 33-38.

Muscarella, C.J., and M.R. Vetsuypens. "A Simple Test of Baron's Model of IPO Underpricing," Southern Methodist University Working Paper 87-14 (1987a).

Muscarella, C.J., and M.R. Vetsuypens. "Initial Public Offerings and Information Asymmetry," Edwin L. Cox School of Business, Southern Methodist University, unpublished (1987b).

Neuberger, B.M., and C.T. Hammond. "A Study of Underwriters' Experience With Unseasoned New Issues," *Journal of Financial and Quantitative Analysis* (1974) pp. 165-77.

Neuberger, B.M., and C.A. LaChapelle. "Unseasoned New Issue Price Performance on Three Tiers: 1975-1980," *Financial Management* (1983) pp. 23-28.

Pugel, T.A., and L.J. White. "An Empirical Analysis of Underwriting Spreads on IPO's," Working Paper 331, Salomon Brothers Center for the Study of Financial Institutions, Graduate School of Business Administration, New York University (September 1984).

Reilly, R.K., and K. Hatfield. "Investor Experience With New Stock Issues," *Financial Analysts Journal* (September/October 1969) pp. 73-80.

Reilly, R.K. "Further Evidence on Short-Run Results for New Issue Investors," *Journal of Financial and Quantitative Analysis* (1973) pp. 83-90.

Reilly, R.K. "New Issues Revisited," *Financial Management* (1978) pp. 28-42.

Ritter, J. "The 'Hot Issue' Market of 1980," *Journal of Business* 57 (1984) pp. 215-40.

Ritter, J. "The Costs of Going Public," University of Michigan Working Paper 487 (1987a).

Ritter, J. "A Theory of Investment Banking Contract Choice," University of Michigan Working Paper 488 (1987b).

Rock, K. "Why New Issues Are Underpriced," *Journal of Financial Economics* 15 (1986) pp. 187-212.

Tinic, S. M. "Anatomy of Initial Public Offers of Common Stock," *Journal of Finance* 43 (1988) pp. 789-822.

Welch, I. "Seasoned Offering, Imitation Costs and the Underpricing of Initial Public Offerings," University of Chicago Working Paper (1988).

Article 17

Capital Market Efficiency: An Update*

Stephen F. LeRoy

Professor, University of California, Santa Barbara, and Visiting Scholar, Federal Reserve Bank of San Francisco. Members of the editorial committee were Adrian Throop, Michael Keeley, and Jonathan Neuberger.

Statistical evidence accumulated in the 20 years following Eugene Fama's (1970) survey raises questions about his conclusion that capital markets are efficient. Stock price volatility has been shown to exceed the volatility consistent with capital market efficiency. Other evidence —for example, the small-firm effect, the January effect, and other calendar-based anomalies of stock prices— points in the same direction. Finally, analysts find it difficult to explain stock prices even after the fact using realized values of variables which, according to efficient capital markets theory, should account for stock price changes.

Economist 1: *"That looks like a $100 bill over there on the sidewalk."*

Economist 2: *"Don't bother going over to check it out. If it were genuine, someone would have picked it up already."*

The theory of efficient capital markets says, most simply, that the prices of financial assets equal the discounted value of the expected cash flows these assets generate. In the context of the stock market, efficiency implies that stock prices equal the discounted value of expected future dividends. Investors are not assumed to form perfectly accurate forecasts of future dividends, but they are assumed to make effective use of whatever information they have. If capital markets are efficient in this sense, changes in stock prices should be associated exclusively with new information leading to revisions in expected future dividends: when dividend prospects improve, stock prices rise, and conversely.

Moreover, since all relevant, publicly available information is discounted in asset prices as soon as it becomes available, investors cannot construct systematically profitable trading rules based only on this information. Thus, in an efficient market there is no motive to buy stock based on favorable information; if the information is in fact favorable, the market already has discounted it. In other words, the $100 bill above could not be genuine; otherwise, it would have been picked up already.

These observations suggest that factors not identifiable with future profitability—fads, nonrational speculative bubbles, investor psychology—should not affect stock prices. In this regard, the stock market selloff on October 19, 1987, offers dramatic evidence that capital markets may not be efficient. On that single day, stock values declined by approximately a half trillion dollars, a magnitude unprecedented in absolute terms. In relative terms the selloff was comparable only to the stock market panic of October 1929 which heralded the Great Depression.

According to the efficient markets theory, the selloff could have been caused only by information made available that day (or over the preceding weekend since October 19, 1987, was a Monday) that justified a downward revision on the order of 22 percent in the present discounted value of expected future dividends. However, no economic information of an even mildly unusual nature was made public that day, let alone information that would drastically increase investors' estimates of the probability of an impending economic cataclysm. It is true that investors were worried about recession, but no more than they usually are. In any event, whatever fears of recession investors had subsequently proved unfounded, as the economy showed virtually no ill effects following the stock market collapse.

Moreover, the partial recovery of stock prices in the days following the selloff can only be reconciled with the efficient markets model if the recovery could be associated with economic news inducing investors to believe that the impending recession would, after all, not be as severe as the news that led to the selloff had indicated. Again, however, no economic news of the requisite importance was reported during the week of October 19.

This is not to say that stock price changes on the order of ten or twenty percent, even over a period as short as several days, are never associated with changes of commensurate magnitude in fundamentals. Following the June 1989 suppression of student protests in China, stock prices in Hong Kong dropped by a magnitude comparable in relative terms to the U.S. selloff in October 1987. The connection between political conditions in China and the role of Hong Kong firms in the Chinese economy is so strong that a stock price change on the order of twenty percent is not an obviously disproportionate response to the news that the Chinese government opted to suppress rather than accommodate the liberalization that the students were advocating. Therefore, there is no clear conflict between market efficiency and the selloff that occurred on the Hong Kong exchange in June 1989.

A single dramatic event like the October 19, 1987, selloff, however, does not invalidate the most important prediction of the efficient markets theory, which is that there should not exist trading rules that allow investors systematically to outperform the market. Research conducted in the 1960s and reported in Fama (1970) generally supported this implication, leading financial economists to conclude that capital market efficiency was corroborated empirically.

The more recent evidence, however, does not substantiate Fama's verdict. Detailed analysis using financial data bases developed in the 1970s, and drawing on a more extensive understanding of the empirical implications of market efficiency than was available in 1970, suggests that the October 19, 1987, selloff was not an isolated episode (although, of course, it was virtually unprecedented in magnitude). Instead, the evidence now suggests that most fluctuations in stock prices cannot be traced to changes in rational forecasts of future dividends, contrary to the prediction of the efficient markets model.

The new evidence arises from two areas of research which developed largely independently. First, analysts realized about fifteen years ago that market efficiency implied an upper bound on the volatility of stock prices. Empirical tests suggest that this bound is violated, indicating that stock prices are more variable than is consistent with market efficiency. Second, beginning about the same time analysts came to realize that stock returns display a variety of systematic patterns that are difficult to explain within a framework of rational optimization. The "variance-bounds" and "anomalies" literatures are surveyed in this paper.

Some economists view the updated evidence on market efficiency as demonstrating that the theory of efficient capital markets is wrong, and that investors are simply not as rational as efficient markets theory assumes. If so, it follows that capital markets are probably not doing a good job of resource allocation. Most economists, however, start out with a strong commitment to the assumption that people act rationally, and these economists will not reject the efficient markets model—and with it, the presumption that capital markets are doing a reasonably good job of allocating capital—unless confronted with absolutely airtight evidence against efficiency. None of the evidence reported in this paper meets such an exacting standard. Therefore those who start out with a strong predisposition in favor of capital market efficiency interpret the recent evidence as perhaps raising questions about the theory and suggesting topics for future research, but not as justifying definitive rejection.

I. The Efficient Markets Model

Contrary to the impression given above, the efficient markets model does not start out assuming that asset values equal the present value of expected future cash flows. Rather, the present-value representation is derived from the more primitive assumption that the rate of return r_{jt} on the j-th stock (more generally, the j-th asset) satisfies:

$$E\left(r_{jt} \mid I_t\right) = \rho \tag{1}$$

Here I_t comprises investors' information at t; $E(.|I_t)$ denotes the mathematical expectation of (.) conditional on I_t; ρ, the expected rate of return on stock, is a positive constant, on the assumption that capital markets are perfect and investors are risk-neutral. Equation (1) says that an investor with information I_t will predict an expected rate of return equal to ρ for any asset. Since this is the same prediction that an uninformed investor would make, the efficient markets model implies that the information set I_t is useless in predicting expected rates of return. In this sense information I_t is "fully reflected" in securities prices.

For example, suppose that I_t contains the history of dividends, earnings, sales, advertising outlay, and costs for firm j up to date t, and possibly also macroeconomic variables like GNP, interest rates, commodity prices, and the money stock. Equation (1) says that no matter what values the variables in I_t take on, asset prices will depend on these values in such a way that the expected rate of return on the j-th asset is always ρ. If so, an investor who knows dividends, earnings, and so on is no better off than an investor who does not know the past history of these variables since the uninformed investor can always predict an expected rate of return of ρ without knowing I_t and is assured that his prediction will coincide with that of the informed investor, who predicts an expected rate of return of ρ for all values of I_t.

If at each date the expected rate of return on each asset is ρ, it follows that the expected rate of return on any portfolio is also ρ, since the expected rate of return on a portfolio is just a weighted average of the expected rates of return on its component securities. Accordingly, no trading rules based on information I_t can generate an expected rate of return greater than ρ. Of course, an investor in possession of information better than "the market's" information I_t could use this information to detect differentials in expected rates of return among the various assets, and consequently could construct profitable trading rules. However, efficient markets theory postulates that there do not exist investors with information better than the market's information, or more realistically, that if such investors exist, they do not affect prices.

Fama (1970) distinguished three versions of market efficiency depending on the specification of the information set I_t. Markets are "weak-form efficient" if I_t comprises past returns alone, "semi-strong-form efficient" if I_t comprises all publicly available information, and "strong-form efficient" if I_t includes insider information as well as publicly-available information.[1] It is clear that strong-form efficiency implies semi-strong form efficiency, which in turn implies weak-form efficiency, since expected returns that cannot be predicted based on a large information set surely cannot be predicted based on a small information set that is contained in the large information set. However, the reverse implications do not follow; a capital market easily could be weak-form efficient but not semi-strong-form efficient, or semi-strong-form efficient but not strong-form efficient.

The efficient markets model (1) says that rates of return on stock are unpredictable. It might appear to follow that the efficient markets model implies that stock prices are completely without structure, but that is not the case. In fact, the efficient markets model turns out to be exactly the same model as the present-value relation with which the efficient capital markets model was identified in the introduction. The derivation of this equivalence follows. Because (one plus) the rate of return is by definition equal to the sum of the dividend yield (d_t/p_t) and the rate of capital gain (p_{t+1}/p_t), (1) can be rewritten as:

$$p_t = \frac{E\left(d_{t+1} + p_{t+1} \mid I_t\right)}{1 + \rho} \tag{2}$$

Substituting $t+1$ for t, (2) becomes:

$$p_{t+1} = \frac{E\left(d_{t+2} + p_{t+2} \mid I_{t+1}\right)}{1 + \rho} \tag{3}$$

Using (3) to eliminate p_{t+1} in (2), the price of stock can be written:[2]

$$p_t = \frac{E_t\left(d_{t+1}\right)}{1 + \rho} + \frac{E_t\left(d_{t+2} + p_{t+2}\right)}{(1 + \rho)^2} \tag{4}$$

Here $E_t(.)$ is used as an abbreviated notation for $E(.|I_t)$. Proceeding similarly $n-1$ times, there results:

$$p_t = \frac{E_t\left(d_{t+1}\right)}{1 + \rho} + \frac{E_t\left(d_{t+2}\right)}{(1+\rho)^2} + \cdots + \frac{E_t\left(d_{t+n-1}\right)}{(1 + \rho)^{n-1}}$$
$$+ \frac{E_t\left(p_{t+n} + d_{t+n}\right)}{(1 + \rho)^n} \tag{5}$$

Assuming that $(1 + \rho)^{-n} E_t(p_{t+n})$ converges to zero as n approaches infinity, (5) becomes the familiar present-value equation:

$$p_t = \frac{E_t(d_{t+1})}{1 + \rho} + \frac{E_t(d_{t+2})}{(1 + \rho)^2} + \frac{E_t(d_{t+3})}{(1 + \rho)^3} + \ldots \quad (6)$$

Further, the proof is completely reversible, implying that if the present-value relation (6) is satisfied, so is the efficient markets model (1). Samuelson (1965, 1973) and Mandelbrot (1966) were the first to state this result and to point out its relevance to efficient-markets theory.

What is striking here is that even though dividend changes in (6) can be partly forecast, the generating equation (1) implies that rates of return cannot be forecast. For example, if "the market" expects dividends to rise, the price of stock will be high relative to dividends now, so that when dividends do rise, no extra-normal return will be generated. Stockholders will earn extra-normal (sub-normal) returns only if dividends increase more (less) than had been expected. Thus if capital markets are efficient, a general expectation of a dividend increase does not imply that stocks should be bought (or, for that matter, sold), since the expected increase is already reflected in market prices.

This similarity between the efficient markets model and the "fundamentalist" model means that the much-publicized feud between Wall Streeters, who analyze stocks by computing discounted cash flows, and efficient marketers, who believe that rates of return cannot be forecast, is largely based on misunderstanding. The fundamentalist model focuses on the predictable part of prices, whereas the efficient markets model focuses on unpredictable returns, but the mathematical equivalence between the two models guarantees that there is no inconsistency.

However, the dispute is not entirely without substance: fundamentalists do not assert that prices are exactly equal to the discounted value of future dividends, but rather that prices fluctuate around the discounted value of future dividends. This apparently trivial difference is essential, since only in the latter case can profits be made by buying stocks that are priced lower than fundamentals justify, and selling stocks that appear to be overpriced. If underpriced and overpriced securities do not exist, as advocates of the efficient markets model maintain, then such trading strategies cannot succeed.

In deriving the expected present-value equation (6) from the efficient capital markets model (1), it was necessary to assume that $(1 + \rho)^{-n} E_t(p_{t+n})$ converges to zero as n

approaches infinity. This convergence assumption means that price is expected to grow more slowly than the rate at which future returns are discounted. Violation of the convergence assumption would mean that there exist speculative bubbles: even though price exceeds the discounted value of expected dividends, investors are willing to hold stocks because they anticipate that price will exceed expected dividends by an even wider margin in the future.

It is known that, in theory, speculative bubbles can exist even in simple models in which agents are assumed to be rational and to have identical preferences and endowments, and in which there is no uncertainty (Gilles-LeRoy 1989). In such countries as Japan, where stocks routinely trade at prices 50 times earnings (although such figures are difficult to interpret because accounting practices are different in Japan from those in the U.S.), it is plausible that speculative bubbles are an important determinant of stock prices. However, the same is probably not true of the U.S., where stocks trade at price-earnings multiples on the order of 10 or 15. It is not easy to devise empirical tests which can reliably detect the presence of bubbles. However, one particularly simple kind of bubble would, if it occurred, result in a sustained downward trend in the dividend-price ratio as stock prices rose without limit. Data for the dividend-price ratio in the U.S. do not display any downward trend. The absence of trend in the dividend-price ratio led West (1988a), for example, to conclude that speculative bubbles are probably not an important component of U.S. stock values.

The expected present-value model often strikes people as highly implausible. Many investors do not even consider dividend levels in their investment decisions. Instead they buy stocks that are believed likely to appreciate. Further, the stocks of many firms which do not pay, and have never paid, dividends command high prices. The proposition that rates of return cannot be forecast, on the other hand, is very appealing: the negation of (1) has the unattractive implication that there exists some information variable known to investors which they can use to construct systematically profitable trading rules. Yet the mathematical equivalence of (1) and (6) (granted the convergence condition just discussed) means that it is logically inconsistent to reject the expected present-value model while at the same time accepting the unpredictability of rates of return.

If the reasonableness of (1) is accepted, it follows that the objections to the logically equivalent (6) cannot be as compelling as they appear at first. It is perfectly natural that investors might exhibit greater awareness of capital gains than dividends, given the greater variability and unpredictability of capital gains. Although most investors do not think much about dividend yields, the hypothesis that capital gains reflect changes in dividend prospects nonetheless still holds. Also, whether a given firm has paid dividends in the past is irrelevant. What is relevant is the firm's capacity to pay dividends in the future, which is governed by the firm's earnings prospects. The expected

present-value equation (6) says only that the value of a firm that investors were absolutely certain would never pay dividends in the future (even a liquidating dividend if the firm were to disband or merge into another firm) would be zero.

II. Market Efficiency and Its Implications for Volatility

The October 19, 1987, episode was not the first time stock prices had dropped sharply in the apparent absence of news of commensurate importance bearing on dividend prospects. October 19 was typical of major stock price changes in this respect, not exceptional: most stock price changes, major or minor, cannot convincingly be associated with contemporaneous changes in investors' expectations of future corporate profits (Cutler, Poterba, and Summers, 1987). To the extent that stock prices frequently fluctuate in response to variables unrelated to dividend prospects, stock prices in some sense should be more volatile than is consistent with market efficiency. This consideration led analysts to ask whether market efficiency could be shown formally to have the implication that stock price volatility should be lower than the volatility of dividends, and if so how this prediction could be tested.

Proponents of market efficiency were skeptical of this approach. They argued that since efficiency implies that prices respond instantaneously to new information, stock price volatility cannot be deemed in any sense "excessive." However, because market efficiency has been shown to imply that stock prices equal the discounted sum of expected future dividends, stock prices will behave like a weighted average of dividends over time, and an average is always less volatile than its components.[3] There is no contradiction, then, between the requirement that stock prices respond quickly to new information and the implication that the volatility of prices is related to that of the underlying dividends stream.

Results of tests of the implications of market efficiency for stock price volatility were circulated in 1975 in my paper with Richard Porter (published in 1981). The timing, incidentally, was not coincidental—our thinking on this topic was prompted by the 1974-1975 stock market drop, the most pronounced in the postwar U.S. economy up to that time. Robert Shiller reported similar volatility results in his 1979 and 1981 papers. These papers used different analytical methods, but the results were the same: stock price volatility is too great to be consistent with market efficiency.

These papers alleging excess volatility of asset prices were well-received by economists sympathetic to the idea that asset price changes are not closely linked to changes in

the expected discounted value of the cash flows to which these assets give title. However, defenders of the efficient markets model were motivated to search for statistical problems with the specific econometric procedures used in the initial papers. They found several serious biases, all of which predisposed the tests to reject market efficiency. The most important papers here are Flavin (1983) and Kleidon (1986). At the same time, new volatility tests were being devised which were free of the biases that attended the initial tests (West, 1988; Mankiw, Romer, and Shapiro, 1985; Campbell and Shiller, 1988a, 1988b; and LeRoy and Parke, 1990). These new tests continued to indicate that asset prices are excessively volatile, although perhaps not by as great a margin as the initial tests suggested.

Lawrence Summers has likened the findings of the volatility tests to that of the statistical tests for a link between smoking and lung disease. Early tests indicating the presence of such a link were found to be contaminated by statistical problems which biased the outcome toward that finding. Nevertheless, subsequent tests, which were free of statistical bias, continued to support the original conclusion of a statistically significant link, although the link was shown not to be as strong as had first been thought.

The volatility test reported below, which is very simple and yet appears econometrically sound, is drawn from LeRoy and Parke (1990). Recall that the efficient markets model says that stock price equals the discounted value of expected dividends:

$$p_t = \frac{E_t(d_{t+1})}{1+\rho} + \frac{E_t(d_{t+2})}{(1+\rho)^2} + \frac{E_t(d_{t+3})}{(1+\rho)^3} + \ldots . \quad (6)$$

Because there is no direct way to measure investors' information, direct observation of $E_t(d_{t+1})$, $E_t(d_{t+2})$, ..., is not possible. This greatly complicates the derivation of the implications of market efficiency for price volatility. However, it is possible to show that the less information investors have, the higher will be the variance of the rate of return (LeRoy, 1989). Consequently, assuming markets are at least weak-form efficient, so that investors' information includes at least past returns, puts a lower bound on the amount of information investors have, therefore implying an upper bound on the variance of the rate of return.[4]

To derive the upper bound on the variance of the rate of return, it is necessary to evaluate this variance when investors predict future dividends using no information other than past returns. It is assumed that dividends follow a geometric random walk:

$$d_{t+1} = d_t \, \epsilon_{t+1} \qquad (7)$$

where the ϵs are constant-mean random variables distributed independently over time. Analysts disagree about the accuracy of the geometric random walk specification. Some evidence shows it to be surprisingly accurate for such a simple specification, while other evidence suggests that in some contexts the geometric random walk specification can be misleading. For the present purpose the most attractive feature of the geometric random walk is its simplicity, which allows a very intuitive development of the variance-bounds relations. More complex characterization of dividend behavior, while allowing greater accuracy, would necessarily complicate the discussion by requiring use of more general analytical methods (Campbell-Shiller, 1988, 1988a).

When markets are at least weak-form efficient the upper bound on the variance of the rate of return on stock is the variance that would occur if investors based their dividend forecasts on past dividend behavior and nothing else. In this case the geometric random walk model implies that the best guess about future dividends is that they equal current dividends, multiplied by a trend term which depends on

the mean value of ϵ. Therefore price will be given by a constant markup applied to current dividends:

$$p_t = k \, d_t \qquad (8)$$

If price is proportional to dividends, the rate of return will equal the dividend growth rate multiplied by a constant which is very near one. To see this, recall the definition of the rate of return r_t as the dividend yield plus the rate of capital gain:

$$r_t = \frac{d_{t+1} + p_{t+1}}{p_t} . \qquad (9)$$

Substituting $p = k \, d_t$ and $p_{t+1} = k d_{t+1}$ into (9) and using (7), we have

$$r_t = \left(\frac{k+1}{k} \right) (1 + \epsilon_{t+1}) - 1. \qquad (10)$$

Because k, the price-dividend ratio, is on the order of 25, the multiplicative constant $(k+1)/k$ is not far from one, and therefore can be ignored. Thus the rate of return approximately equals the dividend growth rate, and the variances of these variables are approximately equal also.

In sum, this decreasing relation between investors' information and return volatility implies that if capital markets are at least weak-form efficient (and if dividends follow a random walk) the variance of the rate of return on stock cannot be greater than the variance of the dividend growth rate.

III. Empirical Results

Chart 1 shows the Standard & Poor's stock price index from 1926 to 1985, adjusted for inflation in commodity prices using the producers' price index. As expected, real stock prices display a pronounced upward trend over time, reflecting corporate retained earnings and, to a lesser extent, new equity issues. A very striking observation from Chart 1 is that stock price volatility has decreased between the 1930s and the 1980s. The decline from 1929 to 1932, the rise in the mid-1930s, and the decline in the years just before World War II were much more pronounced than any change occurring between World War II and the mid-1970s. This decreasing volatility of stock prices goes contrary to a common impression that stock market volatility has increased in recent decades. Another observation is that the October 19, 1987, selloff appears in Chart 1 as only a minor drop at the end of the period, rather than as the cataclysm it in fact was. The reason is that it came after nine months of rapid gains in stock prices, so that annual data show only a small drop from 1986 to 1987.

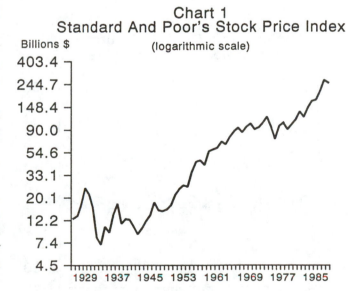

Chart 1
Standard And Poor's Stock Price Index
(logarithmic scale)

Billions $

403.4
244.7
148.4
90.0
54.6
33.1
20.1
12.2
7.4
4.5

1929 1937 1945 1953 1961 1969 1977 1985

Chart 2 displays a simulated rate of return series that is representative of the pattern that would be expected under weak-form market efficiency. To generate the artificial stock prices on which the returns in Chart 2 were based, investors were arbitrarily assumed to be able to forecast dividends with perfect accuracy five years into the future. Beyond that horizon, however, they were assumed to have no information at all. Therefore they were assumed to extrapolate dividends using a constant growth rate, as implied by the geometric random walk. As would be expected in an efficient market, rates of return were higher than normal in years preceding dividend growth that was higher than normal, and lower than normal in years preceding low dividend growth. However, the relevant observation is that the rate of return has lower volatility than the dividend growth rate, conforming to the implication of market efficiency outlined above.

Chart 3 is similar to Chart 2 except that the actual rate of return on stock, rather than the simulated return based on market efficiency, is shown. Several aspects of this diagram are surprising. Most striking is the decrease in the volatility of both the rate of return on stock and the dividend growth rate from the 1930s to the 1980s. This decline in stock price volatility was noted in the discussion of Chart 1. Chart 3 makes clear that the decline in the volatility of dividend growth is even more pronounced than that in return volatility. However, for the purpose of testing the volatility implications of market efficiency, the relevant observation is that over the postwar period the rate of return on stock was much more variable than the dividend growth rate (in the prewar period the difference is not nearly as great). This result is inconsistent with the stock market being weak-form efficient.

The volatility test just presented was chosen because it is easy to motivate intuitively. Because the test depends on strong simplifying assumptions, it may be that the finding of excess volatility arises from a violation of these assumptions rather than of market inefficiency. For example, without the simplifying random walk assumption, it is not necessarily true that the variance of the growth rate of dividends is an upper bound for the variance of the rate of return. Equally important, the version of the expected present-value model used to derive the volatility test incorporated the assumption that the discount rate is constant at ρ. Changing real interest rates over time are therefore a conceivable alternative to market inefficiency as a cause of the apparent excess volatility. However, both of these possibilities have been explored extensively in the variance-bounds literature, and so far, it appears that allowing for these more general specifications does not help explain the excess volatility. Thus, the conclusion that volatility is excessive can be justified in much more general settings than assumed here. The volatility test just reported then should be regarded as a sample from the volatility literature in which simplicity of exposition is purchased at the expense of restrictive specifications.

There are two possible sources of excess volatility in stock prices. First, investors could be overreacting to relevant information; second, they could be reacting to information which is irrelevant according to the efficient markets model. Although there do not appear to exist studies which attempt formally to apportion the excess

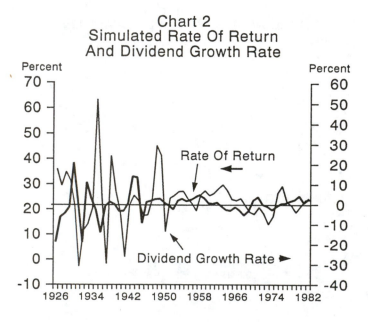

Chart 2
Simulated Rate Of Return
And Dividend Growth Rate

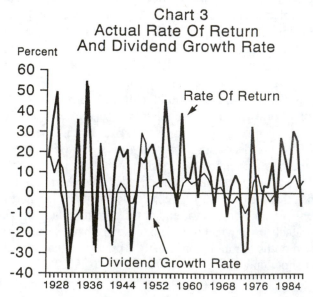

Chart 3
Actual Rate Of Return
And Dividend Growth Rate

volatility between these two sources, it seems likely that both are important.

That investors react to irrelevant information, at least, has been well established. For example, Roll (1984) documented the importance of irrelevant information in determining orange juice futures prices. Efficient markets theory implies that changes in the futures price of orange juice concentrate will reflect changes in the spot price which market participants expect will prevail at the date of the expiration of the futures contract. Roll argued persuasively that the only variable that can plausibly be viewed as giving relevant information about spot prices is weather—specifically, weather forecasts leading market participants to change their estimates of the probability of a freeze in Florida, since a freeze would adversely affect the orange crop.

Other variables which could in principle be relevant, Roll argued, would be expected to have only minor effect in the context of orange juice futures prices since current changes in supply induced by factors other than weather are of secondary importance, inasmuch as these factors do not change abruptly. For example, the number of trees bearing oranges at any time reflects planting decisions made several years earlier. Similarly, it appears unlikely that consumers' income and the prices of such substitutes as apple juice or tomato juice figure in an important way. Thus the efficient markets model predicts that weather should exert a dominant influence on futures prices. Roll verified that low temperatures in Florida were in fact associated with increases in orange juice futures prices, as expected. However, only a few percent of the total variation in futures prices can be explained in this way. In fact, Roll was unable to find any variable at all which correlated significantly with futures prices.

In his Presidential address to the American Finance Association, Roll (1988) reported the results of tests of whether the efficient markets model provides accurate *ex post* explanations for stock prices. He found that, again, irrelevant information appears to be of dominant importance. Even using such data as industry average prices and aggregate stock market indexes, Roll was able to explain *ex post* only a small fraction of the variation in prices of individual stocks.

IV. Asset Pricing Anomalies

There has always existed evidence at odds with the simplest models incorporating market efficiency. Prior to the 1970s, this conflict between theory and evidence usually was dismissed on the grounds that with relatively minor modifications, the efficient markets model could accommodate the contrary observations. For example, analysts identified trading rules that apparently could generate systematic profits, contrary to the efficient markets model. However, when these analysts allowed for brokerage charges, the profits usually evaporated.

More recently, however, analysts have recognized that there exists evidence that is not easy to square with the efficient markets model, even after making reasonable allowance for brokerage charges and other transactions costs. The "P-E anomaly" (Basu 1977, 1983) is the most prominent. It refers to the finding that stocks with low price-earnings ratios generate systematically higher rates of return than do stocks with high P-E ratios. This pattern is difficult to square with any recognizable version of the efficient markets model. In an efficient market, the stock price of successful firms should rise, but only by as much as is consistent with the firms earning normal returns in the future, and similarly with unsuccessful firms.

In contrast, it is easy to relate the P-E anomaly to the excess volatility of stock prices, at least informally. If investors overreact to news, then the stocks of successful firms will be bid to a higher multiple over earnings than is justified by the objective probability of this success continuing in the future. Subsequently the euphoria will wear off, generating low or even negative returns on average. Similarly, investors may be overeager to unburden their portfolios of losers, to the point where these stocks are discounted more than the facts justify. Subsequently such stocks on average generate higher returns than normal as their prospects improve. Correspondingly, this pattern of systematic overreaction to news would be expected to lead to price volatility in excess of that predicted by the efficient markets model. Therefore it is possible that the excess volatility of stock prices is the same thing as the P-E anomaly.

DeBondt and Thaler (1985, 1987) recently have documented a pattern similar to the P-E anomaly. They compared fictional portfolios of "winners"— stocks that had appreciated significantly in the recent past—with similar portfolios of "losers." They found that the losers strongly outperformed the market generally in subsequent years, while winners earned lower returns than the market averages. This result also suggests a pattern of overreaction, although the relation between DeBondt-Thaler's result and the P-E anomaly remains unclear.

Development of large data bases suitable for computerized study of stock prices have led to new anomalies.

Of these, the most striking is the "January effect" (Rozeff and Kinney, 1976; see Thaler, 1987, for a survey). Rozeff and Kinney found that rates of return on stock averaged 3.5 percent in January, whereas in other months returns averaged only 0.5 per cent. Several explanations involving tax-related purchases and sales of stocks have been investigated, but these explanations are not entirely convincing.

Another anomaly is the "small-firm" effect (Banz, 1981) in which small firms appear to earn higher returns than large firms, even when allowance is made for differences in riskiness. A subsequent study (Keim, 1983) showed that the January effect and the small-firm effect may be the same thing: the January effect appears only in samples that give equal weight to large and small firms. Value-weighted samples, in which small firms have much less importance relative to their role in equal-weighted samples, show little evidence of a January effect. This is exactly the pattern that would be expected if small firms account for the January effect.

Still other calendar-based anomalies have surfaced in recent years. Cross (1973), French (1980), and Keim and Stambaugh (1984), among others, have analyzed the "weekend effect," which refers to the observation that stock returns are on average negative from the close of trading on Fridays to the opening of trading on Mondays. Gibbons and Hess (1981) showed that a similar effect exists for bonds. Further, we have the "Wednesday effect": in 1968 the New York Stock Exchange was closed on Wednesdays in order to allow the back offices of brokerage houses to catch up with paperwork. Roll (1986) found that the volatility of stock prices was lower from Tuesday to Thursday when the market was closed on Wednesdays than over two-day periods over which the Exchange was not closed. This puzzle is difficult (although not impossible; see Slezak, 1988) to reconcile with market efficiency, given that as much news about corporate dividends presumably was arriving when the market was closed on Wednesdays as on other weekdays. The implication is that to some extent the trading process itself generates price volatility, a phenomenon clearly inconsistent with market efficiency. Finally, there exists a day-of-the-month effect: stock returns are positive in the days surrounding the turn of the month, but are zero on average for the rest of the month (Ariel, 1985).

Finally, Tinic and West (1984) investigated the seasonal pattern in the risk-return tradeoff. Fama and MacBeth's (1973) paper earlier had verified the prediction from finance theory that high-risk firms earn higher average rates of return than low-risk firms. Motivated by the results on the January effect, Tinic and West investigated the seasonal pattern in the correlation between risk and return which Fama-MacBeth had estimated. They found that this correlation is due entirely to the data for January. Given Keim's result that small firms earn high returns in January, and given the obvious fact that small firms are riskier than large firms, it is not surprising that the correlation between risk and expected return is strongest in January. What is surprising, however, is that the correlation between risk and return is essentially zero for the other eleven months of the year. Inasmuch as investors are risk-averse, this lack of compensation for risk in eleven of the twelve months of the year is not easy to reconcile with market efficiency.

V. Conclusions

Several essentially unrelated types of evidence that capital markets are inefficient have been discussed in this paper. Since it is not easy to think of non-trivial predictions of the efficient markets model that are borne out empirically, the burden of the evidence is negative. (Of course, trivial predictions are borne out. For example, it is true that the sustained upward trend in dividends that has occurred in the U.S. economy is associated with sustained price appreciation, as the efficient markets model predicts.)

How important this conclusion is depends on what lies behind the contrary evidence. The version of capital market efficiency adopted in the variance-bounds test reported above is grossly over-simplified (for example, equation (1) does not allow that investors are risk-averse, and therefore will demand a higher rate of return on high-risk securities than on low-risk securities). If it were to turn out that minor modification of the efficient markets model were sufficient to dispose of the contrary evidence, then the violations of market efficiency would not be important. However, most of the obvious extensions of the efficient markets model have been tried already, largely without success so far. Although it is possible that these extensions of the efficient markets model will succeed in the future, it may at some point be necessary for economists to face the uncongenial task of thinking about a world in which asset prices do not behave according to the precepts of finance and economic theory.

Economists are accustomed to thinking of prices not simply as measuring the amount of wealth that is transferred from one person to another when goods change hands, but also as guiding resource allocation. This is true as much for asset prices as for the prices of consumption goods. To see how this works in the context of asset prices, think of the petroleum market. There exists a large but far from infinite supply of oil reserves in the Middle East and other parts of the world. Other sources of energy exist, but they are at present more expensive than petroleum, at least for such purposes as automobile transportation and heating. However, when the petroleum runs out at some point in the future, the price of petroleum must be high enough to induce energy-users to shift to other energy sources. In the simplest idealized case, the price of petroleum will rise to equality with the alternate energy source just as the last gallon of oil is extracted, so that energy users are induced to shift sources at exactly the right time. Before that day of reckoning, petroleum prices must be rising to guarantee to holders of petroleum reserves a competitive return.[5] In this stylized account, the price of petroleum gives exactly the right signals to users of petroleum: they have adequate incentive to conserve, but are not induced irrationally to squander other resources so as to save petroleum. It follows that a massive program to encourage conservation or reliance on alternative sources is likely to do more harm than good, inasmuch as such a program amounts to fixing a social mechanism that is not broken.

Evidence of capital market inefficiency means that it cannot be taken for granted that asset prices are doing as good a job of rationing resources among alternative users as the foregoing account implies. The existing price of petroleum may not, after all, fully reflect the best information about petroleum reserves, alternative energy technologies, and so forth. Accordingly, the price of petroleum may not be providing the right incentives for conservation and development of alternative technologies.

It is apparent that an extreme interpretation of the evidence against capital market efficiency has the effect of opening the door to a variety of schemes to alter economic institutions. Inasmuch as such schemes generally have met with various degrees of failure in the past, we should not be too quick to jettison capital market efficiency, and with it the idea that prices determined in competitive markets do a reasonably good job of allocating resources. The evidence reviewed here suggests, rather, that economists ought to be aware that the evidence in favor of their way of thinking about the economy is far from clear-cut.

NOTES

* A more detailed version of this paper is found in LeRoy (1989).

1. Although these verbal characterizations of market efficiency are drawn directly from Fama (1970), it is not unambiguously clear that Fama identified market efficiency with the fair-game model (1); see LeRoy (1976, 1989) for discussion.

2. Used here is the rule of iterated expectations, which says that $E(E(d_{t+2} | I_{t+1}) | I_t) = E(d_{t+2} | I_t)$, and similarly for p_{t+2}.

3. Even though future dividends are weighted differently from current dividends because of discounting, and future dividends are not known with certainty, price behaves like an average of dividends over time.

4. The test to be described is known as the "West test" (West, 1988), although the original version of the West test is formally equivalent to one of the volatility tests derived by LeRoy-Porter (1981). (See Gilles-LeRoy, 1988.) West's derivation was independent, and he was the first actually to conduct the test. Also, West was the first to realize that the return volatility test has certain econometric advantages over price volatility tests, particularly for diagrammatic presentation. These advantages justify adoption of the West test here.

In one respect the test reported here differs from that derived by LeRoy-Porter and West. The formal derivation of the West test assumes constant-variance linear processes, which is an unsatisfactory specification in light of the upward trend in stock prices over the past fifty years. In order to correct for scale, Chart 3 instead compares the rate of return with the dividends growth rate. Formal derivation of the validity of this comparison, which is based on the linearization procedure of Campbell-Shiller (1988), is found in LeRoy-Parke (1990).

5. The implication that the prices of exhaustible resources should rise at a rate approximately equal to the real interest rate has been studied by Schmidt (1988). Schmidt found no evidence of rising prices over time, implying that holders of wealth in the form of exhaustible resources earned a zero real rate of return.

REFERENCES

Ariel, Robert A. "A Monthly Effect in Stock Returns," *Journal of Financial Economics* 17: 1985. 161-174.

Banz, Rolf. "The Relationship between Return and Market Value of Common Stock," *Journal of Financial Economics* 9: 1981. 3-18.

Basu, Sanjoy. "Investment Performance of Common Stocks in Relation to their Price-Earnings Ratios: A Test of the Efficient Market Hypothesis," *Journal of Finance* 32: 1977. 663-682.

_____ . "The Relation between Earnings' Yield, Market Value and Returns for NYSE Common Stocks: Further Evidence," *Journal of Financial Economics* 12: 1983. 129-156.

Campbell, John Y. and Robert J. Shiller. "The Dividend-Price Ratio and Expectations of Future Dividends and Discount Factors," *Review of Financial Studies* 1: 1988. 195-228.

_____ . "Stock Prices, Earnings, and Expected Dividends," *Journal of Finance* 43: 1988a. 661-676.

Cross, Frank. "The Behavior of Stock Prices on Fridays and Mondays," *Financial Analysts Journal:* 1973. 67-79.

Cutler, David M., James M. Poterba and Lawrence H. Summers. "What Moves Stock Prices?" reproduced, Harvard University, 1987.

DeBondt, Werner and Richard Thaler. "Does the Stock Market Overreact?" *Journal of Finance* 40: 1985. 793-805.

_____ . "Further Evidence on Investor Overreaction and Stock Market Seasonality," *Journal of Finance* 42: 1987. 557-581.

Fama, Eugene F. "Efficient Capital Markets: A Review of Theory and Empirical Work," *Journal of Finance* 25: 1970. 383-416.

_____ and James D. MacBeth. "Risk, Return and Equilibrium: Empirical Tests," *Journal of Political Economy* 81: 1973. 607-636.

Flavin, Marjorie A. "Excess Volatility in the Financial Markets: A Reassessment of the Empirical Evidence," *Journal of Political Economy* 91: 1983. 929-956.

Gibbons, Michael and Patrick Hess. "Day of the Week Effects and Asset Returns," *Journal of Business* 5: 1981. 579-596.

Gilles, Christian and Stephen F. LeRoy. "Bubbles and Charges," reproduced, University of California, Santa Barbara, 1988.

Grossman, Sanford and Robert J. Shiller. "The Determinants of the Variability of Stock Market Prices," *American Economic Review* 71: 1981. 222-227.

Keim, Donald B. "Size-Related Anomalies and Stock Market Seasonality," *Journal of Financial Economics* 12: 1983. 13-22.

_____ and Robert F. Stambaugh. "A Further Investigation of the Weekend Effect in Stock Returns," *Journal of Finance* 39: 1984. 819-840.

Kleidon, Allan. "Variance Bounds Tests and Stock Price Valuation Models," *Journal of Political Economy:* 1986. 953-1001.

LeRoy, Stephen F. "Efficient Capital Markets: Comment," *Journal of Finance* 3: 1976. 139-141.

_____ . "Efficiency and the Variability of Asset Prices," *American Economic Review* 74: 1984. 183-187.

_____ . "Efficient Capital Markets and Martingales," *Journal of Economic Literature,* 1989.

_____ and William R. Parke. "Stock Price Volatility: Tests Based on the Geometric Random Walk," reproduced, University of California, Santa Barbara, 1990.

LeRoy, Stephen F. and Richard D. Porter. "The Present-Value Relation: Tests Based on Implied Variance Bounds," *Econometrica* 49: 1981. 555-574.

Mandelbrot, Benoit. "Forecasts of Future Prices, Unbiased Markets, and Martingale Models," *Journal of Business* 39: 1966. 242-255.

Mankiw, N. Gregory, David Romer, and Matthew D. Shapiro. "An Unbiased Reexamination of Stock Market Volatility," *Journal of Finance* 40: 1985. 677-687.

Roll, Richard. "Orange Juice and Weather," *American Economic Review* 74: 1984. 861-880.

_____ . "The Hubris Hypothesis of Corporate Takeovers," *Journal of Business* 59: 1986. 197-216.

_____ . "R^2," *Journal of Finance* 43: 1988. 541-566.

Rozeff, Michael S. and William R. Kinney. "Capital Market Seasonality: The Case of Stock Returns," *Journal of Financial Economics* 3: 1976. 379-402.

Samuelson, Paul A. "Proof that Properly Anticipated Prices Fluctuate Randomly," *Industrial Management Review* 6: 1965. 41-49.

_____ . "Proof that Properly Discounted Present Values Vibrate Randomly," *Bell Journal of Economics and Management Science* 4: 1973. 369-374.

Schmidt, Ronald. "Hotelling's Rule Repealed? An Examination of Exhaustible Resource Pricing," *Federal Reserve Bank of San Francisco Economic Review,* Fall, 1988. 41-53.

Shiller, Robert. "The Volatility of Long Term Interest Rates and Expectations Models of the Term Structure," *Journal of Political Economy* 87: 1979. 1190-1209.

_____ . "Do Stock Prices Move Too Much to be Justified by Subsequent Changes in Dividends?" *American Economic Review* 17: 1981. 421-436.

Slezak, Steve L. "The Effect of Market Interruptions on Equilibrium Asset Return Distributions in Dynamic Economies with Asymmetrically Informed Traders," reproduced, University of California, San Diego, 1988.

Thaler, Richard. "Anomalies: The January Effect," *Journal of Economic Perspectives* 1: 1987. 197-201.

Tinic, Seha M. and Richard R. West. "Risk and Return: January vs. the Rest of the Year," *Journal of Financial Economics* 13: 1984. 561-574.

West, Kenneth. "Dividend Innovations and Stock Price Volatility," *Econometrica* 56: 1988. 37-61.

_____ . "Bubbles, Fads and Stock Price Volatility Tests: A Partial Evaluation," *Journal of Finance* 43: 1988a. 639-656.

Article 18

The Equity Risk-Premium Puzzle

Over a long span of U.S. history, a diversified portfolio of common equity has turned out to be an exceptionally good investment, especially when compared with government securities. From 1889 through 1988, the average real (compensated for inflation) rate of return on the Standard and Poor's 500 stock index was about seven percent, compared to 3/4 percent return for government securities. Of course, since equities involve credit risk and government bonds do not, equities ought to pay more on average. However, the advantage of stocks has been very large, larger than seems justifiable on the basis of risk considerations alone.

The magnitude of the equity risk premium has puzzled economists in recent years. This *Letter* considers the nature of the puzzle, a proposed solution, and some implications.

Risk aversion

To explain the equity risk premium, economists rely on a concept called "risk aversion." Since government securities offer a payoff, or return, that is known with certainty, while equities offer a payoff that is uncertain, or risky, investors who are averse to risk are willing to hold equity only if they expect to earn a premium over the return available on government securities. The more risk averse is the investor, the greater the risk premium must be to induce him or her to purchase equities.

To see how risk aversion affects the price of equities, consider the following example. A person is given a choice between two offers, a sure $50.50, or a lottery ticket that offers a fifty-fifty chance of $1 or $100. The expected return on the lottery is $50.50, the same as the first offer. An individual who is not risk averse would be indifferent between receiving a sure $50.50 and the lottery. But a risk averse individual would prefer the first offer of a sure $50.50 to the lottery, even though the lottery has the potential to yield $100.

As risk aversion rises, the individual is willing to settle for a smaller and smaller payment with

certainty instead of the lottery. Economists have estimated the degree of risk aversion of the average individual in the U.S. economy, and have concluded that most people act as if they are risk averse. These estimates of the average degree of risk aversion suggest that in the example above, most people would be indifferent between receiving a sure $2.30 and the lottery with its expected payoff of $50.50.

U.S. government bonds and stocks are analogous to the example described above. Because there is no default risk associated with U.S. government bonds, they offer a sure payoff. Common stock, on the other hand, entitles holders to the uncertain future flows of dividends and capital gains; they are like the lottery in the example above.

The equity risk premium

The chart shows the consecutive ten-year average realized rates of return on stocks (S&P 500 index) and ninety-day Treasury bills for the hundred-year period from 1889 through 1988. Each rate is adjusted for inflation. The ten-year average equity risk premiums for this hundred-year time span, then, are the differences between the rates of return on stocks and Treasury bills in each ten-year period.

Real Rate of Return

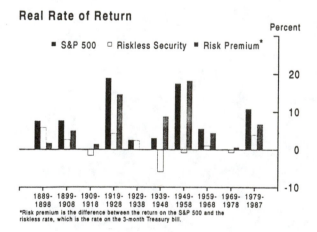

*Risk premium is the difference between the return on the S&P 500 and the riskless rate, which is the rate on the 3-month Treasury bill.

As shown in the chart, the observed risk premium has been quite volatile. This volatility in the *realized* equity risk premium is not surprising, given that the return on equity itself is quite volatile. The realized return on equity has varied from period to period largely as a result of changes in the level of economic activity, inflation, interest rates, and other factors that have a bearing on the performance of the corporate sector of the economy. In the 1960s and '70s, for example, the unexpected increase in inflation, increased uncertainty regarding inflation, and excessive taxation of corporate income may have been important causes of the poor performance of equity and thus the low observed risk premium in those decades.

Where's the puzzle?

Thus, in any given period, a high or low observation for the equity risk premium should not be surprising. But what is surprising about the data presented in the chart is that on average over the hundred-year period, the observed risk premium has been relatively high, given current estimates of the degree of risk aversion among investors.

Economists have attempted to interpret this finding using so-called equilibrium business cycle models. These models analyze macroeconomic phenomena based upon key behavioral assumptions used in microeconomic theory, including utility maximization by individuals and profit maximization by businesses in markets characterized by perfect competition. These models eschew assumptions that institutional rigidities play an important role in macroeconomic developments. Instead, they assume that macroeconomic developments represent the equilibrium outcomes of fundamental economic forces. Of course, use of these models does not deny that institutional factors at times can have important effects.

In a paper published in 1985, economists Rajnish Mehra of the University of California and Edward Prescott of the University of Minnesota and the Federal Reserve Bank of Minneapolis attempt such an interpretation of the equity risk premium. They construct a model in which the degree of risk aversion of the average individual is one of the key determinants of asset yield.

In their model consumption is assumed to follow a path that is very similar to the consumption series of the U.S. economy over time, but in each period there is uncertainty regarding future consumption. Future consumption is financed with income on equity holdings and income from holdings of a riskless asset. The riskless asset provides a stream of income that is certain, while the equity holdings provide an uncertain stream of income.

The premium that is required for people to be indifferent between the two assets depends on their attitudes toward uncertain future consumption. The more people are averse to risk, the larger is the premium they demand for holding risky equity. Thus, the Mehra-Prescott model gives rise to a systematic relationship between an assumed degree of risk aversion and the average equity premiums.

However, at levels of risk aversion estimated by most economists, the Mehra-Prescott model fails to generate the magnitude of the risk premium that is observed historically. In other words, their model suggests that the public would need to be more risk averse than is now believed to be the case to generate the average magnitude of the equity premium we observe from the chart. It is this finding that has been termed the equity risk premium puzzle. A similar puzzle has been recognized by financial market participants regarding the difference between the returns on high-grade (low-risk) bonds and low-grade (high-risk) bonds.

A solution?

In 1988, T. A. Rietz of Northwestern University published a paper "The Equity Risk Premium: A Solution," which reports results that provide a solution to the puzzle using a model specification very similar to the model of Mehra and Prescott. His solution can be summarized as follows. While retaining other features of the Mehra-Prescott model, Rietz introduces the possibility that the output of the economy and the rate of return on equity can fall dramatically. Although this possibility is assumed to be quite remote, equity holders nonetheless face the risk of very low income from equity sometime in the future. This risk has to be compensated for by an increased average rate of return on equity. By introducing the risk of a remotely-possible, catastrophic decline in equity income, Rietz's model gives rise to a large equity risk premium that is comparable to the historically observed value.

End of puzzle?

Rietz's approach has merit, given that the U.S. economy has experienced stock market crashes in which equity prices have fallen drastically, including the one in October 1987. The 1929 stock market crash, in particular, is similar to the one posited by Rietz in that it caused a drastic reduction in the rate of return on equity and thus in consumption opportunities available to individuals. However, the similarity is far from perfect.

First, the magnitude of the crash posited by Rietz is far greater than that of the 1929 crash. The *best* of many bad states (which has probability of one percent, or roughly once in 100 years) assumed by Rietz involves a drastic 25 percent reduction in consumption in a single year! To put this in perspective, we can examine the experience during the Great Depression. The shortfall from trend GNP (that is, the difference between the GNP that would have resulted at three percent annual growth and actual GNP) was 38% over the four year period from 1929 through 1933, and only half of that shortfall is attributed to the fall in consumption. Thus, it took four years for real consumption to decrease by 19 percent (about five percent a year). It is hard to imagine that equity holders perceive themselves facing even a small risk of a decline in equity income as devastating as Rietz assumes.

Moreover, even with this dire scenario, Rietz still needs a very high degree of risk aversion to generate a risk premium that is close to the observed average. To use the earlier example of the lottery, Rietz's assumption concerning the magnitude of risk aversion implies that an average person prefers a certain *$1.08* over the prospect of one dollar or 100 dollars with a fifty-fifty chance. This is much too large compared to many empirical estimates of the relative risk aversion parameter. Thus, Rietz does not appear to have fully resolved the puzzle.

Different opinion

In attempting to explain the average magnitude of the equity risk premium over the past 100 years, economists generally have used some key assumptions that are very strong. For example, in the Mehra and Prescott work, preferences are assumed stable over time. However, Nobel laureate economist James Tobin criticizes the widespread use of utility functions that posit stable preferences.

Specifically, the utility function used by both Mehra and Prescott, and Rietz makes a strong prediction about how an individual makes choices involving risk. They assume that a person who prefers a sure $10 to a lottery that pays either $1 or $100 with a fifty-fifty chance also will prefer a sure $100,000 to another lottery that has a fifty-fifty chance of winning $10,000 or $1,000,000. However, precisely because the awards of the second lottery are 10,000 times larger than the awards in the first example, many individuals might not behave as predicted above. In fact, it is reasonable to expect that their choices might also depend on what they already own.

In addition to changing the way in which risk aversion is modelled, resolution of the equity risk premium puzzle might be feasible only when important institutional factors are considered. For example, some economists have suggested that monetary policy may be an important factor because it influences interest rates, inflation, and thus, the desirability of equity as a portfolio choice. Including institutional factors of this nature also may enhance our ability to examine and understand other economic phenomena, as well as helping to explain the equity risk premium puzzle. In any event, thus far, the puzzle is not completely resolved.

Chan Huh
Economist

Section V
The Bond Market

In the 1980s, one investments issue dominated all others. The emergence of the high-yield (or junk bond) market revolutionized the bond market and had a great impact on other sectors of the financial world. This section focuses on the bond market, with particular attention on the development of the junk bond market. We also consider some recent innovations in the theory of the term structure.

In "The High-Yield Debt Market: 1980–1990," Richard H. Jefferis, Jr. traces the debt market through the 1980s and into the 1990s with the collapse of Drexel. (Drexel Burnham Lambert, led by Michael Milken, was largely responsible for the success of the high-yield/high-risk debt market. Now Drexel is bankrupt and disbanded and Milken has pled guilty to a variety of securities market felonies.) As Jefferis notes, high-yield debt may be in partial eclipse today, but the market succeeded due to basic and persisting economic forces. Therefore, Jefferis believes that risky debt will find a continuing role in a more cautious market.

In "The Truth About Junk Bonds," Sean Becketti considers the three main criticisms raised against junk bonds: they fueled the merger boom, they are responsible for the rise in corporate debt levels, and they have increased financial market volatility. Becketti finds that the evidence does not support these charges. Instead, he argues that junk bonds are similar in character to other financing vehicles.

The term structure of interest rates traces the relationship between the yield on bonds and their maturity. As such, term structure analysis abstracts from other differences besides maturity that might affect the yields on bonds. It does not consider default risk, for example, but it usually focuses on U.S. Treasury bills, notes, and bonds, because these instruments are all free of default risk and are similar in many other respects as well. Peter A. Abken reviews the well-received theories of the term structure in his article "Innovations in Modeling the Term Structure of Interest Rates." As the title implies, Abken also explores new theories of the term structure that attempt to enhance our understanding. While some of the new models of the term structure can be quite complex mathematically, Abken does an excellent job of explaining the intuition of these theories without resorting to mathematics.

Article 19

The High-Yield Debt Market: 1980-1990

by Richard H. Jefferis, Jr.

The February collapse of Drexel Burnham Lambert, which followed five months of turmoil in the junk bond market, signaled the end of a six-year period of sustained growth of that market. Prices of lower-grade bonds declined sharply from September 1989 through February 1990. In the secondary market, some investors found it difficult to locate buyers for their securities. In the primary market, new issues during January 1990 were only one-third of their value a year earlier. New issues during all of 1989 decreased by 11 percent from the 1988 total of $27 billion, while mutual fund investment in high-yield bonds fell from $34 billion to $28 billion.[1] These events, triggered by financial distress in a number of leveraged buyouts that included the slide of the Campeau Corporation into bankruptcy, have engendered predictions of the demise of the modern high-yield market.[2]

This *Economic Commentary* reviews the growth of that market from virtual nonexistence in 1980 to nearly $200 billion by the end of the decade, and assesses the impact of recent events on its viability. Three trends in debt formation that contributed to the rapid expansion of the high-yield market are discussed. The first is the overall growth of the economy, which contributed to the rapid expansion of both equity and debt during the 1980s. The second is the substitution of credit-market debt for bank loans in the balance sheets of middle-market customers who had not previously enjoyed access to the bond market. The third is the wave of leveraged restructuring induced by the Tax Reform Act of 1986.

Volume patterns in the bond market, especially the high-yield market, suggest that the third phenomenon may have played itself out. The tax code, however, still provides both investors and corporations with a strong incentive to elect debt rather than equity as a vehicle for financing new investment. Moreover, the dynamic middle-market customers who fueled the growth of this market prior to 1986 continue to represent profitable lending opportunities. The high-yield market will shrink if investors, shaken by recent events, withdraw their capital, but the economic forces that created the market persist, and it is quite unlikely that high-yield bonds will disappear altogether.

■ Economic Growth and Debt Formation

Between 1980 and 1989, nominal gross national product expanded at an annual rate of 7 percent. Businesses spent $3.6 trillion on new plant and equipment during this period, while outstanding credit-market debt on the balance sheets of domestic nonfinancial corporations increased by $1.2 trillion. Other factors influenced the formation of credit-market debt during the 1980s, but the contribution of economic growth to this phenomenon should not be overlooked.

Did the collapse of Drexel Burnham Lambert in February signal the end of the high-yield debt market? Considering that the economic forces responsible for creating the market remain in place, it is unlikely that junk bonds will disappear any time soon.

FIGURE 1   INVESTMENT AND DEBT FORMATION IN THE 1980s

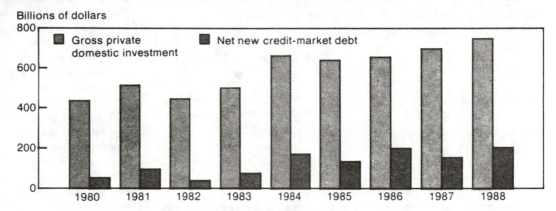

SOURCES: U.S. Department of Commerce, Bureau of Economic Analysis; and Board of Governors of the Federal Reserve System.

FIGURE 2   STANDARD & POOR'S 500 INDEX, 1965-1989

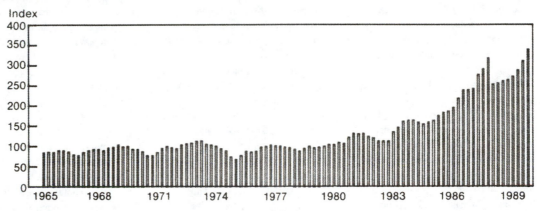

SOURCE: Standard & Poor's Corporation.

Figure 1 shows gross private domestic investment and net new credit-market debt over the course of the decade.[3] As always, new debt formation closely tracks the behavior of investment.[4] (The year of the Tax Reform Act is an obvious exception.) Figure 2 portrays the behavior of equity prices, an indicator of expected future investment opportunities. Equity markets supplied firms with a strong positive signal about the value of investment opportunities throughout the 1980s, contributing to the willingness of businesses to borrow.

■ Credit-Market Debt and Bank Loans

It is convenient for the sake of discussion to partition the decade into three time periods, although the division is somewhat arbitrary. The first period is 1980–1982, which precedes the growth of the high-yield market and serves as a useful reference point. During the second period, between 1983 and 1985, high-yield bonds became a significant component of new corporate lending, capturing an increasing share of a growing debt market from commercial banks. The Tax Reform Act of 1986 marks the beginning of the third period, when the composition of the high-yield market shifted from middle-market firms seeking to finance new investment toward tax-driven restructuring.

Bank loans and corporate bonds make up the bulk of debt on the corporate balance sheet throughout the decade, as they have during the entire postwar period. Balance-sheet data indicate that the combined market share of these two sources of funding remained steady during the 1980s, never varying outside a range of 70 to 75 percent. There was, however, a clear trend toward the use of credit-market debt throughout the decade. Figure 3 shows the steady decline of a composite of bank loans, finance company debt, and mortgage debt relative to security market debt that began in the 1970s.[5]

The share of these items in outstanding debt understates trends in new lending activity. Figure 4 portrays the year-to-year change in outstanding bank loans, corporate bonds, and speculative-grade bonds during the 1980s.[6] Between 1980 and 1982, bank lending accounted for 57 percent of net new corporate credit, while bonds accounted for only 36 percent of that amount. The share of bank lending in net new credit fell by

TABLE 1   CHARACTERISTICS OF HIGH-YIELD ISSUERS
Annual Growth Rates, 1980-1986 (Percent)

Category	High-Yield Firms	Other Firms
Employment	6.7	1.4
Sales	9.3·	6.2
Sales (manufacturing firms)	5.6	3.8
Capital spending	12.4	9.9
Capital spending (manufacturing firms)	10.6	3.8

SOURCE: G. Yago (1988—see footnote 7). All figures are percentages.

half, to 26 percent, between 1983 and 1985, while the share of bonds remained steady at 35 percent. Between 1986 and 1988, bank lending accounted for only 15 percent of new credit, while the share of bonds nearly doubled to 61 percent.

The overall growth in debt, and the substitution of bonds for bank loans, fueled the growth of the high-yield market. New issues of speculative-grade bonds rose from $1.5 billion in 1982 to $15 billion during 1984. During this period, Drexel Burnham Lambert underwrote virtually 100 percent of the new issues. The strategy that proved so successful at Drexel was the marketing of debt, issued by middle-market firms that had previously depended on banks for credit, directly to sophisticated investors. Insurance companies and pension funds provided most of the capital absorbed by the high-yield market between 1982 and 1984. By 1986, the public had become involved more directly through mutual funds.

The leveraged buyouts and leveraged restructurings of recent years have focused attention on a type of high-yield issuer that differs significantly from the representative borrower of 1983–1986. In a broad survey of U.S. industrial firms covering the period 1980–1986, Yago profiles the issuers of high-yield bonds and contrasts these firms with other U.S. industrial companies.[7] Table 1 presents some of the findings from this study. Firms in the sample that used high-yield finance are dynamic enterprises, with growth in

sales, employment, and investment that exceeds that of other industrials. Only 3 percent of the firms in the sample that issued high-yield debt used the proceeds for merger or acquisition activity.

The forces that resulted in the substitution of credit-market debt for bank loans on corporate balance sheets during this period are poorly understood. Plausible explanations include a regulatory burden for banks, conservatism in lending induced by the onus of Third-World debt, and advances in information technology that made it possible for investors to monitor the performance of smaller firms directly, making it unnecessary to rely on banks for those services. The evidence necessary to discriminate among these explanations has not yet been accumulated.

It is, however, possible to dismiss on the basis of currently available evidence at least one other explanation of the substitution of bonds for bank debt. Thrift institutions received significant new investment powers under legislation passed in the early 1980s, which enabled them to invest in high-yield bonds.[8] Some thrifts became active investors in the high-yield market. However, thrift industry investment in high-yield issues, which peaked at a total of $13 billion in 1986, accounted for only 8 percent of outstanding high-yield issues during that year. Thrift holdings of high-yield debt were never a significant portion of either total thrift industry assets or outstanding high-yield debt.

■ The Tax Reform Act of 1986
The biggest year of the decade in the high-yield debt market was not 1988, when leveraged buyout activity reached its zenith, but rather 1986, when the U.S. Congress enacted what may well be the most significant revisions of the tax code in this century. Two features of the Tax Reform Act provide corporations with a strong incentive to substitute debt for equity on the corporate balance sheet. At the corporate level, the curtailment of non-debt tax shields such as the investment tax credit and depreciation allowances eliminated important alternatives to debt for protecting corporate earnings from taxation.[9] At the personal level, the abolishment of preferential treatment for capital gains enhanced the after-tax value of debt relative to equity.[10] The combination of these factors provided a strong impetus for increased leverage between 1986 and 1989.

Financial economists have long believed that the financial structure of corporations is sensitive to the tax environment. When corporate taxes are calculated, interest payments to investors who hold debt are deductible, while dividend payments to investors who hold equity are not. This feature of the tax code provides firms with a powerful incentive to finance investment through the issue of debt. That incentive is mitigated by firms' preference for the flexibility associated with equity (or equivalently, an aversion to the financial distress that may result from excess leverage), and by the availability of tax deductions other than interest payments on debt. Changes in the tax code that reduce the availability of non-debt tax shields tilt the balance between debt and equity in favor of increased debt.

Hard empirical evidence concerning the relationship between the tax code and corporate financial structure has heretofore proved elusive, probably because of measurement problems inherent in financial accounting, and the imprecise timing of tax code revisions. But the Tax Reform Act resulted in such a drastic, instantaneous change in

FIGURE 3   DEBT STRUCTURE OF U.S. NONFINANCIAL CORPORATIONS

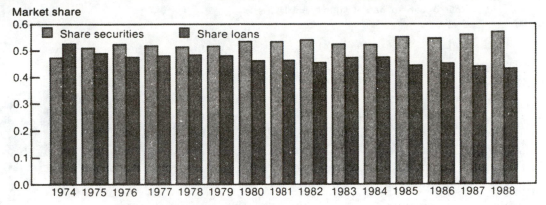

SOURCE: Balance Sheets for the U.S. Economy, Board of Governors of the Federal Reserve System.

FIGURE 4   NET CHANGE IN BONDS AND BANK LOANS ON THE CORPORATE BALANCE SHEET

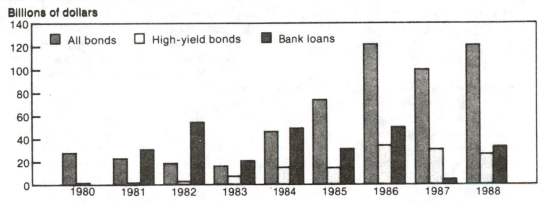

SOURCES: Board of Governors of the Federal Reserve System; and E. Altman (1989—see footnote 14).

the tax environment that it has been possible to detect a response in corporate financial policy. A recent study using a diverse set of U.S. industrial companies documents a $140 increase in outstanding debt in response to each $100 decrease in non-debt tax shields associated with the Tax Reform Act.[11] Moreover, the observed response of individual firms depends on the dividend policy of the firm prior to the change, suggesting that changes in the personal tax code also affected the financial structure of corporations.

It is also possible to observe a response to the Tax Reform Act in aggregate data. The deviation in the relationship between investment activity and debt formation that is apparent in figure 1 has already been noted. Commercial and industrial lending, and new issues of both investment-grade bonds and

speculative-grade bonds, all increased sharply in 1986. Equity repurchases surged the following year: net issues of equity were negative in 1987. The accumulation of debt following tax reform increased the ratio of debt to equity in all nonfinancial corporations from 0.67 to 0.75 between 1985 and 1988.

■ **Leverage, Debt Quality, and Defaults**
The accumulation of debt in the 1980s represents a significant increase in the fixed obligations of corporations. However, during a period when the value of debt on the corporate balance sheet grew by 150 percent, the market value of equity increased by 175 percent, so that the debt-to-equity ratio of nonfinancial corporations actually declined slightly over the past 10 years. As figure 5 shows, debt-to-equity ratios are

currently less than they were during much of the 1970s, a time when stock prices were depressed.[12] Although leverage in U.S. industrial corporations is greater than it was during the 1950s and 1960s, the shift toward more debt in capital structures occurred during the 1970s, not the 1980s.

Nor has there been any widespread decline in debt quality, despite frequent reports to the contrary in the popular press. Moody's Investor Services reports that issues rated Aaa (the firm's highest rating) constituted the most rapidly expanding category of bonds between 1977 and 1989. Issues rated B (the lowest rating for which figures are reported) did take second place in the growth sweepstakes, but by 1989, Aaa issues represented 33 percent of all outstanding issues rated by Moody's, while B-rated issues constituted only 8 per-

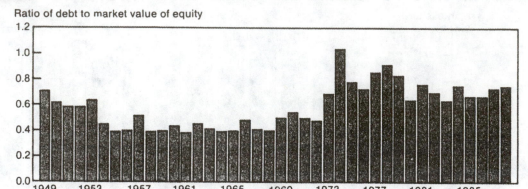

FIGURE 5 LEVERAGE IN NONFINANCIAL CORPORATIONS

Ratio of debt to market value of equity

SOURCE: Balance Sheets for the U.S. Economy, Board of Governors of the Federal Reserve System.

cent of the total.[13] (Recall that the high-yield category was minuscule compared to the investment-grade category at the beginning of the decade.)

This is not to say that high-yield debt is of the same quality as investment-grade debt. Recent defaults among firms that experienced leveraged buyouts during the 1980s have called our attention to a simple fact: high-yield bonds bear high yields because they are riskier than investment-grade bonds. A number of studies report 10-year cumulative default rates on B-rated issues of 30 percent. In contrast, investment-grade issues enjoy cumulative default rates on the order of 1 or 2 percent.[14] The greater default rates associated with high-yield bonds should not surprise investors: Hickman reported a similar discrepancy in default rates for the 1900–1943 period in his 1958 study. (The default rates reported by Hickman are higher than the modern experience for both investment-grade issues and speculative-grade issues. At least part of the difference is attributable to the fact that the Great Depression is included in his sample.)

A feature of default experience that is far more significant than the average default rate is the sensitivity of defaults to overall business conditions. Defaults among high-quality issues are not especially sensitive to economic growth. In contrast, defaults among lower-grade issues are affected significantly by the level of business activity. The implication of this sensitivity is that the onset of a recession is likely to be associated with financial distress among a number of high-yield issuers. The $6 billion in total 1989 defaults, which occurred during a year when economic growth slowed but did not stop, are a reminder of this fact.

The possibility of widespread financial distress among corporate borrowers merits careful consideration from policymakers. Recent analyses of the severe economic depressions that marked the nineteenth century and the first part of the twentieth century suggest that the collapse of credit markets played an important role in these episodes.[15] But the mechanism that induced the collapse of credit appears to have been a significant deflation, or downward revision in expected inflation, which decreased corporate revenues while the value of debt obligations remained fixed, leaving borrowers unable to pay their bills or obtain new credit. The behavior of the money supply and the price level in the United States during the postwar period indicates that this scenario is unlikely, although not impossible.

Moreover, the nonchalant reception that the bankruptcy of Drexel Burnham Lambert received in credit markets suggests that isolated incidents are not apt to trigger a panic.[16]

Conclusion

The spectacular growth of corporate debt during the 1980s was accompanied by the equally spectacular growth of the high-yield bond market. Attributing these phenomena to fads or to greed ignores the fact that neither explanation represents a new force on Wall Street or in the world at large. Financial innovation and the significant restructuring of the U.S. tax code are explanations that hold up much better to careful scrutiny. Recent events are likely to result in increased caution among investors, but the high-yield bond market was created by forces that persist today, and it is unlikely to follow into oblivion the firm credited with its inception.

Footnotes

1. Price and volume statistics were supplied by IDD Information Services.

2. There was an active market in the U.S. for below-investment-grade bonds between 1900 and 1945. See W. Braddock Hickman, *Corporate Bond Quality and Investor Experience.* Princeton: The Princeton University Press and the National Bureau of Economic Research, 1958.

3. Business investment in plant and equipment is taken from table C-54 of the Economic Report of the President, February 1990. Credit-market debt figures are from Balance Sheets for the U.S. Economy, Board of Governors of the Federal Reserve System, October 1989.

4. The difference between investment and credit-market debt is accounted for by retained earnings.

5. The first composite consists of debt created through intermediaries, while the second focuses on securities issued directly by the firm. The appropriate category for some items (mortgage debt and tax-exempt bonds) is not always clear, but the trend is not sensitive to variations in the definition of the two categories.

6. The data for changes in bank loans and outstanding bonds are from Balance Sheets for the U.S. Economy, op. cit. The overall bond category is comprehensive, encompassing private placements, speculative-grade debt, and convertible debt. The speculative-grade debt figures are for public, nonconvertible debt only, as reported in E. Altman, "The Nature of the Market for High-Yield Bonds: Nature of the Market and Effect on Federally Insured Institutions," Washington, D.C.: U.S. Government Printing Office, May 1988. If private placements were included in the speculative-grade debt series, it would be significantly greater.

7. See Glen Yago, Testimony submitted to the U.S. General Accounting Office hearings on high-yield bonds, U.S. General Accounting Office, 1988.

8. The Garn-St Germain Act of 1982 provided thrift institutions with the authority to participate in a wide variety of new investment activities, including investment in high-yield bonds.

9. The elimination of the investment tax credit alone was designed to raise an additional $118 billion in revenue at the corporate level between 1987 and 1991. See Joint Committee on Taxation, "Summary of Conference Agreement on HR 3838, The Tax Reform Act of 1986," August 29, 1986.

10. Prior to 1986, 60 percent of long-term capital gains were exempt from taxation. Individuals currently enjoy a greatly reduced incentive for realizing profits in the form of capital gains rather than interest or dividends.

11. See D. Givoly, C. Hayn, A. Ofer, and O. Sarig, "Taxes and Capital Structure: Evidence from Firms' Response to the Tax Reform Act of 1986," Working Paper, Northwestern University, December 1989. By observing individual firms before and after the Tax Reform Act, these authors are able to circumvent some of the measurement problems that plagued previous studies and document a number of responses to the tax-law revision.

12. The impact of rising equity prices on this relationship is reflected in the value of the Standard & Poor's 500 index, which increased by 210 percent between 1979 and 1989. Equity repurchases explain why the market value of outstanding equity grew less rapidly than equity prices. Figures for debt and equity values are from Balance Sheets for the U.S. Economy, Board of Governors of the Federal Reserve System.

13. "Historical Default Rates of Corporate Bond Issuers: 1970 Through 1988," Moody's Investor Services, July 1989.

14. See E. Altman, "Measuring Corporate Bond Mortality and Performance," *Journal of Finance*, vol. 44 (September 1989), pp. 909-22; P. Asquith, D. Mullins, and E. Wolff, "Original Issue High Yield Bonds: Aging Analyses of Defaults, Exchanges and Calls," *Journal of Finance*, vol. 44 (September 1989), pp. 923-52; and Moody's, op. cit. All of these studies report similar figures.

15. See B. Bernanke, "Nonmonetary Effects of the Financial Crisis in the Propagation of the Great Depression," *American Economic Review*, vol. 63 (1983), pp. 257-76; and Charles Calomiris and R. Glenn Hubbard, "Price Flexibility, Credit Availability, and Economic Fluctuations: Evidence from the United States, 1894-1909," *Quarterly Journal of Economics*, vol. 104 (August 1989), pp. 429-52.

16. Historically, widespread banking panics not accompanied by a severe downward revision in price expectations are quite rare. Runs against individual banks associated with fears of financial weakness (that were often warranted) were much more frequent. See Charles Calomiris and Charles Kahn, "Demandable Debt as the Optimal Banking Contract," Working Paper, Northwestern University, July 1989.

Richard H. Jefferis, Jr. is a visiting scholar at the Federal Reserve Bank of Cleveland.

The views stated herein are those of the author and not necessarily those of the Federal Reserve Bank of Cleveland or of the Board of Governors of the Federal Reserve System.

Article 20

The Truth about Junk Bonds

By Sean Becketti

Junk bonds have been a common element in some of the country's worst financial wrecks this year. The Campeau retailing conglomerate collapsed in January under a heavy debt burden, much of it junk bonds. First Executive Corporation, one of the nation's largest insurance companies, announced a fourth-quarter 1989 loss of $859 million on its junk bond holdings. And Drexel, Burnham, Lambert, the investment bank responsible for the growth of the junk bond market, filed for bankruptcy in February 1990.

These corporate casualties are only the most recent of the problems blamed on junk bonds. For years, some critics have claimed junk bonds are responsible for a host of broader financial market ills. According to these critics, junk bonds fueled the merger mania of the 1980s, caused the rapid growth in the level of corporate debt in recent years, and more generally increased financial market volatility.

If these serious charges are accurate, it may be time for laws or regulations to restrict the use of junk bonds. But if the charges are not accurate,

restricting the use of junk bonds would unnecessarily increase the cost of funds for many businesses.

The truth is that the evidence does not support these extreme charges against junk bonds. To be sure, there may be other concerns about junk bonds, such as whether junk bonds are suitable investments for banks and thrifts. This article does not address concerns such as these. Instead, the article examines whether junk bonds should be blamed for the rise in corporate mergers, corporate debt, and financial market volatility. The first section of the article defines junk bonds. The second section explains why some critics make these accusations against junk bonds, and the third section shows why these charges are not well-founded.

I. What Are Junk Bonds?

A corporation can obtain funds in many ways. It can raise funds by retaining earnings, issuing equity, or floating debt. If it chooses to take on debt, the corporation faces further choices. For short-term finance, it can issue commercial paper or take out bank loans. For intermediate and long-term finance, it can take out

Sean Becketti is a senior economist at the Federal Reserve Bank of Kansas City. Dan Roberts, a research associate at the bank, assisted in the preparation of the article.

bank loans, mortgage property, privately place bonds, or issue marketable corporate bonds. If the corporation chooses to issue marketable bonds, the bonds might be junk bonds.

Junk bonds are corporate bonds with low ratings from a major ratings service. Bond ratings are letter grades that indicate the rating services' opinions of the likelihood of a default. High-rated bonds are called investment-grade bonds, low-rated bonds are called speculative-grade bonds or, less formally, junk bonds.

A bond may receive a low rating for a number of reasons. If the financial condition or business outlook of the company is poor, bonds are rated speculative-grade. Bonds also are rated speculative-grade if the issuing company already has large amounts of debt outstanding. Some bonds are rated speculative-grade because they are subordinated to other debt—that is, their legal claim on the firm's assets in the event of default stands behind the other claims, so-called senior debt.

Junk bonds are traded in a dealer market rather than being listed on an exchange. A small group of investment banks makes a market in these securities; that is, they stand ready to buy or sell junk bonds.[1] Participating investment banks typically make a market in the issues they underwrite and in a limited number of relatively heavily traded issues considered "good credits."

Institutional investors hold the largest share of junk bonds. At the end of 1988, insurance companies, money managers, mutual funds, and pension funds held three-quarters of the face value of the outstanding junk bonds (SEC 1990, p. 22). Individual investors held only 5 percent of the outstanding bonds.

II. Why Are Junk Bonds Criticized?

Junk bonds have been blamed for three financial market ills in recent years: the merger boom, the rise in corporate debt, and the increase in financial market volatility. Critics connect junk bonds with these developments because they occurred simultaneously during the 1980s.

The market for junk bonds was revitalized in the late 1970s and the 1980s after decades of inactivity.[2] In 1977, the investment banking firm of Drexel, Burnham, Lambert began underwriting original-issue junk bonds. From 1977 through 1981, new issues never exceeded $1.5 billion (Chart 1). Then, starting in 1982, junk bond issues enjoyed five years of explosive growth. New issues peaked in 1986 and receded slightly in the last few years to between $25 billion and $30 billion a year. The face value of outstanding junk bonds is currently in the neighborhood of $200 billion, up almost twenty-fold over ten years ago.[3]

As the junk bond market flourished during the last decade, mergers, corporate debt, and financial market volatility also grew. From the end of 1979 through the end of 1989, the value of U.S. mergers grew more than 300 percent.[4] Corporate debt grew over 270 percent.[5] Volatility in U.S. bond markets reached an all-time high in the 1980s. In addition, notable episodes of financial market volatility were the stock market collapses of October 1987 and October 1989.

More than mere coincidence, however, is needed to blame the financial market ills of the 1980s on the growth of the junk bond market. The decade of the 1980s saw the rise of many financial market innovations besides junk bonds—financial futures, program trading, portfolio insurance, and asset-backed securities to name just a few.[6] Why single out junk bonds as the cause of the merger boom, the growth in corporate debt, and financial market volatility?

Some observers suggest that junk bonds caused both the merger boom and the growth in corporate debt by extending credit too freely. According to this argument, corporations unable to borrow in traditional debt markets obtained funds by issuing junk bonds. Some potential acquirers found it easy to float junk bonds to raise

Chart 1
New Issues of Junk Bonds

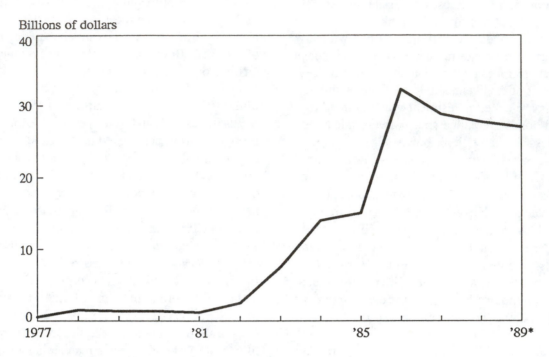

Billions of dollars

*Annualized estimate from data for the first nine months of 1989.

Sources: Perry and Taggart, Jr. 1990 (1977-80); SEC 1990 (1981-89).

the funds for their corporate takeovers. Similarly, some corporate borrowers took advantage of lower credit standards in the junk bond market to go on a debt "binge."[7]

Observers also suggest that the unusual volatility and unpredictability of junk bonds led to higher financial market volatility. This argument is related to the previous one. If, as some critics believe, junk bonds are the result of declining credit standards, then the market for junk bonds is prone to collapse. Investors may initially enjoy high returns, but the borrowers' failure to generate enough earnings to redeem the bonds leads inevitably to defaults. The prospect of these defaults causes frequent shifts in investor portfolios, from junk bonds to safer assets and back again, as investor confidence in

junk bonds ebbs and flows with every change in the financial news. These shifts into and out of junk bonds increase the volatility of returns in other markets, such as the market for investment-grade corporate bonds and the market for equities.[8]

These arguments about the links between junk bonds and other financial market developments imply that junk bonds are qualitatively different from other securities and forms of debt. No one claims that such conventional securities as investment-grade bonds or equity extend funds too freely. Nor are these conventional forms of finance accused of causing excessive financial market volatility. Thus, if junk bonds are responsible for the growth in corporate debt, the merger boom, and the increase in financial market volatility, they must have some special characteristic that sets their behavior very much apart from that of other forms of finance.

III. The Truth about Junk Bonds

This section disputes the idea that junk bonds have special characteristics—the key assumption behind the charges against junk bonds. The section then discusses specific flaws in each of the claims and draws the following conclusions: First, junk bonds played a relatively small role in financing the merger boom of the 1980s. Second, junk bonds are too small a part of the debt market to account for the growth in corporate debt. Third, the timing of the growth in junk bond issues is not closely related to financial market volatility.

Junk bonds are similar to conventional investments

Junk bonds are similar to other, familiar investments with respect to the four principal characteristics of investments: risk, return, liquidity, and control over corporate management.[9] When measuring investments along each of these four dimensions, junk bonds lie between such conventional investments as equities, investment-grade bonds, bank loans, and private placements.[10]

Junk bonds are *riskier* than investment-grade bonds but less risky than equities. Altman (1988) finds that the junk bond default rate, a key component of risk, was 2.2 percent for the years 1970 through 1986, compared with just 0.2 percent for all publicly issued corporate bonds.[11] A more comprehensive measure of risk is the standard deviation of returns. Perry and Taggart (1990) find the standard deviation of monthly returns of junk bonds is greater than that of investment-grade bonds but less than that of equities and of the capital market as a whole.

Junk bond *returns* lie between those of investment-grade bonds and equities. Blume and Keim (1990) find that from January 1977 through December 1988 average monthly junk bond returns were 0.89 percent, higher than the 0.71 percent earned by investment-grade bonds and lower than the 1.14 percent earned by stocks. Perry and Taggart examined the relative performance of various portfolios in the quarters just preceding, during, and just after the seven post-World War II recessions. They found, again, that junk bond returns were intermediate between those of investment-grade bonds and equities.[12]

Junk bonds are more *liquid* than bank loans and private placements but less liquid than equities. Loan contracts and private placements typically contain customized clauses protecting the rights of the investors and restricting the actions of the borrowers. These clauses reduce the marketability of loans and private placements by increasing the cost to third parties of analyzing and valuing the debts and by increasing the frequency of renegotiation. Junk bonds, in contrast, are relatively standardized securities with an established secondary market. Even issues in default have a limited secondary market allowing investors to cut their losses and avoid protracted bankruptcy proceedings.[13] Recent disruptions in the junk bond market, however, are a reminder that the junk bond secondary market is neither as developed nor as liquid as the secondary market for equities.

Junk bonds offer investors more *control over corporate management* than investment-grade bonds but less control than bank loans, private placements, and equities. Some junk bonds contain "equity kickers," that is, options or conversion privileges that let investors obtain an equity share in the borrowing firm. These features give investors the option to participate in the management of the firm.[14] In addition, some junk bonds are sold in strip financing deals, where both bonds and stocks are sold in fixed proportions to investors. In this case, bond holders have voting rights in the management of the firm.[15]

Since junk bonds are not markedly different from other securities, it is hard to understand why they should have any special ability to trigger corporate borrowing sprees. Junk bonds may have cost or tax advantages that allow for some marginal increase in debt. But these advantages are not likely to induce bondholders to invest in junk bonds more recklessly than they do in other debt instruments that are not materially different from junk bonds. Indeed, the bulk of junk bonds are purchased by the same institutional investors who purchase the bulk of private placements, investors who presumably apply the same credit standards to both types of investment.

Again, because junk bonds are similar to traditional financial instruments, it is doubtful they have any special ability to disrupt financial markets. As in any new financial market, the junk bond market may endure brief periods of somewhat greater volatility than average as the market matures and as investors learn how to analyze the investment characteristics of junk bonds. This extra volatility in the junk bond market may be transmitted to other markets as investors adjust their holdings of junk bonds and other securities. However, the fundamental investment characteristics of junk bonds are similar to those of other well-understood securities, such as equities and investment-grade bonds. All of these markets endure episodes of turbulence: the junk bond market does not stand alone in this regard.

In sum, the similarity of junk bonds to conventional financial instruments casts doubt on claims that junk bonds are responsible for the financial market ills of the 1980s. Furthermore, there are specific reasons why junk bonds should not be blamed for these events.

Junk bonds and the merger boom of the 1980s

The junk bond market is too small to have caused the 1980s merger boom. Although a large fraction of the junk bonds issued in the late 1980s were used to finance corporate takeovers, junk bonds accounted for only a small share of merger finance.[16] Even if all junk bonds issued had been used to finance mergers, junk bonds would have accounted for less than 8 percent of the value of U.S. mergers each year. Because not all junk bonds are used to finance mergers, this ratio is a generous upper bound on the junk bond share of merger finance. Moreover, a General Accounting Office study (1988) found that the bulk of the initial financing for tender offers came not from junk bonds but from bank loans. Thus, junk bonds appear to have played a minor role in financing mergers in the 1980s.

Some critics argue that junk bonds were the catalyst for many mergers and, in this way, caused the merger boom despite their small share in merger finance. It is true that junk bonds played a prominent role in several well-publicized mergers, and it is likely that the availability of junk bonds made a few more mergers possible than would have been the case without junk bonds. However, there are many ways to finance a merger. If junk bonds had not been available, mergers that made economic sense would probably have found other forms of finance. Indeed, previous merger booms have occurred without the aid of junk bonds. For example, during the merger wave of the late 1960s—the most recent merger wave prior to the current one and by some measures as significant as the wave of the 1980s—there was no market for original-issue junk bonds. This lack of junk bond financing in no way restrained the 1960s merger wave.

In fact, the merger boom of the 1980s may have helped establish the junk bond market rather than the other way around. The surge in new issues of junk bonds in the late 1980s coincided with the peak in the merger boom. Some part of the demand for debt generated by the merger boom may have increased interest in junk bonds and other innovative debt instruments.

Chart 2
Junk Bond Issues and Stock Market Volatility

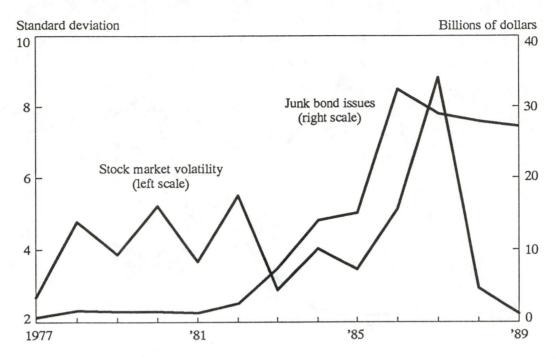

Standard deviation

Billions of dollars

Junk bond issues
(right scale)

Stock market volatility
(left scale)

Note: In this chart, volatility is measured by the annual standard deviation of monthly stock returns of the Standard & Poor's index of 500 stocks.

Sources: See chart 1 (junk bond issues); Center for Research in Security Prices (stock market volatility).

Junk bonds and corporate debt

There is a striking coincidence in the growth of corporate debt and the revitalization of the junk bond market. However, the growth in outstanding junk bonds in the 1980s is not large enough to account directly for the growth in corporate debt. Junk bonds outstanding increased $189 billion from the end of 1979 to the end of 1989. Over the same period, corporate debt increased $1,322 billion. Thus, junk bonds accounted for only 14 percent of the growth in corporate debt.

Furthermore, it is difficult to say that junk bonds were more responsible for the growth in total corporate debt than any another component. During the 1980s, investment-grade bonds

increased more than 100 percent, bank loans grew more than 150 percent, and commercial paper outstanding increased more than 300 percent (Board of Governors of the Federal Reserve System 1990, pp. 35-36). These three forms of debt account for two-thirds of the growth in corporate debt. Clearly, all of these forms of debt played a part in the growth.

Indeed, it is possible that the growth in corporate debt contributed to the growth of the junk bond market, rather than the other way around. A prominent trend in financial markets in the 1980s was the move toward securitization of debt, that is, a move away from intermediated, nonmarketable forms of debt, such as bank loans, and toward marketable securities, such as corporate bonds.[17] Many of the financial innova-

Chart 3
Junk Bond Issues and Bond Market Volatility

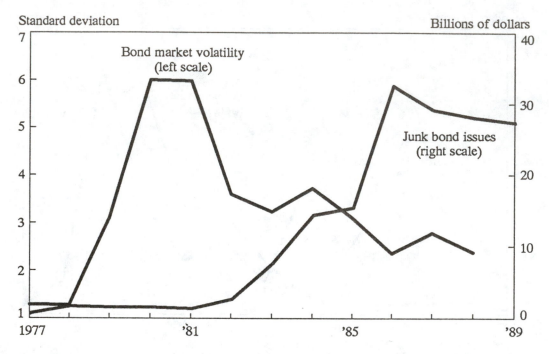

Note: In this chart, volatility is measured by the standard deviation of monthly returns of the Salomon Brothers' Long-Term High-Grade Corporate Bonds Index.

Sources: See chart 2.

tions of the 1980s came to popularity as part of this trend. Junk bonds may be just another reflection of the securitization phenomenon.

Junk bonds and financial market volatility

Financial markets in the late 1980s endured some difficult times—particularly the stock market collapse of October 1987. Some observers claim the growth of the junk bond market increased financial market volatility.

One problem with this claim is the lack of an apparent relationship between the growth of the junk bond market and stock market volatility. Chart 2 shows new issues of junk bonds and stock market volatility from 1981 through 1989.[18] Junk bond issues grew rapidly through 1986 and then leveled off. Stock market volatility was very high in 1987, thanks to the October market collapse, but was unexceptional otherwise.[19] If there were a connection between stock market volatility and the growth of the junk bond market, stock volatility would be high throughout the late 1980s instead of just in 1987.

Furthermore, the growth of the junk bond market and volatility in high-grade corporate bond returns are inversely related. Chart 3 shows new issues of junk bonds again, but this time with the volatility of the Salomon Brothers index of long-term, high-grade corporate bonds.[20] Bond market volatility began the 1980s at record levels and was lower thereafter. If there were a connection between bond market volatility and the growth of the junk bond market, bond volatility would have risen rather than fallen in the late 1980s.[21]

IV. Conclusion

For years, critics have blamed junk bonds for a variety of financial market ills. The merger boom of the 1980s, the rise in corporate debt, and financial market volatility in the 1980s are all traced, by some observers, to junk bonds.

The truth is that the evidence does not support these charges against junk bonds. The key premise in the case against junk bonds—the belief that junk bonds have special properties that upset financial markets—is questionable. While the junk bond market grew at the same time that financial market problems surfaced, this circumstantial link turns out to be unpersuasive. The junk bond market has accounted for only a small part of the merger boom and of the growth in corporate debt, and the growth in the junk bond market is not closely associated with the trends in financial market volatility. Of course, there may be other concerns over junk bonds; for example, it may be inappropriate for banks and thrifts to hold junk bonds. Nevertheless, the three charges against junk bonds examined in this article are not supported by the evidence.

Endnotes

[1] A small number of junk bonds, including some RJR Nabisco issues, are listed on the New York Stock Exchange (SEC 1990, p. 1).

[2] Junk bonds are just low-rated bonds, and low-rated bonds have always been a component of debt markets. In fact, in the 1920s and 1930s, junk bonds accounted for about 17 percent of new issues of corporate bonds on average (Hickman 1958, p. 153). However, the high default rates of the 1930s soured investors on junk bonds, and the market languished until the late 1970s.

[3] The SEC estimates that $204 billion par value registered securities were outstanding as of September 30, 1989. There are no reliable estimates of the market value of these securities (SEC 1990, p. 1). Altman (1987) gives estimates of the value of outstanding junk bonds for earlier years.

[4] This figure is from the database maintained by *Mergers & Acquisitions* magazine. This database tracks mergers of domestic firms with at least $1 million in assets. The value of each merger is recorded as the estimated value of all forms of consideration paid—cash, stocks, bonds, options, etc.—for the acquired company.

[5] There are many ways to measure the increase in corporate indebtedness in the 1980s. Two thorough examinations of this issue are Bernanke and Campbell 1988 and Faust 1990.

[6] Links have been suggested between financial market problems and some of these innovations. For example, program trading and portfolio insurance have been blamed for financial market volatility. However, none of these innovations has been connected with all three financial market developments.

[7] A number of observers make these or similar claims. For examples on the connections between junk bonds and the merger boom, see the comments of Gail I. Hessol, Managing Director for Standard & Poor's, a major securities rating service (Hessol 1988 and *Wall Street Journal* 1990).

To the extent junk bonds caused the merger boom, they also contributed to the growth in corporate debt, since a part of the growth in debt represents the financing of mergers (Clark and Malabre 1988).

[8] Hessol (1988) testified both to the current and prospective risk of junk bonds. In addition, if junk bonds caused the merger boom and the growth of corporate debt, then junk bonds may also have indirectly increased financial market volatility, because some analysts believe that both the merger boom and higher debt affected financial market performance. This point was made in a speech by Rand Araskog, the chairman of ITT Corporation (Clark and Malabre 1988). More recently, some market participants attributed the stock market disruptions of October 1989 to the collapse of the United Airlines buyout.

[9] The similarity of junk bonds to conventional investments does *not* imply that junk bonds are appropriate investments for all investors. For example, junk bonds may not be appropriate for banks and thrifts, just as some other conventional investments—equities, for example—are considered inappropriate investments for banks and thrifts.

[10] Private placements are essentially loans made by nonbanks, typically such institutional investors as insurance companies. They may take the form of either loan contracts or bonds. However, if they are bonds, they are not offered for sale on the public market. Private placements are underwritten by commercial and investment banks.

[11] Junk bonds are, of course, expected to have a higher default rate than investment-grade bonds. That is why they are rated lower than investment-grade bonds. A number of studies attempt to quantify the default risk of junk bonds. Most report annual default rates in the 1 to 3 percent range. Asquith, Mullins, and Wolff (1989) find much higher annual default rates, in the 3 to 9 percent range.

[12] Some observers argue that changes in the nature of junk bond issues make historical evidence on the risk and return of junk bonds an unreliable guide to their future behavior. If these observers are correct, junk bonds could be much riskier and could earn lower returns in the future.

[13] Altman (1989) reports that, on average, junk bonds sell for slightly less than 40 percent of face value at the end of the month in which default takes place.

[14] Equity kickers also allow investors to share in any unexpectedly high profits the firm might earn. This characteristic stands in contrast to traditional bonds where returns are limited to the coupons explicitly offered by the bond. These features not only increase the expected return to bondholders but also serve as a form of call protection since borrowers are more likely to call bonds when profits increase.

[15] Some observers argue that strip financing, along with other forms of junk bond finance, is chosen to reduce the double taxation of corporate dividends while retaining an equity relationship with investors. In other words, according to this view, junk bonds in strip financing function as though they were common stock. The interest paid on the junk bonds is tax deductible to the corporation, in contrast to any dividends paid. Since bondholders and stockholders are the same entities, the net tax burden can be decreased by paying out earnings as coupon payments on the junk bonds rather than as dividends on the common shares.

16 Drexel, Burnham, Lambert estimated that all forms of acquisition financing accounted for 79 percent of junk bond issues in 1987 and 83 percent in 1988. First Boston found that acquisition financing accounted for 76 percent of junk bond issues in 1989 (SEC 1990, p. 20).

17 All forms of corporate debt grew in the 1980s. However, bank loans grew more slowly than bonds, causing them to lose market share to corporate bonds.

18 New issues of junk bonds are compared with the annual standard deviation of monthly returns to see if the growth of the junk bond market increased financial market volatility generally. It might be the case that very short-lived disruptions in the junk bond market caused similarly brief disruptions in other financial markets. That is not the kind of volatility considered here.

The rate of new issues is used to measure the size of the junk bond market in this chart. Essentially the same picture would be produced by using the value of outstanding junk bonds to measure the size of the market.

19 For the post-World War II period, the annual standard deviation of monthly stock returns averaged 3.9 percent. Excluding 1987, the annual standard deviation of monthly stock returns in the 1980s was again 3.9 percent.

20 The Salomon Brothers index includes AAA and AA corporate bonds with maturities of ten years or more. These data end in 1988. In the post-World War II era, the annual standard deviation of this index averaged 1.8 percent. In the 1980s, the annual standard deviation averaged 3.7 percent.

21 Although bond market volatility fell during the 1980s, it remained above its post-World War II average throughout the decade. Some observers maintain that increased corporate leverage in the 1980s, that is, higher ratios of corporate debt to equity, is responsible for this generally higher bond market volatility. Even if this claim is correct, all forms of corporate debt grew in the 1980s, and there is no reason to single out junk bonds as the sole or most important debt component responsible for increased volatility.

References

Altman, Edward I., ed. 1987. "The Anatomy of the High-Yield Bond Market," *Financial Analysts Journal*, July/August.

_____. 1988. "Analyzing Risks and Returns in the High-Yield Bond Market," *Financial Markets and Portfolio Management*.

_____. 1989. "The 'Junk Bond' Default Rate Debate," Working Paper 539, Salomon Brothers Center for the Study of Financial Institutions, New York University, November.

Asquith, P., D. Mullins, and E. Wolff. 1989. "Original Issue High Yield Bonds: Aging Analyses of Defaults, Exchanges, and Calls," *Journal of Finance*. September.

Bernanke, Ben S., and John Y. Campbell. 1988. "Is There a Corporate Debt Crisis?" *Brookings Papers on Economic Activity*.

Blume, Marshall E., and Donald B. Keim. 1990. "Risk and Return Characteristics of Lower-Grade Bonds, 1977-1987," in Edward I. Altman, ed., *The High-Yield Debt Market: Investment Performance and Economic Impact*. Homewood, Ill.: Dow Jones-Irwin.

Board of Governors of the Federal Reserve System. 1990. Balance Sheets for the U.S. Economy 1945-89.

Clark, Jr., Lindley H., and Alfred Malabre, Jr. 1988. "Takeover Trend Helps Push Corporate Debt and Defaults Upward," *Wall Street Journal*. March 15.

Faust, Jon. 1990. "Will Higher Corporate Debt Worsen Future Recessions?" *Economic Review*, Federal Reserve Bank of Kansas City, March/April.

General Accounting Office. 1988. *Financial Markets: Issuers, Purchasers, and Purposes of High Yield, Non-investment Grade Bonds*. Washington: Government Printing Office. February.

Hessol, Gail. 1988. *United States General Accounting Office Hearing on High Yield Bonds*, comments in appendix. General Accounting Office. May, p. 177.

Hickman, W. Braddock. 1958. *Corporate Bond Quality and Investor Experience*. Princeton, N.J.: Princeton University Press.

Perry, Kevin J., and Robert A. Taggart, Jr. 1990. "Development of the Junk Bond Market and Its Role in Portfolio Management and Corporate Finance," in Edward I. Altman, ed., *The High-Yield Debt Market: Investment Performance and Economic Impact*. Homewood, Ill.: Dow Jones-Irwin.

U.S. Securities and Exchange Commission. 1990. *Recent Developments in the High Yield Market*. Staff report, March.

Wall Street Journal. 1990. "Reactions to Milken: Villain or Victim?" April 25.

Article 21

Innovations in Modeling the Term Structure of Interest Rates

Peter A. Abken

				.01
				+.01
				+.02
		1-N		+.01
		91-N		7.38	+.02
		1991-N	10,	7.39	+.02
		1/1991-N	11/0	90	7.41	+.03
9	28,	-N	6 1	15/1991-N	11/08/1990	7.42	+.03
6 3/	3/31/1991-N	8 1/2	1/15/1991-N	11/15/1990	7.42	+.03
9 3/4	03/31/1991-N	14 1/4	11/15/1991-N	11/23/1990	7.42	+.04
12 3/8	04/15/1991-N	7 3/4	11/30/1991-N	11/29/1990	7.41	+.03
9 1/4	04/30/1991-N	7 5/8	12/31/1991-N	12/06/1990	7.39	+.03
8 1/8	05/15/1991-N	8 1/4	12/31/1991-N	12/13/1990	7.37	+.04
14 1/2	05/15/1991-N	11 5/8	01/15/1992-N	12/20/1990	7.39	+.04
8 3/4	05/31/1991-N	8 1/8	01/31/1992-N	12/27/1990WI	7.37	+.06
7 7/8	06/30/1991-N	6 5/8	02/15/1992-N	01/03/1991	7.31	+.02
8 1/4	06/30/1991-N	9 1/8	02/15/1992-N	01/10/1991	7.40	+.02
13 3/4	07/15/1991-N	14 5/8	02/15/1992-N	01/17/1991	7.36	+.03
7 3/4	07/31/1991-N	8 1/2	02/29/1992-N	01/24/1991	7.41	+.04
7 1/2	08/15/1991-N	7 7/8	03/31/1992-N	01/31/1991	7.37	+.01
8 3/4	08/15/1991-N	8 1/2	03/31/1992-N	02/07/1991	7.35	+.03
14 7/8	08/15/1991-N	11 3/4	04/15/1992-N	02/14/1991	7.29	+.02

Economists and market practitioners have long sought to understand interest-rate movements. As a result, a number of term-structure models have been developed over the years. Major advances in option-pricing theory in the 1970s led the way to significant progress. In this article, the author discusses two recent term-structure models that have been highly influential in stimulating further research and are being applied to valuing a wide variety of financial instruments.

The phrase *term structure of interest rates* refers to the relationship between interest rates on bonds of different maturities. It is no doubt familiar to most who peruse the newspaper's financial pages. A precise understanding of what determines the relationships among these interest rates is still lacking, however, despite a voluminous amount of research. The reason for this open-endedness is not hard to grasp: current interest rates to a large extent reflect expectations of future interest rates, as well as all relevant factors that impinge on them.

Financial economists have long sought to characterize, and more importantly to predict, interest-rate movements using mathematical models. These models tend to shape thinking about the term structure even if a formal model is not a conscious part of this process. Policymakers, money managers, and other investors often look to the term structure for clues about the market's expectation regarding future interest rates. To make sense of the array of interest rates determined in financial markets, any such divination usually implicitly or explicitly uses a theory of the term structure. The interest-rate forecasts embedded in the term structure may help to form individual forecasts, upon which all kinds of economic decisions are based. Differences between individual and market outlooks on interest rates may also spur investors and speculators to bet against the market through their trading of bonds. This trading moves bond prices and thus leads to a melding of private information with the public information embodied in the term structure.

Since about the mid-1980s the most important application of term-structure models has been in valuing various kinds of interest-rate options. The most basic of these are bond options, which can be used to hedge the value of bond portfolios against capital losses. Interest-rate caps and swaps are examples of more complex interest-rate contingent claims that can hedge interest payments on debt whose interest rate fluctuates periodically with market rates.[1] Caps and swaps can be viewed as portfolios of bond options and may be valued using term-structure models. Much current financial research centers on refining existing term-structure models and on developing new ones that are easier to use and more accurate in their predictions.

This article begins with a review of the elementary theories of the term structure. These theories—the expectations hypothesis, the liquidity premium hypothesis, and the preferred habitat hypothesis—have been standards in economics since the 1960s and still constitute the core of contemporary textbooks. These theories are no longer "state of the art," however. This article attempts to bridge the gap between the traditional hypotheses of the term structure and more recent, less accessible work stimulated by innovations in options pricing theory since

the early 1970s. Additionally, the discussion of the term-structure models explores the connection between the new modeling "technology" that produced the path-breaking Black-Scholes option-pricing formula published in 1973 and its applicability to pricing bonds, which, like options, are another kind of so-called contingent claim.

Intended as a nonmathematical exposition of both the traditional and recent models of the term structure, this article introduces the term structure by briefly reviewing the three traditional hypotheses as well as the newer models, which are essentially elaborations of the same concepts. Two recent-vintage term-structure models, developed in the mid-1980s, are examined in detail—the Cox-Ingersoll-Ross (1985b) and Ho and Lee (1986) models, which have been highly influential and represent different directions that modeling efforts have taken. To provide a context for these models, related models are also discussed. A brief survey of very recent research shows how these newer models have been extended or applied, and an option pricing example using the Ho and Lee model illustrates an important application of these models.

Whether pricing bonds or contingent claims, all models considered in this article share certain basic principles. The new models explicitly build in uncertainty about the course of future interest rates; they are models of random interest rates. Knowledge of constraints on the behavior of interest-rate movements allows for construction of models that value bonds or interest-rate contingent claims. This article explains how this valuation is accomplished.

The Term Structure under Uncertainty

The term structure of interest rates refers to yields on bonds that are alike in all respects except their time to maturity. Default

The author is an economist in the financial section of the Atlanta Fed's research department.

risk, for example, should be the same across all bonds to allow meaningful comparisons of bond yields spanning the maturity spectrum. Not only because credit risk is absent but also because government bonds offer the broadest range of maturities of all bonds, most analyses of the term structure are conducted using default-free government bonds. The box on page 5 gives some elementary definitions concerning zero-coupon bonds as well as the arithmetic for relating zero-coupon bond prices and yields to maturity. The box on page 12 considers the basic building blocks for the expectations hypothesis and explains how arbitrage forces equality in the holding-period returns on bonds of different maturities. The analysis shown has been conducted in a theoretical world of perfect certainty about future interest rates.

Expectations Hypothesis. Once the future becomes uncertain, investors face interest-rate risk.[2] This risk is irrelevant for investors whose future cash needs exactly match their bonds' maturity dates. The bonds mature at par, and no capital gains or losses are possible. Such a coincidence is the exception rather than the rule, though. If investors need cash sooner, they are necessarily exposed to the possibility of capital loss; that is, newly issued bonds for the same maturity date may bear higher yields, forcing existing bond holders to sell at a discount to match the higher yield. Conversely, if their bonds mature sooner than the time of their cash need, the investors risk reinvesting at a lower yield in a new bond that matures on the desired date. If they had bought a longer-term bond at the outset, no such risk would have been incurred.

In economics the existence of risk implies that the outcome of a decision is not known precisely; however, a range of possible outcomes is known, each of which has some chance—some probability—of occurring. Thus, investors are assumed to know the range of outcomes and, more specifically, the probability distribution for the likelihood that any particular outcome will occur. These and other statistical concepts are fundamental to theories of the term structure because they quantify investors' expectations.

In the expectations hypothesis of the term structure, risk has no effect on investors'

choices. All that matters is their expectation of future interest rates at all maturities. Here the term *expectation* is used in its narrow statistical sense to mean average or mean value for a particular future interest rate. The range of outcomes for an interest rate may be quite wide or quite narrow, but that issue is irrelevant to investors. Investors are said to be "risk neutral."

The expectations theory posits that, regardless of the holding period considered, any possible combination of bonds must offer the same rate of return. This idea, illustrated in the box on page 12 for one- and two-year bonds, works exactly the same way for any other maturity combinations. Any long-term bond yield is the average of the current short-term yield and future expected short-term yields. The essential assumption is that investors care only about holding-period returns and consider all bonds of different maturities as perfect substitutes. All interest rates along the yield curve are therefore linked by arbitrage.

Liquidity Premium Hypothesis. Rather than "risk neutral," investors may be "risk averse," in which case their average sensitivity to bearing risk will be reflected in bond prices. The usual presumption is that longer-term bonds are riskier in the sense that their principal is more exposed to interest-rate fluctuations over time. Specifically, this exposure makes them less liquid (less readily converted to cash by selling them) because they bear a greater potential for capital loss before maturity. Risk-averse investors therefore are believed to require a "liquidity premium" to induce them to hold longer-term bonds willingly. The liquidity premium manifests itself as an increase in the forward rate above the future spot rate, which results in a shifting of the yield curve above the one predicted by the expectations hypothesis. Known as the liquidity premium hypothesis, this concept is a refinement of the expectations hypothesis. The liquidity premium is alternatively known as a *risk premium*, which will be the term used hereafter. To distinguish it, the expectations hypothesis is sometimes called the pure (or risk-neutral) expectations hypothesis.

The liquidity premium hypothesis is rather vague about what determines the risk premi-

Basic Terminology

The basic financial instrument of interest is a zero-coupon bond that promises a fixed payment, which will be assumed to be $1, at a future date.[1] The bond makes no interim payments, that is, it has no coupons. While zeros—Treasury bills and zero-coupon Treasury bonds—trade in the bond markets, many bonds make periodic coupon payments. Because any coupon bond can be decomposed into a zero coupon bond by treating each future coupon payment as well as the repayment of principal as a separate zero coupon, modeling in terms of zeros is not unrealistic.[2] The models to be considered also abstract from credit (or default) risk so that the uncertainty stems only from unknown future interest rates.

A zero-coupon bond is alternatively known as a discount bond because its price is less than its $1 face or par value. Its return is derived strictly from the appreciation in price at the time of maturity. For the sake of simplicity, bonds are assumed to be issued at yearly intervals with maturities in multiples of a year, making the shortest maturity bond a one-year bond. The current date will be time 0.

The bond price, B, is the price at time t, when the bond is purchased, for principal repayment upon maturity at later date T. The difference between t and T is called the bond's time to maturity. Consider a bond with one year to maturity (a one-year bond) issued today at time 0. The bond's yield to maturity, $R(1)$, is determined from the following equation involving the bond's price:

$$1/B(1) = 1 + R(1), \text{ or}$$
$$B(1) = 1/[1 + R(1)].$$

The time to maturity is enclosed in parentheses. If the time to maturity is one year and the yield $R(1)$ is 8 percent, then $B(1)$ is approximately 0.926. The term $R(1)$ is expressed as a simple interest rate. Clearly, yield and bond price are inversely related: as one goes up the other goes down.[3]

Consideration of multiple periods entails compounding of interest. The yield to maturity, $R(n)$, of an n period zero-coupon bond is

$$1/B(n) = [1 + R(n)]^n, \text{ or}$$
$$B(n) = 1/[1 + R(n)]^n.$$

The term $R(n)$ is also expressed as a simple annual interest rate. Plotting the yield to maturity against time to maturity gives the so-called yield curve. The reasons for its shape or structure are the subject of the various hypotheses discussed in the main text.

Notes

[1] Of course, any par value can be used simply by multiplying the bond price by the face amount. For example, a bond promising $10,000 upon maturity would be worth 10,000 times the purchase price of the $1 par value discount bond.

[2] See Bodie, Kane, and Marcus (1989, 420) for a procedure used to infer zero-coupon bond prices from the prices, coupons, and principal payments of coupon bonds.

[3] For a fuller discussion of this terminology as well as the basics concerning the traditional hypotheses of the term structure, the reader is referred to Bodie, Kane, and Marcus (1989). Almost any undergraduate investments or money-and-banking textbook contains some discussion of these topics.

---

um, other than supposing that such a premium is the investor's reward for bearing interest-rate risk. The new models incorporating this hypothesis give more structure to the underlying determinants of the risk premium.

Once risk aversion is assumed to affect interest rates, interpretation of the term structure becomes problematic. Without knowing the size of the risk premium, the expectations hypothesis cannot be used to infer future short-term interest rates. Any forward rate now consists of a risk premium and the expected short-term interest rate. Consider the simple example of deciding between an investment in a sequence of consecutive one-year bonds or an investment in a two-year bond, like that used in the box on page 12. Assume that the one-year yield is 5 percent and the future one-year yield is known to be 7 percent. If the true risk premium were known to be 0.5 percent (or 50 basis points), the two-year yield would be:

$$[5\% + (7\% + 0.5\%)]/2 = 6.25\%,$$

that is, the average of the short rate and the forward rate (which is the sum of the future short rate and the risk premium). The two-year yield is 6.25 percent instead of 6 percent as in the risk-neutral case (where the risk premium is zero). If the risk premium is unknown, all that can be inferred from the current term structure (one- and two-year bond yields) is that the implied forward rate is 7.5 percent. More information is required to disentangle the risk premium from the expected short rate.

For a hypothetical continuum of interest rates along the yield curve, Chart 1 shows the relationship among yield curve, expected short-term interest rates, and forward rates. If the term structure slopes downward—that is, short-term bond yields are above long-term bond yields—one may safely infer that expected short-term rates are lower than the current rate, even if there are risk premia in the forward rates. However, upward-sloping yield curves do not imply that expected short-term rates are rising, since flat or declining expected short-term rates may be sufficiently augmented by rising risk premia to produce rising forward rates. Chart 2 illustrates this phenomenon.[3] These interpretations will be discussed again in the review of recent theoretical models of the term structure.

Preferred Habitat Hypothesis. A third traditional theory is the preferred habitat hypothesis, which posits that interest rates along the yield curve result from market forces in different maturity segments. Sufficiently large risk premia or discrepancies between investors' and market expectations of interest rates may lure investors away from their preferred habitat. Thus, as Franco Modigliani and Richard Sutch (1966) have observed, "risk aversion should not lead investors to prefer to stay short but, instead, should lead them to hedge by staying in their

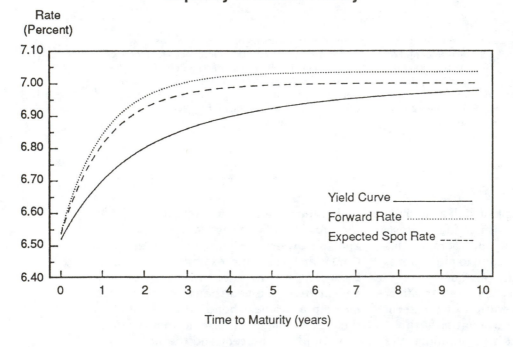

Chart 1.
Liquidity Premium Theory

maturity habitat, unless other maturities (longer or shorter) offer an expected premium sufficient to compensate for the risk and cost of moving out of one's habitat" (184).[4]

Life insurance companies' and pension funds' typical preference for investments in longer-term bonds exemplifies preferred habitats, as does depository institutions' likely penchant for short-term bonds. Life insurance companies and pension funds have relatively predictable long-term liabilities, which they match against investments in long-term bonds and other long-term assets. Similarly, depository institutions tend to fund relatively short-term loans with short-term liabilities. Their bond holdings, therefore, also tend to have short-term maturities.

The supply and demand for bonds within each habitat is assumed to have an impact on interest rates; bonds of different maturities are not considered perfect substitutes. In short, institutional characteristics, not just interest-rate expectations, play a role in determining the term structure. An earlier version of this theory, the market seg-mentation hypothesis, assumed a rigid segmentation of markets, which is now generally regarded as implausible. The preferred habitat hypothesis synthesizes the expectations and market segmentation hypotheses.

Innovations in Modeling the Term Structure

In 1973 Fischer Black and Myron Scholes published their pathbreaking article, "The Pricing of Options and Corporate Liabilities," which transformed not only academic financial research but also actual financial practice. Their celebrated formula allowed academics and practitioners alike to price all kinds of contingent claims.[5] The theory proved to have very broad applications. John C. Cox, Stephen A. Ross, and Mark Rubinstein (1979) have noted that option-pricing theory "applies to a very general class of economic problems—the valuation of contracts where the outcome to each party depends on a

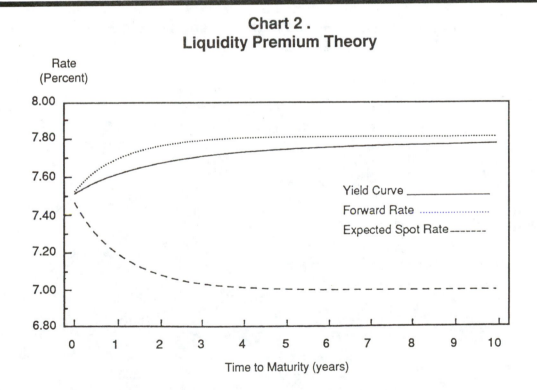

Chart 2 .
Liquidity Premium Theory

Rate (Percent)

Yield Curve ———
Forward Rate ....
Expected Spot Rate - - - - - - -

Time to Maturity (years)

quantifiable uncertain future event" (230). Term structure modeling is one area of financial research that has benefited from the advent of modern option-pricing theory. A detailed review of two general approaches, using two specific models, will develop the connection between option-pricing theory and term-structure modeling. The two models highlight the basic directions of recent research.

The Ho and Lee Model. Proposed by Thomas S.Y. Ho and Sang-Bin Lee in 1986, the Ho and Lee model is a useful starting point in the exposition of term-structure models because it uses what is called a lattice approach. The lattice approach to option pricing explicitly conveys what is meant by a "quantifiable uncertain future event." The basic problem to model is how the price of a zero-coupon bond changes from the present to its future maturity date. Only at the present moment and at the future maturity date is the bond price known with certainty. The Ho and Lee model is one attempt to quantify the

evolution of bond prices over time. As will be illustrated below, this quantification is essential to pricing contingent claims on bonds.

Ho and Lee abstract from the complexities of actual bond price movements by assuming (1) that a bond price moves only at fixed intervals over time (for example, every day or every minute) and (2) that they move either up or down when they change. The up or down price changes have an associated probability of occurring, of, say, 20 percent and 80 percent, respectively. Thus, starting from some known price at the current date, future price changes are restricted to evolve by successive up or down movements, which trace out a tree or lattice pattern.

Chart 3 illustrates the branching process that begins with the initial discount bond price. The initial bond in the example has fifteen months (five quarters) to go before maturity, when it will pay $1. The yield to maturity is assumed to be 9 percent, and the current price is $0.894. The annualized yield to maturity appears in parentheses. Succes-

Chart 3.
Evolution of Bond Prices in the Ho and Lee Model
(yields in parentheses)

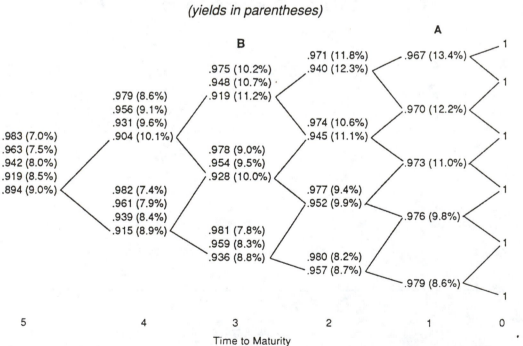

Note: The one-period bond appears at the top of each column; time to maturity increases by one period with each successive row.

sively shorter-term bond prices and yields appear above the 9 percent, fifteen-month bond. Thus, the entire term structure is given in the far left-hand column (five quarters to maturity), starting at the top of the list with a 7 percent, three-month bond that matures (and disappears) in the next column and extending to the longest maturity bond, the 9 percent bond at the bottom of the list. The illustration is therefore given for an upward-sloping term structure.

The tree fans out from the initial price as up and down possibilities proliferate at each future point in time. Each path through the branches to any particular vertex or node in the tree diagram represents a particular succession of up and down price movements. These movements correspond to the realizations of particular "states," which are the possible random outcomes schematically depicted in the tree diagram. After one period elapses from the initial date, two states are possible; after two periods, three states; and so forth. In other words, time is measured horizontally, although states are indicated vertically in the tree diagram. The tree therefore depicts the value of a particular bond in all states as it approaches maturity. In this example, the bond initially has five periods to mature, then four, then three, and so forth. The final branches in the diagram end with $1 in all states, since the bond's value at maturity is known with certainty. The branches link the path of the initial five-quarter bond as it approaches maturity. The shorter-term bonds could also be joined in this fashion to show their progression.

The essential idea behind the evolution of the bond price tree is that the forward rates implied by the initial term structure would actually be the future short-term rates to prevail in the absence of disturbances or shocks causing changes in interest rates. In the Ho and Lee model, bond prices throughout the tree result from perturbations of the initial implied forward rates. Any state price at a given time represents the initial implied forward rate altered by an accumulation of up and down shocks, resulting in a particular position in the tree diagram. Moreover, the size of the price changes, governed by the perturbation function, is restricted in such a way

that no arbitrage profits can be realized; that is, the internal consistency of the model requires that no arbitrary portfolio of discount bonds of different maturities can be formed that earns more than the risk-free rate when the portfolio is perfectly hedged (risk free).

To see how prices are related in the tree diagram, consider any two adjacent state prices. The node marked "A" in Chart 3 is derived as the discounted value of the two certain $1 payoffs at the maturity date, each of which has an equal chance of occurring in this example (that is, the probability is 0.5). The discount factor of 0.967 at node A is in fact the price of a one-period discount bond. This discount factor was computed using Ho and Lee's formula for the perturbation function evaluated at this particular node.[6] All state prices for time 1 are one-period prices. For all earlier periods the bond prices are computed using the same recursive procedure. At node B the price is again the weighted average of two future bond prices times the one-period bond price:

$$(0.5 \times 0.940 + 0.5 \times 0.945) \times 0.975 = 0.919 \, .$$

This calculation represents a discounted expected value since at node B there are two possible future outcomes. Either the bond price rises to 0.945 or falls to 0.940. The average of these is discounted to time 3 using the one-period bond price for time 3. Again, the discount factor is the one-period bond price, 0.975, determined one period earlier (at the top of the bond price list for node B). In summary, the tree diagram represents an expected value calculation, for which the known initial bond price of 0.894 is the final outcome.

At first glance the tree diagram may not seem very useful since the final computation is a bond price that was already known at the outset. However, the important aspect of this exercise is that the various price paths (possible branching patterns) are fully described in the tree. This quantification of a bond's future state prices is essential for contingent claims pricing.

A characteristic of this type of lattice model is that the order of up and down movements does not matter; instead, the cumulative number of up (or down) moves from the initial node determines the price at any future time-state node. Inspection of the tree reveals that, from any interior node, moving rightward first up and then down is identical to moving down, then up. This restriction plays an important role in valuing bonds in this model. Also, the initial upward-sloping term structure retains its slope regardless of its location in future periods, but the levels change. In fact, all interest-rate movements are perfectly correlated in the Ho and Lee model. More complex models that will be considered below avoid this unrealistic feature.

Another drawback of the model is the fact that, depending on the model's parameter values, some bond prices may exceed face value before maturity. This outcome along a price path implies that the bond's interest rate is negative. Peter Ritchken and Kiekie Boenawan (1990) prove that such an occurrence represents an internal inconsistency of the model and show how to modify the model to preclude negative interest rates.

Charts 3 and 4 were produced using the Ritchken-Boenawan modification.

Despite its limitations, the Ho and Lee model has the virtue of clearly and simply illustrating how the current term structure is derived as the discounted expectation of the future bond payoffs. More recent models of this type rectify some of these limitations and consequently are transforming this modeling approach into a more useful tool for applications as well as theory.

A Shift in Risk Aversion. The term-structure movements depicted in Chart 3 are assumed to be generated in a world in which investors do not need to be compensated for bearing interest-rate risk. If investors' preferences shifted to become risk averse with respect to interest-rate risk, what effect would that have on the evolution of bond prices? In general, the expected rate of return for an asset would have to increase for the investor to continue holding that asset willingly. For illustrative purposes, the probability of an upward move was assumed to be the same as the probabil-

Chart 4.
Ho and Lee Model Shift in Risk Aversion Bond Prices
(yields in parentheses)

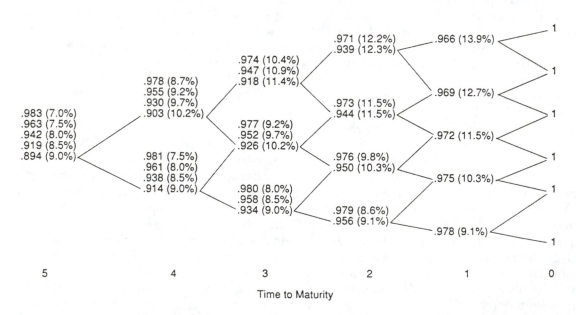

Time to Maturity

Note: The one-period bond appears at the top of each column; time to maturity increases by one period with each successive row.

ity of a downward move in Chart 3. The increase in risk aversion is quantified as an increase in the probability of an upward move from 50 percent to 60 percent. These probabilities are arbitrarily chosen to show the change in the evolution of bond prices. Any increase in the up-move probability would accomplish the same end.[7]

The Ho and Lee model takes the initial term structure as given in the course of valuing future bond prices and contingent claims. Consequently, a shift in preferences is considered to occur after the initial period. Chart 4 gives the new tree diagram, starting with the same initial term structure as Chart 3 and also ending with bond prices equal to par upon maturity in period 5. However, the rate of price appreciation in Chart 4 is always greater (or bond prices are everywhere lower), regardless of the path taken through the tree diagram. The terminal payoff of $1 is the same in both diagrams. The downward shift in prices across all states and times occurs because the discount rates have increased because of the rise in risk aversion. In other words, interest rates are always greater in Chart 4, which reflects the risk premium now included in rates.

The Cox-Ingersoll-Ross Model. The Cox-Ingersoll-Ross model takes an approach to valuing fixed-income securities and their contingent claims that is fundamentally different from Ho and Lee's. The basic difference is that the former is a general equilibrium model, whereas the latter is a partial equilibrium model. Essentially, the Cox-Ingersoll-Ross approach has a deeper theoretical foundation and hence more ambitious goals in terms of economic modeling. The practical distinction is not as sharp at the level of using these models to value bond options.

The Ho and Lee model is a partial equilibrium model in the sense that the initial term structure and the process generating shifts in that structure are assumed to be given outside of the model—that is, they are determined *exogenously*. On the other hand, as will be discussed below, the Cox-Ingersoll-Ross model takes investor preferences and unforecastable shocks to physical investment opportunities as given. That is, term-structure movements themselves are explained within the context of the model; they are explained *endogenously*. The importance of this general equilibrium formulation will become apparent after some preliminary discussion.

The Cox-Ingersoll-Ross model can be stripped of its underlying general equilibrium structure, rendering it a partial equilibrium model. This simplification is a useful starting point for understanding this type of model. In fact, a number of similar models originated at about the same time as the Cox-Ingersoll-Ross model, but these were conceived as partial equilibrium models.[8]

Another difference between the Cox-Ingersoll-Ross and Ho and Lee models is that the former uses continuous-time mathematics, which demands considerably greater technical sophistication than does the discrete-time mathematics of the Ho and Lee model. The use of continuous-time mathematics requires assumptions that all bonds and other financial instruments trade at every moment in time—that is, continuously—and, furthermore, that bonds mature at every moment in time. While highly artificial, this kind of model allows the tools of continuous-time mathematics to deliver pricing formulas for bonds and other financial instruments. In fact, the original Black-Scholes formula was derived using continuous-time mathematics.[9]

The simplest version of the Cox-Ingersoll-Ross model assumes that the term structure can be expressed as a function of one variable, the instantaneous risk-free rate or spot interest rate, that is, the interest rate on a bond that matures at the next "instant" in time. The continuum of bond prices along the term structure is expressed solely as a function of the spot rate and time (or, equivalently, time to maturity). All shocks to the term structure therefore emanate from the spot interest rate, which in fact is a proxy variable for the fundamental uncertainty in the economy. To give more content to this formulation requires appending the full general equilibrium structure of the economy to the model. In contrast, the partial equilibrium model simply posits the instantaneous rate as the source of random fluctuations in the term structure. The spot interest rate is referred to as a "state variable," a variable that summarizes information about uncertainty in the

The Term Structure under Certainty

The question to be answered is, how is the yield on a one-year bond (the "short" rate) related to the yield on a two-year bond (the "long" rate)? Alternatively phrased, for a two-year investment horizon, what governs the decision to select a sequence of two consecutive one-year bonds or one two-year bond? Of course, the answer is that one chooses the alternative that offers the highest yield, but this response must include an important qualification. The choice hinges on what the investor expects the yield will be on the one-year bond to be issued one year hence. Given that expectation, the investor would choose the higher-yielding alternative. However, if there were uncertainty about the future one-year yield, the investor might choose the certain yield on the two-year bond instead. For now we assume that investors hold their expectations with certainty. Certainty means that the expectation will actually be realized in the future.

Investors obviously have strong incentive to seek out the highest return on investments of a given riskiness.[1] This behavior influences the term structure by bidding bond prices, and therefore yields, to a level that reflects the market sentiment about future interest rates. For example, suppose that an investor observes the one-year bond to be currently yielding 5 percent and the two-year bond, 6 percent annually and that the investor believes that the future one-year yield will be 8 percent. To make an investment decision, the investor must determine what the future short rate is implied by market interest rates. For the investor to be indifferent about the investment alternatives over the two-year horizon, the total holding-period rates of return must be equal, that is,

$$2 \times 6\% = 5\% + \text{future short rate};$$
$$\text{future short rate} = 7\%.[2]$$

In other words, the fixed annual yield on the two-year bond summed over two years must equal the sum of the short rate and the expected future short rate. Although the future short rate is not directly observed, it is implied by the one-year and two-year bond rates and is usually referred to as the implied forward rate. In this example assuming certainty about expectations, the forward rate is the same as the expected future short rate.

Given his or her expectation that the future short rate is 8 percent, the investor would rationally choose to buy the current one-year bond and roll over that investment into the future one-year bond. This sequence of bonds would be equivalent to a two-year bond currently offering about 6.5 percent, as compared with the actual yield of 6 percent. The reason that the two-year bond is currently mispriced at 6 percent could be, for example, that investors received news leading them to expect higher inflation a year from now (raising their expected short rate). Their investment choice bids down the price of the two-year bond and hence bids up its yield. Once that yield reaches 6.5 percent, the bond market is back in equilibrium—investors are again indifferent about the investment alternatives. On the other hand, if the expectation were, say, for a 5 percent future one-year bond yield, investors would choose the two-year bond and consequently bid down its yield.

In this example, investors are said to have exploited an arbitrage opportunity. They have profited from the temporarily mispriced two-year bond without taking any risk.[3] Admittedly, this example is highly artificial because expectations are held with certainty; hence, there is by definition no risk. However, this kind of analysis carries over into a more realistic world characterized by uncertainty.

Notes

[1] All bonds are simply assumed to exist and hence no consideration is given to borrowers' behavior, that is, to the decision to issue bonds of particular maturities. Since the discussion applies to default-free bonds—namely, Treasury securities—ignoring the issuer does not detract from the analysis.

[2] Allowing for compounding of interest, the calculation is as follows: $(1.06)^2 = (1.05)(1 + \text{future short rate})$. The future short rate is therefore approxi-

mately 7.0095 percent. Thus, the arithmetic average used in the text is fairly accurate in this example.

[3] For the above example, the arbitrage was indirect since it involved selecting the better investment. A standard arbitrage transaction for this case would entail buying the higher-yielding investment alternative by selling the lower-yielding one; that is, arbitrage profits would be earned with a zero net

investment. Profits are ensured since the yields must eventually equilibrate.

This version of the example assumes that borrowing and lending rates are equal and that the proceeds from selling the lower-yielding bond "short" are immediately and fully available to buy the higher-yielding bond. In general, arbitrage connotes *risklessly* profiting from buying a good at a lower price and selling it at a higher price in the same or another market.

---

economy. More complex models can be constructed by including more state variables, each of which convey independent bits of information about shocks to the term structure. A fuller interpretation of state variables will be possible once general equilibrium models are considered.

The Cox-Ingersoll-Ross model restricts the behavior of the spot rate by supposing that, although random in its movements from one instant in time to another, the spot rate tends to "revert" to a long-term level and never becomes negative. It is prevented from becoming negative because negative real interest rates are not economically meaningful in the context of their model. This restriction alone is not sufficient for a realistic model since the spot rate would exhibit too much variability over time. Thus the assumption of mean reversion was incorporated. Note that the original Ho and Lee model, cast in terms of nominal bond prices and interest rates, does allow negative interest rates and does not have a mean-reversion property.[10]

Valuing a bond using the Cox-Ingersoll-Ross model, like the Ho and Lee or any other valuation model, entails computing the expected value of the discounted payoff. Instead of positing a discrete number of states upon expiration of a bond as in Ho and Lee, the Cox-Ingersoll-Ross model allows for a continuum of outcomes. Again, bond valuation means determining the expected value of the discount factors to be applied in the continuum of states, since the maturity value of a bond is always par. The chief obstacle to making this determination is that the discount factors are unknown for risk-averse investors. Fortunately, the option-pricing methodology that originated with Black and Scholes provides an ingenious solution.

Risk-Neutral Valuation. With certain assumptions, option valuation can be formulated in such a way that knowledge of investors' risk aversion (that is, their discount functions)

becomes irrelevant. This approach applies to many kinds of option-pricing problems though, unfortunately, not directly to term-structure applications for reasons to be discussed shortly. Although step-by-step details pertaining to option valuation are beyond the scope of this article, some background on the manner in which risk aversion is treated in valuation will aid the understanding of term-structure models. If certain assumptions are imposed—continuous trading, continuous price dynamics, and the property of nonsatiation (that is, that investors always prefer to consume more rather than less)—valuation may proceed as if in a risk-neutral world, one in which the discount rates contain no risk premia and thus are observable.[11] Valuation is said to be preference free. This line of reasoning has become known as the Cox-Ross risk-neutrality argument, first expounded in Cox and Ross (1976), and is a useful starting point for considering valuation of interest-rate contingent claims.

The validity of the risk-neutrality argument depends on the construction of a so-called hedge portfolio consisting of the derivative asset (for example, options) and underlying assets (like stocks) that are traded in such a way that the portfolio is without risk. The hedge portfolio would be constructed so that, for instance, a rise in the value of the stock component would be exactly offset by a fall in the value of the option component and vice versa. Because the portfolio is riskless, any funds invested in it would have to earn the risk-free rate of interest; otherwise, arbitrage would be induced between the hedge portfolio and the risk-free asset. The value of the portfolio's components can be determined without regard for risk premia. No matter what the actual degree of risk aversion, the fact that the portfolio is riskless means that the expected rate of return on its components can be assumed to be the riskless rate as well. In other words, the same option price would be derived for any discount rates (if they were known). Thus option pricing proceeds using the preference assumption that makes valuation easiest: risk neutrality.[12]

Allowing for random interest rates complicates the valuation process. The crucial aspect of the risk-neutrality argument is that the stock or underlying asset is itself the state variable and is a traded asset. However, the instantaneous interest rate is not a traded asset and therefore cannot be used directly in constructing a hedge portfolio. Unlike the hedge portfolio used in deriving the Black-Scholes option pricing equation, risk cannot be eliminated in such a way that valuation is preference free.

Nevertheless, the problem of valuing bonds of differing maturity, each of which may require a different and unobservable expected rate of price appreciation (in order to be held willingly by the investor), can be simplified. It is usually assumed that the bond price depends only on the state variables (in this case, the instantaneous interest rate) and time. A hedge portfolio can be formed, but doing so requires knowing something about risk preferences in the economy. In particular, for the Cox-Ingersoll-Ross model forming a riskless hedge portfolio implies that all bonds have the same return-to-risk ratio in equilibrium. That ratio reflects risk preferences. The basic idea is that any two bonds of arbitrary maturity can be traded in such a way (in a hedge portfolio) that they are a perfect substitute for any other bond of arbitrary maturity.

The excess return for a bond of one maturity (over the risk-free rate) relative to that bond's volatility (the standard deviation of its rate of return) must in equilibrium equal the excess return on another bond of different maturity relative to its volatility. This may be expressed mathematically as:

$$\frac{\mu_1 - r}{\sigma_1} = \frac{\mu_2 - r}{\sigma_2} = \lambda(r,t),$$

where μ_1 and μ_2 are the expected bond returns, σ_1 and σ_2 are the bond volatilities, r is the risk-free rate, and λ is the market price of instantaneous interest-rate risk.[13] The function λ can be a function of the state variable

and time (though often it is assumed to be a constant), but it cannot be a function of any bond's maturity since all bonds are related to λ by the above equation. If this relationship did not hold for bonds of any maturity, arbitrage would be possible. Investors would always choose the bond with the highest excess return-to-risk ratio, thereby raising the bond's price and reducing its excess return until the bond's excess return-to-risk ratio equals λ.

Hence, the simplification used in the Cox-Ingersoll-Ross model and other continuous-time term-structure models is that, rather than needing to know the exogenous expected return for each bond, the only exogenous element that needs to be identified is the market price of interest-rate risk, which by hypothesis is shared in common by all bonds.[14] This parameter must be estimated from actual bond price data to use the Cox-Ingersoll-Ross or other similar model. Once the market price of interest-rate risk is estimated, valuation proceeds using risk-neutral pricing methods. The end result is a formula to price bonds of any maturity. In the context of the Cox-Ingersoll-Ross model, the bond price is solely a function of the spot rate of interest and the bond's time to maturity. In more general versions of the model, the bond price is a function of the underlying state variables and time to maturity. To summarize, interest-rate contingent claim pricing does involve making a risk adjustment in arriving at a pricing formula, but valuation is not preference free.

Speaking in terms of risk-neutral valuation in the context of term-structure models is something of a misnomer. Investors are not necessarily risk neutral when λ is zero. They may be risk averse, but, because of the uncertainty resulting from randomness in the spot interest rate (or, more generally, uncertainty stemming from the state variables), their risk aversion is such that they do not require a risk premium. These risk-averse investors' "portfolio decisions are completely myopic being made with no regard for hedging against changes in the state variables [which affect future output and consumption]" (Cox, Ingersoll, and Ross 1981, 783). Consequently, all future payoffs are discounted using risk-free rates, just as in those cases where the Cox-Ross risk neutrality argument applies. In pointing out this subtlety, Cox, Ingersoll, and Ross (1981) chose to call the case in which the factor risk premia are zero the "local expectations hypothesis" rather than the risk-neutral expectations hypothesis.[15]

An Illustration of the Cox-Ingersoll-Ross Model

Charts 5 and 6 are examples of the single-factor Cox-Ingersoll-Ross model, the simplest of their models. Its key features are illustrated in the graphs. The spot interest rate reverts to a long-term rate of 7 percent. Since expected spot rates are above the observed yield curve, any initial spot rate below the long-term rate results in an upward-sloping term structure. Any yield along the term structure can be expressed as a continuous-time average of the current spot rate and the expected spot rates. This relationship has a precise formula in the Cox-Ingersoll-Ross model. The expected spot rates were computed by formula in graphing their curves in Charts 5 and 6. Chart 6 shows a spot rate that is above its long-term rate, and consequently the term structure slopes downward. The rate at which the spot rate reverts to its long-term level is an important parameter that governs how the term structure moves over time. The other critical parameter affecting the term structure is the volatility of the spot rate.

Another feature of the single-factor Cox-Ingersoll-Ross model is that bonds of sufficiently long maturity have yields that are independent of the spot rate. This long-term yield, denoted as the consol rate (the yield on an infinite-maturity bond), appears as a heavy dotted line in all of the relevant charts. As maturity increases, the yield curve approaches this limiting yield "asymptotically," that is, very gradually. In contrast, multifactor models do not have the unrealistic characteristic that long-term bond yields are constant. The model developed by Michael J. Brennan and Eduardo S. Schwartz (1979) and another by Stephen M. Schaefer and Schwartz (1984) are two-factor models that include the consol

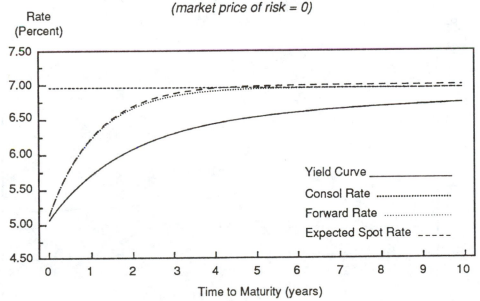

Chart 5.
Cox-Ingersoll-Ross Model
(market price of risk = 0)

rate as an instrumental variable. This kind of model allows randomness to affect the term structure from opposite ends of the maturity spectrum. In fact, Ren-Raw Chen and Louis Scott (1990) have found that allowing for two and three factors greatly improves the fit between term-structure model bond prices and actual market bond prices.

As discussed earlier, risk aversion drives a wedge between forward rates and expected future spot rates. Yet risk aversion is not the only factor that separates forward from expected future spot rates. Charts 5 and 6 show separate forward rates and expected future spot rate curves even though the market price of instantaneous interest-rate risk is zero. This type of discrepancy was first explicated by Stanley Fischer (1975) in considering the effect of inflation on nominal interest rates and then by Scott F. Richard (1978) in his two-factor term-structure model. Terence C. Langetieg (1980) observed that only in a world of certainty, not just risk neutrality, would risk premia be zero.

Cox, Ingersoll, and Ross (1981) gave a comprehensive analysis of the phenomenon,

which arises from a mathematical condition known as Jensen's inequality.[16] A nontechnical explanation is that equality of forward and future expected spot rates implies a particular type of bond pricing equilibrium, one that is not generally compatible with other types. If, for example, the local expectations hypothesis is true and therefore a bond's current price is the expected discounted value of its face value, where the discount factor is a function of all the instantaneous spot rates expected to prevail up to the maturity date, then forward rates cannot equal expected spot rates in equilibrium. In fact, the bond yield implied by equality of forward and expected spot rates is greater than the yield implied by the local expectations hypothesis.

In other words, even for a zero market price of spread risk, forward rates are biased predictors of future expected spot rates for a reason that has nothing to do with risk premia. However, Charts 5 and 6 make it apparent that the discrepancy between forward and expected future spot rates is very small—only a few basis points (based on re-

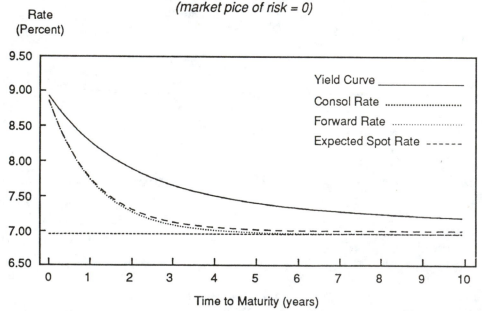

Chart 6.
Cox-Ingersoll-Ross Model
(market pice of risk = 0)

Rate
(Percent)

Yield Curve _____
Consol Rate ....
Forward Rate ....
Expected Spot Rate - - - - - -

Time to Maturity (years)

alistic parameter values for the Cox-Ingersoll-Ross model).[17]

Charts 7 and 8 are based on the same model generating Charts 5 and 6, but the market price of instantaneous interest-rate risk is now negative, giving rise to positive risk premia. The expected spot-rate curve is the same as before; however, the forward-rate curve now rises above its level in the earlier charts because of the effect of risk

Chart 7.
Cox-Ingersoll-Ross Model
(market price of risk = −.05)

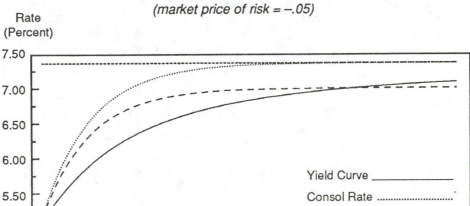

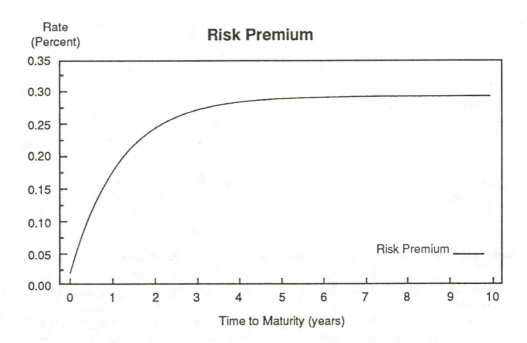

Chart 8.
Cox-Ingersoll-Ross Model
(market price of risk = –.05)

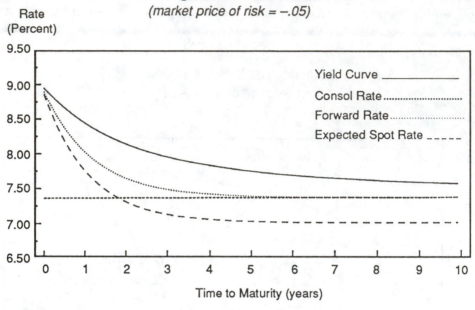

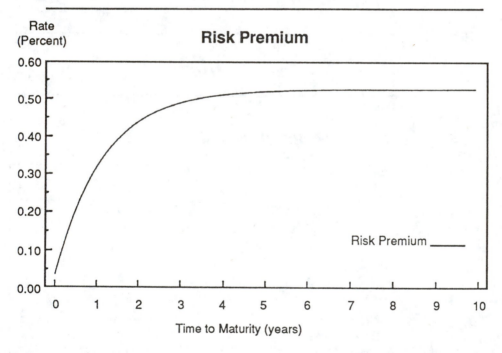

premia. Consequently, the yield curve is higher everywhere in Charts 7 and 8 than it was in Charts 5 and 6.

The risk premium graphed in the inset below the yield curves in Charts 7 and 8 represents the difference between the instantaneous expected rate of return on a bond of a given maturity and the expected rate of return on a bond that is an instant from maturing (the spot interest rate). This is the risk premium concept used by Cox, Ingersoll, and Ross, which they refer to as the term premium. For both upward- and downward-sloping yield curves, the risk premium curve increases with the maturity of the bond. In fact, for this model the risk premium is proportional to the interest elasticity of the bond price. That elasticity rises with the maturity of the bond. In other words, a 1 percent increase (or decrease) in interest rates depresses (or elevates) longer-term bond prices more than shorter-term bond prices. Thus, the Cox-Ingersoll-Ross model gives a risk premium structure similar to that predicted by the liquidity premium hypothesis. The actual interpretation is different, however, and will be discussed in the next section.

Other models give more complex risk premium behavior. For example, a one-factor model proposed by Francis A. Longstaff (1989), which in many respects is similar to the Cox-Ingersoll-Ross model, produces a risk premium that does not simply increase with maturity; that is, it can have a humped pattern as well that may lend greater realism to the model.

General Equilibrium. Up to this point, the risk premium has been simply a quantity that separates forward rates from expected spot rates. Neglecting the effect of Jensen's inequality, the risk premium's impact is the same in the liquidity premium and preferred habitat hypotheses. Cox, Ingersoll, and Ross (1985a, b) allowed a fuller interpretation of the risk premium by embedding their term-structure model in a larger model of the economy. Particularly since the 1970s, economic theory has placed greater emphasis on the rational maximizing behavior of individuals; Cox, Ingersoll, and Ross sought to incorporate such behavior explicitly into a term-structure model (and, more generally, in any model for valuing asset prices).

Individuals in the Cox-Ingersoll-Ross model's hypothetical economy are identical and rational in the sense that they know the structure of the economy and all relevant information for the decisions that they make. They seek continually to achieve the highest level of satisfaction possible, or, in more technical language, they maximize their "utility functions" through time. They are endowed initially with a certain amount of wealth, which they use to invest in the productive processes of the economy, purchase financial assets (which enable them to defer consumption today to a future date), and consume the economy's single output. Whatever output goes unconsumed is invested to produce more future output.

The individual's maximization problem is to decide on the *optimal* amount of each of these activities to undertake. The decisions will depend in part on their attitude toward risk, which is mathematically represented as an element of their utility function. Risk in this hypothetical economy derives partly from shocks to production that change wealth and comsumption over time. A big rise in the price of oil or the occurrence of drought are examples of such shocks. Production is also uncertain because of shocks to technology, which are modeled as the random evolution of a set of state variables. These state variables have no further interpretation, other than being the basic sources of uncertainty.

The optimizing decisions of the investor/consumer result in an economic equilibrium that includes equilibrium asset prices and interest rates. There are many implications of the Cox-Ingersoll-Ross general equilibrium model. The one to be emphasized here is the nature of the risk premium. Any security's rate of return in excess of the risk-free rate depends on its sensitivity to changes in wealth and to changes in each of the state variables. Cox, Ingersoll, and Ross (1985a) give the following interpretation of the risk premium: "Just as we would expect, individuals are willing to accept a lower expected rate of return on securities which tend to pay off more highly when marginal utility is higher. Hence, in equilibrium such securities will have a lower total risk premium" (376). What individuals ultimately care about is the flow of consumption they enjoy over time. Changing their securities portfolios is one way they achieve this goal. When times are lean and consumption is relatively low, the satisfaction from each additional increment to consumption—that is, its marginal utility—is high. (It is assumed that as consumption rises, marginal utility falls, which is to say that additional consumption carries less utility value.) Trading in securities is the method by which individuals smooth consumption (and raise utility). Because they have limited wealth, (in other words, budget constraints), individuals must prefer some securities more than others. In particular, securities that pay most when consumption is low are more valuable than those that pay most when consumption is high. Consequently, securities that yield most in lean times bear higher prices and hence lower risk premia. That is, their return in excess of the risk-free rate will be lower since risk-averse individuals prefer these kinds of securities. In other words, some securities are better at hedging certain kinds of risk than other securities, and the value of such securities will depend on investor preferences.

Risk-neutral consumers/investors do not care about fluctuations in their consumption flows or investment opportunities. As a result, they would not be willing to pay a premium for the hedging characteristics of any security; all securities would earn the risk-free rate in equilibrium. As mentioned above, however, individuals can be risk averse (specifically, by experiencing diminishing marginal utility with respect to consumption or, equivalently, wealth) but not require any risk premia. As Cox, Ingersoll, and Ross (1981) have pointed out, such a combination could occur if changes in the marginal utility of wealth were unaffected by changes in the state variables. Such conditions should be regarded as exceptional, though, and not realistically characteristic of the economy.

The general equilibrium structure provides a more detailed interpretation of a term-structure model. In particular, the one-factor Cox-Ingersoll-Ross model includes the specialized assumption that the risk premium does not depend on wealth but represents the "covariance of changes in the interest rate with percent changes in optimally invested wealth (the 'market portfolio')" (Cox, Ingersoll, and Ross 1985b, 393). In the one-factor model, a single state variable, which is unobservable, summarizes all underlying uncertainty. However, the spot interest rate depends on that state variable; it determines all movements in the spot rate. The state variable represents changes in physical investment opportunities, which in turn account for all variations in wealth. Thus, risk depends on how changes in bond prices determined by the spot rate vary with changes in wealth. Bonds that are better hedges against shifts in investment opportunities (and hence wealth) are more highly valued and carry lower risk premiums. For example, in the one-factor Cox-Ingersoll-Ross model if wealth tends to decline as the spot interest rate rises (the wealth-spot rate covariance is negative), then short-term bonds will carry lower risk premiums than longer-term bonds because they are subject to smaller capital losses. Because long-term bond prices decline more than short-term bond prices in response to a rise in the spot rate, long-term bonds are riskier to include in the wealth portfolio and require a greater risk premium as compensation. Similar reasoning applies to the interpretation of the risk premium arising in more complex multi-factor models. This general equilibrium theory of the risk premium has considerably greater economic content than the comparatively vague notion that investors demand risk premia for illiquid bonds.

The general equilibrium approach of the Cox-Ingersoll-Ross model offers further insights into how underlying economic variables, such as shifts in investment opportunities, affect the term structure. Partial equilibrium models cannot reveal these linkages. In fact, Cox, Ingersoll, and Ross (1985b) make the point that partial equilibrium models can be internally inconsistent. First, there may not be any underlying equilibrium consistent with the assumptions concerning the choice of state variables, such as the spot interest rate, and the way they evolve randomly over time. In other words, the two assumptions may be incompatible. Second, arbitrarily selecting a functional form for the risk premium (for example, assuming that it is constant) may produce a model that implies arbitrage opportunities— a fatal modeling flaw.[18]

From a modeling standpoint, the general equilibrium approach is clearly preferable. In terms of actually implementing a bond pricing model, however, the difference between partial and general equilibrium may not be critical. Even if the general equilibrium model is internally consistent, it may misprice actual bonds as much as a partial equilibrium version. Poor predictions can stem from a misspecification of the actual underlying economy if, for instance, the details of the model are simply too far off. On the other hand, a more complex, realistic model might be impossible to use because essential parameters cannot be reliably estimated given limited data about the actual economy. Simpler models may perform better even if they are internally inconsistent.

Extensions and Variations on Term-Structure Models

Cox, Ingersoll, and Ross (1985b) explore some extensions of their basic model. They show how to incorporate more state variables. This addition results in general equilibrium multifactor models that are similar to the earlier multifactor models of Brennan and Schwartz (1979) and of Schaefer and Schwartz (1984). As more factors are added, the mathematical complexity increases considerably, making these models cumbersome. Simple formulas for pricing bonds are not available; rather, computer-intensive numerical methods must generally be used to obtain bond prices.

Longstaff (1989) attempts to get better performance out of a single-factor general equilibrium model by allowing for nonlinear behavior in the underlying state variable and consequently also in the observable spot interest rate. One impact of this nonlinearity is to make the spot rate revert to its long-term level more slowly from above than from below. Greater flexibility and realism are achieved because the possible theoretical shapes of the term structure are more varied. These attributes may model actual variations in the term structure better than the simple Cox-Ingersoll-Ross model.

Cox, Ingersoll, and Ross (1985b) also show how to adapt their approach to value nominal bonds. Their original model does not include the existence of money or inflation.

They modify the model by incorporating the aggregate price level as another state variable and obtain a nominal bond-pricing formula. Alternatively, they recast the entire model in terms of nominal variables and derive interest-rate and bond-pricing equations similar in form to the real-variable model. In this revised model, the instantaneous nominal interest rate equals the sum of the instantaneous real interest, the expected instantaneous rate of inflation, and a group of terms that arise from the effects of Jensen's inequality. In other words, the so-called Fisher equation, which states that the nominal rate is the sum of the real rate and expected inflation, does not hold (for the same mathematical reason that forward rates do not equal expected future spot rates even when factor risk is zero). Richard's (1978) is an earlier partial equilibrium model that included expected inflation as one of two state variables.[19]

The Cox-Ingersoll-Ross model has been used in a number of recent applications involving the valuation of interest-rate contingent claims. Krishna Ramaswamy and Suresh M. Sundaresan (1986) value floating-rate instruments, which have interest payments that vary with current market rates, using the Cox-Ingersoll-Ross single-factor model. The Cox-Ingersoll-Ross model was adapted to valuing the cash flows from such instruments. Louis O. Scott (1989) prices default-free interest-rate caps using the Vasicek and Cox-Ingersoll-Ross single-factor models. John Hull and Alan White (forthcoming) apply modified versions of the Vasicek and Cox-Ingersoll-Ross models to price bond-options and interest-rate caps, which are derivative instruments designed to hedge floating-rate instruments. Peter A. Abken (1990) uses the Cox-Ingersoll-Ross single-factor model as a component of a model to price default-risky interest-rate caps. Sundaresan (1989) employs the Cox-Ingersoll-Ross model in his valuation model for interest-rate swaps, which are also hedging tools that have numerous forms and applications. A basic use is to convert fixed-rate interest payments into floating-rate payments (or vice versa). Longstaff (forthcoming) extends the Cox-Ingersoll-Ross single-factor model to price options that have payoffs specified in terms of yields rather than prices. His preliminary empirical work demonstrates that the model predicts actual traded yield option prices with greater accuracy than other existing models. Abken (forthcoming) develops a swap valuation model that allows for default risk on the part of parties participating in a swap. The Longstaff yield option model is a component of his model.

The single-factor Ho and Lee model has been extended into both discrete- and continuous-time multifactor models by David Heath, Robert Jarrow, and Andrew Morton (1987, 1988). Like the Ho and Lee model, the Heath-Jarrow-Morton models use all the information in the current term structure, but they do so in a more sophisticated way, avoiding the deficiencies of the Ho and Lee model. In particular, the Heath-Jarrow-Morton models preclude negative interest rates and, since they are multifactor, do not imply perfectly correlated bond-price movements. The models are specified in terms of the evolution of the forward rate rather than the bond price as in Ho and Lee.

Unlike Ho and Lee's, these models are preference free, a characteristic that the authors cite as a major advantage of their method. Still, "fitting" the models to the actual forward-rate curve is problematic, and inaccuracies at this step become relayed into inaccurate bond-option prices. Heath, Jarrow, and Morton (1989) conducted an empirical test of the earlier Heath-Jarrow-Morton (1987) model and found that despite some problems, the test supports the model's validity.

In a similar vein, Philip H. Dybvig (1988) shows how to fuse the Ho and Lee model (or, more generally, models incorporating the information in the current term structure) with single- or multifactor state variable models. He finds that a relatively simple single-factor hybrid model fits the term structure very well over time.

Robert R. Bliss, Jr., and Ehud I. Ronn (1989a) have also extended and refined the Ho and Lee approach by including a set of state variables that affect movements in forward rates (that is, the perturbation function and the risk-neutral probabilities are functions of the state variables). Their modeling

changes effectively prevent the occurrence of negative interest rates as in the Ho and Lee model and allow for a more flexible modeling of interest-rate movements. In Bliss and Ronn (1989b) the authors test their model by valuing actual options on Treasury-bond futures contracts. The results indicate a systematic discrepancy between model predictions of option prices and actual option prices. A possible explanation for the bias (aside from actual options' being mispriced) is that their estimated perturbation functions, based on past observed forward-rate movements, do not sufficiently capture actual movements in forward rates.

Naoki Kishimoto (1989) extends the Ho and Lee model to enable valuation of assets such as stock options, convertible bonds, and junk bonds, for which risk stems not only from future interest-rate changes but also from other factors. The model combines the features of the Ho and Lee term-structure model with the Cox-Ross-Rubinstein method of modeling asset-price risk.

Black, Emanuel Derman, and William Toy (1990) have quite recently developed another variation on the Ho and Lee model. Their model posits a time-varying volatility for the spot interest-rate process and assumes that the spot rate is log-normally distributed, thereby preventing the realization of negative values. Like Ho and Lee's, this model does not give a simple formula for valuing either bonds or interest-rate contingent claims and consequently must be implemented as a computer algorithm.[20]

Contingent Claims Pricing

Having introduced the Ho and Lee model, it is now easy to illustrate how an option can be valued using this model and, by extension, any other term-structure model. Consider a European call option on a discount bond—a three-month Treasury bill. A call is usually specified in terms of a bond's price. The option gives the holder the right to buy the T-bill at a prespecified price upon expiration of the option. To make matters easy, the call is assumed to be European so that it may be exercised only upon expiration, unlike an American option, which can also be exercised earlier. The call in the illustration is assumed to have an 11 percent strike or, equivalently, a strike price of 0.973 (on a hypothetical T-bill with $1 face value). The underlying T-bill matures three months after the option. (Note that the option cannot meaningfully expire at the same time as the T-bill because the bill's price is known with certainty, that is, its price equals its face value.)

The object of this exercise is to determine the value of the call option when it has one year remaining before expiration. The earlier example from Chart 3 gives the state-price evolution for the T-bill that is relevant for this problem. Chart 9 repeats the T-bill price tree but also includes the option prices at each node of the tree. Again, the valuation process starts from the expiration date at time 0. The call option has value only when the T-bill price is above the strike price of 0.973 (or equivalently the annualized bill rate is below 11 percent). Thus, the only positive option payoffs occur for the first two lower entries in the column on the far right. The rest of the computation proceeds exactly as

it did in Chart 3, except that the call option payoff, not the bill price, is used in recursively working back to the initial date. The probability-weighted call option payoffs in the time 0 column are averaged pairwise and discounted using the three-month bill price corresponding to realized state price one period earlier. That bill price, shown in Chart 3, is derived from Ho and Lee's formula, which in turn is based on the initial term structure of interest rates. Repeating the procedure back to the present time at quarter 4 before expiration gives an option price of 0.00101 on a face value of $1. Multiplying by $1 million to be somewhat more realistic gives a call option price of $1,010. This figure can be converted into an interest rate, expressed in basis points (one-hundredths of a percent), by dividing by 25.[21] Therefore, for every $1 million face value of T-bills, the call option would cost 40.4 basis points.

More accurate valuation would be achieved by dividing the time interval to expiration more finely than into four quarters and thereby increasing the number of branches in the binomial tree. Still other models could be used to value the call option; however, the Ho

Chart 9.
Ho and Lee Model Contingent Claim Valuation

Call Option on Three-Month T-Bill Price (Strike = .973 or 11%)
Value One Year before Option Expiration = $1,010 or 40.4 Basis Points

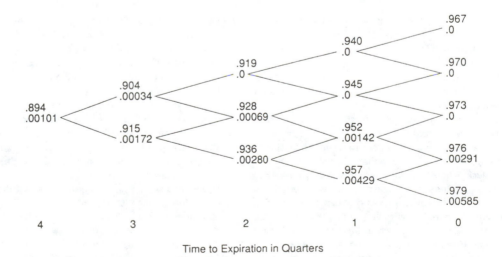

Time to Expiration in Quarters

and Lee model makes the mechanics of valuation fairly transparent.

Cox, Ingersoll, and Ross (1985b) give a closed-form solution for option prices based on their single-factor model.[22] It is similar in form to the Black-Scholes option-pricing formula although more complicated. Farshid Jamshidian (1989) has derived a closed-form solution for pricing bond options based on the single-factor Vasicek model. This formula is much easier to use than the formula of Cox, Ingersoll, and Ross. The choice of which to use is an empirical question that is the subject of current research.

Conclusion

This article has given an introduction to the new types of term-structure models that have appeared in the last fifteen years. These models have evolved not only because of the option-pricing revolution triggered by the Black-Scholes formula and its stimulation of financial research but also as a result of the rational expectations approach in economics and finance. Research in this field has also been motivated by the greater asset-price volatility that has characterized financial markets in recent years. In other words, market demand has been growing for term-structure models to help in the valuation of increasingly complex financial instruments such as interest-rate caps and swaps. It can be expected that financial theory and practice will continue to spur advances in one another.

Much research time and money are currently being devoted to building better term-structure and interest-rate contingent claims pricing models. The benefits of improved modeling have both academic and intellectual significance to financial researchers as well as dollars and cents payoffs to market practitioners. Part of this research effort is devoted to refining existing models to give the best "fit" with actual market bond and option prices. A number of researchers have explored the performance and accuracy of some of the new term-structure models.[23] It is beyond the scope of this article to review their evaluations, but it is important to note that there tend to be trade-offs between ease of use and model accuracy. The type of application may also determine which model is appropriate: a simple single-factor model, for example, may be quite adequate for pricing short-term bond options, while more elaborate multifactor models may be needed for accurate pricing of longer-term options, which require greater precision in term-structure modeling.

Notes

[1] See Abken (1989) for an introduction to interest-rate caps and Wall and Pringle (1988) or Smith, Smithson, and Wakeman (1988) for an introduction to interest-rate swaps.

[2] Although uncertainty is sometimes regarded as connoting risks that are not measurable, risk and uncertainty here are considered synonymous.

[3] The Cox-Ingersoll-Ross term-structure model, which is discussed below, was used to generate these charts.

[4] Modigliani and Sutch also note that similar considerations apply to bond issuers (that is, borrowers).

[5] The Black-Scholes formula performs poorly for valuing options on bonds. The original model assumes (1) that the short-term interest rate is constant (implying that the term structure is always flat) and (2) that the volatility of the asset return on which the option is written is constant. However, the volatility of a bond's rate of return must diminish to zero, because the bond price must equal face value at maturity. The volatility cannot be reasonably assumed to be constant, unlike a stock's. Schaefer and Schwartz (1987) modify the Black-Scholes equation by making a bond's volatility proportional to its duration, which results in a decreasing volatility that reaches zero upon maturity. Hull and White (1989) extend the Schaefer-Schwartz model to relax the assumption of a constant short-term interest rate. These extensions of Black-Scholes are "preference-free" models, which are discussed later in this article. Ball and Torous's (1983) is another influential, though flawed, model in this vein that is a direct antecedent of the Schaefer-Schwartz and Hull-White models.

[6] See Ho and Lee (1986) for the details about the perturbation function and its derivation.

[7] Measuring such a shift in risk aversion would be very difficult, and, to the author's knowledge, has not yet been attempted empirically

[8] These are by Vasicek (1977), Dothan (1978), Courtadon (1982), Richard (1978), Brennan and Schwartz (1979),

and Langetieg (1980). The Cox-Ingersoll-Ross model first circulated in an unpublished manuscript dated July 1977.

[9] See Black (1988) for Black's surprise and amusement at the continuing popularity of his original model with Scholes. He believes that the original model's highly restrictive assumptions limit its usefulness and suggests modifications to make the model perform better.

The Black-Scholes formula can also be derived using discrete-time mathematics. See Cox, Ross, and Rubinstein (1979).

[10] See Dybvig (1988) for an analysis and extension of the Ho and Lee model.

[11] More precisely, "continuous price dynamics" means that the underlying asset price is assumed to follow an Ito process. See Jarrow and Rudd (1983) for an introduction to option pricing.

[12] See Jarrow and Rudd (1983, chap. 7) for a more detailed exposition of the risk-neutrality argument.

[13] The standard deviations in the denominators are actually negative quantities. The bond return standard deviation can be shown to be the product of the negative interest elasticity of the bond price times the positive standard deviation of the spot interest rate. Therefore positive excess return to volatility ratios (and positive risk premia in the term strucure) occur for negative values of $\lambda(r,t)$.

[14] Ingersoll (1987, chaps. 17-18) gives a succinct, though technical, discussion of valuation methods when a model's state variables are not traded assets. See Cox, Ingersoll, and Ross (1981, 772) for the general method of forming a hedge portfolio for their multifactor term-structure model.

[15] For risk-neutral investors, risk premia are zero only in special cases. Cox, Ingersoll, and Ross (1981) show that one case is the trivial one where interest rates are nonrandom (782-83). Another special case requires that the covariance of the bond's return with the marginal utility of wealth is zero. In general this covariance will not be zero and risk premia will exist. These authors also show that a sufficient condition for the local-expectations hypothesis to prevail for risk-averse investors is that they have logarithmic, state-independent utility (783).

[16] In words, Jensen's inequality states that the mathematical expectation of a concave function of a random variable is less than the value of the concave function evaluated at the mean of the random variable. The inequality relationship is reversed for a convex function. See Cox, Ingersoll, and Ross (1981, 776-77) for an analysis of the effect of Jensen's inequality on different forms of the expectations hypothesis. See Fischer (1975, 513) for a simple example of Jensen's inequality that is also pertinent to the term-structure case.

[17] Campbell (1986) argues that the discrepancy between forward and expected future spot rates is mathematically a second-order effect and can be ignored in doing empirical work. Using his linearized framework for analysis of the term structure, the differences among term structure theories studied by Cox, Ingersoll, and Ross (1981) disappear.

[18] See Cox, Ingersoll, and Ross (1985b, 398) for a simple example of how an arbitrage opportunity could arise.

[19] As a future research topic, it might be interesting to extend Richard's model to allow for the impact of monetary policy on the term structure. For example, anticipated inflation could be specified as a function of current or lagged short-term interest rates. This or some other type of reaction function could probably be incorporated as a first step in modeling the effects of monetary policy.

[20] See Hull and White (forthcoming) for the continuous-time formulation of both the Ho and Lee model and the Black-Derman-Toy model. Dybvig (1988) also gives a continuous-time version of Ho and Lee.

[21] The value of a basis point is derived first by dividing $1 million by 10,000 (the number of basis points in 100 percent) to give $100 per basis point per year. The underlying asset, the T-bill, has a three-month maturity; therefore, the value of a basis point per quarter is $25.

[22] A closed-form solution is a formula that is "ready" to evaluate, given the model's parameters. In contrast, many models, such as Ho and Lee or Brennan and Schwartz, require numerical methods to arrive at bond or contingent claim prices.

[23] This work includes that of Marsh and Rosenfeld (1983), Brown and Dybvig (1986), Dietrich-Campbell and Schwartz (1986), Dybvig (1988), Longstaff (1989), Heath, Jarrow, and Morton (1989), Bliss and Ronn (1989a), Pearson and Sun (1989), Buser, Hendershott, and Sanders (1990), Chen and Scott (1990), and Hull and White (forthcoming).

References

Abken, Peter A. "Interest-Rate Caps, Collars, and Floors." Federal Reserve Bank of Atlanta *Economic Review* 6 (November/December 1989): 2-24.

_____. "Valuing Default-Risky Interest-Rate Caps: A Monte Carlo Approach." Federal Reserve Bank of Atlanta Working Paper 90-5, July 1990.

_____. "Valuation of Default-Risky Swaps and Options on Swaps." Federal Reserve Bank of Atlanta working paper, forthcoming.

Ball, Clifford A., and Walter N. Torous. "Bond Price Dynamics and Options." *Journal of Financial and Quantitative Analysis* 18 (December 1983): 517-31.

Black, Fischer. "The Holes in Black-Scholes." *Risk* 1 (March 1988): 30-33.

Black, Fischer, and Myron Scholes. "The Pricing of Options and Corporate Liabilities." *Journal of Political Economy* 81 (May/June 1973): 637-59.

Black, Fischer, Emanuel Derman, and William Toy. "A One-Factor Model of Interest Rates and Its Application to Treasury Bond Options." *Financial Analysts Journal* (January/February 1990): 33-39.

Bliss, Robert R., Jr., and Ehud I. Ronn. "Arbitrage-Based Estimation of Nonstationary Shifts in the Term Structure of Interest Rates." *Journal of Finance* 44 (July 1989a): 591-610.

_____. "A Non-Stationary Trinomial Model for the Valuation of Options on Treasury Bond Futures Contracts." University of Texas at Austin unpublished manuscript, November 1989b.

Bodie, Zvi, Alex Kane, and Alan J. Marcus. *Investments*. Homewood, Ill.: Richard D. Irwin, Inc., 1989.

Brennan, Michael J., and Eduardo S. Schwartz. "A Continuous Time Approach to the Pricing of Bonds." *Journal of Banking and Finance* 3 (July 1979): 133-55.

Brown, Stephen J., and Philip H. Dybvig. "The Empirical Implications of the Cox, Ingersoll, Ross Theory of the Term Structure of Interest Rates." *Journal of Finance* 41 (July 1986): 617-30.

Buser, Stephen A., Patric H. Hendershott, and Anthony B. Sanders. "Determinants of the Value of Call Options on Default-Free Bonds." *Journal of Business* 63 (January 1990): S33-S50.

Campbell, John Y. "A Defense of Traditional Hypotheses about the Term Structure of Interest Rates." *Journal of Finance* 41 (March 1986): 183-93.

Chen, Ren-Raw, and Louis Scott. "Maximum Likelihood Estimation for a Multi-Factor Equilibrium Model of the Term Structure of Interest Rates." University of Georgia unpublished manuscript, April 1990.

Courtadon, Georges. "The Pricing of Options on Default-Free Bonds." *Journal of Financial and Quantitative Analysis* 17 (March 1982): 75-100.

Cox, John C., Jonathan E. Ingersoll, Jr., and Stephen A. Ross. "A Re-Examination of Traditional Hypotheses about the Term Structure of Interest Rates." *Journal of Finance* 36 (September 1981): 769-99.

_____. "An Intertemporal General Equilibrium Model of Asset Prices." *Econometrica* 53 (March 1985a): 363-84.

_____. "A Theory of the Term Structure of Interest Rates." *Econometrica* 53 (March 1985b): 385-408.

Cox, John C., and Stephen A. Ross. "The Valuation of Options for Alternative Stochastic Processes." *Journal of Financial Economics* 3 (January 1976): 145-66.

Cox, John C., Stephen A. Ross, and Mark Rubinstein. "Option Pricing: A Simplified Approach." *Journal of Financial Economics* 7 (September 1979): 229-63.

Dietrich-Campbell, Bruce, and Eduardo Schwartz. "Valuing Debt Options." *Journal of Financial Economics* 16 (July 1986): 321-43.

Dothan, L. Uri. "On the Term Structure of Interest Rates." *Journal of Financial Economics* 6 (January 1978): 59-69.

Dothan, Michael U. *Prices in Financial Markets*. New York: Oxford University Press, 1990.

Dybvig, Philip H. "Bond and Bond Option Pricing Based on the Current Term Structure." Washington University in St. Louis Working Paper, September 1988.

Fischer, Stanley. "The Demand for Index Bonds." *Journal of Political Economy* 83 (June 1975): 509-34.

Heath, David, Robert Jarrow, and Andrew Morton. "Bond Pricing and the Term Structure of Interest Rates: A New Methodology for Contingent Claim Valuation." Cornell University Working Paper, October 1987.

_____. "Bond Pricing and the Term Structure of Interest Rates: A Discrete Time Approximation." Cornell University Working Paper, April 1988.

_____. "Contingent Claim Valuation with a Random Evolution of Interest Rates." Cornell University Working Paper, November 1989.

Ho, Thomas S.Y., and Sang-Bin Lee. "Term Structure Movements and Pricing Interest Rate Contingent Claims." *Journal of Finance* 41 (December 1986): 1011-29.

Hull, John, and Alan White. "An Extension to the Schaefer-Schwartz Bond Option Pricing Model." University of Toronto unpublished manuscript, February 1989.

_____. "Pricing Interest-Rate Derivative Securities." *Review of Financial Studies* 3 (forthcoming).

Ingersoll, Jonathan E., Jr. *Theory of Financial Decision Making*. Totowa, N.J.: Rowman and Littlefield, 1987.

Jamshidian, Farshid. "An Exact Bond Option Formula." *Journal of Finance* 44 (March 1989): 205-9.

Jarrow, Robert A., and Andrew Rudd. *Option Pricing*. Homewood, Ill.: Richard D. Irwin, Inc., 1983.

Kishimoto, Naoki. "Pricing Contingent Claims under Interest Rate and Asset Price Risk." *Journal of Finance* 44 (July 1989): 571-89.

Langetieg, Terence C. "A Multivariate Model of the Term Structure." *Journal of Finance* 35 (March 1980): 71-97.

Longstaff, Francis A. "A Nonlinear General Equilibrium Model of the Term Structure of Interest Rates." *Journal of Financial Economics* 23 (August 1989): 195-224.

_____. "The Valuation of Options on Yields." *Journal of Financial Economics* (forthcoming).

Marsh, Terry A., and Eric R. Rosenfeld. "Stochastic Processes for Interest Rates and Equilibrium Bond Prices." *Journal of Finance* 38 (May 1983): 635-45.

Modigliani, Franco, and Richard Sutch. "Innovations in Interest Rate Policy." *The American Economic Review* 56 (May 1966): 178-97.

Pearson, Neil D., and Tong-Sheng Sun. "A Test of the Cox, Ingersoll, Ross Model of the Term Structure of Interest Rates Using the Method of Maximum Likelihood." Unpublished manuscript, January 1989.

Ramaswamy, Krishna, and Suresh M. Sundaresan. "The Valuation of Floating-Rate Instruments: Theory and Evidence." *Journal of Financial Economics* 17 (December 1986): 251-72.

Richard, Scott F. "An Arbitrage Model of the Term Structure of Interest Rates." *Journal of Financial Economics* 6 (March 1978): 33-57.

Ritchken, Peter, and Kiekie Boenawan. "On Arbitrage-Free Pricing of Interest Rate Contingent Claims." *Journal of Finance* 45 (March 1990): 259-64.

Schaefer, Stephen M., and Eduardo S. Schwartz. "A Two-Factor Model of the Term Structure: An Approximate Solution." *Journal of Financial and Quantitative Analysis* 19 (December 1984): 413-24.

_____. "Time-Dependent Variance and the Pricing of Bond Options." *Journal of Finance* 42 (December 1987): 1113-28.

Scott, Louis O. "Pricing Floating Rate Debt and Related Interest Rate Options." University of Georgia unpublished paper, October 1989.

Smith, Clifford W., Charles W. Smithson, and Lee Macdonald Wakeman. "The Market for Interest Rate Swaps." *Financial Management* 17 (Winter 1988): 34-44.

Sundaresan, Suresh. "Valuation of Swaps." Columbia University Center for the Study of Futures Markets Working Paper 183, April 1989.

Vasicek, Oldrich A. "An Equilibrium Characterization of the Term Structure." *Journal of Financial Economics* 5 (November 1977): 177-88.

Wall, Larry D., and John J. Pringle. "Interest Rate Swaps: A Review of the Issues." Federal Reserve Bank of Atlanta *Economic Review* 73 (November/December 1988): 22-37.

Section VI
Derivative Instruments

In the last ten years, derivative markets have come of age. In finance, a *derivative instrument*, or just a *derivative*, is a financial instrument based on, or derived from, some other more fundamental instrument. For example, a stock option is a derivative instrument because the option gives its owner the right to buy or sell the stock that underlies the option. Similarly, a stock index futures contract is a contract to profit or lose based on the performance of the individual stocks that comprise the stock index. In both cases, the options and futures are derivative, because each is based on some more fundamental financial instrument. There can be no stock option without the stock, and there can be no stock index futures contract without the stock index. This section focuses on some interesting developments in the market for derivatives.

For many years, the stock market has given rise to mutual funds. In essence, a mutual fund is a portfolio of securities with fractions of the portfolio being owned by many investors. If a trader buys a mutual fund, he or she owns a fraction of all of the shares in the mutual fund portfolio. This idea has recently become very popular in the futures market. A commodity fund is like a mutual fund for commodity futures. Traders commit their money to a commodity fund, and the fund trades a portfolio of futures contracts. Edwin J. Elton, Martin J. Gruber, and Joel Rentzler question the attractiveness of commodity funds in their article, "Commodity Funds: Does the Prospectus Really Tell All?" The authors charge that the performance results reported by funds is sometimes misleading. The evidence presented by Elton, Gruber, and Rentzler provides a clear warning to investors attracted to commodity funds.

Richard W. McEnally and Richard J. Rendleman, Jr. offer another warning to investors in their article, "How to Avoid Getting Taken in Listed Stock Options." McEnally and Rendleman actually believe that options trading should be left mainly to professionals. However, for the individual investor determined to trade options, the authors provide some pointers on how to retain as much of the invested funds as possible. A good portion of their advice concerns the relationship between the investor and the broker.

In "Primes and Scores: What They Are and How They Perform," Shreesh Deshpande and Vijay M. Jog explore these new investment vehicles. In essence a Prime and a Score are created by dividing a stock into two investments. In sum, the Prime is a more conservative investment because it receives any dividends paid by the underlying investment. By contrast, the Score holder receives the bulk of any capital gains. By splitting dividend paying stocks into Primes and Scores, investors have the opportunity to make exactly the investment play they wish.

Article 22

Commodity Funds: Does the Prospectus Really Tell All?

By Edwin J. Elton, Martin J. Gruber and Joel Rentzler

Publicly offered commodity funds have not been attractive investments for individual investors either as stand-alone investments or as additions to a portfolio containing stocks and bonds. This was indicated in a study we undertook of commodity fund returns, which we reported on in the *AAII Journal* ("The Risks and Returns of Commodity Funds," by Edwin J. Elton, Martin J. Gruber and Joel C. Rentzler, April 1987).

Despite these results, new funds are a fast-growing part of the investment scene. The natural question arising is: Why do investors continue to choose to purchase commodity funds and why are these funds such a fast-growing segment of investors' portfolios?

One potential explanation is that investors are irrational. But a second and more plausible explanation is that potential investors in a fund are systematically given misleading and biased information and have no ability to evaluate its inaccuracies.

The resolution of this puzzle has important implications for potential commodity fund investors. If the second explanation is indeed supported by research, it should cause prospectus return data to be viewed with extreme caution. This also would apply to other types of limited partnerships, such as those found in real estate, venture capital, and oil and gas.

The Study

Publicly traded commodity funds are offered by prospectus to potential investors. There are clear rules

Edwin J. Elton and Martin J. Gruber are professors of finance in the Graduate School of Business Administration at New York University. Joel Rentzler is an associate professor of finance at Baruch College. This article is based on a paper that originally appeared in the January 1989 Journal of Business.

delineating what must be reported in the prospectus, including information on past performance. In particular, both the commodity pool operator and the commodity trading adviser must provide at least three years of performance history, if available, for all pools and accounts that they have operated or advised during the previous three years. They may also include any period of time longer than three years. It is also worth noting that performance figures cannot end more than three months before the date of the disclosure document.

To examine the accuracy of information available to a potential investor, we took a look at limited partnerships that are offered to the public by prospectus with the investment "opportunity" offered over a specified period of time, usually less than six months. The principal information the potential investor has at the time he makes his decision is the description of the fund and the historical performance of the fund's investment adviser and pool operator, as presented in the prospectus.

In the study, we examined whether the evidence provided in the prospectus has any relationship to the performance of the fund after it goes public. We also examined the discussion of commodity funds by a sample of the financial press to see whether it corrects or reinforces the general conclusion that investors might draw from examining prospectuses.

In order to analyze the performance of public commodity funds compared to prospectus returns, we obtained prospectuses for 77 of the 91 funds examined in our previous study.

Table 1 shows a comparison between the historical returns reported in the prospectuses and the returns on the same set of funds after they went public. The average return shown in the prospectuses was 5.59% per month, or 92% annually. This is much higher than the returns earned by these same funds once they went public. For the first year and the first two years after

Table 1.
Prospectus Returns vs. Returns After Funds Went Public

Public Commodity Funds	Average Monthly Return (%)	Return as % of Average Return of all Prospectuses (%)	No. of Funds With Returns Above Own Prospectus	No. of Funds With Returns Above Average Return of All Prospectuses
First year public	0.23	4.1	2	1
First 2 years public	0.36	6.4	2	1
First 3 years public	0.30	5.4	0	0
First 4 years public	0.54	9.7	0	0

Average monthly return of prospectuses: 5.59%

going public, only one fund in our sample had returns above the average return for all prospectuses. No fund had average performance above the average prospectus return after two years.

We also examined how many funds outperformed the return shown in their own prospectuses. The answer: None after two years, and only two in the first two years after going public.

If prospectus returns are an attempt to convey the average expected return, with some funds having actual performance above that shown in the prospectus and some funds' performance below that shown in the prospectus, they fail to do so. Actual fund performance is almost always substantially below prospectus return.

One possible explanation for the difference in prospectus and public fund return is that performance changed over time—and that the prospectus performance occurred during a period when commodity trading advisers did well and public fund performance occurred during a period when commodity trading advisers did poorly. The funds in our study went public over a 6-year period, so this is unlikely to be the explanation. However, we directly tested for this by comparing commodity fund returns with reported prospectus returns that covered the same time periods. Thus, both the commodity funds and the prospectus returns were subject to the same economic influences. An analysis of the comparison showed that the pattern of returns reported in the prospectuses was very similar to the pattern of returns earned by public funds; at the same time, the public funds earned 2.81% less per month than the returns shown in the prospectus. The results strongly suggest that the difference in public fund return and prospectus return cannot be explained by a different time period or different economic influences.

What Went Wrong?

These results demonstrate that the historical return data reported in the prospectuses of publicly offered commodity funds are not indicative of the return these funds earn once they are public. In fact, the differences in performance figures are so large that the prospectus numbers are seriously misleading. They also show that this discrepancy cannot be accounted for by a different time period for prospectus returns and public fund returns.

The logical question is: What accounts for these return discrepancies?

There are three reasons why we would expect prospectus return figures to be unrepresentative of future performance:

- Transaction costs and management fees: Public funds in general charge larger commissions and management fees than private pools. While the data as reported in the disclosure document would allow the investor to recalculate some or all of the rates of return based on the new expected commissions, these corrected rates of return are often not presented.

- Self-selection: Only commodity advisers with successful track records are likely to go public. To the extent that good performance arose by chance, the superior performance is unlikely to continue over time.

- Control over reported numbers: The adviser can choose the length (in excess of three years) of the performance period placed in the prospectus and, to some extent, the ending date. This allows the most favorable period to be selected.

Why would these explanations cause the differences, and how much of the return differences do they account for?

The first reason that the historical returns reported in the prospectus are not indicative of future performance is that transactions costs and management fees will be different after the public offering than they were before. Some prospectuses include a return figure utilizing the new fee schedule. Other prospectuses contain enough data to allow an investor with a calculator and some time to approximate the returns that would have been earned had the new commission costs and management fees been in existence. However, the time period covered by the transaction and management fee data is often different from, and shorter than, the return history in the prospectus. Furthermore, the level of sophistication needed and the time required to perform the necessary calculations is not insignificant.

We recalculated returns for a sample of 23 prospectuses. If these new fees had been in effect, the average monthly return shown in the prospectus would have been lowered by 0.13%, from 5.59% to 5.46%. Furthermore, only one prospectus had a change in return of more than 0.75%. Thus the change in the fee schedule as reported in the prospectus accounts for only a small part of the difference in returns before and after going public.

The second possible explanation is self-selection. There are a large number of commodity trading advisers registered with the National Futures Association. In 1980, there were 1,866 such advisers, while as of February 1987, there were 2,080. The vast majority of these advisers manage private, as opposed to publicly traded, accounts—in our sample period there were only 94 public funds.

Since the prospectus on any publicly offered account must, by law, contain past performance figures, it is logical that those advisers who have done well over a recent period are the advisers who are going to be selected to manage a public account.

One possible explanation for the results we found is that commodity trading advisers' performance is random and that the ones who are selected as advisers to public funds are the ones who, by pure chance, had a sequence of good returns.

To examine this, we first determined whether the returns shown in the prospectus could have arisen by chance given the actual performance of public commodity funds. Then we examined evidence of randomness.

By law, the disclosure document must include at least 36 months of data, if it exists. The average return shown in the prospectuses over the last 36 months of reported data was 4.14% per month. In our earlier study we found that public commodity funds had an average return of 0.73% per month, with variations around this figure of 11.30% per month. Assuming that the average return is normally distributed, the probability of finding an average monthly return for any fund over a 36-month period higher than 4.14%, is 3.5%. Given the number of advisers managing private pools, we would expect to find more than 65 advisers at any time who have a return greater than 4.14% over the prior 36 months. On the other hand, the number of funds that went public averaged a little over 15 per year over our sample period. Thus, prospectus performance is consistent with the performance we find for public commodity funds if their managers come from the private pools with high performance, and performance is random.

Probably the strongest indication that fund performance is random and, hence, that selection bias accounts for the results is provided by examining the random nature of the relative performance of funds. In our prior study, we showed that there was no predictability in the year-to-year performance of publicly traded commodity funds. This is exactly what would be expected if performance were random and prospectus returns were the return of managers who performed well by chance in the prior period.

The presence of selection bias has implications for other types of investments offered by prospectuses. Due to self-selection by the managers of any type of public offering, the historical data in prospectuses is likely to be highly misleading and an inflated indicator of future performance.

The third explanation for the difference in returns is control over reported numbers. While the number of months of reported performance data must be no less than 36 months if such data exists, the manager is free to present additional data. We would expect, since the prospectus is in a real sense a sales document, that a length of time would be chosen to give the fund managers as high a return as possible.

There are two ways of demonstrating that this is, in fact, the case. There were 77 prospectuses in our sample. Their average reported monthly return for the periods reported in the prospectuses was 5.59%. However, if they had been restricted to reporting a uniform length of the latest 36 months, the average monthly return would have been 4.14%. Of the 77 funds, 69 presented data for more than 36 months. The average monthly return for the added period that was selected voluntarily was 8.85%.

Even more dramatic is the average return reported for the first month in the prospectuses for all funds reporting more than 36 months of data. This is important because funds can choose any starting point they desire. The average return in the starting month was 14.6%, or an annualized rate of better than 400%.

Clearly, allowing the adviser to select the length of the time series to be included in the prospectus leads to an upward bias in the performance figures.

Once again this has connotations for other public offerings. Any time the issuer is allowed to select the time period over which returns are reported, the result is bound to be on average an overstatement of what the future will bring.

The Press as an Information Source

The other source of information on commodity funds

is articles in the financial and popular press. We conducted computer searches for references to commodity funds in business magazines, the New York Times and the Wall Street Journal from June 1979 through February 1987.

Our search of 34 business magazines yielded 28 references to commodity funds. 12 articles discussed general investment in commodity funds and, for the most part, they were highly favorable both in the selection of the numbers they reported and in their general comments on commodity funds. Indeed, some of the statements were stronger than anything contained in any of the disclosure statements.

Nine articles presented general results, five of which were highly favorable. Even those articles that did not present totally favorable results almost always closed with a success story. A typical example is an April 26, 1982, story in Business Week. After explaining that half of the commodity funds suffered losses in 1981, the article states that the most likely reason that the industry is continuing to grow is due to the outstanding performance of some funds. It then goes on to discuss in some detail the performance of Heinhold, which earned a 75% rate of return in the prior year. Articles like this provide biased information to the investor because they almost always discuss the performance of the one to five funds that did well over some time period, and they almost never discuss the funds that did badly. Needless to say, they never caution the reader that there is no evidence that past performance of a commodity fund is related to future performance.

Of the seven remaining articles, four discussed the success of some individual managers, two discussed studies of commodity funds, and one discussed the factors that would lead to a large increase in new money invested in commodity funds.

The data search of the Wall Street Journal and the New York Times produced eight references, excluding the Wall Street Journal's monthly reports on commodity fund performance. Four of these were favorable discussions of funds' usefulness, three were discussions of results, of which only one reported poor performance in the prior year, and one discussed the success of a simple fund.

The search may not have located all articles on commodity funds, but there is no reason to believe it excluded certain types of articles. Anyone reading these articles as a whole would get the impression that commodity funds had excellent performance and were good investments. Although impressions are necessarily subjective, only one article mentioned that a fund had poor performance and dissolved. The overwhelming majority of the articles read like a sales presentation. The newspaper and magazine articles support and reinforce the favorable impression of the prospectuses.

Conclusion

Sales of new publicly offered commodity funds have continued to increase over time despite their poor performance. We believe this growth continues because of the grossly misleading information on performance presented in prospectuses and because of the biased press coverage these funds receive.

This is a general problem with any investment where potential investors are unable to obtain unbiased data on actual performance and must rely on prospectus data and coverage by the financial press. Real estate, oil, gas, and motion-picture limited partnerships are examples of other types of investments where we would expect similar problems to arise.

The implications for individual investors are that they should, at the very least, be very cautious when making an investment decision based on return data provided in commodity fund prospectuses:

- Try to adjust the rates of return as they would have existed had the future commission charges and transaction costs been in effect. Although the effect is small, these returns are more indicative of what the investor would have received had the actual fee schedule been in effect.
- Focus on the return data for the most recent 36 months, and keep in mind that returns beyond 36 months are included at the discretion of the commodity pool operator or commodity fund adviser.
- Finally, and most important, keep in mind the actual performance results of funds that have gone public in the past. The fact that in the past commodity funds have earned less than one-tenth of the returns they reported in their prospectuses after they went public is a warning that every investor should heed.

Article 23

How to Avoid Getting Taken in Listed Stock Options

By Richard W. McEnally and Richard J. Rendleman Jr.

In the stock market crash of 1987, investors lost hundreds of millions of dollars trading in listed stock options. How do we know? We learned as expert witnesses for individual investors who were wiped out in the crash.

One of the most distressing aspects about this experience was that many of these losses were suffered by small investors who were using options trading strategies that they never dreamed would put their wealth at risk. One of the most common laments was "I had no idea I was taking on that much risk."

The 1987 market crash was an extreme market that one hopes will not be repeated. But even in less extreme markets, unwary investors can lose badly with options, not only because of adverse market moves, but also through strategies that gradually eat away their capital.

Our objective is to alert investors to the main pitfalls in trading options—the things your broker never tells you and may not even know himself. We feel that very few people who are not trading options for a living should trade them at all. But if you are going to trade options, you need an understanding of options basics, you should know what can go wrong, and, in particular, you should be able to assess the risks you're assuming.

Options: A Brief Review

A call option gives its owner the right, but not the obligation, to buy a stock or index of stocks at a set price (the exercise price or striking price) at any time before the option's expiration date. A put option carries the right to sell a stock or stock index at a specified price at any time before its expiration. Call options

Richard McEnally and Richard Rendleman are professors of finance at the University of North Carolina's Business School at Chapel Hill.

provide positive payoffs to the investor if the stock price or index value rises above the striking price. Puts provide positive payoffs when the stock or index drops below the exercise price. In these two instances, the options are said to be "in the money," since exercising them creates positive value. If at expiration the price of the underlying stock or index is below the exercise price of a call, or above the exercise price of a put—it is "out of the money"—then the option will be allowed to expire worthless. The buyer loses, but he loses only what was paid for the option.

In practice, it is not necessary for the owner of an option to wait until expiration and exercise in order to realize a profit or loss. "American" options can be exercised prior to expiration, but usually such premature exercise is not the best course of action. Another more common course of action is to sell the option before maturity. This normally results in a larger profit or smaller loss than exercising the option, and it is much simpler.

For every option that is bought, one must be sold. With a call option, the original option seller, known as the "call writer," agrees to sell the stock or index to the option buyer at any time before the option expires. In contrast, the writer of a put agrees to buy the stock or index from the option buyer. In both cases, the interests of the writer are the reverse of those of the buyer: The writer of a call loses when the stock or index rises above the exercise price, and the writer of a put loses when the stock or index falls below the exercise price.

Normally the option writer does not wait to get notification of exercise to close out a written position. Instead, the option is repurchased or covered through a closing transaction. The profit or loss in the transaction is simply the difference between the proceeds from writing the option and the amount that is paid to close out the position. If the option ends up out-of-the-money and is allowed to expire, the writer realizes a profit equal to the initial sales price of the option.

Puts and calls can never be bought on margin; the

full purchase price must be paid to the buyer's broker. Writing options is different. For a call option, if the underlying stock is on deposit with the writer's broker, the writer is said to be "covered." The writer of a call obtains the proceeds when the initial option sale settles. On the other hand, for options on an index, where it's almost impossible for the writer to deposit the index with the broker, or where the writer simply doesn't own the underlying stock, the call writer is said to be "naked." In that case the writer must put up margin based on the value of the underlying stock or index and the price of the option.

To be covered when writing puts, a put writer would have to be short a position in stock—he would have sold shares of stock he did not own. However, few put writers are actually short the stock, and it is almost impossible to short a market index. Accordingly, writers of puts are almost always uncovered, and margin must be made to cover part of the broker's risk exposure.

Writers of both puts and calls can be required to deposit more margin when options move further into the money—as many put writers discovered to their dismay in October 1987.

Option Pricing Theory and Its Implications

In 1973, two finance professors presented a theory of option pricing that has revolutionized the way professional investors approach options trading. The mathematics underlying their model (known as the Black-Scholes model after the professors who developed it) is perhaps the most complex in the entire field of finance, yet the idea behind the model is simple.

The pricing theory recognizes that if option prices are too high, investors find it attractive to write options, thereby driving their prices down. Similarly, if option prices are too low, investors buy options, and their trading activity drives prices up. The model determines the price a typical investor would consider "just right" under ideal market conditions; this is termed the "equilibrium price." At this price, the option position is in equilibrium with the stock market—under ideal market conditions, no investment strategy using options would provide investors with risk-return positions superior to those available in the stock market.

Despite the assumption of ideal market conditions, the model does an outstanding job of describing actual market prices of options. The model's assumption that options are correctly priced has a major implication for individual investors. If an investor could trade options under ideal conditions, he still couldn't consistently win in the options market if he trades at prices according to the model. However, ideal market conditions don't exist in the real world, where investors must pay commissions and taxes, and must post margin.

Therefore, if investors trade at prices according to the model under everyday market conditions, they don't stand a chance of winning consistently in the options trading game.

What You Are Betting On When Trading Options

According to the pricing model, five factors determine the value of an option: the current stock price, the option's striking price, the market's perception of the volatility of the underlying stock price, the time remaining until the option expires, and the market rate of interest. As any of these factors change, the price of the option changes. Changes in the stock price and the market's perception of its volatility can create large, unexpected changes in option prices.

Most investors who buy options understand that they are betting on the future direction of the stock price. Investors who buy calls or write puts are betting that the stock price will go up. Those who write calls or buy puts are betting that the stock price will decline.

However, investors in options are also making a more subtle but highly risky bet on how the market will judge the volatility of the underlying stock or index. A sudden increase in perceived volatility can dramatically increase the prices of both puts and calls, even if the underlying stock or index price never moves. Likewise, as expectations of volatility diminish, option prices will diminish as well.

Taken together, these two bets explain why investors who had written naked put options took such a beating during the October 1987 crash. Not only did put writers lose big when stock prices fell, but they lost even more because the market raised its assessment of volatility.

Why Any Active Options Trading Scheme Will Lose

The options market is a "zero sum game." This means that for every winner there is a loser. It's just like betting on a football game. For every dollar bet on the winning team, an equal amount must be bet on the losing team. The world as a whole cannot get richer by placing bets on football.

The options market is also a zero sum game that is biased against the non-professional investor. Individual investors and retail brokers will most likely be on the losing end of options trading because they are competing against professional investors and floor traders whose only business is to predict stock prices and volatility. These professionals have tremendous analytical resources at their disposal. Many Wall Street firms hire in-house gurus who exclusively conduct mathematical analyses of options markets. These professional investors are likely to be taking the opposite side in many individual investors' options transactions.

Because the options market is a zero sum game, no single options strategy can make us all winners. To win consistently we must bring something special to our trading—even greater analytical capability and insight into markets than the professionals. Without such capability, any options trading strategy is doomed to failure if applied consistently over long periods of time.

Buying Options: The Safest Way to Go

Numerous options strategies are available to investors. The most obvious one is to buy an option. The attractions are obvious: The buyer gets high leverage and known, limited downside risk. For example, suppose IBM is selling for $120. A reasonable price for a call with three months to expiration and an exercise price of $120 would be $6. Puts are a bit cheaper than calls, so a three-month put with an exercise price of $120 might sell for $4. Since exchange-traded puts and calls are written on 100 shares of underlying stock, an investor buying options can take a position in 100 shares of IBM for $400 to $600 and profit from the upside or downside movement of an asset that otherwise would cost $12,000—or $6,000 if bought or sold short on margin. Such leverage of 20:1 to 30:1 is far greater than the 2:1 available with a conventional margin position.

This leverage means the investor who correctly forecasts movements in a stock or market index can do spectacularly well. For example, consider what happened in October 1974 when IBM rose sharply, apparently in response to a rather far-fetched rumor that the Arabs were going to try to take over the company. On October 29, IBM common stock leaped in price from 180¾ to 191¾, a 7% increase. Action in IBM calls was even more impressive. The in-the-money January 160s jumped from 28¾ to 36½, a gain of 27%. The out-of-the-money January 200s went up 33.3%, from 8⅝ to 11½. The at-the-money January 180s did nearly as well, up 32% from 16 to 21⅛. All in all, not bad for a day's work.

Another attractive feature associated with buying options is that you know the maximum loss up front. Returning to the IBM example, the person who buys a call contract can lose only $600, but someone who goes long in the stock could potentially lose the entire $12,000 purchase price. The investor who shorts IBM could, at least in theory, have an infinite loss if IBM rises enough in price. In contrast, buying a put allows the investor to profit if IBM bombs while limiting the maximum loss to $400 if the stock price shoots upward.

Leverage and loss protection don't come free, of course. With the call priced at $6 and the put at $4, IBM stock must rise at least to $126 or fall to $116 before the option buyer walks away with a net profit.

Writing Covered Calls: No Pain, No Gain

Many investors look at the prices of calls and quickly conclude that the way to increase the income of a stock portfolio without taking on additional risks is to write calls against the stock that they hold. At first blush, the math does seem convincing. An investor who owns 100 shares of IBM worth $12,000 might conclude from our example that he could write four three-month call option contracts during the course of the year at a price of $600, pocketing a handy $2,400. If the stock is called away, it is easy enough to buy more at the higher price and re-establish the call-writing program. If its price stays the same, the investor owns the stock and $2,400 to boot, representing a 20% return on a zero appreciation asset. And if the stock goes down, the $2,400 at least cushions the pain.

The problem with this strategy is that covered calls must be written in a market that is reasonably efficient. If investors write call options at efficient market prices, they will earn a fair return given the risks involved. Since writing fully-covered call options tends to reduce the risk of holding stocks, the strategy should reduce expected return, not increase it. To think otherwise denies the risk-return principle of financial markets that, on average, expected return only increases through an increase in risk.

Many call writers fail to realize the importance of large but infrequent price run-ups that account for the 12% or so average annual return investors have come to expect from owning common stocks over the long run. The call writer never gets these large returns. Call writers also forget that writing covered calls, on average, leaves them holding a portfolio of stocks that have depreciated in value. Call writing does lower the downside risk from owning stocks, but it is not as low-risk as investing in Treasury bills. On average, it should yield returns somewhere between Treasury bills and common stocks. And that's exactly what it does.

Naked Writing: What You Don't See Can Hurt You

Covered call writers at least know that the worst outcome will be either giving up profits they would have otherwise made if their stocks rise, or holding stocks they would have held anyway if their stocks fall. Investors who write naked calls and puts have no such comfort. The outcome for option writers, in fact, is that they have an absolute limit on the profit they can make, but the potential for loss is unlimited.

Many option writers do not comprehend just how much risk they are actually taking on. With naked option writing the potential losses are not at all obvious. Naked option writers can lose much more than the initial proceeds from their writing positions.

In our IBM example, for instance, the person who writes the calls exercisable at $120 receives $600 for agreeing to sell 100 shares of the stock at $120 at any time over the next three months. If IBM rises above

Finding an Options Broker: Be Wary

If you are considering options as an investment, you should understand that your broker may not be an objective adviser. Brokers love options for two reasons: The commissions are much higher as a percentage of the trade than commissions on outright common stock trades; and options trading is by necessity an active strategy. No listed options have a life longer than nine months, and the higher-volume, more popular options have much shorter terms to expiration. This means that when you spend money on an options position, the broker has an opportunity to turn the money over again soon and earn another commission. In contrast, when you buy common stock or bonds, the broker may not earn another commission for years.

Brokers frequently point out that the commission on options on a given number of shares is much lower than the commission on the shares themselves. Although this generally is correct, it ignores the fact that most option positions involve more shares of underlying stock than you would trade outright. Moreover, if your strategy is intended to maintain risk at some specific level, such as a risk exposure equivalent to a long-term position in a stock, many trades will be required, and each will generate a commission.

You should be especially wary of a broker who offers guarantees about maximum losses from an options strategy, or who says in so many words, "Don't worry if you don't understand options; I'll handle it." Giving guarantees violates options exchange rules and indicates that the broker has only self-interest in mind. In the options abuses lawsuits that we have consulted on, the biggest problem has been that the customers have not understood the options transactions in which their brokers involved them. Trusting your broker is natural, and even admirable. But in options trading, it is entirely too easy to get in over your head and be unable to stop things before they get out of hand. If your broker does not insist that you have a working knowledge of options, get another broker. And it should go without saying that you should not give your broker a power of attorney or discretion over your account. You should study every transaction before it is executed.

Your broker must also understand the economics of options; sadly, many do not. As a litmus test, ask a prospective broker if he uses the options pricing model described here (the Black-Scholes model) to evaluate options and manage option positions. In addition, ask about how he assesses the immediate risk characteristics of options; the standard is to use deltas, which we also discuss here.

If he is unfamiliar with either of these bare bones basics of options portfolio management, then your broker is not qualified to advise you on options trading.

$120, every dollar of price increase costs the call writer $100 of profit. If IBM rises to $150, the option writer will have a minimum liability of $3,000 and will lose his $600 five times over. Unlike the covered call writer, the naked call writer has no offsetting position in the stock to cushion the loss. Thus, the naked call writer has effectively the same upside risk as if he shorted the stock. Moreover, if IBM does rise above $120, additional margin will be required, and the naked call writer may have to scramble to meet the margin call.

A put writer is in the reverse position. He loses if the stock moves downward significantly; if the stock stays above the striking price, he earns only the initial put premium.

The typical brokerage statement makes the problem worse by giving the option writer an unwarranted feeling of comfort. Suppose an investor buys 100 shares of IBM for $12,000. The risk involved in this position is reasonably clear. Suppose instead that the investor deposits the $12,000 with a broker, writes five put contracts at $400 each for a total of $2,000, and invests the $12,000 plus the $2,000 received from the options in a money market fund. The total value of the account will be shown as $14,000, with a liability of $2,000 for the

options written, leaving a net worth balance of $12,000 —exactly the same numbers as the investor who simply holds one hundred shares of IBM on deposit with the broker.

The $2,000 liability hardly seems intimidating, especially when compared to the $14,000 of safe assets. However, the put writer has effectively taken a long position in IBM that is much more risky than simply buying shares of stock. Suppose IBM drops to $100. The investor who bought 100 shares outright loses $2,000, or 17% of the initial investment. The put writer, on the other hand, has a liability of $10,000 based on five put options now worth $2,000 each, leaving a net worth of only $4,000. He loses 67% of the initial investment. And a margin call will surely be forthcoming.

This pattern of outcomes caused the disasters many investors experienced in the 1987 crash. These investors were writing puts on stocks and indexes in a market that was strongly bullish. The strategy seemed to work well during the first part of the year, giving investors a false sense of security and even encouraging some to increase their exposure before the bottom fell out. The pattern is characteristic of many alluring investment traps. In markets that are moving strongly in one direction or the other, either a call-writing or a put-writing program is going to look very good indeed. But naked option writing is like playing Russian roulette: Anyone who pulls the trigger several times with no bad results and concludes that the pistol isn't loaded can get a rude surprise!

Strategies Involving Pricing "Disparities"

The last strategy we want to review involves positions that attempt to profit from perceived pricing disparities. Standard examples are time spreads, in which the investor buys options with one expiration date and writes otherwise similar options with a different expiration date, and vertical spreads, where the options differ only in the striking price. The objective is to buy options on the relatively underpriced side and write options on the relatively overpriced side, so that as the alleged mispricing corrects itself, the investor makes money.

Such strategies are the height of folly for any investor who is not in intimate contact with the options markets. Even floor traders have trouble making a profit from these positions. Individuals trading without continuous access to quotations are virtually certain to lose.

At least four problems are devastating to such strategies. One relates to correctness of prices, while the others reflect the costs of trading options.

First, the alleged imperfections rarely exist. What may seem to be imperfections are usually incomplete understandings of the considerations that enter into the valuation of options. Others reflect nonsynchronous prices. For example, two settlement (closing) prices reported in the financial press may appear inconsistent with each other, but may simply reflect trades occurring at different times between which the price of the underlying security changed. The options markets may not be perfect at pricing options correctly in a relative sense, but they come close.

Second, the trading strategy must be profitable enough to overcome trading costs. Depending on the options involved and the size of the trade, these costs can range from 1% to 10% of the option's price. In contrast, floor traders, who are the investor's primary competition, pay no commission and only a small clearing fee.

Third, the investor should be aware that there is a "bid" and an "asked" price on all options. This spread, which represents a real cost of trading, can easily run another 5%.

Fourth and finally, a very significant hidden cost is the cost of competing against floor traders, market makers and sophisticated "upstairs traders" who have immediate access to new information and can trade almost as fast. Although this cost is difficult to measure, it means the deck is very much stacked against the individual investor.

A Word About Risk: Deltas

A common defense of the put-writing programs that got so many investors in hot water in 1987 is that no one could reasonably have anticipated the magnitude of the October market drop. We are sympathetic to this argument, but only to a point. The essence of prudent investment is to manage a portfolio so that if a disaster does occur, the damage will be tolerable.

Portfolios containing options positions require a means of assessing exposure to adverse developments. Professional option traders routinely use a device called "delta" for monitoring their risk. Individual investors, or their brokers, can also implement the technique once they understand it.

The delta of an option is nothing more than an estimate of immediate risk measured in terms of equivalent shares of underlying stock. That is, it indicates how many shares of the underlying stock the option buyer or writer would have to be long or short in order to have the same risk as is represented by the option position.

Let's return to the example involving five put option contracts on IBM exercisable at $120 when the stock is also at $120. These options are "at-the-money." As an approximation, the delta of an at-the-money put option contract is −50 to the buyer; each option contract should provide as much immediate price action as a short position in 50 shares of stock. As long as this put is close to the money, a sudden, small change in the price of the stock will change the value of the option by about half as much, but in the opposite direction. If the stock drops $1 per share, or $100 for every 100 shares, the put should increase in value by $0.50 per share of underlying stock, or $50 per option contract. An investor could also earn $50 by shorting 50 shares of stock. Therefore, the position that results from buying these five puts has roughly the same price action as shorting 250 shares of stock.

For the investor who has written the five put contracts, the risk exposure is the opposite to that of the buyer—it is approximately the same as a long position in 250 shares of stock. The writer's immediate downside risk is the same as if he had borrowed $30,000 to buy 250 shares of IBM at a price of $120 per share (250 × $120 = $30,000)—and that represents a lot of leverage on the initial $12,000 investment. Unfortunately, this implicit leverage will never show up on the investor's brokerage statement, and it will become even larger if the stock price begins to fall.

You can work out deltas on a hand-held calculator or personal computer programmed to perform basic options calculations. Such calculations are indispensable for anyone trading options. However, even without actually calculating deltas, several generalizations are possible:

- The delta associated with buying an at-the-money call or writing a put is approximately 50; the delta for writing such calls or buying puts is −50.
- Option positions involving buying a call or writing a put that are well in-the-money have a delta approaching 100; the delta for writing such calls or buying puts is −100.
- When option positions get well out-of-the-money, their deltas approach zero.

These observations help explain how so many investors got caught in the put-writing trap in October 1987. For the most part, they were writing puts that were well out-of-the-money at the time they were written. Such options have small deltas and, thus, the risk expressed in equivalent long positions in the underlying stock or index was also small. However, as the market dropped and these puts became increasingly in-the-money, their deltas and the associated risk became greater. Once they were well in-the-money, as many of them must have been by October 19, the deltas were close to −100 and the risk had increased by orders of magnitude. These put writers were like novice skiers who start down what seems a very slight slope, only to discover that the farther they go the steeper it gets. Unfortunately for the put writers, there was a precipice near the bottom!

One of the messages here is that you must continually monitor option positions. What starts out as a fairly innocuous position can degenerate into something far more dangerous. Options are not for the investor who cannot stay on top of positions or who cannot alter positions as their risk profile changes.

When the investor has more than one position in a stock or index—some long or short positions combined with options, say, or several options on the same underlying stock—deltas need to be aggregated over all the positions. Professional options traders and most brokerage houses trading options for their own account routinely use what is called a "risk equivalency statement." These statements work out the equivalent risk of each position and come down to a bottom line that gives the net equivalent position in the stock or index. At a minimum, these investors reassess the risks in options daily, but some do continuing re-evaluations during each trading day.

To our knowledge, no brokers provide retail customers with such statements. However, the technology is available and if enough customers insisted, these statements could be provided. While they may not be necessary for simple positions, they should be regarded as essential for complex trading strategies and naked option writing.

If You Must Trade Options ...

We hope you've gotten the message by now: Trading in options is best left to the professionals. But if you must trade options, here are a few ways to keep from getting taken.

- Never engage in any options trading program that you do not thoroughly understand. If the risks get out of hand you will never know it until it's too late.
- Use options only as a portfolio management tool to achieve a pattern of payoffs that best suits your tolerance for risk. Buy call options if you might otherwise be inclined to buy stock on margin but wish to limit your losses in the event the stock price heads south. Buy puts as an alternative to shorting stock if the risk of outright short positions bothers you. But remember, these strategies can get costly if continued for a long period of time. Alternatively, write fully-covered calls if you prefer the pattern of payoffs such a strategy provides over the outright purchase of stock. But there's no magic in this strategy either. When engaging in any of these strategies, remember that you are not likely to earn an above-average return in relation to the risks you are taking. In fact, you are likely to come out a little behind, since you must pay transaction costs to execute trades. However, if this type of investing makes you feel better from a risk-return point of view, by all means do it.
- Don't get involved in high-turnover trading strategies that attempt to take advantage of price discrepancies in the options market. Likewise, avoid strategies such as writing time spreads that purport to take advantage of the natural decline in option prices over time. No options trading strategy will always make money for everyone. In the long run, the only people who benefit from this type of trading are your broker and the professional traders who are likely to be taking the opposite side of your transactions.
- Don't allow your money to be "managed" with options by anyone who lacks a working knowledge of the Black-Scholes pricing model, deltas and other theoretical tools for managing options portfolios.
- If you trade options actively, insist that you be provided with periodic risk equivalency statements that estimate how much stock-equivalent risk is present in your options portfolio. This statement should also estimate how much this risk could change in the event of an adverse stock price movement and how much an adverse change in the market's perception of the underlying stock's or index's volatility would change the value of your portfolio.
- If your broker or any other money manager makes any guarantee whatsoever about the maximum losses that could occur in any options-writing strategy, report this individual immediately to the appropriate options exchange and the National Association of Securities Dealers.
- Never give a stock broker a power of attorney to trade stock options on your behalf.

Article 24

Primes and Scores: What They Are and How They Perform

By Shreesh Deshpande and Vijay M. Jog

Since 1983, the Americus Shareowner Service Corp. (ASSC) has sponsored unit investment trusts—the Americus Trusts—for shares of selected firms listed on the New York Stock Exchange and the American Stock Exchange.

These trusts provide investors with two new types of securities, known by their acronyms Prime (for Prescribed Right to Income and Maximum Equity) and Score (for Special Claim on Residual Equity). The introduction of Primes and Scores represents another addition to the investor's portfolio choice.

The Financial Innovation

Primes and Scores are created by "stripping" the common stock of selected firms. More specifically, the ASSC invites shareowners of the selected firms to submit their shares to the Trust (also known by the acronym USIT, for unit share investment trust) in a one-for-one exchange for Trust Units.

Each Trust Unit is designed to permit the holder to separate it into two distinct parts, the Prime and the Score. The Prime entitles the holder, for the duration of the Trust, to all dividends on the underlying common stock as well as price appreciation up to a prespecified maximum, referred to as the termination claim. The Score entitles the holder to any capital gains above the termination claim.

This stripping of the original common share (hence the term "stripped common") into the Prime and Score allows Unit holders to separate the potential for capital appreciation above a specified dollar level from the right to receive dividends and all other attributes of share ownership.

Shreesh Deshpande is an assistant professor in the School of Business at the University of San Diego. Vijay Jog is an associate professor in the School of Business at Carleton University, Ottawa, Canada.

When the Trust is formed, a prospectus is issued that specifies the rights of the holders of the Prime and Score for possible events that may affect the underlying stock. These events include rights offerings, stock splits, mergers and tender offers. In general, the Prime components are entitled to all rights inherent in a share of stock held by the Trust except, of course, the limitation on its potential for capital appreciation beyond the termination claim.

There are four primary rights belonging to Prime holders:

- They will receive all cash dividends paid on the stock (less Trust expenses), all non-cash distributions on the stock that are taxable and have a fair value of less than 5% of the net asset value of the Trust, and any subscription rights, warrants or other rights issued to holders of the stock (or any money received by the Trustee from their sale).
- They may direct the vote of the stock held by the Trust.
- Upon acquiring an equal number of Score components, they can redeem such components as recombined Units on any date after the date of initial issuance of Units at the net asset value per Unit determined as of the next succeeding time of valuation.
- Each Prime component will receive, at termination of the Trust, the net asset value per Unit in underlying common shares up to the termination claim.

If the underlying common shares receive additional shares either due to a stock dividend or a stock split, and the value of the distribution is 5% or more of the net asset value of the Trust Unit, the additional shares are held in the Trust. The termination claim determines how the stock held by the Trust will be distributed between Prime and Score component holders as it establishes the maximum dollar value that Prime component holders can receive at the termination of the Trust.

The possibility of a tender offer for the underlying common stock is, of course, a major concern for Prime and Score holders. Under the terms of the Trust agreement, the Trustee is required to reject any offer to purchase or exchange securities pursuant to a tender offer, whether friendly or hostile, for any of the stock, except in the case of a reorganization of a firm where its shareholders are entitled to vote. In the event of an involuntary exchange or purchase, any cash received is to be added to the Trust's assets and held without interest until the termination date. At that time, the termination claim would decide the sharing of the Unit value of the Trust between the Prime and the Score.

It should be noted that a holder of an individual component is capable of taking advantage of the tender offer by redeeming the Trust Unit. However, the component holder will have to obtain a matching number of complementary components that may or may not be available for purchase. Moreover, a Unit holder may be delayed from taking advantage of the tender offer due to the period of time that it takes to receive underlying shares upon redemption of a Unit.

The creation of a "stripped" common stock is illustrated by the Exxon Americus Trust, which was launched on August 16, 1985, for the shares of Exxon Corp. Individuals who owned Exxon common shares, which were then trading at around $52 per share, could exchange them up to a pre-specified maximum (in this case, 5% of the outstanding stock) for Trust Units by submitting their shares to the Americus Trust. The Trust is scheduled to be terminated on September 20, 1990, with a fixed termination claim of $60. An important feature of the Trust is that at any point during the life of the Trust, a holder of either the Prime or the Score can purchase the complementary part and recombine them to form a Unit. The Unit can then be "put" to the Trust in exchange for the Exxon common shares. There can be no assurance, of course, that such complementary components can be acquired at the time a holder wishes.

For its role in the formation and continual management of the Trust, the ASSC charges a deposit fee ranging from $0.28 to $0.78 per share to investors at the initial transfer of shares into units, and an annual fee of roughly $0.05 per share to the Unit holders.

Primes, Scores, and Units are listed and traded primarily on the American Stock Exchange. There is active secondary market trading of Primes and Scores, indicating that they have gained a fair measure of acceptance.

Investment Attributes

By design, Primes and Scores offer investors the opportunity to channel funds into the security that matches their risk requirements and where their tax exposure can be minimized.

As is apparent in their payoff structures, the Primes and Scores will likely attract investors who would prefer one or the other security instead of holding both

(which is equivalent to holding the common stock). This ability to hold the preferential security is noted in various Americus Trust prospectuses. For instance, the Trust prospectus for the Exxon shares states that "many depositing Unit holders will separate their Units and sell one of the two components, thereby enabling them to concentrate their investment in those aspects of share ownership that more appropriately suit their individual investment objectives." Investors preferring stable (low risk) dividend income and typically facing low taxes on dividends should consider investing in Primes. On the other hand, a Score represents a high risk, high expected return instrument whose payoff is taxed at the capital gains rate when realized.

Some relevant tax aspects of Units, Primes and Scores are as follows:
• First, no gain or loss would be recognized upon the deposit of shares in exchange for Units and the redemption of Units for shares of common stock.
• Second, for the purpose of determining a gain or loss on the sale of a Prime or Score, the cost basis of the component sold would be determined on the date of sale in proportion to the relative market values of the two components at that time.
• Finally, when common shares are exchanged for Units, the holding period for the Unit owner (or the two components) will include the prior holding period of the exchanged shares. If Units, Primes or Scores are purchased in the secondary market, then the holding period for the investment begins at the purchase date.

The tax consequences of exchanging a common share for a Unit can be illustrated by the following example. Assume that an investor buys a share of common stock for $52 and exchanges it for an Americus Unit, consisting of one Prime and one Score. At the time of conversion, Scores are trading for $7 and Primes for $45. After six months, the common stock is at $75, with the Prime selling at $51.75 and the Score at $23.25. If the investor elects to sell his Score, his market profit will be $16.25 ($23.25 − $7.00). However, the tax on the profits would be calculated based on the allocation of cost between the Score and the Prime as a ratio of the relative market values of the two components when the first component is sold, which in this instance is 31% ($23.25/$75). This will result in a taxable gain of only $7.21 ($23.25 × 31%). In essence, the higher basis for the appreciated Score translates into a generally lower effective tax liability for the Score component. A more complete description of the tax rules can be found in "A Way to Get More Out of Stocks You Already Own," published by the ASSC (located at 15 West 39th St., New York, N.Y. 10018; 212/575-8670).

The Existing Americus Trusts

The first Trust was launched by the ASSC on Octo-

Table 1.
The Americus Trusts

Americus Trust*	Prospectus Date	Termination Date	Termination Claim	Initial Termination-Price Ratio**
Exxon	Aug. 16, 1985	Sept. 20, 1990	$ 60	1.157
American Home	Dec. 1, 1986	Dec. 20, 1991	90	1.136
Du Pont	Dec. 22, 1986	Mar. 27, 1992	110	1.250
Bristol-Myers	Jan. 12, 1987	Feb. 14, 1992	110	1.252
AT&T (series 2)	Jan. 12, 1987	Feb. 14, 1992	30	1.182
Merck	Mar. 23, 1987	April 14, 1992	200	1.221
Amoco	Mar. 30, 1987	Mar. 30, 1992	105	1.277
General Electric	April 9, 1987	May 11, 1992	140	1.290
Dow Chemicals	April 14, 1987	May 18, 1992	110	1.325
Kodak	April 20, 1987	April 15, 1992	92	1.258
Union Pacific	April 27, 1987	April 15, 1992	87	1.252
Ford	April 27, 1987	June 30, 1992	104	1.263
Procter & Gamble	May 4, 1987	June 1, 1992	105	1.261
Chevron	May 11, 1987	July 1, 1992	75	1.258
Atl. Richfield	May 11, 1987	July 1, 1992	116	1.256
GTE	May 26, 1987	July 15, 1992	44	1.257
Sears, Roebuck	May 26, 1987	July 15, 1992	64	1.258
General Motors	June 1, 1987	June 30, 1992	107	1.255
Mobil	June 8, 1987	June 30, 1992	60	1.244
Xerox	June 8, 1987	July 15, 1992	97	1.260
Philip Morris	June 15, 1987	July 27, 1992	110	1.255
Coca-Cola	June 15, 1987	July 15, 1992	56	1.258
Hewlett-Packard	June 22, 1987	July 27, 1992	90	1.446
Johnson & Johnson	June 22, 1987	June 30, 1992	118	1.262
IBM	June 29, 1987	June 30, 1992	210	1.264
American Express	June 29, 1987	Aug. 24, 1992	50	1.384

*The first Trust, launched Oct. 23, 1983, was the AT&T pre-divestiture Americus Trust, and it was terminated on Oct. 24, 1988.

**Ratio of the termination claim to the price of underlying common stock taken approximately one week prior to the Trust launch date.

ber 23, 1983, and was based on the pre-divestiture AT&T stock. It terminated on October 24, 1988. Subsequent to the AT&T divestiture, the Primes and Scores of the first Trust were claims to a portfolio of common stocks (AT&T and the seven new Bells).

Since the first Trust, ASSC formed 26 additional Trusts through April 1988 (the end of our study period). The planned total is 30 Trusts, one for each of the 30 stocks in the Dow Jones index, with remaining Trusts to be formed in the future. All Trusts have a projected time span of five years; the majority of those currently outstanding are scheduled to expire in 1992.

Table 1 indicates the termination dates and claims for each of the 26 Trusts. The termination claims range from $30 for AT&T post-divestiture stock to $210 for IBM. A comparison of the termination claim to the contemporaneous stock price determines whether the Score security is "in-the-money." It should be noted that the stock price used for this comparison must be adjusted for stock splits, if any, in the time period after the Trust launch. If the adjusted stock price is greater than the termination claim, then the Score is in-the-money, which means the Score would receive a payoff

at termination.

The last column in Table 1 shows the ratio of the termination claim to the price of common stock when the Trust was initiated (labelled Initial Termination-Price Ratio). The average ratio is 1.261, which implies that, on average, stock prices must rise by about 26% from the stock price when the Trust was launched for the Score security to receive a payoff at termination (to be in-the-money). Of course, investors evaluating Scores should determine the current termination-price ratio (termination claim divided by current stock price) for an idea of how close the Score is to being in-the money.

Risks and Returns

How do these instruments perform in terms of risk and return?

One indication of their price behavior is provided by two contrasting Trusts. Figures 1 and 2 on p. 19 depict the price trends of the Prime, Score and common stock (adjusted for splits) for Exxon and American Home Products. The termination claim is shown as a dashed line, and amounts to $60 for Exxon and $90 for American Home.

In the case of Exxon, as the common stock price crossed the termination claim, the price of the Prime reached the upperbound of $60 (around March 1987). It is evident from Figure 1 that once the common stock price is above the termination claim, the Prime security has almost no price variation, and all common stock price changes are reflected in the Score prices.

The situation for American Home Products in Figure 2 is in contrast to Exxon. Here, the common stock price has, for the most part, remained below the termination claim, meaning that the Score has been "out-of-the-money" over almost the entire time period, and has therefore remained at low price levels.

There are considerable differences in risk between Primes and Scores, which are clearly indicated by looking at their betas. Beta is a measure of market risk; a beta of 1 indicates that the security moves parallel with the market, while a beta above 1 indicates that when the market moves up, the security will move up to an even greater extent and when the market declines, the security will decline to an even greater extent. Table 2 shows the betas for the Primes and Scores, and for the underlying stock.

The results of Table 2 are not surprising. Primes are a low-risk claim primarily on the dividend stream of the underlying common stock. Their betas average 0.45, implying that a 10% rise in the stock market would result, on average, in only a 4.5% rise in the typical Prime, while a 10% drop in the market would cause only a 4.5% drop (on average).

Scores, on the other hand, are a claim on price appreciation over and above the fixed termination claim. Their betas average an exceptionally high 5.06, which implies that a 10% stock market rise will, on average, result in a 50.6% rise in the typical Score, while a 10% market drop will result in a 50.6% drop (on average).

The very high betas of many Scores are due in part to the October 1987 crash, when common stock prices for many firms fell below their respective Trust termination claims. When adjusted common stock prices are below their termination claims, Scores are out-of-the-money and are much more volatile than in-the-money Scores.

What could investors have returned by investing in a portfolio of Primes or Scores? This was measured by determining the ending wealth (as of March 1, 1988) of $1 that was invested on December 31, 1986, in separate portfolios of Primes and Scores. The portfolio consisted of Primes and Scores in existence at the time; as more Trusts were created, the portfolio was adjusted to reflect their addition, so that by August 1987 all 26 securities were included; for comparison, $1 was invested in a common stock portfolio of the 26 firms. The ending wealth for common stock and Primes includes all dividend payments, while for the Score (which does not receive dividends) it represents price gains or losses only. The results: $1 would have grown to $1.12 for the common stock, $1.14 for the Prime and $0.81 for the Score. The Score portfolio fared the worst due to the October 1987 downturn, which affected the Prime portfolio much less.

Ending wealth values were also determined using August 13, 1987, as a starting date, which is when all 26 securities were traded. The results: $1 would have shrunk to $0.79 for the common stock, $0.99 for the Prime and $0.37 for the Score.

Finally, to examine the impact of the October 1987 crash, a "post-crash" portfolio investment was simulated with a starting date of October 30, 1987. The ending value of $1 invested for this time period was $1.04 for the common stock, $1.18 for the Prime and $0.61 for the Score. The relative positions of the portfolios are similar to the previous two time periods, but it is interesting to note how well the Prime portfolio performed. The implication is that as the market recovered after October 1987 and common stock prices rebounded, the upturn seems to have been captured in Prime price increases to a larger extent in comparison to the corresponding Scores. This would happen only when common stock prices are far below the termination claim levels of the respective Trusts, as is certainly true during the five months after October 1987.

Conclusions and Summary

The creation of the Primes and Scores currently traded have expanded the set of securities available for individual investors. Moreover, in contrast to some other innovative financial products, both Primes and Scores have excellent liquidity, since the securities are listed on the Amex.

In terms of risk and return, a Prime has lower risk and expected return when compared to the Score and the underlying common stock. The Score offers the potential for much higher returns, but at much greater risk. The unique advantage of the Prime and Score components is that they allow investors to target their investment to the security that best fits their needs in

Table 2.
Betas for Americus Primes and Scores
(Based on data from 11/87 through 4/88)

	Common	Prime	Score
Exxon	1.27	0.21	3.69
American Home	0.89	0.34	4.44
Du Pont	0.97	0.39	5.12
Bristol-Myers	1.24	0.50	6.08
AT&T	1.11	0.37	4.17
Merck	0.94	0.39	3.50
Amoco	0.85	0.40	4.92
GE	1.28	0.66	7.35
Dow	1.10	0.46	4.57
Kodak	1.10	0.46	5.65
Union Pacific	1.09	0.43	5.26
Ford	1.00	0.32	4.27
Procter & Gamble	0.91	0.42	3.67
Chevron	1.11	0.45	6.75
Atlantic Richfield	0.85	0.35	4.92
GTE	0.79	0.11	6.04
Sears	1.24	0.64	6.45
GM	1.00	0.44	6.98
Mobil	1.15	0.43	6.14
Xerox	0.97	0.56	5.22
Philip Morris	0.91	0.32	3.30
Coca-Cola	1.11	0.51	4.28
Hewlett-Packard	1.45	0.61	4.56
Johnson & Johnson	1.13	0.53	4.14
IBM	0.98	0.65	3.97
American Express	1.40	0.77	6.04
Average	1.07	0.45	5.06

terms of risk and aftertax return.

In summary, the stripping of common shares into Primes and Scores allows investors to:

- Increase dividend yields (but forego most of the capital gains) by investing in less volatile Primes;
- Increase short-term profit potential due to inherent leverage by investing in Scores (instead of common shares);
- Move between common shares, Primes, and Scores to increase gains from market timing; and
- Employ Primes and Scores to effectively reduce tax exposure.

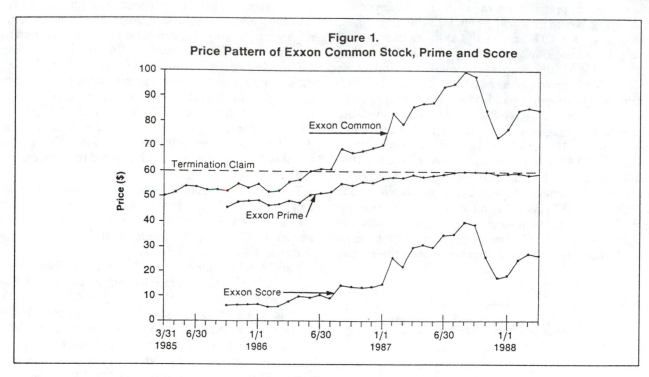

Figure 1.
Price Pattern of Exxon Common Stock, Prime and Score

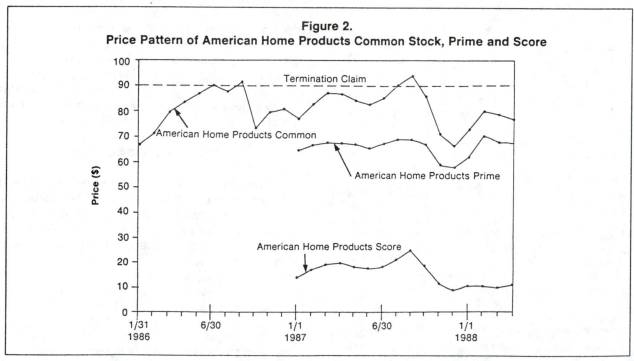

Figure 2.
Price Pattern of American Home Products Common Stock, Prime and Score

Section VII
Global Investing

As articles in previous sections have illustrated, investing today is becoming more global than ever before. Securities markets abroad are developing very quickly, particularly in Japan, Europe, and Australia. With ever-improving communications, capital flows from country to country with increasing ease. These developments act to knit diverse financial markets into one all-encompassing market. While markets around the world are not yet fully unified, major steps have already been taken toward that end. The articles in this section focus on the expanding international character of world securities markets.

In "Globalization in the Financial Services Industry," Christine Pavel and John N. McElravey survey the current status of globalization in financial services. They also examine how future movements toward globalization are likely to proceed. They find that globalization has already been achieved to a large extent for wholesale banking markets, and they foresee an increasing pace to globalization, particularly in Europe.

As world securities markets become more integrated, prices in those markets become more tightly linked. For example, if funds can flow effortlessly between Tokyo and New York, then investment opportunities with the same risk level in the two financial centers must have the same expected return. By contrast, if capital cannot flow freely, there will be no economic pressure to drive the two expected returns into equality. While this simple account does not do justice to some of the complexities, we are seeing freer financial flows and a tighter integration of prices across world markets. Reuven Glick, in "Global Interest Rate Linkages," considers some of the complexities for world money and bond markets. One of the main complexities is foreign exchange rates. As Glick explains, foreign exchange rates are intimately related to differential inflation rates across countries.

One of the main impediments to freer world trade is the diversity of currencies, necessitating billions of dollars of transactions in foreign exchange every day. These foreign exchange transactions are costly and involve risk. Costs arise from transactions as currencies must be exchanged into a foreign currency. Risks arise because one party may default, and it is difficult for the injured party to pursue remedies in a foreign land. In his article, "Reducing the Costs and Risks of Trading Foreign Exchange," Brian J. Cody suggests ways for dealing with these problems. Cody focuses on various types of *netting arrangements*. In a netting arrangement, currency flows between countries are avoided, because the central banks merely adjust their records to show offsets for the currencies that would be received. As Cody explains, these netting arrangements can reduce transaction costs and the risks associated with foreign exchange transactions.

Article 25

Globalization in the financial services industry

The pace has been most rapid at the wholesale, bank-to-bank and bank-to-multinational level; at the retail customer level, globalization will soon quicken, particularly in Europe.

Christine Pavel and John N. McElravey

Globalization can be defined as the act or state of becoming worldwide in scope or application. Apart from this geographical application, globalization can also be defined as becoming universal. For the financial services industry, this second meaning implies both a harmonization of rules and a reduction of barriers that will allow for the free flow of capital and permit all firms to compete in all markets.

This article looks at how global the financial services industry already is, and will likely become, by examining the nature and trends of globalization in the industry. It will also draw lessons from global nonfinancial industries and from recent geographic expansion of banking firms within the United States.

Financial globalization is being driven by advances in data processing and telecommunications, liberalization of restrictions on cross-border capital flows, deregulation of domestic capital markets, and greater competition among these markets for a share of the world's trading volume. It is growing rapidly, but primarily at the intermediary, rather than the customer, level. Its effects are felt at the customer level mainly because prices and interest rates are influenced by worldwide economic and financial conditions, rather than because direct customer access to suppliers has increased. However, globalization at the customer level will soon become apparent, at least in Europe after 1992, when European Community banking firms will be allowed to cross national borders.

Trends in other industries and lessons from interstate banking in the United States suggest that as financial globalization progresses, financial services will become more integrated, more competitive, and more concentrated. Also, firms that survive will become more efficient, and consumers of financial services will benefit considerably. Reciprocity is likely to be an important factor for those countries not already part of a regional compact, as it has been for interstate banking to proceed in the United States.

International commercial banking

The international banking market consists of the foreign sector of domestic banking markets and the unregulated offshore markets. It has undergone important structural changes over the last decade.

Like domestic banking, international banking involves lending and deposit taking. The primary distinction between the two types of banking lies in their customer bases. Since 1982, international lending and deposit taking have both been growing at roughly 15 percent annually. At year-end 1988, foreign loans and foreign liabilities at the world's banks each totalled more than $5 trillion. The extent, nature, and growth of international banking, however, are not the same in all countries.

When she wrote this article, Christine Pavel was an ecnomist at the Federal Reserve Bank of Chicago. She is now an assistant vice president at Citicorp North America Inc. John N. McElravey is an associate economist at the Federal Reserve Bank of Chicago.

Figures 1 and 2 show the ten countries whose banks have the largest shares of foreign banking assets and liabilities. Combined, these ten countries account for nearly three-quarters of all foreign assets and liabilities. Nearly half of all foreign banking assets and liabilities are held by banks in the United Kingdom, Japan, the United States, and Switzerland, up from 47 percent in 1982. This increase is almost entirely due to the meteoric rise in foreign lending by Japanese banks.

Perhaps the most notable event in international banking has been the rapid growth of Japanese banks. This extraordinary growth can be traced to deregulation in Japan, as well as to its banks' high market capitalization, the country's high savings rate, and its large current account surplus. Japanese foreign exchange controls and restrictions on capital outflows were removed in 1980. This allowed the banks' industrial customers to go directly to the capital markets for financing. The loss of some of their best customers, along with deposit rate deregulation and stiffer competition from other types of institutions, reduced profits.[1] To improve their profitability and to service Japanese nonfinancial firms that had expanded overseas, Japanese banks moved into new markets abroad. While a large part of the business of Japanese banks abroad is with Japanese firms, Japanese banks have been very successful lending to foreign industrial firms because of a competitive advantage conferred by a more favorable regulatory environment. Japan's capital requirements have been relatively easy, allowing banks to hold assets at 25 to 30 times book capital.[2] Japan's share of all foreign assets and liabilities rose from 4 percent in 1982 to more than 14 percent in 1988, surpassing the U.S. and second only to the U.K.

While many banks have significant international operations, only a few are truly international in scope. More than one-half of the total banking assets and liabilities in Switzerland, nearly one-half of total banking assets and liabilities in the United Kingdom, and over one-quarter of total banking assets and liabilities in France are foreign. In contrast, less than 25 percent of the balance sheets of German, Japanese, and U.S. banks consist of foreign assets and liabilities.

The United Kingdom and Switzerland have long been international financial centers. For more than 100 years Swiss bankers have been raising loans for foreigners. The largest Swiss banks, in fact, try to maintain a 50–50 split between their foreign and domestic assets for strategic and marketing reasons.[3] Deregulation, or the lack of regulation in some cases,

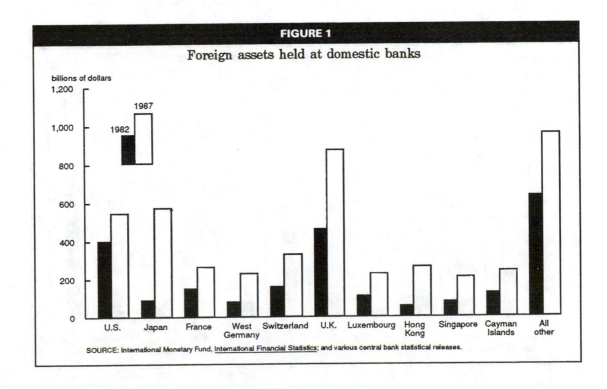

FIGURE 1

Foreign assets held at domestic banks

billions of dollars

SOURCE: International Monetary Fund, International Financial Statistics; and various central bank statistical releases.

and the restructuring of the British financial system have made London a powerful international financial center. More than half of all banking institutions in the U.K. are foreign-owned, and 59 percent of all assets of banks in the U.K. are denominated in foreign currency.[4]

At the aggregate level, the proportion of bank assets that are claims on foreigners is roughly equivalent to the proportion of liabilities that are claims of foreigners. This is not true of individual countries. Some countries' banks lend more to foreigners than they borrow from them. Foreign assets of German banks are almost twice the size of foreign liabilities, and Swiss banks hold about 34 percent more foreign assets than liabilities. For banks in these countries, the combination of international orientation and their country's high domestic saving rates makes them strong net lenders. Banks in the United States, Japan, and France, however, have more foreign liabilities than foreign assets, although in each case the difference is less than 5 percent.

U.S. banks have not always been net foreign borrowers. In 1982, foreign deposits at U.S. banks accounted for less than 13 percent of total liabilities, while foreign assets accounted for over 20 percent of total assets. Foreign deposits at U.S. banks have more than doubled over the 1982–87 period, growing far

more rapidly than domestic deposits. Foreign assets increased only 37 percent over that time and more slowly than domestic assets. This is due largely to the reduction in LDC lending and to the writing down of LDC loans by U.S. banks.

Foreign deposit growth also outpaced domestic deposit growth at Japanese banks. In 1982, foreign deposits accounted for 9 percent of total liabilities, and by 1987, they accounted for 18 percent. Similarly Japanese banks booked foreign assets about twice as fast as domestic assets over the 1982–87 period.

Offshore banking centers

A considerable portion of international banking activity occurs in unregulated offshore banking centers commonly known as the Euromarkets.[5] The Euromarkets, unlike the domestic markets, are virtually free of regulation. Euromarkets consist of Eurocurrency deposits, Eurobonds, and Euro-commercial paper. Eurocurrency deposits are bank deposits denominated in a foreign currency, and account for 86 percent of banks' foreign-owned deposits.

The development of Eurocurrency deposits marked the inauguration of the Euromarket in the mid-1950s. Eurocurrency deposits grew at a moderate rate until the mid-1960s when they began to grow more rapidly.[6] At that

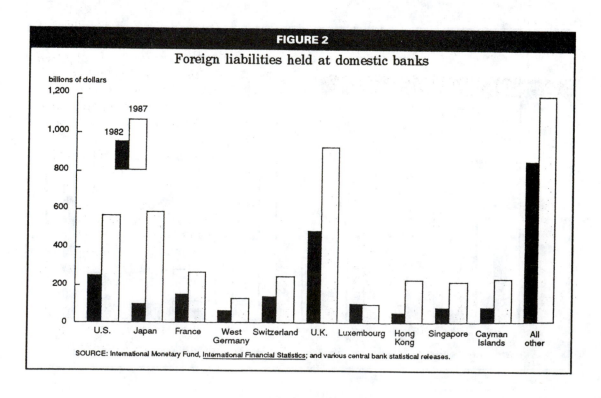

FIGURE 2

Foreign liabilities held at domestic banks

billions of dollars

SOURCE: International Monetary Fund, International Financial Statistics; and various central bank statistical releases.

time, the U.S. government imposed severe controls on the movement of capital, which "deflected a substantial amount of borrowing demand to the young Eurodollar market."[7] These U.S. capital controls were dismantled in 1974, but the oil crisis of the 1970s helped to fuel the continued growth of the Eurocurrency market. The U.S. oil embargo made oil-exporting countries fearful of placing their funds in domestic branches of U.S. banks. In the late 1970s and early 1980s, high interest rates bolstered the growth of Eurocurrency deposits, which are free of interest-rate ceilings and not subject to reserve requirements or deposit insurance premiums. From 1975 to 1980, Eurocurrency deposits grew over threefold.

Since 1980, Eurocurrency deposits have continued to grow quite rapidly, reaching a gross value of $4.5 trillion outstanding in 1987 and a net value of nearly $2.6 trillion (net of interbank claims). Eurodollar deposits, however, have not grown as rapidly. During the early 1980s, Eurodollars represented over 80 percent of all Eurocurrency deposits outstanding, but by 1987, they represented only 66 percent (see Figure 3). The declining importance of Eurodollar deposits can be explained, at least partially, by the decline in the cost of holding noninterest-bearing reserves against domestic deposits in the United States.[8]

Many Eurocenters have developed throughout the world. They have developed where local governments allow them to thrive, i.e., where regulation is favorable to offshore markets. Consequently, some countries with relatively small domestic financial markets, such as the Bahamas, have become important Eurocenters. Similarly, some countries with major domestic financial markets have no or very small offshore markets. In the United States, for example, the offshore market was prohibited until 1981 when International Banking Facilities (IBFs) were authorized.

Japan did not permit an offshore market to develop until late in 1986. Until then the "Asian dollar" market consisted primarily of the Eurocenters of Singapore, Bahrain, and Hong Kong. Now Japan's offshore market is about $400 billion in size, over twice as large as the U.S. offshore market, but still smaller than that in the United Kingdom.[9]

The interbank market

The international lending activities of most banks, aside from the money centers, are concentrated heavily in the area of providing a variety of credit facilities to banks in other countries. Consequently, a large proportion of banks' foreign assets and liabilities are claims on or claims of foreign banks. Eighty percent of all foreign assets are claims on other banks.[10] This ratio varies somewhat by country; however, since 1982, it has been increasing for all the major industrialized countries.

Similarly, nearly 80 percent of all banks' foreign liabilities are claims of other banks.[11] In Japan, 99 percent of all foreign liabilities at banks are deposits of foreign banks. Swiss banks are the exception, where only 28 percent of foreign liabilities are claims of banks.

The Swiss have a long history of providing banking services directly to foreign corporate and individual customers, which explains their relatively low proportion of interbank claims. A favorable legal and regulatory climate aided the development of a system that caters to foreigners, especially those wishing to shelter income from taxes. Confidentiality is recognized as a right of the bank customer, and stiff penalties can be imposed on bank officials who violate that right. In effect, no information about a client can be given to any third party.[12]

Since a very large portion of foreign deposits are Eurocurrency deposits, it is no surprise that about half of all Eurocurrency deposits are interbank claims. Eurocurrency

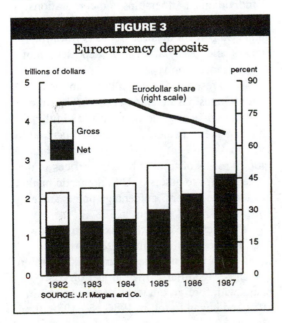

FIGURE 3

Eurocurrency deposits

trillions of dollars | percent

Eurodollar share (right scale)

Gross

Net

1982 1983 1984 1985 1986 1987
SOURCE: J.P. Morgan and Co.

deposits are frequently re-lent to other, often smaller, banks in the interbank market.[13]

The Japanese have become very large borrowers in the interbank market in response to domestic restrictions on prices and volumes of certain activities. Japanese banks operating overseas have been funding their activities by borrowing domestically (from nonresidents) in one market (e.g., the U.K.), and lending the funds through the interbank market to affiliates in other countries (e.g., the U.S.).[14]

Foreign exchange trading

Foreign exchange (forex) trading is another important international banking activity. Informal estimates place daily foreign exchange trading at $400 billion.[15] Like the loan markets, forex markets are primarily interbank markets. The primary players involved in the United States are the large money center and regional commercial banks, Edge Act corporations, and U.S. branches and agencies of foreign banks. Forex trading also involves some large nonbank financial firms, primarily large investment banks and foreign exchange brokers. However, according to the Federal Reserve Bank of New York's *U.S. Foreign Exchange Market Survey* for April 1989, 82 percent of the forex trading volume of banks was with other banks. Foreign exchange trading in New York grew at about 40 percent annually since 1986 to reach more than $130 billion by April 1989. In contrast, foreign trade (imports plus exports) has been growing at only about 6 percent annually since 1982 (3 percent on an inflation-adjusted basis).

The German mark is the most actively traded currency, followed by the Japanese yen, British pound, Swiss franc, and Canadian dollar. Since 1986, however, the German mark has lost some ground to the Japanese yen and the Swiss franc.[16]

The explosion of forex trading can, at least partly, be explained by the high rate of growth in cross-border financial transactions. Capital and foreign exchange controls were reduced or eliminated in a number of countries during the 1980s.

An international banking presence

There are several ways that commercial banks engage in international banking activities—through representative offices, agencies, foreign branches, and foreign sub-

sidiary banks and affiliates. In addition, in the United States, commercial banks may operate International Banking Facilities (IBFs) and Edge Act corporations, which unlike the other means, do not involve a physical presence abroad. The primary difference among these types of foreign offices centers on how customer needs are met (often because of regulation). For example, agencies of foreign banks are essentially branches that cannot accept deposits from the general public, while branches, as well as subsidiary banks, can offer a full range of banking services.

U.S. branches and agencies of foreign banks devote well over half of their assets to loans, about the same proportion as the domestic offices of U.S. commercial banks. U.S. commercial banks, however, hold a much larger proportion of their assets in securities and a much smaller proportion in customer's liability on acceptances.[17] This latter situation reflects the international trade financings of U.S. foreign offices.

U.S. offices of foreign banks compete with domestic banks primarily in commercial lending and, to a lesser extent, in real estate lending.[18] However, a significant portion of the commercial loans held at U.S. offices of foreign banks were purchased from U.S. banks, rather than originated by the foreign offices themselves.[19]

Both U.S. offices of foreign banks and domestic offices of U.S. commercial banks primarily fund their operations with deposits of individuals, partnerships and corporations (IPC).[20] Offices of foreign banks currently gather 23 percent of these deposits from foreigners, and nearly all of these deposits are of the nontransaction type.

The presence of foreign banks in the United States has been increasing. The ratio of foreign offices to domestic offices in the United States has increased from 2.8 percent in 1981 to 4.4 percent in 1987. Similarly, the ratio of assets of foreign banking offices in the United States to assets of U.S. domestic banks has increased over 5 percentage points since 1981 to nearly 21 percent in 1987.[21]

The presence of U.S. banks abroad, however, has been falling since 1985. At that time, U.S. banks operated nearly 1,000 foreign branches.[22] Similarly, the number of U.S. banks with foreign branches peaked at 163 in 1982 and began to fall in 1986. By 1988, the number of banks with foreign branches had fallen to 147. On an inflation-adjusted basis, total assets of foreign branches of U.S. banks fell 12 percent since 1983 to $506 billion in 1988. The number of IBFs and Edge Act Corporations has also been waning. Edge Acts numbered 146 in 1984 and were down to 112 by 1988.[23] This retrenchment reflects the lessening attractiveness of foreign operations as losses on LDC loans have mounted.

Implications of Europe after 1992

The presence of foreign banking firms in European domestic markets will likely increase over the next few years as the 12 European Community states become, at least economically, a "United States of Europe." The EC plans to issue a single license that will allow banks to expand their networks throughout the Community, governed by their home country's regulations.[24]

Since banking powers will be determined by the rules of the home country, banks from countries with more liberal banking laws operating in countries with more restrictive banking laws will have an advantage over their domestic competitors. Consequently, the most efficient form of banking will prevail. Countries with more fragmented banking systems will need to liberalize for their banks to compete with banks from countries with universal banking.

While reciprocity will not be important for nations within the EC, it will be an issue for banks from countries outside the EC, especially those from Japan and the U.S. As financial services companies in Europe begin to operate with fewer restrictions, there will be competitive pressure on the U.S. and Japan to remove the barriers between commercial and investment banking. To be most efficient, firms operating in various markets want similar powers in each market. The EC, as previously noted, solved this problem with a Community banking license. Thus, the EC's efforts at regulatory harmonization may hasten the demise of Glass-Steagall in the U.S. and Article 65 in Japan.[25]

The implications for European banking will be similar to the experience in the United States following the introduction of interstate banking in the early to mid-1980s. Since that time, the U.S. commercial banking industry has been consolidating on nationwide, re-gional, and statewide bases through mergers and acquisitions. Acquiring firms tend to be large, profitable organizations with expertise in operating geographically dispersed networks, while targets tend to be smaller, although still relatively large firms, in attractive banking markets. Large, poorly-capitalized firms will also find themselves to be potential takeover targets.

What these lessons imply for Europe in 1992 is that the largest and strongest organizations with the managerial talent to operate a geographically dispersed organization will become Europe-wide firms, while smaller firms will have a more regional focus and others will survive as niche players. In addition, just as different state laws have slowed the process of nationwide banking in the United States, language and cultural barriers will slow the process in Europe as well. The overall result of a more globally integrated financial sector in Europe, and elsewhere, will be that the organizations that survive will be more efficient, and customers will be better served. Also, it is very likely that the 1992 experience will improve European banks' ability to compete outside of Europe.

Size is not, and will not be, a sufficient ingredient for survival. In general, firms in protected industries, such as airlines, tend to be inefficient. Large banking organizations based in states with restrictive branching and multibank holding company laws tended to be less efficient than their peers in states that allow branches and, therefore, more competition. In addition, commercial banking organizations that operated in unit banking states had little expertise in operating a decentralized organization, and tended to focus primarily on large commercial customers. Consequently, these banking firms have not acquired banks far from home.

The process of consolidation has already begun within European countries and within Europe as firms prepare for a single European banking market. Unlike the Unites States' experience of outright mergers and acquisitions, however, the European experience centers on forming "partnerships." Partnerships have been formed Europe-wide, even though the most recent directive on commercial banking permits branching, because of the difficulties in managing an organization that spans several cultures and languages. Apparently, financial services firms want to get their feet wet first, rather than plunge into European banking and risk drowning before 1992 arrives. But also, until regulations among countries become more uniform, partnerships and joint ventures allow financial firms to arbitrage regulations.

The formation of partnerships and joint ventures is not only a European phenomenon. Indeed, U.S. firms have entered into such agreements with European and Japanese companies. For example, Wells Fargo and Nikko Securities have formed a joint venture to operate a global investment management firm, and Merrill Lynch and Société Générale are discussing a partnership to develop a French asset-backed securities market.

The experience of nonfinancial firms suggests that this arrangement can be a good way to establish an international presence. For example, in 1984, Toyota and General Motors entered into a joint manufacturing venture in California. Through this venture, the Japanese were able to acquaint themselves with American workers and suppliers before opening their own plants in the U.S. Since then, Toyota has opened two more manufacturing plants on its own in North America, and there is speculation in the auto industry that they will buy GM's share of the joint venture once the agreement ends in 1996.[26]

Another case of international expansion through joint ventures can be found in the petroleum industry. Oil companies from some oil-producing countries have been quite active in recent years buying stakes in refining and marketing operations in the United States and Europe. These acquisitions give producers an outlet for their crude in important retail markets, and refiners get a reliable source. Saudi Arabia purchased a 50 percent stake in Texaco's eastern and Gulf Coast refining and marketing operations in November 1988. The state-owned oil companies from Kuwait and Venezuela have joint ventures with European oil companies as well.[27] If joint ventures between financial services firms are as successful as nonfinancial ones have been, then global financial integration will benefit.

International securities markets

International securities include securities that are issued outside the issuer's home coun-try. Some of these securities trade on foreign exchanges. Issuance and trading of international securities have grown considerably since 1986, as has the amount of such securities outstanding.

Greater demand for international financing is stimulating important changes in financial markets, especially in Europe. Regulations and procedures designed to shield domestic markets from foreign competition are gradually being dismantled. London's position as an international market was strengthened by the lack of sophistication of many other European markets. Greater demand for equity financing in Europe has been encouraged by private companies, and by governments privatizing large public-sector corporations. These measures to deregulate and, therefore, improve the efficiency, regulatory organizations, and settlement procedures are a response to competition from other markets, and the explosion of securities trading in the 1980s.[28]

It is estimated that the world bond markets at the end of 1988 consisted of about $9.8 trillion of publicly issued bonds outstanding, a nearly $2 trillion increase since 1986.[29] At year-end 1988, two-thirds of all bonds outstanding were obligations of central governments, their agencies, and state and local governments. This figure varies considerably across countries. Over two-thirds of bonds denominated in the U.S. dollar and the Japanese yen are government obligations, but less than one-third of bonds denominated in the German mark are government obligations, and only 10 percent of bonds denominated in the Swiss franc represent government debt.[30]

The international bond market includes foreign bonds, Eurobonds, and Euro-commercial paper. Foreign bonds are bonds issued in a foreign country and denominated in that country's currency. Eurobonds are long-term bonds issued and sold outside the country of the currency in which they are denominated. Similarly, Euro-commercial paper is a short-term debt instrument that is issued and sold outside the country of the currency in which it is denominated.

The Japanese are the biggest issuers of Eurobonds because it is easier and cheaper than issuing corporate bonds in Japan. Japanese companies issued 21 percent of all Eurobonds in 1988.[31] Ministry of Finance (MOF) regulations and the underwriting oligopoly of the four largest Japanese securities firms keep the issuance cost in the domestic bond market higher than in the Euromarket. The ministry would like to bring this bond market activity back to Japan, so it has been slowly liberalizing the rules for issuing yen bonds and samurai bonds (yen bonds issued by foreigners in Japan). So far, the impact of these changes has been small.[32]

International bonds accounted for almost 10 percent of bonds outstanding at the end of 1988 and over three-quarters are denominated in the U.S. dollar, Japanese yen, German mark and U.K. sterling (see Figure 4). These countries represent four of the largest economies and financial markets in the world.

The importance of international bond markets has increased considerably for many countries. As Table 1 shows, international bonds account for nearly half of all bonds denominated in the Swiss franc and over one-third of all bonds denominated in the Australian dollar. International bonds account for over 21 percent of bonds denominated in the British pound, up dramatically from less than 1 percent in 1980. The rise in importance of international bonds for these currencies can, at least in part, be explained by the budget surpluses in the countries in which these currencies are denominated and, therefore, the slower growth in the debt obligations of these countries' governments.

The value of world equity markets, at $9.6 trillion in 1988, is about equal to the value of world bond markets. Three countries—the United States, Japan, and the United Kingdom—account for three quarters of the total capitalization on world equity markets, and they account for nearly half of the 15,000 equity issues listed on the world's stock exchanges (see Figure 5).

American, Japanese, and British equity markets are the largest and most active. American and British markets are very open to foreign investors, but significant barriers to foreign competitors still exist in Japan.

Stocks have, historically, played a relatively minor role in corporate financing in many European countries. Various regulatory and traditional barriers to entry made these bourses financial backwaters. The stock exchanges in Switzerland, West Germany, France, and Italy have only recently taken steps to modernize in order to compete against exchanges in the U.S. and the U.K. It was estimated that about 20 percent of daily trad-

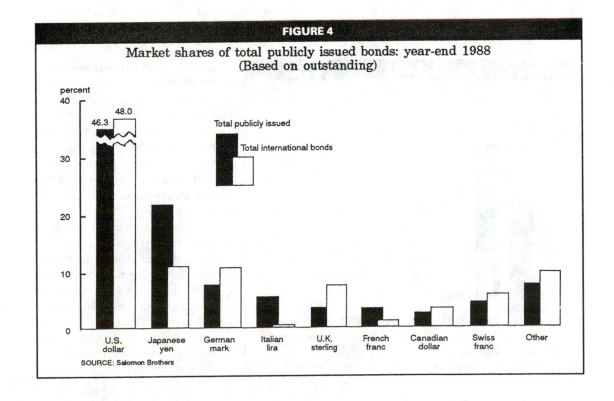

FIGURE 4

Market shares of total publicly issued bonds: year-end 1988
(Based on outstanding)

percent

Total publicly issued

Total international bonds

46.3   48.0

U.S. dollar | Japanese yen | German mark | Italian lira | U.K. sterling | French franc | Canadian dollar | Swiss franc | Other

SOURCE: Salomon Brothers

TABLE 1

International shares of the world's major bond markets
(Percent based on outstanding)

	1980	1985	1988
U.S. dollar	4.4	8.8	10.5
Japanese yen	1.6	3.2	5.0
German mark	12.6	11.2	14.2
U.K. sterling	0.9	9.4	21.3
Canadian dollar	3.1	5.5	13.7
Swiss franc	27.3	42.3	49.2
Australian dollar	n.a.	9.5	36.2

SOURCE: Salomon Brothers

ing in French equities was done in London in 1988.[33] French regulators hope that their improvements will lure some of that trading back to Paris.

West German equity markets, until recently, provided a good illustration of the kinds of barriers that keep stock exchanges small, inefficient, and illiquid. Access to the stock exchange was effectively controlled by the largest banks, which have a monopoly on brokerage. Under this arrangement, small firms were kept from issuing equity, thus remaining captive loan clients. Large German firms have traditionally relied more heavily on bank credit and bonds than on equity to finance growth. The integration of banking and commerce in Germany has contributed to this reliance. German banks, "through their equity holdings, exert significant ownership control over industrial firms."[34]

The fragmented structure of the West German system, which consists of eight independent exchanges each with its own interests, also helped check development. Over the last several years, though, rivalries between the exchanges have been somewhat buried, and they have been working to improve their integration and cooperation. One way is through computer links between exchanges to facilitate trading. A transaction that cannot be executed immediately at one of the smaller exchanges can be forwarded to Frankfurt to be completed. Overall, German liberalization efforts have been moderately successful, adding about 90 new companies to the stock exchange between 1984 and 1988.[35]

Active institutional investors, such as pension funds, which have a major position in the U.S. markets, have no tradition in the German equity market. Billions of marks in pension funds are on the balance sheets of German companies, treated as long-term loans from employees.[36] Freeing these funds in a deregulated and restructured market could have a profound effect on Germany's domestic equity markets.

Issuance of international securities

The issuance of international securities was mixed in 1988. Issuance of international bonds was relatively strong, while issuance of international equities, at $7.7 billion in 1988, was off considerably from 1987, but almost triple 1985 issuance.[37]

The contraction of international equities was driven by investors, and reflects their caution. Following the stock market crash in October 1987, portfolio managers reportedly focussed, and have continued to focus, on low-risk assets and on domestic issues.[38] Lower volatility of share prices on the world's major

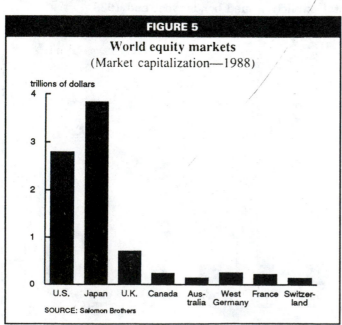

FIGURE 5

World equity markets
(Market capitalization—1988)

trillions of dollars

SOURCE: Salomon Brothers

exchanges, however, would likely aid a rebound in the appetite for and in the issuance of international equities.

Some important structural changes took place in international financial markets between 1985 and 1987. A sharp increase in issuance for the U.K. translated into substantially greater market share of international equity issuance, from 3.7 percent in 1985 to 33.0 percent in 1987. This increased share of international activity reflects the deregulation and restructuring of the London markets that occurred in the fall of 1986, improving their place as an international marketplace for securities. Even with the retrenchment in 1988, London maintained its leading role, with twice the issuance of second-place U.S.[39]

Over this same three-year period, Switzerland's international equity issuance translated into a substantially smaller market share, falling from 40.7 percent to 6.0 percent. This sharp decline in market share, from undisputed leader to fourth, reveals Switzerland's failure to keep pace with deregulation in other countries. For years, a cartel system dominated by its three big banks has set prices and practices in the stock markets. It is only recently that competition from markets abroad has forced the cartel to liberalize its system.[40]

In contrast to the international equities markets, issuance of international bonds was very strong in 1988, following a sharp contraction in 1987 entirely due to a 25.5 percent decline in Eurobond issuance.[41] Eurobonds account for about 80 percent of international bond issues, and nearly two-thirds of all international issues are denominated in three currencies—the U.S. dollar, Swiss franc, and the Deutschemark. Nearly 60 percent of international bonds are issued by borrowers in Japan, the United Kingdom, the United States, France, Canada, and Germany.

The long-time importance of the United States and the U.S. dollar in the international bond market has been dwindling. In 1985, 54 percent of all Eurobonds were denominated in U.S. dollars, but by 1988 only 42 percent were in U.S. dollars.

Similarly, U.S. borrowers issued 24 percent of all international bonds in 1985, but issued only 8 percent in 1988. The impetus behind this decline lies in part with the investors who prefer low-risk securities and are leery of U.S. bonds because of the perceived increase in "event risk" associated with restructurings and leveraged buyouts. Also, no doubt, developments such as the adoption of Rule 415 by the Securities and Exchange Commission (shelf registration) have encouraged U.S. firms to issue domestic securities by making it less costly to do so.

Trading in international securities

The United States is a major center of international securities trading. Foreign transactions in U.S. markets exceed U.S. transactions in foreign markets by a ratio of almost 7 to 1. This is a result of several factors. The United States has the largest and most developed securities markets in the world. U.S. equity markets are virtually free of controls on foreign involvement. SEC regulations on disclosure dissipate much uncertainty concerning the issuers of publicly listed securities in the United States while less, or inadequate, regulation in other countries makes investments more risky in those foreign markets. The market for U.S. Treasury securities has also been very attractive to foreign investors. In fact, large purchases of these securities by the Japanese have helped finance the U.S. government budget deficit.

Both foreign transactions in U.S. markets and U.S. transactions in foreign markets have been increasing at a very rapid pace. Foreign transactions in U.S. equity securities in U.S. markets plus such transactions in foreign equities in U.S. markets grew at almost 50 percent annually to exceed $670 billion in 1987.[42] Foreign transactions in U.S. stocks on U.S. equity markets have been increasing faster than domestic transactions; in 1988, foreign transactions accounted for 13 percent of the value of transactions on U.S. markets, up from 10 percent in 1986 (see Table 2).

Foreign transactions have increased in securities markets abroad as well; however, they have not, in general, kept pace with domestic trading. Consequently, foreign transactions as a percentage of all transactions has declined over the 1986-88 period for Japan, Canada, Germany, and the United Kingdom. Nevertheless, transactions by U.S. residents in foreign equity markets were estimated at about $188 billion in 1987, nearly 12 times as much as in 1982.[43]

TABLE 2

Foreign transactions in domestic equity markets: Share of domestic trading
(Percent of total volume)

	1985	1988
Japan	8.7	6.5
Canada	29.5	21.6
Germany	29.9	8.7
U.S.	9.7	13.1
U.K.	37.3	20.8
France	38.0	43.5
Switzerland	4.6	6.3

SOURCE: Salomon Brothers

Foreign transactions in U.S. bonds and foreign bonds in U.S. markets in 1988 increased to more than 13 times their 1982 level (see Figure 6). This trading boom was fueled mainly by growth in transactions for U.S. Treasury bonds, which accounted for about 84 percent of total foreign bond transactions in 1988, up from 63 percent in 1982. These transactions in U.S. Treasury bonds accounted for almost three-quarters of all foreign securities transactions in U.S. markets in 1988.

Bond transactions in other countries by nonresidents also increased dramatically. In Germany, for example, the value of such transactions increased by 300 percent over the 1985-88 period and now account for over half of the value of all transactions in German bond markets.[44] Foreign bond transactions by U.S. residents reached an estimated $380 billion in 1987, six times greater than the 1982 figure.

Derivative products

Globalization has affected derivative financial products in two ways. First, it has spurred the creation and rapid growth of internationally-related financial products, such as Eurodollar futures and options and foreign currency futures and options as well as futures and options on domestic securities that trade globally, such as U.S. Treasury securities. Trading hours on some U.S. futures and options exchanges have been expanded to support cross-border trading of underlying assets, such as Treasury securities. Second, globalization has lead to the establishment of futures and options exchanges worldwide. Once the exclusive domain of U.S. markets, especially in Chicago, financial derivative products are now traded in significant volumes throughout Europe and Asia.

The number of futures contracts on Eurodollar CDs and on foreign currencies as well as the number of open positions has increased rapidly (see Figure 7). The number of futures contracts on Eurodollar CDs traded worldwide increased almost 70 percent annually since 1983 to reach over 25 million in 1988. This compares with a 20 to 25 percent annual growth rate for Eurodollars.[45] Similarly, nearly 40 million futures and options contracts on various foreign currencies were traded worldwide in 1988, up from 14 million in 1983. This growth rate is roughly equivalent to that of forex trading.

The rapid increase in the volume of trading of internationally-linked futures and options contracts has largely benefited U.S. exchanges, which are the largest and sometimes the only exchanges where such products are traded. Nevertheless, the share of exchange traded futures and options volume commanded by the U.S. exchanges has dropped from 98 percent in 1983 to about 80 percent in 1988.

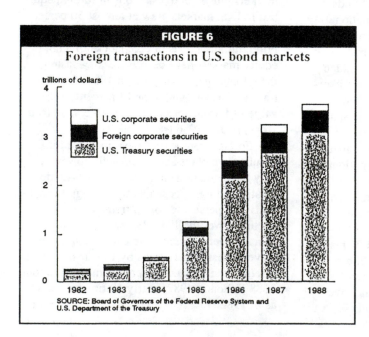

FIGURE 6

Foreign transactions in U.S. bond markets

trillions of dollars

- ☐ U.S. corporate securities
- ■ Foreign corporate securities
- ▨ U.S. Treasury securities

1982 1983 1984 1985 1986 1987 1988

SOURCE: Board of Governors of the Federal Reserve System and U.S. Department of the Treasury

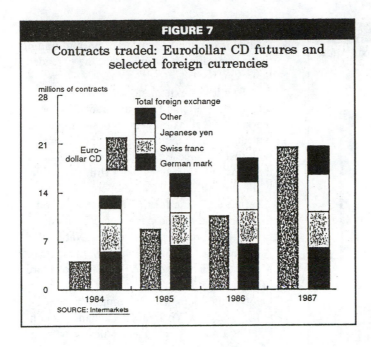

FIGURE 7

Contracts traded: Eurodollar CD futures and selected foreign currencies

millions of contracts

Total foreign exchange
Other
Japanese yen
Swiss franc
German mark

Euro-dollar CD

SOURCE: Intermarkets

These 18 percentage points were primarily lost to European and Japanese exchanges.

In the past four years, 20 new exchanges have been established, bringing the total to 72.[46] Many of these new exchanges are in Europe. In addition, foreign membership at many exchanges is considerable. For example, over two-thirds of LIFFE's (London International Financial Futures Exchange) membership is based outside of the United Kingdom.[47]

Two notable additions to futures and options trading are Switzerland and West Germany. The Swiss Options and Financial Futures Exchange (SOFFEX) was established in March 1988, and is the world's first fully-automated, computer-based exchange.[48] SOFFEX trades index options on the Swiss Market Index, which consists of 24 stocks traded on the three main stock exchanges in Geneva, Zurich, and Basle. Critics of the system contend that there is a lack of liquidity on the underlying stocks, thus limiting its effectiveness. Swiss banks control brokerage and can match trades internally with their own clients. This leaves a small amount for open trading on the exchange.[49]

The Germans will begin trading futures and options in 1990. The exchange will trade bond and stock-index futures, and options on 14 high-turnover German stocks. Trading will be executed entirely by computer, as on its Swiss counterpart. The main reason the government approved the new exchange was competition from London for business that the Germans felt should be in Frankfurt. LIFFE began trading futures on West German government bonds in September 1988, and, as of year-end 1989, it was the second most active contract on the exchange, trading about 20,000 contracts daily. It has been estimated that anywhere from 30 to 70 percent of this London-based trading is accounted for by the German business community.[50]

When an exchange is established, its product line usually includes a domestic government bond contract, a stock index futures contract, and, sometimes, a domestic/foreign currency futures or option contract. Therefore, the number of contracts listed on foreign exchanges that compete with contracts on U.S. exchanges is small relative to the number of contracts traded throughout the world.

The U.S. exchanges' most formidable competitors are LIFFE and SIMEX (Singapore International Monetary Exchange). LIFFE competes with U.S. exchanges for trading volume in U.S. Treasury bond futures and options and in Eurodollar futures and options. SIMEX also competes for trading volume in Eurodollar futures as well as in Deutschemark and Japanese yen futures. But the SIMEX contracts are also complements to U.S. contracts in that a contract opened on the U.S. (Singapore) exchange can be closed on the Singapore (U.S.) exchange.

As shown in Figure 8, LIFFE commands less than 3 percent of trading volume in T-bond futures and options and Eurodollar options. Similarly, less than 3 percent of all Deutschemark futures trading occurs on SIMEX. LIFFE and SIMEX, however, are much more significant competitors for Eurodollar futures volume. SIMEX accounts for 7.5 percent of trading volume and LIFFE accounts for 6.5 percent.

Furthermore, in only three years, SIMEX managed to capture over 50 percent of the annual trading volume in the yen futures contract. The relatively greater success of SIMEX with the yen contract reflects the importance

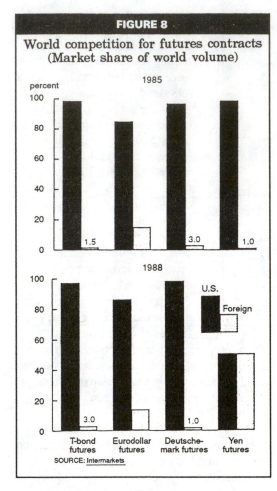

FIGURE 8

World competition for futures contracts
(Market share of world volume)

SOURCE: Intermarkets

of trading in the same time zone as one side of a foreign exchange transaction. In June 1989, a yen/dollar futures contract was launched in Tokyo, along with a Eurodollar contract. The experience of SIMEX suggests that the yen contract will attract market share away from SIMEX rather than from the CME because Singapore and Tokyo are in the same time zone. The above experiences suggest that once deutschemark futures begin trading on the German exchange, some proportion now traded in London will move to Germany.

24-hour trading

True 24-hour trading exists in only a few markets, and is most valuable for assets whose investors span several time zones. Major currencies are traded around the clock in at least seven major money centers. Precious metals, especially gold bullion, and oil, which trade in New York, London and Singapore, are traded 24 hours a day. U.S. Treasury bonds are traded around the clock as well, but overseas markets are thin. Twenty percent of the busi-

ness at the French futures exchange in Paris (Matif) is conducted outside of normal trading hours, indicating how important the extended hours can be.[51]

To a lesser extent, stocks of about 200 major multinational firms are traded in foreign markets as well as in their domestic markets, but foreign trading volume does not compare with that in domestic markets. One reason is that most information about a firm is revealed while domestic markets are open.

In preparation for the increase in round-the-clock trading and due to perceived competition from foreign exchanges, the National Association of Securities Dealers, the Chicago Mercantile Exchange, and the Chicago Board of Trade have made plans to extend their normal trading hours through computerized systems. The New York Stock Exchange is considering trading stocks electronically outside of normal trading hours, and the Cincinnati Stock Exchange and the CBOE are planning 24-hour electronic trading systems. The trading hours for foreign currency options on the Philadelphia Stock Exchange begin at 7:45 a.m. (Eastern Standard Time) to encompass more of the London business day.

International investment banking

As financial markets become more globally integrated, foreign investment banks are attempting to play larger roles in domestic markets. Overall, they are meeting with mixed results.

Foreign investment banks in the United States

Foreign-based investment banks have made some inroads into U.S. domestic capital markets. For the first time, two foreign firms ranked among the top ten advisers for U.S. mergers and acquisitions in the first quarter of 1989. Kleinwort Benson and S.G. Warburg, ranked sixth and seventh, respectively, according to the value of deals.[52] They placed ahead of Merrill Lynch and Kidder Peabody. No Japanese firms ranked among the top M&A advisers, although Fuji Bank of Japan has an ownership interest in Kleinwort Benson.

The Japanese are making a concerted effort to penetrate the U.S. investment banking market, but they have met with little success. The Big Four—Nomura Securities, Daiwa Securities, Nikko Securities, and Yamaichi

Securities Company—expanded in the United States in the mid-1980s, but have scaled back personnel due to unprofitable U.S. operations. Two of the Big Four—Nomura and Yamachi—have been trying to model their U.S. operations as identifiable Wall Street companies, and not just subsidiaries of Tokyo firms, by their appointment of Americans to head their U.S. operations. Nomura's strengths have been its primary dealership in U.S. government securities and U.S. stock trading unit, primarily for Japanese purchase. Nomura's weaknesses, however, are its lack of financial product development and its trading skills.

The Japanese have been more successful in U.S. derivative markets. In April 1988, Nikko Securities became the first Japanese securities firm to acquire a clearing membership at the Chicago Board of Trade (CBOT). Since then, fifteen others have joined the CBOT. The Chicago Mercantile Exchange (CME) has seventeen Japanese companies as members. Nikko, Daiwa, and Yamaichi are members of both the CBOT and CME. Recently, Nomura announced a cooperative agreement with Refco, one of the world's largest futures merchants. Consummation of the deal will assist Nomura in learning futures trading.

U.S. investment banks' activities abroad

Merger and acquisition activity has been slowing in the United States, prompting Wall Street firms to look to foreign markets. According to a 1988 survey, U.S. firms accounted for slightly more than half of all cross-border merger and acquisition activity. The most active U.S. investment banks were Shearson Lehman Hutton (57 deals), Goldman Sachs (46), and First Boston (34).[53]

U.S. investment banks represented about 12 percent of all mergers and acquisitions for European clients in 1988. The most active U.S. firms in this category were Security Pacific Group (37 deals), Shearson Lehman Hutton (26), and Goldman Sachs (22). Security Pacific has acquired two foreign investment banks, one Canadian and one British.[54]

U.S. firms expect to find some business in Asia as well. The newly formed investment bank, Wasserstein Perella, for example, recently dispatched merger and acquisition teams to Japan to set up the Tokyo joint venture, Nomura Wasserstein Perella.

In the area of securities underwriting, U.S. firms are quite strong. Seven of the top ten underwriters of debt and equity securities worldwide are U.S. firms; however, only three U.S. firms rank among the top underwriters of non-U.S. securities. Merrill Lynch was the top underwriter of all debt and equity offerings worldwide during the first half of 1989.[55]

The strength of U.S. firms abroad lies primarily in Europe. Foreign securities firms in Tokyo have found it difficult to establish themselves. Thirty-six of the 51 Tokyo branches of foreign securities houses lost a total of $164 million for the six months ending March 1989.[56] As a result of these losses, many foreign firms have cut back their Tokyo operations, concentrating on a particular product or service. Twenty-two out of the 115 Tokyo stock exchange members are foreign firms. Another 29 foreign securities houses have opened branch offices in Tokyo. Nevertheless, the Big Four dominate the Tokyo exchange, accounting for almost 50 percent of daily business. The foreign firms account for only 4.5 percent of this daily business.[57]

Three American investment banks, Salomon Brothers, Merrill Lynch, and First Boston, have been able to develop profitable operations in the Tokyo market. All three American firms attribute their success in part to a well-trained staff, and to hiring Japanese college graduates to fill positions. Salomon posted a $53.6 million pretax profit as of March 31, 1989. It also made a $300 million capital infusion, which has helped to make Salomon a challenger to the Big Four in bond trading.[58]

The U.S. government has been pressuring for greater access for U.S. firms to Japanese capital markets since 1984. For instance, Japanese government securities are predominantly sold through closed syndicates, in which foreign firms account for only about 8 percent of the total. Change has been slower than foreign investment banks and governments would like, but some progress has been made. The Japanese sold 40 percent of its 10-year bonds at an open auction in April 1989.[59]

Conclusion

Financial markets and financial services are becoming more globally integrated. As businesses expand into new markets around the world, there is greater demand for financing to follow them. All major areas of international finance have grown far more rapidly than foreign trade in recent years. Trading of securities in U.S. markets by nonresidents, trading volume of foreign currency futures and options, and foreign exchange trading have been growing at 40 percent or more a year. This rapid growth of international financial transactions reflects the growth in cross-border capital flows.

The major markets for domestic as well as international financial services are the United States, Japan, and the United Kingdom, although it is beginning to make more sense to talk about the dominant markets as the United States, Japan, and Europe. The reduction of regulatory barriers and harmonization of rules among countries have allowed more firms to compete in more markets around the world. These markets are also competing against each other for a share of the world's trading volume.

Today, a very large part of financial globalization involves financial intermediaries dealing with other, foreign, financial interme-

diaries. Consequently, prices in one market are affected by conditions in other markets, but, with a few exceptions, of which commercial lending is the most notable, customers do not have direct access to more suppliers. Again, this could change as Europe moves toward economic and financial unification.

Lessons from industries such as automobiles and petroleum, as well as lessons from geographic expansion in the United States, indicate that the financial services industry will become more consolidated, with firms from a handful of countries garnering substantial market share. International joint ventures will be common and often precursors to outright acquisitions. For smaller firms to survive as global competitors, they will have to find and service a market niche.

As the financial services industry and financial markets become more globally integrated, the most efficient and best organized firms will prevail. Also, countries with the most efficient—but not necessarily the least—regulation will become the world's major international financial centers.

FOOTNOTES

[1] "Japanese Finance," Survey, *The Economist*, December 10, 1988, pp. 3 and 10.

[2] Ibid.

[3] Thomas H. Hanley, et. al., "The Swiss Banks: Universal Banks Poised to Prosper as Global Deregulation Unfolds," *Salomon Brothers Stock Research*, June 1986.

[4] See David T. Llewellyn, *Competition, Diversification, and Structural Change in the British Financial System*, 1989, unpublished xerox, p. 1.

[5] Christopher M. Korth, "International Financial Markets," in William H. Baughn and Donald R. Mandich, eds., *The International Banking Handbook*, Dow Jones-Irwin, 1983, pp. 9-13.

[6] During the Cold War, the U.S. dollar was the only universally accepted currency, and the Russians wanted to maintain their international reserves in dollars, but not at American banks for fear that the U.S government might freeze the funds. Therefore, the Russians found some British, French and German banks that would accept deposits in dollars. See Korth, p. 11.

[7] Christopher M. Korth, "The Eurocurrency Markets," in Baughn and Mandich, p. 26.

[8] Herbert L. Baer and Christine A. Pavel, "Does regulation drive innovation?," *Economic Perspectives*. Vol. 12, No. 2, March/April 1988, pp. 3-15, Federal Reserve Bank of Chicago.

[9] "Japanese banking booms offshore," *The Economist*, November 26, 1988, p. 87.

[10] *International Financial Statistics*, International Monetary Fund, various years.

[11] Ibid.

[12] This does not apply in criminal cases, bankruptcy, or debt collection. The disclosure of secret information to foreign authorities is not allowed, unless provided for in an international treaty. In such a case, which is an exception, the foreign authorities could obtain only the information available to Swiss authorities under similar circumstances. See Peat, Marwick, Mitchell & Co., *Banking in Switzerland*, 1979, pp. 35-6.

[13] Eurobanks have specific rates at which they are prepared either to borrow or lend Eurofunds. In London, this rate is known as LIBOR (the London Interbank Offer Rate). LIBOR dominates the Eurocurrency market.

[14] Henry S. Terrell, Robert S. Dohner, and Barbara R. Lowrey, "The Activities of Japanese Banks in the United

Kingdom and in the United States, 1980-88," *Federal Reserve Bulletin*, February 1990, p. 43.

[15]Michael R. Sesit and Craig Torres, "What if They Traded All Day and Nobody Came?," *Wall Street Journal*, June 14, 1989, p. C1.

[16]*U.S. Foreign Exchange Market Survey*, Federal Reserve Bank of New York, April 1989, pp. 5-7.

[17]"Report of Assets and Liabilities of U.S. Branches and Agencies of Foreign Banks," Table 4.30, *Federal Reserve Bulletin*, June 1989, Board of Governors of the Federal Reserve System; and *Annual Statistical Digest*, Board of Governors of the Federal Reserve System, Table 68.

[18]Ibid.

[19]*Senior Loan Officer Opinion Survey on Bank Lending Practices for August 1989*, Board of Governors of the Federal Reserve System.

[20]See footnote 17.

[21]*Annual Report*, Board of Governors of the Federal Reserve System, Banking Supervision and Regulation Section, various years; authors' calculations from Report of Condition and Income tapes, Board of Governors of the Federal Reserve System, various years.

[22]Ibid.

[23]Ibid.

[24]"European banking: Cheque list," *The Economist*, June 24, 1989, pp. 74-5.

[25]The Glass-Steagall Act is the law that separates commercial banking from investment banking in the U.S. Article 65 is its Japanese equivalent.

[26]James B. Treece, with John Hoerr, "Shaking Up Detroit," *Business Week*, August 14, 1989, pp. 74-80.

[27]*Standard and Poor's Oil Industry Survey*, August 3, 1989, p. 26.

[28]"European Stock Exchanges," *A supplement to Euromoney*, August 1987, pp. 2-5.

[29]Rosario Benvides, "How Big is the World Bond Market?—1989 Update" *International Bond Markets*, Salomon Brothers, June 24, 1989.

[30]Ibid.

[31]"Look east, young Eurobond," *The Economist*, September 16, 1989, pp. 83-4; "Japanese paper fills the void," *A supplement to Euromoney*, March 1989, p. 2.

[32]See *The Economist*, Sept. 16, 1989, pp. 83-4.

[33]"La grande boum," *The Economist*, October 1, 1988, pp. 83-4.

[34]Christine M. Cumming and Lawrence M. Sweet, "Financial Structure of the G-7 Countries: How Does the United States Compare?," Federal Reserve Bank of New York, *Quarterly Review*, Winter 1987/88, pp. 15-16.

[35]"Sweeping away Frankfurt's old-fashioned habits," *The Economist*, January 28, 1989, pp. 73-4.

[36]Ibid.

[37]*Financial Market Trends*, OECD, February 1989, pp.85-6.

[38]Ibid.

[39]Ibid.

[40]"A smooth run for Switzerland's big banks," *The Economist*, June 17, 1989, pp. 87-8.

[41]*World Financial Markets*, J.P. Morgan & Co., November 29, 1988.

[42]"Foreign Transactions in Securities," Table 3.24, *Federal Reserve Bulletin*, June 1989, Board of Governors of the Federal Reserve System.

[43]Ibid.

[44]Various central bank statistical releases.

[45]The underlying instrument is worth $1 million.

[46]"US exchanges fight for market share," *A supplement to Euromoney*, July 1989, p. 9.

[47]Elizabeth R. Thagard, "London's Jump," *Intermarkets*, May 1989, p. 22.

[48]See *A supplement to Euromoney*, August 1987, p. 28.

[49]Ginger Szala, "Financial walls tumble for German investors," *Futures*, January 1990, p. 44.

[50]Ibid., p. 42.

[51]See Thagard, p. 23.

[52]Ted Weissberg, "Wall Street Seeks Global Merger Market: IDD's First-quarter M&A Rankings," *Investment Dealers Digest*, May 8, 1989, pp. 17-21.

[53]"The World Champions of M&A," *Euromoney*, February 1989, pp. 96-102.

[54]Ibid.

[55]Philip Maher, "Merrill Lynch Holds on to Top International Spot," *Investment Dealers Digest*, July 10, 1989, pp. 23-25.

[56]"Japan proving tough for foreign brokerage," *Chicago Tribune*, September 11, 1989, section 4, pp. 1-2

[57]Ibid.

[58]Ibid.

[59]Ibid.

Article 26

Global Interest Rate Linkages

Long-term interest rates in Germany, Japan, and the U.S. rose more or less in tandem in the early part of this year. The 10-year government bond rate in Germany rose from an average of 7.3 percent in December to an average of 8.6 percent in April; the comparable interest rate in Japan rose from 5.8 percent to 7.3 percent during the same period; and in the United States, the rise was from 7.8 percent to 8.8 percent. During most of this period the dollar appreciated against the yen and depreciated against the DM.

These trends have created concern about the apparent sensitivity of U.S. interest rates to events affecting interest rates abroad. To the extent that such sensitivity exists, many observers argue that the effectiveness of monetary policy in controlling domestic interest rates and inflation may be affected. This *Letter* discusses the mechanisms through which foreign "shocks" may affect interest rates in the United States, and attempts to interpret recent events within this analytical framework.

Exchange rates and interest rates

Financial capital has become highly mobile across international borders. Consequently, a change in the level of interest rates in one country can cause cross-border movements of funds which affect exchange rates and the level of interest rates in other countries. The way in which exchange rates and interest rates change, however, depends on the factors that caused interest rates abroad to change in the first place.

These factors can be categorized as either "nominal" or "real," corresponding to the two determinants of the level of long-term interest rates: respectively, the expected rate of inflation and the "real" interest rate, which is determined by the real supply of and demand for credit. Accordingly, the effects of developments in one country on exchange rates and other countries'

domestic interest rates depend on whether interest rate rises abroad are due to "nominal shocks," such as changes in inflationary expectations, or to "real shocks," such as changes in saving or investment behavior.

To understand the recent trends in U.S. and foreign interest rates and changes in the value of the dollar, then, it is useful to consider separately the effects of the two kinds of shocks to foreign interest rates: first, an increase in foreign inflation expectations, and second, an increase in the (actual or anticipated) real demand for capital abroad. In this analysis, Germany and the U.S. represent the foreign and domestic countries, respectively, although the results are generally applicable to all other countries as well.

This analysis focuses on the near-term effects of the shock on the relative *demands* for different assets, and assumes that the *supplies* of domestic and foreign assets are given. It rules out consideration of changes in money supplies associated with possible monetary policy responses. In addition, financial capital is assumed to be perfectly mobile between countries. This rules out any barriers to asset flows, such as capital controls or taxes.

Increase in foreign inflation

A permanent rise in expected German inflation is an example of a pure "nominal" shock; it has no effect on the world equilibrium real rate of return. A rise in German inflation expectations initially will reduce the anticipated real return to holding German assets *from the point of view of German investors*. Assuming that changes in German inflation have at most a negligible effect on U.S. inflation (because German goods represent only a small share of the basket of goods consumed by U.S. residents), returns on U.S. assets will not be affected, and the decline in real German asset returns will induce a shift in demand away from German assets towards those denominated in dollars, which offer a relatively higher real return.

This shift in asset demand will cause the German nominal interest rate to rise until the anticipated real return on German assets is restored back to the world equilibrium real rate. (As long as the change in foreign inflation expectations leaves the equilibrium world real interest rate unchanged, U.S. as well as foreign equilibrium *real* interest rates will be unchanged.) Moreover, because U.S. inflation expectations are assumed not to be affected by the rise in German inflation expectations, U.S. nominal interest rates will remain constant. Instead, the increase in the demand for dollar-denominated assets will cause the current value of the Deutsche mark (DM) to depreciate against the dollar.

In response to a permanent increase in expected German inflation, the DM will be expected to depreciate in the future at the same rate as German inflation. Accordingly, in equilibrium, the expected rate of nominal depreciation of the DM will exactly offset the rise in the nominal spread between German and U.S. interest rates, leaving the real interest rate spread at its initial level (zero, assuming that capital is perfectly mobile internationally and that U.S. and German assets are perfect substitutes).

The result that U.S. nominal interest rates remain unaffected by a change in German expected inflation is independent of the degree of asset substitutability between German and U.S. assets. If U.S. and foreign assets are less than perfect substitutes, U.S. residents will demand a premium to hold more German assets in their portfolios. This premium will raise the effective nominal return for investing in German assets (that is, the nominal yield abroad plus the expected depreciation of the DM) relative to U.S. nominal interest rates. But there is no reason for the size of the premium to change with a change in inflation expectations. Thus, U.S. rates should be unaffected by a change in German inflation expectations even if German and U.S. assets are imperfect substitutes.

In sum, flexible exchange rates generally insulate the nominal interest return on U.S. assets from a foreign nominal shock. In this case, foreign nomi-

nal interest rates and the exchange rate bear the entire burden of the adjustment.

Increase in foreign demand

Consider next an increase in (actual or expected) real investment demand in Germany. Such a shift in demand raises the demand for capital in Germany, and causes German real interest rates to rise relative to U.S. real rates. Moreover, because this shift in real investment demand tends to raise the demand for German goods by more than that for U.S. goods, the DM will be expected to appreciate against the dollar in real terms (assuming the shift in investment demand is expected to be permanent).

From the point of view of U.S. investors, then, the effective real dollar return to investing in German assets (that is, the higher German yield plus the expected appreciation of the DM) initially will rise above the real return available on dollar-denominated assets. Consequently, investors will shift their demand away from U.S. assets, and U.S. real and nominal yields will rise.

Assuming that the shift in foreign demand is permanent, but no further shifts occur, in the long run, German and U.S. real interest rates will be equalized (as long as capital is perfectly mobile, and U.S. and German assets are perfect substitutes, so that there is no risk premium). In this new equilibrium, both the world real interest rate and the real exchange value of the DM will be permanently higher.

The magnitudes of the changes in the levels of the real interest rate and the real exchange rate will depend in part on the sensitivities of U.S. aggregate demand to changes in these variables. For example, if U.S. demand is very sensitive to the interest rate, but not very sensitive to the exchange rate, small changes in the interest rate and large changes in the exchange rate will be necessary to restore equilibrium. Consequently, an increase in German investment demand would lead to a relatively small rise in the equilibrium real interest rate and a relatively large rise in the equilibrium real value of the DM against the dollar.

Assuming the money supply in each country remains constant, the rise in real (and nominal) interest rates associated with the increase in

German investment demand raises the opportunity cost of holding money and reduces money demand. As residents in each country attempt to reduce their money holdings by spending these balances on goods, national price levels will rise unless the monetary authorities respond by decreasing the money supply.

In sum, then, a floating exchange rate does not insulate either the U.S. price level or U.S. real and nominal interest rates from a real shock emanating abroad.

Interpreting recent events
Many observers argue that differences in inflation rates across countries have been the dominant force influencing the spreads between U.S. and foreign interest rates in recent years. In this environment, changes in the value of the dollar to a large extent have insulated U.S. interest rates from developments abroad. When U.S. inflation was rising relative to inflation abroad from 1985 through 1987, the dollar was weak and the U.S.-foreign yield spread widened to reflect the expected depreciation of the dollar. In 1988 when inflation rates abroad began to converge with that in the U.S., U.S.-foreign yield spreads narrowed, and the dollar strengthened.

Currently, most economists are forecasting higher inflation in Japan because of its booming economy and in West Germany because of the anticipated financial strain of rebuilding East Germany. To the extent investors believe that the rate of inflation will be higher in Japan and Germany than in the U.S., the dollar should be stronger against both the yen and DM.

However, recent developments do not accord perfectly with this pattern, implying that inflation fears may not be the whole story. First, although the dollar has been rising against the yen, it has been falling against the DM. Second, despite these changes in the value of the dollar, U.S. interest rates apparently have not been insulated from the rise in foreign interest rates; instead, U.S. rates have risen more or less simultaneously with those abroad.

These observations suggest that recent financial market developments may be due in part to real

forces. Anticipated efforts by West Germany to improve the infrastructure and productive facilities of East Germany, and possibly other countries in Eastern Europe, can be expected to increase the real demand for credit, real interest rates, and the level of the DM in the future. And although little actual investment has taken place as yet, the *expectation* of higher German investment demand in the future could be influencing current real rates and exchange rates. Thus, the anticipated greater competition for funds could explain why U.S. interest rates have risen recently together with foreign interest rates. It also could explain why the dollar has depreciated against the DM, but not against the yen.

One should not put too much weight on this explanation, however, since other, independent factors also may have been at work. For example, it is possible that U.S. inflation expectations rose independently in the first part of the year. This may explain why U.S. nominal interest rates rose simultaneously with foreign rates. The concern about Japan's political future as a result of the January elections and the Tokyo stock market adjustment may have contributed to the weakness of the yen.

Important distinction
In any case, this analysis suggests that it is important to distinguish between nominal and real shocks when interpreting developments in international markets. The response of U.S. interest rates to foreign shocks depends critically on whether the shock is nominal or real in nature. Changes in the value of the dollar generally will insulate U.S. nominal interest rates from foreign nominal shocks, such as an increase in foreign inflation expectations. However, the dollar will not insulate U.S. rates from a foreign real shock, such as an exogenous increase in real capital demand abroad (as long as international capital is sufficiently mobile). In this case, any real demand shift abroad will affect the world equilibrium real interest rate. U.S. nominal interest rates will be affected accordingly.

Reuven Glick
Research Officer

Article 27

Reducing the Costs and Risks of Trading Foreign Exchange

Brian J. Cody*

A U.S. exporter who has received Deutsche marks from a German firm wants to exchange his mark receipts for dollars. A chief financial officer of a U.S. corporation wants to purchase Spanish pesetas in order to buy corporate stock on the Madrid stock market. A foreign exchange speculator wants to increase his holdings of French francs because he believes that the franc's value will appreciate in the near future.

*Brian J. Cody is a Senior Economist in the Macroeconomics Section of the Research Department, Federal Reserve Bank of Philadelphia.

Thousands of trades like these generate the business that underlies the enormous flow of funds each day between institutions participating in the foreign exchange market. The volume of global foreign exchange trading has doubled in the last three years, according to surveys by the Bank of England, the Federal Reserve Bank of New York, and other central banks. The surveys estimate the average daily turnover in the New York market as of April 1989 at $129 billion, up 120 percent compared to March 1986. This daily turnover is roughly 21 times the average daily value of stocks traded on the New York Stock Exchange in 1989.

This enormous volume of foreign exchange contracts is arranged between foreign exchange brokers and traders at financial and nonfinancial institutions throughout the world. The volume reflects a wide variety of transactions involving flows of international capital and goods.

To market participants, however, these transactions involve costs and financial risks. Accordingly, private financial institutions, as well as the world's central banks, have been studying payment arrangements that allow netting of transactions between institutions. Netting will undoubtedly cut the transaction costs of foreign exchange trading. More important, if properly implemented, netting arrangements should both reduce credit and liquidity risks to all participating financial institutions and enhance the soundness of the entire payments system.

BILATERAL NETTING ARRANGEMENTS

The basic idea behind netting arrangements is simple. Consider two friends who owe each other money. The debts could be settled by each friend paying the other the full amount owed. However, the friends could save on their transaction costs if the one owing more money simply subtracted the amount owed to her and paid the net amount to her friend.

Each day, individual banks and other financial institutions engage in hundreds of trades in the foreign exchange market. Like the two friends, these institutions are reducing their transaction costs by netting their foreign exchange payments. The only difference is that, because each institution arranges hundreds of transactions in all the major currencies in a single day, the potential savings are much larger.

Consider three banks with foreign exchange departments: Rhinebank, Floyds, and Countibank. On a particular Monday, the institutions have arranged a total of eight transactions in the spot foreign exchange market.[1] Each interbank transaction involves the exchange of one currency for another. These transfers could be generated by the flow of goods (exporters selling foreign exchange receipts), financial instruments (a firm buying foreign securities), or exchange rate speculation (speculators betting on exchange rate movements).

Figure 1 depicts the spot foreign exchange transactions occurring between Rhinebank, Floyds, and Countibank. Rhinebank and Floyds engage in four transactions with each other—twice trading Deutsche marks (DMs) for dollars, once trading dollars for pounds sterling (£s), and once trading £s for DMs. Countibank engages in a total of four transactions, two each with Rhinebank and Floyds.

When these obligations are settled, Rhinebank will process 12 transactions, making four payments to Floyds and two to Countibank—one for each foreign exchange contract—and receiving as many payments from each. Floyds would also process 12 transactions. Since it had arranged four contracts, Countibank would process eight transactions. If they were to adopt a netting arrangement, these three banks could cut their transaction costs (the back-office expenses of processing the trades, as well as a per-item charge on payment messages sent over the wire-transfer network) by reducing the number of payments and receipts they have to process on any particular day.

---

[1]Spot foreign exchange settlements typically occur two business days from the trade date. The New York Fed's foreign exchange survey reports that spot transactions accounted for 63.9 percent of all foreign exchange trading reported by New York banks in April 1989. Foreign exchange swaps, forward contracts, options, and futures accounted for the remaining portion. For complete results, see "Summary of Results of U.S. Foreign Exchange Market Survey Conducted in April 1989," Federal Reserve Bank of New York, September 13, 1989; "The Market for Foreign Exchange in London," Bank of England *Quarterly Bulletin* (November 1989) pp. 531-35; and "Survey of Foreign Exchange Market Activity," Bank for International Settlements, Monetary and Economic Department (February 1990).

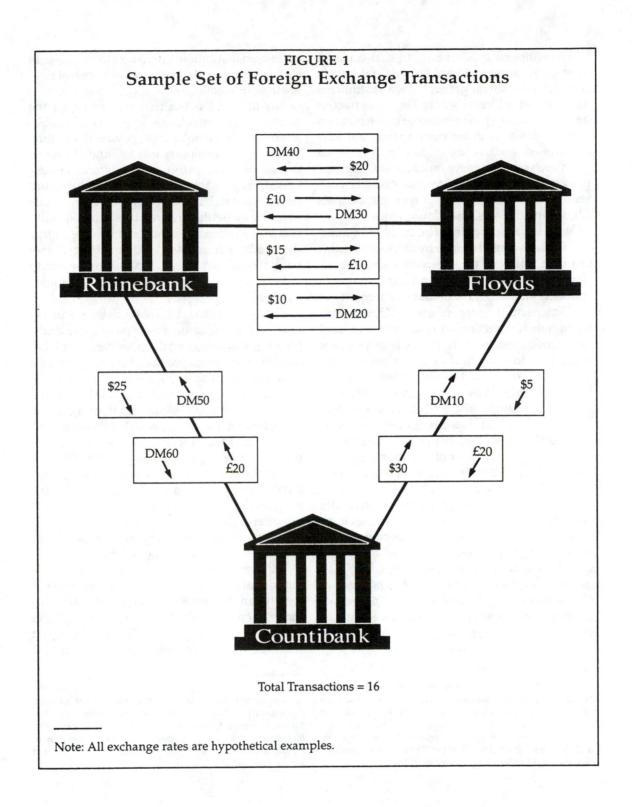

FIGURE 1
Sample Set of Foreign Exchange Transactions

Total Transactions = 16

Note: All exchange rates are hypothetical examples.

The simplest type of netting that could be arranged among the banks is *bilateral netting*. In a bilateral arrangement, two institutions agree, either informally or in a legal contract, to net the currency payments due to the other on a particular day. After netting, only one payment in each currency is due to or received from each counterparty on each day. Figure 2 presents the payments flows that result from a series of bilateral netting arrangements between Rhinebank, Floyds, and Countibank.

With bilateral netting, the number of transactions falls considerably, by 50 percent in this example. Bilateral arrangements tend to benefit institutions that engage in a large number of transactions with a particular counterparty or trading partner. For example, Countibank, though its transaction costs are reduced, does not benefit as much as the other banks because it engages in only half as many transactions with Rhinebank and Floyds as these banks do between themselves.

The most tangible benefit of bilateral netting to these institutions is the reduction in transaction costs. However, banks also incur additional costs in the form of additional risk, because there is typically a delay of two business days between the time when a trade is arranged and the moment when the currencies actually change hands. This lag exposes institutions to the risk that their expected foreign exchange receipts will be delayed more than two days or might never be received. What's more, it is typical for payments to be made at the beginning of the delivery day in one currency before other funds are received later in that day in another currency.[2] Netting can

reduce an institution's exposure to this risk. In fact, bilateral netting can provide several risk-reduction benefits.

Liquidity risk is the risk that although the debtor will eventually make good on his obligation, he will not make payment on time because of a temporary lack of funds in terms of one or more currencies. Bilateral netting agreements unambiguously reduce exposure to liquidity risk in the foreign exchange market. Before netting, Floyds faced the liquidity risk that Rhinebank would not be able to pay the US$25 million it owed. After netting, Rhinebank would owe only US$5 million on net to Floyds, substantially reducing Floyds' liquidity risk.

Credit risk is the risk that a debtor will default on his obligation, never paying the creditor. For instance, Floyds faces credit risk because there is a chance that, between the time its deals with Rhinebank are arranged and the actual exchanges occur, Rhinebank will declare bankruptcy and default on its obligations. Credit exposure, which equals total expected foreign exchange receipts, is one measure of the credit risk borne by an institution. Figure 2 shows the dollar amount of each bank's apparent credit exposure in the three currencies before and after bilateral netting. Whether a bilateral netting arrangement reduces the participants' actual credit exposure depends on how the banks view the netted payments.

If the gross foreign exchange obligations—the individual foreign exchange contracts—are not legally satisfied until final payment is actually made, then the banks are said to be engaged in *bilateral payments netting*.[3] This arrangement leaves an institution's credit exposure unchanged

---

[2]Other terms are sometimes used to describe aspects of credit risk, such as "settlement risk," which can contain elements of credit and liquidity risk, and "replacement cost risk." For a more detailed discussion, see "Report on Netting Schemes," Group of Experts on Payments Systems of the Central Banks of the Group of Ten Countries, Bank for International Settlements (February 1989).

[3]Payment netting can be either an informal or a formal agreement to net the amount of the gross liabilities. The formal agreement, which is legally binding, is known as *binding payments netting*. In both cases, the parties remain legally bound for the gross transactions, not the net amounts.

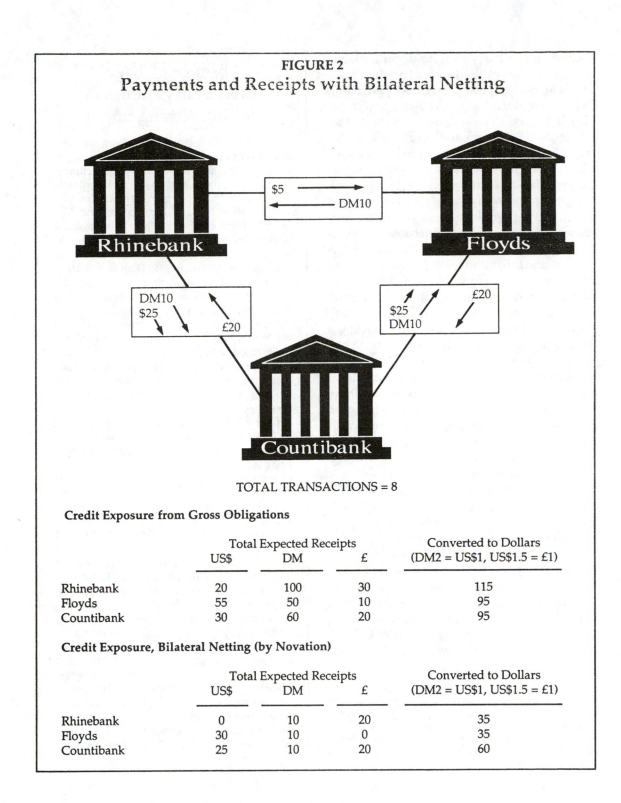

FIGURE 2
Payments and Receipts with Bilateral Netting

Rhinebank

$5 →
← DM10

Floyds

DM10
$25
£20

$25
DM10
£20

Countibank

TOTAL TRANSACTIONS = 8

Credit Exposure from Gross Obligations

| | Total Expected Receipts | | | Converted to Dollars |
	US$	DM	£	(DM2 = US$1, US$1.5 = £1)
Rhinebank	20	100	30	115
Floyds	55	50	10	95
Countibank	30	60	20	95

Credit Exposure, Bilateral Netting (by Novation)

| | Total Expected Receipts | | | Converted to Dollars |
	US$	DM	£	(DM2 = US$1, US$1.5 = £1)
Rhinebank	0	10	20	35
Floyds	30	10	0	35
Countibank	25	10	20	60

because, if one party were to default, the netting agreement would dissolve back into agreements in terms of gross, not netted, obligations. Reconsider Rhinebank and Floyds. On net, Floyds expects to receive an equivalent of $35 million from Rhinebank and Countibank. Floyds' credit exposure would appear to have fallen to $35 million from an original exposure of $95 million. If Rhinebank were to declare bankruptcy before Wednesday's payments were made, Floyds would be legally bound to its gross obligations with Rhinebank. It would have to pay Rhinebank US$20 million, DM30 million, and £10 million. With regard to Rhinebank's gross obligations to Floyds, however, Floyds would become just another unsecured creditor to the failed institution and would probably not receive complete payment for the gross amounts owed by Rhinebank.[4]

In fact, there is a danger that bilateral payments netting could actually *increase* credit risk if an institution were mistakenly to treat its net obligations, rather than its underlying gross positions, as the measure of its true credit exposure. Institutions routinely set limits on the credit exposure they are willing to accept with respect to individual parties. If a bilateral netting arrangement leads traders to underestimate their true credit exposure, they might continue arranging deals even though they had exceeded their credit exposure limit.

Bilateral *netting by novation* is a way of reducing credit exposure. As in payments netting, two institutions engaged in netting by novation calculate their net obligations in each currency. Unlike payments netting, netting by novation legally discharges the gross obligations and replaces them with a new (novated)

---

[4]Floyds might have "rights of set-off" in this case that would, in effect, allow it to net its liabilities to a counterparty with its claims on that counterparty. The existence and scope of such rights vary among countries, however, and are not discussed in detail here. See "Report on Netting Schemes," pp. 13-14.

Absence of Legal Precedents Hampers Netting Arrangements

One impediment to establishing arrangements for netting by novation is their uncertain legality. Netting by novation replaces original gross obligations with new contracts requiring only the payment of net amounts.

No nation has any legal precedents upholding these contracts. The closest case we have is a 1975 British case involving not financial firms but two airlines: Air France and the now-defunct British Eagle. Both were part of a multilateral netting system operated by the International Air Transport Association. The Association acted as a clearinghouse, settling debts among individual airlines on a net basis. When British Eagle went under, its liquidator tried to recover the gross obligations owed to Eagle by Air France. Air France contended its obligation was limited to the net amount it owed to the clearinghouse. The court decided in favor of Air France and thus supported the legality of the netting contracts.

Of course, the details of the airline case differ from those in foreign exchange transactions, and the precedent applies only in one country, the United Kingdom. Courts around the world could rule differently on the enforceability of foreign exchange clearinghouse contracts. Should this happen, each financial firm involved in a bankruptcy situation would seek disposition of the case in the court most favorable to its interest. For instance, a British bank forced to liquidate could try to have its case against a French bank tried in France, where it might feel the netting contract has less chance of being enforced.

Netting systems are trying to overcome the uncertainties surrounding the legality of foreign exchange netting arrangements. One such system, FXNET, has developed agreement language it believes will stand in several legal jurisdictions, including the United States, Japan, and Switzerland. (For more information on these contracts, see *FXNET Legal Documentation*, Volumes 1 & 2, April 21, 1989.)

agreement for the net amount (see *Absence of Legal Precedents Hampers Netting Arrangements*). If an institution were to fail and, most importantly, the bankruptcy courts accepted the novated contracts as binding, the parties would be responsible for only the net amounts of the contracts, not the original gross obligations. Consequently, netting by novation effectively reduces each institution's credit exposure to the netted amounts. So in this case, Floyds' credit exposure, when expressed in dollars, really is reduced to $35 million.

In sum, bilateral netting arrangements—payments netting and netting by novation—can substantially reduce the transaction costs and liquidity risk incurred by the netting parties. While all netting institutions will benefit, the degree of cost and liquidity-risk reduction depends directly on the number and magnitude of foreign exchange contracts maturing on a particular day. While bilateral payments netting has the potential to reduce credit exposure, netting by novation will undoubtedly reduce this risk.

MULTILATERAL NETTING

Another form of netting—*multilateral netting*—can further cut the transaction costs of foreign exchange trading, as well as potentially reduce liquidity and credit risk. Multilateral netting involves some agreement that directs how individual parties will net as a group and share the risk of default of any participant. The presence of this agreement provides multilateral netting with the additional feature of potentially reducing *systemic risk*—the risk that a default at one institution could trip otherwise solvent institutions into default.

Several multilateral netting proposals suggest the use of an institution that stands between individual banks. In these cases, multilateral foreign exchange netting is a system in which financial institutions engaged in foreign exchange transactions net their gross obligations with a central counterparty. This facility functions as the clearinghouse for the interbank transactions. This central counterparty would also function as the settlement agent for the system, initiating the final settlement for the participating institutions. It can be organized under various structures, including a partnership of members who clear or an independent agency that agrees to act in this capacity. The netting strategy works the same as in bilateral netting, except that the institutions make or receive only one payment in each currency to or from this third party.

With multilateral netting, once two institutions arrange a foreign exchange contract, they notify the central counterparty of their deal. Once the central authority verifies the contract, the original gross obligations between the institutions are replaced by agreements between the individual banks and the central authority. As subsequent transactions are recorded, each bank accumulates a net position with the central authority. At the end of trading, no matter how many institutions it deals with each day, a bank makes or receives only one net payment in each currency to or from the clearinghouse.

Multilateral netting reduces transaction costs and liquidity risk... Figure 3 presents the payments flows resulting from the multilateral netting of payments between the three banks and the central counterparty in our example. Based on the set of underlying obligations, Countibank will process no payments or receipts in any currency, since on net it is square with the central authority. Multilateral netting also reduces liquidity risk. On net, Rhinebank is owed only £20 million, and Floyds only US$30 million, from the central counterparty.

...But Credit Risk May Not Be Reduced. The ability of a multilateral netting arrangement to reduce credit risk depends on the structure of the agreement. *Multilateral payments* netting takes essentially the same form as its bilateral cousin. While the individual banks accumulate net balances against the central counterparty, the original gross obligations

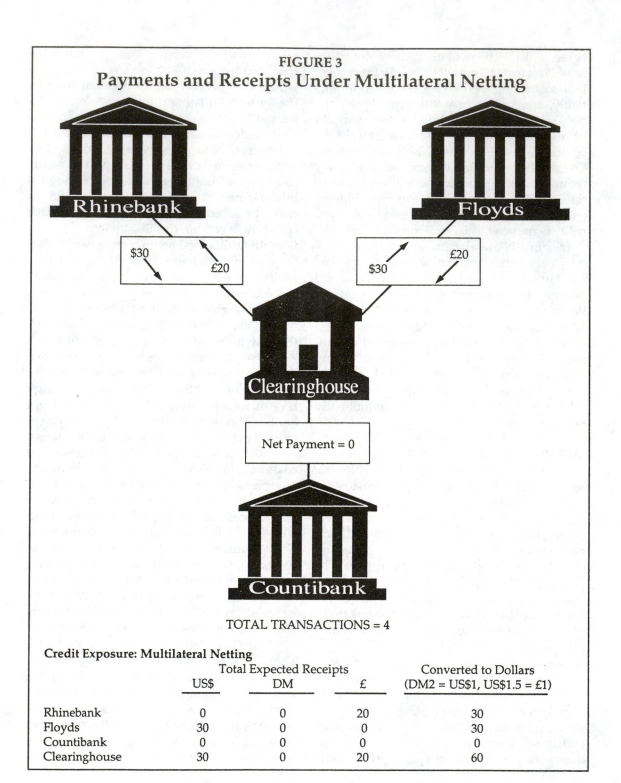

FIGURE 3
Payments and Receipts Under Multilateral Netting

Rhinebank

Floyds

$30   £20

$30   £20

Clearinghouse

Net Payment = 0

Countibank

TOTAL TRANSACTIONS = 4

Credit Exposure: Multilateral Netting

| | Total Expected Receipts | | | Converted to Dollars |
	US$	DM	£	(DM2 = US$1, US$1.5 = £1)
Rhinebank	0	0	20	30
Floyds	30	0	0	30
Countibank	0	0	0	0
Clearinghouse	30	0	20	60

remain in effect until final net payments are received. If one institution were to default, this netting system would require all transactions involving the defaulting institution to be removed from the clearinghouse's books. Once the obligations with the defaulting institution are "unwound" into their original bilateral obligations, new net positions would be calculated between the solvent institutions and the clearinghouse.[5] Any transaction with the defaulting institution must then be settled on a bilateral basis between that institution and the particular trading partner.

There Is a Way to Reduce Credit Risk... In contrast to payments netting, *multilateral netting by novation and substitution* reduces credit risk. Under this system, once the institutions notify the central authority of their foreign exchange contract, new agreements between each of the individual banks and the central counterparty are substituted for that original obligation between the two banks. These new (novated) agreements legally take the place of the original contract. If one of the institutions were to default, the netted obligations of the other institutions with respect to the central authority would remain in effect. Those arising from trades with the defaulting bank would not be unwound.

---

[5]The New York Clearing House for Interbank Payments System (CHIPS) currently would "unwind" obligations should any institution default. On June 4, 1986, the New York Fed conducted a survey of the transactions passing through CHIPS on a "typical" day. The survey found that foreign exchange transactions accounted for 72.6 percent of the system's 28 billion transactions. CHIPS is developing a new payment finality program that would eliminate the risk of transactions being unwound should an institution fail to meet its obligations. The program calls for the 140 U.S. and foreign banks in CHIPS to pledge about $4 billion in U.S. government securities as collateral that would be sold to cover the transactions of an institution that could not settle by the normal close of business. See "Large-Dollar Payment Flows From New York," Federal Reserve Bank of New York *Quarterly Review* (Winter 1987-88) and "Members of Chips Agree to Share Payment Risks," *American Banker*, March 19, 1990.

If Rhinebank were to default, Countibank would not have to make or receive any payments with respect to either the clearinghouse or Rhinebank because its net position was zero. Likewise, Floyds' obligation to the central authority would also be unchanged. It would receive US$30 million and owe the central counterparty £20 million. Thus, this form of netting reduces each bank's credit exposure from the amount of the gross liabilities to the net position against the clearinghouse. In other words, the central counterparty bears the credit exposure in this system; that is, it would still be obligated to pay Rhinebank £20 million, even if Rhinebank were to default on its payment.

...and Systemic Risk May Be Reduced. Prior to the default of Rhinebank, Countibank had no obligation with respect to the clearinghouse since its net position was zero. If multilateral payments netting were in effect, then after the default and unwinding of Rhinebank's transactions, Countibank would not only have to make payments directly to Rhinebank—its original gross obligations—but it would also have liabilities to the clearinghouse. If Countibank could not meet these obligations, it too would have to default. Multilateral payments netting provides no mechanism to prevent the failure of one institution from infecting other institutions in the payments system. Thus, multilateral payments netting would not help reduce systemic risk. Multilateral netting by novation and substitution, however, can reduce systemic risk. Since the system does not unwind transactions if a party fails, the clearinghouse essentially shields the other institutions from the failed party and absorbs the systemic risk. In terms of our previous example, the clearinghouse would still pay Floyds US$30 million, even though it had received no funds from the bankrupt Rhinebank.

The risk shield of multilateral netting by novation and substitution, however, is only as strong as the capital position of the central counterparty. That is, the degree of reduction in systemic risk depends entirely on the central agent's ability to fulfill its payment obligations even if one or more of its debtors default. If the clearinghouse could not sustain the loss, the netted amounts could possibly be unwound into the gross obligations. Without sufficient capital, then, multilateral netting by novation and substitution provides no advantage over multilateral payments netting.

Say the central agent is organized and capitalized by a consortium of financial institutions. These institutions would reduce systemic risk by pooling the risk and sharing it among themselves. They would bear the cost of supplying the needed funds to pay off the clearinghouse's debts should a member institution fail. If an independent institution serves as the central counterparty, it must have either sufficient funds or lines of credit on which it can draw should one of its debtors fail.

Securing the necessary financial capital is crucial to the success of any multilateral netting arrangement, and it can be costly. But it is just one of the many costs of establishing and maintaining such a system. There are financial, legal, and computer costs as well. In fact, many of these costs are incurred even in bilateral netting arrangements. Ultimately, the desirability of any netting system hinges on its risk-reduction benefits outweighing all these costs.

CURRENT EFFORTS TO DESIGN NETTING ARRANGEMENTS

Facing tremendously expanded activity in the foreign exchange market, financial institutions are finding the use of netting schemes increasingly desirable to control transaction costs and reduce risk. As a result, a number of competing bilateral and multilateral foreign exchange netting systems are being developed. Some are already in operation; others are on the drawing board.[6]

The FXNET netting system—a London-based limited partnership—currently provides a bilateral netting by novation system in London and New York for participating institutions. FXNET has designed the computer facilities and supporting legal documents used by individual institutions that arrange bilateral netting agreements on these markets.

International Clearing Systems, INC. (ICSI), a wholly owned subsidiary of the Options Clearing Corporation, is developing a multilateral netting by novation and substitution arrangement.[7] This plan envisions foreign exchange clearinghouses as self-regulating organizations, with rules and bylaws written and administered by their participants and owners. These financial institutions would be responsible for funding the clearinghouse.

The Euronetting project, currently being developed under the direction of the Banca Commerciale Italiana, would also provide netting by novation and substitution.[8] Its central clearinghouse is envisioned as a legal corporation capitalized by a top tier of paying agents or banks. The handful of top-tier banks

---

[6]Summaries of some of these projects are presented in "Banking and Payment Services: Official Papers of an International Symposium Sponsored by the Board of Governors of the Federal Reserve System," *Payment Systems Worldwide* 1 (Spring 1990).

[7]See ICSI, "Netting of Foreign Exchange Trades and Other Obligations: An Illustration of the Use of On-line, Real Time Clearance and Settlement Systems for the Quantification and Control of Risk in Financial Markets," a submission to the Office of Technology Assessment, United States Congress, for its study *Clearing and Settlement of Financial Instruments Worldwide* (February 1989). The Options Clearing Corporation (OCC) currently operates such a clearinghouse for options, including foreign exchange options, traded on U.S. securities exchanges. The OCC is owned by the Chicago Board Options Exchange, the American Stock Exchange, the Philadelphia Stock Exchange, the Pacific Stock Exchange, and the Mid-West Stock Exchange.

[8]See Renato Polo, "A Perspective on the Euronetting Project," *Payment Systems Worldwide* 1 (Spring 1990) pp. 46-47.

would be responsible for maintaining the clearinghouse accounts, transferring funds among correspondent banks, and supplying needed capital if a member institution fails.

The Society for Worldwide Interbank Financial Telecommunication (SWIFT), the world standard for interbank financial communications, is developing a new service called ACCORD. This service will match (unofficially net) foreign exchange transactions between institutions and advise institutions of opportunities to net their foreign exchange payments. As such, ACCORD would operate as an information service and would not be legally responsible for arranging netting agreements between institutions. Introduction of this service is planned for 1990.

Central banks have been studying private financial institutions' efforts to develop foreign exchange netting arrangements.[9] Their interests include establishing safe systems, limiting their risk exposure, and ensuring proper regulation. As with any financial market innovation, netting arrangements might raise new supervisory and regulatory issues. For instance, central bankers are aware that there is a natural tendency for markets to move from a more to a less strictly regulated environment.[10] The regulation of payments systems in major financial centers, such as those in the United States or Europe, could drive systems to less regulated or completely unregulated centers, such as those in the Caribbean.

CONCLUSION

The use and continued development of foreign exchange netting arrangements offer the potential to improve the efficiency and reduce the costs of dealing in the rapidly expanding foreign exchange market. While these systems will undoubtedly reduce transaction costs, their ability to reduce the various risks—liquidity, credit, and systemic—depends on the legal structure of the system. The work of central banks and private institutions on these netting schemes should help ensure a more efficient and less risky foreign exchange market.

[9]For more information, see *Payment Systems in Eleven Developed Countries*, prepared under the aegis of the Bank for International Settlements by the Central Banks of the Group of Ten Countries and Switzerland (May 1989); and Federal Reserve Governor Wayne Angell, "Cooperative Approaches to Reducing Risks in Global Financial Markets: Issues and Policies," May 14, 1990. The views of the Group of Experts on Payments Systems from the G-10 central banks concerning netting arrangements are expressed in "Report on Netting Schemes," Group of Experts on Payments Systems of the Central Banks of the Group of Ten Countries, Bank for International Settlements (February 1989).

[10]Speaking before an international symposium, Tommaso Padoa-Schioppa, Deputy Director General of the Banca d'Italia, stated, "For instance, the recent initiatives to reduce systemic risk on Fedwire and CHIPS could be undermined by the shift of some of the dollar payments to 'offshore' clearing systems" (from "Payment Systems: A New Ground for Central-Bank Cooperation," speech before the International Symposium on Banking and Payment Service, sponsored by the Board of Governors of the Federal Reserve System, June 9, 1989, p. 16).

Section VIII
The Investor–Broker Relationship

For individual investors, all access to securities markets is mediated by a broker, so the relationship with a broker is crucial. In television advertisements, brokerage firms portray the relationship as one of mutual interest in which the broker assists the individual investor in building retirement security, investing for a child's college education, or getting the money for a down payment on a home. In the real world, the relationship between the investor and broker often becomes adversarial. In essence, the broker is a salesperson, and the broker's compensation depends upon getting the investor to trade. Frequent trading is costly, however, and investors sometimes lose all hope of investment profit because they are induced to trade too frequently and they burn up their investment funds in brokerage fees. This section considers problems that arise in the investor-broker relationship.

One of the most frequent problems that arises between an investor and a broker is the allegation of *churning*. Churning occurs when a broker improperly induces an investor to trade too frequently. Excessive trading generates transaction costs that enrich the broker at the customer's expense and ensure that the customer has no chance of investment success. In their paper, "Guidelines for Detecting Churning in an Account," Seth C. Anderson, Sue L. Visscher, and Donald A. Winslow discuss why churning occurs and how to identify it.

When a dispute between a customer and a brokerage firm arises that cannot be settled between the two parties, the disagreement is almost always subjected to arbitration. Henry Sanchez, Jr. discusses arbitration in his paper, "Resolving Broker Disputes: The Arbitration Process." As Sanchez points out, churning is a typical kind of dispute that leads to arbitration between the broker and customer. In addition, customers sometimes charge that brokers have led them into investments that are unsuitably risky or inappropriate for the customer's level of income. As Sanchez shows, there is a potential mine field of disputes that customers should be aware of as they seek to establish a relationship with a broker.

The Securities Investor Protection Corporation (SIPC) is a non-profit industry organization designed to protect customers' funds in brokerage firm bankruptcies. However, in his article, "SIPC: What Happens if Your Brokerage Firm Fails?" Henry Sanchez, Jr. points out that the SIPC does not insure customers' funds against fraud. Therefore, the protection is much more limited than some customers may think. Sanchez discusses the structure of the SIPC and details the services that the corporation actually provides.

Article 28

Guidelines for Detecting Churning in an Account

By Seth C. Anderson, Sue L. Visscher & Donald A. Winslow

Charges of churning are often leveled against brokerage firms' customer representatives when an investment account has been actively traded and the returns are unsatisfactory, given the objectives of the account.

There are numerous complex issues involved in the legal concept of churning and the associated liability of brokers. One key issue is whether the broker has "controlled" the account to a significant degree, but this issue of control is relatively straightforward.

Another major issue, and one of the most difficult ones, is the determination of whether a particular account has been the subject of excessive trading. This article focuses on the issue of excessive trading and its effects on portfolio returns, and a benchmark for the determination of excessive trading will be described. The benchmark should provide a useful guideline for individual investors in assessing the performance of their own broker, if they are relying on him to manage their portfolios. The benchmark may also serve as a guideline for individuals who make their own investment decisions, to judge if they are trading excessively to the detriment of their bottom-line return.

The Causes of Churning

The root cause of broker churning lies in the compensation structure of the securities industry. Securities brokerage firms generate profits by charging commissions on transactions conducted in customer accounts. Approximately 30% to 50% of the commissions paid to

Seth C. Anderson is a finance professor at Auburn University, Alabama. Sue L. Visscher is a finance professor at the University of Toledo, Ohio. Donald A. Winslow is a law professor at the University of Kentucky, Lexington.

Reprinted with permission from Volume 68 of the North Carolina Law Review. Copyright ©1989 by the North Carolina Law Review Association.

the firm by customers are passed on to the individual brokers. These transaction commissions are generally the only compensation that brokers receive; therefore, they have a tremendous incentive to increase the frequency of trading in their customers' accounts.

On the other hand, full service brokers are also expected to dispense investment advice to customers and to help them maximize the value of their accounts subject to their risk preferences. In fact, many large brokerage firms spend a substantial amount of money advertising the notion that their brokers offer superior investment advice. However, since the broker's compensation depends only on transaction volume, the financial incentive may bias the broker's judgment in interpreting and implementing the firm's investment advice. The broker and the firm both receive a short-term benefit from increased trading activity in a customer's account, even when the customer's investments are performing poorly and are being consumed by increased commissions.

The broad antifraud provisions in the federal securities laws provide the most commonly used basis for determining churning liability. The Securities and Exchange Commission holds that by "hanging out his shingle," a broker gives an implied warranty that he will treat his customers fairly and honestly. That implied warranty of fiduciary responsibility is violated when a broker churns a customer account.

One measure used by the courts to detect excessive trading is the turnover ratio. This ratio compares the total cost of securities purchased for an account within a specific time period (usually one year) to the average amount invested in the account. This can be converted into a percentage turnover rate by multiplying by 100. The ratio is based on the value of securities traded, and not the number of times each security is traded. For instance, a ratio of 1 (or 100%) implies one complete portfolio turnover in one year. This does not necessarily mean that every security in the portfolio was traded once during the year; instead, it means that the value of securities traded during the year was equal to the total value of the portfolio.

One securities lawyer writing in the area of churning has proposed a 2-4-6 rule as a measure of excessive trading. Under this rule, if the annual turnover ratio exceeds 2 (implying two complete portfolio turnovers in a year, or a turnover rate of 200%), possible churning is indicated; if it exceeds 4, churning is presumed; and if it exceeds 6, the presumption of churning becomes conclusive. Such a blanket rule, however, does not consider the customer's risk and return objectives. Unless such qualitative factors are considered, court decisions appear to be very inconsistent: Some decisions have found very high turnover ratios to be acceptable for accounts with a high-risk strategy, while other decisions have found low turnover ratios to constitute churning in accounts with a low-risk strategy.

Another possible measure, which we apply here, is to examine a sample of mutual funds as surrogates for customer investment accounts with different risk-return objectives. The professional investment managers of mutual funds are presumed to trade the fund accounts in order to maximize return for a given level of risk. Since the compensation for mutual fund managers is not based on trading volume, there is little incentive for excessive trading. The trading activity of mutual funds, therefore, should reflect the volume necessary to attempt to achieve the original investment goals and can be used as a benchmark for the turnover of individual broker-managed customer accounts with similar investment goals.

Mutual Fund Turnover Patterns

For this study, mutual funds were divided into nine primary categories, covering a wide spectrum of goals, from high-risk aggressive growth funds to lower-risk income funds. Ten funds from each category were randomly selected, and their turnover rates over a recent five-year period were averaged. The fund types and their average turnover rates are reported in Table 1, along with an indication of the range of turnover rates.

Turnover rates for mutual funds are computed by dividing the lesser of purchases or sales for the fiscal year by the monthly average value of the securities owned by the fund during the year. The result is expressed as a percentage, with 100% implying a complete portfolio turnover within one year.

All of the average turnover rates for the mutual fund categories are less than 200%. The table also provides a variability figure, which measures the average amount by which a majority of fund rates varied around the average fund rate. This figure can provide investors with an idea of the likelihood of various other turnover rates—in particular, rates that may be higher than the average. Assuming a normal distribution of turnover rates, fully 84% of all funds in a single category will have turnover rates that do not exceed the average plus the variability; 98% of all funds in a single category will have turnover rates that do not exceed the average plus two times the variability; and virtually all funds in a single category will have turnover rates that do not exceed the average plus three times the variability.

For example, according to Table 1, there is almost no chance at all that a fund investing in either international or small company securities would ever have a turnover rate greater than 200%, since in this study virtually all funds in these two categories had rates that fell below this level. There is less than a 2% chance that funds investing in securities with a predominantly income objective (equity-income and income) would have turnover rates exceeding 200%. And there is almost no chance that higher-risk funds investing for capital gains (option-income, aggressive growth and growth-income) would have a turnover rate exceeding 300%.

This mutual fund turnover data can be used as a benchmark against which to judge turnover for portfolios of individual stocks. Since the average turnover rates of most of the categories are significantly different from each other, it is very important that the individual investor's investment objectives are identified and matched with one of the mutual fund categories in terms of expected risk and return. For example, the goal of saving for children's college expenses might be matched with a moderate level of risk and return that either a balanced or equity-income mutual fund might indicate. There is only a 2% chance that such a mutual fund would have a turnover rate exceeding 200%; therefore, if the turnover rate of the individual investor's broker-managed investment portfolio exceeds 200%, the possibility of churning certainly exists. An investor following his own advice should reassess his investment strategy in this situation, also.

The Bottom-Line Impact of Excessive Trading

The detection of excessive trading is not only important in terms of assessing whether a broker is improperly churning an account, but it is also important in terms of the effect on the expected portfolio return. Commissions on full-service accounts and even on discount broker accounts run significantly higher than the cost mutual funds pay to trade. Therefore, the same turnover ratio in a broker-managed account and a mutual fund account with exactly the same composition of securities will leave the broker-managed account with a lower return.

For example, consider a scenario in which an investor invests $40,000 for one year, half in a mutual fund account and half in a broker-managed account with the same expected degree of risk. Suppose that both accounts have a turnover ratio of 200%. This means that

Table 1.
Turnover Rates for Various Mutual Fund Categories

Fund Category	Average Turnover Rate(%)	Average Variability*(%)	Maximum Turnover of 84% of Funds in Category(%)	Maximum Turnover of 98% of Funds in Category(%)	Maximum Turnover of Virtually All Funds in Category(%)
Option-Income	143	68	211	279	347
Aggressive Growth	130	70	200	270	340
Growth	106	62	168	230	292
Balanced	81	61	142	203	264
Equity-Income	76	61	137	198	259
Growth-Income	67	88	155	243	331
Income	63	49	112	161	210
International	59	42	101	143	185
Small Company	56	37	93	130	167

*Indicates the range of rates (around the average) for the majority of funds.

on average each security is bought and sold twice. Suppose that the stocks in each account average $20 per share, so that there are 1,000 shares in each account. The broker-managed account charges a $0.60 per share commission on each purchase and sale, and the mutual fund has deducted from the portfolio value $0.10 per share per transaction. Each account earns a 12% return before transaction costs, or $2,400. The total transaction costs for the mutual fund would be $400 ($0.10 × 4 × 1,000), producing a net return of $2,000. The total commission paid by the broker-managed account would be $2,400 ($0.60 × 4 × 1,000), completely eliminating the return.

The difference in transaction costs indicates that broker-managed accounts should have lower turnover rates than mutual funds with similar investment objectives. In fact, the number of shares that could be bought and sold in the broker-managed account in the above

scenario could not exceed 333—a portfolio turnover rate of 33.3%—in order for the portfolio returns net of transactions costs to be equal. Of course, in order to determine the total impact on portfolio return, the mutual fund sales and management fees and any other broker-managed account fees should also be considered.

The turnover rates of the various categories of mutual funds are benchmarks for reasonable activity levels in portfolios with similar investment objectives. Turnover rates in individual stock portfolios that are much higher are certainly a cause for concern. If the portfolio is being managed or advised by a broker, the investor should consider switching brokers. And if the investor is managing his own account, he should take a long hard look at his investment strategy to determine whether the excessive trading and its accompanying costs are really justified.

Article 29

Resolving Broker Disputes: The Arbitration Process

By Henry Sanchez Jr.

Recent cases decided by the United States Supreme Court have placed virtually all investor claims against their brokers into the arbitration forum. Prior to two major Supreme Court decisions in 1987 and 1989 that allow for compulsory arbitration of investor claims, brokerage customers could have most of their securities claims heard in the court system; only upon voluntarily submitting to arbitration could their cases be heard in that forum.

Since the Supreme Court's decisions, the Securities and Exchange Commission has responded by rescinding its rule requiring the disclosure that customers can go to court when arbitration clauses are used in customer agreements. In addition, the National Association of Securities Dealers and the New York Stock Exchange have instituted numerous rule changes as they relate to their arbitration proceedings. Finally, Congress has held hearings discussing the merits of securities arbitration in an effort to decide whether changes to the federal securities laws are necessary. Brokerage firm customers who have signed customer agreements containing arbitration clauses will now find it almost impossible to have their claims against their brokers heard in state or federal courts.

While these events have served to reduce the options available to investors who are engaged in disputes against their brokers, the results are not necessarily all bad for investors. Data released by the SEC suggests that investors receive a higher percentage of their claimed amount of damages against brokers in the arbitration forum than in the courts. This suggests that many investors may be better off in arbitration than in court. This article will explore some of these findings and discuss the arbitration system in general.

Henry Sanchez Jr. is a senior associate in the law firm of Butler, Burnette and Pappas, Tampa, Florida. He was formerly with the Securities and Exchange Commission.

Arbitration Provisions in Customer Agreements

When an investor opens a securities trading account with a brokerage firm, there is usually a clause in the customer agreement stating that disputes between the investor and the broker or brokerage firm will be heard in arbitration. The typical arbitration clause in a customer's agreement reads basically as follows:

Any controversy arising out of or relating to this contract or the breach thereof, shall be settled by arbitration, in accordance with the rules then attaining, of either the American Arbitration Association or the Board of Arbitration of the New York Stock Exchange or the National Association of Securities Dealers.

There may be additional provisions relating to the state in which the arbitration shall be heard and the number of members on an arbitration panel. Investors should read these provisions carefully so that they may determine their rights in the event of a future dispute with their broker.

Some investors may have signed customer agreements prior to 1987 that contain language excluding arbitration of certain claims against their brokers. In those instances, investors may be able to have certain claims heard in courts rather than in the arbitration forum. The law in these cases is changing, and courts consequently may or may not honor the exclusionary language for customer agreements signed before the 1987 and 1989 cases. However, for agreements signed after these cases, it is clear that the brokerage firm and the customer will be bound by the language of the agreement, absent fraud or other grounds to void the contract.

Many investors may feel that they must sign these agreements if they want the brokerage firm's services. Some have argued that the printed form customer agreements are "contracts of adhesion," a contract in which the weaker party has no choice regarding the terms of the contract if that party wishes to receive the services offered by the stronger party. However, no court has ever found that these arbitration clauses are void as contracts of adhesion. In the securities industry, if a potential customer attempts to cross out the arbitration clause, it is possible that the brokerage firm will refuse to open the account, but firm policies vary.

Typical Broker Disputes: Churning

Most investor claims against brokers center on two charges: the churning of customer accounts by brokers and brokers placing customers into unsuitable investments.

Churning is excessive trading by a broker in order to generate commissions without regard to a customer's interests. Under SEC, NASD, and NYSE rules, transactions involving the purchase or sale of securities that are excessive in size or in frequency, in view of the financial resources and character of the customer, are considered to be manipulative, deceptive, and fraudulent.

There is no one particular formula used to determine whether there is excessive trading in a customer's account. There are, however, signs investors should be aware of that will alert them to the possible churning of their accounts. For example, if the investor has not authorized his broker in writing to trade in the account at the broker's discretion (a "discretionary" account), the broker must receive authorization to conduct all trades. If the broker is repeatedly contacting the investor with recommendations, it may be that the broker is attempting to generate transactions in the account that, naturally, will generate commissions for that broker. In a churning case, these recommendations will be for buy and sell transactions within the account itself, not for additional investments and, therefore, there will be no real change in the overall size or value of the investor's portfolio. Of course, churning occurs in discretionary accounts as well.

By measuring the volume of trading (excluding additional monies invested in the account) relative to the account size, an investor can determine the "turnover rate" of his account. An excessive "turnover rate" is a factor indicative of churning. The "turnover rate" is determined by dividing the total cost of purchases by the average monthly size of the account. An annual "turnover rate" of four, five or six times will be indicative of churning.

Also included within the definition of churning is a trading scheme known as "in-and-out" trading. In-and-out trading is the sale of all or part of an investor's portfolio with the proceeds immediately reinvested in other securities followed in a short period by the sale of the newly acquired securities. Another factor to look at is the proportion of the broker's commission as compared to the size of the account and as compared to the broker's total income.

For those investors purchasing and selling options, excessive trading is more difficult to prove due to the nature of options trading. Options trading ordinarily involves more frequent transactions due to the particular trading characteristics of options.

Claims of Unsuitability

In addition to churning, unsuitability claims against brokers are often the basis of arbitration claims. An unsuitable investment is one that, in light of the customer's disclosed objectives and background, the broker knows or reasonably believes to be inappropriate. The difference between an unsuitability claim and a churning claim is that the analysis in an unsuitability claim focuses on the quality of the investment, while in a churning claim, the focus is on the quantity of activity in an account, and the quality is disregarded.

Under the NASD and NYSE rules, recommendations by brokers to customers for purchases, sales or exchanges of securities should be made with reasonable grounds to believe that the recommendation is suitable for that customer, based on the customer's financial situation and needs as revealed to the broker when the relationship was initially established. In addition, a broker should have a reasonable basis for making recommendations to investors. This means that the broker must know or should know the characteristics of the securities being recommended and their effect on the investor's investment objectives.

How does an investor know when a broker is getting him into an unsuitable investment? There is no specific answer to this question. Each investor's objectives and needs vary and they must be clearly communicated to the broker. While this can be done orally, it is far better to do it in writing. The larger brokerage firms provide forms or questionnaires in order to document investors' objectives.

There are, however, some generalizations that can be made regarding unsuitable investments:
- Retirees should not be in risky investments, such as options or futures, if they are depending on their investments for security through their retirement years. These funds should be in conservative investments such as dividend-paying stocks and bonds.
- Investments in new ventures or limited partnerships should be made only after consulting with an expert independent from the transaction.
- If an investor is asked to invest more than that person can afford to lose, that investment is unsuitable.
- Investors with trading accounts must be aware that such accounts are, generally, unsuitable for long-term investment or for persons with limited resources.
- Investors with margin accounts (where they borrow

funds to invest) must also be aware that these accounts are, generally, unsuitable for long-term investments.

While churning and unsuitable investments are the most typical claims against brokers, other claims against brokers are also commonly made, including unauthorized trading, negligence, failure of a broker to execute a customer's order, margin violations, and fraudulent misrepresentations or omissions related to purchases or sales of securities.

In some instances, not only is the broker liable to the customer, but the firm may also be liable. These instances arise generally in cases where the brokerage firm fails to adequately supervise the activities of its brokers. This means that each brokerage firm should have procedures for brokers to follow, and each firm must be diligent in making sure those procedures are followed.

Resolving Disputes Within the Firm

Needless to say, it is far better to discover that there is a problem earlier rather than later. The best place to detect possible churning and other violations, including unauthorized trading and failure to properly execute a customer's order, is in the broker's own confirmation and monthly statements to investors. Investors should keep all documents related to their account in an organized manner. By reviewing each statement an investor will be aware of all transactions in that account. This is especially important for investors with discretionary accounts because their brokers can, and will, conduct transactions in those accounts without first notifying the investor; the confirmation statement may be the only notification an investor receives that a discretionary transaction took place.

Any problems with the statement should be immediately brought to the attention of the broker. If an unauthorized trade has been made, the broker should be contacted within several days after receiving the confirmation statement. Other problems should be brought to the broker's attention within several weeks, before the next monthly statement is received. If a satisfactory explanation is not given, then the office manager should be contacted. In cases where the investor fails to complain about excessive trading or fails to question statements disclosed on that customer's confirmation or monthly statement from the broker, claims of churning and unsuitability may be successfully defended by the broker or the firm.

Brokerage customers should always attempt to have their disputes with brokers initially resolved through the brokerage firm's client grievance resolution process. If contact with the local office manager fails to resolve the problem, the head of the firm's Compliance Department should be contacted. If the brokerage firm is too small to have a Compliance Department, or if the local office manager does not satisfy inquiries, the regional manager or the firm's president should be contacted. Any correspondence to the brokerage firm should be sent by registered or certified mail, return receipt requested.

Failing resolution at the firm level, complaints can be lodged with the SEC, state securities administrators, the NASD, and the NYSE. The major drawback to filing a complaint with a state or other regulatory agency is that the investigatory processes can be slow and, if there is a complaint pending with one of these agencies, an arbitration claim probably cannot be heard until finalization of the investigation.

Turning to Outside Forums

Investors who cannot resolve their disputes by contacting the brokerage firm will turn either to the courts or to arbitration.

If an investor begins an action against a broker in court and there is an existing executed customer agreement containing an arbitration clause, the broker and the brokerage firm can compel arbitration based on that contract. If there exists no arbitration clause compelling arbitration and the customer wishes to bring a claim against the broker in arbitration, the broker must submit to arbitration under the rules of the NASD and NYSE. In addition, in the case of a custodial-type account naming a third party beneficiary, the beneficiary is generally bound by the arbitration provisions of the agreement.

Where a pre-existing agreement to arbitrate does not exist, the investor has a choice between arbitration and litigation. The choice is not always a simple one because the circumstances of each case vary.

An investor must consider several factors in deciding between arbitration and litigation. These factors also come into play in deciding whether to bring a claim at all. They include:

- Whether or not a violation occurred. In general, problems that involve clerical errors can usually be resolved at the firm level.
- The amount of loss. There are several ways to measure this, the simplest being the original account size minus the current account size. Other formulations take into account the time value of money. There are procedures in the arbitration process that allow for resolution of small claims—under $10,000.
- The severity of the violation. Although rare, arbitrators will award attorney's fees and punitive damages in instances where the broker has clearly gone haywire.
- The costs of bringing a claim. These costs vary greatly, depending on the complexity of the case, but could include: filing fees, attorney's fees (if any),

travel expenses, expert witness fees and their costs, and other miscellaneous costs.

- The likelihood of recovery on a claim. This is simply an assessment of whether the investor has a solid case.

An Overview of the Arbitration Process

Most arbitration cases are heard before a panel from the National Association of Securities Dealers, the American Stock Exchange, the New York Stock Exchange or the American Arbitration Association.

The theory behind arbitration is that it is a faster system and less costly to the parties. According to a study conducted by the accounting firm of Deloitte Haskins & Sells (now Deloitte & Touche) at the request of the NYSE, data gathered from brokerage firms supported the conclusion that arbitrated cases are resolved more quickly and at lower legal costs to brokerage firms than litigation. Presumably, investors would incur lower legal costs through arbitration as well. The study also indicated that investors who used arbitration appeared to recover slightly greater amounts than those who went through the complete litigation process, although the difference, according to the SEC, is not statistically significant. Thus, the study indicates that litigation costs for both brokerage firms and, by inference, investors, are significantly more than costs in arbitration.

Arbitrations take place outside of the court system. However, arbitration awards are legally binding and may be set aside only in extremely rare circumstances. Also, in the case of voluntary submission to arbitration, once arbitration is used as a method of determining a dispute, the participants, in general, give up their right to pursue their claim in the courts.

Procedures in each forum vary. The choices of arbitration forums are typically set forth in the arbitration clause of the customer's agreement. These choices generally include the NASD, the NYSE, the ASE and the American Arbitration Association.

A key factor to keep in mind when choosing from one of these forums is where the arbitration hearing will be held. Investors should check with the appropriate forum to see where they hold the arbitrations. Investors bringing claims may have to travel long distances for a hearing. Generally, NASD arbitrations are heard in fairly large cities throughout the country on a regular basis. In contrast, most NYSE arbitrations are held in New York.

After an investor has decided that a violation has occurred and that a claim in arbitration will be made, the investor should contact the appropriate forum to obtain a copy of the arbitration rules and other necessary documents for filing the arbitration claim. Filing fees vary for the claims in each forum.

Typical Arbitration Procedures

While procedures vary for each forum, the NASD's arbitration procedure can provide investors with a good idea of what to expect.

The arbitrators are chosen from a pool of individuals in the community where the arbitration will be heard. The arbitrators themselves are either considered to be "public" or "industry" arbitrators. Public arbitrators are individuals with no current or recent prior employment with brokerage firms. They also include certain attorneys, who, although they may have brokerage firms as their clients, work on brokerage matters less than a certain percentage of their total amount of working time. Industry arbitrators are those arbitrators that currently are, or within the recent past were, employed by brokerage firms.

In claims involving demands for $10,000 or more, the arbitration panel will consist of two public arbitrators and one industry arbitrator, unless the investor requests otherwise. Once the arbitrators are chosen by the Director of Arbitration, any party has the right to request that an arbitrator be removed by filing a written notice of challenge with the Director of Arbitration. The parties are entitled to challenge one arbitrator for no reason whatsoever, and an unlimited number of arbitrators for cause.

An arbitration is commenced by filing a Statement of Claim with the entity that will administer the arbitration. The person or entity filing the Statement of Claim is called the Claimant. In an arbitration to be heard before the NASD, the Statement of Claim is filed with the Director of Arbitration in New York. The signed brokerage agreement, along with pertinent supporting materials as exhibits, must be included with the Statement of Claim, along with the filing fee. Filing fees are determined by the size of the claim. The Statement of Claim need not be drafted as a formal litigation-type document; it may be in letter form. The arbitration rules for each forum will indicate what should be stated in the Statement of Claim, but this will include:

- A specification of the relevant facts,
- The remedies sought by the investor,
- Whether a hearing is requested and the desired location of the hearing.

There is a small claim procedure for claims of $10,000 or less. In these cases, if the Claimant does not request a hearing, one arbitrator will be selected to decide the claim solely based upon the parties' written submissions. The arbitrator in the small claims proceeding may, at his request, have a hearing or require parties to submit additional documents.

Once the customer's claim is filed with the Director of Arbitration of the NASD, the Director of Arbitration will inform the opposing party (the Respondent) and forward copies of all documents filed by the Claimant.

The Respondent has 20 calendar days in the case of a small claim arbitration, and 20 business days in all other arbitrations, to provide an answer to that complaint, unless an extension of time has been granted by the Director of Arbitration. At this point, the Respondent may assert a related counterclaim or may file a claim against a party not yet a party to the action, but necessary to the action. If there is a counterclaim contained in the Respondent's answer, the Claimant has 10 calendar days in the case of a small claim arbitration, and 10 business days in all other arbitrations, to file a reply to such counterclaims.

Sufficient copies of all documents filed by all parties must be supplied so that all other parties and the Director of Arbitration receive a copy. There is a limited discovery procedure in NASD arbitrations permitting the parties to request certain documentation from the other parties. Documents that investors can request include all brokerage firm documents in the investor's file, as well as documents on the investor kept by the broker. (Brokerage firms and brokers usually keep separate files on customers.)

Arbitrations heard under the jurisdiction of the NASD are assigned to a staff attorney who will organize the file, contact potential arbitrators and schedule a date for the hearing. Arbitration hearings are semiformal proceedings. The parties present their cases in a manner similar to that presented in court. However, there are no formal requirements that the rules of evidence used in courts be followed.

After each party presents its case, the arbitrators sign a written award that is sent to the parties. The awards are made publicly available. The arbitrators are not required to write opinions or provide reasons for their award but may do so on their own or upon written request received no later than the hearing date.

It is possible that once a complaint has been filed with the office manager (prior to filing a formal claim against the broker) or after an arbitration claim has been filed, the broker and/or the brokerage firm may seek to settle the matter. In addition to all the other matters to consider, an investor must decide whether the settlement is satisfactory in light of the claim itself, the likelihood of recovery in a full-blown action, the costs of bringing the claim and all other factors pertinent to the investor. When considering a settlement, investors should keep in mind that although the arbitrators do have the power to award attorney's fees, costs of the action, and punitive damages, these are rarely given.

Is a Lawyer Necessary?

Representation by an attorney is not necessary in arbitration. However, complicated issues and a large amount of damages indicate that an attorney should be consulted. Even if the investor does not decide to hire an attorney, he or she should at least have obtained an independent assessment of the matter. In choosing an attorney for representation, investors should keep in mind that although knowledge of the securities laws is not always required in simple matters, such knowledge is necessary where there are complex securities law issues. Local bar associations and local libraries can assist investors in searching for an attorney.

Not having an attorney present at an arbitration proceeding is not necessarily fatal to the party because the rules of evidence applicable in courts do not apply in arbitration. Consequently, the arbitrators are free to determine the manner of proceeding and will listen to requests from the parties regarding the claim. In fact, an arbitration can go forward even if one of the parties is not present at the scheduled hearing.

If an attorney is hired, fees are levied in a variety of ways. Some attorneys will work on a contingency basis, receiving up to 33⅓% of damages collected. Others work on an hourly basis, with hourly charges ranging between about $100 and $350, plus expenses. A typical straightforward arbitration case could cost between $4,000 and $5,000. Sometimes where a small claim is involved, a flat fee can be arranged. However, fees vary tremendously depending on the complexity of the case and the size of the claim.

Conclusion

Claims between investors and their brokers will most likely find their way to an arbitration forum. This article is intended to give general information about the process and should not be relied upon as a complete in-depth analysis of arbitration procedures. If an investor believes that a claim exists against a broker, that investor has a number of important decisions to make as to how to proceed. Arbitration may not be the perfect way to resolve a dispute with a broker, but it is certainly the current system of choice.

Article 30

SIPC: What Happens If Your Brokerage Firm Fails?

By Henry Sanchez Jr.

Brokerage firms routinely point out to new customers that they are members of the Securities Investor Protection Corp.—the SIPC. This is done primarily to reassure investors that they are "insured."

But what does it mean to a customer that a brokerage firm is "insured" by the SIPC? Misconceptions about this term abound. For instance, most investors are probably aware that they are not protected by SIPC for losses resulting from downturns in the market.

But many investors may not be aware that SIPC insurance does not cover losses that are due to a broker's fraudulent, manipulative or deceptive selling schemes. Instead, protection against fraud by brokers can be found under the federal and state securities laws. The federal law requires issuers to provide sufficient information to individual investors so that they can make fully informed decisions, and it ensures that investors can bring claims against brokers for restitution of losses caused by the fraudulent, manipulative or deceptive selling schemes of brokers.

What, then, does SIPC cover? This article describes what SIPC does insure, and it explains what you can expect should you find your brokerage firm under an SIPC proceeding.

What is SIPC?

SIPC, which was created under the Securities Investor Protection Act of 1970, protects investors from losses due to the financial difficulties of brokerage firms, including brokerage firm bankruptcies. It is not a governmental agency or entity, but rather a non-profit corporation that is fully supported by the assessments charged

Henry Sanchez Jr. is a senior associate in the law firm of Butler, Burnette and Pappas, Tampa, Fla. He was formerly with the Securities and Exchange Commission.

to the members by SIPC. The assessments are determined by the board of directors and charged directly to each member firm.

SIPC is subject to the supervision of the Securities and Exchange Commission (SEC), which is authorized to examine and inspect SIPC and to require periodic reports. In fact, the SEC is authorized to apply to a federal district court for an order requiring SIPC to discharge its obligations for the benefit of investors.

SIPC was set up as part of an effort to provide greater protection for customers of registered brokers and dealers and members of national securities exchanges, to restore investor confidence in the capital markets and to upgrade the financial responsibility requirements for registered brokers and dealers.

Before SIPC, an investor could lose all of the cash or securities held in his account if the brokerage firm went bankrupt or closed due to financial failure. Although the securities exchanges had their own trust funds established for the protection of investors, these funds were totally inadequate to handle the financial problems of brokerage firms and fully protect their customers.

All broker-dealers are required to be members of SIPC unless they fit into one of the following exceptions:

- The firm principally conducts its business outside of the United States;
- The firm's business consists exclusively of: the distribution of shares of mutual funds, the sale of variable annuities, the business of insurance, or the furnishing of investment advice to investment companies or insurance company separate accounts; and
- The firm is a government securities broker who is a member of a national securities exchange and is registered with the SEC under a provision of law that does not confer SIPC membership.

Membership in SIPC by brokerage firms can be compared to membership in the Federal Deposit Insurance

Corporation by banks, which protects customers' funds up to $100,000. Most bank depositors choose a bank because of the rates it provides and the services it offers. Similarly, investors should not choose a brokerage firm based solely upon the fact that it is a member of SIPC; other factors, such as the reputation and professionalism of the firm, should also be examined.

Unlike the FSLIC and the FDIC, SIPC is relatively healthy financially. In its most recent annual report submitted to the SEC (and which is available to the public by writing to the SIPC at: 805 15th St. N.W., Washington, D.C., 20005), chairman James Stearns wrote that SIPC had a very low number of new customer protection proceedings in the past year: There were six new proceedings filed in 1989, with four proceedings involving an aggregate of fewer than 50 customer claims. The report goes on to state that SIPC has $472 million in its fund, which is the highest level in SIPC's history.

What SIPC Can Do

SIPC is required to maintain a fund for customer protection against brokerage failures. Should those funds be inadequate in a particular situation, SIPC can borrow against the U.S. Treasury up to $1 billion. The SEC can issue promissory notes and the subsequent purchase of such notes by the U.S. Treasury Department results in funds going to SIPC.

Proceedings under the Securities Investor Protection Act, in which SIPC files for the protection of customer accounts, can only be initiated by SIPC; brokerage firm customers have no right to bring these proceedings on their own, and they cannot request or compel SIPC to bring a proceeding against a member firm. Instead, if a customer believes that a brokerage firm is in financial trouble, the SEC's Office of Financial Responsibility in the Division of Market Regulation should be notified.

Proceedings brought by SIPC are in the form of liquidation proceedings, akin to bankruptcy. In fact, the brokerage firm is often referred to as the "debtor" in the liquidation proceedings.

Once SIPC determines that a member brokerage firm has failed or is in danger of failing to meet its financial obligations, SIPC may seek a protective decree to protect the firm's customers from its failure.

Once a protective decree is issued by the court, a trustee designated by SIPC is appointed to liquidate the brokerage firm. At that point, claims against the firm must be filed directly with the trustee and the trustee causes the distribution of customers' property in accordance with the governing laws. In limited situations involving small claims, SIPC may pay the claims to the customers directly.

The customers of a firm that is under an SIPC proceeding do not have the option of receiving cash in lieu of securities. Instead, SIPC attempts to leave the customer in the same position as if the broker remained in business. If there is no problem with the brokerage firm's account documentation, the trustee may attempt to arrange for the transfer of some or all of the customers' accounts to another SIPC member. This transfer requires the prior approval of SIPC, but not the consent of any customer.

In these situations, the customers' trading activities are only temporarily disrupted. The problem with this procedure, however, is that it may take several weeks to effectuate the transfers, thus subjecting customers to market risk during that time period with the inability to sell the securities involved.

How Long Does It Take?

There is no specific time frame in which a liquidation proceeding will be completed. According to SIPC, most customers can expect to receive their property in their accounts in one to three months from the date of the filing of the protective decree. Obviously, where the debtor brokerage firms' records are accurate and complete, deliveries of securities and cash can begin and be completed much sooner than where firms have incomplete or inaccurate files.

In cases where the files are incomplete or inaccurate, there can be delays of several months. These delays can be extended if it appears that the principals of the firm or the firm itself were involved in fraudulent activities.

Finally, some delays may be caused by the fact that certain stock certificates must be transferred with specific instructions to the transfer agents.

Accounts using options face somewhat different procedures, since these are wasting assets that must be carefully monitored during the life of the option. If SIPC files for a liquidation proceeding against a broker with customers that have options positions, all "standardized" options positions (exchange-traded options) can be closed, with the exception of covered short positions when the broker has caused the cover to be deposited with the Options Clearing Corporation or its correspondent broker (the broker on the other side of the options position). In these situations, the customer must attempt to find out whether the short option cover was deposited with the Options Clearing Corporation or the correspondent broker; this information can be obtained from the Options Clearing Corporation in Chicago.

Where it is not possible to transfer the customers' accounts to other SIPC members, the customers will receive from the trustee all of the securities in their accounts registered in their names or such securities that are in the process of being registered in the customers' names and that are not in negotiable form. The customers will then receive all remaining cash and securities held by the brokerage firm, on a pro rata basis. If the customers' accounts are not fully reimbursed, SIPC then will provide its own funds to satisfy any remaining claims of the customers up to the maximum of $500,000, which includes a maximum of up to $100,000 on claims for cash in customer accounts. If a customer has sold a security prior to the initiation of the liquidation proceeding, that customer may make a claim for cash up to the $100,000 limit. Finally, if there are any remaining assets of the brokerage firm after the payment of all liquidation expenses, these assets may be available to the customers to satisfy any remaining portion of their claims on a pro rata basis with other creditors.

You may want to note that, during the liquidation process, a distinction is made between securities held by the brokerage firm in the customer's name that are not in negotiable form ("customer name securities") and securities held in "street name," which are securities held in the customer's account for the customer's benefit, but that are registered with the transfer agent in the brokerage firm's name. Customer name securities are excluded from the liquidation proceeding and are treated as if they were merely held by the debtor broker-dealer for the benefit of the customer. Consequently, Customer name securities are not distributed to customers through the liquidation proceeding, which distributes the firm's assets; instead, they are transferred directly.

When Is a "Customer" Not a "Customer"?

To receive SIPC protection, it is important that customers of broker-dealers actually are "customers" as defined under the regulations governing SIPC. Under these rules, a person may be a customer with regard to some, but not all, of the claims. A person qualifies as a customer of the brokerage firm that is being liquidated if the broker received, acquired, or held the customer's securities in the ordinary course of business, either with a view to sale or for safekeeping. The term "customer" also includes any person who has a claim against the brokerage firm arising out of sales or conversions of securities, and any person who has deposited cash with the brokerage firm for the purpose of purchasing securities. The loan of money or securities to a broker, that is clearly not for the purpose of investing or trading in securities, does not make the lender a customer of the brokerage firm. In this case, the person is a general creditor of the brokerage firm.

The definition of "customer" under the Securities Investor Protection Act does not include persons whose claims arise out of transactions with foreign subsidiaries of SIPC member firms or whose claims are for cash or securities that are part of the capital of the brokerage firm or are subordinated to the claims of creditors of the brokerage firm. In addition, SIPC funds cannot be used to pay claims of customers who are general partners, officers or directors of the brokerage firm; or, the beneficial owner of 5% or more of any class of equity security of the brokerage firm (other than certain non-convertible preferred stocks); or a limited partner with a participation of 5% or more in the net assets or net profits of the brokerage firm; or someone with the power to exercise a controlling influence over the management of the brokerage firm; or a broker or dealer or bank acting for itself rather than for its own customer or customers.

If customers have cash balances in their trading accounts, those cash balances are protected if the cash is deposited or left in the account for the purpose of purchasing securities. Cash balances left in the accounts solely for the purpose of earning interest are not protected. Nevertheless, SIPC makes the assumption that cash balances left in securities accounts are for the purpose of purchasing securities and substantial evidence is required to rebut this presumption.

How Do Customers Become Involved?

Investors are notified of liquidation proceedings by the trustee appointed by the court once SIPC has filed for a protective decree. The trustee must send notice of the commencement of the liquidation proceedings to each person who was a customer of the failed brokerage firm within the last 12 months; the notice is sent to the addresses of customers as they are provided in the books and records of the brokerage firm. The trustee also must place a notice in one or more newspaper of general circulation in the form and manner prescribed by the court.

All creditors of the brokerage firm are also notified by the trustee.

A customer with a claim to cash or securities in an account at a failed brokerage firm involved in a liquidation proceeding must be careful to follow the time deadlines. Only where the court grants a reasonable, fixed extension of time for the filing of a statement of claim by the United States, by a state or political subdivision thereof, or by an infant or incompetent person without a guardian, may the time period be extended. No claim of a customer or other creditor of the failed brokerage firm that is received by the trustee after the expiration of six months beginning on the date of publication of notice can be allowed. This six-month time bar is automatic and acts as an absolute bar to a customer's claim.

In order to be fully protected, however, the court may fix a time period within which customer claims must be filed. This time period will not exceed 60 days after publication of notice, and it may be for such shorter time period as the court orders. After the 60-day period, the trustee has the option of either paying to the customers the value of the securities on the date the petition was filed by SIPC or distributing the securities to the customer, whichever is the most economical of the two.

This may sound confusing, but it is an important distinction: A brokerage firm customer is fully protected if the claim is filed within the time period that is set by the court, but if the claim is filed after the time period set by the court, but before the expiration of six months, the customer is protected only to the extent that the trustee determines it most economical to the estate of the debtor brokerage firm. The reason for the distinction is that Congress wanted to protect SIPC against speculation by customers who would withhold their claims for a longer time period in order to determine whether a change in market conditions would give them a more valuable distribution.

Filing a Claim

Once a customer receives notice of the liquidation proceeding, that customer must file with the trustee a written statement of claim. Unlike a bankruptcy proceeding, however, the customer need not file a formal proof of claim. When filing statements of claim, customers must be careful to include everything in the account. If a statement of claim is filed within the appropriate time period, but does not include everything in the account, amendments to the claim after the expiration of the six-month time period are not allowed. In addition, when a customer files a statement of claim with the trustee, the customer should be careful to include all supporting documentation to substantiate that claim. This documentation includes, but may not be limited to: customer account agreements, margin agreements, confirmation statements and monthly statements.

It is important that a customer filing a statement of claim assures that the trustee actually receives the claim.

Consequently, customers filing claims should do so in some manner as to receive confirmation of delivery, such as a return receipt confirming delivery to the trustee.

Customers with margin accounts, or customers who have purchased securities but have not received them into their account at the time liquidation proceedings commence, must make payment to the trustee within 60 days after publication of the notice for the liquidation proceeding. For margin account customers who do not have a cash balance in the account, if there is a margin requirement during the time period, the trustee is required to sell some of the securities in the account to satisfy the margin debt.

Conclusion

SIPC has broad powers to protect customers by rapidly moving to file for liquidation of failing brokerage firms. By and large, these protections result in the least amount of disruption in the customer's trading of securities.

However, customers who fail to file their claims on time once notice of a liquidation proceeding has been served upon them will lose their investments. Customers must be careful to follow the time deadlines that are set.

Finally, SIPC does not protect customers from loss in value of their securities due to market conditions, nor does it protect against the fraudulent activities of brokers. Restitution for fraud may only be found in the federal or state securities laws.

Sources

An Overview of Securities Markets

"What Securities Markets Do—And for Whom," Chapter 2 of U.S. Congress, Office of Technology Assessment, *Electronic Bulls & Bears: U.S. Securities Markets & Information Technology*, OTA-CIT-469 (Washington, DC: U.S. Government Printing Office, September 1990).

"How Technology is Transforming Securities Markets," Chapter 7 of U.S. Congress, Office of Technology Assessment, *Electronic Bulls & Bears: U.S. Securities Markets & Information Technology*, OTA-CIT-469 (Washington, DC: U.S. Government Printing Office, September 1990).

Herbert L. Baer and Douglas D. Evanoff, "Payments System Issues in Financial Markets That Never Sleep," Federal Reserve Bank of Chicago *Economic Perspectives*, 14:6, Nov./Dec. 1990, pp. 2-15.

Debt, Inflation, and Macroeconomic Forecasts

Frank E. Morris, "The Changing American Attitude Toward Debt, and its Consequences," Federal Reserve Bank of Boston *New England Economic Review*, May/June 1990, pp. 34-39.

Adrian W. Throop, "The Costs of Anticipated Inflation," Federal Reserve Bank of San Francisco *Weekly Letter*, July 29, 1990, pp. 1-3.

Adrian W. Throop, "Oil Prices and Inflation," Federal Reserve Bank of San Francisco *Weekly Letter*, October 5, 1990, pp. 1-3.

David P. Ely and Kenneth J. Robinson, "The Stock Market and Inflation: A Synthesis of the Theory and Evidence," Federal Reserve Bank of Dallas *Economic Review*, March 1989, pp. 17-29.

Gerald H. Anderson and John J. Erceg, "Forecasting Turning Points With Leading Indicators," Federal Reserve Bank of Cleveland *Economic Commentary*, October 1, 1989, pp. 1-4.

Leonard Mills, "Can Stock Prices Reliably Predict Recessions?," Federal Reserve Bank of Philadelphia *Business Review*, September/October 1988, pp. 3-14.

Equity Market Linkages and Market Volatility

Sean Becketti and Gordon H. Sellon, Jr., "Has Financial Market Volatility Increased?," Federal Reserve Bank of Kansas City Economic Review, June 1989, pp. 17-30.

"The Operation of Stock Markets," Chapter 3 of U.S. Congress, Office of Technology Assessment, *Electronic Bulls & Bears: U.S. Securities Markets & Information Technology*, OTA-CIT-469 (Washington, DC: U.S. Government Printing Office, September 1990).

George Sofianos, "Margin Requirements on Equity Instruments," Federal Reserve Bank of New York *Quarterly Review*, 13:2, Summer 1988, pp. 47-60.

James T. Moser, "Circuit Breakers," Federal Reserve Bank of Chicago *Economic Perspectives*, 14:5, September/October 1990, pp. 2-13.

The Stock Market

Marc Reinganum, "Investment Characteristics of Stock Market Winners," American Association of Individual Investors *AAII Journal*, 11:8, September 1989, pp. 8-11.

Robert Schweitzer, "How Do Stock Returns React to Special Events?," Federal Reserve Bank of Philadelphia *Business Review*, July/August 1989, pp. 17-29.

Anthony Saunders, "Why Are So Many New Stock Issues Underpriced?," Federal Reserve Bank of Philadelphia *Business Review*, March/April 1990, pp. 3-12.

Stephen F. Leroy, "Capital Market Efficiency: An Update," Federal Reserve Bank of San Francisco *Economic Review*, Spring 1990, pp. 29-40.

Chan Huh, "The Equity Risk-Premium Puzzle," Federal Reserve Bank of San Francisco *Weekly Letter*, April 13, 1990, pp. 1-3.

The Bond Market

Richard H. Jefferis, Jr., "The High-Yield Debt Market: 1980-1990," Federal Reserve Bank of Cleveland *Economic Commentary*, April 1, 1990, pp. 1-6.

Sean Becketti, "The Truth About Junk Bonds," Federal Reserve Bank of Kansas City *Economic Review*, July/August 1990, pp. 45-54.

Peter A. Abken, "Innovations in Modeling the Term Structure of Interest Rates," Federal Reserve Bank of Atlanta *Economic Review*, 75:4, July/August 1990, pp. 2-27.

Derivative Instruments

Edwin J. Elton, Martin J. Gruber, and Joel Rentzler, "Commodity Funds: Does the Prospectus Really Tell All?" American Association of Individual Investors *AAII Journal*, 11:9, October 1989, pp. 8-11.

Richard W. McEnally and Richard J. Rendleman, Jr., "How to Avoid Getting Taken in Listed Stock Options," American Association of Individual Investors *AAII Journal*, 12:2, February 1990, pp. 8-13.

Shreesh Deshpande and Vijay M. Jog, "Primes and Scores: What They Are and How They Perform," American Association of Individual Investors *AAII Journal*, 11:7, August 1989, pp. 15-20.

Global Investing

Christine Pavel and John N. McElravey, "Globalization in the Financial Services Industry," Federal Reserve Bank of Chicago *Economic Perspectives*, 14:3, May/June 1990, pp. 3-18.

Reuven Glick, "Global Interest Rate Linkages," Federal Reserve Bank of San Francisco *Weekly Letter*, May 25, 1990, pp. 1-3.

Brian J. Cody, "Reducing The Costs and Risk of Trading Foreign Exchange," Federal Reserve Bank of Philadelphia *Business Review*, November/December 1990, pp. 13-23.

The Investor–Broker Relationship

Seth C. Anderson, Sue L. Visscher, and Donald A. Winslow, "Guidelines for Detecting Churning in an Account," American Association of Individual Investors *AAII Journal*, 11:9, October 1989, pp. 8–11.

Henry Sanchez, Jr., "Resolving Broker Disputes: The Arbitration Process," American Association of Individual Investors *AAII Journal*, 12:2, February 1990, pp. 15–19.

Henry Sanchez, Jr. "SIPC: What Happens if Your Brokerage Firm Fails?" American Association of Individual Investors *AAII Journal*, 12:10, November 1990, pp. 13–16.

RANDALL LIBRARY-UNCW

3 0490 0473845 4